STUDIES IN JAINA HISTORY AND CULTURE

The past ten years have seen the interest in Jainism increasing, with this previously little-known Indian religion assuming a significant place in Study of Religious. This timely collection presents original research from a cross-section of eminent scholars on varied aspects of Jaina Studies. The volume crosses disciplinary boundaries with a range of empirical and textual studies on Jainism and the Jains. Topics that are covered include the role of women in Jain society, Jaina law and property, and sectarian Jain traditions. *Studies in Jaina History and Culture* is a stimulating and representative snapshot of the current state of Jaina Studies that will interest students and academics involved in the study of religion or South Asian cultures.

Peter Flügel is Chair of the Centre of Jaina Studies at the Department of the Study of Religions in the School of Oriental and African Studies, University of London. He has published extensively on the history and anthropology of contemporary Jain schools and sects, Jain stūpas, Jaina–Vaiṣṇava syncretism, and the social history of the Jain tradition. He is the editor of the *International Journal of Jain Studies* http://www.soas.ac.uk/ijjs

STUDIES IN JAINA HISTORY AND CULTURE

Disputes and dialogues

Edited by Peter Flügel

MOTILAL BANARSIDASS PUBLISHERS
PRIVATE LIMITED • DELHI

Routledge
Taylor & Francis Group
LONDON AND NEW YORK

Also available at

MOTILAL BANARSIDASS

41 UA Bungalow Road, Jawahar Nagar, Delhi-110007
8 Mahalaxmi Chamber, 22 Bhulabhai Desai Road, Mumbai-400026
203 Royapettah High Road, Mylapore, Chennai-600004
236, 9th Main III Block, Jayanagar, Bengaluru-560011
8 Camac Street, Kolkata-700017
Ashok Rajpath, Patna-800004
Chowk, Varanasi-221001

Reprint, 2017

First published 2006
by Routledge
2 Park Square, Milton Park, Abingdon, Oxon OX14 4RN

Simultaneously published in the USA and Canada
by Routledge
711 Third Avenue, New York, NY 10017

Routledge is an imprint of the Taylor & Francis Group, an informa business

First issued in paperback 2013

Typeset in Times New Roman by
Newgen Imaging Systems (P) Ltd, Chennai, India

British Library Cataloguing in Publication Data
A catalogue record for this book is available
from the British Library

Library of Congress Cataloging in Publication Data
A catalog record for this book has been requested

ISBN : 978-81-208-4089-8

Digitally Printed at Replika Press Pvt. Ltd.

IN MEMORY OF JULIA LESLIE (1948–2004)

CONTENTS

FIGURES

TABLES

CONTRIBUTORS

Piotr Balcerowicz is Lecturer at the Oriental Institute, Warsaw University, Poland, where he teaches Sanskrit and lectures on Indian philosophy as well as on intercultural relations and contemporary history and cultures of Asia. He organized four international conferences on Indology and is the editor of a number of Indological books. He published extensively on Indian philosophy, but also on the Middle East and Central Asia (approx. 70 papers in Polish, English, and German). He authored five books on Indian philosophy, Jainism, and history of Afghanistan.

Willem Bollée studied Classical Philology and Indology. He was a collaborator at the Critical Pali Dictionary in Copenhagen and Hamburg, Assistant Professor of Indo-European Linguistics at Münster University and, after his Habilitation, Professor of Indology at Heidelberg University. Among his books are the *Kuṇālajātaka* (1970), *Studien zum Sūyagaḍa* I–II (1977–88), *Bṛhatkalpabhāṣya* (3 vols, 1998) and *The Story of Paesi* (2002, 2nd edition, 2005) and many articles.

John E. Cort is Professor of Asian and Comparative Religions at Denison University in Granville, Ohio, USA. He is the author of *Jains in the World: Religious Values and Ideology in India* (New York: OUP, 1998) as well as several dozen articles on Jainism, and on South Asian religion, culture, and society. He also edited *Open Boundaries: Jain Communities and Cultures in Indian History* (Albany: SUNY, 2001), and the late Kendall W. Folkert's *Scripture and Community: Collected Essays on the Jains* (Atlanta: Scholars Press, 1993).

Paul Dundas is Reader in Sanskrit in the School of Literatures, Languages and Cultures, University of Edinburgh. Among his extensive publications on various facets of Jainism is *The Jains* (second revised and expanded edition Routledge 2002; Italian translation 2005). His monograph *History, Scripture and Controversy in a Medieval Jain Sect* is forthcoming from Routledge.

Peter Flügel is Chair of the Centre of Jaina Studies at the Department of the Study of Religions in the School of Oriental and African Studies, University of

London. He has published extensively on the history and anthropology of contemporary Jain schools and sects, Jain stūpas, Jaina–Vaiṣṇava syncretism, and the social history of the Jain tradition. He is the editor of the *International Journal of Jain Studies* http://www.soas.ac.uk/ijjs

Sherry E. Fohr is a Visiting Assistant Professor at Converse College. She received her PhD from the Department of Religious Studies at the University of Virginia and conducted research in India with Jain nuns with a Fulbright-Hays fellowship.

Sin Fujinaga is Professor of Ethics in the Minayonojo National College of Technology. He studied Jainism under the guidance of late Professor UNO Astusi, Hiroshima University and Muni Jambuvijayaji in India. He has written one book and nearly fifty papers on Jainism. Presently he serves as editor of the *Journal for Jaina Studies*.

Julia A. B. Hegewald is heading an interdisciplinary research group on Jainism in Karnataka at the South Asia Institute of the University of Heidelberg, Germany (Emmy Noether-Programm, DFG). She studied at the School of Oriental and African Studies (SOAS) in London and was Research Fellow in Indian Architecture at University College Oxford. She has published extensively on Jainism and on South Asian art and architecture.

M. Whitney Kelting is Assistant Professor of Religion at Northeastern University in Boston, Massachusetts. Her book *Singing to the Jinas: Jain Laywomen, Mandal Singing and the Negotiations of Jain Devotion* (New York: OUP, 2001) examines the role of devotional singing in contemporary Jain laywomen's theology and praxis.

Werner Menski is Professor of South Asian Laws at SOAS, University of London and author of several books on South Asian and Hindu law, including *Hindu Law: Beyond Tradition and Modernity* (New Delhi: OUP, 2003). He first studied Jainism in Germany during the 1970s and is currently project leader of the AHRC project on "Jaina law and identity" at SOAS.

Olle Qvarnström is Professor of Indic Religions at the Department of History of Religions, Lund University, Sweden. Recent publications include: *The Yogaśāstra of Hemacandra: A Twelfth Century Handbook on Jainism,* (Cambridge, MA: Harvard University Press, 2002), and *Jainism and Early Buddhism. Essays in Honour of Padmanbh* S. Jaini. Ed. by O. Qvarnström (Berkeley: Asian Humanities Press, 2003).

Josephine Reynell is a Research Associate at the International Gender Studies Centre, Department of International Development, Queen Elizabeth House, University of Oxford. She received her PhD from the University of Cambridge.

She is also an Associate of the Centre for Jaina Studies at SOAS. She teaches anthropology for the Institute of Human Sciences at the University of Oxford and is Director of Studies for Human Sciences at Lady Margaret Hall. She has taught part-time for Oxford Brookes University and on the Women's Studies MA at Ruskin College for mature students. She is beginning research on the Jain diaspora in the UK.

Emma Salter is Associate Lecturer with the Open University and teaches philosophy and religious studies at a sixth form college in north England. She was awarded a doctorate by Cardiff University, UK in 2003 for her ethnographic study of the devotees of Śrīmad Rājacandra. She has contributed to *The New Lion Handbook: The World's Religions* (Oxford: Lion Hudson, 2005).

Royce Wiles is currently working in the research library of the Afghanistan Research and Evaluation Unit (AREU) in Kabul, Afghanistan. He is also helping with the restoration of other academic libraries in the city including the library of the Museum of Kabul. He studied Sanskrit and Jain Prakrits in Canberra with L. A. Schwarzschild and J. W. de Jong and in Pune with A. M. Ghatage.

Kristi L. Wiley is a Visiting Lecturer in the Department of South and Southeast Asian Studies at the University of California, Berkeley. She received her PhD from the University of California, Berkeley. She teaches Sanskrit and courses on religion in South Asia. She is the author of the *Historical Dictionary of Jainism* (Lanham, Maryland: Scarecrow Press, 2004). Her research has focused on aspects of Jainism associated with *karma* theory.

FOREWORD

This volume of essays is clear proof that the study of Jainism has assumed its rightful place in the academic study of Indian religion. Indeed, it is hard to imagine a more vibrant field today in Indian religious studies than this once-neglected area. Written by scholars in North America, Europe, and Asia, the essays deal with diverse topics, ranging from the history of the *Jain saṁgha*, to subtle points of philosophy and doctrine; they are written by anthropologists concerned with contemporary practice and art historians who see in ancient monuments evidence of religious change. They also reflect trends both new and old: some of the essays involve a close reading of texts in a continuation of the best of nineteenth-century philology, whereas others speak a more contemporary language and deal with issues that are newer to academic debates, for example, the role of women in the religious community, defining personhood, and structures of authority. Together, the essays offer a comprehensive picture of Jainism. They allow us to see Jain studies today as a lively field that engages scholars of many different disciplines on issues that span the entire range of scholarly debates in religious studies. The next challenge for all of us will be to make use of the insights gained from scholarship on Jainism to achieve a broader understanding of Indian religions as a whole. "Jainology," as a relative newcomer on the academic scene, can learn from "Buddhology," its better-established older sister. There is everything to be gained by communicating between our "ologies," and much to be lost by the creation of artificial boundaries. The study of Jainism must now be an integral part of the study of Indian religions, as the study of Indian religions must be an integral part of the academic study of religion. Volumes such as the present one will go a long way toward generating an awareness of the importance of the study of Jainism for the larger scholarly community.

Phyllis Granoff
New Haven
April 2005

PREFACE

Most contributions to this first volume of the Routledge Advances in Jaina Studies series emerged from research papers presented at the annual Jaina Studies Workshop at the London School of Oriental and African Studies between 1999 and 2002, notably John E. Cort's third Annual Jain Lecture on March 16, 2002, "A Fifteenth Century Digambar Mystic and His Contemporary Followers: Tāraṇ Taraṇ Svāmī and the Tāraṇ Svāmī Panth." The contributions of Piotr Balcerowicz, Willem Bollée, and Royce Wiles were solicited especially for this volume. Willem Bollée's article "Adda or the oldest extant dispute between Jains and heretics (Sūyagaḍa 2, 6): Part One" is also published in Jambū-jyoti (Munivara Jambūvijaya Festschrift), Edited by M. A. Dhaky and J. B. Shah, 48–84 (Ahmedabad: Shardaben Chimanbhai Educational Research Centre, 2004). Part Two of this article appeared in the Journal of Indian Philosophy 27 (1999) 411–37. No attempt was made to impose a homogeneous style on the contributions to this book.

Peter Flügel
London
February 2003

Part I

ORTHODOXY AND HERESY

1

ADDA OR THE OLDEST EXTANT DISPUTE BETWEEN JAINS AND HERETICS (SŪYAGAḌA 2,6)

Part one[1]

Willem Bollée

The Sūyagaḍa is the second oldest book of the Śvetāmbara Jain canon. It has preserved in deliberately vague formulation doctrines of heterodox teachers in Mahāvīra's times. A first English translation was made by Hermann Jacobi in 1895. The text is introduced by the Nijjutti which is not a proper commentary but an aide mémoire for the teacher in a religious class and contains basic points to be treated. The first word commentary is the *cūrṇi* in Prākrit followed by the *ṭīkā* in Sanskrit.

Śīlâṅka introduces this lecture with 17 Nijjutti stanzas,[2] only the first four of which occur *pratīka*-wise in Cū and are dealt with there. They commence with the *nikṣepa* of *adda*, the title of the lecture.

N 184. *nāmaṃ ṭhavaṇā addaṃ davv'-addaṃ c'eva hoi bhāv'-addaṃ /*
eso khalu addassa u nikkhevo cau-viho hoi //

d: V: *nikkhevŏ cauvviho*[3]

N 185. *udag'-addaṃ sār'-addaṃ chavi-y'-adda vas'-adda taha siles'-addaṃ /*
eyaṃ davv'-addaṃ khalu bhāveṇaṃ hoi rāg'-addaṃ //

N 186. *ega-bhavie ya baddhâue ya a(b)himuhie ya nāma-goe ya /*
ee tiṇṇi pagārā davv'-Adde honti nāyavvā //

a: thus read with MSS in T; C: *bhaviya-baddhāuya*; TV: *bhaviya-baddhāue*; – b: thus read with MSS in T; TV: *abhimuhae*

N 187. *Adda-pure Adda-su(y)o nāmeṇaṃ Addao tti aṇ-agāro /*
tatto samuṭṭhiyam iṇaṃ ajjhayaṇaṃ Addaijjaṃ ti //

N 188. *kāmaṃ duvālas'-aṅgaṃ Jiṇa-vayaṇaṃ sāsayaṃ mahā-bhāgaṃ /*

savv'-ajjhayaṇāī tahā savv'-akkhara-saṃnivāyā ya //

N 189. *taha vi ya koī attho uppajjai taṃmi taṃmi samayaṃmi /*
puvva-bhaṇio aṇumao ya hoi Isibhāsiesu jahā //

(N 184) Adda ('wet') can be looked upon as a designation, a figural representation, from a material and from a figurative point of view: this fourfold *nikṣepa* of *adda* does exist, no doubt (*khalu*).

As is usual, the Nijjutti first nikṣepizes the title of the lecture, but for the details we mainly depend on Śīlâṅka, because for the Cuṇṇi we only have C with its many textual corruptions at our disposal.

Though I do not understand Jinadāsa's remark here,[4] a hint can be drawn from him to the correct etymology of Addaya, namely, one born under the asterism Ārdra, as mentioned by Pāṇini (4,3,28).[5]

(N 185) "Moist" in a material sense is moist with water (1), moist by nature (2), moist on the surface (3), oily (4) and sticky (5). Moist in a figurative sense is full of love-feeling.

Subsequently Śīlâṅka gives the following examples for *davv'-adda*: mud (1), Gmelina arborea (?), Sochal salt and the like[6] (2), camphor, red Aśoka[7] etc. (3), smeared with a fatty substance (as marrow)[8] (4) and pillars, walls etc. smeared with hard mortar[9] (5).

(N 186) The quantity of life bound by a form of existence, the future name and the family – these are the three kinds of material *adda* one should know.

As to Śīlâṅka, *dravyârdra* pertaining to Prince Ārdraka can also be taken differently – according to Aṇuog § 491,[10] that is, namely concerning a soul which immediately after returning from a heaven[11] is reborn in the person of Ārdraka-kumāra whose quantity of life, name and sex are the immaterial counterpart to *dravyârdra*.[12]

(N 187) In Addapura there lived a vagrant ascetic named Addaya, the son of Adda. After him, viz. Addaya, this lecture obtained its name.

(N 188) The Jina's word, namely, the twelve *Aṅga*s, indeed is everlasting and eminent, (and) so are all their lectures and all combinations of syllables.

(N 189) Nevertheless some truth appears this very moment as was said earlier and approved of in the *Isibhāsiyāiṃ*.

As the stanza begins with *taha vi ya* a preceding *jai vi* is expected. Here apparently a stanza has dropped out which Śīlâṅka still had before him as he glosses the words *jai vi* by *yady api sarvam apîdaṃ dravyârthataḥ śāsvatam.*

Isibhāsiyesu: the 28th lecture of this text is called *Addaijj' ajjhayaṇaṃ*. Besides, the Cuṇṇi on Aṇuog § 266 as well as Samav 23 mention our lecture and in Ṭ II 136b 7 it says *tathā pūrvam apy asāv artho 'nyam uddiśyôkto 'numataś ca bhavati Ṛṣibhāṣiteṣûttarādhyayanâdiṣu yathā*. Utt 31,16 mentions the 23 lectures of the Sūyagaḍa and Śāntisūri 616a 5 quotes Āvaśyaka-saṃgrahaṇī 36 (ĀvNHar 658a 12) enumerating the titles of the Sūy II lectures. Jinadāsa only tells us the Adda story, but does not comment on the following N stanzas.

N 190. *ajj'-Addaeṇa Gosāla-bhikkhu-bambha-vvaī-ti-daṇḍiṇaṃ /*
jaha hatthi-tāvasāṇaṃ kahiyaṃ iṇam-o tahā voccaṃ //

b: thus read m.c. for all edd.: *bambhavaī*; – d: T: *vucchaṃ*

N 191. *gāme Vasanta-purae Sāmaio gharaṇi-sahiŏ nikkhanto /*
bhikkhā-yariyā-diṭṭhā ohāsiya bhatta vehāsaṃ //

N 192. *saṃvega-samāvanno māī bhattaṃ caittu diya-loe /*
caiūṇaṃ Adda-pure Adda-suyo Addao jāo //

N 193. *pīī ya doṇha dūo pucchaṇam Abhayassa paṭṭhave so vi /*
teṇâvi samma-diṭṭhi tti hojja paḍimā rahaṃmi gayā //

N 194. *daṭṭhuṃ saṃbuddho rakkhio ya āsāṇa vāhaṇa palāo /*
pavvāvanto dhario rajjaṃ na karei, ko anno ? //

c: thus to be corrected in Bollée 1995: 136

N 195. *a-gaṇinto nikkhanto viharai paḍimāĕ dārigā-vario /*
su-yaraṇa-vasu-hārāo ranno kahaṇaṃ ca devīe //

c: thus v.l. in Ṭ for the metrically faulty: *suvaṇṇa-vasu* read by VT

N 196. *taṃ nei piyā tīse pucchaṇa kahaṇaṃ ca varaṇa-dovāre /*
jāṇāhi pāya-bimbaṃ āgamaṇaṃ kahaṇa niggamaṇaṃ //

N 197. *paḍimâgaya-ssamīve sa-parīvārā a-bhikkha paḍivayaṇaṃ /*
bhogā suyāṇa pucchaṇa suya-bādha puṇṇe ya niggamaṇaṃ //

N 198. *Rāyagihâgama corā rāya-bhayā-kahaṇa tesi dikkhā ya /*
Gosāla-bhikkhu-baṃbhī ti-daṇḍiyā tāvase[hi saha] vā(y)o //

d: thus read m.c. against VT and accordingly correct Bollée 1995: 136

N 199. *vāe parāiittā savve vi ya saraṇam abbhuvagayā te /*
Addaga-sahiyā savve Jiṇa-vīra-sagāsĕ nikkhantā //

N 200. *na dukkaraṃ vā nara-pāsa-moyaṇaṃ*
gayassa mattassa vaṇaṃmi rāyaṃ
jahā u cattâvalieṇa tantuṇā
su-dukkaraṃ me paḍihāi moyaṇaṃ

a: thus MSS in T for: *ṇaṃ*; – c: all prints: *vattâ-*

(N 190) That discussion of the monk Gosāla, the brahmin renouncer, the Tridaṇḍin and the elephant ascetic with the venerable Addaka I shall recount just as it happened.

Ti-daṇḍīṇaṃ: at Ṭ II 154 b 4 Śīlâṅka holds the speaker of Sūy 2,6,46 to be an *eka-daṇḍin*; see my note on that stanza.

(N 191) In the village of Vasantapura, Sāmāiya and his wife went forth into homelessness. Seen a-begging she was solicited (by him and therefore brought herself) to refuse food and hang herself.

Vasanta-purae: Ṭ II 137 b 1 *Magadhā-janapade Vasanta-purako grāmaḥ.* modern Basantpur, north of Purnia, Bihar (Jain 1984: 428).

Ohāsiya: Sa. **avabhāṣita* (Bollée 1994, s.v.).

Bhatta vehāsaṃ: Ṭ II 137 b 7 *bhakta-pratyākhyāna-pūrvakam ātmôdbandhanam akāri*. Mahāvīra disapproved of violent deaths, but made an exception for hanging in extreme circumstances (Settar 1990: 16 and 22 where our reference, and its combination with terminal fasting, is not dealt with, however).

(N 192) Panic-stricken (and) subject to illusion (he renounced) food,
(died and) was reborn in heaven. After ending that course he was reborn as Addaya, the son of Adda, in Addapura.

Māī: *ācāryasyânivedyâivâsau māyāvī* (Ṭ II 137 b 9). After this stanza Śīlâṅka's word commentary is silent till N 200. From N 195–199 the *nijjutti*'s character as a teacher's aid of memory in a religion class becomes particularly clear. My rendering tries to mirror this style, but more than once cannot but be tentative.

(N 193) Affection between the two. Messenger. He put a question to Abhaya. In the idea that there might be a sudden comprehensive intuition (for Abhaya) a statue secretly travelled with this very (messenger).

Rahaṃsi: iyara-divase Abhayassa ḍhukko. Abhaya-kumāra-sattaṃ pāhuḍaṃ uvaṇei bhaṇio ya, jahā Adda-kumāro añjaliṃ karei, teṇa pāhuḍaṃ paḍiṭṭhiyaṃ dūo ya sakkārio. Abhayo vi pariṇāmiyāe buddhīe pariṇāmeūṇa so bhava-siddhīo jo mae saddhiṃ pīiṃ karei. Evaṃ saṃkappeūṇa paḍimā kārijjai. Taṃ mañjūsāe choḍhuṃ acchai. So dūo annayâvi āpucchai. Teṇa tassa mañjūsāe (paḍimā) appiyā bhaṇio ya eso, jahā kumāro bhaṇṇai eyaṃ mañjūsaṃ rahasse ugghāḍejjāsi, mā mahā-yaṇa-majjhe, jahā na koi pecchei (Cū 415,7 sqq.).

As Ṭ II passes over these details of the statue story, he already may have read and not understood *rahaṃmi*. In this word the metre requires a long second syllable.

(N 194) At (its) sight he did receive a revelation and though guarded he made off riding horses. Renouncing the world though held back, he did not rule. Who else (would)?

> *Āsāṇa vāhaṇa: aśva-vāhanikayā vinirgataḥ* (Ṭ II 138a 14). Cf. N 197 *suyāṇa pucchaṇa*.

(N 195) Disregarding (a deity's warning) he fled the world, but remained under a layman's vow. (Then) he was sought in marriage by a young woman. Streams of golden gifts. Telling the king and queen.

(N 196) It was he whom her father brought her. Question and story about the way of choosing. You must recognize him by a disk on his feet/the shape of his feet. His arrival. Story. His renouncing wordly life.

(N 197) Near the man with the layman's vow she was constantly surrounded by others. The answer. Enjoyments. A children's questioṇ. The tying up by his son and his leaving into homelessness when (the twelve years' period) had come to an end.

(N 198) At his return to Rāyagiha (his former guardians had become) dacoits out of fear of the king. Their story and renunciation. The dispute with a Gosāla and a Buddhist monk, a brahmin, a Tri-daṇḍin and an ascetic.

(N 199) After being besieged in a religious dispute all of Ārdraka's companions sought spiritual refuge with Mahāvīra and left worldly existence.

(N 200) It is not difficult to free himself from the fetters of men for a mad elephant in the jungle, Oh king, but how to free myself from a thread turned around me as on a spindle seemed very difficult to me.

> *Jahā: etat tu me pratibhāti duṣkaraṃ yac catatrâvalitena (!) tantunā baddhasya mama pratimocanam* (Ṭ II 139 a 14). The very rare word *catta*, Sa. *cāttra* probably designates the skewer in D. Schlingloff's exemplary description of cotton manufacture in India.
>
> (Schlingloff 1974: 86)

According to Śīlâṅka, in Vasantapuraka, a place in Magadha, there lived a layman named Sāmāyika who after hearing a sermon of his teacher Dharmaghoṣa[13] renounced the world as did his wife. Once he happened to see her on his almsround and wanted her. She, however, refused and, realizing that he would pursue her in his passion, stopped taking food and eventually hanged herself. Disconcerted he, too, without telling his *ācārya* stopped eating, died and reached heaven like she had before him. Then he was reborn as Ārdraka, son of Ārdraka, in Ārdrapura,[14] whereas she obtained rebirth as a Sheth's daughter in Vasantapura.[15]

One day Ārdraka betakes himself with an older attendant (*mahattama*)[16] to King Śreṇika in order to present him as his father's *paramamitra* with valuable gifts. When Ārdraka hears that Śreṇika has a worthy (*yogya*) son, he begs his attendant to offer this Prince Abhaya, that is Ārdraka Jr, presents of himself. This is done the day after the *durbar* in the royal palace. Abhaya kindly accepts the homage (?).[17] When Ārdraka is back home, return presents from the King arrive and from Abhaya a representation of the first Tīrthaṇkara, the sight of which reminds Ārdraka of his previous existences, inter alia, one as a deity. Not satisfied even by heavenly enjoyments, earthly ones interest him even less. His father was worried and therefore had him guarded by 500 Rājputs. Nevertheless, riding on horse-back (? *aśva-vāhanikā*)[18] he manages to flee and subsequently renounce the world though a deity tries to prevent him and warn him of a danger.

When he reached Vasantapura and is exercising *kāyôtsarga* under the eleventh layman's vow[19] he is seen by the Sheth's daughter who wants to marry him. Then the deity rains six and a half *koṭi* of gold for the girl and prevents[20] the king from seizing it only by letting arise snakes, etc. When wooed later she wants to be given only to that man in connection with whom there had been a gold rain and whom she will know by a foot mark (*pāda-gatâbhijñāna*). This happens to be when Ārdraka, who had continued wandering, returns after twelve years, is recognized and, pursued by the woman, remembers the deity's warning, yet breaks his vow by an act of fate[21] and becomes entangled with her. After the birth of a son Ārdraka wants to go his way again while the woman begins to earn a living for herself and her son by spinning cotton (*karpāsa-kartana*). The son wraps his father up in twelve threads in order to persuade him to stay with his mother which the man then does for many years. Subsequently, Ārdraka goes to Rājagṛha. Yet on his way he falls in with the 500 Rājputs who after Ārdraka's flight had not dared return to the king and subsisted on dacoity in a jungle stronghold. Ārdraka instructs them and they become monks. On their entering the capital Gośālaka, the elephant ascetics and brahmins[22] are defeated in a dispute which establishes the connection with the theme of the canonical text below. When Ārdraka betakes himself to the king, an elephant tied up *vāri-chūḍhao* sees him and wants to be freed by Ārdraka's *teya-pabhāva*, but is destroyed (*naṭṭho*, Cū ibid.). Ārdraka then speaks N 200 where, however, the mad jungle elephant does not fit the Cū story. In Ṭ, Ārdraka tells this episode to the king who asks him *kathaṃ tvad-darśanato hastī nirgalaḥ saṃvṛtta iti* and the reply is *mahān Bhagavataḥ prabhāvaḥ* (Ṭ; II 139a 13), which also diverges from N 200.

Then follows the main text of verses in *triṣṭubh*s. In this metre the fifth syllable is in priciple *anceps*, but in the Indian editions used here it is most times long,[23] a fact I have not indicated just as I have left out the *ta-śruti* or substituted it by *y*.

The first two stanzas of the canon text are spoken by Gośālaka.

2,6,1
purā-kaḍaṃ, Adda, imaṃ suṇeha:
eg'-anta-yārī samaṇe pur'āsī
se bhikkhuṇo uvanettā aṇ-ege
āikkhai 'ṇhiṃ puḍho vitthareṇaṃ

a: thus J; TV: *suṇeha-m-*; - d: T: *āikkhatiṇhiṃ*, V: *āikkhaeṇhiṃ*, J: *āikkhateṇhaṃ*

HEAR, ADDA, WHAT HE [MAHĀVĪRA] DID LONG AGO:
AT FIRST HE WAS A SOLITARY MONK, THEN HE INITIATED
MANY MONKS AND NOW HE TEACHES THE *DHAMMA* TO
EACH OF THEM.

Purā-kaḍaṃ: sarvair api Tīrthakaraiḥ kṛtaṃ pure-kaḍam (Cū 417,6), *pūrvaṃ yad anena bhavat-tīrthakṛtā kṛtaṃ* (Ṭ II 139 b 8 sq.).

Suṇeha: see Pi § 503 *in fine*. In Sanskrit, the use of the indicative *pro imperativo* is restricted to the first person (Speijer 1886: 276).

Eg'-anta-yārī: the Ṭīkā tradition uniformly reads *meganta*°. As an enjambment of the a-*pāda* is out of the question and *(m)e* does not fit in the b-*pāda* nor does Śīlâṅka comment on it, we may assume a scribal error analogous with the many cases in Dasav and Utt where *suṇeha me* occurs, especially at the beginning of a lecture, like at Utt 1,1 = Dasav 8,1 *āṇupuvviṃ suṇeha me*; Utt 20,38 where *suṇehi me* is to be read instead of Charpentier's *muṇehi*, or Utt 35,1 *suṇeha me egamaṇā* (thus read m.c.). – This stanza portrays the Jain monk's full responsibility for his destiny and control of his life, his original isolation and independence, which mirror the state of the soul as conceived by Jainism (Dundas 2002: 42 with parallels), but is also the old Buddhist ideal (Suttanipāta 35 sqq.).

Aṇ-ege: acc. masc. pl., as in Pāli. This form should be added in Pi § 435.
Āikkhai: also at Sūy 2,1,30 (cf. Pāli *ācikkhati*, BHS *ācikṣati*).

2,6,2
sā 'jīviyā paṭṭhaviyā 'thireṇaṃ
sabhā-gao gaṇao bhikkhu-majjhe
āikkhamāṇo bahu-janna-m-atthaṃ
na saṃdhayāi avareṇā puvvaṃ

d: TVJ: *saṃdhayāī*

THIS IS THE WAY OF LIFE ADOPTED BY AN INCONSTANT
MAN: BY GOING AMONG (OTHER) MONKS FROM HIS GAṆA
INTO AN ASSEMBLY AND TEACHING MASS SALVATION
HE BEHAVES DIFFERENTLY FROM THE PAST.

Ājīviyā: the use of this word by the Ājīvika Gosāla can hardly be by chance. According to Śīlâṅka, Gosāla here accuses the Jains of hypocrisy respectively renunciation of principles: 'Thinking "ordinary people do not respect a person living alone" for opportunist reasons he (Mahāvīra) has surrounded himself with many followers.' A saying in Ṭ underpins this reproach.[24]

Sabhā-gao etc.: 'to stand up in a crowd of men, surrounded by monks, and to teach his doctrines for the benefit of many people' (Jac.) following Ṭ II 140 a 5 *sabhāyāṃ gataḥ – sa-deva-manuja-parṣadi vyavasthitaḥ* this being also possible. Here as in Vinaya I 5,12 we can still see traces of the Vedic reluctance (Āraṇyakas) to divulgate secret knowledge. – *Gaṇao: gaṇaśo bahuśo 'n-ekaśaḥ* (Ṭ *loc. cit.*), which *gaṇatas* can hardly mean. Or is *gaṇa(t)o* a copyist's error for *gaṇaso* ? This remains unclear; it was left out in Jac.'s rendering.

Bahu-janna-°: Pā. bahujañña for which PED refers to *bāhu-°* (in one idiomatic expression only). – Cū 418,2 *janāya hitaṃ janyaṃ bahu-janāya bahu-janyaṃ taṃ cârthaṃ kathayati*, Ṭ II 140 a 6 *bahu-janebhyo hitaḥ artho bahu-janyo 'rthas*. – Because of this adjective *atthaṃ* in my opinion is the object of *āikkhamāṇo* and not a postposition, as Jac. seems to think; but cf. stanza 4.

Saṃdhayāi: metrically conditioned form for which Cū 418,3 reads *saṃdhāyati*, Ṭ II 140 a 7 *saṃdhatte*. For *-āva-* > *-ā-* see Pi § 165.

2,6,3
eg'-anta-m-eva-m-aduvā vi iṇhiṃ,
do v' anna-m-annaṃ na samei jamhā
puvviṃ ca iṇhiṃ ca aṇ-āgayaṃ vā
eg'-anta-m-eva paḍisaṃdhayāi

a: VT and Basham 1951: 53 n. 3: *evaṃ aduvā*; J: *eva aduvā*; – read: *viy'* ? – V: *eṇhiṃ*; – b: J: *samenti*; – d: VT and Basham l.c.: *evaṃ paḍi°*

(HE SHOULD LIVE) EITHER IN SOLITUDE OR (AS HE DOES) NOW, BECAUSE THESE TWO (MODES) EXCLUDE EACH OTHER.

(Adda speaks:)

HE COMBINES THE PAST WITH THE PRESENT AND THE FUTURE (BY LIVING) ALONE.

c = Utt 12,32 a (with *ca* instead of *vā* and the variant *puvviṃ ca pacchā ca tah'eva majjhe*)

Eg'-anta: yadi ekanta-cāritvaṃ śobhanam, etad evâtyantaṃ kartavyam abhaviṣyat (Cū 418,6, similarly Ṭ). In unpolished dialogue style it is difficult to tell an adjective from a case form with no ending.[25]

Vi: for *viy'* ? Unclear comments. Cū *l.c.* continues: *uta manyase idaṃ mahā-parivāra-vṛttaṃ sādhu(ṃ) tad idam ādāv evâcaraṇīyam āsīt.*

Puvviṃ: according to Pi § 103 not corresponding to Sa. *pūrvam* (though the text of Sūy 1,3,4,4 reads *puvvaṃ*), but to Sa. **pūrvīm* like *saddhiṃ* equals Ved. *sadhrīm*. However, cf. BHS *pūrvi* m.c. for *pūrve* as an adjective.

2,6,4

samecca logaṃ tasa-thāvarāṇaṃ
khemaṃ-kare samaṇe māhaṇe vā
āikkhamāṇo vi sahassa-majjhe
eg'-antayaṃ sārayaī tahacce

a: thus J and Pi § 591 for CTV: *samicca*

A ŚRAMAṆA OR BRAHMIN WHO UNDERSTANDS THE LIVING BEINGS – THE MOVING AND NON-MOVING ONES – ONE WHO MAKES (HIS FELLOW BEINGS) FEEL AT PEACE AND SECURE – TRULY SHOWS HIMSELF TO BE A MONK EVEN WHEN TEACHING AMIDST (A) THOUSAND(S).

Khemaṃ-kare: at Sūy 2,1,13 used of the *rāja* (Bollée 1977: 135).

Tahacce: other occurrences of this word, which is not found in PSM and APSŚK, seem restricted to Sūy 1,13,7 and 1,15,18. In the latter instance and in our place here Jac. rendered it by '(remaining in the same) mental disposition (as before)', presumably following the commentaries. Cū 419,5 and Ṭ II 141 a 7 sq. explain it by *tathârca* equalling *arcā* (which in Sa. means 'worship' or 'idol' [MW]) with *leśyā* 'mental disposition' or *śarīra* and thus revealing their ignorance. *Tahacca* corresponds in meaning to Pā. *tathatta* and to BHS *tathātva*. The apparent development of -cc- < -tv- which Pischel (§§ S 281 and 299) and Roth (1983: 157) assumed was repeatedly shown improbable by Norman (1990 CP I: 12) not only for absolutives but also for *caccara*. In the case of *tahacca* I think we have to do with a contamination of **tahatta* and *sacca*.

2,6,5
dhammaṃ kahantassa u n'atthi doso
khantassa dantassa jiy'-indiyassa
bhāsāĕ dose ya vivajjagassa
guṇe ya bhāsāya nisevagassa

a: CJ: *kahentassa*; – b: J: *jitêndassa*; – c: VTJ: *bhāsāya*

IT IS NO OFFENCE, WHEN A QUIET AND RESTRAINED
MAN WHO IS IN CONTROL OF HIS SENSES AND DOES NOT
USE SPEECH FOR NEGATIVE PURPOSES, BUT RATHER EMPLOYS
IT POSITIVELY, PROFESSES HIS *DHARMA*.

b = ĀyārN 231 a; – c: cf. Dasav 7,56 ab
U: = Sa. *tu* in the sense of *api* according to Śīlâṅka.

2,6,6
maha-vvae pañca aṇuvvae ya
tah'eva pañcâsava saṃvare ya
vira(y)iṃ iha-ssāmaṇiyaṃmi panne
lavâvasakkī "samaṇe" ti bemi

c: V: *puṇṇe* (following Śīlâṅka's cty. *pūrṇe*)

WHO KNOWS THE FIVE MAJOR AND THE FIVE MINOR
VOWS AS WELL AS THE FIVE INFLUXES AND THE WAYS
TO WARD THEM OFF; WHO KNOWS THE OBSERVANCES A
MONK IN THIS WORLD SHOULD KEEP; WHO PUSHES OFF
(KARMIC) ATOMS, – HE IS A TRUE MONK. THUS I SAY.

d: cf. 20 d

Pañcâsava: I follow Śīlâṅka (*āśravān*, Ṭ II 141 b 7) and Jacobi (Cū is unclear) taking °*āsava* as an acc. pl. m. -*ā* with m.c. shortened ending,[26] as otherwise the second *ya* has no function.

Panne: Ṭ has this reading also in his text, but Śīlâṅka must have read *puṇṇe* in his exemplar, for he sankritizes *pūrṇe* – *kṛtsne saṃyame vidhātavye*, but mentions *prājña* as a *pāṭha*. Jacobi translates 'blessed (life of Śramaṇas)' which would correspond to *puṇye* in Sa.; as to this he gives no explanation. In this way the sentence made up of the *pāda*s a-c lacks a verb, which Śīlâṅka supplies with *prajñāpitavān* and *pratipāditavān*, respectively, and Jacobi by 'he teaches.' Perhaps the commentator objected to *panne*, because *prājña* resp. *prajña* (thus Cū 419,11) seems to be used only absolutely ('wise') resp. ifc. in Sa. and Pāli, though otherwise in the latter two languages an accusative of the object at deverbative nouns at least is known,[27] if not as frequent as in Vedic.[28] The appearance of the *varia lectio* may have been caused by assimilation in the pronunciation of *a* and *u*.

Lavâvasakkī: see Bollée 1988: 63 note on 1,2,2,20.

2,6,7
sīôdagaṃ sevau bīya-kāyaṃ
āhāya-kammaṃ taha itthiyāo
eg'-anta-cāriss' iha amha dhamme
tavassiṇo nâbhisamei pāvaṃ

d: J: *ṇo 'hisameti*

(Gosāla speaks:)

IN OUR FAITH NO EVIL (KARMAN) ARISES FOR AN ASCETIC
WHO DRINKS UNBOILED WATER, EATS SEEDS (OR)
FOOD PREPARED ESPECIALLY FOR ALMS RECEIVERS, OR
ENJOYS WOMEN, AS LONG AS HE LIVES ALONE IN THIS
WORLD.

Āhāya-kammaṃ: this form proves the new etymology **āghāta-karman* '(food) for which killing has taken place' proposed by R. P. Jain (1983: 65 sqq.). Such food as alms has always been forbidden to Jain and Buddhist monks in so far as the animal was killed especially for them.[29] The strict attitude concerning *ahiṃsā* may have accompanied the conversion of Rājputs in western India in the seventh to eighth century CE,[30] a psychologically understandable phenomenon. Many Jains still consider themselves of Rājput origin.[31]

Eg'-anta.: cf. Basham 1951: 115 'We have here a definite indication of lonely wanderers, not gathered in communities, living according to the ascetic rules laid down by Gosāla.'

Iha-°: after the caesura, but should belong to the preceding part of the *pāda*.

Abhisamei: sambandham upayāti (Ṭ II 142 a 12). In the sense of 'to come up, appear' *abhisamaiti* and *abhisameti* do not occur in Sa. and Pā., respectively.

2,6,8
sīôdagaṃ vā taha bīya-kāyaṃ
āhāya-kammaṃ taha itthiyāo
eyāī jāṇa – paḍisevamāṇā
agāriṇo a-ssamaṇā bhavanti

c: TVJ: *jāṇaṃ*

(Adda speaks:)

(ASCETICS,) WHO USE UNBOILED WATER OR SEEDS,
FOOD ESPECIALLY PREPARED FOR ALMS RECEIVERS OR
WHO ENJOY WOMEN – KNOW THESE THINGS ! – ARE LAYMEN,
NOT MONKS.

Sīôdagaṃ, etc.: with regard to this the Jains originally sided with the Ājīvikas, as Sūy 1,3,4,1 sqq. show.

Jāṇa: Ṭ II 142b 1: *jānīhi*. *jāṇa* is found also in Āyār 1,3,1,1.

2,6,9

biyā ya sīôdaga itthiyāo
paḍisevamāṇā samaṇā bhavanti
agāriṇo vi samaṇā bhavantu;
sevanti ū te vi taha-ppagāraṃ

a: TVJ: *siyā ya bīodaga*; – b: thus J; TV: *bhavantu*; – d: T: *u taṃ 'vi*, V: *ū taṃ pi*, J: *sevanti jaṃ te vi.*

IF (*ya*) THOSE WHO USE SEEDS AND UNBOILED WATER,
AND ENJOY WOMEN ARE MONKS, THEN ALSO LAYMEN
MUST BE MONKS AS THEY, TOO, PRACTISE SUCH A REGIMEN.

Cū has a lacuna here: *pratīka*, comment and stanza number 677 are left out. Śīlâṅka explains: *syād etad bhavadīyaṃ mataṃ yathā: te ekânta-cāriṇaḥ (...) kathaṃ te na tapasvina ity etad āśaṇkyârdraka āha: yadi bījâdy-upabhogino 'pi śramaṇā ity evaṃ bhavatâbhyupagamyate, evaṃ tarhi (...)*. Though *siyā* is typical for Jainism, it seems to me an early copyist's error influenced by the next stanza.

U: *tu-r-avadhāraṇe* (Ṭ II 142 b 6). A restriction, however, does not fit here, rather a reason or a confirmation. *U*, therefore, may stand here for *va* = *eva*.

2,6,10

je yâvi bīôdaga-bhoi bhikkhū
bhikkhaṃ c' ihaṃ jāyai jīviy'-aṭṭhī
te nāi-saṃjoga-m-avi ppahāya
kāyôvagā n' anta-karā bhavanti

a: C: *je yāvi sītôdagam eva* (emended as: *bīodaga bhoti*) *bhikkhū*; – b: C *ca iha*; TVJ *vihaṃ* (Ṭ II 142b 8: *bhikṣāṃ ca*); – d: J: *'ṇantakarā*

BESIDES, MONKS WHO USE SEEDS AND UNBOILED WATER,
AND, SEEKING THEIR SUSTENANCE IN THIS WORLD,
GO FOR ALMSFOOD WILL REINCARNATE (AND) DO NOT
SET AN END (TO *SAṀSĀRA*), EVEN THOUGH GIVING UP THE
CONTACT WITH / SEPARATING THEMSELVES FROM THEIR
RELATIVES.

c = 21 c

Bīôdaga-°: probably read: *sīôdaga-*. (cf. Cū 421,1).

Cū 420,14: *koī ṇamm itthīo pariharati loka-rava-bhīto – bālo vṛddho vā – na dharma-yogyo vā strī-varjam api sītôdaga-bhojī nāma bhikkhū bhikṣāṃ ca iha tāva ke jīvato dhyāna-nimittaṃ jīvit'-aṭṭhatā evaṃ-prakārā. Nātīṇa saṃjogo nāti-saṃjogo pūrvâpara-saṃbandhâdi, api padârthâdiṣu nāti-saṃyogam iti duppajja haṇijjaṃ. Mumukṣavo 'pi santaḥ kāyopakā eva bhavanti, anantaṃ kurvantîty an-anta-karāḥ karmaṇāṃ saṃsārasya bhavasya duḥkhānām evêty arthaḥ.*

Bhikkhaṃ, etc.: cf. Dasav 9,1,6 *jo vā visaṃ khāyai jīviy'-aṭṭhī*, which passage in the same metre Śīlâṅka may have had in mind when reading *vihaṃ* (though *c* and *v* are easily interchanged of course), but he does not comment on it and in fact it makes no sense here. Jacobi, too, passes over this word. I therefore adopted the Cū reading. – Another hint at a possible connection with the above Dasav passage is the sg. *jāyai* required by the metre as against *jayanti*. The short plural forms *-bhoi bhikkhū* may have contributed to *jāyai*.

Kāyôvagā: cf. SN II 24,26 *bālo kāyassa bhedā kāy' ūpago hoti.*

2,6,11

imaṃ vayaṃ tu tumã pāu-kuvvaṃ
pāvāiṇo garihasi savva(m) eva
pāvāiṇo u puḍho kiṭṭayantā
sayaṃ sayaṃ diṭṭhĩ karenti pāu

a: C: thus corrected for originally: *evaṃ vāī tumaṃ*; – b: J: *garahasi*; TVJ: *savva*; – c: V: *pāvāiṇo puḍhŏ puḍhŏ kiṭṭ°*; – d: V: *karonti*; – J: *pāuṃ*

(Gosāla speaks:)

BUT IF YOU ADVANCE SUCH AN OPINION, YOU CATEGORICALLY REPROACH ALL WHO PROFESS A RELIGIOUS LIFE.

(Adda speaks:)

EVERY SINGLE PERSON, HOWEVER, WHO PROFESSES A RELIGIOUS LIFE, PRAISES HIS OWN PERSUASION AND MAKES IT PUBLICLY KNOWN.

Vayaṃ: vāī corrected as *vayaṃ* (Cū 421,4) resp. *vācaṃ* (Ṭ II 143 a 6). For this reading there are therefore two, for the interpretation several possibilities all supposing not very satisfactory presumptions, e.g. *vaiṃ* requires an unfound Old Indian etymon **vācī*, the *-ā-* of which became *-a-* in a pretonic position (Pi § 413).[32] Furthermore, for Pā. *vacī* PED only gives Sn 472 and for the rest takes this form to be a compound form of *vaco*. *Vayaṃ* could also be an accusative and equal Sa. *vacas*, also in Pā. (Geiger/ Norman 1994: § 99), yet apparently in both middle Indo-Aryan canonical languages only the instr. of this word occurs, in Pā. also *vaco* ~ Amg. *vao*. Finally, the Amg. equivalent of Sa. *vrata* could be considered which, however, semantically does not fit here very well.

Pāu-kuvvaṃ: in the canonical seniors *pāu-karai* is restricted to Sūy and Utt and has for objects *dhammaṃ* (Sūy 1,2,2,7 and 1,12,19), *viṇayaṃ* (Utt 1,1) and *āyāraṃ* (Utt 11,1). Old Pāli (e.g. Sn 316 with *dhammaṃ*) is no help to our problem either and the same holds true for *imaṃ*, which is acc. sg. mfn. (Pi § 430).

Pāvāiṇo: 'philosophers' (Jac.); *pravadana-śīlā prāvādukāḥ* (Cū 421,7), similarly Śīlâṅka. This word, as well as semantically in fact also the four preceding stanzas, must probably be connected with Āyār 1,4,2 and 3, esp. 1,4,2,6, where *pāvāuyā* are addressed, and with 1,4,3,2* *pāvāiyā* and Sūy 2,2,80 *pāvāuyā*. Schubring renders the Āyār references by 'Widerredner' and gives as their etymon JHS *prāvādika* and *prāvāduka* resp.; cf. Pā. *pǎvadati* 'to dispute'(PED). Sa. *pravādin* has a short first syllable and a slightly different meaning.

Puḍho: cf. 1,1,3,13 cd *puḍho pāvāuyā savve akkhāyāro sayaṃ sayaṃ*.

2,6,12

te anna-m-annassa u garahamāṇā,
akkhanti bho ! samaṇā māhaṇā ya
sao ya atthi a-sao ya n'atthi
garahāmŏ diṭṭhiṃ, na garahāmŏ kiṃci

a: C: thus corrected for originally: *aṇṇamaṇṇassa tu te*; – J: °*assa vi gara*°; – b: J: *akkhanti u sam*°

ŚRAMAṆAS AND BRĀHMAṆAS, SIR, CRITICIZE EACH
OTHER: THE OWN SIDE IS (RIGHT), THE OPPONENT (WRONG).
WE ONLY CENSURE A WRONG VIEW, (BUT OTHERWISE)
WE DO NOT CENSURE ANYTHING.

Akkhanti: ākhyānti (Cū 421,11), *ācakṣate* (Ṭ II 143 a 12). Formally, Jinadāsa is right (cf. Pi § 492), semantically there is no difference here.

Sao etc.: '(The truth, they say,) is all on their side [. . .]' (Jac.). *Svam ātmīya-vacanam ity arthaḥ, tasmāt sutaṃ śreyo 'sti nirvāṇam ity arthaḥ* (Cū 421,11 sq.), *svata iti svakīye pakṣe svâbhyupagame 'sti puṇyaṃ tat-kāryaṃ ca svargâpavargâdikam asti* (Ṭ II 143 a 14 sq.). I have not found any parallels. Formally *sao* can equal Sa. *satas* as well, as is shown by 1,13,1 c (also *triṣṭubh*-metre): *sao ya dhammaṃ a-sao a-sīlaṃ santiṃ a-santiṃ karissāmi pāum*. – In Pā. the gen. sg. *sato* is not found apparently (PED, Geiger).

Garahāmŏ etc.: 'But we blame only the wrong doctrines and not at all (those who entertain them)' (Jac.)

Diṭṭhiṃ: at Cū 421,14 referable particularly to the Buddhists, as to which Jinadāsa may rather have had his own times in view than the past of the text. In the d *pāda* either the object must be supplied which is hard here or one must render the second *garahāmo* by 'to call names' and take *kiṃci* as a predicative attribute of the object (which, however, is missing then also) as apparently the commentators do: *tān nanu kiṃca garahāmo?* Jinadāsa asks and replies on Adda's behalf: *na, yathā tvaṃ, pāpa-dṛṣṭiḥ mithyā-dṛṣṭiḥ mūḍho mūrkhaḥ a-jānako vêti* (Cū 421,14) and similarly Śīlâṅka: *na kaṃcid (!)*[33] *garhāmaḥ kāṇa-kuṇṭhôdghaṭṭanâdi-prakāreṇa*[34] – Controversies abounding in invectives during religious disputes occurred not only long ago. Thus von Glasenapp

(1928: 14) wrote about Dayânand Sarasvatī, who originally was a follower of Śaṅkara and later founded the Ārya-samāj: "*Mit seiner gewaltigen Stimme suchte er bei seinen endlosen Redekämpfen die Gegner niederzuschreien und sparte auch nicht mit Schimpfworten, wenn es galt, sich ihrer zu erwehren.*"[35]

2,6,13
na kiṃci rūveṇ' abhidhārayāmo
sa-diṭṭhi-maggaṃ tu karemu pāuṃ
magge ime kiṭṭiĕ āriehiṃ
aṇ-uttare sap-purisehĩ añjū

b: J: *saṃ diṭṭhimaggaṃ tu karemo*

BY NO MEANS DO WE CRITICIZE (A PERSON'S) PRIVATE QUALITIES, BUT WE (ONLY) PROCLAIM OUR OWN RELIGIOUS WAY. THIS WAY, THE UNEXCELLED (AND) STRAIGHT ONE, HAS BEEN RECOMMENDED BY NOBLE MEN, BY GOOD PEOPLE.

Na kiṃci etc.: 'We do not detract from anybody because of his personal qualities' (Jac.). Śīlâṅka explains the opening words by *na kañcana śramaṇaṃ brāhmaṇaṃ vā* (Ṭ II 143 b 10 sq.), cf. note on prec. stanza.

Rūveṇa: according to Cū 422,1 apparently a physical quality by which one reviles a person is meant, 'as when someone says to another who makes a mistake: One-eye ! Humpback ! Leper !'[36] or reviles him as to his origin: 'He is doing the work of a Caṇḍāla.'[37] In the same way (one should not say): 'Bloody Tridaṇḍin, damned sophist![38] What you preach here is wrong. What does the stupid Kapila think how the soul does act ?' etc.[39] Further, the Buddhists, too, are being abused[40] and their doctrine of the *skandha*s attacked. At Ṭ II 143 b 11 the gloss on *rūveṇa* is restricted to insult because of bodily parts provoking abhorrence, or caste or the (ab)use of caste marks.[41]

Abhidhārayāmo: vācam bemi (Cū 422,7), *garhaṇâbuddhyôdghaṭṭayāmaḥ* (Ṭ II 143 b 11 sq.). The verb, which has a counterpart in Pāli and BHS, there means 'to uphold, maintain' (CPD) resp. 'to support; assist' (BHSD), in Sa. also 'to resist' (MW).[42] In our passage, however, it can hardly be anything but equivalent to *garahai*, cf. Ved. *abhibharati* 'to lay or throw upon (as a fault or blame)' (MW); for the semantic development cf. *jugupsati* as a desiderative of *GUP*.

Magge etc.: 'I have been told the supreme, right path by worthy, good men' (Jac.).

Ime: nom. m. sg. (Pi § 430).

Āriyehiṃ: sarva-jñais tyājya-dharma-dūra-vartibhiḥ (Ṭ II 144 a 3). According to Leumann (1921: 40) "das Beiwort *edel* fehlt bei Mahāvīra and others – im Gegensatz zum Buddha," but Śīlâṅka apparently does relate it to Arhats and the same is the case, I would say, with Āyār 1,2,2,3 *esa magge āriyehiṃ paveie*. At SN III 4,15 *ariyā* are equalled to *sap-purisā*.

Aṇuttare: cf. DN II 246,6* *esa maggo ujū*[43] *maggo esa maggo an-uttaro.*

2,6,14
uḍḍhaṃ ahe yaṃ tiriyaṃ disāsu
tasā ya je thāvara je ya pāṇā
bhūyâbhisaṅkāĕ duguñchamāṇo
no garahaī vusimaṃ kiṃci loe

a: J: *ahe ya*; – c: T: *bhūyâhisaṃkābhi*, V: *bhayâhisaṃkābhi*; TVJ: *duguñchamāṇā*

A (PERSON) LEADING A MONK'S LIFE AND DREADING
TO HARM (OTHER) BEINGS – BEINGS THAT MOVE BEYOND,
UNDER AND HORIZONTALLY IN THE DIRECTIONS
AND SUCH AS DO NOT DO THAT – BY NO MEANS CRITICIZES
ANYTHING IN THE WORLD.

a: cf. PiṇḍaN 363; – c = 1,14,20 a

Bhūyâbhisaṅkāe: saṅkâlaye aṇṇāṇe ca (Cū 423,2), *bhūtaṃ – sadbhūtaṃ tathyaṃ tatrâbhiśaṅkayā* (Ṭ II 144 a 8 sq.) which Śīlâṅka follows up by the right explanation.

Vusimaṃ: 'well-controlled' (Jac.), 'sage' (Caillat 1991: 86 and 88). Mme Caillat suggests '*vusimaṃ* could have been an old equivalent of *tīrthakṛt*, a "fordmaker", or a "sage", with PSM connecting the word with Sa. *bṛsī* 'a pad, (esp.) the seat of an ascetic' + *-ma(nt)-*. Thus the image would be that the monk use his seat as a raft to cross *saṃsāra*. Rafts for crossing rivers have of course been employed from time immemorial.[44]

Kiṃci loe: savva-loe tti trailokye pāsaṇḍa-loke vā (Cū 423,3). Mme Caillat (1991: 88) reads *kiṃci*, but translates "the *v(usimaṃ)* does not blame (anybody) in the world" perhaps thinking of *kaṃci* in 2,6,12.

(Gosāla speaks:)

2,6,15
āgantagâgārĕ ārām'-ăgāre
samaṇe u bhīe na uvei vāsaṃ
dakkhā hu santi bahave maṇussā
ūṇâirittā ya lavālavā ya

a: C: *āgantāre*, TV: *āgantagāre*, J: *āgantāgāre*; – c: J: *maṇūsā*

IN A HOSTEL OR HOSPICE IN A GARDEN, HOWEVER,
YOUR SOLICITOUS MONK WON'T STAY, FOR THERE ARE
MANY CLEVER PEOPLE (THERE), SOME OF WHOM ARE
TOO LITTLE COMMUNICATIVE, OTHERS TOO VOLUBLE.

Āganta° etc.: the metrically wrong traditions may have been brought in from Āyār 1,8,2,3 *āgantāre ārāmâgāre.*[45] Cū yields little here, but Śīlâṅka's comment runs *āgantukānāṃ – kārpaṭikâdīnām agāram āgantâgāraṃ* (Ṭ II 144 b 6 sq.). My conjecture restores the metre, and the compound has a counterpart in Pā. *āgantukâgāra* (SN IV 219,9 and V 51,24).

Uvei vāsaṃ: vāsam upaiti (Ṭ II 144 b 8). The idiom once occurs in Pāli: *tattha yo samaṇo vā brāhmaṇo vā vāsaṃ upeti* (SN IV 348,19), but of Buddhist monks apparently *vāsaṃ upagacchati* was used (see PTC). Ṭ obviously read *tattha* before *na*. Cf. note on vs. 16 infra.

Dakkhā: nipunāḥ prabhūta-śāstra-viśāradāḥ (Ṭ II 144 b 9); strikingly, the Śākyas are not mentioned in first instance here.

Ūṇâirittā: 'lower or nobler men' (Jac.). Cū 423, 6 sq. here comments *kiṃcid ūṇeṇa kecid atiriktā jattha ūṇā atiriktā vā, tattha samādhi atthi* (?) and Ṭ II 144 b 11 *"nyūnāḥ" svato 'vamā hīnā jāty-ādy-atiriktā vā; tābhyām parājitasya mahāṃcchāyābhraṃśaḥ.*[46] Against Śīlâṅka's interpretation it can be said that the monk does not belong to this world and as such stands outside the system of upper and lower classes.

Lavālavā: 'talkative or silent men' (Jac.).[47] Our commentators' glosses run *japa-lapa vyaktāyāṃ vāci "lapālapa" iti vīpsā bhṛśaṃ-lapā lapālapā vā, jahā dava-davâdi turitaṃ vā gaccha gaccha vā; uktaṃ hi: "deva-devassa." Athâpi yaṃ evaṃ vaḍa-vaḍâdi kiṃ evaṃ lavalavesi ?* (Cū 423,7 sq.); *lapā – vācālāḥ ghoṣitâneka-tarka-vicitra-daṇḍakāḥ tathā a-lapā – mauna-vratikā niṣṭhita-yogāḥ (!) guḍikâdi-yuktā vā, yad-vaśād abhidheya-viṣayā vāg eva na pravartate* (Ṭ II 144 b 12 sq.). Though the item mentioned last is an interesting piece of information about ascetics with a vow of silence who, if they were not completely bound by it, helped themselves by a pebble or so in their mouth 'so that no word by which contents can be intimated was produced' – a Jain monk would have little to fear from a silent ascetic. I would therefore like to agree with Jinadāsa and take *lavālava* in an intensive sense, in our passage also with metrically required *-ā-*.[48] *Lapalapa* is not found in Sa.- nor is *lapa*, for that matter – but it does occur in Pāli.[49] The meaning of the last line is, I believe, that the monk on the one hand can incur harm at the hands of an interlocutor who expresses himself too briefly and thus may provoke dubiosities, and on the other hand, by being washed away from his own persuasion into heresy by a flux of arguments an adversary might come up with.

2,6,16
mehāviṇo sikkhiya buddhimantā
suttehi atthehi ya nicchaya-nnā
pucchiṃsu mā ṇe aṇ-agāra anne
ii saṅkamāṇo na uvei tattha

b: J: *nicchaya-ṇṇū*; – c: J: *aṇagāra ege*

WITH THE UNEASY IDEA 'SOME RECLUSE OR OTHER (OF THOSE WHO ARE) WISE; HAVE FINISHED THEIR TRAINING;

OBTAINED INSIGHT AND ARE WELL ACQUAINTED WITH YOUR SCRIPTURES AND THEIR MEANING MIGHT ASK ME QUESTIONS' HE DOES NOT GO THERE.

d = 18 d

Sikkhiya: śikṣitā aṇ-egāṇi vyākaraṇa-Sāṃkhya-Viśeṣika-Bauddhâjīvika-Nyāyâdīṇi śāstrāṇi (Cū 423,9), *śikṣāṃ grāhitāḥ śikṣitāḥ* (Ṭ II 145a 1). The final syllable of *sikkhiya*, handed down as short in all editions, is metrically anceps and therefore the *lectio difficilior* here. On this basis the form would have to be taken in an absolute sense though as such remarkable in the present context; cf. *thavara* in 14b, where according to the rules *thavarā* could be expected without prejudice to the metre.

Suttehi etc.: *"sūtre" sūtra-viṣaye viniścaya-jñāḥ tathā artha viṣaye ca niścaya-jñā yathâvasthita-sūtrârtha-vedina ity arthaḥ* (Ṭ II 145a 1f.). For the loc. *-hi* – stated by Pi § 363 to occur only in Apabhraṃśa – see Lüders 1952: § 220 (cf. note on vs. 22). Jacobi renders as '(. . .) men, who are well versed in the sacred texts and their meaning'. Thus the monks of other denominations[50] apparently knew the Jain *sūtras* so well, that Mahāvīra's disciples did not like to enter into a discussion with them (and should not do so, Sūy 1,1,4,2; Āyār 2,3,2,17; Uvās 58 < Schubring 2000: § 163).[51]

Passages like these seem to corroborate Schubring's thesis regarding the grounds for the disappearance of the Puvvas.[52] In the Pāli canon, however, not only the heretical doctrines are somehow discernible (as against the Sūyagaḍa – the remainder of the Puvvas), but even the names of the teachers are mentioned. Furthermore, it may be asked, if only by mere accident Vaddhamāna and Gotama never met.

Pucchiṃsu mā: for the aorist as prohibitive tense cf. Pāli, e.g. MN I 387,22 *mā maṃ etaṃ pucchi.*

Ṇe: in Pi § 431 and Geiger/Norman 1994: § 107 only given as acc.pl. of *(e)ṇa/ena*, but Pi § 415 mentions it also as acc. sg. of the personal pronoun of the first person, though in brackets, which may mean that he had not found the form in the texts.

Na uvei: upagacchati (Ṭ II 145a 3); cf. note ad vs. 15 supra.

(Adda speaks:)

2,6,17
no 'kāma-kiccā na ya bāla-kiccā
rāyâbhiyogeṇa kuo bha(y)eṇaṃ
viyāgarejjā pasiṇaṃ na vâvi
sa-kāma-kicceṇ' iha āriyāṇaṃ

a: thus CT; VJ: *nākāmakiccā*; – c: VT: *viyāgarejja*

HE SHOULD REPLY TO (A) QUESTION(S) OR NOT (AS THE CASE MAY BE), BUT NEITHER DO SO EAGERLY NOR

RASHLY NOR ON THE KING'S ORDERS OR BECAUSE HE IS AFRAID, YET WORTHY PEOPLE'S QUESTIONS HE SHOULD BE PLEASED TO ANSWER.

No 'kāma°: notwithstanding the uniform tradition of *no 'kāma.* in Cū and Ṭ which, however, omit the *avagraha*, a reading *nâkāma°* can be concluded from the commentaries. I have therefore kept *no*, cf. Sūy 1,1,1,16.[53]

Kuo bhayeṇaṃ: '(nor) from fear of anybody', which Jacobi can hardly have meant in the sense of *kuo ci* like the interrogative pronoun that can be used instead of the indefinite one in familiar German.[54]

Viyāgarejjā: at Ṭ II 145a 12ff. several times sanskritized as *vyāgṛṇīyāḍ*

Pasiṇaṃ: sg. or plur. (see Lüders 1954: 143ff. referred to by Geiger/ Norman 1994: 71, but some reject an acc. plur. masc. *-aṃ*).

Na vâvi: Ṭ II 145a 13: *na ca – nâiva*.

Sa-kāma-kicceṇa: sanskritized *sva-kāma-kṛtyena* (Ṭ II 145b 1), but as a pendant of *a-kāma-°* in the a-*pāda* I would prefer *sa-°*.

Āriyāṇaṃ: āryāṇāṃ sarva-heya-dharma-dūra-vartināṃ tad-upakārāya dharma-deśanāṃ vyāgṛṇīyād asau (Ṭ II 145b 2f.). This and the next stanza show that *ā*. means: fellow believers. Thereby, however, Adda recognizes Gosāla's reproach as correct.

2,6,18

gantā ca tattha aduvā a-gantā
viyāgarejjā samiy' āsu-panne
aṇ-āriyā daṃsaṇao parittā
ii saṅkamāṇo na uvei tattha

a: VJ: *tatthā*

WHETHER HE GOES THERE OR NOT, QUICK-WITTED HE WILL GIVE CORRECT ANSWERS/EXPLANATIONS. FEARING LEST THEY BE HERETICS BECAUSE THEY HAVE TURNED AWAY FROM THE (RIGHT) BELIEF HE DOES NOT GO TO THEM.

d = 16 d

Gantā: taken by Śīlâṅka (Ṭ II 145b 4) and Jacobi to pertain to the monk's pupils (*vineya*), who in my opinion are not meant here, at any rate not by Gosāla.

Samiy': 'impartially' (Jac.), *samatayā – sama-dṛṣṭitayā* (Ṭ II 145b 6). The latter sanskritization is impossible; formally and semantically, however, *samyak* and *samakam* would do.[55] Cf. Sūy 1,2,2,6 *samiyā dhammaṃ udāhare muṇī*; Āyār 1,7,8,14 *samiyā āhare muṇī* and Sūy 1,2,2,8 *pāṇā (. . .) samayaṃ samīhiyā* with *samiyaṃ uvehāe* as a Cū variant and *samayaṃ tatth' uvehāe* in Āyār 1,3,3,1.

Āsu-panne: 'the wise man' (Jac.), *sarva-jña* (Ṭ II 145b 6). With the exception of Āyār 1,7,1,3 (prose) I have only found references of this compound in *triṣṭubh* metre.[56] It seems to be absent in Pāli and Sa.

Parittā: 'men have fallen (from...)' (Jac.), *pari – samantād itāḥ – gatāḥ prabhraṣṭāḥ* (Ṭ II 145b 8). *Paritta* may be best taken as a ppp. of *pra* √*RIC* 'leer werden' [pwb] (to become empty), i.e. approximately 'without'. This meaning is not attested in Sa. and Pāli.

2,6,19
paṇṇaṃ jahā vaṇie ūday'-aṭṭhī
āyassa heuṃ pagarei saṅgaṃ
ta(y)-ūvame samaṇe Nāya-putte
icc eva me hoi maī viyakkā

a: VJ: *uday'*; – c: V: *tayovame*; J: *tauvame*; – d: V: *viyakko*

(Gosāla speaks:)

THE *śramaṇa* NĀYAPUTTA ACTS JUST AS A PROFIT-ORIENTED MERCHANT PROCURES GOODS FOR HIS INCOME (AND) THEREBY A KARMIC BOND/DEPENDENCE (FROM OTHERS). THIS IS MY VIEW AND OPINION.

b ≠ 21 d

Right from the start Gosāla's attack was directed against Mahāvīra's alleged inconsequence: the fact that he first lived alone and then decided to go into the public eye surrounded by monks and to proclaim his teaching (vss. 1–2).

Jacobi's rendering of the first line runs: 'As a merchant desirous of gain (shows) his wares and attracts a crowd to do business (. . .)', which involves the assumption of a hard zeugma or a complementary verb to *paṇṇaṃ* as provided by the commentaries.[57] *Prakaroti* means 'vollbringen, ausfuühren, bewirken, veranstalten, machen, anfertigen; s. aneignen, nehmen (*dārān* ein Weib)' (pwb) as far as concerns the meanings possible here. The doctrine, which is not expressed clearly, represents Mahāvīra's true doctrine; the asyndetically connected words *paṇṇaṃ* and *saṅgaṃ* share the notion of binding and form a unity of contrasts – the material and the spiritual – which their chiastic position underlines.

Paṇṇaṃ: glossed by Śīlâṅka inter alia as camphor, aloe, musk and amber.[58]

Ūday'-aṭṭhī: cf. Pā. *uday'-atthika* (AṅguttaraN II 199,20) where the Jain Śākya Vappa complains to the Buddha that he is like a merchant making every effort to sell his goods yet does not realize any profit. As a disciple Mahāvīra's he would believe himself *seyyathâpi (...) puriso uday'-atthiko assa paṇīyaṃ poseyya so udayaṃ c'eva na labheyya*. The commercial simile may be typical of the Jains and testifies to the great age of their professional activity (cf. also vs. 21).

Āyassa heuṃ: cf. *bahu-janna-m-atthaṃ* in vs. 2.

Pagarei saṅgaṃ: "ṣaṃja saṃge" ṣaṃjanaṃ saktir vā saṃgaḥ (Cū 425,7; *pagarei* is not glossed), *mahā-jana-saṅgaṃ vidhatte* (Ṭ II 146a 12). See further infra at vs. 21.

Viyakkā: in Pāli and Sa. only masc.

Nāya-putte: see note on 2,1,13 (Bollée 1977: 139) and on the Nāga tribe see Kosambi 1963: 33.

2,6,20

navaṃ na kujjā, vihuṇe purāṇaṃ
ciccâmaiṃ tāi ya sâha evaṃ:
eyāvayā bambha-vaya tti vuttā
tassôday'-aṭṭhĭ 'samaṇe' tti bemi

b: V: *tāi yam āha*, J: *tāyati sâha*; – c: Cū 426,1: *etāvato*, T: *etovayā*, J: *ettāvayā*; – TVJ: *bambhava(t)i tti*; – J: *vutte*

(Adda speaks:)

HE DOES NOT EFFECT NEW (KARMAN) AND CASTS OFF OLD (KARMAN) BY GIVING UP WRONG VIEWS. THEREFORE (*sa*) THE SAINT SPOKE ACCORDINGLY: IN THIS RESPECT THEY ARE CALLED MEN OF EXCELLENT VOWS. "ONLY HE WHO STRIVES AT THIS GAIN IS A MONK." THUS I SAY.

Navaṃ etc.: here Cū 425,12f. quotes DasavN 383 (...) *nāṇī navaṃ na bandhai.*[59]

Vihuṇe: vidhūnayati – apanayati (Ṭ II 146b 3).

Tā(y)i: apparently connected by Jinadāsa with √ *TṚ*: *tīrṇo vi parān tāretîti* (Cū 425,11f.). Śīlâṅka, however, glosses *trāyī – Bhagavān sarvasya paritrāṇa-śīlo (. . .) tāyī vā mokṣaṃ prati; aya-vaya-maya-paya-caya-t a y a-naya gatāv ity asya rūpaṃ.*[60] Jacobi ('who protects others') follows the latter and renders *tāyi* by 'saviour', but Schubring first started from *tyāginaḥ* (Schubring 1926: 133 note 7; 2004: 2b 1f.), and later (Dasaveyālia, Isibhāsiyāiṃ) changed his mind in favour of *trāyin* (see Alsdorf 1965: 5). The etymological identity of *tāi(ṇ)*, Pāli *tādin* and Sa. *tādṛś* can be proved by Utt 23,10 *guṇavantāṇa tāiṇaṃ* and Petavatthu *guṇavantesu tādīsu*. See further Roth 1968: 46ff.

Sa eva – Bhagavān eva – āha, yathā vimati-parityāgena mokṣa-gamana – śīlo bhavati (Ṭ II 146b 5ff.).

Eyāvayā etc.: 'Herein is contained the vow (leading to) Brahman (i.e. Mokṣa)' (Jac.). *Etāvato* (Cū 426,1), *etāvatā saṃdarbheṇa* (Ṭ II 146b 6).

Bambha-vaya: brahmaṇaḥ padaṃ brahma-padaṃ vā brahma-vrataṃ vā (Cū 426,1), *brahmaṇo – mokṣasya vrataṃ brahma-vrataṃ* (Ṭ, l.c.). Though the first explanation can also be defended – *brahma-pada* occurs in Sa. 'Brahmas Stätte' (PWB), here perhaps in the sense of 'excellent way'.[61] *Pada* is used in Pāli as a synonym of *patha* (PED, s.v.) – I consider the second one more probable. The word occurs also with *-vv-*, e.g. MahānisīhaBh 1794. – Cf. also Āyār 2,16,2 *aṇ-anta-samaya*, for which see Bollée 1990: 32.

Tassa etc.: 'this is the gain which a Śramaṇa is desirous of. Thus I say' (Jac.).

2,6,21
[sam]ārabhãte vaṇiyā bhūya-gāmaṃ
pariggahaṃ c'eva mamāyamāṇā
te nāi-saṃjoga-m-avi ppahāya
āyassa heuṃ pagaranti saṅgaṃ

a: C: *samārabhante hi vaṇiyā*; – b: J: *mamāyamīṇā*; – d: J: *pakarenti*

MERCHANTS KILL MANY LIVING BEINGS AND EVEN
THOUGH GIVING UP THE CONTACT WITH / SEPARATING
THEMSELVES FROM THEIR RELATIVES THEY ACQUIRE PROPERTY;
(IN DOING SO) THEY TAKE UP A (KARMATIC) BOND
MERELY FOR THE SAKE OF MATERIAL GAIN.

b: cf. Āyār 1,2,5,3 where between *pariggahaṃ* and *a-mamāyamāṇe* the metre requires a short syllable like *tu* or *ca*; – c = 10 c; – d ≠ 19 b

Ārabhãte, etc.: Jacobi takes this form as a sg. and renders 'a merchant kills (. . .)'. On account of their business activities with many waggons, draught-animals and camels merchants kill living beings.[62]

Pariggahaṃ: du-padaṃ[63] *caup-padaṃ dhanaṃ dhaṇṇa-hiraṇṇa-suvaṇṇâ(d)i* (Cū 426,4, similarly Ṭ). Sustaining a family compels the laymen to strive for property.

Pagaranti saṅgaṃ: bhṛśaṃ karenti prakarenti; saktiṃ saṅgaṃ (thus read in stead of *saṃyaṃ*, Cū 426,7), *sambandhaṃ kurvanti* (Ṭ II 146 b 12). Cf. Āyār 1,1,7,6 *ārambha-sattā pakarenti saṅgaṃ* '(. . . . those are involved in sin who . . .) and engaging in acts, are addicted to worldliness' (Jac.), '. . . .der Betätigung ergeben wirken sie Verknüpfung [mit der Welt]' (Schubring 1926: 72; 2004: 83).

2,6,22
vitt'-esiṇo mehuṇa-saṃpagāḍhā
te bhoyaṇ'-aṭṭhā vaṇiyā vayanti,
vayaṃ tu kāmesu ajjhovavannā
aṇ-āriyā pema-rasesu giddhā

PROPERTY-MINDED AND ENGAGING IN SEXUAL RELATIONS
THESE MERCHANTS SAY (THEY BEHAVE THUS) TO EARN THEIR
LIVING (or: WANDER AROUND FOR PLEASURE).
WE, HOWEVER, (BELIEVE THAT THEY ARE) GIVEN
TO THE PLEASURES OF THE SENSES, NOT (SERIOUS) BELIEVERS
(AND) LUSTFUL.

Mehuṇa°: why this and *pema-rasesu giddhā* should be particularly characteristics of merchants is not clear. Does *vaṇiyā* in fact stands for (Jain) laymen? Then the reason why these characteristics are mentioned here would become understandable for many souls are destroyed in sexual intercourse.[64] Chiastically as to the a-*pāda* here property and disregard for living beings are taken up once more in vs. 23 a.

Jinadāsa then admonishes those who live in that way by means of several quotations citing the first: *śiśnôdara-kṛte, Pārtha !* (426,9f.) in Cū 86,7f. ad Āyār 1,2,5,5, introduced by *bhaṇiyaṃ ca loge vi* and completed as follows: *pṛthivīṃ jetum icchasi / jaya śiśnôdaram, Pārtha! tatas te pṛthivī jitā*. The first *pāda* reminds us of Mbh (cr. ed.) 1,164,13 b *p. j. icchatā* and the last one of Mbh 5,148,4 a *tatas te pṛthivī-pālāḥ*.

Vayanti: vrajanti (Cū 426,8), to which Śīlâṅka adds: *vadanti vā* (Ṭ II 147a 1), perhaps because Āyār 1,1,7,6 *ārambhamāṇā viṇayaṃ vayanti / chandôvaṇīyā* ∪ *ajjhovavannā / ārambha-sattā pakarenti saṅgaṃ*.

2,6,23
ārambhagaṃ c'eva pariggahaṃ ca
a-viussiyā nissiya āya-daṇḍā
tesiṃ ca se udae, jaṃ vayāsī,
caur'-ant' aṇ-antāya duhāya, nêha

THEY NEITHER GIVE UP KILLING NOR PROPERTY,
BUT STICK TO IT. THEY ARE INCONSIDERATE, BUT THEIR
GAIN WHICH YOU MENTIONED (WILL SERVE) THEM ONLY
TO ENDLESS DISTRESS IN THE (WHOLE) SQUARE (WORLD),
NOT ONLY HERE.

A-viussiyā: 'they do not abstain from (. . .)' (Jac.), *avosiriuṃ* (Cū 427,1), *a-vyutsṛjya – a-parityajya* (Ṭ II 147a 4). If anywhere, it is with this rare form that the occasional parallelism of verse numbers is remarkable, in this case 1,1,2,23 *je u tattha viussanti, saṃsāraṃ te viussiyā*,[65] where I should now like to translate: 'wer damit aber aufhört, beendet für sich den Saṃsāra'. Cf. also Theragāthā 784 *a-vyosita*.[66]

Nissiyā: for this form cf. *sikkhiya* in vs. 16.

Āya-daṇḍā: see my comment at 1,2,3,9 (Bollée 1988: 75f.).

Vayāsī: according to Pi § 516 = *avādīḥ*, but cf. Pāli *avacāsi* (Geiger/Norman 1994, § 165.1); *vayāsī* points to vs. 19.

Caur'-ant': for this notion see Schubring 2000: § 103. Jacobi translates the second line as: 'and their gain of which you spoke, will be the endless Circle of Births and pains manifold'. Perhaps he wanted to read: *-antā ya duhā ya*.

Nêha: Jacobi here remarks: "*Nehā* or *nedhā*. According to Śīlâṅka it is *na iha*: 'not even here (do they find the profit they seek)'. I think it maybe the Prākṛt equivalent of *anekadhā* or it could stand for *snehāḥ*, in which case the meaning would be: love's (reward will be) pain". *Faute de mieux* I have followed the commentator, as Jacobi did not convince me.

2,6,24
ṇ'-egant'-aṇ-accantiya ūdae so
vayanti te do vi guṇôdayaṃmi.

se ūdae sâi-m-aṇanta-patte
tam ūdayaṃ sāhae tāi nāī

a: CT: *ṇeganta ṇaccantiva* thus corrected in C for original: *ṇaccantiya*, V: *neganti naccanti ya*; – TV: *odae*; J: *udaye se*; – c: VTJ: *udae*; – d: VT: *udayaṃ*, J: *uddayaṃ*; TV: *sāhayai*, J: *sāhati*

THIS GAIN OF THEIRS IS UNCERTAIN AND NOT WITHOUT AN END. THEY EXPERIENCE (THESE) QUALITIES, BOTH OF THEM, (ONLY) IN THE BEGINNING. THE GAIN ACQUIRED THROUGH HIM (i.e. MAHĀVĪRA), HOWEVER, HAS A BEGINNING, BUT NO END. THE SAINT (AND) GUIDE/NĀYA GIVES AWAY HIS GAIN.

N'egant': ṇ'eganti ṇ'accanti ity ādi, ekântena bhavatîty ekântikaḥ (...) ātyantikaḥ sarva-kāla-bhāvī (Ṭ II 147a 9f.). For the seventh syllable *-a* see vs. 16 (*sikkhiya*).

Vayanti etc.: (...) *tad-vido vadanti tau ca dvāv api bhāvau vigata-guṇôdayau bhavataḥ* (Ṭ II 147a 11; similarly Cū 427, 5 f. where *guṇa* is glossed *pagāra*). Jacobi saw that this interpretation cannot be correct, yet to read *guṇe 'dayammi*, as he does, is not necessary for *guṇo°* can represent *guṇā + ū*. or *guṇ' ū°*. The a-*pāda*, too, reads *odae* for *ūdae*. *Vayanti* ~ *vrajanti*, as in vs. 22.

Se udae: put chiastically and thus in a certain contrast with *ūdae so*.

Sāhaye etc.: 'the saviour and sage shares his profit (with others)' (Jac.). *Sāhaye: ākhyāti silāhati* (Cū 427,7), *kathayati ślāghate vā* (Ṭ II 147a 14). As to the form, *sāhaye* (thus to be read m.c.) can correspond to *ślāghate* or *ślāghayati* as well as to *sādhate* or *sādhayati*. The verb last mentioned has many meanings, inter alia, 'to grant, bestow, yield' [MW] and these appeared better to me.

Tāi nāī: ṇātîti jñātiḥ kulī (Cū 427, 8), *jñātī jñātāḥ kṣatriyā jñātaṃ vā vastujātaṃ vidyate yasya sa jñātī, vidita-samasta-vedya ity arthaḥ* (Ṭ II 147b 2f.). Though his gloss is otherwise wrong yet Śīlâṅka makes us suppose that we might read *Nāe* and consider this to be short for *Nāyaputte*, cf. Dasav 6,21 *na so pariġġaho vutto Nāyaputteṇa tāiṇā*. Nevertheless I would prefer to take *nāe* ~ Pāli *nāgo* ~ Sa. *nāyakaḥ*, as in Suttanipāta 522 *(...vimutto) nāgo tādi pavuccati tathattā*' (...being completely released.) Such a one is rightly called "nāga".' (Norman 1992: 57).

2,6,25
a-hiṃsayaṃ savva-payâṇukampī
dhamme ṭhiyaṃ kamma-vivega-heuṃ
tam āya-daṇḍehĩ samāyarantā
a-bohie te paḍirūvă eyaṃ

HE DOES NOT HARM ANYONE, HAS PITY ON ALL BEINGS, IS OF UNSHAKEABLE FAITH (AND) MAKES THAT HIS ACTIONS ARE JUDGED CORRECTLY. HE WHO PUTS HIM ON A PAR (?) WITH INCONSIDERATE PEOPLE IS A MODEL OF FOLLY.

Savva-payâṇukampī: ~ī uniform reading for which, if correct, cf. Edgerton, BHSG 10.54; otherwise the ending might be emended *-iṃ* though nasalisation in MSS equals lengthening of the preceding vowel.

Dhamme ṭhiyaṃ: this expression is found also in Pāli, e.g. Sn 250, 327 etc.[67] Cū 427,11 *dasa-vidhe dhamme*,[68] Ṭ II 147b 9 *paramârtha-bhūte*.

Kamma°: '(who) causes the truth of the Law to be known' (Jac.).

Taṃ etc.: 'him you would equal to those wicked men' (Jac.).

Āya-daṇḍehĩ: see at 1,2,3,9.

Samāyarantā: samācaranti iti samaṃ ācarantā samācarantā, tulyaṃ kurvantā ity arthaḥ; samānayanto vā samānaṃ kurvantā ity arthaḥ (Cū 427,13), *samācaranta – ātma-kalpaṃ kurvanti vaṇig-ādibhir udāharaṇaiḥ* (Ṭ II 147b 10). Sa. *samācarati* means 1. 'to act or conduct oneself towards' (loc.); 2. 'to practise, do; 3. to associate with' (instr.; MW). In Pāli only the second meaning is testified to, but at our place, only the causative of the third meaning, if at all, would make sense. A possible alternative may be a derivation from √ *KAR: samākaroti* means 'to bring together, unite' (MW). That would fit exactly, though the verb seems to occur in Vedic only and not at all in Pāli. *Samāyaranta*, however, cannot be anything else but a nom. pl. and therefore it is not clear to me, why Jacobi could separate it from *te* in the d-*pāda*.

A-bohie etc.: 'This is the outcome of your folly' (Jac.).

Quotations in the commentaries

As noticed elsewhere[69] Mbh quotations can present readings rejected in the critical edition.

aya-vaya-maya-paya-caya-taya-ṇaya gatau (Ṭ II 146b 5 ad Sūy 2,6,20) = 147b 1 ad Sūy 2,6,24. Cf. Hemacandra 1979: 101 (790ff.)

aśoka-vṛkṣaḥ sura-puṣpa-vṛṣṭir divya-dhvaniś câmaram āsanaṃ ca bhā-maṇḍalaṃ dundubhirāta-patraṃ sat-prātihāryāṇi Jinêśvarāṇām (Cū 418,4 ad Sūy 2,6,2) *ahiṃsā satyam a-steyaṃ brahmacaryam a-lubdhatā* (Ṭ II 142b 1 ad Sūy 2,6,8). Quotation of Mbh 14 App. 4. 2214.

āśvade śīghra-bhāve ca (Cū 426,12 ad Sūy 2,6,22)

udaiga pakkheve (Cū 426,2 ad Sūy 2,6,20)

kamu icchāyāṃ (Cū 424,3 ad Sūy 2,6,17)

citte tāyitavye (Cū 428,6 ad Sūy 2,6,25)

cira-saṃsaṭṭho 'si me, Goyamā (Cū 424,7 ad Sūy 2,6,17). Quotation of Viy 14,7 [*saṃsiṭṭhe*].

chatraṃ chātraṃ pātraṃ vastraṃ yaṣṭiṃ ca carcayati bhikṣuḥ veṣeṇa parikareṇa ca kiyatâpi vinā na bhikṣâpi (Ṭ II 139b 14f. ad Sūy 2,6,2)

jahiṃ jassa jaṃ vavasiyaṃ (Cū 421,13 ad Sūy 2,6,12)
tvaci bhogāḥ sukhaṃ māṃse (Cū 414,1 ad SūyN 185)
diṭṭhaṃ miyaṃ a-saṃdiddhaṃ (Cū 419,8 ad Sūy 2,6,5). Quotation of Dasav 8,48a.
deva-devassa (Cū 423,8 ad Sūy 2,6,15)
navaṃ na kujjā vihuṇe purāṇaṃ (Cū 425,12 ad Sūy 2,6,20)
nāṇaṃ sikkhai nāṇaṃ guṇei nāṇeṇa kuṇai kiccāiṃ nāṇī navaṃ na bandhei, etc. (Cū 425,12 f. ad Sūy 2,6,20). Quotation of DasavN 383 [*bandhai*].
pāeṇa khīṇa-davvā (Cū 423,14 ad Sūy 2,6,16)
Brahmā lūna-śirā Harir dṛśi sarug vyālupta-śiśno Haraḥ, Sūryo 'py ullikhito 'nalo' py akhila-bhuk Somaḥ kalaṅkâṅkitaḥ / svar-nātho 'pi visaṃsthulaḥ khalu vapuḥ-saṃsthair upasthaiḥ kṛtaḥ, san-mārga-skhalanād bhavanti vipadaḥ prāyaḥ prabhūnām api // (Ṭ II 143b 12 ff. ad Sūy 2,6,13)
Bhagavaṃ pañca-mahavvaya-gutto indiya-sãvuḍo ya virao ya / annesiṃ pi tam-eva ya dhammaṃ desei gāhei // (Cū 419,12 f. ad Sūy 2,6,6)
mana puvvaṅgamā [?] (Cū 428,5 ad Sūy 2,6,25)
rāga-dveṣau vinirjitya kim araṇye kariṣyasi? atha no nirjitāv etau kim araṇye kariṣyasi? (Ṭ II 141a 10 f. ad Sūy 2,6,4)
vidyā-vinaya-sampanne brāhmaṇe <gavi hastini> (Cū 424,2f. ad Sūy 2,6,16). Quotation of Mbh 6,27,18ab.
viṣayā vinivartante nirāhārasya dehinaḥ (Cū 426,12 ad Sūy 2,6,22). Quotation of Mbh 6,24,59ab = 12,197,16ab.
śaṅke praharṣa-tulā (Cū 425,1 ad Sūy 2,6,18)
śiśnôdara-kṛte, Pārtha ! (Cū 426,9 f. ad Sūy 2,6,22. The complete *śloka* is found Cū 86,7 f. ad Āyār 1,2,5,5. Cf. Mbh 3,2,61a)
ṣañja saṅge (Cū 425,7 ad Sūy 2,6,19)
sukhāni dattvā sukhāni (Cū 420,6 ad Sūy 2,6,7)

Notes

1 Part two appeared in the *Journal of Indian Philosophy* 27 (1999) 411–437. The abbreviations for the titles of Indian texts are those adopted for my *Studien zum Sūyagaḍa*: C = *pratīkas* in Jinadāsa's Cūrṇī [1950]; T = Sūy text in Śīlâṅka's commentary vol. II [1953]; V = Vaidya's ed. [1928]; J = Jambūvijaya's ed. [1978]; Cū = Cūrṇī, Ṭ = Ṭīkā.
2 Minor variants are noted in Bollée 1995: 135f.
3 This "correction" of T by Vaidya, just as his adoption of T's reading at N 198 d, shows the correctness of Alsdorf's remark in his Itthīparinnā paper (Alsdorf 1974: 194 note 5).
4 *Vatthā ṇa khiva-m-addeṇa vaṇṇ'-addaṃ citta-kammâdisu ārdakaṃ likhitam Ārdrānakṣatraṃ likhitam* (Cū 413, 12 sq.).
5 See Hilka 1910: 33.
6 *Śrīparṇī-sovarcalâdikam* (Ṭ II 136 a 2).
7 *Muktā-phala-raktâśokâdikam* (Ṭ ibid.).
8 *Vasayôpaliptaṃ vasârdram* (Ṭ II 136 a 3).
9 *Vajra-lepâdy-upaliptaṃ stambha-kuḍyâdikam* (l.c.).
10 *Tattha negama-saṃgaha-vavahārā ti-vihaṃ saṃkhaṃ icchanti, taṃ jahā: ekkabhaviyaṃ baddhâuyaṃ abhimuha-nāma-gottaṃ ca.*

11 The particulars of this process, which *stricto sensu* seems to contradict Buddhist conceptions, are told by Buddhaghosa with regard to the future Buddha, but will represent a common Indian idea as the Tusita-devatā who form the setting see off the reincarnand in the Nandavana. Sumaṅgalavilāsinī 430, 11 states *sabba-devalokesu hi Nandavanaṃ atthi yeva*. Thus beings enjoying their positive karman in other *devalokas* will leave these in the same way (see Bollée, Physical aspects of some Mahāpuruṣas [in press in WZKS Hg (2005)]).

12 *Ekena bhavena yo jīvaḥ svargâder āgatya (...) āsannataro baddhâyuākaḥ (...) āsannatamo' bhimukha-nāma-giotro yo' nantara-samayam evârdrakatvena samutpatsyate – ete ca trayo'pi prakārā dravyârdrake draṣ ṭavyāḥ* (Ṭ II 136a 6sqq.).

13 In another context (ĀvCū 526,4 and in a stanza from a longer metrical quotation in the *vṛtti* I 69 a 1 on Āyā 1,1,7,1*) mentioned as the teacher of Jiyasattu, Rājā of vasantapura. I do not understand why this prince in PrPN I, p. 288 no. 15 should probably be identical with a ruler of Rāyagiha of that name in Nirayāv 4, 1, as suggested by Chandra and Mehata at no. 38. A Jiyasattu of Vasantapura is also found at ĀvCū 498,6 and 503, 6.

14 For the formation cf., for example, Prince Selaga of Selagapura in Nāyā 1,5. Localisations like these naturally are of little importance for the historicity of Sūy 2,6 as already Basham 1951: 54 remarked.

15 Here Jinadāsa's version diverges in that the nun is reborn in a foreign country (*meccha-visaye*) as Addaya, son of Prince Addaga and his queen Dhāriṇī, whereas Sāmāyika returns to this world as a Sheth's daughter in Vasantapura (Cū 415, 2 sq.).

16 Cū 415,4 sqq. only speaks of a *dūta*.

17 *Abhaya-kumāreṇâpi pariṇāmikyā buddhyā pariṇāmitam* (Ṭ 138 a 5 sq.).

18 Derivate of *aśva-vāhana* 'das Reiten zu Pferd' (Schmidt, *Nachträge*).

19 Cū 416,7 reads *sāvaga-paḍimā* instead of *uvāsaga-* (see Schubring 2000: § 163). Thus the layman is completely put on an equal footing with the monks. At Ṭ II 138 b3 it reads *anytara-pratimā-pratipannaḥ kāyôtsarga-vyavasthitaḥ*.

20 Read *vidhṛto* instead of *vighṛto* at Ṭ II 138 b5.

21 *Thathāvidha-karmôdayāe câvaśyaṃ-bhāvi-bhavitavyatā-niyogena ca*, Ṭ II 138b13.

22 Called *dhijjāti* in Cū 417,2; see Bollée 1977: 112 and 1988: 279. The word in question seems to be first a term of abuse used by Brahmins for non-brahmins who returned the invective as a nickname for the former. Even Brahmins who had become Buddhist monks sometimes could not abstain from their old habit as stated Udāna 28, 11, where we hear of the brahmin *bhikkhu* Pilinda-Vaccha's custom of addressing his *confratres* by *vasala-vāda*.

23 Even if this results in an impossible form like the imperative *jāṇaṃ* in vs. 8.

24 *Ekākī viharaṃl lokikaiḥ paribhūyata iti matvā loka-pânkti-nimittaṃ mahān parikaraḥ kṛtaḥ* (on *loka-pa[ṅ]kti* see Bollée 1977: 151), *thatā côcyate: "chattraṃ chāttraṃ pātraṃ vastraṃ yaṣ ṭiṃ ca carcayati bhikṣuḥ / veṣena parikareṇa ca kiyatâpi vinā na bhikṣâpi*" // (Ṭ II 139 b13 sqq.).

25 As to this see Jacobi's remark on Utt 1,7 and *infra* Sūy 2,6,6.

26 Cf. BHSG § 8.94.

27 Speijer 1886: § 52; Sen 1953 § 16.

28 Speyer 1896: §25.

29 See e.g. Alsdorf 1962: 5 sqq.

30 See e.g. K. C. Jain 1963: 17f.

31 Granoff 1989: 204; Dundas 2002: 148.

32 At the references mentioned in Pi §§ 56b and 409 *vayam* corresponds to Sa. *vayas*.

33 Yet cf. *kiñcid* at Ṭ II 143 b10.

34 *Udghaṭṭana* must have an extended conception of 'outbreak (of violence or passion)' (MW), namely, 'passionate utterance, abuse', cf. *ghaṭṭe* 'to hurt with words, speak of malignantly' (MW).

35 'At his endless duels of words he tried to shout down his opponents with his formidable voice and was profuse in invectives when it was necessary to withstand them'.

36 Cf. Āyār 2,4,2,1.
37 Cf. Āyār 2,4,1,8.
38 This translation of *parivrājaka* follows Seidenstücker 1920: 125.
39 *Rūvam iti yathā loko lokaṃ kasmiṃścid aparādhe ākrośati: 'Kāṇaḥ! kubjaḥ! kodhi' (Sa. Kuṣṭhī)! vêti jātyā vêti 'Caṇḍāla-karma karoti.' Nâivaṃ kiṃcid rūpeṇa "Tridaṇḍika duṣṭha! Parivrājaka duṣṭha ! Idam te durdṛṣṭam śāsanaṃ. Tena mūrkha-Kapilena kiṃ dṛṣṭam, yena kartā kṣetrajñaḥ?"*
40 *He kaṣāya-kaṇṭha!* (Cū 422,5).
41 *Jugupsitâṅgâvayavôdghaṭṭanena jātyā tal-liṅga-grahaṇôdghaṭṭanena vā.*
42 Following this meaning Jacobi translates Utt 2,21 'sitting there he should brave all dangers.' He may have read similarly to Charpentier *tattha se ciṭṭhamāṇassa uvasaggâbhidhārae*, yet I do not understand his construction then. Śāntisūri reads *uvasagge 'bhidhārae*, which does not solve the difficulty. Only his reading *uvasaggabhayaṃ bhave* allows for a harmony with *ciṭṭhamāṇassa* (thus also Alsdorf in a marginal jotting in his personal copy of Charpentier). The latest Utt edition, the one made by Puṇyavijaya and Bhojak (Bombay, 1977), in the b-*pāda* has the traditional version of the European edition. – The only other reference for *abhidhārayai* I have found seems to me just as suspect: Dasav 5,2,25 a monk is recommended to visit every house on his almsround and *nīyaṃ kulaṃ aīkamma ūsaḍhaṃ nâbhidhārae*, which Schubring renders by 'he should not pass by a lowly house and go only to a noble one'. As to the meaning this no doubt is correct, just as Haribhadra paraphrases the verb by *yāyāt*. Then one should either assume a meaning 'to patronize' – which in fact would reverse things – or read *abhidhāvae*.
43 Thus read for *uju* in the PTS ed.
44 See, for example, Hornell 1920: 174 sq.
45 In the Āyār chapter containing his analysis, p. 61, Schubring expresses himself to the effect that this line starts with prose. In his working copy, however, he later emended the text as follows: *āgant' ārāmâgāre gāme nagare vi egayā vāso.*
46 *Chāyā-bhraṃśa iti* 'loss of face'.
47 Similarly Basham 1951: 53.
48 Otherwise these formations have an *-ā-* in the joint of the compound; for examples from Pāli see PED s.v. *kiccā-kiccā* and Geiger/Norman 1994: § 33; for Sa., Wackernagel 1905: 148 (§ 61) and Debrunner 1957: 44; and for both, Hoffmann 1975: 113–119.
49 Mahāniddesa 226,28 in the form *lapaka-lapaka*, in Vism 26,3 also as *lapa-lapa*, used of a talkative monk.
50 Buddhists, inter alios (Cū 423,12).
51 Interdictions of intercourse with heterodox people occur in Hinduism, for example, Viṣṇupurāṇa 3,18,79 and 96ff.
52 See Schubring 2000, § 38; Alsdorf 1974: 253; Dhaky 1997: 5; Bollée 1998: 365.
53 The verse number parallel 1,2,1,17 contains *no* . . . *na* 'not at all'.
54 See Drosdowski 1984: § 579.
55 Cf. Milindapanha 82, 31ff.
56 Sūy 1,5,1,2; 1,6,3; 1,6,7; 1,6,25; 1,14,4; Utt 4,6.
57 *Ghettūṇa* (Cū 425,7) ~ *gṛhītvā* (Ṭ II 146a 12).
58 *Karpūrâgaru-kastūrikâmbarâdikaṃ*, Ṭ II 146a 11.
59 Cū: *bandhei*.
60 Quotation from unknown source.
61 For *brahma* in this sense see Zaehner 1969: 214.
62 *Kraya-vikrayârthaṃ śakaṭa-yāna-vāhanôṣṭra-maṇḍalikâdibhir anuṣṭhānaiḥ* (Ṭ II 146b9).
63 On slavery in India see, for example, Jain 1984: 140ff.
64 See Bollée 1977: 30.

65 Bollée 1977: 99.
66 Sa. *vyavasita*: *vyavasyati*.
67 See PTC s.v. *ṭhita*, p. 230b line 15 from bottom.
68 Cf. Ṭhā 10,945 (Suttâgame I 304,23) *dasa-vihe samaṇa-dhamme pannatte taṃ jahā khantī, muttī*, etc.
69 Bollée 1977: 71 n. 80.

Bibliography and abbreviations

Alsdorf, Ludwig. 1962. *Beiträge zur Geschichte von Vegetarismus und Rinderverehrung in Indien*. Akademie der Wissenschaften und der Literatur in Mainz. Abhandlungen der Geistes- und Sozialwissenschaftlichen Klasse Nr. 6 1961. Wiesbaden: Steiner Verlag.

—— 1965. *Les Études Jaina*. Paris: Collège de France.

—— 1974. *Kleine Schriften*. Wiesbaden: Steiner Verlag.

Amg. = Ardhamāgadhī

AnguttaraN = Anguttara Nikāya

Aṇuog = *Aṇuogadārāiṃ* see *Nandisuttaṃ*

APSŚK = Ānanda Sāgara Sūri. 1954. *Alpa-paricita-saiddhāntika-śabda-kośa*. Surat: Devchand Lalbhai Jain Pustakoddhara Fund.

ĀvCū = Āvassaya Cuṇṇi

ĀvNHar = Āvassaya Nijjutti by Haribhadra

Āyār = Āyāraṅga

Basham, Arthur L. 1951. *History and Doctrines of the Ājīvikas*. London: Luzac.

BHSD = Edgerton, Franklin. 1953. *Buddhist Hybrid Sanskrit Grammar and Dictionary*. Vol. II: Dictionary. New Haven, CT: Yale University Press.

BHSG = Edgerton, Franklin. 1953. *Buddhist Hybrid Sanskrit Grammar and Dictionary*. Vol. I: Grammar. New Haven, CT: Yale University Press.

Bollée, Willem. 1977. *Studien zum Sūyagaḍa* I. Wiesbaden: Franz Steiner Verlag.

—— 1988. *Studien zum Sūyagaḍa II*. Stuttgart: Franz Steiner Verlag.

—— 1990. "Āyāraṅga 2,16 and Sūyagaḍa 1,16." *Journal of Indian Philosophy* 18: 29–52.

—— 1994. *Materials for an Edition and Study of the Piṇḍa- and Oha-Nijjuttis of the Śvetâmbara Jain tradition*. Part 2: Preliminary Text and Glossary. Stuttgart: Franz Steiner Verlag.

—— 1995. *The Nijjuttis on the Seniors of the Śvetâmbara Siddhânta: Āyārânga, Dasaveyāliya, Uttarajjhāyā and Sūyagaḍa*. Stuttgart: Franz Steiner Verlag.

—— 1998. "Review of M. A. Dhaky, Arhat Pārśva and Dharaṇendra Nexus. Delhi, 1997." *Bulletin D'Études Indiennes* 16: 365 ff.

CPD = *Critical Pāli Dictionary*. 1925. Begun by V. Trenckner. Copenhagen: Royal Danish Academy of Letters and Sciences.

Dasav = Dasaveyāliya

Debrunner, Albert. 1957. *Nachträge zu Wackernagels Altindische Grammatik II,1*. Göttingen: Vandenhoeck und Ruprecht.

Dhaky, Madhusudan. 1997. *Arhat Pārśva and Dharanendra Nexus*. Ahmedabad: Lalbhai Dalpatbhai Institute of Indology.

DN = Dīgha Nikāya

Drosdowski, Günther (ed.). 1984. *Grammatik der Deutschen Gegenwartsprache*. Mannheim: Duden Verlag.

Dundas, Paul. 2002. *The Jains*. 2nd Revised Edition. London: Routledge.
Geiger, Wilhelm. 1994. *A Pali Grammar*. Revised and edited by Kenneth R. Norman. Oxford: Pali Text Society.
Glasenapp, Helmuth von. 1928. "Religiöse Reformbewegungen im heutigen Indien." *Morgenland. Darstellungen aus Geschichte und Kultur des Ostens*. Heft 17. Leipzig.
Granoff, Phyllis. 1989. "Religious Biography and Clan History among the Śvetâmbara Jains in North India." *East and West* 39: 195–215.
Hemacandra. 1979. *Dhātupārāyaṇa*. Ed. by Muni Candravijaya. Palitana.
Hilka, Alfons. 1910. *Die altindischen Personennamen*. Breslau: Verlag von M. und H. Marcus.
Hoffmann, Karl. 1976. *Aufsätze zur Indoiranistik I*. Edited by Johanna Narten. Wiesbaden: Ludwich Reichert Verlag.
Hornell, J. 1920. "The Origins and Ethnological Significance of Indian Boat Designs." *Memoirs of the Asiatic Society of Bengal*. Vol. VII, 3. Calcutta: Asiatic Society.
Jac. = Jacobi, Hermann 1895. *Jaina Sūtras II*. SBE. XLV. Oxford: Clarendon Press.
Jain, Jagdish C. 1984. *Life in Ancient India as Depicted in the Jain Canon and Commentaries*. 2nd revised and enlarged edition. Delhi: Munshiram Manoharlal.
Jain, Kailash C. 1963. *Jainism in Rajasthan*. Sholapur: Jaina Samskrti Samrakshaka Sangha.
JHS = Jain Hybrid Sanskrit
Kapadia, Hiralal R. 1933. "Prohibition of Flesh-Eating in Jainism." *Review of Philosophy and Religion* IV: 232–239.
Kosambi, Damodar D. 1963. "The Autochthonous Element in the Mahābhārata." *Journal of the American Oriental Society* 84: 34–44.
Leumann, Ernst 1921. *Untersuchungen zur Geschichte des Buddhismus* VI. München = "Buddha and Mahāvīra." *Zeitschrift für Buddhismus* 4, 1–3 (1921) 1–22, 129–152, 233–254.
Mbh = Mahābhārata
MW = Monier Williams. 1899. *Sanskrit-English Dictionary*. Oxford: Oxford University Press.
N = Nijjutti
Nandisuttaṃ and Aṇuogaddārāiṃ. 1968. Jaina Āgama Series. Vol. 1. Bombay.
Nāyā = Nāyādhammakahāo
Norman, Kenneth R. 1990–2001 *Collected Papers I-VII*. Oxford: Pali Text Society. do. 1992 *The Group of Discourses*. Vol. 2. Oxford: Pali Text Society.
Pā = Pāli
PED = Rhys Davids, T. W. and W. Stede. 1921–3. *Pāli-English Dictionary*. London: Pali Text Society.
Pi = Pischel, Richard. 1981. *Grammar of the Prakrit Languages*. Translated from German by Subhadra Jhā. 2nd revised edition. Delhi: Motilal Banarsidas.
PrPN = Mehta, Mohan Lal and K. Rishabh Chandra. 1970–1972. *Prakrit Proper Names*. Vol. I–II. Ahmedabad: L. D. Institute.
PSM = Seṭh, Paṇḍit Haragovinda Dās Trikamcand. 1928. *Pāia-Sadda-Mahaṇṇavo (Prākṛta-Śabda-Mahārṇavaḥ)*. Dillī: Vīr Sevā Mandir. (Reprint: Motīlāl Banārasīdās, 1986).
Roth, Gustav. 1968. " 'A Saint like that' and 'A Saviour' in Prakrit, Pali, Sanskrit and Tibetan Literature." *Śrī Mahāvīr Jaina Golden Jubilee Volume* I, English section. Bombay: Mahāvīr Jain Vidyālaya.
—— 1983 *Mallī-Jñāta, das achte Kapitel des Nāyādhammakahāo im sechsten Aṅga des Śvetāmbara Jainakanons herausgegeben, übersetzt und erläutert*. Wiesbaden: Franz Steiner Verlag.

Sa = Sanskrit
Samav = *Samavāyâṅgam*. 1918. Mehesana: Āgamôdayasamiti.
Schlingloff, Dieter. 1974. "Cotton-Manufacture in Ancient India." *JESHO* XVII, 1: 81–96.
Schmidt, Richard. 1928. *Nachträge zum Sanskrit-Wörterbuch in kürzerer Fassung von Otto Böhtlingk*. Leipzig: Harrassowitz.
Schubring, Walther. 1926. *Worte Mahāvīras*. Göttingen: Vandenhoeck und Ruprecht. (translated from the German into English with much added material by Willem Bollée and Jayandra Soni. Ahmedabad: L. D. Institute, 2004).
—— 1935. *Die Lehre der Jainas*. Berlin: Walter De Gruyter.
—— 2000. *The Doctrine of the Jainas*. (translation of prec. c. with three indices enlarged and added by Willem Bollée and Jayandra Soni). Delhi: Motilal Banarsidas.
Seidenstücker, Karl. 1920. see *Udāna*.
Settar, Shadakshari. 1990. *Pursuing Death*. Dharwad: Institute of Indian Art History, Karnatak University.
Sen, Sukumāra. 1953. "Historical Syntax of Middle Indo-Arya." *Indian Linguistics* XIII: 355–473.
Sn = Suttanipāta
SN = Samyutta Nikāya
Speijer, Jacob S. 1886. *Sanskrit Syntax*. Leiden: E. J. Brill.
Speyer, Jacob S. 1896. *Vedische- und Sanskritsyntax*. Straßburg: Grundriss der Indo-arischen Philologie und Altertumskunde I 6.
Sūtrakṛtâṅgacūrṇī. 1950. Ṛṣabdevjī Keśarīmaljī Śvetâmbar Saṃsthā. Ratlam.
Sūtrakṛtâṅgam II. 1953. Goḍīpārśva Jaina Grantha-mālā 7. Bombay.
Sūy = *Sūyagaḍaṃgasuttaṃ*. 1978. Ed. Muni Jambūvijaya. Jaina Āgama Series 2. Bombay: Mahāvīra Jaina Vidyālaya.
Udāna. 1920. Das Buch der feierlichen Worte des Erhabenen. Übersetzt von Karl Seidenstücker. Augsburg.
Utt = *Uttarâdhyayanāni*. 1937. Ātmavallabhagranthâvali 12.
Viy = Viyāhapannatti
Wackernagel, Jakob. 1905. *Altindische Grammatik II,1*. Göttingen: Vandenhoeck und Ruprecht. Reprint 1957.
WZKS = Wiener Zeitschrift für die Kunde Südasiens und Archiv für indische Philosophie.
Yamazaki, Moriichi and Yumi Ousaka. 1997. *Uttarajjhāyā Word Index and Reverse Word Index*. Philologica Asiatica Monograph Series 11. Tokyo: The Chūō Academic Research Institute.
Zaehner, R.C. 1969. *The Bhagavadgītā*. Oxford: Clarendon Press.

2

THE LATER FORTUNES OF JAMĀLI

Paul Dundas

Those of us in the English-speaking world who commenced serious research into the history and practice of the Jain religion twenty or so years ago were of necessity autodidacts to a large extent. The reason for this was that there were virtually no academic specialists in the subject at whose feet one could sit and little by way of available instruction which went beyond that already provided by what in one's darker and more frustrated moods often seemed to be, with a few exceptions, an uninspiring and repetitive secondary literature primarily concerned with the metaphysical basics of Jainism. The gaining of some sort of foothold and orientation within a huge, diverse and largely unexplored primary literature was by no means straightforward and methods had to be devised to get beyond the existing textbooks. I for one decided that a possible strategy might be to investigate the various sectarian controversies which had preoccupied the Jain community in its early period, on the assumption that it is generally in the area of internal dispute that religions expose both their cherished preoccupations and also possible inconsistencies in their structure.

To this end, it seemed an obvious course of action to consider the early Jain heretics, know in Prākrit as the *pavayaṇa-nihṇaga*, 'concealers of the doctrine', seven of which are listed at *Sthānāṅga Sūtra* 587 and who according to tradition arose in Mahāvīra's lifetime and the immediate centuries after his death, in the expectation that here would be fruitful and extensive ancient source material on Jain disputes and, in the nature of heresies such as Arianism in Christianity (cf. Wiles 1994), a continuing vein of dissent and contention which would inevitably resurface at various times in Jainism's history. It was with some surprise, then, that I quickly realised that with the exception of Jamāli, the first of these so-called heretics, the ancient scriptural texts had very little to say on the subject of the *nihnava* ('concealments', heresies; for the original sense, see Brough 1996: 77–78) and that Leumann's paper of 1885, which amplified the exiguous canonical material with some of the early commentarial and postcanonical literature, had been virtually the first and last serious scholarly word on the subject (Leumann 1885 and cf. Balbir 1993: 146). In the light of this, I decided to pay no further attention to the subject of the *nihnava*.

However, my interest in this subject was revived in 1998 by two papers delivered at a conference held in Lund to honour Professor P. S. Jaini. One of these papers (for the second by Professor Johannes Bronkhorst, see Bronkhorst 2003) presented by Professor Georg von Simson drew attention to what he styled the principle of 'characterizing by contrast', a form of narrative parallelism which could throw light on the structures of the biographies of the Buddha and the *Mahābhārata* hero Bhīṣma by reference to a rival, antipathetic character. So, as in the *Mahābhārata* the impetuosity of the young and ambitious Karṇa, who demands the generalship of the Pāṇḍava army, highlights and contrasts with the qualities of the older and more temperate Bhīṣma, in similar manner the Buddha's evil and jealous cousin Devadatta, who led a breakaway from the monastic community (one which, if the Chinese pilgrims are to be believed, was still in existence well into the common era; see Deeg 1999) to restore what he saw as the exclusively ascetic orientation of the path, points through contrast to the imperturbable nature of the great teacher and the correctness of the 'middle way' preached by him which viewed asceticism as an objectionable extreme (Simson 2003). In the light of this intriguing structural possibility identified by von Simson and the fact that there are certain similarities, if only at a superficial level, between the lives of the Buddha and the twenty fourth Jina Mahāvīra, it seemed legitimate to consider whether there might be any Jain equivalent of Devadatta. An obvious candidate would appear to be the first 'concealer of the doctrine', Jamāli, according to tradition Mahāvīra's nephew (in some versions also son-in-law; see below) who as described in the *Bhagavatī Sūtra* attempted to reformulate a principle of Jain teaching and then led some monks away from the main ascetic community.

Yet an examination of traditional biographies of Mahāvīra demonstrates that Jamāli plays little part in the overall trajectory of the narrative and contemporary understanding by Jains today does not assign him any marked role as some sort of stock villain in a well-known story. All textual accounts concur that Jamāli's misconception of the teaching was easily demonstrated to be false by Mahāvīra and his chief disciple, that the community of monks briefly under his influence melted away and abandoned its leader and that after a period of preaching he died alone. Jamāli's personality only momentarily contrasts with that of Mahāvīra and the episode of his heresy and its overturning does not play any major structural role in the biography of the Jina. Although one later source asserts, albeit on no obvious authority, that Jamāli was the leader of the Ājīvika sect,[1] there is no record of any sectarian movement claiming descent from him. Furthermore, no memory even of the name of Jamāli is preserved amongst the Digambara Jains, with only the Śvetāmbaras recording a narrative version of his life (Leumann 1998: 306).

In fact, as we shall see, the Śvetāmbaras eventually came to be interested more in the moral deviation which Jamāli came to represent and the karmic destiny which ensued from it rather than the details and implications of the heretical teaching which he advocated. In this short study I propose to consider the fortunes of Jamāli in respect to the manner in which he is portrayed in the canonical and commentarial sources and his transformation into a flawed ethical type and exemplar of hostility towards one's teacher. I will then draw attention to the dispute which developed during the sixteenth and seventeeth centuries concerning the karmic consequences set up by Jamāli's actions and the nature of the rebirths which he experienced after his solitary and unrepentant death.

Jamāli's portrayal in *Bhagavatī Sūtra* 9.33

The only extended source for Jamāli in the scriptural canon is provided by *Bhagavatī Sūtra* (henceforth *Bhagavatī*) 9.33, although there is evidence that a narrative relating to him occurred elsewhere within a now lost version.[2] This section of what is the largest of the scriptural texts, which may in its earliest part date from the first century BCE but in its totality is no doubt several centuries later (Ohira 1994: 5–39), I will now proceed to summarise, following the text given on pp. 455–482 of the Jaina Āgama Series edition of Dośī.

Jamāli is a mighty and rich *kṣatriya*, or member of the warrior class, from the city of Kṣatriyakuṇḍa, living a life of luxury and with eight beautiful wives, who is intrigued by the excitement aroused prior to what he learns will be a sermon preached by Mahāvīra at the Bahuśāla shrine (*ceiya*) outside the city of Brāhmaṇakuṇḍa. He goes to the shrine in a regal fashion, riding a chariot with parasol and martial retinue and pays homage to Mahāvīra. Moved by the Jina's sermon, he resolves to renounce, a course of action for which he is described as being suited in every way. However, his mother is deeply dismayed at his decision and a debate ensues in which the pleasures of the householder's life and the difficulties of the ascetic path are made clear to Jamāli by his parents. However, eventually they acquiesce and give their permission. A lavish preparation for renunciation ensues, with begging bowl and ascetic's whisk being bought at great expense and a barber hired at high price to crop Jamāli's hair so that only four tufts are left and what has been cut off being anointed, perfumed and worshipped (*accittā*) by his mother who then places it in a jewelled casket as a future devotional focus (*darisaṇe*) on holidays and festivals. Thereupon, finely dressed, anointed and attended by glamorous young men and women, Jamāli is taken in a palanquin through streets thronged with onlookers and is formally presented to Mahāvīra by his parents. Then, 'as in the case of the brahman Ṛṣabhadatta' (see below), Jamāli pays homage to Mahāvīra, abandons his fine accoutrements, pulls out his remaining hair and renounces with 500 men to begin the career of an ascetic.

Subsequently, after much fasting and scriptural study, 'developing himself through various acts of austerity' (*vicittehiṃ tavokammehiṃ appāṇaṃ bhāvemāṇe*), Jamāli petitions Mahāvīra to allow him to separate from the larger community to wander with the 500 monks who had renounced with him. The Jina makes no reply even when asked three times and so leaving his master Jamāli goes forth from the vicinity of the Bahuśāla shrine to wander through the countryside with the 500 monks. One day, while outside Śrāvastī, Jamāli falls ill of a fever brought on by of the poor quality of the food he has consumed during his austerities and asks his monastic followers for a bed to be spread for him. On enquiring as to whether the bed was made (*kaḍe*) or being made (*kajjai*), they reply that 'the bed was not made (but) being made' (*ṇo khalu... ṇaṃ sejjāsaṃthārae kaḍe kajjai*). Recalling Mahāvīra's teaching (stated at the very beginning of the *Bhagavatī*) that something which is in the process of moving has actually moved, Jamāli sees directly (*paccakkhaṃ*) that the bed which was in the process of being made has not actually been made and judges this to be a decisive counter-example undermining the Jina's teaching and subverting his authority.

Persuading some of his followers of the force of his insight, but rejected by others, Jamāli goes to confront Mahāvīra, now at the famous Pūrṇabhadra shrine outside Campā, claiming omniscience and equal status with him. Mahāvīra's disciple Gautama challenges Jamāli and asks him to answer questions about the universe and the soul (*jīva*) in respect to whether they are eternal or non-eternal. Jamāli is unable to provide the correct answer, whereupon Mahāvīra states that even his less advanced followers are able to confirm that the world and the soul are simultaneously both eternal in the sense of being unchanging and non-eternal through being subject to temporal and locational modifications. Jamāli does not accept this and withdraws from Mahāvīra's presence, continuing for a long time to follow the ascetic path and to seduce both himself and others 'through preaching what was untrue and his excessive preoccupation with falsehood' (*asabbhāvubbhāvaṇāhiṃ micchattābhinivesehi ya*).

Finally, he fasts to death 'without having confessed and repented' (*aṇāloiya-paḍikkaṃte*), to be reborn in the Lāntaka heaven as one of the class of gods known as Kilbiṣaka for the lengthy time period of thirteen *sāgaropamas*.[3] On being questioned by Gautama about his 'bad pupil' (*kusisse*), Mahāvīra describes the nature and heavenly location of the Kilbiṣaka gods, confirming that Jamāli was born amongst them because of his hostility to his teacher and the community. Those who are hostile to the teacher, the preceptor, the monastic clan (*kula*), the monastic group (*gaṇa*) and the community, who defame and calumniate the teacher and preceptor, who seduce themselves and others through preaching what is untrue and through obsessive preoccupation with falsity and live many years on the ascetic path, eventually die unconfessed and unrepenting and are reborn as Kilbiṣaka gods. After falling from that state when their time runs out, 'they wander through *saṃsāra* taking up to four (or) five existences among hellbeings, animals, men and gods and achieve liberation (that is to say) are then awakened and make an end' (*jāva cattāri paṃca neraiya-tirikkhajoṇiya-maṇussa-devabhavaggahaṇāiṃ saṃsāraṃ aṇupariyaṭṭittā tao pacchā sijjhaṃti bujjhaṃti jāva aṃtaṃ kareṃti*). Some (*atthegatiyā*), however, 'wander through the beginningless, endless[4] and lengthy four-pointed[5] forest of *saṃsāra*' (*aṇādīyaṃ aṇavadaggaṃ dīhamaddhaṃ cāuraṃta-saṃsārakaṃtāraṃ aṇupariyaṭṭaṃti*).

Mahāvīra predicts that Jamāli, in accord with his behaviour as both enemy of his teacher and community and rigorous ascetic, after exhausting his period of time amongst the Kilbiṣaka gods, will wander through *saṃsāra*, 'taking up to five existences amongst animals, men and gods, and then will attain deliverance which will bring his sufferings to an end' (*jāva paṃca tirikkhajoṇiya-maṇussa-devabhavaggahaṇāiṃ saṃsāraṃ aṇupariyaṭṭittā tao pacchā sijjhihiti jāva aṃtam kāhiti*).

Comments on *Bhagavatī* 9.33

Certain observations and expansions can be made with regard to the story of Jamāli as just summarised.

(1) The name Jamāli is slightly odd in appearance. However, as Bollée has shown, it is most easily to be taken as the equivalent of Sanskrit *Yama-ari*, 'enemy of Yama, the god of death' (Bollée 1994: 66), with r > l signifying an eastern provenance. Bollée also suggests a possible Vaiṣṇava (and thus possibly a Western?) connection for the name. However, equivalent epithets such as Yamāntaka tend to relate more normally to manifestations of Śiva.

(2) The text specifies that stereotyped passages found in the first *upāṅga* text of the canon, the *Aupapātika Sūtra*, are to be inserted (*jahā Uvavāie*) to flesh out the description of the events prior to Jamāli becoming a monk. This section itself became a stereotyped passage, paradigmatic of the renunciation of wealthy young males as envisaged in early Jainism, incorporated into the story of Megha at *Jñātṛdharmakathāḥ* 1.[6] The reference to Jamāli's mother worshipping his cut hair and placing it in a casket for future devotional use is reminiscent of the preservation and worship of physical relics, specific evidence for which is generally difficult to find in early Jainism.

(3) The description of Jamāli's post-renunciatory career makes clear that he undoubtedly led a life of austerities in accord with the stipulation of the Jain path, but also that he left Mahāvīra and assumed the role of a teacher without specific authorisation. His demand when he had fallen ill that a bed be made for him thus infringes correct monastic practice which would normally expect that attentive service (*vaiyāvṛttya*) be offered by one's fellow monks. Furthermore, illness in Jainism is regarded as being the result of some sort of excess (Deo 1954–1955: 209–210), which in Jamāli's case might be taken as overintense practice of austerities.

(4) The teaching challenged by Jamāli is famously enunciated at the beginning of the *Bhagavatī* where a series of nine doublets taking the form of present participle and past participle asserts the position that any action which is actually under way is equivalent to having been completed. The *Bhagavatī* invokes this principle sporadically in various contexts, some relating to monastic practice, others to ontology (Ohira 1994: 149).

The principle is not one which seems to have been much referred to by later Jain philosophers. It is, however, deployed as an explanatory mechanism by the thirteenth century karma theorist Devendra Sūri in his autocommentary on verse 25 of his *Caturtha Karmagrantha* where he invokes the expression *gṛhyamāṇaṃ gṛhītam*, 'what is being taken is taken', a variant of *calemāṇe caliaṃ*, 'what is in motion has moved', of *Bhagavatī* 1.1 and *kaḍemāṇe kaḍaṃ*, 'what is being done is done', of *Bhagavatī* 9.33, with reference to the physical appropriation of atoms in the formation of the material (*audārika*) body (cf. Mahetā 1999: 95–96). *Bhagavatī* 9.33 does not provide any broader context for the teaching and Jamāli's misconception of it is not specifically refuted. In effect, Jamāli seems to represent a type of naive empiricist, not dissimilar to King Prasenajit criticised in the *Rājapraśnīya Sūtra*, in that he appeals to direct experience alone to justify the implausibility of a doctrinal principle (Dundas 2002: 94).

The only developed modern interpretations of the nature of Jamāli's heretical teaching and the Jain tenet which he reformulates have been provided by Ohira and, most recently, Bronkhorst, who does not draw on the former's work. Ohira bases her interpretation primarily on canonical material, whereas Bronkhorst largely refers to Jinabhadra's *Viśeṣāvasyakabhāṣya* (sixth century) and the canonical commentator Śīlāṅka (ninth century).

Ohira (1994: 149–150) holds that the tenet challenged by Jamāli, namely that what is being done is actually done, represents a genuine difficulty in the analysis of action as located in time, in that the nature of action may in fact change during a period of time. She argues that the principle is most easily 'applicable to problems involving volitional action in the field of ethical conduct' and that the Jain theoreticians subsequently applied the principle to other areas. Ohira concludes that as far as the nature of action is concerned, Jamāli was correct in his criticisms.

Bronkhorst cites Jinabhadra's interpretation of Jamāli's heresy as relating to the possibility of something emerging from an existent or non-existent entity and thus being located in a broader nexus of ontological issues involving production which orthodox Jainism found objectionable. He also refers to Śīlāṅka's argument that Jamāli failed to grasp the principle that what is being made is made in actuality operates in accord with the worldly standpoint (*vyavahāranaya*), thus misunderstanding how ordinary usage works. Bronkhorst interprets Jamāli's heresy and the response by Gautama and Mahāvīra about the nature of the universe and soul as linked and suggests the possibility that *anekāntavāda*, the doctrine of the multiple nature of reality, has been developed in response to the problem of the production of entities (Bronkhorst 1999: 61–66).

(5) The Kilbiṣaka gods amongst whom Jamāli is reborn are the equivalent of the lowermost stratum of human society. The highest of their three classes is located in the Lāntaka heaven (Schubring 2000: 246).[7]

The text of the option presented by *Bhagavatī* 9.33 concerning the rebirth of those who cease to Kilbiṣaka gods is not entirely certain. The general statement by Mahāvīra about the rebirth of those who are hostile to their teachers has the word *jāva* (~ Sanskrit *yāvat*) before the words *cattāri paṃca* to give the apparent sense of 'up to four (or) five rebirths'.[8] The equivalent passage referring specially to Jamāli according to Dośī's Jaina Āgama Series edition reads *jāva paṃca*, with *cattāri* given only as a variant, whereas the recent edition by Muni Dīparatnasāgara has *cattāri paṃca*, that is, without *jāva*, as does the 1953 Sthānakvāsī edition of Pupphabhikkhū, the 1974 Terāpanthī edition of Muni Nathmal and Lalwani's text of 1985. The *jāva* which occurs later in both sentences in fact functions as an abbreviation marker, indicating that stereotyped or previously given material has to be supplied. Only the Terāpanthī edition specifically inserts the wording of this material.[9]

It is undoubtedly important for later Jain discussants that Jamāli's destiny as predicted by Mahāvīra is finite in that he will attain liberation and put an end to his sufferings.[10]

The structure of *Bhagavatī* 9

The extensive *Bhagavatī* has generally been mined by scholarship without reference to the overall structure and coherence of its constituent parts. This clearly composite scripture's recent students, most notably Deleu, have certainly been sensitive to the fact that conscious organisational principles were deployed by the monastic editors (Deleu 1970: 45–69), yet the possible implications of this for the interpretation of *Bhagavatī* 9 have not been adequately pursued. Here I wish briefly to draw attention to the manner in which the story of Jamāli can convey meaning not only by being detached from its moorings and treated simply as evidence of a possible trend in early Indian thought but by being situated more firmly in its scriptural context as a component of *Bhagavatī* 9 with some connections to the other sections of that chapter.

It would certainly appear to be natural to locate the central significance of Jamāli's career exclusively in the heretical teaching he is described as propounding and so concentrate upon this, as do Ohira and Bronkhorst in their treatment of *Bhagavatī* 9.33. However, that is certainly not the approach taken in the commentary by the eleventh century Abhayadeva Sūri. This highly authoritative exegete devotes a great deal of space to elucidating the passage describing Jamāli's progress towards renunciation, including his abandonment of what is effectively a kingly way of life, and relatively little to the issues involved in his teaching. Furthermore, a focussed reading of the ninth chapter of the *Bhagavatī* as a whole (rather than merely the portion of section 33 which deals with Jamāli) suggests that there is a single important theme under consideration throughout, namely the nature of omniscience and those who have attained it, which binds the various sections together and imposes a degree of unity.

Chapter 9 of the *Bhagavatī* commences, as do the other chapters of this scripture, with a verse summing up by catchwords in standard *niryukti* style the various topics dealt with in each *uddeśaka*, or section. These are respectively seven: the continent of Jambūdvīpa, the planetary bodies above it, the intermediate continents in the Lavaṇa Ocean, those who have learnt and activated the doctrine without hearing it from the appropriate people, Gaṅgeya (an ascetic follower of Mahāvīra's predecessor Pārśva), the city of Kuṇḍagrāma and the killing of living beings.

The first three of these topics, constituting *Bhagavatī* 9. 1–30, involve answers given at Mithilā and Rājagṛha by Mahāvīra to questions asked by Gautama concerning terrestrial and celestial geography. The specific and detailed answers given by Mahāvīra can be viewed as guarantors of his status as a fully enlightened being and clearly serve to establish his unimpeachable omniscient authority at the outset of *Bhagavatī* 9.

The next *uddeśaka, Bhagavatī* 9.31, links up with the foregoing by discussing the nature of authority, its source and those who are connected with it. Mahāvīra describes how after the 'destruction-calming' (*khaovasama*) of knowledge-concealing karma and various other types of karma, an individual can gain an understanding of the teaching 'without hearing' (*asoccā*) it from one of the ten kinds of people who know (Deleu 1970: 108–109) and also gain wisdom, become a monk, practise asceticism of various kinds, ward off karma and eventually, after eliminating karma completely, gain omniscience. However, this particular type of person has only a limited capacity to proclaim the teaching and to initiate monks, although he will eventually attain liberation. Equally, the individual who actually hears the doctrine from one of the ten kinds of people who know and follows the same trajectory of career can proclaim the doctrine and teach pupils who are then able to form a preceptorial lineage.

The setting of the next *uddeśaka, Bhagavatī* 9.32, is the vicinity of Vāṇiyagrāma where Gaṅgeya, a follower of Pārśva, questions Mahāvīra about the dynamics of rebirth for the four main types of living creatures, with particular reference to the various hells. Mention is made of Pārśva's teaching about the eternity of the world, with Mahāvīra asserting that through his own attainment of omniscience he gained an understanding of this truth independently (*asoccā*). He confirms that human beings are reborn as result of their own various activities. Gaṅgeya is converted on the textual model of another follower of Pārśva, Kālāśa Vaiśyaputra (Deleu 1970: 162–163 and Ohira 1994: 136).

The setting of the next *uddeśaka, Bhagavatī* 9.33, is located near Brāhmaṇakuṇḍagrāma, which seems to refer to the district of the city of Kuṇḍagrāma inhabited by brahmans. At this location Mahāvīra has homage paid to him by Ṛṣabhadatta and his wife Devānandā. The latter is declared to be Mahāvīra's mother, a reference to the episode of the transfer of the embryo prior to the Jina's birth in a *kṣatriya* family (Dundas 2002: 26); a contrasting link might also be made with the grief of Jamāli's mother in the following section. Ṛṣabhadatta and Devānandā both renounce in the manner of another brahman, Skandaka Kātyāyana, described in *Bhagavatī* 2.1, and eventually reach the goal of the path. The rest of the section deals with Jamāli who lives in the *kṣatriya* quarter in the city of Kuṇḍagrāma.[11] This develops as described earlier. Mahāvīra's reference to the various stages of Jamāli's rebirths in heavens both alludes to his own omniscience and points back to *Bhagavatī* 9.32 which deals with the possible rebirth for hellbeings, animals, men and gods, concluding that individuals are reborn through morally positive (*subha*), morally negative (*asubha*) and mixed (*subhāsubha*) karma.

The final commentarial statement on this section by Abhayadeva Sūri deals with the issue of why Mahāvīra, who as an omniscient being must have known what would ensue, nonetheless still initiated Jamāli. One possible answer is that it is difficult to overcome (*laṅgh*) things which happen of necessity. Alternatively, it could be argued Mahāvīra saw some particular quality in Jamāli. As Abhayadeva Sūri puts it, the omniscient do not act purposelessly with regard to anything.

The final *uddeśaka*, *Bhagavatī* 9.34, deals with the nature of violence, demonstrating that in killing one living creature, many entities are destroyed in conjunction. Such violence is caused by enmity. The section concludes by describing how lower forms of life and plants breathe each other in, effectively a kind of violence. Similar violence is caused by air bodies blowing as wind through the leaves of a tree and causing it to fall. Although Deleu does not see any connection between 9.34 and the *uddeśaka* preceding (Deleu 1970: 60), its discussion of the nature of completed action in terms of violence provides an obvious link with the teaching disputed by Jamāli. Furthermore, it connects directly to the theme of omniscience, since ability to pass authoritative judgment on unseen entities such as air bodies is of necessity restricted to the omniscient.

The Jamāli *uddeśaka* of the *Bhagavatī* 9.33 can be regarded as making its point by means of a foregrounding throughout of the issues of enlightenment and concomitant correct understanding of the nature of reality, already established with reference to Mahāvīra at the beginning of the chapter as central source of authority on the Jain path. For Jamāli claimed to be an omniscient *kevalin*, the equal of Mahāvīra, in the same way as another 'dubious' figure to be described later in the *Bhagavatī*, Makkhali Gosāla, and thus can be regarded as a limited type of teacher of the type described at 9.31. Gautama's ignoring of Jamāli's teaching and his posing to him of counter-questions about the nature of the universe and the soul automatically put the discussion within the framework of omniscience and also alludes to the episode of Gaṅgeya at 9.32 where Mahāvīra refers to his independent discovery of this truth. The only commentary we have on this passage, that of Abhayadeva Sūri, specifically contrasts Jamāli and Gaṅgeya which suggests that at least one highly authoritative reader interpreted the passage intertextually in conjunction with the preceding section. There is also reference to the episode of the brahman Skandaka Kātyāyana at *Bhagavatī* 2.1 who was converted by Mahāvīra's teaching about the nature of the universe and the soul and the description of whose renunciation was to be a paradigmatic stereotyped passage for the conversion of those of high class at other comparable parts of the text, as, for example, in the case of Ṛṣabhadatta's renunciation at the beginning of *Bhagavatī* 9.33 which in turn serves as the model for that of Jamāli.

The intensity of Jamāli's intellectual delusion is thus confirmed by his failure to grasp a teaching which served to convert two individuals who were not members of the Jain community. The overall context of *Bhagavatī* 9.33 relates most clearly to the establishment of the fact that Jamāli is an imperfect (*chadmastha*) and self-appointed teacher. It is clear that Mahāvīra and Gautama do not specifically disprove Jamāli (cf. Ohira 1994: 148), and a reading of this section in the light of the whole chapter suggests that Jamāli is a negative exemplar not so much because of the precise nature of his teaching as through his refusal to accept the authority of the omniscient Mahāvīra. As such, he provides a paradigmatic example of a type of misguided and unauthorised teacher challenging details of scripture (and thus in von Simson's terms a type of contrasting characterisation) whose ambiguous identity as in certain respects both Jain and non-Jain was increasingly to preoccupy later Śvetāmbara Jain intellectuals, as sectarian splits developed within the community at a later period.

The development of the story of Jamāli

An expansion of the *Bhagavatī* version of the story of Jamāli in terms both of protagonists and refutation of the heretical teaching can be found in the *Āvaśyaka Cūrṇi* (pp. 416–420) of Jinadāsa (seventh century). The location of the story of the first *pavayaṇaniṇhaga* in Jainism within this text is significant in that it occurs after the story of the seventh *pavayaṇaniṇhaga* Goṣṭhāmāhila. As with the other heretics, the only canonical reference to Goṣṭhāmāhila is *Sthānāṅga Sūtra* 587 which gives a list of designated teachings and the names of teachers and places of origin correlated with them. The full significance of Goṣṭhāmāhila's teaching is adumbrated for the first time by the *Āvaśyaka* commentarial literature where it is said to involve a modification of Jain doctrine, positing a situation where the soul is merely 'touched' by karmic matter and not bound by it, a notion which recalls *Bhagavatī* 9.34, the *uddeśaka* immediately following the Jamāli section, which describes somebody who kills as being 'touched' by enmity. In the case of both these teachers, there occurs what seems from an analytical perspective to be little more than a readjustment of a detail of standard doctrine, rather than any major reframing of the basic premises of the path as a whole. Yet, as Jainism developed, the doctrinaire position of many orthodox members of the community was that rejection of just a small fragment of the teaching was tantamount to rejection of the entirety.[12]

With regard to the early part of Jamāli's career, the *Āvaśyaka Cūrṇi* describes itself as being in accord with the *Bhagavatī*, but in fact introduces a significant novelty. Not only is Jamāli said to be the son of Mahāvīra's eldest sister Sudarśanā and so his nephew, he is also presented as the husband of the Jina's daughter Anavadyāṃgī, more normally called Priyadarśanā and thus his son-in-law.[13] As in the *Bhagavatī*, the *Āvaśyaka Cūrṇi* depicts Jamāli as realising on the basis of direct experience of one particular case that Mahāvīra's teachings are false. However, while some monks of his group believed his interpretation, others did not and the text switches from Prākrit to Sanskrit to show how the orthodox teaching of *calemāṇe calitaṃ*, 'something in the process of moving has moved' is correct, with specific reference to the operation of karmic matter and employing the analogy of the production of a woven cloth (*paṭa*).[14] Jamāli refuses to accept the force of this and his monks leave him, returning to Mahāvīra.

The focus of the narrative shifts to Priyadarśanā, who following her husband, renounced with a thousand nuns and then joined his breakaway community. Her mistaken acceptance of Jamāli's heresy through love for him is overturned when after performing the ceremony of *caityavandana* she visits the house of the potter Ḍhaṃka. Informed by Priyadarśaṇā of Jamāli's teaching, he knows that she is mistaken, but tells her that he does not understand the issue in detail (*visesataraṃ*). Later, while Priyadarśanā was carrying out the necessary ascetic duty of 'study at the appropriate time of the day' (*sajjhāya-porisī*), Ḍhaṃka was engaged in manufacturing (*? uvvattaṃteṇaṃ*) dishes. A spark of fire flew (from his kiln?) which burnt the top part of Priyadarsanā's robe (*saṃghāḍī*). She indignantly told the potter that it had been burnt and he retorted by invoking what must logically be her view derived from Jamāli, namely that 'something being burnt is not burnt' (*dajjhamāṇe adaḍḍhe*). So in that case how can her garment be burnt since only a part of it has been affected? Priyadarśanā gained understanding (*saṃbuddhā*) with regard to that matter and went to Jamāli to explain it. He, however, did not understand it and so with her followers Priyadarśanā rejoined Mahāvīra. The rest of the section follows the *Bhagavatī*'s account of Jamāli's lack of repentance and we hear no more of his erstwhile wife.

Close approximations to the *Āvaśyaka Cūrṇi*'s version, with generally somewhat lengthier consideration of the philosophical issue at stake, were to be deployed by several later Śvetāmbara writers, most notably Hemacandra (1089–1172) in his *Triṣaṣṭiśalākāpuruṣacarita* 10.8.28–108 (Johnson's translation, vol 6. pp. 197–198), Jinapati Sūri (1153–1220) in his commentary on Jineśvara Sūri's *Pañcaliṅgīprakaraṇa* (pp. 33a–44b) and Jinakuśala Sūri (1280–1332) in his commentary on Jinadatta Sūri's *Caityavandanakulaka* (pp. 55–58).[15] Predictably, they repeat the *Āvaśyaka Cūrṇi*'s claim that Jamāli was Mahāvīra's son-in-law. Schubring (2000: 33) notes that this fact is not actually mentioned in the two canonical biographies of Mahāvīra, namely book two of the *Ācārāṅga Sūtra* and the *Jinacarita* section of the *Kalpa Sūtra*,[16] nor in the *Bhagavatī*, and he cites the *Āvaśyaka* literature as the authority, claiming that Jamāli's name had been suppressed in the earlier texts. Deleu, who is, as we have seen, commendably aware of some connections between sections in *Bhagavatī* 9, argues for something similar, claiming that the two episodes in *Bhagavatī* 9.33 'are linked up to oppose Jamāli, the heretical monk of kṣatriya birth, whose relationship with [Mahāvīra] the text expressly conceals, and Devāṇandā, the righteous nun of brāhmaṇa birth who [Mahāvīra] says is his real mother' (Deleu 1970: 60).

Here we have an example of how an acceptance of Jain tradition can distort a critical understanding of Jain history. The particular relationship between Mahāvīra and Jamāli, which Schubring and Deleu claim has been 'hushed up' in the early biographical literature of the Jina, does not in textual form predate the *Āvaśyaka* commentary literature, although it is understandable how invoking such a family tie would give added point to the story. Furthermore, through Jamāli's supposed marriage with his mother's brother's daughter, there occurs a clear instance of cross-cousin marriage, a practice normally associated with the south of India and so generally styled Dravidian. Trautmann (1974) has drawn attention to the fact that cross-cousin marriage of the Dravidian pattern has been a constant feature of family alliances in western India (which of course is and was non-Dravidian ethnically) and that any sources which describe it (in fact he only adduces one of Jain provenance) cannot be of eastern origin, even though their subject matter is located in that region, because there is no obvious evidence of cross-cousin marriage being or having both practised in the Ganges basin.

Thus the conclusion must be that the story of Jamāli's marital relationship with Mahāvīra cannot be based on historical actuality, let alone involve, as claimed with regard to the *Bhagavatī*, some sort of suppression of information, but rather reflects the western Indian provenance of the *Āvaśyaka Cūrṇi*. It might be going too far to suggest that the whole story of Jamāli has been anachronistically linked with Mahāvīra by the redactors of a scriptural tradition whose centre of operations was in western India, but it might instil caution with regard to accepting everything in the Jain scriptures as being of an original eastern origin (cf. Tieken 2001: 587).

The emergence of Jamāli as a type and the question of his rebirths

The *Āvaśyaka Cūrṇi* (p. 418) explains *Bahuraya*, the name of Jamāli's heresy according to *Sthānāṅga Sūtra* 587, as signifying that 'many were delighted by his belief' (*etāe diṭṭhīe bahue jīvā ratā*).[17] However, there seems to be no evidence of any distinctive sect which perpetuated the master's insight. The early common era collections of Prākrit commentarial verses refer to Jamāli as emblematic of a type inimical to the Jain community, but make no obvious reference to his teachings. According to *Sūtrakṛtāṇga Niryukti* v. 125, 'The man of devious arguments who undermines with devious mind what has come down through succession of teachers will die as Jamāli died'.[18] This verse was often quoted by later writers as a warning against selfishly causing strife in the Śvetāmbara Jain community.[19] *Bṛhatkalpabhāṣya* v. 1324 is similar in tone: 'But whatever ignorant man having traduced that same (true) path, by (following) his own logic resorts to what is the wrong path is like the unperturbed (?) Jamāli'.[20] Another influential text from a later period, Śānti Sūri's (tenth century) *Ceiyavaṃdaṇamahābhāsa* v. 131 again characterises Jamāli as the epitome of all negative tendencies: 'The man who despises the community, considers himself learned and adopts what is bad (nonetheless) contrives to think of himself as different from people, just like Jamāli'.[21]

A still later writer, Jinamaṇḍana Gaṇi (fifteenth century) sums up in his *Śrāddhaguṇavivaraṇa* (p. 52a) what had become the standard image of Jamāli as an *abhiniviṣṭa*, a man in the grip of an obsession who 'as a rule attempts to establish a teaching of his own making through failing to consider the fundamentals of Jain philosophy'.[22]

As mentioned earlier, *Bhagavatī* 9.33 describes Mahāvīra's confirmation that those who have been born as Kilbiṣaka gods will after subsequent rebirth experience a maximum of five births in the four possible types of existence and then achieve deliverance, while others will continue to be reborn throughout *saṃsāra*. Jamāli, asserts Mahāvīra, will fall into the first category, apart from the fact that he will be reborn only amongst animals, gods and men, not amongst hellbeings. The later narratives of Jamāli are not uniform in reproducing this prediction. The *Āvaśyaka Cūrṇi* only refers to the heretic's birth as a god and says nothing about his future existences. Siddharṣi (ninth–tenth centuries) in his commentary called *Heyopadeya* on *Upadeśamālā* v. 459 has Jamāli bringing to conclusion a period as a Kilbiṣaka god and endless existence (*kilbiṣakadevatvaṃ bhavam cānantaṃ nivartitavān*). Vardhamāna (eleventh century), however, another commentator on the *Upadeśamālā*, describes in the same manner as the *Bhagavatī* how Jamāli will experience four or five existences as animal, human and god before attaining deliverance. Hemacandra in the *Triṣaṣṭiśalākāpuruṣacarita* has him undergoing five rebirths (Johnson's translation, vol. 6: 198). Jinapati Sūri (see previous section) simply describes the heretic as experiencing various (*anyānya*) existences after ceasing to be a god, while Jinakuśala Sūri (see previous section) gives no information at all about his post-Kilbiṣika destiny.

It can be said that medieval Śvetāmbara tradition became increasingly more preoccupied with the precise characteristics of Jamāli's rebirth destiny than with any possible ramifications of his heretical teaching. Succinct evidence for this can be seen in a question posed in the *Hīrapraśnottarāṇi*, a collection compiled by Kīrtivijaya in the second decade of the seventeenth century comprising answers provided by the great teacher Hīravijaya Sūri to various problems and a key source for assessing what issues members of the important Śvetāmbara subsect, the Tapā Gaccha, found difficult or controversial at that time. The question is put simply (p. 17): on the basis of the evidence of three textual sources, the *Bhagavatī*, the *Karṇikāvṛtti* commentary on the *Upadeśamālā* and the *Vīracaritra*, how many existences did Jamāli experience? The answer is even simpler: these texts show that he experienced fifteen existences.[23]

In his *Vicāraratnākara* (pp. 42b–43b) the afore-mentioned Kīrtivijaya expands on this. He describes how some 'contemporary pseudo-scholars' (*ādhunikāḥ paṇḍitamanyāḥ*) appeal to scripture in order to form the conclusion that Jamāli underwent endless (*ananta*) existences. The specific scriptural reference adduced by them is from *Nandī Sūtra* 116–117 which asserts that throughout all periods, past, present and future, the result of 'damaging' or 'disrupting' (*virāhaṇā*) the scriptural canon (*duvālāsaṃgaṃ gaṇipiḍagaṃ*) through promulgating something contrary to it in terms of wording, meaning or both is to wander through 'four pointed' (*cāuraṃta*) *saṃsāra*. By contrast, a respectful attitude (*arāhaṇā*) towards scripture enables one to get beyond *saṃsāra*.[24]

Those who argue on this basis, claims Kīrtivijaya, fail to understand the point (*tātparya*) of the scriptural passage. Although the commentary has given Jamāli as an example of wandering through four-pointed *saṃsāra* on the grounds of his damaging scripture through wilfully misreading it,[25] this example is in fact partial (*ekadeśena*), that being no complete correlation (*sarvātmanā tulyatvam*) of the example and the point which is to be derived from the example (*dārṣṭāntika*). In the same way as the simile 'her face is like the delightful moon' is incomplete as an index of a woman's beauty,[26] the example of Jamāli simply relates to wandering through *saṃsāra*, not to the 'fourpointed forest' (*cāuraṃtaṃ kaṃtāraṃ*) of *saṃsāra*. Wandering through *saṃsāra* for Jamāli is completed by (*saṃpannam*) fifteen existences. If the example of Jamāli is not taken as partial but as a totality (*sarvātmanā*), then contradiction with the *Bhagavatī* would be involved (*saṃpanīpadyate*), for the scripture states that he will experience only four or five existences in respect to three stages of rebirth (*gati*) and does not refer to limitless (*ananta*) existences.[27]

Kīrtivijaya's discussion bears witness to the fact that by the early seventeenth century the nature of Jamāli's karmic destiny had come to be a factor in the dispute between the rival Sāgara and Vijaya lineages of the Tapā Gaccha. While it goes without saying that practical issues of power and authority were involved, a central feature of the dispute as intellectually constituted revolved around the moral status of those who did not belong to the Tapā Gaccha and the uprightness or otherwise of teachers who promulgated paths different from orthodox Jainism, with Jamāli functioning as a possible primordial example of such an individual (Balbir 1999 and Dundas forthcoming).

Dharmasāgara, who flourished in the second half of the sixteenth century, is clearly the individual who is being criticised by Kīrtivijaya in the *Vicāraratnākara*. His highly controversial *Sarvajñaśataka*, 'One Hundred Verses on the Omniscent Ones', a work proscribed by the leaders of the Tapā Gaccha for its intolerant stance, strongly reasserts (vv. 103–104 with autocommentary) the view of the *Bhagavatī* that Jamāli was in the grip of false doctrine through irrational obsession and a promulgater of what is contrary to scripture (*utsūtra*) in that he misrepresented the words of the teachings. As an agent of disrespect (*āśātanā*) towards the Jinas, Dharmasāgara claims against what would appear to be the specific statement of the *Bhagavatī*, that Jamāli must on such grounds inevitably be *anantasaṃsārin*, an individual who will be reborn for an 'endless' period of time (see below), rather than having his existences restricted to fifteen, albeit eventually attaining deliverance after this. This judgement fits into the broader strategy directed by Dharmasāgara at what he perceives to be false teachers and self-appointed leaders of sectarian splits.

I will now give a highly condensed account of the salient points of Dharmasāgara's argument and then demonstrate how they were countered in the second half of the seventeeth century by Yaśovijaya, the main representative of the irenic wing of the Tapā Gaccha. Of necessity, I will omit the fine detail of what is often a rather involved argument.

Dharmasāgara on Jamāli's rebirths

The root verses of the *Sarvajñaśataka* are composed in Prākrit. Verse 103 runs as follows: 'The obsessive (*abhiṇivesī*) who is deeply involved in disrespect towards the Jinas and their teachings (*āsāyaṇā*) is certainly an ocean of suffering brought about by endless (*ananta*) saṃsāra, as in the example of Jamāli'.[28]

In his Sanskrit autocommentary, Dharmasāgara provides as supporting scriptural authority *Gacchācāra* v. 31 which prescribes endless (*ananta*) *saṃsāra* for monks who have set out on the wrong path (*unmārga*, glossed as *nihnavamārga*, the 'path of concealing the doctrine') and those who destroy the true path.[29] He then refers to the fact that the term *ananta*, literally 'without end', is in actuality divided into gradations, from the lowest (*jaghanya*) upward; in other words, *ananta* does not literally mean 'endless'.[30] Dharmasāgara claims that since ascribing to the Jina what has not been preached by him is the worst sort of fault, the consequence must be commensurate in intensity. Therefore at the maximum (*utkṛṣṭatayā*) the length of rebirth in *saṃsāra* experienced by such an individual as, for example, Jamāli, who evinced great disrespect (*āśatanā*) towards the Jina and his words, can be said in technical terms to consist of 'half a *pudgala-parāvartta* less a part' (*deśonāpārddha-pudgala-parāvartta*). Given that a *pudgala-parāvartta* represents 'the time required by a soul to absorb as karman at least once all the atoms of the universe and release them after they have come to fruition' (Tatia 1958: 291), a soul such as that of Jamāli, who represents a standard exemplification of an enemy of the doctrine, can be regarded as condemned to a vast period of rebirth, albeit not a literally endless one, for eventually he will gain deliverance, as is clearly stated in the *Bhagavatī*.[31] Dharmasāgara backs up this judgement by reference to the authoritative Śīlāṅka (ninth century) who in commenting on *Sūtrakṛtāṅga Niryukti* v. 125 (referred to earlier) uses the analogy of a pot revolving on a mechanical waterwheel (*araghaṭṭaghaṭīyantra*) to describe the rebirth destiny of such an individual who misrepresents the doctrine which has descended through the teacher lineage (cf. Bollée 1977: 113, n. 35).

Dharmasāgara clarifies the context of this analogy by claiming that it applies to whoever experiences a particularly long (*drāghīyasī*) period of *saṃsāra* through repeated rebirth amongst one-sensed creatures and the rest. This is confirmed by reference to Haribhadra (sixth century) who describes at *Upadeśapada* v. 16 how the fault of carelessness in respect to one's surroundings (*pramāda*) as a result of ignorance leads to long 'life-duration' (*kāyasthiti*) amongst one-sensed creatures.[32] Municandra (eleventh–twelfth centuries), the commentator on this verse, expands it by reference to the analogy of the waterwheel. Dharmasāgara then goes on to quote *Nandī Sūtra* 116–117 (also cited by Kīrtivijaya in his *Vicāraratnākara*; see above) which refers to the consequence of harming the scriptural canon as being wandering through four-pointed *saṃsāra*, and the eleventh century Malayagiri's commentary thereon which invokes Jamāli as an example of someone who damages the scriptures through reading them differently (*anyathā sūtraṃ paṭhati*) because of obsession (*abhiniveśa*). This position is clinched by Dharmasāgara by reference to a verse from the *Pañcasaṃgraha* (eleventh century): 'He who does not approve of one word of scripture, even though approving of the rest, is of false belief like Jamāli'.[33] If in the light of these various authoritative references Jamāli, who has evinced massive disrespect towards the word of the Jinas, were not to be *anantasaṃsārin* but rather one whose rebirths are delimited to a mere fifteen, then, Dharmasāgara claims, there would be massive inconsistency.

Dharmasāgara goes on to deal with the issue of possible discrepancy between some of the textual accounts of Jamāli's fate by reference to the standard description in *Bhagavatī* 9.33 and Siddharṣi's commentary on *Upadeśamālā* v. 459. The *Upadeśamālā*, which describes Jamāli as abandoning a kingdom and becoming leader of the Ājīvikas (see note 1), does not provide any details about his fate. Siddharṣi's commentary, which Dharmasāgara specifically dates to the Vikrama era year 720 (i.e. 663 CE) and so confirms as an old but non-canonical authority, describes Jamāli as first being reborn as a Kilbiṣaka god because of the intense austerity he had performed and as thereafter experiencing endless rebirth (*bhavaṃ cānantaṃ nivartitavān*) until he attained deliverance.[34] The *Bhagavatī*, however, refers to 'four (or) five' (*cattāri paṃca*) animal, human and god existences prior to final deliverance (which demonstrates that Dharmasāgara is not following the reading of the Jaina Āgama Series edition). In reply to the obvious objection that the meaning of the scriptural passage does not signify endless rebirths, however that is interpreted, Dharmasāgara states that the numerical expression 'four (or) five' relates sequentially (*krameṇa*) to moving (*trasa*) and stationary (*sthāvara*) types of life and thus gives a total of nine when comprising all *jīvas* (namely one-sensed earth-, water-, fire-, wind-, tree-life forms, and two-sensed, three-sensed, four-sensed and five-sensed creatures). Rebirth amongst humans and gods certainly relates to the five-sensed category, but rebirth amongst animals, Dharmasāgara claims by applying the term to lower forms of life, involves all nine categories and is 'endless' for those expressing contempt towards the Jinas and their teachings. This, he claims, is the position in authoritative scripture in general.

Dharmasāgara goes on to explain the implication of the foregoing. It is normally an accepted principle that those who are enemies of their teachers wander endlessly in *saṃsāra* among the nine possible types of life in the four states of rebirth (animal, hellbeing, human and god). However, *Bhagavatī* 9.33 has to be taken separately as describing a special case because it states that Jamāli through his own specific and unique destiny (*tathābhavyatva*) will be reborn among only three of these states, that is, with the exception of that of hellbeings. So an individual can through fate be reborn among the gods, and among the hellbeings also, without being reborn in animal and human state.[35] However, taking birth amongst animals and human beings is necessary to bring about endless wandering throughout *saṃsāra* and subsequent deliverance. Thus the expression 'taking birth amongst animals amid the nine states of existence', which is how Dharmasāgara interprets Mahāvīra's prediction of Jamāli's destiny in *Bhagavatī* 9.33, must be regarded as denoting such endless wandering. In actuality, Dharmasāgara claims, reference to animal rebirths also conventionally (*samayabhāṣayā*) denotes endless existences.[36]

In addition, there is evidence of a more unambiguous account of Jamāli's fortunes. Dharmasāgara refers to a manuscript of the Jamāli section of *Bhagavatī* 9.33

which does not contain the word 'four' (and thus is in accord with Jaina Āgama Series reading), so that the reference is simply to rebirth among the five types of life defined as one-sensed to five-sensed. The account of Jamāli given by Hemacandra in his *Triṣaṣṭiśalalākāpuruṣacarita* seems to reflect this, describing him as falling from heaven, then wandering for five times (*pañcakṛtvaḥ*) among animals, men and gods. Dharmasāgara interprets this as meaning rebirth five times amongst animals only and suggests that since Jamāli has indulged in great disrespect towards the Jinas and their teachings, his fate could unquestionably involve a endless period of time in that even if one is reborn five times amongst animals, one could still experience endless rebirths multiplied endless times.

Furthermore, Dharmasāgara continues, the general applicability (*prayoga*) of the scriptural statement about Jamāli wandering through *saṃsāra* has of necessity to relate to endless existences. For such a general point relating to a predestined soul (*bhavya*) whose deliverance is imminent after a brief period of finite existences does not occur in any authoritative text. What is being indicated is that Jamāli, having ceased his period of existence among the Kilbiṣaka gods, thereupon experienced some low and contemptible human births not conducive to following Jainism, being subsequently reborn among minute (*sūkṣma*) one-sensed creatures.[37] It is impossible, indeed against scripture, that somebody who has erred as Jamāli did in being inimical to his teacher will, immediately on ceasing to be a Kilbiṣaka god, re-enter the Jain path. Thus what is stated about Jamāli's wandering through *saṃsāra* in the *Bhagavatī* and other authoritative sources (*sāmānyasūtram*) can be said to be consistent. The more radical statement of the *Bhagavatī* that some wander for ever through beginningless and endless four-pointed *saṃsāra* must be understood as referring to the souls called *abhavya*, who are doomed to eternal rebirth because of their innate negative propensities, since there is no mention in the text of their gaining of deliverance.

Dharmasāgara then attacks the possibility that the number 'five' mentioned in the *Bhagavatī* should be multiplied by the three rebirth states to give a total of fifteen existences for Jamāli, which was Hīravijaya's Sūri's conclusion recorded in the *Hīrapraśnottarāṇi* (see above). Leaving aside the problem of the word 'four' also occurring in the *Bhagavatī* (here Dharmasāgara does not refer to the manuscript he has previously adduced) and thus the possibility of differing calculations of the relevant numbers, how would the five existences be divided up? Would it be two existences as animal, two as god and one as human? Or three as animal, one as human and one as god? Or what? There is no reference in any authoritative text which would make such a calculation valid.

Dharmasāgara argues that the general example of scripture which prescribes the period of rebirth for delinquents must hold good. Otherwise Marīci, the grandson of Ṛṣabha the first Jina of this time cycle who is ultimately reborn as the final Jina Mahāvīra, would have taken birth for an incalculable (*asaṅkhyeya*) number of existences among one-sensed creatures simply as a result of an ill-judged statement (*durvacana*) which ultimately led to the promulgation by his pupil Kapila of the heretical Sāṃkhya doctrine. On the other hand,

Prince Subāhu, who honoured the word of the Jinas yet subsequently experienced sixteen rebirths, would suffer more than Jamāli who actually traduced the word of the Jinas.[38]

Dharmasāgara insists that indifference to the incorrect view that Jamāli attained liberation after a mere fifteen existences would entail that disrespect towards the Jinas has no consequence. Anybody aware of this would have no sense of fear and so engage in inappropriate behaviour. In fact, the teaching of those who speak what is contrary to the scriptures unquestionably results in endless *saṃsāra* and so liberation from rebirth has to be far distant for those guilty of this fault. Rejection of even a fraction of what has been spoken by the Jinas implies contempt for the entire scriptural canon because it involves lack of trust (*pratyaya*) in the authoritative teachers.[39] It cannot be claimed that Jamāli could simultaneously reject the proposition 'what is being made is made' and maintain his faith in all the other teachings. This would be tantamount to claiming that he could have contradictory means of gaining knowledge (*upayoga*).

Yaśovijaya's response to Dharmasāgara

Yaśovijaya's (1624–1688) reply to Dharmasāgara's argument about Jamāli occurs in his *Dharmaparīkṣā* (pp. 203–231) and is a component of a broader argument concerning the nature of the upright heretic, that individual who, while not following all the specifications of the Jain path, nonetheless advocates a morally blameless soteriological path which does not substantially deviate from that of the Jains. Yaśovijaya deals with Dharmasāgara's points in reverse order of their occurrence in the *Sarvajñaśataka* and as he frequently matches his opponent in complexity and minutiae of detail. I provide here only the gist of his position on the subject of Jamāli's rebirths.

As we saw, the scriptural commentator Śīlāṅka asserted that Jamāli will wander through *saṃsāra* endlessly in the same way as a pot revolves on a mechanical water wheel. Yaśovijaya argues that to interpret this as signifying repeated rebirth in the four possible states of existence is the result of misreading the scriptures. He criticises those who rely on Śīlāṅka's statement alone as a proof, claiming that it could equally well establish what Dharmasāgara does not and, because of the testimony of *Bhagavatī* 9.33, cannot accept, namely Jamāli's rebirth in all four states of rebirth.

In broad terms, since rebirth in the various states of existence is different in respect to every person, why can there not be a diffferent trajectory of rebirth in terms of difference of will (*adhyavasāya*) exercised by an individual?[40] Yaśovijaya claims that if, as is stated by *Gacchācāra* v. 31, one of the main proof texts used by Dharmasāgara, there is endless *saṃsāra* for those who preach what is contrary to the scriptures, then by following another authoritative source, *Upadeśapada* vv. 422–423,[41] there also would have to be endless *saṃsāra* for monks of lax behaviour (*pārśvastha*).[42] However, that there is difference in that respect is conveyed through the fact that the respective mental activity (*pariṇāma*) informing action is not the same. Moreover, if one understands that the analogy of the waterwheel used with reference to wandering through *saṃsāra* implies the endlessness of the process, then one would also have to accept that there is endless *saṃsāra* also for those addicted to sexual activity in the same manner as for those who teach matters contrary to the scriptures. For the analogy must operate with regard to them as well, as can be seen when Śīlāṅka uses it in his commentary on *Ācārāṅga Sūtra* 1.3.2.2.[43] In actuality, this analogy is used in many places and cannot have the burden of significance ascribed to it by Dharmasāgara.

Yaśovijaya also claims that Dharmasāgara has overinterpreted *Bhagavatī* 9.33's description of Jamāli's rebirths in insisting that the words 'four (or) five' refer to types of existences (*jāti*), such as two-sensed and one-sensed. In doing so, he flouts the basic rules of grammar which would by this reading of the text require the locative case. Furthermore, if endless *saṃsāra* for Jamāli were to be intended by the *sūtra*, then the wording would have to be phrased differently and contain the expression 'endless'. Similarly, the account of the destiny of the Ājīvika leader Makkhali Gosāla, described in chapter thirteen of the *Bhagavatī*, would require to be reformulated.[44] How could there be endless rebirth among nine types (*jāti*), since there could in actuality be completion of the whole process after nine occasions? Generalisations about being reborn among every type of creature (*vyakti*) are not derived from literal words (*akṣara*) and are incompatible (*bādhita*) with the examples of all the animals, gods and humans who are reborn in this way. What is the point of resorting to the scriptures for an explanation, as Dharmasāgara repeatedly does, when one has already idiosyncratically established one's interpretation upon the presupposition of fixed endless rebirth? This, claims Yaśovijaya, is itself disrespect for the Jinas.

Yaśovijaya then discusses Hemacandra's description of Jamāli being reborn five times amongst animals, men and gods.[45] According to Dharmasāgara, the sense of this must be that Jamāli will be reborn five times amongst animals, with the necessary implication that he will be subjected to endless rebirths in other states. Yaśovijaya rejects this on linguistic grounds. The word 'five' can only be taken with the whole of the following compound, so that the overall sense is 'having been reborn five times amongst animals, humans and gods'. There is no authority for Jamāli being reborn amongst lower forms of life nor is there any warranty for the idea that he gains liberation after a particularly long time period of time. Predestination (*tathābhavyatva*), already referred to by Dharmasāgara, determines the specific nature of one's rebirth and there is no point in comparing the destinies of other individuals recorded in Jain legend who seem to have suffered more than Jamāli despite their piety. Yaśovijaya invokes as a counter-example in this respect the figure of Dṛḍhaprahārin, a byword for evil actions in Jain tradition, who nonetheless gained liberation.[46] Furthermore, scriptural texts which do not mention liberation can not be taken, as Dharmasāgara claims, as referring to the *abhavya*, the type of individual who will never gain release, since that is easily contradicted by reference to other passages in the *Bhagavatī*.[47]

Yaśovijaya is untroubled by Dharmasāgara's strictures about the force of the expression 'four (or) five', adducing evidence to show that the expression can simply have the sense of 'five', as Hemacandra and others interpret with reference to Jamāli. It is noteworthy, however, that Yaśovijaya does not specifically refer to the conclusion of earlier Tapā Gaccha teachers such as Hīravijaya Sūri and Kīrtivijaya that Jamāli's rebirths were fifteen in number, but simply points to grammatical authority for taking 'five' with each component of the compound 'animals, men and gods'.

In the final stages of his riposte Yaśovijaya addresses the issue of textual sources. He quotes the *Doghaṭṭī* commentary on the *Upadeśamālā* which describes Jamāli being reborn four or five times amongst animals, humans and gods and is thus in accord with the words of scripture as evinced in *Bhagavatī* 9.33.[48] He then refers to Siddharṣi's commentary on the *Upadeśamālā*, showing that different manuscripts of this text give different accounts of Jamāli's fate, with one stating that he underwent endless existences and so being viewed by Dharmasāgara as vindication of his position.

Yaśovijaya asserts that on the basis of this evidence those who are qualified and of a neutral disposition (*madhyasthagītārthāḥ*) interpret the situation as follows. According to many texts, most notably the *Bhagavatī*, Jamāli is known to have experienced a delimited number of rebirths, whereas by following particular readings of Siddharṣi's commentary on the *Upadeśamālā* he can be said to have experienced endless existences. In other words, the textual evidence adduced by Dharmasāgara is exiguous. Although it might be held that the real situation is only to be understood by those who already know the truth about reality, one can nonetheless conclude that there is at the least partial agreement between the differing accounts and that one must accept the good faith of the learned. As Yaśovijaya puts it, texts are not to be tortured on the wheel of negative preconceived ideas.[49]

Conclusion

Dharmasāgara and Yaśovijaya offer two different intepretations of a scriptural passage in *Bhagavatī* 9.33. For the former, the passage's purport, after some creative interpretation and reliance on restricted evidence, can only be that Jamāli's disrespect for his teacher and the Jain doctrine is such that he must be reborn for a vast period of time in low forms of existence before achieving liberation. For Yaśovijaya, the scriptural passage does not have to be taken too far from its literal sense to establish that Jamāli only experienced a relatively short number of rebirths to expiate his misdemeanour. This disagreement is itself a component of the dispute within the Tapā Gaccha concerning the moral status of non-Jain teachers and Jain teachers who promulgate sectarian versions of Jainism.

We have seen that if the figure of Jamāli never entirely disappears from Śvetāmbara Jainism, he is not so much associated with a particular teaching as deemed to be an exemplar of a moral failing which manifested itself most markedly in challenging Mahāvīra's omniscience. So the disagreement between monastic intellectuals of the Tapā Gaccha in the sixteenth and seventeenth centuries turned around the rebirth status of Jamāli as an example of a type who develops hostile tendencies towards his teacher, not his possible loss of status as a Jain through his false teaching; for he never challenged the ascetic ideology at the basis of the Jain path. Similarly, the modern monk Nyayavijaya (1998: 207) can in his recent extensive survey of Jain teaching and philosophy simply describe Jamāli as being an example of *abhiniveśa-mithyātva*, someone who obsessively follows false doctrine, without deeming it necessary to delineate in any way the nature of the false doctrine to which he subscribed.

Recent students of heresy have drawn attention to the manner in which medieval Christian heretics, while deviant in terms of items of practice or belief, nonetheless broadly endorsed the dominant discourse of the Christian church (Berlinerblau 2001: 347–351). Although the term 'heretic' cannot be fully mapped on to the conceptual world of traditional Indian soteriologies, Jamāli might be held by the religious historian to represent heresy as just described, in that he is both a participant within normative Jainism as represented by the scriptures through his full espousal of the ascetic path and at the same time outside it through his attempt to reconfigure an aspect of the authoritative teachings.[50]

For the Jain devotee, however, the significance of Jamāli must lie in the fact that whatever his moral turpitude, his eventual deliverance from rebirth and attainment of liberation are prophesied as inevitable by Mahāvīra. Representative in this respect not so much of irredeemable evil but of the possibility of purging the effects of one's errors and eventually gaining the goal of the path, as even Dharmasāgara had to admit, the story of Jamāli is in its totality a means of inculcating optimism even in the midst of the indignities of rebirth.[51]

Notes

1 *Upadeśamālā* v. 459: *Ājivagagaṇaneyā rajjasiriṃ payahiūṇa ya Jamālī/hiyam appaṇo kariṃto na ya vayaṇijje iha paḍaṃto.*

2 A mnemonic verse quoted by *Sthānāṅga Sūtra* 755 (p. 310 of Jambūvijaya's Jaina Āgama Series edition) refers to Jamāli as being the subject of the sixth chapter of the *Antakṛddaśāḥ*, a judgment not borne out by inspection of the text as transmitted.

3 For the *sāgaropama* as a length of time, see Schubring 2000: 226.

4 For the expression *aṇavadagga*, see Burrow 1979: 42–43.

5 The expression *cāuraṃta* (elsewhere sometimes *cauraṃta*) refers to the four possible types of existence.

6 This was noted long ago by Leumann 1997: 534–535 and more recently by Ohira 1994: 148.

7 *Sthānāṅga Sūtra* 355 specifies four reasons for being reborn as a Kilbiṣaka god, one of which is teaching what is contrary to the path (*ummaggadesanā*). For the dimensions of the Lāntaka heaven and its location as the fourth *vimāna*, see Kirfel 1967: 211, 297.

8 The expression *jāva cattāri paṃca* occurs elsewhere in the *Bhagavatī* and the *Jīvābhigama Sūtra*, as pointed out by Yaśovijaya, *Dharmaparīkṣā* (see later), p. 224.

9 The specific inserted wordings are *muccaṃti pariṇivvāyaṃti savvadukkhāṇaṃ and bujjhihiti muccihiti parinṇivvāhiti savvadukkhāṇaṃ.*

10 Bhatt 1983: 112 regards the *mokṣa*-indicating phrase of the type *savvadukkhāṇam aṃtaṃ karehiti* as 'on the whole' connected in the *Bhagavatī* with laymen.

11 Note that the three locations mentioned in *Bhagavatī* 9.32 and 9.33 are connected with the three classes of brahman, warrior and merchant.

12 See note 33. Of course, both Jamāli and Goṣṭhāmāhila are presented as viewing their teachings as representing a major challenge to the Jina's doctrine.

13 Cf. *Uttarādhayana Niryukti* v. 167. Verses 2825 and 2832 of Jinabhadra's *Viśeṣāvaśyabhāṣya*, a text approximately contemporary with the *Āvasyaka Cūrṇi*, refer to Priyadarśanā following Jamāli out of love for her husband and then rejoining Mahāvīra (Mehta and Chandra 1970: 456).

14 *Āvasyaka Cūrṇi* p. 417 suggests that the issue disputed by Jamāli turned around the identification of the precise instant in the process of production when an object could be deemed to have come into being. The general response to this is that if an object which is to be involved in movement were not to be regarded as having moved at the very first instant of a succession of instants, then it would be difficult to argue that it had moved at the second and subsequent instants. A cloth comes into being when the first thread is deployed at the precise time of the beginning of the action bringing it into being. If it were not to come into being at that instant, then that action would be pointless because it would not have any result. For since an action has as its aim producing what is to be produced, and as something which has not arisen at that particular initial instant would certainly not arise at later instants, what particular physical manifestation would those and subsequent actions take in respect to an entity, in that it is being argued that it does not come into being through an initial action but through the later ones? Jamāli's position logically entails non-origination and the non-efficacy of action and time. Cf. Ohira's interpretation given above.

15 Hemacandra in a brief disproof of Jamāli's position argues for the significance of the name of an object being mentioned even when it has just begun to be made. 'If an object is not said to be completed in the first instant, it does not come into existence at another moment because of the non-distinction between moments' (Johnson's translation, p. 195).

Jinapati Sūri discusses the nature of difference between entities, describing (v. 226) the unreflecting view that something being made is not made as 'standard' (*laukika*). If, Jinapati Sūri suggests (v. 229), there is complete difference between something which has been made and what is being made through their being unconnected, how could the thought of the object being made manifest itself, because it would be continually non-existent throughout? Jinapati Sūri appeals (vv. 24–25) to the two levels of truths structure which here would locate 'being made' and 'made' as separate on the transactional *vyavahāra* level but non-different on the more profound *niścaya* level.

Jinakuśala Sūri depicts Jamāli as basing his position on the likelihood of an infinite regress (*anavasthā*) of initial instants with regard to the performance of an action. This is rejected on the grounds that it would undermine cause and effect.

16 Tieken (2001) argues for the chronological priority of the *Jinacarita*.

17 Cf. *Uttarādhyayana Niryukti* v. 165: *bahu-raya Jamāli-pabhavā*. The alternative *Āvaśyaka CūrṇI* explanation (*bahusu samaesu kajjasiddhiṃ paḍucca ratā saktā bahuratā*) fancifully plays on the nature of Jamāli's teaching that an act only comes into being over the course of many instants.

18 *āyariyaparaṃparaeṇa āgayaṃ jo u cheyabuddhīe/kovei cheyavādī Jamāliṇāsaṃ sa ṇāsihii*.

19 Cf. the eleventh–twelfth century Municandra's *Pākṣikasaptati* v. 53, the twelfth century Prabodhacandra's commentary on Jinadatta Sūri's *Sandehadolavalīprakaraṇa* pp. 41b–42a and the fourteenth-century Dharmakīrti's commentary on Devendra Sūri's *Caityavandanabhāṣya* p. 337 v. 47.

20 *jo puṇa tam eva maggaṃ dūseuṃ apaṇḍio satakkāe / ummaggaṃ paḍivajjai akoviyappā Jamālīva.*

21 *saṅghaṃ avamannaṃto jāṇagamāṇī jaṇo asaggāhī / kaham avi bhinnaṃ mannai Jamālipamuhāṇam appāṇaṃ.*

22 *abhiniviṣṭo hi pumān prāyas tattvādivicārabahirbhāvena svāṅgīkṛtam eva samarthayate.* According to Yaśovijaya (see later), *Pratimāśataka* p. 149, Mahāvīra, who was well aware of Jamāli's nature, responded with silence rather than specific rejection when he asked for permission to leave his teacher, on the grounds that 'true words used to guide one who is of undisciplined behaviour have untruth as their result' (*avinīte hi satyavācah prayogo 'pi phalato 'satya eva*).

23 The *Karṇikāvṛtti* on the *Upadeśamālā* was written by Udayaprabha Sūri in 1243 (Sandesara 1953: 71 and 187–188), while the Vīracarita could be the tenth book of Hemacandra's *Triśaṣṭiśalākāpuruṣacarita* (Johnson's translation, volume 6) or the Prākrit *kāvya* by Guṇacandra (a monk in the lineage of the eleventh century teacher Abhayadeva Sūri) referred to by Yaśovijaya, *Dharmaparīkṣā* p. 225.

24 Text from the Jain Āgama Series edition p. 47:

> *icceiyaṃ duvalāsaṃgaṃ gaṇipiḍagaṃ tīe kāle aṇaṃtā jīvā āṇāe virāhettā cāuraṃtaṃ saṃsārakaṃtāraṃ aṇupariyaṭṭiṃsu. icceiyaṃ duvalāsaṃgaṃ gaṇipiḍagam paduppaṇṇakāle parittā jīvā āṇāe virāhettā cāuraṃtaṃ saṃsārakaṃtāraṃ aṇupariyaṭṭaṃti. icceiyaṃ duvalāsaṃgaṃ gaṇipiḍagaṃ aṇāgate kāle aṇaṃtā jīvā āṇāe virāhettā cāuraṃtaṃ saṃsārakaṃtāraṃ aṇupariyaṭṭissaṃti.*
>
> *icceiyaṃ duvalāsaṃgaṃ gaṇipiḍagaṃ tīe kāle aṇaṃtā jīvā āṇāe virāhettā cāuraṃtaṃ saṃsārakaṃtāraṃ vitivaiṃsu. icceiyaṃ duvalāsaṃgaṃ gaṇipiḍagam paduppaṇṇakāle parittā jīvā āṇāe virāhettā cāuraṃtaṃ saṃsārakaṃtāraṃ vitivayaṃti. icceiyaṃ duvalāsaṃgaṃ gaṇipiḍagaṃ aṇāgate kāle aṇaṃtā jīvā āṇāe virāhettā cāuraṃtaṃ saṃsārakaṃtāraṃ vitivatissaṃti.*

Kīrtivijaya abbreviates the second section.

25 See Haribhadra's commentary on the *Nandī Sūtra*, p. 94.

26 The description by Gerow 1971: 153 of 'partial' (*ekadeśin*) simile suggests that Kīrtivijaya's point is that the expression 'the girl's face is like the moon' requires a wider range of similes to give a complete description of her body.

27 In quoting the *Bhagavatī*, Kīrtivijaya's omits the *jāva* found in the Jaina Āgama Series edition.

28 *so 'bhiṇivesī ṇiamā aṇaṃtasaṃsāradukkhasalilaṇihī/āsāyaṇāi bahalo jahā Jamālī taovaṇayao.*

29 *ummaggamaggasaṃpaṭṭhiāṇa sāhūṇa Goyamā ṇūṇaṃ/saṃsāro a aṇamto hoi a sammaggaṇāsīṇaṃ.*

The *Gacchācāra* belongs to the *prakīrṇaka* category of scripture and is clearly one of the younger texts of the Śvetāmbara canon.

30 This subtlety was well known to medieval Jain karma theory. See *Caturtha Karmagrantha* of Devendra Sūri v. 79 and cf. Mahetā 1999: 259–261 who sets out the various gradations involved.

31 Tatia 1994: 304 defines (s.v.) *ardhapudgala-parivartana* as 'half the time it takes all karmic particles to undergo their complete course of binding and falling from the soul.' On p. 35 he gives a fuller definition:

> Those who are destined to attain liberation are capable of achieving the prerequisite enlightened world view through suppressing, eliminating or partially suppressing and partially eliminating the view deluding karma. Once they do this, they have a set period of time before achieving liberation. The maximum span of this period is equal to half the time it takes for a soul

to bind and release all the karmic particles scattered in the cosmos (something it has done an infinite number of times in its beginningless career).

For canonical occurrences of this notion, cf. Deleu 1970: 182–185 and 184 where *poggala-pariyaṭṭa* is rendered by 'atomic regroupment'. Ohira 1994: 91 explains *pudgala-parivartanā* as the 'time cycle for a *jīva* in taking in and out the total matters in the universe.' For remaining in *saṃsāra* for half a *poggala-pariyaṭṭa*, see Deleu 1970: 193. The expression *deśona*, 'less a part' would seem to imply 'just under' and possibly refers to the period of life lived or karma exhausted immediately before the fixed period of time comes into play.

32 *eaṃ puṇa evaṃ khalu aṇṇāṇapamāyadosao ṇeaṃ / jaha dīhā kāyaṭhiī bhaṇiā egiṃdiāīṇaṃ.*

33 *eyam akkharaṃ pi jo na roei suttaṇidiṭṭhaṃ / sesaṃ roaṃto vi hu micchādiṭṭhī Jamāli vva.* Jamāli's heresy effectively turned around one syllable, a privative 'a' added to the second component of the formula *kaḍemāne kaḍe*. For the *Pañcasaṃgraha* of Candrarṣi, see Mahetā and Kāpaḍiā 1968: 123–126. An edition of Pañcasaṃgraha is not available to me.

For a similar sentiment to that of the *Pañcasaṃgraha*, see Hemacandra, *Triṣaṣṭiśalākāpuruṣacarita* 10.8 (Johnson's translation, vol. 6: 195): 'The Arhats do not speak falsely, devoid of love and hate. There is not an atom of error, obscured perception, et cetera, in their words'; Jinapati Sūri on *Pañcaliṅgīprakaraṇa* p. 43a v. 268: *vīropadiṣṭaikapadāpalāpāt saṅghe Jamālir bata durbhago 'bhūt / vyaṅgaḥ pumān aṅgulimātrabhaṅgāt kim aṅga maṅgalyapadaṃ labheta*; and Jinakuśala Sūri on *Caityavandanakulaka* p. 57a v. 56: *śraddadhāty arhatāṃ yo nākṣaramātram api śrutam / mithyātvaṃ yāto so 'vaśyaṃ durgatiṃ ca tataḥ param.*

34 Scholarship generally dates Siddharṣi to around 870–920.

35 Dharmasāgara states at *Sarvajñaśataka*, p. 268, that the expression *cāuraṃta* is an epithet of *saṃsāra* and need not literally refer to the four locations of rebirth (*gati*). Not all those designated *anantasaṃsārin* are reborn in the four *gati*. Everyone's rebirth is different because of *tathābhavyatva*.

36 Dharmasāgara states at *Sarvajñaśataka*, p. 268, that the minimum requirement for being *anantasaṃsārin* is animal and human rebirth, otherwise it would be impossible to be *anantasaṃsārin* and also subsequently achieve deliverance.

37 Dharmasāgara cites *Daśavaikālika Sūtra* 5.2.47–48:

> And when he is to be born as a god and come to existence as a [Kilbiṣaka] god, he does not know which of his deeds results in this. When his life there has come to an end, he will be born with impediment in his speech, then in one of the hells or as an animal, where it is very difficult to attain enlightenment.
> (Schubring 1977: 214–215)

38 For Marīci and Kapila, see Hemacandra, *Triṣaṣṭiśalākāpuruṣacarita* (Johnson's translation, volume 1): 3–8. The nature of the relationship between the two and its relevance to the case of Jamāli is discussed by Dharmasāgara, *Sarvajñaśataka* v. 104 with autocommentary. For Prince Subāhu, see Mehta and Chandra 1972: 823–824.

39 Cf. note 33.

40 For *adhyavasāya*, see Glasenapp 1991: 94 s.v.

41 *sīyalavihārao khalu bhagavaṃtāsāyaṇā ṇiogeṇa/tatto bhavo aṇaṃto kilesabahulo jao bhaṇiyam.*

titthayarapavayaṇasuyaṃ āyariyaṃ gaṇaharaṃ mahiḍḍhīyaṃ/āsāyaṃto bahuso aṇaṃtasaṃsārio hoti.

42 Here Yaśovijaya refers to but does not quote the *Mahāniśītha Sūtra*.

43 See p. 106 of Jambūvijaya's edition of the *Ācārāṅga Sūtra*. The *sūtra* specifically talks about the one who lives through violence (*ārambhopajīvī*). Destruction of life forms is, of course, a consequence of sexual congress according to Jain prescription.

44 Yaśovijaya proposes the rephrasings *tiriyamaṇussadevesu aṇaṃtāiṃ bhavaggahaṇāiṃ saṃsāram aṇupariaṭṭittā pacchā sijjhissai* and *jahā Gosāle Maṃkhaliputte taheva ṇeraiavajjaṃ saṃsāram aṇupariaṭṭittā tao pacchā sijjhissai.*

45 *cyutvā tataḥ pañcakṛtvo bhrāntvā tiryagnṛnākiṣu / avāptabodhir nirvāṇaṃ Jamāliḥ samavāpsyati.* See *Triṣaṣṭiśalākāpuruṣacarita*, Johnson's translation, vol. 6: 198.

46 Dṛḍhaprahārin was a merciless cutthroat prior to becoming a Jain monk. See Mehta and Chandra 1970: 354.

47 Yaśovijaya, *Dharmaparīkṣā*, pp. 222–223, refers to the case of the layman Śaṅkha described at *Bhagavatī* 12.1.

48 The *Doghaṭṭī* commentary was written by Ratnaprabha Sūri in 1182 (Caudharī 1973: 324 and Sandesara 1953: 188). There is a Gujarati translation of this work by Hemasāgara Sūri, Muṃbaī: Ānanda Hemagranthamālāvalī 1975, but I have not had access to it.

49 Yaśovijaya provides a Gujarati summing up of his position, intended for general dissemination, in his *101 Bolsaṃgrah*. See Vijayaśilacandrasūri 1995: 28–32.

50 The early seventeeth century *Senapraśna*, p. 42, states that the various heretics (*nihnava*) are still members of the Jain community (*svapakṣa*).

51 Cf. the location of a lost, possibly original version of the story of Jamāli in the *Antakṛddaśāḥ* (see note 2), a text describing those who attained liberation.

Bibliography

Primary sources

Ācārāṅga Sūtra with the commentary of Śīlāṅka. *Ācārāṅgasūtraṃ Sūtrakrtāṅgasūtraṃ ca*, ed. Muni Jambūvijaya. Delhi: Motilal Banarsidass, 1978.

Āvaśyaka Cūrṇi of Jinadāsa, Ratlām: Ṛṣabhdevjī Keśarmaljī Śvetāmbarsaṃsthā, 1928.

Bhagavatī Sūtra. Aṃgasuttāṇl Vol. 2, ed. Muni Nathmal. Ladnun: Jain Viswa Bharati, saṃvat 2031 [CE 1974].

Bhagavatī Sūtra. K. C. Lalwani, *Sudharma Svāmī's Bhagavatī Sūtra*, Vol. IV (Śatakas 9–11), Prakrit Text with English Translation. Calcutta: Jain Bhawan, 1985.

Bhagavatī Sūtra. Suttāgame Vol. 1, ed. Pupphabhikkhū, Gurgāṃv 1953: 384–939.

Bhagavatī Sūtra. Viyāhapaṇṇattisuttaṃ (prathamo bhāgaḥ), ed. Paṇḍit Becardās Jīvrāj Dośī, Jaina-Āgama-Granthamālā Vol. 4, 1. Bambaī: Mahāvīr Jain Vidyalaya, 1974.

Bhagavatī Sūtra with the commentary of Abhayadeva Sūri, *Aṃgasuttāṇi (saṭīkam)*, Vol. 5, ed. Muni Dīparatnasāgara. Ahmadābād: Āgama Ārādhanā Kendra, saṃvat 2056 [CE 1999].

Bṛhatkalpabhāṣya, in Willem B. Bollée (ed.), *Bhadrabāhu Bṛhat-Kalpa-Niryukti and Sanghadāsa Bṛhat-Kalpa-Bhāṣya*, Part 1. Stuttgart: Franz Steiner, 1998.

Caityavandanabhāṣya of Devendra Sūri with the commentary of Dharmakīrti. Muṃbaī: Jinaśāsana Ārādhanā Ṭrasṭ, sam. 2045 [CE 1988].

Caityavandanakulaka of Jinadatta Sūri with the commentary of Jinakuśala Sūri. Bombay: Shri Jinduttsuri Prachin Pustakoddhar Fund, 1920.

Caturtha Karmagrantha of Devendra Sūri, in *Catvāraḥ Karmagranthāḥ*, Ācāryadevaśrīmadvijayapremasūrīśvarakarmasāhityajainagranthamālā Vol. 12. Piṇḍvāḍā: Bhāratīya-Prācya-Tattva-Prakāśan-Samiti, saṃvat 2032 [CE 1975].

Ceiyavaṃdaṇamahābhāsa of Śānti Sūri. Mumbai: Jina Śāsana Ārādhanā Ṭrasṭ, saṃvat 2043 [CE 1986].

Dharmaparīkṣā of Yaśovijaya. Muṃbaī: Aṃdherī Gujarātī Jain Saṃgh, saṃvat 2043 [CE 1986].

Hīrapraśnottarāṇi compiled by Kīrtivijaya Gaṇin. Muṃbaī: Jina Śāsana Ārādhanā Ṭrasṭ, saṃvat 2045 [CE 1988].

Jñātṛdharmakathāḥ. Nayādhammakaihāo (Jñātādharmakathāṅgasūtram), Jaina Āgama Series 5, 1, ed. Muni Jambūvijaya. Baṃbai: Śrī Mahavīra Jain Vidyālaya, 1989.

Nandī Sūtra. Namdisuttaṃ Aṇuogaddārāiṃ ca, ed. Muni Puṇyavijaya. Bambaī: Jaina Āgama Granthamalā, 1968.

Nandī Sūtra with the commentary of Haribhadra, ed. Muni Puṇyavijaya. Varanasi/ Ahmedabad: Prakrit Text Society, 1966.

Pākṣikasaptati of Municandra, ed. Muni Lābhasāgara. Kapaḍvaṃj: Āgamoddhārak Granthamālā, saṃvat 2028 [CE 1971].

Pañcaliṅgīprakaraṇa of Jineśvara Sūri with the commentary of Jinapati Sūri. Bombay: Shri Jinduttsuri Prachin Pustakoddhar Fund, 1919.

Pratimāśataka of Yaśovijaya, ed. Muni Ajitaśekharavijaya. Ahmedabad: Divya Darśan Ṭrasṭ, samvat 2044 [CE 1987].

Sandehadolāvalīprakaraṇa of Jinadatta Sūri with the commentary of Prabodhacandra Gaṇin. Jetaran: Sheth Chhaganlal Hirachand, 1918.

Sarvajñaśataka of Dharmasāgara, ed. Muni Lābhasāgara. Kapaḍvaṃj: Āgamoddhāraka Granthamālā, samvat 2024 [CE 1967].

Senapraśna compiled by Śubhavijaya Gaṇin. Muṃbaī: Devcand Lalbhāī Jain Pustakoddhār Granthamālā, 1919.

Śrāddhaguṇavivaraṇa of Jinamaṇḍana Gaṇin. Muṃbaī: Jinaśāsana Ārādhanā Ṭrasṭ, 1988.

Sthānāṅga Sūtra. Ṭhāṇaṃgasuttaṃ Samavāyaṃsuttaṃ ca, ed. Muni Jambūvijaya, Jaina Āgama Granthamala Vol. 3. Bambaī: Mahāvīr Jain Vidyālaya, 1985.

Sūtrakṛtāṅga Niryukti, in W. B. Bollée (ed.), *The Nijjuttis on the Seniors of the Śvetāmbara Siddhānta: Āyāranga, Dasaveyāliya, Uttarajjhāyā and Sūyagaḍa*. Stuttgart: Franz Steiner, 1995.

Triṣaṣṭiśalākāpuruṣacarita of Hemacandra, trans. Helen W. Johnson, *The Deeds of the Sixty-Three Illustrious Men*, Vol. 1. Baroda: Gaekwad's Oriental Series, 1931.

Triṣaṣṭiśalākāpuruṣacarita of Hemacandra, trans. Helen W. Johnson, *The Deeds of the Sixty-Three Illustrious Men*, Vol. 6. Baroda: Gaekwad's Oriental Series, 1962.

Upadeśamālā of Dharmadāsa Gaṇin, with the commentaries of Vardhamāna Sūri and Siddharṣi Gaṇin. Mumbaī: Jinaśāsana Ārādhanā Ṭrasṭ, 1991.

Upadeśapada of Haribhadra with the commentary of Municandra. Muṃbaī: Jinaśāsana Ārādhanā Ṭrast, saṃvat 2046 [CE 1989].

Uttarādhyayana Niryukti, in W. B. Bollée (ed.), *The Nijjuttis on the Seniors of the Śvetāmbara Siddhānta: Āyāranga, Dasaveyāliya, Uttarajjhāyā and Sūyagaḍa*. Stuttgart: Franz Steiner, 1995.

Vicāraratnākara of Kīrtivijaya Gaṇin, ed. Vijayadāna Sūri. Bhāvanagar: Devcandra Lālbhāī Jain Pustakoddhār Saṃsthā, 1927.

Secondary sources

Balbir, Nalini. 1993. *Āvaśyaka-Studien. Introduction générale et Traductions*. Stuttgart: Franz Steiner.

——. 1999. 'About a Jain Polemical Work of the 17th Century'. N. K. Wagle and O. Qvarnström (ed.), *Approaches to Jaina Studies: Philosophy, Logic, Rituals and Symbols*. University of Toronto: Centre for South Asian Studies: 1–18.

Berlinerblau, Jacques. 2001. 'Towards a Sociology of Heresy, Orthodoxy and Doxa'. *History of Religions* 40: 327–351.

Bhatt, Bansidhar. 1983. 'Stratification in *Śatakas* 1–20 of the *Viyāhapannatti*'. *Indologica Taurinensia* 11: 109–118.

Bollée, W. B. 1977. *Studien zum Sūyagaḍa* 1. Wiesbaden: Franz Steiner.

——. 1994. 'Notes on Middle Indo-Aryan Vocabulary IV'. N. N. Bhattacharyya (ed.), *Jainism and Prakrit in Ancient and Medieval India*. New Delhi: Manohar: 63–70.

Bronkhorst, Johannes. 1999. *Langage et réalité: sur un épisode de la pensée indienne*. Turnhout: Brepols.

——. 2003. 'Jainism's First Heretic and the Origin of Anekānta-vāda'. Olle Qvarnström (ed.), *Jainism and Early Buddhism*: 95–111.

Brough, John. 1996. 'The meaning of *ni-hnu* in the Brāhmaṇas'. Reprinted in John Brough, *Collected Papers*, Minoru Hara and J. C. Wright (ed.). London: School of Oriental and African Studies, University of London: 74–78.

Burrow, Thomas. 1979. *The Problem of Shwa in Sanskrit*. Oxford: Clarendon Press.

Caudhurī, Gulābcandra. 1973. *Jain Sāhitya kā Bṛhad Itihās*, Vol. 6. Vārāṇasī: Parśvanāth Vidyāsram Śodh Saṃsthān.

Deeg, Max. 1999. 'The Saṅgha of Devadatta: Fiction and History of a Heresy in the Buddhist Tradition'. *Journal of the International College for Advanced Buddhist Studies* 2: 183–218.

Deleu, Jozef. 1970. *Viyāhapannatti (Bhagavaī). The Fifth Anga of the Jaina Canon. Introduction, Critical Analysis, Commentary and Indexes*. Brugge: De Tempel.

Deo, S. B. 1954–1955. *History of Jaina Monachism from Inscriptions and Literature*. Poona: Bulletin of the Deccan College Research Institute, Vol. 16.

Dundas, Paul. 2002. *The Jains* (second revised and enlarged edition). London and New York: Routledge.

——. 2007. *Sudharman's Heirs: History, Scripture and Controversy in a Medieval Jain Sect*. Oxford: Routledge.

Gerow, Edwin. 1971. *A Glossary of Indian Figures of Speech*. The Hague and Paris: Mouton.

Glasenapp, Helmuth von. 1991. *Doctrine of Karman in Jain Philosophy*. Varanasi: P. V. Research Institute.

Kirfel, Wilhelm. 1967. *Die Kosmographie der Inder. Nach Quellen dargestellt*. Hildesheim: Georg Olms.

Leumann, Ernst. 1885. 'Die alten Berichte von den Schismen der Jaina', *Indische Studien* 17: 91–135.

——. 1998. *Kleine Schriften*. Nalini Balbir (ed.). Stuttgart: Franz Steiner.

Mahetā, Dhīrajlāl Ḍahyālāl. 1999. *Ācārya Śrī Devendrasūrīśvarajī viracit Ṣadaśītī Nāmā Caturth Karmagranth*. Surat: Jaindharm Prasāraṇ Ṭrasṭ.

Mahetā, Mohanlāl and Kāpaḍiā, Hirālāl. 1968. *Jain Sāhitya kā Bṛhad Itihās*, Vol. 4. Vārāṇasī: Pārśvanāth Vidyāśram Śodh Saṃsthān.

Mehta, Mohan Lal and Chandra, K. Rishabh. 1970. *Prakrit Proper Names*, Part 1. Ahmedabad: L. D. Institute of Indology.

——. 1972. *Prakrit Proper Names*, Part 2. Ahmedabad: L. D. Institute of Indology.

Nyayavijaya, Muni. 1998. *Jain Philosophy and Religion*, trans. N. J. Shah. Delhi: Motilal Banarsidass.

Ohira, Suzuko. 1994. *A Study of the Bhagavatīsūtra. A Chronological Analysis*. Ahmedabad: Prakrit Text Society.

Qvarnström, Olle. 2003. *Jainism and Early Buddhism: Essays in Honor of Padmanabh S. Jaini*. Fremont: Asian Humanities Press.

Sandesara, Bhogilal J. 1953. *Literary Circle of Mahamatya Vastupala and its Contribution to Sanskrit Literature*. Bombay: Bharatiya Vidya Bhavan.

Schubring, Walther. 1977. *Kleine Schriften*. Wiesbaden: Franz Steiner.

——. *The Doctrine of the Jainas Described after the Old Sources* (second revised edition). Delhi: Motilal Banarsidass.

Simson, Georg von. 2003. 'Characterizing by Contrast: The Case of the Buddha and Devadatta, Bhīṣma and Karṇa'. Olle Qvarnström (ed.), *Jainism and Early Buddhism*: 621–635.

Tatia, Nathmal. 1951. *Studies in Jaina Philosophy*. Varanasi: P. V. Research Institute.

——. 1994. *That Which Is. Tattvārtha Sūtra*. San Francisco, CA, London and Pymble: HarperCollins.

Tieken, Herman. 2001. 'The Arrangement of the *Śrutaskandha* of the *Āyāraṃga*', *Journal of Indian Philosophy* 29: 575–588.

Trautmann, Thomas R. 1974. 'Cross-Cousin Marriage in Ancient North India?' Thomas R. Trautmann (ed.), *Kinship and History in South Asia*. Ann Arbor, MI: Center for South and Southeast Asian Studies, The University of Michigan: 61–103.

Vijayaśīlacandrasūri. 1995. 'Mahopādhyāya ŚrīYaśovijayajīgaṇikṛt 101 Bolsaṃgrah.' *Anusaṃdhān* 7: 22–42.

Wiles, Maurice. 1994. *Archetypal Heresy: Arianism through the Centuries*. Oxford: Clarendon.

3

THE DATING OF THE JAINA COUNCILS

Do scholarly presentations reflect the traditional sources?

Royce Wiles

The oldest manuscripts of Śvetāmbara canonical texts are palm-leaf ones from the eleventh to twelfth centuries CE. As shown by Hoernle (*Uvāsagadasāo* 1880–90), Alsdorf (1965: 42), Bollée (1977–1988) and by my own doctoral work on the *Nirayāvaliyā* (Wiles 2000) there is, in all likelihood, only one recension of most, if not all, Śvetāmbara canonical texts.[1] A definitive interpretation of the material available on the history of the Śvetāmbara 'canon'[2] has not yet been written, however, current views on this are summarized in the standard scholarly accounts of Jainism (Dundas 1992: 53–70, Jaini 1979: 42–88, Schubring 1935 §37–56). Since the first descriptions of the canon by Jacobi (1879) and Weber (1883–1885), the most original contribution to the description of this history has been the work of Kapadia (1941) who provided citations of evidence from the primary source materials. Here I wish to query a consistent feature of scholarly presentations about the redacting councils to which the Śvetāmbara canon is attributed, namely a recurring weakness to adequately identify and examine the sources upon which these scholarly presentations are based, especially the bases for the dating of the councils. I want to show that current scholarly accounts do not adequately represent the sources.

According to the Śvetāmbara tradition, the final council of Valabhī under Devarddhigaṇin was critical to the recension of the extant canon transmitted to us. I will therefore focus more attention on it, and present only an outline of the material on the other councils.

Bhadrabāhu and the council of Pāṭaliputra

Dundas gives a clear version of the current scholarly opinion on the first council:

> The first recitation [of the Jaina scriptural canon] is supposed to have been held at Pataliputra (modern Patna) 160 years after Mahavira's

> death, as a result of which knowledge of the twelve-limbed canon was deemed to be imperfect and, with the subsequent disappearance of the *Drishtivada*, it was officially reduced to eleven limbs.
>
> (Dundas 1992: 62)

Dundas adds further down the page that 'the earliest accounts of any of the recitations date from the second half of the seventh century...' (Dundas 1992: 62). What is not stated however, is that the date just indicated – 160 AV – does *not* come down to us from the second half of the seventh century. According to my readings, the date of 160 AV is based (solely?) on Hemacandra's *Pariśiṣṭaparvan* (9.112) which was written during v.s. 1216–1229.

Most scholarly accounts of the first council, at Pāṭaliputra, demonstrate a failure to accurately present information about the original sources. Schubring includes material on the first council in his epitome of the Jaina lineage of teachers, his version is based on Hemacandra's *Pariśiṣṭaparvan*, which he dates to v.s. 1216–1229 (Schubring 1935 (§23): 34 = 1962: 45). Although Schubring does remind us that Hemacandra's account would have been based on earlier literary sources, in particular the *Āvassaya* literature, he does not make explicit here that Hemacandra's comments in *Pariśiṣṭaparvan* 9.55–67, can only be matched with the *Āvassaya-cuṇṇi* version, that is, to my knowledge there is no other identified early source for information on the Pāṭaliputra council.

When Jaini (1979: 5, n. 6) cursorily mentions the Pāṭaliputra council he cites no direct references to Prākrit sources, nor does he give an explicit date for it. Further on he does imply a date, when he gives Bhadrabāhu's era as 'circa 300 BC' (ibid., p. 50), however, he does not attempt to justify or discuss that date. Only Kapadia appears to have had access to the *Āvaśyaka-cūrṇi* and he cites an extract which is clear and unequivocal:

> At that time there was a famine of twelve years. [The Jaina mendicants] lived here and there on the coast, then, [after the famine] they met again in Pāṭaliputra. From some they gathered chapters and pieces [of texts] and so put together the eleven Aṅgas. The *Diṭṭhivāda* did not survive. Bhadrabāhu was living in Nepal, he knew the fourteen Pūrvas. The *saṅgha* sent emissaries to him to say: 'Teach [us] the *Diṭṭhivāda*.' They went and related that edict from the *saṅgha*. He replied to them: 'Because of the famine I could not begin the *mahāprāṇa* [practice], now I have undertaken it.' So he did not go. The emissaries returned and told the *saṅgha* this. They sent more emissaries [to ask]: 'What is the punishment for someone who disobeys an order of the *saṅgha*?' They went and said that. He said: 'That one is to be expelled.' He then said to them: 'Do not expel me, send intelligent [students], I will give seven instructions.'[3]

Given the close similarity between the wording of the *Āvaśyaka-cūrṇi* account and that of Hemacandra,[4] it seems that here Hemacandra has indeed closely followed the *cūrṇi* version, making it more intelligible in the process. What is highly significant is that no date is offered by the *cūrṇi* passage.

Apart from the *Āvassaya-cuṇṇi* and the – probably derivative – account in Hemacandra's *Pariśiṣṭaparvan*, I have not come across other citations of original sources for information on this first council. The *Āvassaya-cuṇṇi* is written in Prākrit and is certainly ancient, it preserves much otherwise unrecorded information, and is generally dated between *Saṃvat* 650 and 750 = 593–693 CE (Balbir 1993: 1, 81). If the *Āvassaya-cuṇṇi* is the sole original source of information on the first council, in my opinion that needs to be stated in scholarly accounts, instead of those accounts simply repeating earlier statements without adequate reference to any textual basis for their assertions. Similarly, if the date of the first council is based solely on Hemacandra's work then that also needs to be stated by scholars.

The councils of Mathurā (under Skandila), Valabhī I (Nāgārjuna) and Valabhī II (Devarddhigaṇin)

Accounts of the history of the Jaina Āgamas almost always refer to the redacting work of the two Jaina Ācāryas Skandila and Nāgārjuna and to Devarddhigaṇin Kṣamāśramaṇa. These three individuals are all cited as having ensured the transmission of the teaching of the Jina Mahāvīra at different 'councils', in spite of that teaching being endangered by times of famine. Devarddhigaṇin is held to have been directly responsible for causing the teachings gathered by the two earlier Ācāryas (Skandila and Nāgārjuna) to be written down. Sometimes datings are also offered for these individuals and their work. However, on examining the textual references used to justify these statements the evidence for the composite account they present is at best extremely weak, particularly with regard to datings. Later I will attempt to demonstrate how accounts of this aspect of the canonical texts of the Śvetāmbara Jainas rarely indicate the severely limited foundations upon which they are based. Few scholars have examined original sources, instead most accounts have repeated received information uncritically, often obscuring the speculative nature of the basic information.

First I will give a survey of scholarly accounts of the final redaction of the Jaina Āgamas, to show the evolution of received scholarly opinion on the place of the teachers mentioned earlier in the history of the Āgama. I will then examine the textual bases cited as evidence, to test those scholarly accounts.

Scholarly accounts of the Jaina councils

The first printed account of the events surrounding the editing of the Jaina Āgama was published by Jacobi in the introduction to his landmark edition of the *Kalpasūtra* (1879). Jacobi quotes what he refers to as a 'common and old tradition' that the ultimate redaction of the Śvetāmbara Jaina canonical works was made by Devarddhigaṇin Kṣamāśramaṇa in 980 AV (Jacobi converts this date to

454 or 514 CE): Devarddhigaṇin saw the Āgamas almost being lost and so had them written down by the *saṅgha* of Valabhī. Jacobi continues:

> Devarddhigaṇin, the Buddhaghoṣa of the Jainas, has most probably arranged the whole of the traditional Jaina literature, which he gathered in the Āgamas from books and from the mouth of living theologians. He was nearly too late for his task. For in many cases, fragments only of books were left, and he put them together to make up a book as he thought best.[5]
>
> (*Kalpasūtra* 1879: 15–16)

Jacobi provides three references to back up his account: (1) his notes on *Kalpasūtra* §148, (2) Jinaprabhamuni's *Sandehaviṣauṣadhī* and (3) Padmamandiragiri's *Ṛṣimaṇḍalaprakaraṇa* (*Saṃvat* 1553) – each of these will be taken up in turn when the traditional sources for information on the councils are examined later. For now it is enough for my purposes to show that Jacobi, ever a careful scholar, has stated explicitly the basis for his conclusions.

The next account of the creation of the Jaina canon was by Weber (1883–1885: 218), cited here in the English translation by Smyth (1888):

> the transmission was only oral; for which, according to tradition, writing was not substituted till eight centuries later, in the year 980 Vīra [converted by Weber to 543 CE (p. 220, n. 1)]. This was effected by a council in Valabhī under the presidence of Devarddhigaṇi Kṣamāśramaṇa; though others state that this ensued 13 years after (993 Vīra [556 CE]) at the hands of a council in Mathurā under śrī Skandilācārya. In connection with this the statement may be placed that in the year 980 the Valabhī king Dhruvasena commanded that the *Kalpasūtram* should be recited publicly. Herein a special participation of the king in the work is indicated, be it in that of Devarddhigaṇi or in that of Skandila, to whom by this act he gave decisive support.

Weber is clearly depending on Jacobi, but disagreeing with the date conversions, he does not cite any sources or information other than those given already by Jacobi. He places Devarddhigaṇin at the Valabhī council prior to a Mathurā council under Skandila.

Not until Charpentier (1922: 1, 15–17) do we have another overview of the academic interpretation of this element of Jaina history. Charpentier summarizes earlier views in the introduction to his edition of the *Uttarādhyayana*. His version is:

> A famous teacher, Devarddhigaṇin, called the *kṣamāśramaṇa*, who saw that the sacred lore was in danger of becoming obsolete – no doubt because of the scarcity of manuscripts – convoked a second great Council at Valabhī. This is said to have taken place in 980 or 993 AV, and seems to have been connected in some way with a public recitation of

> the *Jinacaritra*, or 'Life of Mahāvīra' before king Dhruvasena of Ānandapura (a town not mentioned elsewhere). Now, as king Dhruvasena I of Valabhī is supposed to have succeeded to the throne in 526 AD, and 993–526 is = 467 (BC), the actual year of Mahāvīra's death, I think we are entitled to assume, that this was the real date of the Council of Valabhī, and that it was in some way protected by Dhruvasena. Devarddhigaṇin, the president of the council, no doubt took down from the members all the scriptures considered as canonical that did not at that time exist in written form, and we need not doubt that the whole external form of the Siddhānta dates from about 526 AD.

There are quite a few problems with Charpentier's account. According to his footnote (page 16, n. 1) he is basing his comments on the commentaries cited by Jacobi in his 1879 edition of the *Kalpasūtra* (page 270 to be specific). As will be shown later, those commentaries are far from definite in their interpretation of the old dates, and they date from several hundred years after the events to which they refer. In my opinion Charpentier has gone too far in his assumptions to link Dhruvasena to the council. This will be seen later when the commentary passages in question are considered.

In 1926 Schubring's *Worte Mahāvīras* appeared. The opening twenty-six pages of this important collection of translations from Jaina canonical texts deals with the canon of the Śvetāmbara Jainas:

> It was probably in the first quarter of the sixth century [500–525 CE] that the city of Vaḷā, called Valabhī in Sanskrit, on the Kāṭhiāwāḍ peninsula in Gujarat, was witness to a religious conference of the 'white' Jainas. Under the presidency of Devarddhi, one of their principals, in the convocations of the believers an attempt was made to settle and copy down the wording of the sacred texts. Therewith were the testaments of the teaching of Mahāvīra, almost a thousand years – according to the tradition – after the passing away of the master, saved from the steady advance of decay. Since then the Canon of the white-robed has in essence remained unchanged.[6]

The date suggested for the council under Devarddhigaṇin is 500–525 CE. Importantly, no citations at all are brought forward to justify this. The main point I want to make here is that the account of the council is presented without any substantiating evidence that would allow readers to judge the tradition's reliability for themselves, or even ascertain how definite or not, it might be. The account by Guérinot (1926: 72) repeats the now standard view, also without giving any sources. In both of these scholarly accounts the 'facts' have become self-evident and need not be backed up with original citations or even references to them.

Winternitz, paving the way for his brief (but still indispensible) tour through Jaina literature, provides a summary history of the Councils, but, like the other accounts cited so far, he does not give any references to original sources (1933: 2, 431–435). In the section on canonical history Winternitz cites Weber, Jacobi and von Glasenapp (1925) yet only speaks of one council in Valabhī, and makes no mention of Skandila (the position of the Jaina teacher Nāgārjuna has not even been referred to by Western scholars yet).

Schubring (1935: 55, n. 4) is again brief, but at least cites Jacobi while adding a reference to a note by Bhandarkar (*Report*, 1883–1884: 129) – first pointed out by von Glasenapp (1925: 466, n. 9) – that the council in Mathurā under Skandila occurred earlier than Devarddhi's work in Valabhī. Again, however, there are no new original sources and Jacobi's work of fifty years earlier is repeated (although without the date equivalents).[7] This seems to have remained a settled matter for Schubring, in 1959 he wrote the following (although his phrasing, as usual, is careful): 'The authoritative texts of the Śvetāmbaras... in their oldest portions date from the 3rd to 2nd century BCE. The canon was collected at a council in Kathiawar (Gujarat) in the 6th cent.'[8] The remarks of all the preceding scholars have ultimately been based on a single source, Jacobi's work of 1879. A new contribution was only made in 1941 in Kapadia's *A history of the canonical literature of the Jainas*. This was the first account since Jacobi to provide citations from traditional sources as evidence.[9] For this reason it has been the basis for the more careful account of Jaini (1979: 51–52) and has influenced Folkert (1993: 46, n. 6, see later) and Dundas (1992), as well as the 'revised German edition' of Schubring (1962: 2000).[10]

The section of Kapadia's work relevant here is the chapter, 'Redaction of the Jaina canon.' Kapadia (1941: 61) says: 'So Skandila summoned a council of Jaina saints at Mathurā and made up the *kāliyasuya* by taking note of whatever could be gathered from them'. Disappointingly, Kapadia adds baldly: 'It appears that this happened sometime between Vīra *Saṃvat* 827 and 840' (1941: n. 4). There is no additional information, nor are original sources cited to give any idea where this date came from. Kapadia also notes (pp. 61–62) that there was a similar project under Nāgārjuna[11] in Valabhī.

Kapadia's summary account cites the texts listed later (in the same sequence) and although he is providing much new information, his account lacks any sense of chronology. I have added the currently accepted dates for these texts (sources for dates are given below when the texts are taken up individually):

Nandīsūtra-cūrṇi	676 CE
Bhadreśvara's *Kahāvalī*	*c.*1150–1200 CE
Hemacandra's *Yogaśāstra* auto-commentary	1088–1172 CE
Malayagiri's commentary on *Joīsakaraṇḍaga*	*c.*1093–1193 CE
Samayasundara's *Sāmācārīśataka*	*c.*1630 CE

Kapadia does not mention dates for any of these and he presents them all as equally valid. He is after all interested in the events recorded in the tradition and is not concerned about dates. For most scholars his presentation is uncritical in that regard but at least he made the original citations available for the first time. His important contribution was published in India during the second World War and that may have limited its impact. It has only recently been reprinted (2000). Renou in his account of the Jaina canon, for example, shows no sign of familiarity with the new information provided (1951: 2, 633).

The more recent accounts of P. S. Jaini (1979: 51–52) and Folkert (1993) are based on Kapadia and can be cited from Folkert's summary (1993: 46):

> The Jains themselves point to three significant councils at which their texts were at issue. The first is placed at Mathurā, ca. 350 CE, under the leadership of Skandila. The second is placed at Valabhī, in Saurashtra, at about the same time, under Nāgārjuna. The third council is again placed at Valabhī, ca. 500 CE, under Devarddhigaṇin. The function of the first two councils apparently was to commit to writing the texts subscribed to by the Śvetāmbara monastic groups (*gacchas*) represented at each. The third council appears to have produced a uniform version of those texts, noting certain important variants, and to have seen that copies were made and delivered to major Jain centers.

As Folkert suggests in a footnote, European scholars have not had access to the original materials, this may explain why scholarly presentations of the councils and statements about the redaction of the canon have not been seriously reexamined.

The final account to be presented here is that of Dundas (1992: 61–64) who has provided the most recent comprehensive account of Śvetāmbara traditions of the transmission of their scriptures.[12] Dundas's account is perhaps the best contemporary formulation of the academic position regarding the councils (p. 62):

> The first recitation [of the teachings] is supposed to have been held in Pataliputra (modern Patna) 160 years after Mahavira's death.... The second recitation took place 827 years after Mahavira but, on this occasion, was held at two places simultaneously, at Mathura in the north under the auspices of Skandila and at Valabhī in the west under the auspices of Nagarjuna.... The final recitation held at Valabhī in the first half of the fifth century was convened by Devarddhiganin and the accounts of it stress that, to avoid the complete disappearance of the scriptures, the canon was redacted in manuscript form.

What none of these scholarly accounts of the councils makes clear is the late date of the sources on which they are based. Certainly the statements made reflect the Śvetāmbara tradition, but they exclude the notable equivocations present in the tradition, equivocations which take away any element of certainty about the dating of these events. If we now turn to the original sources for information on the councils it will be seen that the scholarly views expressed earlier are considerably more definite than the tradition itself. A few scholars have raised doubts about the datings but none has highlighted the lateness of the sources for the datings, for example Ohira (1994: 3 (§7)) in her study of the *Viyāhapaṇṇatti*, simply questioned the dating of the third council ('the Third Canonical Council [was] held in Valabhī (453 AD or 466 AD according to tradition) which is again disputable'.

Accounts of the council of Valabhī in Śvetāmbara texts

Based on the citations of Jacobi and Kapadia mentioned earlier, I will now turn to the original sources concerning the events of the councils and the redacting of the canon. The extracts are taken up here in approximate chronological order.[13] The information relied on by scholars is largely from the commentary literature, only two sources (§1 and §2) are not from there, and those two are the most undetailed.

The following textual sources will be examined:

§1 Devavācaka, *Nandīsūtra* (*Therāvalī*)
§2 *Kalpasūtra, Jinacaritra*, section 148
§3 Jinadāsagaṇi, *Nandīsūtra-cūrṇi* (676 CE) (plus the *Āyāra-* and *Daśāśrutaskandha-cūrṇis*)
§4 Haribhadra (700–770 CE) *Laghuvṛtti on Nandīsūtra*
§5 Śīlāṅka (9th century) *Āyāraṭīkā*
§6 Śāntyācārya Vādivetāla (d. saṃ. 1096 [1039]?), *Śiṣyahitā on Uttarādhyayana*
§7 Hemacandra (1088–1172), *Yogaśāstra* commentary
§8 Malayagiri (*c.*1093–1193) *ṭīkā* on the *Prakīrṇaka* entitled *Joisakaraṇḍaga*
§9 Bhadreśvara (*c.*1150–1200) *Kahāvalī*
§10 Jinaprabhamuni (1307) *Sandehaviṣauṣadhī*, commentary on *Kalpasūtra*
§11 Vinayavijaya (1559) *Subodhikā*, commentary on *Kalpasūtra*
§12 Dharmasāgara (1571), *Kiraṇāvalī* or *Vyākhānapaddhati*, city on *Kalpasūtra*
§13 Samayasundara (*c.*1630), *Sāmācārīśataka*
§14 Samayasundara (1642), *Kalpalatā*, commentary on *Kalpasūtra*
§15 Lakṣmīvallabha (<1835 CE) *Kalpadruma*, commentary on *Kalpasūtra*

§1 Devavācaka

The *Nandīsūtra* as transmitted to us has at its beginning a list of elders (*Sthavirāvalī*) which is attributed to Devavācaka.[14] This is the earliest source to name the teachers Skandila and Nāgārjuna and link them (vaguely) with the transmission of the teachings. The very careful scholar Muni Jambūvijaya has shown that the *Nandīsūtra* itself was known to Mallavādin (fifth century) in a form different to the one it has now.[15] There is, however, no way of knowing if the *Sthavirāvalī* dates from an older version of the *Nandīsūtra* or the newer one. Since the *Nandīsūtra-cūrṇi*, which comments on these verses is dated 676 CE

(*Nandīsūtra* 1966b: 83) it is enough for my purposes to say that the *Sthavirāvalī* was written before then.

At the start of the *Nandīsūtra* a sequence of forty or so verses praises Mahāvīra and the *saṅgha*, gives a list of the ford-makers and the *gaṇadharas*, before praising the teaching of Mahāvīra, and finally the list of elders (verses 23–43). The verses naming the teachers Skandila and Nāgārjuna are:

> I bow down to him Skandilācārya, whose method of explanation (*aṇuyoga*) is even now spreading in half of Bhārata, whose fame has spread to many cities. Then I bow down to Himavanta, who has prowess as great as the Himālaya, has great fortitude and valour, the bearer of limitless spiritual study. We bow down to Himavanta Kṣamāśramaṇa [and] Ācārya Nāgārjuna, bearers of the mode of explanation of the *kāliya* texts, bearers too of the Pūrvas. I bow down to Vācaka Nāgārjuna, endowed with tenderness and mildness, who attained the state of Vācaka in due course, transmitter of the flood of scripture. I bow to the pupil of Nāgārjuna, Ācārya Bhūtadiṇṇa, whose colour is like excellent purified gold, a *campaka* flower, the heart of a choice blooming lotus, whose heart is compassionate toward souls capable of liberation, skilled in the virtue of compassion, wise, foremost in half of Bhārata, foremost amongst experts in all kinds of spiritual study, the best expert who expounds the scriptures, delighter of the line of the Nāgila clan, forward in the benefitting of beings, up-rooter of the danger of existence. I bow to Lohitya, who knows well what is eternal and what is not, who always bears the meaning of scriptures well-understood, the actuality of developing those of good nature [?][16]

Whether or not Skandila and Nāgārjuna are the spiritual forefathers of Devarddhigaṇi need not detain us here. The verses place the names Skandila and Nāgārjuna firmly in the lineage of expounders of the texts, but no hint of dates is given. All that is established here is that these teachers existed before 676 CE (the date of the *Nandīsūtra-cūrṇi*).

§2 Kalpasūtra *§148*

This is the key passage for Western scholars' statements, since it, or rather Jacobi's comments about this passage in the introduction to his edition (1879), are the ultimate source of the scholarly views presented in the section about the date of the redacting council. First, the passage, which comes at the end of one section and just after the description of the death of Mahāvīra:

> *samaṇassa bhagavao Mahāvīrassa jāva savva-dukkha-ppahīṇassa nava vāsa-sayāiṃ viikkaṃtāiṃ, dasamassa ya vāsa-sayassa ayaṃ asīime*

> *saṃvacchare kāle gacchai. vāyāṇ'aṃtare puna: ayaṃ teṇaue saṃvacchare kāle gacchai iti [variant dīsai*].[17]
>
> (*Kalpasūtra* 1879: 67)
>
> Since the time that the Venerable Ascetic Mahāvīra died, etc. (all down to) freed from all pains, nine centuries have elapsed, and of the tenth century this is the eightieth year [= 980 AV]. Another redaction has ninety-third year (instead of eightieth [= 993 AV]).[18]
>
> (*Kalpasūtra* 1884: 270)

So 980 or 993 years have passed since the death of Mahāvīra. But the brief passage does not say to what event the reference is made: the text does not indicate in any way what happened after the lapse of that number of years, likely candidates however could reasonably be the composition of the *Kalpasūtra* itself or its redaction.

In 1879 Jacobi took this statement to refer to Devarddhigaṇin: 'It needs hardly be remarked that the passages containing the dates 980 and 993 AV do not refer to the author [of the *Kalpasūtra*, Bhadrabāhu], but to Devarddhigaṇin, the editor of the *Kalpasūtra*' (p. 23). In Jacobi's footnote to his translation he also listed this as the first option (1884: 270, n. 1, the other options will be dealt with later when the commentaries are presented). The passage just cited – or rather the combined remarks by the later commentators about it – is at the heart of Jacobi's 1879 statements about the dates for the redacting councils cited earlier. *In the text itself*, however, there is no mention of Mathurā, Valabhī, Skandila, Nāgārjuna or Devarddhigaṇin, those associations are only made later in commentary literature (extracts §10 onwards).

§3 Jinadāsa Nandī-cūrṇi

The colophon to the *cūrṇi* on the *Nandīsūtra* is dated Śaka 598 [676 CE].[19] Since the verses have been translated under extract §1 earlier, only the *cūrṇi* comments on those are given here.

> The verse [no. 32] 'Whose [mode of explanation]': How then his mode of explanation? It is said, there was a time of profound and difficult famine for twelve years, because [the ascetics] were again and again (*aṇṇaṇṇato = anyānya-taḥ*?) lapsing [from the rules][20] for the sake of food, scriptural learning (*suta*) perished through the absence of understanding (*gahaṇa*), text-work (*guṇaṇā*), [and] *aṇuppeha* [?]. Then in the time of plentiful food in Mathurā there was a great meeting of ascetics with the faithful, headed by Ācārya Khandila, saying: 'Who remembers whatever [let them recount that for us].' Thus the *Kāliyasuta* [texts] were gathered. Because this was done in Mathurā it is said to be the Mathurā recension. And that approved by the Ācārya Khandila was done

in his presence and is said to be the mode of explanation. The rest is easy.

Others say: that scriptural learning (*suta*) was not destroyed, but in that very difficult famine the other main bearers of the mode of explanation perished. Only the teacher Khandila remained.[21] In Mathurā the mode of explanation was again set forth for the ascetics, therefore it is called the Mathurā recension, the mode of explanation in his presence it is said.[22]

The only contribution of the *cūrṇi* on v. 34 is that Nāgārjuna was the pupil of Himavanta.

[Verse 35] *cūrṇi*: 'In due course' by grasping the texts [beginning with] '*Sāmādiyā*...' and so on: and in time, with the turn of those ahead, succeeding the person [ahead of him], he attained the stage of *vācaka*. He directs the flood of scripture, the pouring out [of scripture?]. The rest is easy.

This is the oldest dated source for the account of the councils: the teachers' names are mentioned, but there is no indication at all of their dates.

Two other sources in the ancient layer of the *cūrṇi*s can be treated here (I cite these references from Mehta and Chandra (1970–1972, Nāgajjuṇa sv): the *Āyāra-cuṇṇi*, (also ascribed to Jinadāsa, 593–693 CE, see Balbir 1993: 1, 81) mentions the two names: Nāgārjuna (*Āyāraṅga-cuṇṇi* 1941: 219, 232, 237, 244, 313) and Devarddhigaṇin (page 207). Another (unascribed?) *cūrṇi* on the *Daśāśrutaskandha* mentions the name Nāgajjuṇa (*Nāgajjuṇiyā tu evaṃ paḍaṃti evaṃ tu guṇappehī aguṇā'navvijjae* (*Āyāradasāo* 1954: 204)).[23] These occurrences which add nothing to what we know, merely confirm the continuity of the tradition. The references which follow all echo this information, until we get to the commentary speculations (§10 and so on which follows).

§4–8

Because of their brevity and derivative nature, these text references can be treated together. Reference §4 is by Haribhadra (700–770 CE) in the *Laghuvṛtti* on the *Nandīsūtra* (cited here from the edition of Puṇyavijaya (1966b: 16f.)).[24] Because Haribhadra is merely re-presenting the *cūrṇi* version in Sanskrit his passages need not be examined in detail. He adds nothing to the previous entries, but merely transmits that information in the more widely known Sanskrit. Reference §5 comes in the ninth century when Śīlaṅka, an important Śvetāmbara commentator, refers in his commentary on the *Āyāraṅga* to Nāgajjuṇa (**Āyāraṅga* 1916: 303). This is hardly a major reference, but does show the continuity of the tradition through the ninth century and that the earlier information was available. Similar is reference §6 by Śāntyācārya Vādivetāla (he died in *Saṃvat* 1096 [1039]?).

In his *Uttarādhyayana* commentary entitled *Śiṣyahitā* (*Uttarādhyayana* 1933: 149) he refers to the name Nāgarjuṇa.

The great Hemacandra (1088–1172) in his *Yogaśāstra* commentary (1926 or 1939 edition p. 207) seems to re-present the version from the *cūrṇi* or from Haribhadra, and merely says that the Āgamas were written down by Skandila and Nāgārjuna and others fearing that because of a famine the teachings would be lost.[25] The major later commentator Malayagiri (*c.*1093–1193) provides the eighth reference, in his commentary on the *Joisakaraṇḍaga* (1928: 41) he gives only the traditional account.[26] While in his commentary on the *Nandīsūtra* he adds that Skandila was a 'Disciple of preceptor Sīha of the Baṃbhaddīvā branch.'

§9 Bhadreśvara Sūri, Kahāvalī

This work has been dated by Jacobi (1932: xii–xiii) to the twelfth century *Saṃvat*.[27] Jacobi offers further comment: 'Bhadreśvara's tales are, as a rule, but a more elegant version of the *kathānakas* contained in the *cūrṇis* and *ṭīkās*' (p. xii). 'Bhadreśvara's work has few literary merits. It is scarcely more than a collection of disconnected materials for the history of the Śvetāmbara church, culled from the ample literature of *cūrṇis* and *ṭīkās*' (p. xiii). So this extract cannot be used as evidence, seeming to rely as it does on the earlier sources already cited.[28]

§10 Jinaprabhamuni, Sandehaviṣauṣadhī.

It is of vital significance that none of the citations up to this point has given any indication of the dates of the teachers. This extract is the first indication of a tradition of dating. Jinaprabhamuni completed the *Sandehaviṣauṣadhī*, a commentary on the *Kalpasūtra*, on *Āśvina sudi 8, Saṃvat 1364*, or 1307 CE. This is the first of several comments on the extract given at §2 earlier. Jacobi makes it clear that he has not seen the '*cūrṇi*' on the *Kalpasūtra* but he thinks all the Sanskrit commentators are deriving their information from it (*Kalpasūtra* 1879: 25).[29] This may explain his trust of the commentatorial tradition here, that is, the antiquity of the *cūrṇis* supposedly vouching for the authenticity of the tradition. A lengthy extract is cited by Jacobi (1879: 114–115) from a manuscript supplied by Bühler (presumably from Bühler's personal collection (Jacobi 1879: 25–26)).[30] In the passage cited by Jacobi (and then concisely paraphrased by him) we are presented with the following options for the meaning of the dates given in the *Kalpasūtra* text. The first choices relate to the year 980, which is explained as the number of years to have elapsed: (1) since the passing away of Mahāvīra and the composition of the *Kalpasūtra* by Bhadrabāhu, (2) since Devarddhi saw the teachings in danger and set them down, or (3) since the death of the son of king Dhruvasena, though some say that was 1080 years ago, (4) the year 993 could be the number of years since *Pajjusaṇā* was moved from the fifth to the fourth of *Bhādrapada*.

The traditions available to Jinaprabhamuni did not allow him to decide, he relegates the option of the council dating to second place. This is the earliest source to link a date with the redacting council of Devarddhigaṇin, it does so cautiously and qualifies all its options with *bahuśrutā vā yathāvad vidanti*, 'the learned know how it was.' This passage is the oldest source I have found for the dating repeated in the scholarly accounts presented in the first section earlier, although not one of those accounts communicated clearly the lack of definiteness, nor the other choices for the meaning of the date given in the tradition, nor even the fact that this option for the date's meaning is not recorded before 1307 CE.

§11 Vinayavijaya, Subodhikā

This commentary on the *Kalpasūtra* (as yet unpublished), is also cited by Jacobi (1879: 116–117). It was written in *Saṃvat* 1616 [1559]. Once again this passage relates to extract §2.[31] The commentator begins by stating that he is having to rely on earlier commentators. He then presents two choices, the first is that this verse was written by Devarddhigaṇin himself to show when the *Kalpasūtra* was written, that is, the writing down of the canon was in 980, so the *Kalpasūtra* was also written down then. He then cites a Prākrit verse stating that 980 years after Mahāvīra in the town of Valabhī, Devarddhigaṇin wrote down the teachings. The second option is that 980 was when the *Kalpasūtra* was first read aloud in Ānanda[pūra]. He then goes on to present the traditions about the date being 993 etc. This commentator, while giving the Devarddhi option first, nevertheless says, 'the omniscient ones know the reality [of it, ie. what the truth is]' *tattvam punaḥ kevalino vidanti*. The tradition is not firm and the dating is being offered a thousand years after the relevant event.

§12 Dharmasāgara, Kiraṇāvalī *or* Vyākhānapaddhati

This commentary on the *Kalpasūtra* by Dharmasāgara, *Kiraṇāvalī* or *Vyākhānapaddhati*, was written in *Saṃvat* 1628 [1571]. This is still unpublished but was cited by Jacobi (1879: 115–116).[32] The opening line of the relevant section shows that the writer of the *cūrṇi* used by Dharmasāgara has not commented on this line: *yady api cūrṇikāreṇa kuto'pi kāraṇāṃ na vyākhyātam*. He is relying on a statement in an old and worn commentary, *avāpta-jīrṇa-ṭīkaikadeśa*. He repeats the Devarddhigaṇin option. Once more the overall tone is uncertainty and we are told 'to find out the truth from the learned', *tattvam tu bahuśruta-gamyam*, and 'to ask the experts in scripture or those knowing the innermost details of the teachings' *tattvaṃ tu śrutadhara-gamyam praṣṭavyā vā pravacana-rahasya-vidaḥ*. Even the oldest commentators then are consistently representing the traditional interpretations as uncertain, surely there should be some sign of this uncertainty in modern interpretations of this evidence.

§13–14 Samayasundara, Sāmācārīśataka *and* Kalpalatā

Before turning to the final commentary on the *Kalpasūtra* passage we have a statement by Samayasundara, who lived around 1630 CE. In his *Sāmācārīśataka* he repeats the statements of the earlier sources, apparently on the basis of the *Nandīsūtra-cūrṇi*, without adding anything new.[33] The same author is responsible for the next citation, in his *Kalpalatā*, a commentary on the *Kalpasūtra* written sometime before *Saṃvat* 1699 [1642]: '[I]n 980 VN at the end of the second famine, a council of monks met under [Khandila's] chairmanship in Mahurā to redact the canon' (*Kalpasūtra* *1939: 107). Jacobi says 'The comment of the *Kalpalatā* is a mere abstract of the *Sandehaviṣauṣadhī* [extract §10]' (1879: 115). This means Samayasundara is likely to have based his comments on that text, therefore neither of these quotations from him qualify as an independent confirmation of the tradition.

§15 Lakṣmīvallabha's Kalpadruma

This final dated text, is a commentary on the *Kalpasūtra* written sometime before 1835 CE. The mention of the names here shows the tradition of commenting continued, but this text is too late as a source to be of interest here. Already by the 1500s the commentaries were merely repeating earlier accounts.

Conclusion about the dates of the Jaina redacting councils

The original sources containing information about the redacting teachers and their activity can be divided into those which provide a date and those which do not. None of the sources before Jinaprabhamuni's *Sandehaviṣauṣadhī* of 1307 give any indication of a date for the redactions, while the statements from 1307 onwards are consistently tentative and qualified. Accordingly, there is no justification for scholarly accounts to link the councils with the suggested datings in anything but the most preliminary way. Certainly to present these dates as unquestionably well established facts is misleading.

A tradition about something happening in 980 (or 993) AV is certainly found in the *Kalpasūtra* (§2 cited earlier). What the dates refer to is not clear, as Jacobi (1884: 270, n. 1) states in the footnote to his translation:

> The commentators confess that there was no fixed tradition, and bring forward the following four facts, which are applied at will to either date:

1 The council of Valabhī under the presidency of Devarddhi, who caused the Siddhānta to be written in books.
2 The council of Mathurā under the presidency of Skandila, who seems to have revised the Siddhānta.
3 The public reading of the *Kalpasūtra* before king Dhruvasena . . .
4 The removal of *Pajjusaṇā* by Kālākācārya from the fifth to the fourth *Bhādrapada*.

Jacobi cited – from manuscript sources – four commentators on *Kalpasūtra* §148 and another text, Padmamandiragiri's *Ṛṣimaṇḍalaprakaraṇa* (*Saṃvat* 1553) (*Kalpasūtra* 1879: 114–118). These turn out to be the sources of the four alternatives he gives earlier. What is notable about these works as sources is that they are not definite even about what event is being dated, that is, they present alternatives, and three suggest that readers look elsewhere for clarification: *bahuśrutā vā yathāvad vidanti* (*Sandehaviṣauṣadhī*), *tattvaṃ tu śrutadharagamyam praṣṭavyā vā pravacanarahasyavidaḥ* (*Kiraṇāvalī*) and *tattvam punaḥ kevalino vidanti* (*Subodhikā*), which shows there was no clear traditional information on which to base a judgement.

A second notable feature is the late date of these commentaries. Listing them here using Jacobi's dates (1879: 25–36), which are in general supported by Velankar (1944), we have:

1307	Jinaprabhamuni, *Sandehaviṣauṣadhī* (completed *Saṃvat* 1364)
1496	Padmandiragiri, *Ṛṣimaṇḍalaprakaraṇa* (*Saṃvat* 1553)
1559[34]	Vinayavijaya, *Subodhikā* (*Saṃvat* 1616)
1571	Dharmasāgara, *Kiraṇāvalī* or *Vyākhānapaddhati* (*Saṃvat* 1628)
<1835[35]	Lakṣmīvallabha, *Kalpadruma*

'[T]he common and old tradition' referred to by Jacobi, turns out to be neither so common nor so old. We cannot blame Jacobi if his early remarks (1879) have not been tempered by the qualification given in his footnote to the translation of *Kalpasūtra* §148 (1884). Remarks in the introduction to a truly pioneering translation are more likely to be widely read than a footnote deep in the English version of a Jaina religious text. His later more qualified remarks have not been taken up by scholars, who have instead relied on his earlier – perhaps overconfident – assertion linking Devarddhigaṇin with the date 980/993 AV. The continued overstatement of the case for accepting these datings for more than a century however cannot be defended.

Kapadia, the only other scholar to publish original source passages, was vague when he connected the references detailing the councils to the dates 980/993 AV. He cited the *Nandīsūtra-cūrṇi* text and added as a footnote 'It appears that this happened sometime between Vīra *Saṃvat* 827 and 840' (1941: 61, n. 4). He then cited a text linking the dates with Devarddhigaṇin – text §14 earlier – but that text is dated from 1642 and hardly authoritative in this matter.

In the sources that have come to light so far, references about the activities of Skandila, Nāgārjuna and Devarddhigaṇin are straightforward, if vague, for the most part. The passages suggesting the date for their activities appear only in the later commentatorial traditions, where they are presented with indications that the tradition is not definite on this point. The misrepresentation of these matters as definite, when the tradition clearly indicates that they are not definite, is what I hope to correct in the standard accounts of the history of the councils in the transmission of the Jaina canon. We can certainly say that the tradition speaks of councils, and I endorse the versions of Folkert and Dundas cited earlier, with the addition of the information that *late* traditions ascribe those councils to 980 (or 993) AV.

Notes

1 Presumably the editing of the texts, or at least the majority of them, was completed sometime prior to the great commentator Abhayadeva (fl. 1058–1071 according to the dates of his commentaries on the *Uvavāiya* and *Viyāhapaṇṇatti, Saṃvat* 1115 and *Saṃvat* 1128 respectively (Velankar 1944: 64a, 290a)).

2 Other problematic aspects of the Śvetāmbara 'canon', its contents etc., are dealt with by Kapadia (1941), Jaini (1979: 47–77), Bruhn (1987) and Folkert (1993: 87).

3 *Āvāśyaka-cūrṇi* (*1928–1929: 2, 187, cited here from Kapadia 1941: 72, n. 1): *tammi ya kāle bārasavariso dukkālo uvaṭṭhito/saṃjatā ito ito ya samuddatīre acchittā puṇar avi Pāḍaliputte militā/tesiṃ aṇṇassa uddesao, aṇṇassa khaṇḍaṃ, evaṃ saṅghāḍitehiṃ ekkārasa Aṅgāṇi saṅghātitāṇi, Diṭṭhivādo natthi/Nepālavattaṇīe ya Bhaddabāhusāmī acchanti coddasapuvvī, tesiṃ saṅgheṇaṃ patthavito saṅghāḍao 'Diṭṭhivādaṃ vāehi' tti/gato, niveditaṃ saṅghakajjaṃ taṃ, te bhaṇanti – dukkālanimittaṃ mahāpāṇam na paviṭṭho mi, iyāṇiṃ paviṭṭho mi, to na jāti vāyaṇaṃ dātuṃ paḍiniyattehiṃ saṅghassa akkhātaṃ. tehi aṇṇo vi saṅghāḍao visajjito – jo saṅghassa āṇaṃ atikkamati tassa ko daṇḍo? te gatā, kahitaṃ, to akkhāi – ugghāḍijjai/te bhaṇanti – mā ugghāḍeha, peseha mehavī, satta pāḍipucchagāṇi demi.*

4 *Pariśiṣṭaparvan* (9.55–9.67, pp. 244–245): *itaś ca tasmin duṣkāle karāle kālarātrivat/nirvāhārthaṃ sādhusaṅghas tīraṃ nīranidher yayau // 55 // aguṇyamānaṃ tu sadā sādhūnāṃ vismṛtaṃ śrutam/anabhyasanato naśyaty adhītaṃ dhīmatām api // 56 // saṅgho 'tha Pāṭalīputre duṣkālānte 'khilo 'milat / yad Aṅgādhyayanoddeśādy āsīd yasya tad ādade // 57 // tataś caikādaśāṅgāni śrīsaṅgho 'melayat tadā/Dṛṣṭivādanimittaṃ ca tasthau kiñcid vicintayan // 58 // Nepāladeśamārgasthaṃ Bhadrabāhuṃ ca pūrviṇam/jñātvā saṅghaḥ samāhvātuṃ tataḥ praiśīn munidvayam // 59 // gatvā natvā munī tau tam ity ūcāte kṛtāñjalī/samādiśati vaḥ saṅghas tatrāgamanahetave // 60 // so 'py vāca mahāprāṇaṃ dhyānam ārabdham asti yat/sādhyaṃ dvādaśabhir varṣair nāgamiṣyāmy ahaṃ tataḥ // 61 // mahāprāṇe hi niṣpanne kārye kasmiṃścid āgate/sarvapūrvāṇi guṇyante sūtrārthabhyāṃ muhūrtataḥ // 62 // tadvacas tau munī gatvā saṅghasyāśaṃsatām atha / saṅgho 'py aparam āhūyādideśeti munidvayaṃ // 63 // gatvā vācyaḥ sa ācāryo yaḥ śrīsaṅghasya śāsanam / na karoti bhavet tasya daṇḍaḥ ka iti śaṃsa naḥ // 64 // saṅghabāhyaḥ sa kartavya iti vakti yadā sa tu / tarhi taddaṇḍayogyo 'sīty ācāryo vācya uccakaiḥ // 65 // tābhyāṃ gatvā tathaivokta ācāryo 'py evam ūcivān / maivaṃ karotu bhagavān saṅghaḥ kiṃ tu karotv adaḥ // 66 // mayi prasādaṃ kurvāṇaḥ srīsaṅghaḥ prahiṇotv iha / śiṣyān medhāvinas tebhyaḥ sapta dāsyāmi vācanāḥ // 67 //* Schubring has paraphrased this passage (1935 §23), there is also the translation of the entire *Pariśiṣṭaparvan* by R. C. C. Fynes, 1998 in which this passage is translated on pp. 193–194.

5 In a footnote Jacobi added:

> About 30 years earlier, between 410 and 432 AD, Buddhaghoṣa caused the Buddhist *piṭakas* and *arthakathās* to be written down 'for the more lasting stability of faith.' As the redaction of the Buddhist works in Ceylon and that of the Jaina works in Guzerat occurred about the same time, it may be inferred either that the Jainas adopted that measure from the Bauddhas, or that it was in the 5th century that writing was more generally made use of in India for literary purposes.
>
> (*Kalpasūtra* 1879: 16, n. 1)

Perhaps a desire to see the Jaina and Buddhist moves as contemporaneous has led Jacobi to state the case for linking the councils with the date 980 so strongly.

6 Schubring 1926: [1]:

> Es wird im ersten Viertel unseres sechsten Jahrhunderts gewesen sein, daß die Stadt Vaḷā, im Sanskrit Valabhī gennant, auf der Halbinsel Kāṭhiāwaḍ in Gujarat, Zeugin einer geistlichen Tagung der, weißen Jainas wurde. Unter dem Vorsitz Devarddhis, eines ihrer Häupter, wurde in Versammlungen der Gläubigen der Wortlaut der heiligen Texte festzuhalten versucht und der handschriflichen Vervielfältigung zugeführt. Damit waren die Zeugnisse von Mahāvīras Lehre, fast tausend Jahre – so will es die Überlieferung – nach dem Hinscheiden des Meisters, vor dem Fortschreiten der Verflüchtingung gerettet. Seitdem besteht der Kanon der Weißgewandeten im Wesentlichen unverändert.

7 'Im Jahre 980 nach Mahāvīra, nach anderer Überlieferung 993, fand zu Valabhī (heute Vala) auf Kathiawar unter dem Vorsitz des Gaṇin Devarddhi eine Mönchsversammlung statt mit dem Ziele, die heiligen Bücher zu vervielfältigen.'

8 Schubring (1959: 669), translation by John Cort in Folkert (1993: 47, n. 9): 'Die für die Shvetāmbaras verbindlichen Werke... stammen in ihren ältesten Teilen aus dem 3. bis 2. Jh. vChr. Zum Kanon wurden sie in einem Konzil auf Kathiawar (Gujarat) Ende des 6. Jh. gesammelt.'

9 Kapadia's account, and even his citations, are also reproduced by India-based authors, for example, Ratnaprabha and Kanu Chhotalal Jain *Śramaṇa Bhagavān Mahāvīra* (1942–1951) in v. 5, pt. 1 pp. 215–216. For 'Yugapradhāna Nāgārjuna' there is a brief mention in this work (p. 317), but it seems to be a reworking of Kapadia's information, with the addition of an (unsourced) date for Nāgārjuna's death VN. This is a confused and confusing publication offering unsourced extracts with translations. Derivative accounts almost entirely based on the early pioneers continue to be published in India, for example, Muni Uttam Kamal Jain in *Jaina sects and schools* (Delhi: Concept), (1975: 44–45) but he misleadingly adds a citation from *Epigraphia Indica* (XVI, 17) purporting to indicate a date for the council of Valabhī, when in fact there is no mention there of the council. (I am grateful to Peter Flügel for pointing out this reference.)

10 This point being one of the few cases where the English version is better than the original German. In that it follows Kapadia's account (1962: 77, n. 4).

11 This seems to be the first mention of the Jaina teacher Nāgārjuna in scholarly accounts. The references in Jaina commentaries to the two traditions of reading, the tradition of Valabhī or the tradition of Mathurā are dealt with in the text.

12 Jagdishchandra Jain's versions have not been used. He prints the following contradictory statements a few lines apart: '... after the redaction of the canon in these councils, ācārya Skandila and Nāgārjunasūri could not get an opportunity to meet each other and hence the two different versions remained unreconciled.' 'The council of Valabhī was attended by both Ārya Skandila and Nagārjunasūri' (Jain 1984: 40).

13 In each case I think it vitally necessary to cite extensively the text of each source. Not paying attention to the original sources has been a major contributing reason to the inexact scholarly position now holding sway. Even in India the original sources are extremely difficult to locate, for example, the old commentaries cited by Jacobi in 1879 have still not been published to my knowledge, that is, Jinaprabhamuni's *Sandehaviṣauṣadhī*, Vinayavijaya's *Kiraṇāvalī/Vyākhānapaddhati*, Samayasundara's *Kalpalatā*.

14 Puṇyavijaya has examined material about the links between the writer of the *Nandīsūtra*, Devavācaka and Devarddhigaṇi Kṣamāśramaṇa (Puṇyavijaya 1961: 29–31), although he cites Devendra Sūri (author of the *Navyakarmagranthas*) using 'Devarddhi-vācaka' and 'Devarddhi-kṣamāśramaṇa' several times while citing *Nandīsūtra* readings – which may strengthen the case for separating the two authors

since Jaina authors tend to be careful about epithets and honorifics – he prefers not to decide on whether there was one author or two (see also *Nandīsūtra* 1966a: 5).

15 Mallavādin (1966–1988), see the Sanskrit *Prākkathana*, page 24.

16 *Nandīsūtra* (1968: 1–8): *jesi imo aṇuogo payarai ajjāvi aḍḍhabharahammi/bahunagaraniggayajase te vande Khandilāyarie // 33 // tato Himavantamahantavikkamaṃ dhiparakkamam aṇantaṃ/sajjhāyamaṇantadharam Himavantaṃ vandimo sirasā // 34 // Kāliyasuyaaṇuogassa dhārae dhārae ya puvvāṇaṃ/Himavanta-khamāsaṇe vande Nāgagjjuṇāyarie // 35 // miu-maddava-saṃpaṇṇe aṇupuvviṃ vāyagattaṇaṃ patte/ohasuyasamāyarae Nāgajjuṇavāyae vande // 36 // vara-kaṇagativiya-campaya-vimaula-vara-kamala-gabbha-sari-vaṇṇe/bhaviya-jaṇa-hiyaya-daie dayā-guṇa-visārae dhīre // 37 // aḍḍhabharaha-ppahāṇe bahu-viha-sajjhāya-sumuṇiya-pahāṇe / aṇuoiya-vara-vasahe Ṇāila-kula-vaṃsa-ṇandikare // 38 // bhūahiyayappa-gabbhe vande haṃ Bhūyadiṇṇam āyarie/bhava-bhaya-voccayakare sīse Ṇāgajjuṇa-risīṇaṃ // 39 // visesayaṃ sumuṇiya-ṇiccāṇiccaṃ sumuṇiya-sutta-'ttha-dhārayaṃ ṇiccaṃ // vande haṃ Lohiccaṃ sabbhāvubbhāvaṇātaccaṃ // 40 //.*

17 Jacobi's oldest dated manuscript was Vikrama 1484 [1427 CE], presumably on paper (1879: 28). Muni Puṇyavijaya's edition of the *Kalpasūtra* (1952) is based on six manuscripts, including five on palm leaf, one from Khambhāt dated *Saṃvat* 1247 [1190]. His text for this passage is: *samaṇassa ṇaṃ bhagavao Mahāvīrassa jāva savvadukkhappahīṇassa nava vāsasayāiṃ viikkantāīṃ, dasamassa ya vāsasayassa ayaṃ asīime saṃvaccharekāle gacchai / vāyaṇangare puṇa ayaṃ teṇaue saṃvaccharekāle gacchai iti dīsai / 147 //.*

18 Stevenson's version, in his presentation of the *Kalpasūtra*, need not detain us. Jacobi's comments on its unreliability (*Kalpasūtra* 1879: 27) were echoed by Winternitz (1933:2, 462, n. 1).

19 *Śakarājño paccasu varṣaśateṣu vyatikrānteṣu aṣṭanavateṣu Nandyadhyayanacūrnī samāptā ti //* (*Nandīsūtra* 1966b: 8, 83); Schubring prefers '677' (1935: 43).

20 The *Pāia-sadda-mahaṇṇavo* gives for *phiḍia: bhraṃśa-prāpta naṣṭa, cyuta; atikrānta, ullaṅghita*. The commentary on the *Nandisūtra* known as the *Viṣama-pada-ṭippanakam*, glosses this as *nirgatānāṃ* (*Nandīsūtra* 1966b: 182) while Kapadia's text (1941: 61, n. 3) gives *aṇṇato ṭhitāṇaṃ* probably using *Nandīsūtra-cūrṇi* 1928.

21 Reading *saṃthare* with Kapadia's citation (1928: 61, n. 3).

22 *Nandīsūtra (1966b: p. 9 line 19–p. 11 line 7): jesi imo aṇuogo payarai ajjāvi aḍḍhabharahammi / bahu-nagara-niggaya-jase te vande Khaṇḍilāyarie // 32 // jesi imo. gāhā/ kahaṃ puṇa tesiṃ aṇuogoṇ ucyate bārasa-saṃvaccharie mahante dubbhikkha-kāle bhattaṭṭhā aṇṇaṇṇato phiḍitāṇaṃ gahaṇa-guṇaṇā-'ṇuppehābhāvato sute vippaṇaṭṭhe puṇo subhikkha-kāle jāte Madhurāe mahante sāhu-samudae Khandilāyariya-ppamuha-saṅgheṇa 'jo jaṃ saṃbharati' tti evaṃ saṅghaḍitaṃ Kāliyasutaṃ / jamhā ya etaṃ Madhurāe kataṃ tamhā Mādhurā vāyaṇā bhaṇṇati / sā ya Khandilāyariya-sammaye tti kātuṃ tass'antiyo aṇuogo bhaṇṇati / sesaṃ kaṇṭhaṃ / aṇṇe bhaṇanti – jahā sutaṃ ṇa ṇatthaṃ, tammi dubbhikkha-kāle je aṇṇo pahāṇā aṇuyogadharā te vinaṭṭhā, ege Khandilāyarie saṃdhare, teṇa Madhurāe aṇuyogo puṇo sādhūṇaṃ pavattito tti Madhurā vāyaṇā bhaṇṇati, tassamtio ya aṇiyogo bhaṇṇati // 32 //... midu-maddava-saṃpaṇṇe aṇupuvviṃ vāyagattaṇaṃ patte/oha-suya-samāyāre Ṇāgajjuṇavāyae vande // 35 // midu-maddava. gāhā / 'aṇupuvvī' sāmādiyādisutaggahaṇeṇa, kālato ya purima-pariyāyattaṇeṇa purisāṇupuvvito ya vāyagattaṇaṃ patto, ohasutaṃ ca ussaggo, taṃ ca āyarati/sesaṃ kaṇṭhaṃ // 35 // Ṇāgajjuṇa vāyagassa sīso Bhūtadiṇṇe āyarito / tassimā guṇa-kittaṇā tihiṃ gāhāhiṃ...*

23 A more complete list of these internal citations is given by Puṇyavijaya (1961: 31–32) although he omits the occurrence on p. 244. The use of the respectful term Bhadanta makes Puṇyavijaya think the unnamed *cūrṇi* writer was of the line of Nāgārjuna, or at least identifying with his lineage.

24 *Nandīsūtra (1966b: 13): jesi imo aṇuogo payarai ajjā vi aḍḍhabharahammi/bahunagaraniggayajase te vande Khaṇḍilāyarie // 33 // jesi. gādhā/Vyākhyā – yeṣām ayam anuyogaḥ pracarati adyāpy ardhabharate Vaitāḍhyādārataḥ / bahunagareṣu nirgataṃ – prasiddhaṃ yaśo yeṣāṃ te bahu-nagara-nirgata-yaṣasaḥ tān vande siṅghavācaka-śiṣyān Skandilācāryān/kahaṃ puṇa tesiṃ aṇuogoṇ ucyate, bārasa-saṃvaccharie mahante dubbikkhe kāle bhattaṭṭhā phiḍiyāṇaṃ gahaṇa-guṇaṇā-'ṇuppehā'bhāvato sutte vippaṇaṭṭhe puṇo subhikkhe kāle jāte mahurāe mahante samudae Khandilāyariya-ppamuhasaṅgheṇa "jo jaṃ saṃbharahī" tti evaṃ saṅgahaḍitaṃ Kāliyasuyaṃ/jamhā eyaṃ Mahurāte kayaṃ tamhā Māhurā vāyāṇā bhannati / sā ya Khandilāyariya-sammata tti kāuṃ tassaṃtio aṇuogo bhaṇṇati/anne bhaṇanti jahā – suyaṃ ṇo ṇaṭṭhaṃ, tammi dubbhikkha-kāle je anne pahāṇā aṇuogodharā te viṇaṭṭhā/ege Khandilāyarie sandhare/teṇa Mahurāe puṇo aṇuogo pavattio tti Māhurā vāyaṇā bhannai/tassaṃtio ya aṇuogo bhaṇć ṇai tti gāthārthaṇ // 33 // tatto Himavanta-mahanta-vikkamaṃ dhī-parakkamamaṇantaṃ/ sajjhāyamaṇantadharaṃ Himavantaṃ vandimo sirasā // 34 //... kāliyasuyaaṇuogassa dhārae dhārae ya puvvāṇaṃ/himavantakhamāsae vande Ṇāgajjuṇāyarie // 35 // kāliya. gāhā / Vyākhyā – kālikaśrutānuyogasya dhārakān / dhārakāṃś ca 'pūrvāṇā' utpādādīć nām/himavatkṣamāśramaṇān vande/tathaitacchiṣyān eva vande Nāgārjunācāryani iti gāthārthaḥ // 35 // kimbhūtānn.*

25 *Jinavacanaṃ ca duṣṣamā-kāla-vaśād uccinna-prāyam iti matvā bhagavadbhir Nāgārjuna-Skandalācārya-prabhṛtibhiḥ pustakeṣu nyastam* (cited by Kapadia 1941: 62, n. 2).

26 *iha hi Skandilācārya-pravṛttau duṣṣamānubhāvato durbhikṣapravṛttyā sādhūnāṃ paṭhanaguṇanādikaṃ sarvam apy aneśat / tato durbhikṣātikrame subhikṣapravṛttau dvayoṇ saṅghayor melāpako'bhavat / tad yathā – eko Valabhyām eko Mathurāyāṃ / tatra ca sūtrarthasaṅghaṭane parasparaṃ vācanābhedo jātaḥ /* (cited by Kapadia 1941: 62, n. 3).

27 Jacobi knew of only one palm leaf manuscript of the text and that was of indifferent quality: 'There are two Bhadreśvara-Sūris in Peterson's Index of Authors in the *4th Report*. The first in the list is probably the author of the *Kahāvalī*, in the second half of the 12th century of the *Saṃvat* era [c. 1100–1150 CE]' (Jacobi 1932: xii).

28 Bhadreśvara also names Nāgajjuṇa in his *Kahāvalī: atthi Mahurā'urīe suyasamiddho Khandilo nāma Sūri, tahā Valahi nayarie Nāgajjuṇo nāma Sūri/tehi ya jāe bārasavarisie dukkāle nivvaḍabhāvao viphuṭṭhim (?) kāūṇa pesiyā disodisiṃ sāhavo/gamiuṃ ca kahavi dutthaṃ te puṇo miliyā sugāie/jāva sajjhāyanti tāva khaṇḍukhuruḍīhūyaṃ puvvāhiyaṃ/tato mā suyavocchittī hou tti pāraddho sūrīhiṃ siddhantuddhāro/tattha vi jaṃ na vīsarīyam taṃ taheva saṇṭhaviyaṃ/pamhuṭṭhāṇaṃ uṇa puvvavarāvaḍantasuttatthāṇusārao kayā saṅghaḍaṇā* (cited by Kapadia (1941: 62, n. 1) from a manuscript).

29 From notes by Puṇyavijaya (*Nandīsūtra* 1966b: Prastāvanā) and Velankar (1944: 75) there is clearly more than one *cūrṇi* on the *Kalpasūtra*, however without access to more materials I cannot clarify the situation beyond saying that the following texts have been referred to by earlier authors: (1) *Kalpa-cūrṇi* (*Nandīsūtra* 1966b: Prastāvanā 6–7) – (2) *Kalpa-viśeṣa-cūrṇi* (*Nandīsūtra* 1966b: Prastāvanā 6–7) – (3) *Kalpasūtrasya cūrṇī Niryukti-garbhā* (printed *Kalpasūtra* 1952: 83–[115]) Prakrit prose around 67 verses, this is probably the same as the '*Niryukti* by Bhadrabāhu... 68 gāthās' (Velankar 1944: 75b). It begins: *saṃbodho sattamāsiyaṃ phāseṭṭā* verses begin *Pajjosamaṇāe akkharāiṃ*. It makes no comment on §148 (= §147 in Puṇyavijaya's edition) but jumps from a comment on the preceding passage to §201 – (4?) *Cūrṇi*, 700 *granthas* (Velankar 1944: 75b) – In addition Puṇyavijaya cites a *Kalpacūrṇi* (different from the *Daśāśrutaskandhacūrṇi*) which ends: *tao ya ārāhaṇāto chiṇṇasaṃsārī bhavati saṃsārasaṃtatiṃ chettuṃ mokkhaṃ pāvatīti. Kalpacūrṇī samāptā. granthāgram 5300 pratyakṣaragaṇanayā nirṇītam. [sarvagranthāgram 14784]* (*Nandīsūtra* 1966a: Prastāvanā, 7). He also cites a *Kalpaviśeṣacūrṇi* ending: *Kappavisesacuṇṇī samatteti.*

However the *Niryukti* embedded in a *cūrṇi* published by him in *Kalpasūtra* 1952 does not end like this and so is presumably another *cūrṇi*.

30 nava vāsa-sayāiṃ ti *śrīVīranirvṛter navasu varṣaśateṣv aśītyadhikeṣu [980] vyatīteṣv iyaṃ vācanā jāte 'ty arthe vyākhyāyamāne na tathā vicāracāturīcañcūnāṃ cetasi prītir, asya sūtrasyaśrīVardhamānānantaraṃ saptatyadhikavarṣaśateno'tpannenaśrīBhadrabāhusvāmipraṇītatvāt tasmād iyati kāle gate iyaṃ vācanā pustakeṣu nyaste 'ti sambhāvyate. śrīDevarddhikṣamāśramaṇair hiśrīVīranirvāṇān navasu varṣaśateṣv aśītyuttareṣu [980] atīteṣu granthān vyavacchidyamānān dṛṣṭvā sarvagranthānām ādime Nandyadhyayane sthavirāvalīlakṣaṇaṃ namaskāraṃ vidhāya granthāḥ pustakeṣu likhitā ity ata evā'tra granthe sthavirāvalīprānte Devarddhikṣamāśramaṇasya namaskāraṃ vakṣyate, pūrvaṃ tu guruśiṣyāṇāṃ śrutādhyayanādhyāpanavyavahāraḥ pustakanirapekṣa evā"sīt. kecit tv idam āhur, yad iyatkālātikrame Dhruvasenanṛpasya putramaraṇārtasya samādhim ādhātum Ānandapure sampratikāle Mahāsthānākhyayā rūḍhe sabhāsamakṣam ayaṃ grantho vācayitum ārabdha iti. samaṇassa ṇam bhagavao Mahāvīrassa jāva savva-dukkha-ppahīṇassa Dhuvaseṇarāiṇo putta-maraṇe ege vāsa-sahasse asīti-vāsāhie vatikkaṃte ity [1080] api kvadicādarśeṣu dṛṣṭam, bahuśrutā vā yathāvad vidanti. trinavatiyutanavaśatapakṣe [993] tv iyatā kālena pañcamyāś caturthyām paryuṣaṇāparva pravavṛte: teṇauya-nava-saehiṃ samaikkaṃtehi Vaddhamāṇāo / pajjusavaṇa-cautthī Kālayasūrīhiṃto ṭhaviyā // vīsahi diṇehi kappo paṃcaga-hāṇī ya kappa-ṭhavaṇā ya / nava-saya-teṇauehiṃ vucchinnā saṃgha-āṇāe // Sāla[va]haṇeṇa raṇṇā saṃghāeseṇa kārio bhayavaṃ / pajjūsavaṇa-cautthī cāummāsaṃ caudasīe // caumāsaga paḍikamaṇaṃ pakkhiya-divasammi cauviho saṃgho / nava-saya-teṇauehiṃ āyaraṇaṃ taṃ pamāṇaṃti // iti Tīrthodgārādiṣu bhaṇanāt.* This commentary was published in **Kalpasūtra*: 1913.

31 *yady api etasya sūtrasya vyaktatayā bhāvārtho na jñāyate, tathā' pi, yathā pūrvaṭīkākārair vyākhyātaṃ, tathā vyākhyāyate. tathā hi: atra kecid vadanti, yat Kalpasūtrasya pustakalikhanakālajñāpanāya (MS jñānānāṃ paya) idaṃ sūtraṃ śrīDevarddhigaṇikṣamāśramaṇair likhitaṃ. tathā cā'yam artho yathāśrīVīranirvāṇād aśītyadhikanavavarṣaśātikrame pustakārūḍhaḥ siddhānto jātas, tadā Kalpo'pi pustakārūḍho'pi jātaṇ iti. tatho'uktam:* Valahī-puraṃmi nayare Devaḍḍhi-ppamuha-sayala-saṃghehiṃ / putthe āgama lihio nava ya asīyāo Vīrāo // *anye vadanti: navaśataaśītivarṣe [sic] Vīrāt Senāṅgajārtham Ānande saṅghasamakṣam mamahaṃ (!?) prārabdhaṃ vācayituṃ vijñaiḥ, ityādy antarvācyavacanāt: śrīVīranirvāṇād aśītyadhikanavaśatavarṣātikrame Kalpasya sabhāsamakṣaṃ vācanā jātā, tāṃ jñāpayitum idaṃ sūtraṃ nyastam iti, tattvam punaḥ kevalino vidanti.* vāyaṇaṃtare puṇe'*tyādi vācanāntare punar ayaṃ trinavatitamaḥ saṃvatsaraḥ kāle gacchatī'ti dṛśyate. atra kecit vadanti vācanāntare ko'rthaḥ? pratyuttaraṃ (MS pratyaṃtare):.* teṇaue tti *dṛśyate; yat Kalpasya pustake likhanam parṣadi vācanaṃ vā aśītyadhikanavavarṣaśatātikrame iti kvacitpustake likhitaṃ, tat pustakāntare trinavatyadhika navavarṣaśatātikrame iti dṛśyate, itibhāvaḥ. anye punar vadanti: ayam aśītitamaḥ saṃć vatsara iti ko'rthaḥ? pustake Kalpalikhanasya hetubhūtaḥ ayaṃ śrīVīrād daśaṃśatasya aśītitamasaṃvatsaralakṣaṇakālo gacchatī'ti.* vāyaṇaṃtare *ko'rthaḥ? ekasyāḥ pustakalikhanarūpāyā vācanāyā anyat parṣadi vācanarūpaṃ yad vācanāntaraṃ tasya punar hetubhūto daśamaśatasya ayaṃ trinavatitamaḥ saṃvatsaraḥ. tathā cā'yam arthaḥ: navaśatāśītitamavarṣe Kalpasya pustake likhanaṃ navaśatatrinavatitamavarṣe ca parṣadvācane'ti tatho'ktaṃ śrīMunisundarasūribhiḥ svakṛtastotraratnakośe: vīrāt trinandāṅkaśarady acīkarat tvaccaityapūte Dhruvasenabhūpatiḥ / yasmin mahaiḥ saṃsadi Kalpavācanām ādyāṃ, tad Ānandapuram na kaḥ stute? // pustakalikhanakālas tu yatho'ktaḥ pratīta eva:* Valahīpuraṃmi nayare *ityādivacanāt: tattvam punaḥ kevalino vidanti.*

32 *yady api cūrṇikāreṇa kuto'pi kāraṇān na vyākhyātam, avāptajīrṇaṭīkaikadeśe tv asyā vācanāyā ity evaṃ vyākhātam; tathā'pi aśītyadhikanavaśate varṣātikrame*

sarvān granthān vyavacchidyamānān dṛṣṭvā pustakeṣu nyasadbhiḥ śrīDevarddhigaṇikṣamāśramaṇaiḥ śrīKalpasūtrasyā'pi vācanā pustake nyaste 'ti kecit sambhāvayanti. tathā punar iyatkālātikrame Dhruvasenanṛpasya putramaraṇārtasya samādhiṃ ādhātum, Ānandapure sabhāsamakṣaṃ śrīKalpavācanā'py ajanī 'ti kecit; tattvaṃ tu bahuśrutagamyam iti. trinavatiyutanavaśatapakṣe tu: teṇaua-nava-saehiṃ samaikkaṃtehi Vaddhamāṇāo // pajjosavaṇa-cautthī Kālagasūrīhiṃto ṭhaviyā // *ityādi sammatim udbhāvye 'yatkālātikrame bhādrasitacaturthyām paryuṣaṇāparvapravṛttir iti kecid vyākhyānayanti. evaṃ vyākhyāne kriyamāṇe śatrusaṃśayanirāsaka-Gardabhillocchedakāri-Kālakasūrito'yam bhinna eva sampadyate. na cai'vam, yataḥ prabhāvakacaritraKālakācāryakathāprabhṛtigrantheṣv eka evo'ktaḥ. tathā Kalpacūrṇi-Niśīthacūrṇyādiṣu tu BalamitraBhānumitrayor mātulena paryuṣaṇāparva caturthyām pravartitam; BalamitraBhānu (mitra)Tīrthodgāraprakīrṇādiṣu śrīVīrajinaVikramādityarājñor antarālavartināv api Vikramādityapratyāsannāv uktau; tatrā'pi kiyatkālavartināv api Vikramādi-tyakālabhāvināv api sambhavataḥ, tathā śālavāhana Vikramādityaprabandhādiṣu tayor yuddhasaṃgatiś ca. kiṃ ca, cūrṇikārā api: katham idānīm aparvarūpāyāṃ caturthyām paryuṣaṇe'? 'ti śiṣyanodanāyāṃ: yugapradhānaKālikasūrivacanād eve'ty evam uttaraṃ dattavantaḥ, na punaḥ:* vāya-ṇaṃtare puṇa ayaṃ teṇaue saṃvacchare kāle gacchai tti *pravacanavacanene'ty ādi svayam eva"locyam. tasmād: aśītipakṣe Dhruvasenanṛpā(nu)grahāt Paryuṣaṇākalpaḥ parṣadi vācayitum ārabdhaḥ, trinavatipakṣe tu pañcakāpekṣayā kālanaiyatyena parṣadi Kalpasūtravācane pravacanamaryādābhaṅga iti paryālocanayā: 1) abhivard-hite varṣe viṃśatyā dinair gṛhijñātaparyuṣaṇā, 2) pañcakahānyā svābhigṛhīta-paryuṣaṇā ce'ty ubhayam api vyucchedya saṅghādeśād ekai'va vācanā caramapañcake vyavasthāpite'ti vastugatyā vyākhyānīkriyata iti vastugatyā vyākhyāne kriyamāṇe parṣadvācanāṭaḥ pañcakahānyādivyavacchedenai'va caramapañcake yā vācanā sā vācanāntaram ity arthasaṃgatir api. kecit tu vicāryamāṇaṃ yad aśītipakṣe tad eva vācanāntareṇa trinavatipakṣe'pi yuktisaṃgataṃ dṛśyate. katham anyathā,* ii dīsai tti *akathayayiṣyatṇ? tattvaṃ tu śrutadharagamyam praṣṭavyā vā pravacanarahasyavidaḥ.*

33 *Śrīdevarddhigaṇikṣamāśramaṇena śrīvīrādaśītyadhikanavaśata (980) varṣe jātena dvādaśavarṣīyadurbhikṣavaśād bahutarasādhuvyāpattau bahuśrutavicchittau ca jātāyāṃ... bhaviṣyad bhavyalokopakārāya śrutabhaktaye ca śrīsaṅghāgrahād mṛtāviśiṣṭatadākālīnasarvasādhūn Valabhyāmākārya tanmukhādavicchinnāvaśiṣṭān nyūnādhikān truṭitāntruṭitānāgamālāpakānanukrameṇa svamatyā saṅkalyya pustakār-ūḍhāḥ kṛtāḥ / tataḥ mūlato gaṇadharabhāṣitānāmapi āgamānāṃ kartā śrīdevarddhi-gaṇikṣamāśramaṇa eva jātaḥ /* (cited by Kapadia 1941: 63, n. 1, repeated by Jaini 1979: 52, n. 17).

34 Dated to *Saṃvat* 1696 [1639] (Velankar 1944: 77).

35 Jacobi was not able to give a date for this work, but Velankar refers to it as the *Kalpadrumakalikā*, and says it was composed during the reign of Jinasaubhāgyasūri, who became Sūri in *Saṃvat* 1892 [1835] (Velankar 1944: 78a).

Bibliography

* indicates volumes I have not been able to physically consult.

Primary sources

Āyāradasāo

1954 *Śrī Daśāśrutaskandha: mūla-niryukti-cūrṇi*. Bhāvnagar: Vikrama Saṃvat 2011 [1954]. (Maṇivijayajī Gaṇī Granthamālā)

Āyāraṅga-sutta

1916 **Śrīmadgaṇadharavarasudharmasvāmipraṇītaṃ Śrutakevalibhadrabāhusvāmidṛbdhaniryuktiyuktaṃ, Śrīmacchīlaṅkācāryavihitavivṛtiyutaṃ [part 2 °vivaraṇayutaṃ] Śrīācārāṅgasūtram*. Mahesana: Āgamodayasamitiḥ, Vīrasaṃvat 2442. Vikramasaṃvat 1972–1973. Krāīṣṭa 1916. 2 v.

Āyāraṅga-cuṇṇi

1941 *Śrīācārāṅgacūrṇiḥ*/Bahuśrutakiṃvadantyā Śrījinadāsagaṇivaryavihitā [edited by Sāgarānanda]. Mālavadeśāntargataratnapurīya (Ratalāmagata): Śrīṛṣabhadevajīkeśarīmalajī Śvetāmbarasaṃsthā, Vikramasya Saṃvat 1998. Śrīvīrasya 2468. Krāiṣṭasya 1941.

Āvaśyaka-cūrṇi

1928–1929 **Śrīmad Gaṇadhara-Gautama-Svāmi-sandṛbdhaṃ... Śrīmad-Bhadrabāḥu-Svāmi-sūtrita-Niryukti-yutaṃ Śrīmaj-Jinadāsa-Gaṇi-Mahattara-kṛtayā Curṇyā sametaṃ Śrīmad-Āvaśyaka-sūtraṃ* [edited by Sāgarānanda]. Indore: Jaina-bandhu Press, 1928–29. 2 v. This is the only printed edition.

Kalpasūtra

1879 *Jinacaritra* in *The Kalpasûtra of Bhadrabâhu edited with an introduction, notes and a Prākṛit-Saṃskṛit glossary* by Hermann Jacobi. Leipzig: F. A. Brockhaus, 1879. (Abhandlungen für die Kunde des Morgenlandes; 7, 1).

1884 [Translation] *Gaina Sûtras: translated from Prākrit* by Hermann Jacobi. Part I: The Ā*k*ârâṅga Sûtra. The Kalpa Sûtra. Oxford: Clarendon Press, 1884. (Sacred Books of the East; 22).

1913 *[*Kalpasūtra* with Jinaprabha's *Sandehaviṣauṣadhī*]. Jāmnagara: Hīralāl Haṃsarāj, 1913. [Velankar 1944: 74b]

1939 *[*Kalpasūtra Kalpalatā*, with Samayasundara Gaṇi's *Kālikācārya kathā*]. Bombay: Jinadattasūri Prācīna Pustakoddhāra, 1939. 4, 196 p.

1952 *Kalpasūtra: mūla pāṭha, cūrṇi, niryukti tathā Śrī Pṛthvīcandrasūrikṛta ṭippaṇa, pāṭhāntarā Gujarātī bhāṣāntara tathā bhāṣāntaramāṃ ādharā śabdono koṣa*, Sampādaka Puṇyavijayajī; Gujarātī bhāṣāntara tathā adharā śabdhono koṣa Becaradāsa Jīvarāja Dośī. Amadāvāda: Sārābhāī Maṇilāla Navāba, Vikrama Saṃvat 2008. Īsvī San. 1952. (Śrī Jaina Kalā-sāhitya saṃśodhaka kāryālaya sirija; naṃ 5).

Mallavādin

1966–1988 *Dvādaśāraṃ Nayacakram: Tārkikaśiromaṇijinaśāsanavādiprabhāvakācāryapravara-Śrīmallavādikṣamāśramaṇapraṇītaṃ: Ācārya Śrīsiṃhasūrigaṇivādikṣamāśramaṇaviracitayā Nyāyāgamānusāriṇyā vṛttyā samalaṅkṛtaṃ: ṭippaṇādibhiḥ pariṣkṛtaḥ*/Sampādakaḥ... Muni Jambūvijaya. Prathamāvṛttiḥ. Bhāvanagarasthā: Śrījaina-Ātmānandasabhā, Vīrasaṃvat 2492–2514: Vikrama Saṃvat 2022–2044: Īsvī san 1966–1988: Ātmasaṃvat 70–92. 3 v. (Śrī-Ātmānandajainagrantharatnamālā 92, 94, 95).

Nandisūtra

1966a *Nandīsuttaṃ: Sirijiṇadāsagaṇimahattaraiviraiyāe Cuṇṇīe saṃjuyaṃ* Saṃśodhakaḥ sampādakaś ca Munipuṇyavijayaḥ. Vārāṇasī: Prākṛta Grantha Pariṣad, Vīrasaṃvat 2492 [1966]. (Prākṛtagranthapariṣad granthāṅka; 9).

1966b *Nandisūtram: Śrī-Śrīcandrācāryakṛtadurgapadavyākhyā-ajñātakartṛkaviṣamapadaparyāyābhyāṃ samalaṅkṛtayā Ācāryaśrīharibhadrasūrikṛtayā Vṛttyā sahitam*, Saṃśodhakaḥ sampādakaś ca Munipuṇyavijayaḥ. Vārāṇasī: Prākṛta Grantha Pariṣad, Vīrasaṃvat 2493 [1966]. (Prākṛtagranthapariṣad Granthāṅka 10).

1968 *Nandisuttaṃ: Siridevavāyagaviraiyaṃ. Aṇuogaddārāiṃ ca: Siriajjarakkhiyatheraviraiyāiṃ* Sampādakāḥ Puṇyavijayo Muniḥ; Dalasukha Mālavaṇiyā, Amṛtalāla Mohanalāla Bhojaka ity etau ca. Bambaī: Śrī Mahāvīra Jaina Vidyālaya, Vīra saṃvat 2494 [1968]. (Jaina-Āgama-Granthamālā; Granthāṅka 1).

Nandīsūtra-cūrṇi

1928 **Nandī Cūrṇi with Haribhadra's Vṛtti*, edited by Sāgarānanda Sūri. Ratalāma: Ṛṣabhadevajī Keśarīmalajī Śvetāmbara Saṃsthā, Vikrama Saṃvat 1984 [1928].

Pariśiṣṭaparvan

1932 *Sthavirāvalīcarita or Pariśiṣṭaparvan, being an appendix of the Triṣaṣṭi-śalākāpuruṣacarita*, by Hemacandra; edited by Hermann Jacobi. 2nd ed. Calcutta: Asiatic Society of Bengal.

Uttarādhyayanasūtra

1921–1922 *The Uttarādhyāyanasūtra being the first Mūlasūtra of the Śvetāmbara Jains: edited with an introduction, critical notes and a commentary/* by Jarl Charpentier. Uppsala: Appelbergs Boktryckeri Aktiebolag, 1922. (Archives d'Études Orientales; v.18).

1933 **Śrīmanti Uttarādhyayanāni: Jinadāsagaṇimahattara kṛtayā Curṇyā sametāni* edited by Sāgarānanda. Ratnapura [Ratlām]: Śrīṛṣabhadevajī Keśarīmalajītyabhidhā Śrīśvetāmbarasaṃsthā, Vīra Saṃvat 2459. Vikrama Saṃvat 1989. Krāiṣṭa san 1933.

Uvāsagadasāo

1880–1890 *The Uvāsagadasāo, or, The religious profession of an Uvāsaga, expounded in ten lectures, being the Seventh Anga of the Jains, edited in the original Prākrit with the Sanskrit commentary of Abhayadeva and English translation* by A. F. Rudolf Hoernle...2 v. Calcutta: Asiatic Society of Bengal, 1890, 1880. (Bibliotheca Indica work 105.)

Secondary sources

Alsdorf, Ludwig 1965. *Les études jaina: état présent et tâches futures*. Paris: Collège de France.

Balbir, Nalini. 1993. *Āvaśyaka-Studien: introduction générale et traductions*. Stuttgart: Franz Steiner. 2 v. (Alt- und Neu-Indische Studien; 45, 1).

Bollée, Willem B. 1977–1988. *Studien zum Sūyagaḍa: die Jainas und die anderen Weltanschauungen vor der Zeitenwende: Textteile, Nijjutti, Übersetzung und Anmerkungen*. Wiesbaden: Franz Steiner, 2 v. (Schriftenreihe des Südasien-Instituts der Universität Heidelberg; Band 24, 31).

BORI Cat. = Descriptive catalogue of the government collections of manuscripts deposited at the Bhandarkar Oriental Research Institute. v. 17: Jaina literature and philosophy. Āgamika literature 1935–54. Compiled by Hiralal Rasikdas Kapadia. Poona: Bhandarkar Oriental Research Institute.

Bruhn, Klaus. 1987. 'Das Kanonproblem bei den Jainas', in *Kanon und Zensur: Beiträge zur Archäologie der literarischen Kommunikation, II*. München: Fink, pp. 100–112.

Charpentier, Jarl. 1921–1922, see Uttarādhyayana 1921–1922.

Dundas, Paul. 1992. *The Jains*. London: Routledge, 1992.

Fynes, Richard C. C. 1998. *The Lives of the Jain Elders*. Oxford: Oxford University Press.

Folkert, Kendall W. 1993. *Scripture and Community: Collected Essays on the Jains*. Edited by John E. Cort. Atlanta, GA: Scholars Press, 1993.

Glasenapp, Helmuth von. 1925. *Der Jainismus: eine indische Erlösungsreligion*. Berlin: Georg Olms. [Reprint: 1984. Hildesheim: Georg Olms.]

Guérinot, A.-A. 1926. *La religion djaïna*. Paris.

Jacobi, Hermann. 1932, see *Pariśiṣṭaparvan* mentioned earlier.

Jaini, Padmanabh S. 1979. *The Jaina Path of Purification*. Berkeley, CA: University of California Press. xii, 327 p. [Reprint: Delhi: Motilal Banarsidass, 1990.]

Jain, Jagdish Chandra. 1984. *Life in Ancient India: As Depicted in the Jain Canon and Commentaries, 6th century BC to 17th century AD*. 2nd revised and enlarged edition New Delhi: Munshiram Manoharlal, 1984. 1st ed. 1947.

Kapadia, Hiralal Rasikdas. 1941. *A History of the Canonical Literature of the Jainas*. Gopipura, Surat: Hiralal Rasikdas Kapadia. [Reprint: Ahmedabad: Sharadaben Chimanbhai Educational Research Centre, 2000. (Shree Shwetambar Murtipujak Jaina Boarding Series; vol . 17).]

Mālavaṇiyā, Dalasukha and Mohanalāla Mehtā. 1966. *Jaina sāhitya kā bṛhad itihāsa* Sampādaka Dalasukha Mālavaṇiyā Mohanalāla Mehatā. Vārāṇasī: Pārśvanātha Vidyāśrama Śodha Saṃsthāna. (Pārśvanātha Vidyāśrama Granthamālā). Volume 2. *Aṅgabāhya Āgama.* Lekhaka Jagadīśacandra Jaina va Mohanalāla Mehatā.

Mehta, Mohanlal and K. Rishabh Chandra. 1970–1972. *Prakrit proper names*. Compiled by Mohanlal Mehta and K. Rishabh Chandra; edited by Dalsukh Malvania. Ahmedabad: L. D. Institute of Indology, 2 v. (L. D. series; 28, 37).

Ohira, Suzuko. 1994. *A study of the Bhagavatīsūtra: a chronological analysis*. Ahmedabad: Prakrit Text Society 1994.

Puṇyavijaya, Muni 1961. 'Jaina āgamadhara aura Prākṛta vāṅmaya: Jaina Āgamadhara sthavīra aura ācārya'. Originally an address to the Akhila Bhāratīya Prācyavidyāpariṣad (Śrīnagar), Prākṛta aura Jainadharma vibhāga, 14–16 October 1961. Reprinted in *Jñānāñjali: Pūjya Muni Puṇyavijayajī Abhinandana Grantha*. pp. [19]–61 (Hindī section). Baḍodara: Sāgara Gaccha Jaina Upāśraya, Vīra Nirvāṇa Saṃvat. 2595. Vikram Saṃvat 2025. Īsvī San.

Renou, Louis. 1951. *L'inde classique: manuel des études indiennes*. Paris: École Française d'Extrême-Orient. (Tome III).

Schubring, Walther. 1926. *Worte Mahāvīras: Kritische Übersetzungen aus dem Kanon der Jaina*. Göttingen: Vandenhoeck & Ruprecht.

——. 1935. *Die Lehre der Jainas nach den alten Quellen dargestellt*. Berlin: Walther de Gruyter, 1935. (*Grundriss der indo-arischen Philologie und Altertumskunde*; Band 3 Heft 7.) [Abridged translation: *The doctrine of the Jainas: described after the old sources*. Translated from the revised German edition by Wolfgang Beurlen. Delhi: Motilal Banarsidass, 1962. 2nd rev. ed. 2000.]

——. 1959. 'Jinismus', in *Die Religion in Geschichte und Gegenwart*, 3rd ed., pp. 668–670. Tübingen: J. C. B. Mohr Paul Siebeck.

Smyth 1888–1892, see Weber, Albrecht. 1883–1885.

Velankar, Hari Damodar. 1944. *Jinaratnakośa: An Alphabetical Register of Jain Works and Authors. Volume 1 Works* [no more published]. Poona: Bhandarkar Oriental Research Institute. (Government Oriental Series Class C; no. 4).

Weber, Albrecht. 1883–1885. 'Ueber die heiligen Schriften der Jaina.' *Indische Studien* (1883–1885) 16: 211–479; 17: 1–90. [Reprint. Hildesheim: Georg Olms, 1973. Reduced size.] [Translated by Herbert Weir Smyth (1857–1937): 'Weber's Sacred literature of the Jains.' *Indian Antiquary* (1888–92) 17–21. Separately printed Bombay, 1893. pp. 1–143.]

Wiles, Royce. 2000. *The Nirayāvaliyasuyakkhandha: Critical Edition, Translation and Notes*. PhD. thesis, Australian National University, Canberra. (published version forthcoming).

Winternitz, Moritz. 1933. *A History of Indian Literature. Volume 2: Buddhist Literature and Jaina Literature*. Translated from the original German by S. [V.] Ketkar and H. Kohn and revised by the author. Calcutta. [Reprint: New York: Russell & Russell [1971].]

Part II

THE QUESTION OF OMNISCIENCE AND JAINA LOGIC

4

THE JAIN–MĪMĀṂSĀ DEBATE ON OMNISCIENCE

Olle Qvarnström

Introduction

A central theme of research within the history of religious philosophy has been the debate concerning reason and revelation, which had its roots in the Greco-Roman tradition on the one side, and the Judeo-Christian tradition on the other. Initiated in the second and third century of the common era by authors such as Celsos, Porphyrius and Emperor Julian,[1] it came to dominate medieval scholasticism and was brought to the fore after the Renaissance as a result of the development of natural science and biblical criticism, among other things. Today, the debate has re-emerged, and grown in momentum as well as complexity, largely due to Islamic and Christian fundamentalism.[2]

The result, as one might expect, has been the production of a plethora of scholarly studies that have looked at the question of reason vs. revelation from numerous angles of vision.[3] To date, however, judging from the content of these studies, the scholarly community has not adequately attended the fact that, in certain respects, a similar debate took place in India. This debate originated from a religious conflict that arose between the followers of the Vedic tradition, on the one hand, and those of various non-Vedic traditions, on the other. As with the debate in the West, the Indic controversy thus had a double heritage and stemmed from an irreconcilable antagonism between those who held that man was doomed to ignorance and thus fully dependent upon revelatory scripture and those who held that man was not only predetermined for knowledge, but capable of acquiring it through his own natural faculties.

The controversy in India differed, however, in several respect from that in the West. One principal difference was that whereas the Western controversy consisted of an encounter between two fundamentally incompatible worldviews, and thus extended from radical opposition to attempts at reconciliation, the Indic controversy involved traditions that had mutually influenced one another and thus shared fundamental values, including a common cognitive universe and *lingua franca*.[4] Moreover, the most ancient sciences in India – ritual science and linguistics (including grammar, semantics, phonetics and prosody) – as well as geometry and mathematics were all intimately connected to the Vedic religion. Because of this, the Indic debate was not marked by the same opposition or need of synthesis.

The central question at issue was similar to the one that many medieval Jewish, Christian and Muslim thinkers grappled with relative to Greek philosophy: What constitutes the source of all knowledge? A set of truths, insights and injunctions that man acquires through non-human revelation; or, a set of truths, insights and injunctions that man acquires through his own natural faculties? Or phrased differently: Does man acquire valid knowledge by means of non-human revelation or is he capable of apprehending it directly by means of his own natural faculties?

In terms of the Indian debate, this question concerned the very foundation of the Vedic and non-Vedic traditions and was largely responsible for the emergence of Brāhmaṇical systematic theology as well as Buddhist and Jain logic and epistemology. Ultimately, it came to revolve around the issue of omniscience (*sarvajñatā*). In contrast to the Western debate, however, those on the side of omniscience were not monotheists arguing the cause of an omniscient God in heaven, but Buddhist and Jain 'atheists' who were claiming the possibility of omniscience in human beings.[5] The debate reached its height during the seventh and eighth centuries when the well-known Mīmāṃsā theologian, Kumārila,[6] made a final effort to defend his Bhaṭṭa school from the epistemological critique of the Buddhists.[7] In the words of Kumārila, although the Mīmāṃsā tradition had gradually descended into materialism (*lokāyata*), through his efforts it would be restored to the path of orthodoxy (*āstikapatha*) once again.[8] Adopting his opponents' terminology, Kumārila thus contrasted the allegedly personal omniscience of the Buddha with the non-personal, that is, authorless (*apauruṣeya*), Veda.[9]

In contrast to the Jain tradition, but not unlike Christian, Muslim and Jewish ecclesiastics, Kumārila and the Mīmāṃsakas viewed man as intrinsically flawed, impaired by defects such as attachment, desire, etc., and thus incapable of distinguishing between right and wrong, *dharma* and *adharma*. Only the Veda, consisting of words that were eternal (i.e. not created by a fallible author), could bridge the insurmountable gulf between man and the imperceptible reality of the Veda, thus informing him of his duties or *dharma*. Even religious traditions such as Sāṃkhya and Yoga, which entertained identical doctrines to those of the Veda, were nonetheless deemed unauthoritative due to their human origin. Decried as 'wolves in sheep's clothing', they were said to provide merely 'the appearance of dharma' (*dharmābhāsa*), and nothing more.[10]

This declaration, stemming from one of the most prominent thinkers of the Brāhmaṇical tradition, was the outcome of a long and complex historical development, originating with the religious polemics between Vedic and non-Vedic traditions as confirmed in the canonical scriptures of the Buddhists and Jains.[11] But it was, above all, the critique leveled at Kumārila and his predecessors by the Buddhist philosophers, Dignāga and Dharmakīrti, that constituted the primary impetus for Kumārila's philosophical repudiation of the idea of an omniscient being in his *Ślokavārttika* and *Bṛhaṭṭīkā*.[12] The challenge of Jain philosophers both prior to and contemporary with Kumārila – philosophers such as Samantabhadra and Akalaṅka – are also thought to have played a significant role in compelling Kumārila to systematize and refine his arguments with respect to the doctrine of human omniscience.[13] Along with their criticism of Brāhmaṇical theology, the Buddhists and the Jains were occupied with composing texts which validated the omniscience of their respective founders and discussed the epistemology and structure of omniscience as well.[14]

The debate on human omniscience was related to the concept of *dharma*, in terms of its definition as well as the means by which it could be validated and known.[15] According to Kumārila, mankind could receive valid instruction regarding right and wrong conduct only through the injunctions (*vidhi*) and prohibitions (*pratiṣedha*) of Vedic revelation,[16] and not via perceptual or inferential proof. By definition, *dharma* was that which had the Veda as it sole authority[17] and the Veda had been revealed neither by man nor a supreme God. It was beginningless (*anādi*), authorless (*apauruṣeya*), and of self-sufficient validity (*svataḥprāmāṇya*).[18] In response to Kumārila, the eighth century Mahāyāna Buddhist philosopher, Śāntarakṣita,[19] and his Śvetāmbara Jain colleague, Haribhadra,[20] composed texts which sacrilegiously argued that man was already in possession of everything knowable, including *dharma*. It remained only for him to uncover the truth that resided within himself, thus realizing his inherent omniscience.

The main arguments advanced by Haribhadra and Śāntarakṣita, in support of an omniscient being and in criticism of the Veda as an absolute authority, were later used by their respective co-religionists, such as Vidyānanda (ninth century) and Ratnakīrti (eleventh century), in an ongoing effort to refute Kumārila and the Mīmāṃsakas.[21] Hence, in order to fully appreciate the arguments propounded by these later writers, it is first necessary to understand the philosophical and religious nuances of the original debate.

Over the years we have seen the completion of a few extensive studies that systematically examine the Buddhist contribution to the debate on omniscience,[22] most remarkably, the Jain contribution has more or less escaped the eye of historians of religion and Indologists alike.[23] Consequently, no attempt has thus far been made to integrate the Buddhist and Jain doctrines of omniscience into a broader Indological religious and cultural context.

The first major Śvetāmbara Jain response to Kumārila's criticism of an omniscient being (*sarvajña*) appears to be the *Śāstravārtāsamuccaya* and *Sarvajñasiddhi* of Haribhadra (eighth century).[24] By undertaking an examination of the former text along with its professed autocommentary, the *Dikpradā*, this article constitutes a small beginning step in the direction of such a comprehensive effort.

The *Śāstravārtāsamuccaya* or 'Summary of the Main Topics of the Philosophical Treatises' belongs to Haribhadra's doxographical writings. These consist of texts that thematically describe the Jain faith in relation to that of different opponents – be they philosophers, as in the *Śāstravārtāsamuccaya*,[25] or ordinary people, as in the *Lokatattvanirṇaya* and *Aṣṭakaprakaraṇa*; or, deliver summaries of entire systems of philosophy, including his own, as in the

Ṣaḍdarśanasamuccaya.[26] In the *Śāstravārtāsamuccaya*, Haribhadra puts himself in the *vāda*-tradition (i.e. the tradition of debate), whereas in his *Sarvajñasiddhi* he argues with the Mīmāṃsakas from within the *pramāṇa* tradition of logic and epistemology.[27]

In what follows, I intend to paraphrase the relevant section in the *Śāstravārtāsamuccaya* in light of the *Dikpradā*, and thereafter comment upon some of its fundamental tenets.

The *Śāstravārtāsamuccaya* of Haribhadra (vv. 580–626)

Haribhadra's account of the Jain-Mīmāṃsā debate is organized in terms of two diametrically opposite propositions which bring the polemics to a close – one negating and the other affirming the existence of an omniscient being. The first proposition states that *dharma* and *adharma* can only be established on the basis of the tradition known as Veda. The second attributes the establishment of *dharma* and *adharma* to any person capable of directly perceiving objects residing beyond the reach of the senses (*atīndriyadarśin*). The main narrative structure of the text may thus be divided into four parts, the first two consisting of the position of the proponent (*pūrvapakṣa*) and the latter two, that of the opponent (*uttarapakṣa*).

In the first part, the Mīmāṃsakas advance the argument that it is not possible to prove the existence of an omniscient being (*sarvajña*) (whose word would serve as a valid means of cognition) through the five means of valid cognition (*pramāṇa*), namely perception (*pratyakṣa*), inference (*anumāna*), analogy (*upamāna*), verbal testimony (*āgama*), or presumption (*arthāpatti*), and that this fact constitutes evidence of his non-existence (*abhāvapramāṇatā*). Regarding the first three means of cognition, the Mīmāṃsakas point out that in the absence of an inherent mark (*liṅga*) identifying an omniscient being, perception, along with inference and analogy, are all invalidated. Since the very object of perception is unestablished, knowledge drawn from either a characteristic mark, or a correspondence between things with the same properties, is not achievable. As for the remaining two, Mīmāṃsakas argue that the presence of an omniscient being cannot be proven either on the basis of the Jain tradition, since it stands in opposition to the prescriptive statements (*codanā*) of the Veda, or by presumption, since everything, including the teaching of *dharma*, can be explained without positing the existence of an omniscient being.

Because of the apparent insufficiency of the valid means of cognition to solidly establish the existence of an omniscient being, the Mīmāṃsakas reject the notion entirely. Instead, they argue that the establishment of *dharma* and *adharma* rests entirely upon the Veda, which is considered trustworthy (*āpta*) (not being subject to human error), without origin (*apauruṣeya*), and having as its object that which is beyond the senses.

In the second part of Haribhadra's text, the Mīmāṃsakas continue to develop their thesis in favour of the Veda as the exclusive source of *dharma*. Veda, they argue, is accessible to all. Consequently, there is no reason to suppose the existence of a being capable of seeing beyond the senses (*atīndriyārthadraṣṭṛ*), as the accurate knower and direct instrument (*sākṣātkaraṇa*) of *dharma* and *adharma*. *Dharma*, as a cosmic and moral principle, is represented, on the one hand, in sacrifice (*iṣṭā*), pious liberality (*pūrta*), castes and stages of life (*varṇāśrama*), and on the other hand, in activities such as meditation (*dhyāna*). The former results in enjoyment (*bhoga*), the latter in liberation (*mokṣa*) or the highest good (*śreyas*).

In the third section of the *Śāstravārtāsamuccaya*, Haribhadra calls upon his co-religionists to answer the Mīmāṃsaka claim that it is not possible to prove the existence of an omniscient being on the basis of the valid means of cognition.

Regarding perception, the Jains argue that, regardless of how the Mīmāṃsakas define the term, the existence of an omniscient being cannot be unequivocally ruled out. If perception is defined as including all objects (*sarvārthaviṣaya*), it must necessarily include an omniscient being, and if it is defined as the opposite, that is, *asarvārthaviṣaya*, an omniscient being may still exist, even though he is not perceivable by the material senses. Furthermore, *dharma*, understood as prescriptive statements and the intrinsic characteristic of a person, *is* perceptible to the senses, since it exists as an object of knowledge (*jñeya*). The existence of an omniscient being may therefore be inferred from the perception of *dharma*, defined in this specific sense.

Such a being's existence could also be confirmed on the basis of the Jain scriptures (*āgama*), since the idea of omniscience is a result of their prescriptive statements. Like perception, these [Jain] scriptures contain intrinsic validity (*svataḥprāmāṇya*), and are eternal like the Veda (*śruti*). Moreover, when one attains omniscience as a result of an immediate experience of *dharma*, and that experience is subsequently confirmed by other persons who have had the same experience, there is analogy. Finally, even on the basis of a scripture that deals with the transcendent (*atīndriyatva*), one may presume the existence of an omniscient being. Otherwise, there would be no hope for an unenlightened person (*chadmastha*) who, while incapable of experiencing the transcendent, still has confidence in the scripture (*śāstra*).

Having pronounced all means of valid cognition as incapable of disproving the existence of an omniscient being, the Jains continue their critique in the fourth and final part of Haribhadra's *Śāstravārtāsamuccaya* by questioning the Veda as the source of *dharma* and knowledge. In their view, the Veda is not to be considered authoritative merely by virtue of its ancient heritage or claims of an unbroken tradition. Its succession may have been broken and its custodians narrow-minded (*arvāgdarśin*) and thus ignorant of *dharma* and unqualified to elucidate the transcendental subject matter of the Veda. In addition, there is no consensus regarding the meaning of Vedic (*veda-*) as opposed to mundane (*laukika-*) words (*pada*). This being the case, it would be theoretically possible to acquire 'knowledge' based on a wrong cognition (*viparyaya*).

The wise, among whom the Jains include themselves, thus raise doubts regarding which words in the Veda belong to which category. Couched in more Christian terms, the doubt concerns whether the Bible is identical with the words of God or the words of God exist in the Bible. In support of the Buddhist logician, Dharmakīrti,[28] the Jains suggest that the only way to resolve this problem is to consult someone who has experienced the area of life to which some of these words refer. An ordinary human being is wholly inexperienced in this regard and is consequently unqualified to know the Veda either by himself or from anyone else, since ordinary human beings are impeded by desire, attachment, etc.

Furthermore, the Veda does not explain itself. How then, wonder the Jains, does one acquire knowledge of the Veda. Again resorting to Dharmakīrti,[29] Haribhadra points out that the phrase, *agnihotraṃ juhuyāt svargakāma*, 'He who is desirous of heaven should present an oblation into the sacred fire', could just as well mean that one should consume dog meat! If the Word of the Veda (*śabda*) boasts a transcendental status and simultaneously purports to reveal its own meaning (*arthaprakāśa*), this contradicts its claim of being eternal and unchanging. And even if it were capable of revealing its own meaning, it might still generate a false cognition. Consequently, a word cannot be understood and evaluated without paying attention to the convention (*saṅketa*) that informs its meaning. It could be correct (in accordance with reality), incorrect or create confusion (*śaṅka*) due to a multiplicity of meanings, everyone being occupied with his own explanation (*vyākhyā*).

Given this point of view, it is illogical to maintain, as do the Mīmāṃsakas, that an exposition (*vyākhyā*), such as that of Jaimini, has the same ontological status as the Veda itself. Commentaries often contradict one another, and it is impossible to determine whether one particular exposition or *vyākhyā* is correct or construed (*sādhutvakalpitātva*). Neither can the correctness of a particular exposition be established on the basis of confirmation by other means of valid cognition, such as perception, since Kumārila and his colleagues have declared these incapable of comprehending objects that lie beyond the reach of the senses. Therefore, Haribhadra and the Jains consider Jaimini's elucidation of the Veda to be nothing more than a personal interpretation.

Furthermore say the Jains, logic dictates that the Veda could not be without some origin (*apauruṣeya*), nor some organ of speech, and still be possible to comprehend. And yet if an organ of speech is admitted, it would necessarily have to be part of creation (*laukika*) and not transcendent and beginningless. On the other hand, even assuming that the Veda somehow revealed itself without the necessity of an organ of speech, one could logically still doubt its words, since these may stem from some invisible author – possibly even a demon (*piśācakartṛ*). Only someone who is able to directly perceive the transcendent could bring one's doubt concerning the non-personal origin of the Veda to an end, according to the Jains. The world does not testify to its origin and the Vedic priests may all be ignorant, propagating false doctrines, like the Persians (*pārsika*) who advocate mother-marriage (*mātṛvivāha*).[30]

In reality, only an omniscient being is capable of determining whether the Veda has an origin or not. Arguments such as that of not remembering an author have no weight as evidence. The fact that a text has an author does not necessarily devaluate its status, neither does the occurrence of different recensions. Furthermore, the apparent efficacy of Vedic mantras cannot serve as proof that the Veda is uncreated. Playing on the name of Kumārila's predecessor, Śabara, the Jains declare that even the words of a savage or *śābara* may have efficacy: The entire world might simply be misled.

The final argument propounded by Haribhadra draws on the opponent's own scripture. According to the Jains, even the Veda refers to an all-knowing person (*sarvavid*): a great soul (*mahātman*) who has the capacity to see beyond the objects of the senses, and is thus singularly qualified to correctly understand the informative statements (*arthavāda*), etc., of the Veda. The Jains obviously consider their own omniscient being, the revealer of the one true 'Āryaveda',[31] to be such a great soul. Thus Haribhadra concludes his fictive debate between Mīmāṃsā and Jainism by declaring that 'It is in no way possible to decisively establish *dharma* and *adharma* other than from an all-inclusive doctrine (*āgama*) revealed (*abhivyakta*) by an omniscient being (*sarvajña*).'

Concluding remarks

The Jain–Mīmāṃsaka debate on omniscience, as delineated in the *Śāstravārtāsamuccaya* and *Dikpradā* of Haribhadra, stands as the culmination of a development that began more than a millenium earlier. In essence, it concerned the question of whether or not *dharma* was an object of perception. The denial of omniscience thus amounted to the denial of a direct, perceptual knowledge of *dharma*, whereas its acceptance allowed for the possibility that man could himself acquire knowledge of good and evil. The former position was held by Kumārila and the Mīmāṃsakas, the latter by Haribhadra and the Jains.

Both the Mīmāṃsakas and the Jains held that the source of all knowledge resided beyond the objects of the senses (*atīndriya*) and was identical to *dharma*. Furthermore, both believed that the human mind was a major source of distortion,[32] incapable of directly experiencing *dharma*.

Haribhadra and the Jains therefore cherished the idea of omniscience conceived as an inherent faculty that enabled the human being to cognize everything, including that which was beyond the senses.[33] Such a cognition was thought to take place in the Self (*jīva*), independent of the mind and the senses, and constituted, accordingly, a direct means of acquiring valid knowledge of *dharma*. The Mīmāṃsakas notion of perception as the apprehension of an existing object by the mind and senses[34] was classified by the Jains, beginning with Umāsvāti,[35] as sensory knowledge (*mati*) and put in the same category as scriptural knowledge (*śruta*). Both were viewed as indirect means (*parokṣa*) of knowledge (*pramāṇa*), whereas direct knowledge (*pratyakṣa*) was said to occur through omniscience.[36] Haribhadra and the Jains thus opposed the claim made by the Mīmāṃsakas that *pratyakṣa* disproved the existence of an omniscient being.

Kumārila and the Mīmāṃsakas, on the other hand, advocated Vedic revelation (*śruti*) as the only means by which man could know right from wrong. Kumārila was, however, not opposed to every type of omniscience: 'If there is an omniscient [person] who knows everything through the six means of valid cognition (*pramāṇa*), how can he be refuted?'[37] An omniscient being whose omniscience was independent of the six means of knowing was, however, not conceivable.[38] Omniscience as a cognitive faculty *sui generis* was accordingly rejected.[39]

Faith – as either a secular and intellectual trust in the impersonal Veda and the efficacy of sacrifice (*śraddhā*), or a personal trust (*bhakti*) in the omniscient Jina and his words (*āgama*)[40] – was a necessary condition in both Mīmāṃsā and Jainism. However, it was not considered instrumental in bringing about heavenly existence or liberation.[41]

The question thus remained, was the source of knowledge or *dharma* revealed by direct personal experience,[42] or was it revealed by itself and codified in the non-personal Veda? Was revelation personal or impersonal? Was it located within man or outside of him? Was it directly attainable through the non-activity (*nivṛtti*) of self-realization (*ātmajñāna*) or indirectly accessible through a variety of [ritual and intellectual] activities (*pravṛtti*)?[43]

The debate over whether or not man was capable of having a direct experience of *dharma*, however, had more than philosophical consequences. It had serious political overtones as well, since the claim of directly experiencing *dharma* constituted a threat to the privileges of the priestly class who subsisted on the administration of the revealed word of the Vedas. This situation parallels in some measure the perceived threat of Christian and Sufi mystics by those who administered the Word of God in the Bible and Koran. Although in the Vedic tradition the killing of a brahmin was considered a mortal sin, legend has it that Kumārila, previously a Buddhist, launched a 'holy war' against the members of his former faith, including his now-rejected teacher, persecuting and even killing the 'blasphemers' for alleging that they had achieved a direct experience of *dharma*.[44]

In addition to his debate with Kumārila on the *possibility* of omniscience, Haribhadra was involved in a second polemic concerning the *exact definition* of omniscience with fellow Jains, Buddhists and Sāṃkhyites – each faction claiming their founder to be a superman (*mahāpuruṣa*) and true god (*mahādeva*).[45]

The opposing positions held by Jainism and Mīmāṃsā on the question of omniscience was transmitted through the centuries by Indian doxographers, thus emphasizing the importance of the debate. This is evident in the thirteenth century *Sarvadarśanasaṃgraha* of Mādhava, whose description of *Ārhatadarśana* includes, for the sake of contrast, a resumé of the Mīmāṃsā criticism of an omniscient being.[46]

Although we are unable to determine the degree to which Haribhadra's ideas influenced the Mīmāṃsā tradition, legend has it that on his death-bed Kumārila conceded that, after all, the Jains had contributed some valuable insights.[47]

Notes

1 See Neumann 1880, Hoffmann 1987 and Harnack 1916, respectively.
2 See, for example, Stenberg 1996; Marty and Appleby 1993.

3 For an introduction, see Gilson 1938; Helm 1999; Brooke 1991; Watt 1985; Sirat 1985.

4 On Jain attitudes towards the Sanskrit language, see Dundas 1996; on sociolinguistic attitudes in Jainism, see Deshpande 1993: 9ff.

5 In his article on the omniscience of Mahāvīra and the Buddha, Padmanabh S. Jaini (1974) concludes that from the *Māṇḍukya Upaniṣad* onwards, the term *sarvajña* was exclusively employed to describe the *īśvara* of philosophical systems (*darśana*) such as Yoga, Vaiśeṣika and Nyāya, as well as the Purāṇic trinity, Brahmā, Viṣṇu and Śiva. The term was also used metaphorically as a synonym for *brahmajña* or *ātmajña*, 'the knower of the Self'. However, it appears that no passage in the entire Brāhmaṇical literature refers to human omniscience in the primary sense of the word. Jaini further notes that the term *sarvajña*, like the terms *jina* and *arhat*, was adopted by the Buddhists from the Jains. According to Jaini (1977), not all souls were thought to be capable of reaching omniscience, since some lacked the appropriate inherent disposition. Apart from stray references in the Jain canonical scriptures (Schubring 1962: 202), the earliest systematic differentiation between souls that were capable of liberation (*bhavya*) and those that were not (*abhavya*) is found in Umāsvāti's *Tattvārthasūtra* (II.7). In most cases, however, these terms refer to someone, often a student, who is either qualified or unqualified for the Jain teaching, and do not indicate any lacking of inherent capacity. See, for example, Haribhadra's *Yogadṛṣṭisamuccaya* (vv. 225–226) and *Lokatattvanirṇaya* (vv. 2–7).

6 On Kumārila (seventh century AD) and the Mīmāṃsā tradition, see Verpoorten 1987. According to Parpola (1981: 155), who subscribed to the view of Jacobi (1911), subsequent to Kumārila and Śaṅkara, the Mīmāṃsā school was divided into two mutually exclusive philosophies, Mīmāṃsā and Vedānta. However, the Jain as well as Buddhist traditions attest to an earlier division. In the sixth century *Dvātriṃśikā* of Siddhasena, one chapter, designated in the colophon as *Vedavāda*, is devoted to pre-Śaṅkara Vedānta philosophy. And according to the Jain tradition, this same *Dvātriṃśikā* originally included a description of Mīmāṃsā as well. See Qvarnström (2003b). The earliest Buddhist text which distinguishes between Mīmāṃsā and Vedānta as independent systematic philosophies appears to be Bhavya's *Madhyamakahṛdayakārikā* and *Tarkajvālā*, which include separate chapters on (pre-Śaṅkara) Vedānta (VIII) and Mīmāṃsā (IX). See Qvarnström 1989; Kawasaki 1992.

7 For a summary of Kumārila's arguments, see Verpoorten 1987: 22–37.

8 *Ślokavārttika* I.10. This argument is echoed in the ninth and tenth century doxographical work, the *Sarvasiddhāntasaṃgraha*, where it is said that Kumārila established the path of the Veda (*vedamārga*), which had been decimated by the Buddhists and other nihilists. In diametric opposition to this view, the tenth century Jain author Siddharṣi, in his *Upamitibhavaprapañcakathā*, declared that Mīmāṃsā was in no way a philosophical system and that it had even been preceded by the Materialists. See Handiqui 1949: 225–226.

9 As observed by Jayatilleke (1963: 192) and Clooney (1990: 215, n. 64), the idea of the Veda as *apauruṣeya* most likely developed in response to the Buddhist claim of a human source of all knowledge. However, there were also strong, internal reasons for introducing the idea of *apauruṣeya* as well as the beginningless (*anādi*) and self-sufficient validity (*svataḥprāmāṇya*) of the Veda. See Bronkhorst 2001.

10 *Tantravārttika*, p. 124 (tr.).

11 See, for example, *Tevijjasutta* of the *Dīghanikāya* and *Uttarajjhayaṇa* (ch. 25).

12 See Verpoorten 1987: 23ff. As a result of the criticism leveled at Mīmāṃsā in the *Pramāṇasamuccaya*, Kumārila vehemently attacked Dignāga in his *Ślokavārttika* (Hattori 1968: 15–16, Iyengar 1927), and as a consequence of Dharmakīrti's criticism, Kumārila composed the *Bṛhaṭṭīkā* (Raja 1991: 109). The *Bṛhaṭṭīkā*, which according to Frauwallner is the last work of Kumārila, composed c. AD 630, is only indirectly accessible through Śāntarakṣita's *Tattvasaṃgraha* (Frauwallner 1962, Verpoorten 1987: 30).

For a summary of Kumārila's critique of omniscience in the *Ślokavārttika*, see D'sa 1980: 192–195.

13 Kumārila's criticism of an omniscient being in the *Ślokavārttika* and *Bṛhaṭṭīkā*, which is mainly directed against the Buddhists, also constitutes one of the few responses to Jain doctrines from Brāhmaṇical systematic theologians. The other principal response is found in the *Brahmasūtrabhāṣya* of Śaṅkara. According to Pathak (1893, 1930), Kumārila attacked Samantabhadra (*Āptamīmāṃsā*) and Akalaṅka (*Siddhiviniścaya*) in his *Ślokavārttika*. Akalaṅka is then said to have been defended by his pupil Prabhācandra (*Prameyakamalamārtaṇḍa*), and by Vidyānanda (*Aṣṭasahasrī*). In his argumentation, however, Pathak presents no textual evidence in support of his thesis. On Akalaṅka's theory of omniscience, see Fujinaga 2000.

14 See, for example, the *Āptamīmāṃsā* of Samantabhadra, and the *Sanmatitarka* of Siddhasena Divākara, both from the fifth and sixth century AD. For Mahāyāna Buddhist texts dating from this period, see the *Sarvajñatāsiddhi* chapter of Mātrceṭa's *Varṇārhavarṇastotra* (Hartmann 1987), and the *Sarvajñatāsiddhinirdeśa* chapter of Bhavya's *Madhyamakahṛdayakārikā* and *Tarkajvālā*, though directed towards the Jain notion of omniscience (Kawasaki 1992). For further references, see Būhnemann 1980: vi–viii.

15 In this context, Dharmakīrti and his *Pramāṇavārttika* and *Pramāṇaviniścaya* was of particular importance, arguing for the possibility of a yogic perception or insight into *dharma*. See Steinkellner 1978: 126ff.; Bühnemann 1980: vii. For an elaborate discussion on the concept of *dharma* in Jainism, see Qvarnström (2004) scheduled to appear in a special issue of the *Journal of Indian Philosophy*, edited by Patrick Olivelle and Phyllis Granoff.

16 Ślokavārttika II: 242f.

17 *Tantravārttika*, p. 104 (tr.).

18 On these three concepts, see Bronkhorst 2001.

19 See the *Tattvasaṃgraha* of Śāntarakṣita (vv. 2848ff., 3128ff.) along with the commentary, *Pañjikā*, by Kamalaśīla. For the dates of Śāntarakṣita, see Frauwallner 1933: 238–240; 1937: 65–74. Haribhadra refers in the auto-commentary on *Śāstravārtāsamuccaya* 296 to Śāntarakṣita's *Tattvasaṃgraha* 958 and 1083: *yad uktaṃ sūkṣmabuddhinā śāntarakṣitena nāsato bhāvakartṛtvaṃ tadavasthāntaraṃ na saḥ //*. Bhattacharyya (ref. to in Winternitz 1983: 460, n. 1) was, however, wrong in identifying Haribhadra with one *ācārya sūri*, alluded to in the *Tattvasaṃgraha* 124 and 126. The textual passage, which could refer to any Jain author, reads: *na hetur astīti vadan sahetukaṃ nanu pratijñāṃ svayam eva sād(h)ayet / athāpi hetuḥ praṇayālaso bhavet pratijñayā kevalayāsya kiṃ bhaved iti ācāryasūripādaiḥ*.

20 See the *Sarvajñasiddhi* and *Śāstravārtāsamuccaya* of Haribhadra. Within the Digambara Jain tradition, the *Siddhiviniścaya* (ch. 8) of Akalaṅka (eighth century) appears to be the first text denouncing Kumārila and his denial of human omniscience. Akalaṅka does not, however, criticize the Mīmāṃsakas as extensively and systematically as does Haribhadra in the earlier mentioned works. Some scholars hold that Akalaṅka was known to Haribhadra, basing their contention upon the following quotation from the latter's *Anekāntajayapatākā: akalaṅkanyāyānusāri cetoharaṃ vacaḥ* (Kapadia 1947: 253). In my opinion, however, it is more likely that *akalaṅka* connotes 'perfect logic'. Singh (1974: 144) notices, however, that Akalaṅka in his *Nyāyaviniścaya* (p. 294) quotes from Haribhadra's *Yogabindu* (v. 431).

21 See Vidyānanda's *Āptaparīkṣā* and *Aṣṭasahasrī*, and Ratnakīrti's *Sarvajñasiddhi*. Other Jain texts criticizing Kumārila and the Mīmāṃsakas are, for example, Siddharṣi's *Upamitibhavaprapañcākathā* (tenth century), Prabhācandra's *Prameyakamalamārtaṇḍa* (eleventh century), and Anantakīrti's *Bṛhat-* and *Laghusarvajñasiddhi* (eleventh century).

22 See, for example, Eltschinger 1977, 1978; Hartmann 1987; Griffiths 1990: 85; Kawasaki 1992.

23 There are some exceptions (even though they do not analyze the *Śāstravārtāsamuccaya* and *Sarvajñasiddhi* of Haribhadra), for example, Pathak 1893, 1931; Solomon 1962; Singh 1974; Jaini 1974.

24 The *Śāstravārtāsamuccaya* may safely be ascribed to Haribhadra, the author of the *Anekāntajayapatākā*, and thus belongs to the eighth century AD (Handiqui 1947: xl, l–li, Qvarnström 1999). Two commentaries remain extant: the *Syādvādakalpalatā*, a voluminous commentary written by Yaśovijaya, the scholarly seventeenth century Śvetāmbara monk; and, the presumably much earlier *Dikpradā*, ascribed to Haribhadra himself. A close reading of the latter text, however, does not provide decisive internal evidence establishing that the *Dikpradā* and *Śāstravārtāsamuccaya* were written by the same author. And the external evidence is similarly inconclusive. The *Dikpradā*, for example, is not mentioned in the *Anekāntajayapatākā*; nor does it contain Haribhadra's blueprint, or *viraha* (Williams 1965). At this stage, it appears safest to leave open the question of the *Dikpradā's* authorship in the hope that future research will uncover a definitive answer. Regarding the relationship between Haribhadra and Kumārila, the only representative of the Mīmāṃsā tradition referred to in the *Śāstravārtāsamuccaya* is Jaimini (v. 612). The *Dikpradā*, however, mentions Kumārila in connection with a partial quote from the *Ślokavārttika* (II.95cd: *tasmād ālokavad vede sarvasādhāraṇe sati //*) which occurs in the *Śāstravārtāsamuccaya* (585ab) and then reappears in the *Dikpradā*. Another 'echo' from the *Ślokavārttika* is found in *Śāstravārtāsamuccaya* 583cd: *pramāṇapañcakāvṛttes tatrābhāvapramāṇatā //*. Cf. *Ślokavārttika* IV, *abhāvapariccheda*, v.1: *pramāṇapañcakaṃ yatra vasturūpe na jāyate / vastusattāvabodhārthaṃ tatrābhāvapramāṇatā //*. This verse is quoted in full by Haribhadra in his *Ṣaḍdarśanasamuccaya*, v. 76. The paucity of references to Kumārila and/or his works in the *Śāstravārtāsamuccaya* and *Dikpradā* may be accounted for as being characteristic of the doxographical genre or *samuccaya*, since the *Aṣṭakaprakaraṇa*, *Ṣaḍdarśanasamuccaya* and *Lokatattvanirṇaya* of Haribhadra display the same feature. Even in a late doxographical work, such as the thirteenth century *Sarvadarśanasaṃgraha* of Mādhava, the chapter describing Jainism (*Ārhatadarśana*) in relation to the teachings of the followers of Kumārila (*tutātita*), only contains a few quotations from the *Ślokavārttika*. Finally, Haribhadra's reply to Kumārila's critique may be viewed as a more general response, since Kumārila's criticism of a *sarvajña* mainly was directed against Buddhist doctrine. From a chronological point of view, Haribhadra seems to have been a contemporary of Śāntarakṣita, whose *Tattvasaṃgraha* (958 and 1083) is quoted in the *Dikpradā* ad *Śāstravārtāsamuccaya* 296 (see note above). On the date of Haribhadra, see Qvarnström 1999. For manuscripts of the *Śāstravārtāsamuccaya* and *Dikpradā*, see Velankar 1944: 383.

25 The debate on human omniscience versus scriptural revelation in the *Śāstravārtāsamuccaya* is discussed in the section entitled 'the discourse on liberation' (*mokṣavāda*).

26 On Haribhadra, the doxographer, and his Buddhist and Jain precursors, see Qvarnström 1999.

27 *Śāstravārtāsamuccaya* (581–583) seems to have borrowed verses from the *Sarvajñasiddhi* (11–13).

28 *Pramāṇavārttika* III. 318.

29 *Pramāṇavārttika* III. 318cd–319ab.

30 Buddhist texts also compare practices found in the Veda with incestuous practices attributed to the Persians. See Halbfass (1983: 14, n. 68).

31 According to the *Vasudevahiṇḍī* (sixth century), which was known to Haribhadra, the Ārya Vedas were composed by Bharata, the first Jain 'universal emperor' of this world.

After a time, brāhmins, such as Sulasā and Yājñavalkya, composed the Anārya Vedas. See Jain 1977: 12.

32 Bronkhorst 1997: 365ff.; Qvarnström 2003a.

33 See Haribhadra's *Yogadṛṣṭisamuccaya* 101; *Yogabindu* 412; Shah 1967: 233. On Kumārila's refusal of supernatural perception or *yogipratyakṣa*, see *Ślokavārttika* IV: 26–28; Verpoorten 1987: 25f. According to Kumārila, Yoga texts belong to that category of traditional texts or *smṛtis* which, despite the incorporation of Vedic doctrines, should not be followed. See *Tantravārttika*, p. 165 (tr.).

34 *Mīmāṃsā Sūtra* I.1.4; *Ślokavārttika* IV (*pratyakṣasūtra*).

35 *Tattvārthasūtra* I. 9–14.

36 See Soni 2000.

37 *Ślokavārttika* II: 111cd (quoted from D'sa 1980: 193).

38 *Ślokavārttika* II: 112cd (D'sa 1980: 193).

39 See Shah 1967: 233.

40 See Haribhadra's *Yogadṛṣṭisamuccaya* 110.

41 On the concepts of *śraddhā* and *bhakti*, see Hara 1964.

42 Cf. the *Yogaśāstra* and *Svopajnavṛtti* II.12.

43 *Tantravārttika*, p. 236 (tr.).

44 Walker 1968: 571.

45 See *Yogabindu* (3, 17–18, 31, 425–437); *Yogadṛṣṭisamuccaya* (102–109, 140–147).

46 Mādhava's summary of Mīmāṃsā in the *Sarvadarśanasaṃgraha* is based upon the *Śabarabhāṣya* (Verpoorten 1987: 10, n. 54). The chapter on Jainism (*Ārhatadarśana*) includes, in addition, several quotations from the *Ślokavārttika* (II: 117, etc.), and summarizes, according to Mādhava, the teaching of the followers of Kumārila (*tathā coktam tautātitaiḥ*).

47 Cowell and Gough (1904: 84, n. 9).

Bibliography

Primary sources

Āptamīmāṃsā *of Samantabhadra*

Ed. with the *Vṛtti* of Vasunandin by Gajādharial Jain, Benares: Sanātana Jaina Granthamālā, 1914.

Āptaparīkṣā *of Vidyānanda*

Ed. by Darabārilāla Jaina Koṭhiyā, Sahāranapura: Vīra Seva Mandira, 1949.

Aṣṭakaprakaraṇa *of Haribhadrasūri*

The *Aṣṭakaprakaraṇa* with Abhayadeva's *Vṛtti* and Jineśvara's *Vivṛtti*. Sanskrit text publ. by M. Bhagubhai, Ahmedabad, 1911.

Aṣṭasahasrī *of Vidyānanda*

Text publ. by Nāthāraṅgaji Gāṃdhī, Bombay: Nirṇaya Sāgara Press, 1915.

Āvaśyakacūrṇi *of Jinadāsa*

Ed. by Rishabhdeo Kesharimar. 2 Vols. Ratlam 1928, 1929.

Bṛhatsarvajñasiddhi *of Anantakīrti*

Ed. by K. Bharmapa Nitve. *Laghīyastrayādisaṃgraha*... Māṇikacandradigambarajainagranthamālā 1, Kolhapur-Bombay, 1915.

Dīghanikāya

Pāli text ed. by T. W. Rhys Davids and J. E. Carpenter, London: Pāli Text Society, 1890–1911.

Tr. from the Pāli by T. W. Rhys Davids as *Dialogues of the Buddha*, London: Pāli Text Society, 1899.

Dvātriṃśikā *of Siddhasena Divākara*

Dvātriṃśikās of Siddhasena. Ed. by S. C. Vidyabhusana. Arrah 1915. Re-issued by A. N. Upadhye in Siddhasena's *Nyāyāvatāra* and Other Works (including the *Dvātriṃśikā* and *Sammaisutta*), Bombay: Jaina Sāhitya Vikāsa Maṇḍala, 1971.

Ed. with the *Nyāyāvatāra* and *Sanmatitarka* by Anandasagara. Jainadharmaprasāraka Sabhā. Bhavnagar 1909.

Laghusarvajñasiddhi *of Anantakīrti*

Ed. by K. Bharmapa Nitve. *Laghīyastrayādisaṃgraha*... Māṇikacandradigambarajainagranthamālā 1. Kolhapur-Bombay, 1915.

Lokatattvanirṇaya *of Haribhadra*

Ed. and tr. into Italian by L. Suali as 'Il «Lokatattvanirṇaya» di Haribhadra', *Giornale della Società Asiatica Italiana* 10. Firenze 1905: 263–319.

Mīmāṃsā Sūtra *of Jaimini*

Tr. by G. Jha, with the *Bhāṣya* of Śabara. 3 Vols. Gaekwad Oriental Series 66, 70, 73, Baroda 1973–1974.

Nyāyaviniścaya *of Akalaṅka*

Akalaṅkagranthatrayam. Ed. by M. K. Shastri. Saraswati Oriental Series 8, Ahmedabad: Sanchalaka-Singhi Jaina Granthamala, 1939.

Prameyakamalamārtaṇḍa *of Prabhācandra*

Ed. by M. K. Jain, Bombay: Nirnayasagar Press, 1941.

Ṣaḍdarśanasamuccaya *of Haribhadrasūri*

Ed. by F. L. Pullè as 'Shaṭdarçanasamuccayasūtraṃ', *Giornale della Società Asiatica Italiana*, 1 (1887): 47–73.
Ed. and tr. into English by Qvarnström 1999.

Sanmatitarkaprakaraṇa *of Siddhasena*

Ed. with the the commentary of Abhayadevasūri by Sukhlāl Sanghāvi and Becardās Dośi. Ahmedabad, 1985.

Sarvadarśanasaṃgraha *of Sāyaṇa Mādhava*

Ed. by V. S. Abhyankar, Poona: Ānandāśrama Sanskrit Series 51, 1951.
Tr. by E. B. Cowell and A. E. Gough, London: Kegan Paul, Trench, Trūbner & Co, 1904.

Sarvajñasiddhi *of Haribhadrasūri*

Sanskrit text along with the *Hiṃsāṣṭaka*, its *Svopajña Avacūri* and *Aindrastuti.* Publ. by R. K. Saṃsthā, Rutlam, 1924.
Ed. by Muni Hemacandravijaya, Jaipur, 1963.

Sarvajñasiddhi *of Ratnakīrti*

Ed. and tr. by Gudrun Bühnemann as *Der Allwissende Buddha. Ein Beweis und seine Probleme. Ratnakīrtis Sarvajñasiddhi*. Wiener Studien zur Tibetologie und Buddhismuskunde, heft 4. Hrsg. von E. Steinkellner, Wien: Arbeitskreis für Tibetische und Buddhistische Studien, Universität Wien, 1980.

Śāstravārtāsamuccaya *of Haribhadrasūri*

Sanskrit text ed. by K. K. Dixit, Ahmedabad: L. D. Institute of Indology, 1969.

Śāstravārtāsamuccaya *and* Dikpradā *of Haribhadrasūri*

Śāstravārtāsamuccaya by Śrī-Haribhadra-Sūri with his own Commentary named *Dikpradā*, Bombay: Nirnaya-Sagar Press, 1929.

Ślokavārttika *of Kumārila*

Ed. with the *Nyāyaratnākara* of Pārthasārathi Miśra by D. Śastri. Benares, 1978.
Tr. into English by G. Jha, with Extracts from the Commentaries, 'Kāśika' of Sucarita Miśra and 'Nyāyaratnākara' of Pārthasārathi Miśra Delhi 1983 (1 ed. Bibliotheca Indica 146. Calcutta 1900–1908).

Syādvādakalpalatā *of Yaśovijaya*

Text publ. by Chaukhambha Orientalia. Vols. 1–7, Varanasi 1977–1989.

Tantravārttika *of Kumārila*

Ed. with the *Śabarabhāṣya* and *Ṭupṭīkā* of Kumārila by K. V. Abhyankar and G. A. Joshi. *Mīmāṃsādarśanam*, Vols. II–VII. Ānandāśrama Series 97, Trivandrum 1970–1974.
Tr. into English by G. Jha, Delhi, 1983 (1 ed. Bibliotheca Indica 161. Calcutta 1903–1924).

Tattvārthasūtra *of Umāsvāti*

Ed. and tr. by H. Jacobi as *Eine Jaina-Dogmatik. Umāsvāti's Tattvārthādhigama Sūtra*. Leipzig, 1906.
——. *Tattvārthasūtra* together with the combined commentaries of Umāsvāti/ Umāsvāmī, Pūjyapāda and Siddhasenagaṇi. Ed. and tr. by N. Tatia as *That Which Is,* NewYork: Harper Collins Publishers, 1994.

Tattvasaṃgraha *of Śāntarakṣita*

Ed. by D. Śastri, with the Commentary 'Pañjikā' of Kamalaśīla. 2 Vols., Varanasi Benares, 1982.
Tr. into English by G. Jha, with the Commentary of Kamalaśīla. Baroda, 1970–1974.

Triṣaṣṭiśalākāpuruṣacaritra *of Hemacandra*

Tr. by H. Johnson as *The Lives of Sixty-three Illustrious Persons*. 6 vols., Baroda: Oriental Institute, 1931–1962.

Upamitibhavaprapañcakathā *of Siddharṣi*

Ed. by P. Peterson and H. Jacobi, Bibliotheca Indica. 144, Calcutta: The Asiatic Society of Bengal, 1899–1910.

Uttarajjhayaṇa *(Uttarādhyayana)*

Ed. by J. Charpentier. *Archives D'Études Orientales* 21–22, Upsala, 1922.
Tr. by H. Jacobi. *Jaina Sūtras*. Sacred Books of the East XLV: 1–232, Oxford: Clarendon Press, 1895.

Vasudevahiṇḍī *of Saṅghadāsagaṇi*

Ed. by Muni Caturavijaya and Muni Puṇyavijaya, Gandhinagar, 1989.

Yogabindu *of Haribhadrasūri*

Sanskrit text and tr. by K. K, Dixit. Lalbhai Dalpatbhai Series 19, Ahmedabad, 1968.

Yogadṛṣṭisamuccaya *and* Yogaviṃśika *of Haribhadrasūri*

Sanskrit text and tr. by K. K. Dixit, Lalbhai Dalpatbhai Series 27, Ahmedabad, 1970.

Yogaśāstra *of Hemacandra*

Yogaśāstraṃ Svopajñavṛttivibhūṣitam. Sanskrit text ed. by Mūni Jambūvijaya. Vols. I–III, Bombay: Jaina Sāhitya Vikāsa Maṇḍala, 1977, 1981, 1986.

Translated into English by O. Qvarnström as *The Yogaśāstra of Hemacandra. A Twelfth Century Handbook on Jainism.* Harvard Oriental Series, Vol. 60. Cambridge, MA: Harvard University Press, 2002.

Secondary sources

Bronkhorst, J. (1997) 'Philosophy and Vedic Exegesis in the Mīmāṃsā', in Eli Franco and Karin Preisendanz (eds), *Beyond Orientalism: The Work of Wilhelm Halbfass and its Impact on Indian and Cross-Cultural Studies*, Poznan: Studies in the Philosophy of the Sciences and the Humanities, Vol. 59, 359–371, Amsterdam – Atlanta: Rodopi.

Bronkhorst, J. (2001) 'The origin of Mīmāṃsā as a School of Thought: A Hypothesis', in Klaus Karttunen and Petteri Koskikallio (eds), *Vidyārṇavavandanam: Essays in Honour of Asko Parpola*, Helsinki: Finnish Oriental Society, 83–103.

Brooke, John H. (1991) *Science and Religion: Some Historical Perspectives*, Cambridge: Cambridge University Press.

Bühnemann, Gudrun. (1980) See *Sarvajñasiddhi* of Ratnakīrti.

Clooney, Francis X. (1990) *Thinking Ritually. Rediscovering the Pūrva Mīmāṃsā of Jaimini*, publications of the De Nobili Research Library, 17. Vienna.

Cowell, E. B. and Gough, A. E. (1904) See *Sarvadarśanasaṃgraha.*

Deshpande, Madhav M. (1993) *Sanskrit & Prakrit. Sociolinguistic Issues*, Delhi: Motilal Banarsidass.

D'sa, F. X. (1980) *Śabdaprāmāṇyam in Śabara and Kumārila. Towards a Study of the Mīmāṃsā Experience of Language*, publications of the De Nobili Research Library, Vol. VII. Ed. G. Oberhammer. Vienna.

Dundas, Paul. (1996) 'Jain Attitudes towards the Sanskrit Language', in Jan E. M. Houben (ed.), *Ideology and Status of Sanskrit,* 137–156, Leiden/New York/Köln: E. J. Brill.

Eltschinger, V. (1977) 'Bhāvaviveka et Dharmakīrti sur āgama et contre la Mīmāṃsā (2)', *Asiatische Studien/Études Asiatiques*, LI/4: 1095–1104.

——. (1978) 'Bhāvaviveka et Dharmakīrti sur āgama et contre la Mīmāṃsā (1)', *Asiatische Studien/Études Asiatiques*, LII/1: 57–84.

Frauwallner, Erich. (1962) 'Kumārila's Bṛhaṭṭīkā', *Wiener Zeitschrift für die Kunde Südund Ostasiens*, VI: 78–90.

Fujinaga, Sin. (2000) 'Akalaṅka's Theory on Sarvajña: Proving the Existence of Omniscience', *Indian Culture and Logic* (Fukuoka), 10: 717–730.

Gilson, Etienne. (1938) *Reason and Revelation in the Middle Ages*, New York: Charles Scribner's Sons.

Griffiths, P. (1990) 'Omniscience in the Mahāyānasūtrālaṅkāra and its Commentaries', *Indo-Iranian Journal*, 33: 85–120.

Halbfass, W. (1983) 'Kumārila on Ahiṃsā and Dharma', *Studien zur Indologie und Iranistik*, 9: 1–26, Reinbek: Verlag für Orientalistische Fachpublikationen.

——. (1988) *India and Europe*, Albany, NY: State University of New York Press.

Handiqui, K. K. (1949) *Yaśastilaka and Indian Culture*, Jīvarāja Jaina Granthamālā, no. 2, Sholapur: Jaina Saṃskṛti Saṃrakshaka Sangha.

Hara, M. (1964) 'Bhakti and Śraddhā', *Indo-Iranian Journal* VII, 2/3: 124–145.

Harnack, A. von. (1916) *Porphyrius, Gegen die Christen, 15 Bücher, Zeugnisse, Fragmente und Referate*, Berlin: Abh. d. kgl. preuss. Akad. d. Wiss., Phil. -Hist. kl.

Hartmann, J.-U. (1987) *Das Varṇārhavarṇastotra des Mātṛceṭa*, Göttingen: Vandenhoeck & Ruprecht

Hattori, M. (1968) *Dignāga, On Perception, being the Pratyakṣapariccheda of Dignāga's Pramāṇasamuccaya*, Cambridge, MA: Harvard University Press.

Helm, P. (1999) *Faith and Reason*, Oxford: Oxford University Press.

Hoffmann, Joseph R. (1987) *Celsus. On the True Doctrine. A Discourse Against the Christians*, tr. with a General Introduction by Joseph R. Hoffmann, New York/Oxford: Oxford University Press.

Iyengar, R. (1927) 'Kumārila and Dignāga', *Indian Historical Quarterly*, 3: 603–606.

Jacobi, H. (1911) 'The Dates of the Philosophical Sūtras of the Brahmans,' *Journal of the American Oriental Society*, 31: 1–29.

Jain, J. (1977) *The Vasudevahiṇḍī. An Authentic Jain Version of the Bṛhatkathā*, L.D. Series 59, Ahmedabad: L.D. Institute of Indology, 1977.

Jaini, P. S. (1974), 'On the Sarvajñatva (Omniscience) of Mahāvīra and the Buddha', in L. Cousins *et al.* (eds), *Buddhist Studies in Honour of I. B. Horner*, 71–90, Dordrecht: D. Reidel Publishing Company.

——. (1977) 'Bhavyatva and Abhavyatva: A Jaina doctrine of "Predestination"', in A. N. Upadhye *et al.* (eds), *Mahāvīra and His Teachings (2,500 Nirvāṇa Anniversary Volume)*, 95–111, Bombay: Bhagavān Mahāvīra 2500th Nirvāṇa Mahotsava Samiti.

Jayatilleke, K. N. (1963) *Early Buddhist Theory of Knowledge*, London: Allen and Unwin Ltd.

Kapadia, H. R. (ed.) (1947) *The Anekāntajayapatākā of Haribhadra Sūri. With his own Commentary and Municandra Sūri's Supercommentary*. Vol. II, Baroda: Baroda Oriental Institute.

Kawasaki, S. N. (1992) *Issai-chi shiso no kenkyū* ('Studies in the Idea of Omniscience'). Tokyo: Shun Ju Sha co.

Marty, M. E. and Appleby, R. S. (eds) (1993) *Fundamentalisms and Society: Reclaiming the Sciences, the Family and Education*, Chicago, IL: Chicago University Press.

Mironow, N. D. (1911) 'Janickija Zamytki' ('Notes on Jain Studies') *Bulletin de l'Académie Impériale des Sciences de St.-Pétersbourg*, 349–354 (Siddharṣi), 501–508 (Devabhadra), tr. from Russian by E. Grinstead.

Mynster, Lars. (1990) *Kejser Julian mod Galilæerne*. Oversat og kommenteret af Lars Mynster, København: Museum Tusculanums Forlag.

Nakamura, H. (1983) *A History of Early Vedānta Philosophy*, Delhi: Motilal Banarsidass.

NCC = *New Catalogus Catalogorum*. Eds. V. Raghavan, K. Kunjunni Raja *et al.* Madras 1949.

Neumann, K. J. (1880) *Kaiser Julians Bücher gegen die Christen, nach ihrer Wiederherstellung übersetzt*, Leipzig.

Parpola, Asko (1981) 'On the Formation of the Mīmāṃsā and the Problems concerning Jaimini, with Particular Reference to the Teacher Quotations and the Vedic Schools', *Wiener Zeitschrift für die Kunde Südasiens*, 25: 145–177.

——. (1994). 'On the formation of the Mīmāṃsā and the problems concerning Jaimini, with particular reference to the teacher quotations and the Vedic schools (Part II)', *Wiener Zeitschrift für die Kunde Südasiens*, 38: 293–308.

Pathak, K. B. (1893) 'The Position of Kumārila in Digambara Jaina Literature', in E. D. Morgan (ed.) *Transactions of the Ninth International Congress of Orientalists*, Vol. I, London: Printed for the Committee of the Congress, 22 Albemarle Street.

Pathak, K. B. (1930) 'Śāntarakṣita's Reference to Kumārila's Attacks on Samantabhadra and Akalaṅkadeva', *Annals of the Bhandarkar Oriental Research Institute*, XI: 155–164.

——. (1931) 'Kumārila's Verses attacking the Jaina and Buddhist Notions of an Omniscient Being', *Annals of the Bhandarkar Oriental Research Institute*, XII: 123–131.

Qvarnström, O. (1989) *Hindu Philosophy in Buddhist Perspective. The Vedāntatattvaviniścaya Chapter of Bhavya's Madhyamakahṛdayakārikā*, Lund: Almqvist Wiksell International.

——. (1999) 'Haribhadra and the Beginnings of Doxography in India', in O. Qvarnström and N. K. Wagle (eds), *Approaches to Jaina Studies: Philosophy, Logic, Rituals and Symbols*, 169–210, South Asian Studies Papers, no. 11, University of Toronto, Centre for South Asian Studies.

——. (2002) See *Yogaśāstra*.

——. (2003a) 'Losing One's Mind and becoming Enlightened. Some Remarks on the Concept of Yoga in Śvetāmbara Jainism and its relation to the Nāth Siddha tradition,' in I. Whicher and D. Carpenter (eds), *Yoga: The Indian Tradition* 130–142, London and New York: RoutledgeCurzon.

——. (2003b) 'Early Vedānta Philosophy preserved by the Jain Tradition: The Vedavādadvātriṃśikā of Siddhasena Divākara', in O. Qvarnström (ed.), *Jainism and Early Buddhism. Essays in Honour of Padmanabh S. Jaini*, Berkeley, CA: Asian Humanities Press.

——. (2004) 'Dharma in Jainism', *Journal of Indian Philosophy*, 32/5–6: 599–610.

Raja, K. Kunjunni. (1991) 'On the Dates of Śaṃkara and Maṇḍana', *Adyar Library Bulletin*, 55: 104–116.

Schubring, Walter. (1962) *The Doctrine of the Jainas*, Delhi: Motilal Banarsidass. (1 edn, *Die Lehre der Jainas*, Berlin and Leipzig 1935.)

Shah, N. G. (1967) *Akalaṅka's Criticism of Dharmakīrti's Philosophy*, Ahmedabad: L. D. Institute of Indology.

Singh, R. (1974) *The Jaina Concept of Omniscience*. L.D. Series 43, Ahmedabad: L. D. Institute of Indology.

Sirat, C. (1985) *A History of Jewish Philosophy in the Middle Ages*, Cambridge: Cambridge University Press.

Solomon, E. A. (1962) 'The Problem of Omniscience', *Adyar Library Bulletin*, 26: 36–77.

Soni, J. (1996) *The Notion of Āpta in Jaina Philosophy*. The 1995 Roop Lal Jain Lecture, Centre for South Asian Studies, University of Toronto.

——. (2000) 'Basic Jaina Epistemology', *Philosophy East & West*, 50/3: 367–377.

Steinkellner, E. (1978) 'Yogische Erkenntnis als Problem im Buddhismus' *Transzendenzerfahrung, Vollzugshorizont des Heils*. Hrsg. von G. Oberhammer, 121–134, Wien.

Stenberg, L. (1996) *The Islamization of Science. Four Muslim Positions Developing an Islamic Modernity*, Stockholm: Almqvist & Wiksell International.

Velankar, H. D. (1944) *Jina-ratna-kośa*, Poona: Bhandarkar Research Institute.

Verpoorten, J.-M. (1987) *Mīmāṃsā Literature*. A History of Indian Literature VI: 5. Ed. J. Gonda. Wiesbaden: Otto Harrassowitz.

Walker, B. (1968) *Hindu World*, Vol. I. Delhi Motilal Banarsidass.

Watt, W. M. (1985) *Islamic Philosophy and Theology: An Extended Survey*, Edinburgh: Edinburgh University Press.

Williams, R. (1965) 'Haribhadra', *Bulletin of the School of Oriental and African Studies*, 28/1: 101–111.

Winternitz, M. (1983) *A History of Indian Literature*, Vol. 2, Buddhist Literature and Jain Literature. A New Authoritative tr. by V. Srinivasa Sarma, Delhi: Motilal Banarsidass. (1 edn, *Geschichte der indischen Literatur*, Bd. 2, Leipzig 1920.)

5

WHY MUST THERE BE AN OMNISCIENT IN JAINISM?

Sin Fujinaga

1. It is a well-known fact that the Jains deny the existence of God as a creator of this universe while the Hindus admit such existence. According to Jainism this universe has no beginning and no end, so no being has created it. On the other hand, the Jains are very eager to establish the existence of an omniscient person. Such a person is denied in the Hindu tradition. The Jain saviors or *tīrthaṃkara*s are sometimes called *bhagavān*, a Lord. This word does not indicate a creator but rather means a respected person with all-pervading knowledge. Generally speaking, the omniscience of the *tīrthaṃkara*s is such that they grasp each and every thing of the universe not only in the present time, but in the past and the future also. The view on the omniscience of *tīrthaṃkara*s, however, is not ubiquitous in the Jaina tradition. Kundakunda remarks, "From the practical point of view an omniscient Lord perceives and knows all, while from the real point of view he perceives and knows his own soul."[1] Buddhism, another non-Hindu school of Indian philosophy, maintains that the founder Buddha is omniscient. In the Pāli canon, the Buddha is sometimes described with the word *savvaññu* or *sabbavid*, both of which mean omniscient.[2] But he is also said to recognize only the religious truth of *dharma*, more precisely, the four noble truths, *caturāryasatya*. This means that the omniscient Buddha does not need to know details of matters such as the number of insects in this world. Opposed to these two traditions, the Hindu schools do not admit any kind of omniscient person. Especially the Mīmāṃsakas fiercely attack the notion of omniscience because for them the (non-personal) *Veda*s are the ultimate authority on things in this universe.

In the history of Indian philosophy, these three schools, that is, the Jains, the Buddhists, and the Mīmāṃsakas attack each other and proclaim their own views on omniscience. Historically speaking, a Jain philosopher, Samantabhadra who must have lived in the sixth century of CE, is the first person who tried to establish the existence of an omniscient person by using the method of inference (*anumāna*).[3] From the Mīmāṃsaka side, Kumārila attacked Samantabhadra's position in his *Ślokavārtika*, while the famous Buddhist philosopher Dharmakīrti also criticized the notion of an omniscient person proclaimed by the Jain philosopher in his *Pramāṇavārttika*.[4]

Most of the books or papers which deal with Jain epistemology discuss omniscience at some length following the line of K. B. Pathak (1892, 1931) who must have been the first modern scholar to investigate the topic of omniscience in Jainism. Pathak showed that Kumārila attacked not only the Jain notion of omniscience but also that of the Buddhists. E. A. Solomon (1962) deals with omniscience not only in Jain literature but also in Hindu literature and Buddhist canons. Jaini (1974/2001) also discusses the omniscience of Mahāvīra and the Buddha. Singh (1974) is the only book in English whose main topic is omniscience in Jainism. But he does not refer to the reason why there must be an omniscient in Jainism. The second volume of Jain (1994) contains some discussion on the omniscient in Jainism as well as Buddhism. However, even in this book, we cannot find any argument about the necessity of the all-knowing person. Readers of this volume will find that Olle Qvarnström discusses how the Jain philosopher Haribhadra attacked Kumārila's notion of omniscience.[5]

In this chapter we shall see how the Jains tried to show the possibility of an all-knowing person, and we shall discuss why the Jains are so eager to establish the omniscience of the savior on the basis of some Prākrit and Sanskrit treatises such as the *Rājapraseṇīya*, and *Āptamīmāṃsā*.

2. Before discussing the attempts to prove the existence of the omniscience in Jainism, we shall have a brief view at Jain epistemology. The Jains admit the two kinds of valid method of knowledge (*pramāṇa*): *pratyakṣa* and *parokṣa*. The former means direct cognition or perception and the latter includes indirect or inference, scripture. In Jain epistemology the term *pratyakṣa* refers to the omniscience also because it grasps objects directly. It is also important to realize that in early times perception was categorized as a part of *parokṣa* while later Jain philosophers considered it as direct cognition. Samantabhadra uses the word *pratyakṣa* in two meanings: direct cognition including omniscience as well as perception.[6]

The Jain philosopher Samantabhadra tried to prove the existence of an omniscient person in his main work *Āptamīmāṃsā*, which means the examination of the reliable person. He first shows the possibility of complete annihilation of karmic matter:

> In some person there must be a total destruction of the spiritual deficiencies and of the physical veilings (that act as the cause of these deficiencies), for there must be a case where such destruction is most complete of all; this is just as by an employment of appropriate means it is possible to make in a physical substance a total destruction of the extraneous as well as organic impurities which it had happened to accumulate.[7]

It must be noted in this verse that Samantabhadra does not discuss the possibility of destruction of all the *karma*s but rather of those that hinder the power of ecognition (*ghātikarma*).

In the next verse, he shows the possibility of the existence of an omniscient person by the following syllogism: "The objects that are minute, concealed or distant must be amenable to somebody's perception, because they are amenable to inferential knowledge, similar to fire etc."[8]

What Samantabhadra intends in this verse seems to be as follows: we can infer the existence of fire on a remote mountain by seeing smoke from that mountain. At the same time, this fire is directly perceived by someone else, that is a person at that spot. This assumption can be applied to any object that we cannot see directly; a germ on the skin, a pebble in someone's fist and so on. A germ is not perceived directly by us, but by inference we know that it exists somewhere: by perceiving pus from the wound we can know that there are germs while someone can perceive it directly through a microscope. A pebble in someone's fist is perceptible for that person and the other person can infer the existence of it by perceiving the special form of the fist. It must be also admitted, for Samantabhadra, that all things in the universe are objects of inference. Thus, they are objects of perception, that is perceived by someone. This means that there must be somebody who can recognize all things. This is the omniscient person. To formulate this argument:

> Whatever exists in this universe must be object of perception (*pratijñā*). Because (whatever exists in this universe must be object of inference. And incomplete all) the object of inference must be perceived by someone (*hetu*). Like fire on a remote mountain (*dṛṣṭānta*).

In the strict sense, however, Samantabhadra's argument does not establish the existence of an omniscient person. First, we must realize that all the things in this universe can be divided into two groups: that which can be perceived directly and that which cannot be perceived directly. Samantabhadra suggests only that some person may perceive that which we cannot perceive. Moreover, the person who perceives the fire is not always the same person who can perceive other things directly.

It should be noticed here that this argument does not match Samantabhadra's final purpose. He intends to demonstrate that only the *tīrthaṃkara* is omniscient and not persons of other schools such as the Buddha in Buddhism. Therefore, Samantabhadra tries to prove his view by two sets of inference again:

> And such an omniscient person are you alone (because your) utterance
> is neither in conflict with logic nor with the scripture.
> For the proof of such an absence of the conflict, it is circumstance that
> your thoughts are never contradicted with what is well established.[9]

In the first syllogism Samantabhadra proclaims that only the Jain *tīrthaṃkara* is omniscient, he who has destroyed all hindrances and recognizes all the things in this universe. The reason for this is that he preaches in accordance with logic and the scriptures. The second syllogism shows why there is no conflict between the preachings and logic or the scriptures. It is so, because what he preaches is not denied by what is commonly admitted as authentic.

With these verses, Samantabhadra has posited that only a Jain *tīrthaṃkara* can be possessed of omniscient knowledge in the sense of knowing all the things in the universe not only in the present but even in the past as well as in the future.[10] As we have seen, his attempts were not successful because he only shows that all the things are objects of inference as well as those of perception but does not show that one and the same person can perceive all the objects. Even then it remains true that he introduced the method of inference into the discussion on the omniscience. Samantabhadra must be the first person to do so not only in Jainism but also in Indian philosophy because, to our knowledge, before him no one tried to establish the existence or non-existence of the all-knowing person.

Most Jain philosophers after Samantabhadra, both Śvetāmbaras and Digambaras, adopt the argument which Samantabhadra showed in his *Āptamīmāṃsā*, for example, Akalaṅka (*c.*720–760 CE). In establishing the existence of the *kevalin* he fundamentally follows Samantabhadra. To enforce the latter's arguments the former shows some concrete instances such as perfect knowledge of an astronomer. But what is new and more important is that he introduces the concept of *suniścita-asambhavad-bādhaka-pramāṇa* (SABP) as a reason to establish the existence of omniscience. The Sanskrit notion SABP means the well-known fact that "we have no valid methods of knowing to deny the existence of omniscience."[11]

Hemacandra (1088/9–1173), another philosophical giant of the Jain tradition, combines the traditional idea of *sarvajña* with that of Samantabhadra and Akalaṅka when he discusses the concept of omniscience in his *Pramāṇamīmāṃsā*. According to him: "That which is independent and supreme (i.e. omniscience) is the manifestation of the nature of *ātman* when all the veiling *karma*s are completely annihilated."[12]

In this definition of omniscience Hemacandra clearly mentions the relationship between omniscience and *karma*. When one destroys the veiling *karma*s completely, then the soul will have its innate nature in which omniscience is included. To prove the existence of omniscience, Hemacandra proposes two reasons: The possibility of the final end of the progressive development of knowledge, and the non-existence of any methods to deny it.[13]

Here Hemacandra follows the line directed by Samantabhadra and Akalaṅka. But, he has elaborated the arguments on the existence of omniscience by checking SABP one by one.[14]

Besides these three philosophers, many other Jain philosophers have attempted to prove the existence of omniscience. Vādidevasūri (1087–1170) in the Śvetāmbara tradition and Dharmabhūṣaṇa (*c.*1358–1418) in the Digambara tradition are good examples of such philosophers.[15] From Samantabhadra onwards, the history of Jain epistemology is, in a sense, the history of establishing the possibility of omniscience. Other schools in Indian philosophy were never concerned with this topic more avidly than the Jains.

Now, a question arises: why are the Jain philosophers so eager to establish the existence of the omniscient person who knows each and everything in this universe? Their enthusiasm, in my understanding, must have a close relationship with the concept of *bhavya* or the possibility of emancipation.

3. Though the concept of *bhavya* occurs, as Prof. P. S. Jaini points out,[16] even in the Jain *āgama*s, we shall focus on how Samantabhadra discusses this topic in relation with the idea of omniscience. The tenth chapter of *Āptamīmāṃsā* deals with the way to liberation or *mokṣa*. First Samantabhadra criticizes his opponent's position:

> If you maintain that the bondage necessarily results from even slight ignorance, then no one would not be omniscient because of infinite number of objects to be known. On the other hand, if you say that we can reach *mokṣa* even with slight knowledge, even then there must be the contradicted state (i.e., bondage) which resulted from massive ignorance.[17]

In verse 98, Samantabhadra expresses his own position on this topic.

> Ignorance causes a person to be bound when he or she is suffering from delusion. But, ignorance does not do so if the person is free from delusion. Moreover, one may reach *mokṣa* with slight knowledge if there is no influence of delusion. But, it is not so in the case of a person under its effect.[18]

This means that to reach *mokṣa* we need not destroy all the *karma*s but what we have to do is to demolish *mohanīya karma*s. As Shah (1999: 87) clearly mentions, this opinion does not go with traditional Jain understanding of the relation between *karma* and *mokṣa*. In the traditional Jain theory, *mokṣa* means total annihilation of *karma*. A person with a slight knowledge has not yet destroyed his/her *karma* completely. Thus he / she must remain in *saṃsāra*. The Buddhist philosopher Dharmakīrti attacks this theory proposed by Samantabhadra.[19]

One may ask: why do we have different experiences such as attachments in this world? Are those experiences predestinated by a supreme God?[20] To this Samantabhadra answers:

> Occurrence of attachment and others is of various types owing to the variety of bondage by *karma*. And *karma* or bondage by *karma* occurs to *jīva* because of *jīva*'s own reasons.[21]

Here, Samantabhadra clearly mentions the cause of our experiences and its variety. Someone may have attachment to something while another shows indifference to mundane matters or affairs. Such different attitudes originate from the different kinds of bondage which are caused by *karma*s. In its turn, *karma*s arise due to a *jīva* itself. A certain *karma* occurs because of a certain modification which occurred in a *jīva* previously. There is a cause–effect relation in one and the same *jīva*. Fundamentally, any foreign causes which may affect one's conditions cannot be supposed in Samantabhadra's theory.

Now *mokṣa* itself, according to this theory, can be regarded as a result and naturally must have its cause. Then what is the fundamental or first cause of *mokṣa*? Samantabhadra explains:

> For you, Mahāvīra, there are two types of *jīva*s: pure ones and impure ones. These two capacities, purity and impurity, are just as cookability and non-cookability of beans. For their manifestation, purity has its beginning while impurity is beginningless. This nature of purity or impurity is not in the scope of logic.[22]

According to this statement, Mahāvīra teaches us that *jīva*s can be classified into two categories: *śuddhi* or pure ones and *aśuddhi* or impure ones. Here, the words *śuddhi* and *aśuddhi* are synonyms for *bhavya* and *abhavya* respectively. 'The pure ones' are those who have the ability to reach the final liberation, and 'the impure ones' are those who are destined to remain in this mundane world forever. In other words, not all the *jīva*s can reach *mokṣa*.[23] Samantabhadra compares these capacities of the soul with those of beans: some of them become soft and edible when they are stewed but others remain hard even when we stew them for a long time. It is interesting to point out the fact that we cannot distinguish an edible bean from a non edible one by their appearance. At first, all the beans look the same to us, they must be hard before they are boiled. Once they are boiled, some beans will show their own nature and become soft while the others remain hard as before. In the same manner, we cannot know whether a person has the capacity to obtain *mokṣa* or not. Having undertaken austerities or *tapas* which heats us up, to someone its own nature will appear and he or she will be liberated. But, the others will stay in the chain of reincarnations and remain in this world to suffer pain. Things which remain in the same condition are beginningless while things which newly occur have a beginning. Therefore, Samantabhadra says "*sādy-anādī tayor vyaktī* (Their manifestation, purity has its beginning while impurity is beginningless)."

The most important point in Samantabhadra's remarks mentioned above is that the purity or impurity of a person cannot be known through inference (*atarka-gocara*). No ordinary person is capable to tell that such and such person will be liberated in the future, and the others will not. One cannot know the possibility of liberation of a certain person even through inference. We cannot recognize by perception what cannot be inferred.[24] This implies that the hallmark of liberation cannot be perceived. Then who can realize liberation? One possible answer to this question is this: only the omniscient person does. This omniscient one, however, must be that person who knows each and everything in this universe. The Buddha who, as mentioned earlier, realizes only the religious matters or *dharma*s would not tell us about our liberation in the future. Only the Jain omniscient who realizes all the matter in this world can do so.

4. As mentioned earlier, even in the Śvetāmbara *āgama*s the topic of the omniscience is often referred to. Among many references we find notions similar to Samantabhadra argument. The *Rāyapaseṇīya*, the second *upāṅga* in Śvetāmbara *āgama*s, mainly consists of the dialogue between a Jain monk Kesī and a materialist king Paesī. The former belongs to a school derived from Pārśvanātha[25] and the latter is converted to Jainism at the end of the dialogue. First, the king Paesī denies the existence of a soul or *jīva*, but through the elevated explanation of Kesī, the king inclines to the view that a soul exists and that it is different from a body or matter. Even then the king asks the monk to show the soul in real form like a fruit which we can see. To this, Kesī replies; "Oh, king Paesī, we, persons with imperfect knowledge, cannot realize nor perceive things in the categories at all."[26] The ten categories are (1) principle of motion, (2) principle of stop, (3) space (4) a soul separated from the body, (5) atom, (6) voice, (7) smell, (8) wind, (9) if a person can be a jina or not, (10) if a person is able to annihilate all the miseries or not.[27] The last two alternatives refer to the possibility of one's emancipation or *mokṣa* because a Jina will destroy all the *karma*s and the one who annihilates all the miseries or pains can reach the state of *mokṣa*.

In these passages the monk Kesī clearly mentions that we ordinary human beings cannot realize whether a person will get final beatitude or not. Then who does know it? Kesī continues; "Indeed, an *araha* or *Jina* to whom the supreme knowledge and vision have occurred and who is omniscient can clearly realize and perceive these things."[28] This means that the omniscient Jina or *tīrthaṃkara* can recognize whether a person can attain the emancipation or *mokṣa*. Thus in the Śvetāmbara tradition too the omniscient person or *tīrthaṃkara* is regarded as the only one that can tell who has the possibility of *mokṣa* or not.

The *Rāyapaseṇīya sutta* in which the earlier discussion happens belongs to a new stratum in the history of Śvetāmbara *āgama*s.[29] Even then it must have reached the present form before the sixth century. With these facts it will be concluded that at least in the sixth century Śvetāmbara Jains were of the opinion that only the omniscient one can know whether a certain person can reach *mokṣa* or not.

5. The final goal of all religious activities, at least in traditional Indian thoughts, is to reach *mokṣa*. The Jains, however, maintain that only the way showed by the Jain saviors can lead us to the final goal. We cannot reach the goal by performing sacrifice as some Hindu schools proclaim. On the way to the goal we must perform various kinds of austerities by fasting and so on. But, such austerities do not take everyone to *mokṣa*. As we have seen earlier, according to Jainism we cannot realize ourselves whether we have the possibility of *mokṣa* or not. If there is nothing to assure us of the possibility, then we do feel uneasy about pursuing our way. With the existence of a supreme being this uneasiness can be dispelled. Such a supreme being need not tell us of the possibilities of *mokṣa* and cannot know only religious matter, but must recognize everything in

this universe including the possibilities of all the *jīvas*. Thus, we can concentrate on wending our way to the final goal.

Notes

1 *Jāṇadi passadi savvaṃ vavahāraṇeṇa kevalī bhavagavaṃ / kevalaṇāṇī jāṇadi passadi ṇiyameṇa appāṇaṃ //* (*Niyamasāra* v. 158).

2 See, for example, *Jātaka* p. 77.

3 The earliest mentioning of omniscience in Jain literature must be that found in Āyā I, 3, 4. Post-canonical philosophers such as Kundakunda, and Umāsvāti also refer to this topic. But they did not establish that fact by means of inference. After Samantabhadra, as we will see, many Jain philosophers discussed the existence of an omniscient person.

4 Pathak (1892) has established that Samantabhadra was prior to Kumārila. Dharmakīrti's attack on Samantabhadra's philosophy is discussed in Fujinaga 2000. The historical priority of Kumārila to Dharmakīrti is not clearly established. It is also extremely probable that these three philosophers were contemporary with each other.

5 See his essay "The Jain-Mīmāṃsā Debate on Omniscience" in this volume.

6 See Fujinaga 1999.

7 ĀM 4: *doṣāvaraṇayor hānir niḥśeṣā'sty atiśāyanāt / kvacid yathā svahetubhyo bahirantarmalakṣayaḥ* // English translation is based on Shah (1999: 3).

8 ĀM 5abc: *sūkṣmāntaritadūrārthāḥ pratyakṣāḥ kasyacid yathā / anumeyatvato 'gnyādir...* // English translation is based on Shah (1999: 4).

9 ĀM 6: *sa tvam evāsi nirdoṣo yuktiśāstrāvirodhivāk / avirudho yad iṣṭaṃ te prasiddhena na bādhyate* // English translation is based on Shah (1999: 4). The Sanskrit text clearly shows that "you" in this verse refers to a single person. According to the Jain doctrine, however, there must be more than one omniscient person, at least 24 *tīrthaṃkaras*. Thus, in a sense, Samantabhadra's argument in this verse does not go with traditional doctrine of Jainism. It also must be noted that the two syllogisms in this verse have no example (*dṛṣṭānta*).

10 Thus the Buddha cannot be an omniscient.

11 The topic of SABP has not been discussed thoroughly so far in spite of its importance in the history of Jaina epistemology. It is, however, too wide and deep to argue here, so we shall deal with this topic on another occasion.

12 PM S. XV: *tat sarvathāvaraṇvilaye cetanasya svarūpāvirbhāvo mukhyaṃ kevalaṃ.*

13 Cf. PM S. XVI, XVII: *prajñātiśayaviśrāntyādisiddhes tatsiddhiḥ. bādhakābhāvāc ca.*

14 For the details of Hemacandra's discussion on SABP, see PM §§ 59–63.

15 Vādideva discusses omniscience in his *Pramāṇanayatattvāloka* II-24–27 and auto-commentary on them while §§ 21–27 of *Nyāyadīpikā* show Dharmabhūṣaṇa's position on omniscience.

16 Jaini (1977/ 2000: 95–109).

17 ĀM 96: *ajñānāccet dhurvo bandho jñeyānantyān na kevalī / jñānastokād vimokṣaś ced ajñānād bahuto 'nyathā* // See also Shah (1999: 84).

18 ĀM 98: *ajñānān mohino bandho nājñānād vītamohatāḥ / jñānastokāc mokṣaḥ syād amohān mohino 'nyathā* // See also Shah (1999: 85).

19 For the attack of Dharmakīrti on Samantabhadra's position, see Fujinaga (2000).

20 Cf. *Aṣṭasahasrī* on ĀM 99 (p. 267).

21 ĀM. 99abc: *kāmādiprabhavaś citraḥ karmabandhānurūpataḥ / tac ca karma svahetubhyo...* // Shah (1999: 85) understands that the word *sva* refers to *karma*. Cf. ĀM 4 in which the phrase *svahetubhyas* occurs in.

22 ĀM. 99d–100: *te śuddhyaśuddhitaḥ // śuddhyaśuddhī punaḥ śaktī te pākyāpākyaśaktivat/ sādyanādī tayor vyaktī svabhāvo 'tarkagocaraḥ //*

23 *Vṛtti* of Vasunandin on ĀM 99: *ata eva na sarveṣāṃ mokṣaḥ.*

24 In this context inference represents the whole *parokṣa*.
25 Kesī is called *pāsāvvaccijjo* (*Rāyapaseṇīya sutta* 7, p. 5) and refers to himself as *aṃhaṃ samaṇāṇaṃ niggaṃthāṇaṃ*... (do. 20, p. 18).
26 *Rāyapaseṇīya sutta* 30 (p. 33). *eva khalu Paesī! dasaṭṭhāṇāiṃ chaumatthe maṇusse sabbhāveṇāṃ na jāṇāi na pāsai.*
27 do. (p. 34). 9) *ayaṃ jiṇe bhavissai vā no bhavissai*, 10) *ayaṃ savvadukkhāṇaṃ antaṃ karissai vā no vā.* See also *Sthānāṅgasūtra*, p. 337.
28 do. *eyāṇi ceva uppannanāṇadaṃsaṇadhare arahājiṇe kevalī savvabhāveṇaṃ jāṇai pāsai.*
29 For the position of the *Rāyapaseṇīya sutta* in the Jain *āgama*s, see Dixit (1971: 4).

Bibliography

Primary sources and abbreviations

ĀM = *Āptamīmāṃsā* of Samantabhadra with *vṛtti* of Vasunandin, ed. by G. Jain. Benares (Sanātana Jaina Granthamālā 7) 1914.

Aṣṭasahasrī, of Vidyānada on *Aṣṭaśatī* of Akalaṅka, ed. by Baṃsīdhar. Sholapur (Gandhī Nāthārarājī Jaina Granthamālā) 1914.

Aṣṭaśatī, of Akalaṅka, see *Aṣasahasrī*.

Āyā = *Ācārāṅgasūtram* and *Sūtrakṛtāṅgasūtram*, ed. by Sāgarānanda, re-ed. by Muni Jambūvijaya. Delhi etc. (Lālā Sundarlāl Jain Āgamagranthamālā Vol. I) 1978.

The Jātaka together with its commentary, ed. by V. Fausbøll. Vol. I. Oxford (Pali Text Society) 1990.

Mīmāṃsā Ślokavārttika, of Kumārila, ed. by D. D. Shastri. Varanasi (Prachyabharati Series 10) 1978.

Niyamasāra, of Kundakunda, ed. and tr. by U. Jain. Lucknow (The Sacred Books of the Jainas Vol. IX) 1931.

Nyāyādīpikā, of Dharmabhūṣaṇa, ed. by D. Jain. Delhi (Vīrasevamandira Granthamālā no. 4) 1968.

PM = *Pramāṇamīmāṃsa*, of Hemacandra, ed. by Sukhlāl Saṅghavī *et al.* Ahmedabad–Calcutta (Siṅghī Jaina Granthmālā 9) 1939.

Pramāṇanayatattvāloka, of Vādidevasūri with auto-commentary *Syādvādaratnākara*, ed. by Motilāl. Poona 1926–1930. [Reprinted: Bhāratīya Buk Dārpreśan, Dilli 1988.]

Pramāṇavārttika, of Dharmakīrti, ed. by Dwarikadas Shastri. Varanasi (Baudha Bharati Series 3) 1968.

Rāyapaseṇīyasutta, ed. by R. C. Tripathi. Ahmedabad 1936.

Sthānāṅgasūtram and Samavāyāṅga Sūtram, ed. by Sāgarānanda, re-ed. by Muni Jambūvijaya. Delhi etc. (Lālā Sundarlāl Jain Āgamagranthamālā Vol. II) 1985.

Secondary sources

Bollée, Willem, 2002, *The Story of Paesi* (*Paesi-kahāṇayaṃ*). Wiesbaden: Steiner Verlag (Beiträge zur Kenntnis südasiatischer Sprachen und Literaturen 8).

Dixit, K. K., 1971, *Jaina Ontology*. Ahmedabad: C. D. Institute (Lalbhai Dalpatbhai Series 31).

Fujinaga, S., 1999, "Samantabhadra's Epistemology: Combining Jaina Ideas with the Ideas of Other Schools," in N. K. Wagle and O. Qvarnström, eds, *Approaches to Jaina Studies: Philosophy, Logic, Rituals and Symbols*. Toronto (University of Toronto: Centre for South Asian Studies) pp. 131–137.

Fujinaga, S., 2000, "Determining Which Jaina Philosopher was the Object of Dharmakīrti's Criticisms," in *Philosophy East and West*. Vol. 50, No. 3. pp. 378–385.

Jain, P. K., 1994, *Bhāratīya Darśan meṃ Sarvajñavād*. Delhi.

Jaini, P. S., 1974, "On the *Sarvajñatva* (Omniscience) of Mahāvīra and the Buddha," in L. Cousins, ed., *Buddhist Studies in Honor of I. B. Horner*, Dordrecht (Reidel). [reprinted in *Collected Papers on Buddhist Studies*. Delhi (Motilal Banarsidass) 2001. pp. 97–121].

——1977, "*Bhavyatva* and *Abhavyatva*: A Jaina Doctrine of 'Predestination'," in *Mahāvīra and His Teachings (2,500 Nirvāṇa Anniversary Volume)*, Bombay. [reprinted in *Collected Papers on Jaina Studies*. Delhi (Motilal Banarsidass) 2000. pp. 95–109].

Pathak, B. K., 1892, "The Position of Kumārila in Digambara Jaina Literature," in *The Transactions of the Ninth International Oriental Congress*. pp. 186–214.

——1931, "Kumālira's Verses Attacking the Jain and Buddhist Notions of an Omniscient being," in *Annal of Bhandarkar Oriental Institute* Vol. XII, No. 2. pp. 123–130.

Shah, N. J., 1999, *Samantabhadra's* Āptamīmāṃsā *Critique of an Authority, along with English Translation, Introduction, Notes and Akalaṅka's Sanskrit Commentary Aṣṭaśatī*. Ahmedabad (Sanskrit-Sanskriti Granthamālā 7).

Singh, R. J., 1974, *The Jaina Concept of Omniscience*. Ahmedabad (L. D. Series 43).

Solomon, E. A., 1962, "The Problem of Omniscience (Sarvajña)," in *The Adyar Library Bulletin* Vol. XXVI, No. 1–2. pp. 36–77.

6

IMPLICATIONS OF THE BUDDHIST–JAINA DISPUTE OVER THE FALLACIOUS EXAMPLE IN *NYĀYA-BINDU* AND *NYĀYÂVATĀRA-VIVṚTI**

Piotr Balcerowicz

From the times of Aristotle, to whom the idea seemed so obvious and natural that he eventually failed to spare anywhere in his voluminous oeuvre even a single word of explanation on it, and of Alexander, his commentator, who was the first to point out its significance explicitly,[1] the benefits of symbolic expressions in logic,[2] or formal logic to be more precise, have not been questioned seriously by any sane student ever since. It has been unanimously determined that the predominant idea underlying the usage of symbols in logic lies in the desire, first, to make the student 'aware, that the validity of the processes of analysis does not depend upon the interpretation of the symbols which are employed, but solely upon the laws of their combination',[3] and, secondly, to render 'every logical proposition, whether categorical or hypothetical, capable of exact and rigorous expression',[4] not to mention a certain amount of intellectual gratification derived from 'the symmetry of their analytical expression, harmony and consistency',[5] notwithstanding the simple fact that 'in the beginning the use of letters is a mystery, which seems to have no purpose except mystification'.[6] The distinct advantage of the first two requirements, that is the recognition of class and general notion as a universal point of reference and univocality in the use of names, that jointly enable us to arrive autonomously at specific universally applicable, contents- and context-independent 'elementary laws of thought'[7] and draw valid conclusions autonomously with reference to the contents of premises, was recognised relatively early by Alexander:

> In the discipline [of logic], letters are used in order to make us aware, that conclusion does not depend on contents, but on [syllogistic] figures, on relation of premisses and on [syllogistic] modes, because it is not the

> very contents that is important for syllogistic inference, but the arrangement itself. Accordingly, letters are employed [to represent] general notions and to show, that conclusion will always follow and from any assumption.[8]

Two additional considerations that are taken for granted and speak in favour of the method resting upon the employment of symbols in formal logic were added in one breath at the moment of formulating the first theory to represent formal logic with the help of symbolic means that remain at the disposal of algebra, the result of which is symbolic logic, or mathematical logic or logistic: the need for a necessary instrument, or methods, or 'aids' (or, to intimate the name of the 'symbolic culprit' anew, τὸ ὄ ργανον) to facilitate the progress of scientific discovery, on the one hand, and, on the other, the demand of the discipline of the intellect.[9]

Our list of benefits can be further extended with two more features, that is, that of concision and manageability as well as amenability to and capability of expressing abstract concepts absent from natural language.[10] Every student of philosophic Sanskrit knows how indefinite or imprecise – and logically unsatisfactory – the conjunctions *ca* or *vā* (especially in negated sentences) in the natural language can be, how their meaning in certain contexts may overlap and how much intuitive their interpretation sometimes is. Conspicuous examples are furnished, for instance, by the problem of *catuṣ-koṭi*, wherein the first hemstitch of one of its formulations *naîva svataḥ prasiddhir na parasparataḥ para-pramāṇair vā*[11] could theoretically be represented in a number of ways (p stands for *svataḥ prasiddhir*, q for *parasparataḥ prasiddhir*, and r for *para-pramāṇair prasiddhir*): (1) $\sim p \wedge \sim q \vee r$, (2) $\sim p \wedge \sim q \vee r$, (3) $\sim p \wedge \sim q \vee \sim r$, (4) $\sim p \vee \sim q \vee \sim r$, (5) $\sim p \wedge \sim (q \vee r)$ or (6) $\sim p \vee \sim (q \vee r)$ etc., but it is the reader who intensionally interprets it not as an alternative (the usual meaning of *vā*) but as a disjunction (7) $\sim p \wedge \sim q \wedge \sim r$. The inadequacy of, say, such ambiguous words as 'and' or 'or', or its equivalents, to express certain abstract relations, that are not present in the natural language but are easily definable with the help of truth tables (1110, 0111 and 0110) in the two-value logic and can be represented with symbols ($p|q$, $p \vee q$, p,q), is well-known.[12]

Having said that, could such a symbolic and formalised language have any drawback? Apart from the earlier-quoted remark uttered jokingly by Bertrand Russell, two crucial disadvantages can be seen in the way any formalised language, alongside symbols as its corollaries, operates 'at the expense, where necessary, of brevity and facility of communication'.[13]

But there is one more to be mentioned, of extralogical consequence and of sociological import. However, before I come to speak of it, let us consider what actually happens when, say, Dharmakīrti avails himself of examples of proof formulas or of the fallacies of proof formula? Notoriously, Indian logicians did not use symbols in the proper sense. In which sense does he then use sentences that stand for proof formulas? While formulating an inference for others, does he refer to a particular situation or does he articulate general rules? The question indeed seems rather trivial. A good example of a reasoning of universal denotation is the one provided by Dharmakīrti: 'Thus is the formulation of the logical reason based on [essential] identity: whatever is existent, is without exception impermanent, for instance the pot – this is the simple (unqualified) formulation of the logical reason based on [essential] identity,'[14] with the thesis and the logical reason having most broadly conceivable universal reference: *sarvam anityam, sattvāt* ('everything is impermanent, because it is existent').[15] But we have countless instances when Dharmakīrti, and Indian logicians in general, draws inference with regard to a very particular situation ('here, on this particular spot') following a general rule of invariable concomitance, for example: 'The formulation of the logical reason based on effect is [as follows]: wherever there is smoke, there is fire, for instance in the kitchen, etc. And there is smoke here, [* hence there is fire here],'[16] where the implied thesis (or conclusion) **astîhâgniḥ* ('there is fire here') pertains to an individual case.[17] But even then, in both earlier cases these formulations instantiate only some ideal patterns, or semi-symbolic formulas, even though no symbolic expressions occur in the formulations. That is clear from Dharmakīrti's commentary itself, when the general rule is first stated and than instantiated, or applied to a particular case, for example:

> If *x*-s are observed, *y* – characterised by (i.e. dependent on) these (*x*-s) [previously] unobserved – is observed, and [*y*] is not observed, even if one of *x*-s is absent, [then] *y* is the effect of *x*; and [in this case] this [effect] is smoke.[18]

Clearly, Dharmakīrti – and Indian logicians in general – does not use symbols; however, particular terms such as *ghaṭa*, *ākāśa*, *paramâṇu*, *śabda*, etc., stand for certain classes of objects, for example the class of material perceptible things (*mūrta* = *pratyakṣâdy-anupalabdha*), the class of imperceptible things (*amūrta*), the class of produced things (*kṛtaka*), etc. His formulations are 'replaceable', namely they stand for general symbols, and the actual contents of a proposition is rather secondary; being of exemplary, illustrative character, its meaning is hardly of any relevance. However, their meaning is not entirely irrelevant: such semi-variables, for example *ghaṭa*, that occur in proof formulas denote a particular class, for example either the class of material perceptible things (*mūrta*) or the class of produced things (*kṛtaka*), and its particular denotation range is determined by the context. Thus, intensional logic possesses some indistinct aspects of extensionality.

A good exemplification of this is furnished by a comparison of two varieties of the fallacious example found in Śaṅkarasvāmin's *Nyāya-praveśa* (NP) and in Dharmakīrti's *Nyāya-bindu* (NB). The former avails himself of one and the same sentence word for word (*nityaḥ śabdo 'mūrtatvāt paramâṇuvat*) to exemplify two different kinds of *dṛṣṭântâbhāsa*, namely of *sādhana-dharmâsiddha* (of the *sādharmya* type) and *sādhyâvyāvṛtta* (of the *vaidharmya* type), the only difference being in stating the invariable concomitance (*vyāpti*) either in the positive manner (*yad amūrtaṁ tan nityaṁ dṛṣṭaṁ* – 'whatever is imperceptible is experienced to be permanent') or negative manner (*yad anityaṁ tan mūrtaṁ dṛṣṭaṁ* – 'whatever is impermanent is experienced to be perceptible').[19] However, Dharmakīrti, in explicating two divisions of the fallacious example, namely *sādhya-vikala* and *sādhyâvyatirekin*, that correspond to Śaṅkarasvāmin's *sādhana-dharmâsiddha* and *sādhyâvyāvṛtta* respectively, employs partly the same sentence, but changes the essential element in the reasoning: the statement of the object that serves as an example. The result is that we have two different examples that can be interchanged ([S1] *karmavat* and [V1] *paramâṇuvat*).[20]

I have expressed earlier the conviction that the actual contents of a proposition is *rather secondary* instead of saying it is *of no relevance*, inasmuch as the contents of a proposition is indeed entirely irrelevant structurally to the way a proof formula is formulated (its role is to exemplify certain ontological and logical relations), but, on the other hand, it does play a certain role, since it conveys some ideas, being formulated with verbal means. I agree, all these remarks are perhaps not particularly original and are, at least intuitively, taken for granted by every student of Indian epistemology. Why, then, am I saying all this? To repeat my previous question: is there, thus, any advantage in using no symbols? Apparently there is, though it is not of logical nature, and I shall try to demonstrate this on the following pages.

As it is well-known to the student of Buddhist thought, in the third chapter of *Nyāya-bindu* we come across Dharmakīrti's exposition of nine fallacies of the example based on similarity (*sādharmya-dṛṣṭântâbhāsa*) as well as the complementary ninefold division of the fallacy of the example based on dissimilarity (*vaidharmya-dṛṣṭântâbhāsa*). Further, within both ninefold divisions of fallacious examples we can observe that each of them can be naturally divided into three sub-classes of three structurally similar elements. Accordingly, the complete enumeration runs as follows:

[S] fallacious examples based on similarity (*sādharmya-dṛṣṭântâbhāsa*):

- [SA] lacking *x*:
  - [S1] the fallacious example lacking the probandum (*sādhya-vikala*),
  - [S2] the fallacious example lacking the probans (*sādhana-vikala*),
  - [S3] the fallacious example lacking both the probandum and the probans (*sādhya-sādhana-vikala*),
- [SB] in which the property of *x* is doubtful:
  - [S4] the fallacious example in which the property of the probandum is doubtful (*sandigdha-sādhya-dharma*),
  - [S5] the fallacious example in which the property of the probans is doubtful (*sandigdha-sādhana-dharma*),
  - [S6] the fallacious example in which the property of the probandum and the probans is doubtful (*sandigdha-sādhya-sādhana-dharma*),

[SC] with positive concomitance characterised by *x*:

[S7] the fallacious example without positive concomitance (*ananvaya*),

[S8] the fallacious example with unindicated positive concomitance (*apradarśitânvaya*),

[S9] the fallacious example with inverted positive concomitance (*viparītânvaya*);

[V] fallacious examples based on dissimilarity (*vaidharmya-dṛṣṭântâbhāsa*):

[VA] lacking negative concomitance with *x*:

[V1] the fallacious example lacking negative concomitance with the probandum (*sādhyâvyatirekin*),

[V2] the fallacious example lacking negative concomitance with the probans (*sādhanâvyatirekin*),

[V3] the fallacious example lacking negative concomitance with the probandum and the probans (*sādhya-sādhanâvyatirekin*),

[VB] in which negative concomitance with *x* is doubtful:

[V4] the fallacious example in which negative concomitance with the probandum is doubtful (*sandigdha-sādhya-vyatireka*),

[V5] the fallacious example in which negative concomitance with the probans is doubtful (*sandigdha-sādhana-vyatireka*),

[V6] the fallacious example in which negative concomitance both with the probandum and with the probans is doubtful (*sandigdha-sādhya-sādhana-vyatireka*),

[VC] with negative concomitance characterised by *x*:

[V7] the fallacious example without negative concomitance (*avyatireka*),

[V8] the fallacious example with unindicated negative concomitance (*apradarśita-vyatireka*),

[V9] the fallacious example with inverted negative concomitance (*viparīta-vyatireka*).[21]

Noteworthy is the fact that Dharmakīrti's typology, along with illustrations for each of the entries, is followed in each and every detail – with a few exceptions – in the classification found in Siddharṣigaṇi's *Nyāyâvatāra-vivṛti* (NAV) – a Jaina epistemic treatise, the significance of which exceeds perhaps even the philosophic import of the *Nyāyâvatāra* aphorisms, despite the subservient function it was predestined to perform, being a commentary thereupon. The juxtaposition presented in the following two tables (Tables 6.1 and 6.2) will clearly show such a dependence. I have single-underlined phrases found in NB that are basically identical with NAV. I have *double-underlined* the portions that can be either reconstructed on the basis of NB or NBṬ or supplied from corresponding sections of NAV. I use a broken underline to mark synonymous (but not identical) expressions in NB and NAV.

Table 6.1 Sādharmya-dṛṣṭântâbhāsa

#	*Variety of the fallacious example*	*Nyāya-bindu of Dharmakīrti*	*Nyāyâvatāra-vivṛti (on NA 24) of Siddharṣigaṇi*
[S1]	*sādhya-vikala* lacking the probandum	*nityaḥ śabdo 'mūrtatvāt, karmavat* (NB 3.124). Speech element is impermanent, because it is imperceptible, like action.	*bhrāntam anumānaṁ, pramāṇatvāt, pratyakṣavat.* Inference is erroneous, because it is a cognitive criterion, like perception.
[S2]	*sādhana-vikala* lacking the probans	*nityaḥ śabdo 'mūrtatvāt, paramānuvat* (NB 3.124). Speech element is impermanent, because it is imperceptible, like infinitesimal atom.	*jāgrat-saṁvedanaṁ bhrāntaṁ, pramāṇatvāt, svapna-saṁvedanavat.* The sensation of a person in the waking state is erroneous, because it is a cognitive criterion, like the sensation in dream.
[S3]	*sādhya-sādhana-vikala* lacking both the probandum and the probans	*nityaḥ śabdo 'mūrtatvād, ghaṭavat* (NB 3.124). Speech element is impermanent, because it is imperceptible, like pot.	*nâsti sarva-jñaḥ, pratyakṣâdy-anupalabdhatvād, ghaṭavat* There is no omniscient person (*sc.* omniscient person is non-existent), because he is not comprehended through perception, etc., like a pot.
[S4]	*sandigdha-sādhya-dharma* in which the property of the probandum is doubtful	*rāgâdimān ayaṁ vacanād rathyā-puruṣavat* (NB 3.125). This [particular person] is endowed with passion, because he speaks, like a person in the street.	*vīta-rāgo 'yaṁ, maraṇa-dharmatvād, rathyā-puruṣavat.* This [particular person] is dispassionate, because he is mortal, like a person in the street.
[S5]	*sandigdha-sādhana-dharma* in which the property of the probans is doubtful	*maraṇa-dharmâyaṁ puruṣo rāgâdimattvād, rathyā-puruṣavat* (NB 3.125). This particular person is mortal, because he is endowed with passion, like a person in the street.	*maraṇa-dharmâyaṁ puruṣo, rāgâdimattvād, rathyā-puruṣavat.* This particular person is mortal, because he is passionate, like a person in the street.

[S6]	*sandigdha-sādhya-sādhana-dharma* in which the property of the probandum and the probans is doubtful	*asarva-jño 'yaṁ rāgâdimattvād, rathyā-purṣavat* (NB 3.125). This [particular person] is not omniscient, because he is endowed with passion, like a person in the street.	*asarva-jño 'yaṁ, rāgâdimattvād, rathyā-puruṣavat.* This [particular person] is not omniscient, because he is passionate, like a person in the street.
[S7]	*ananvaya* without positive concomitance	[**rāgâdimān ayaṁ, vaktṛtvād,*[22]] *yathā yo vaktā sa rāgâdimān, iṣṭa-puruṣavat* (NB 3.126). [This particular person is endowed with passion, because he is a speaker (*sc*. talks),] for instance whoever is a speaker is endowed with passion, like any selected person.	*rāgâdimān vivakṣitaḥ puruṣo, vaktṛtvād, iṣṭa-puruṣavat.* A particular person in question is dispassionate, because he is a speaker (sc. talks), like any selected person.
[S8]	*apradarśitânvaya* with unindicated positive concomitance	*anityaḥ śabdaḥ kṛtakatvād ghaṭavat* (NB 3.126). Speech element is impermanent, because it is produced, like pot.	*anityaḥ śabdaḥ, kṛtakatvād, ghaṭavat.* Speech element is impermanent, because it is produced, like pot.
[S9]	*viparītânvaya* with inverted positive concomitance	[**Anityaḥ śabdaḥ, kṛtakatvād* ,] *yad anityaṁ tat kṛtakam* [**ghaṭavat*[23]] (NB 3.127). [Speech element is impermanent, because it is produced;] whatever is impermanent is produced, [like pot].	*anityaḥ śabdaḥ, kṛtakatvād, yad anityaṁ tat kṛtakam ghaṭavat* [Speech element is impermanent, because it is produced; whatever is impermanent is produced, like pot.

Table 6.2 Vaidharmya-dṛṣṭântâbhāsa

#	*Variety*	*Nyāya-bindu*	*Nyāyâvatāra-vivṛti (on NA 25) of Siddharṣigaṇi*
[V1]	*sādhyâvyatirekin* lacking negative concomitance with the probandum	[**nityaḥ śabdo 'mūrtatvāt,*[24]] *paramāṇuvat* (NB 3.129) [Speech element is impermanent, because it is imperceptible,] like infinitesimal atom	*bhrāntam anumānam, pramāṇatvāt; yat punar bhrāntaṁ na bhavati na tat pramāṇaṁ, tad yathā svapna-jñānam* Inference is erroneous, because it is a cognitive criterion, whatever is not erroneous, however, is not a cognitive criterion, like cognition in dream
[V2]	*sādhanâvyatirekin* lacking negative concomitance with the probans	[**nityaḥ śabdo 'mūrtatvāt,*[25]] *karmavat* (NB 3.129). Speech element is impermanent, because it is imperceptible, like action	*nirvikalpakaṁ pratyakṣaṁ, pramāṇatvāt; yat punaḥ savikalpakaṁ na tat pramāṇaṁ, tad yathânumānam* Perception is non-conceptual, because it is a cognitive criterion, whatever is accompanied by a conceptualisation, however, is not a cognitive criterion, like inference
[V3]	*sādhya-sādhanâvyatirekin* lacking negative concomitance with the probandum and the probans	[**nityaḥ śabdo 'mūrtatvāt,*[26]] *ākāśavat* (NB 3.129). Speech element is permanent, because it is imperceptible, like space	*nityânityaḥ śabdaḥ, sattvāt; yaḥ punar na nityânityaḥ sa na san, tad yathā ghaṭaḥ* The speech element is [both] permanent and impermanent, because it is existent, whatever is not [both] permanent and impermanent, however, is not existent, like a pot
[V4]	*sandigdha-sādhya-vyatireka*	*asarva-jñāḥ kapilâdayo 'nāptā vā, avidyamāna-sarva-jñatâptatā-liṅga-bhūta-pramāṇâtiśaya-śāsanatvāt; yaḥ sarva-jña āpto vā sa jyotir-jñānâdikam upadiṣṭavān. yathā – ṛṣabha-vardhamānâdir iti* (NB 3.130). Kapila and others are neither omniscient nor authoritative persons,	*asarva-jñā anāptā vā kapilâdayo, ārya-satya-catuṣṭayâpratipādakatvāt; yaḥ punaḥ sarva-jña āpto vā 'sāv ārya-satya-catuṣṭayaṁ pratyapīpadat, tad yathā śauddhôdaniḥ.* Kapila and others are neither omniscient nor authoritative persons, because they do not teach the four noble truths, whoever is

		because [their] teaching is the best cognitive criterion as the proof that they have no omniscience or authority, whoever is an omniscient or an authoritative person, he teaches astrology, etc., like Ṛṣabha, Vardhamāna and other [Jinas]	an omniscient and an authoritative person, however, he teaches the four noble truths, like the Buddha.
[V5]	*sandigdha-sādhana-vyatireka* in which negative concomitance with the probandum is doubtful	*na trayīvidā brāhmaṇena grāhya-vacanaḥ kaścit vivakṣitaḥ puruṣo rāgâdimattvāt, ye grāhya-vacanaḥ* na te rāgâdimantaḥ *tad yathā gautamâdayo dharma-śastrāṇāṁ praṇetāraḥ* (NB 3.131) A particular person in question is not such whose statements could be trusted by a Brahmin learned in the three Vedas, because he is endowed with passion, etc., those whose statements can be trusted are not endowed with passion, etc., like Gautama and others, who are promulgators of *Dharma-śāstra*	*anādeya-vākyaḥ kaścid vivakṣitaḥ puruṣo rāgâdimattvāt; yaḥ punar ādeya-vākyo, na sarāgâdimāṁs, tad yathā sugataḥ* A particular person in question is untrustworthy, because he is endowed with passion, etc., whoever is trustworthy, however, is not endowed with passion, etc., like the Buddha.
[V6]	*sandigdha-sādhya-sādhana-vyatireka* in which negative concomitance both with the probandum and with the probans is doubtful	*avīta-rāgāḥ kapilâdayaḥ. parigrahâgraha-yogāt; yo vīta-rāgo na tasya parigrahâgrahaḥ, yatharṣabhâdeḥ* (NB 3.132). Kapila and others are not dispassionate, because they are endowed with covetousness and greed, whoever is dispassionate, he does not have covetousness and greed, like Ṛṣabha.	*na vīta-rāgāḥ kapilâdayaḥ, karuṇâspadeṣv apy akaruṇâparīta-cittatayâdatta-nijaka-māṁsa-śakalatvāt; ye punar vīta-rāgās te karuṇâspadeṣu karuṇā-parīta-cittatayā datta-nija-māṁsa-śakalās, tad yathā bodhi-sattvāḥ.* Kapila and others are not dispassionate, because – inasmuch as [their] consciousness is not filled with compassion – they have not offered any bits of their own flesh even to the abodes of compassion (*sc.* to hungry beings who deserved compassion), those, however, who are dispassionate, inasmuch as their consciousness

(*Continued*)

Table 6.2 Continued

#	*Variety*	*Nyāya-bindu*	*Nyāyâvatâra-vivṛti (on NA 25) of Siddharṣigaṇi*
			is filled with compassion, offered bits of their own flesh to the abodes of compassion (*sc.* to hungry beings who deserved compassion), like Bodhisattvas.
[V7]	*avyatireka* without negative concomitance	*avīta-rāgo 'yaṁ vaktṛtvāt; yatrâvīta-rāgat vaṁ nâsti, sa vaktā. yathôpala-khaṇḍaayaṁ, iti* (NB 3.133). This [person] is not dispassionate, because he is a speaker (*sc.* talks), [a person], in whom there is no dispassionateness, is a speaker (*sc.* talks), like a bit of stone.	*Avīta-rāgaḥ kaścid vivakṣitaḥ puruṣo, vaktṛtvāt; yaḥ punar vīta-rāgo, na sa vaktā, yathôpala-khaṇḍaḥ.* A particular person in question is not dispassionate, because he is a speaker (*sc.* talks), whoever is dispassionate, however, is not a speaker (sc. does not talk), like a bit of stone.
[V8]	*apradarśita-vyatireka* with unindicated negative concomitance	*anityaḥ śabdaḥ kṛtakatvād, ākāśavat (NB 3.134).* Speech element is impermanent, because it is produced, like space	*anityaḥ śabdaḥ kṛtakatvād, ākāśavat* Speech element is impermanent, because it is produced, like space.
[V9]	*viparīta-vyatireka* with inverted negative concomitance	[**anityaḥ śabdaḥ, kṛtakatvād, yad akṛtakaṁ tan nityaṁ bhavati*, [**ākāśavat*[27]] (NB 3.135). [Speech element is impermanent, because it is produced,] whatever is not produced is permanent, [like space.]	[**anityaḥ śabdaḥ, kṛtakatvād, yad akṛtakaṁ tan nityaṁ bhavati, yathākâśam.* Speech element is impermanent, because it is produced, whatever is not produced is permanent, like space.

As far similarities in wording in both texts are concerned, the exceptions, that is, passages where Siddharṣigaṇi does not follow in his illustrations those of Dharmakīrti at all, can easily be seen in the tables: [S1] *sādhya-vikala-dṛṣṭân-tâbhāsa*, [S2] *sādhana-vikala-dṛṣṭântâbhāsa*, [V1] *sādhyâvyatireki-dṛṣṭântâb-hāsa* and [V2] *sādhanâvyatireki-dṛṣṭântâbhāsa*.

In some other cases Siddharṣigaṇi's classification follows Dharmakīrti's typology in general, but varies in wording so insignificantly that the differences can be altogether discarded. Thus [S7] in the *ananvaya* type of fallacious example and in Siddharṣigaṇi's expression *vivakṣitaḥ puruṣaḥ* is tantamount to Dharmakīrti's *ayam*. That is also the case in [V7] the *avyatireka* type of fallacious example (*ayam = kaścid vivakṣitaḥ puruṣaḥ*), whereas the invariable concomitance is expressed in quite a similar way, barring different position of the negative clause (*yatrâvīta-rāgatvaṁ nâsti sa vaktā, yaḥ punar vīta-rāgo, na sa vaktā*). In [V4] *sandigdha-sādhya-vyatireka- dṛṣṭântâbhāsa* the second predicate *anāptā vā* is interchanged with the subject *kapilâdayaḥ*; the verb forms *upadiṣṭavān* (Dharmakīrti) and *pratyapīpadat* (Siddharṣigaṇi) are identical in meaning, likewise the pronouns *sa* (Dharmakīrti) and *asau* (Siddharṣigaṇi); the significant difference being the logical reason, that is the realm of supernatural teaching in the invariable concomitance and the example respectively: *avidyamāna-sarva-jñatâptatā-liṅga-bhūta-pramāṇâtiśaya-śāsanatvāt, jyotir-jñānâdikam, vardhamānâdiḥ* (Dharmakīrti) and *ārya-satya-catuṣṭayâpratyapīpadakatvāt, śauddhôdaniḥ* (Siddharṣigaṇi). In [V5] *sandigdha-sādhana-vyatireka-dṛṣṭântâb-hāsa* the negation in the statement of the thesis is expressed either by the particle *na* (Dharmakīrti) or by the alpha-privativum *a-°* (Siddharṣigaṇi), while the compounds *grāhya-vacanaḥ* (Dharmakīrti) and *°-ādeya-vākyaḥ* (Siddharṣigaṇi) are identical in meaning; the only difference in the expression of the invariable concomitance is the number, namely plural *ye… te* (Dharmakīrti) and singular *yaḥ… sa* (Siddharṣigaṇi); Siddharṣigaṇi does omit the phrase *trayīvidā brāhmaṇena*; the only significant difference being the example *gautamâdayo dharma-śastrāṇāṁ praṇetāraḥ* (Dharmakīrti) and *sugataḥ* (Siddharṣigaṇi). In [V9] the *viparīta-vyatireka* type the example is indicated either by the suffix *°-vat* (Dharmakīrti) or by relative indeclinable *yathā* (Siddharṣigaṇi).

In two instances the similarities in Dharmakīrti's and Siddharṣigaṇi's formulations are partial, thus in [S3] *sādhya-sādhana-vikala-dṛṣṭântâbhāsa* and in [S4] *sandigdha-sādhya-dharma-dṛṣṭântâbhāsa* only the example is identical, namely *ghaṭavat* and *rathyā-puruṣavat*, respectively, and the compound element *°-rāga-°* and pronoun *ayam* in [S4]. In [V3] *sādhya-sādhanâvyatireki-dṛṣṭântâbhāsa* the subject of the thesis *śabdaḥ* is the same, whereas the predicate *nitya* (or *nitya-°*) partly overlaps. In [V6] *sandigdha-sādhya-sādhana-vyatireka-dṛṣṭântâbhāsa* only the theses of Dharmakīrti and Siddharṣigaṇi are identical, the negations being expressed either by the alpha-privativum *a-°* (Dharmakīrti) or by the particle *na* (Siddharṣigaṇi).

The large number of similarities or identical formulations alone is so ample that it leaves no doubt as regards the indebtedness of Siddharṣigaṇi to Dharmakīrti in this respect. That is the first point I wished to make: Dharmakīrti's typology has been practically accepted by NAV *en bloc*. A solitary case of parallelism in choosing illustrations of fallacious examples might be claimed to be nothing but coincidental, but the situation when Siddharṣigaṇi's choice of expressions in most cases coincides with that of Dharmakīrti and the eighteenfold division of *dṛṣṭântâbhāsa* is identical in both cases, it can by no means be a matter of coincidence. Further, my thesis is corroborated additionally by the way Siddharṣigaṇi makes the selection of three proof formulas that are not mentioned by Dharmakīrti *in extenso* but in a terse, incomplete form to be supplemented from the context of preceding *sūtra*s, namely [S7], [S9] and [V9]. When we reconstruct the proof formulas to complete formulations (for details see respective notes 22, 23, 27), as intended by Dharmakīrti – that is, [S7] [**rāgâdimān ayaṁ, vaktṛtvād,*] *yathā yo vaktā sa rāgâdimān, iṣṭa-puruṣavat*, [S9] [**anityaḥ śabdaḥ, kṛtakatvāt,*] *yad anityaṁ tat kṛtakam* [**ghaṭavat*], [V9] [**anityaḥ śabdaḥ, kṛtakatvāt,*] *yad akṛtakaṁ tan nityaṁ bhavati*, [**ākāśavat*] – it turns out that they correspond virtually in every detail to the examples given by Siddharṣigaṇi.

There is at least one more reason to believe that Siddharṣigaṇi follows Dharmakīrti in his typology. Commenting upon [V4] he classifies the *sandigdha-sādhya-vyatireka* type as reducible, on extra-logical grounds, to be exact, to [V1] the *sādhyâvyatirekin* variety. The only reason for singling it out as a separate variety is the need to take into consideration the opinion of some people 'lacking the recognition' of certain substantial facts, to whom a particular case of a fallacious example lacking negative concomitance with the probandum 'appears to be [the fallacious example] in which negative concomitance with the probandum is doubtful'.[28] As a commentator, he was obviously restrained by the contents of Siddhasena Mahāmati's *Nyāyâvatāra*.[29] However NA 25[30] may be similarly taken to enforce the acceptance of the whole [VA] class (namely [V1], [V2], [V3]) as well as only some types of the [VB] class (namely one or more out of [V4], [V5], [V6]), but not necessarily all of them.[31] As the text stands, NA 25 does not urge one to distinguish separately the *sandigdha-sādhya-vyatireka* type.

Having examined the varieties of fallacious examples as illustrated by Dharmakīrti and Siddharṣigaṇi, we can easily notice a couple of regularities. What is conspicuous is the almost complete absence of any similarity in the [A] sub-category of [S] and [V], namely in [SA] (i.e. [S1], [S2], [S3]) and in [VA] (i.e. [V1], [V2], [V3]). There is a lot of correspondence in the [B] sub-category – namely [SB] (i.e. [S4], [S5], [S6]) and [VB] (i.e. [V4], [V5], [V6]) – in the exposition of both authors, although the comparison betrays certain differences, whereas the [C] sub-category – namely [SC] (i.e. [S7], [S8], [S9]) and [VC] (i.e. [V7], [V8], [V9]) – is altogether identical in NB and in NAV.

The question what factors could account for this evident incongruity in treating Dharmakīrti's sub-categories by Siddharṣigaṇi, if there is any, arises. Why does Siddharṣigaṇi quote certain Dharmakīrti's reasonings *in extenso*, whereas he diverges from the Dharmakīrti's formulations in other cases?

Examining the varieties [S7], [S8], [S9], [V7], [V8] and [V9], Siddharṣigaṇi enters into a polemical discussion with an opponent, nay, he openly disputes the status of a separate fallacious example of the six types, attempting to prove them to be misconceived and faulty solely either due to the defects of the logical reason (*hetu*) or due to the incompetence of the speaker, but not because of their deficient nature being a separate and independent category of the fallacy of the example. The appropriate sections of NAV are introduced respectively as follows:

> And now [a doubt is raised]: "Some [thinkers] have taught an additional triad of fallacies of the example, as well, namely [S7] [the fallacious example] without positive concomitance, [S8] [the fallacious example] with unindicated positive concomitance and [S9] [the fallacious example] with inverted positive concomitance." '[32]

and

> Other [thinkers], inasmuch as they are [such kind of people] who speak without deliberation, have demonstrated three additional fallacies of the example, as well, namely: [V7] [the fallacious example] without negative concomitance, [V8] [the fallacious example] with unindicated negative concomitance and [V9] [the fallacious example] with inverted negative concomitance.[33]

In the light of what has been said on the foregoing pages there can be no doubt regarding the identity of the opponent, referred to by Siddharṣigaṇi as 'others' (*paraiḥ*). To dispute the antagonistic standpoint, in this case Dharmakīrti's tradition, the easiest way would be simply to cite either the rival thesis and the name of its advocate. General practice of philosophic discourse in India, however, has it that it was enough to hear even the incipit alone to identify Dharmakīrti as the adversary. On the other hand, to interpolate or alter in any other way the opponent's statements was not advisable methodologically for a variety of reasons. A modified quotation might no longer be an unambiguous indication of its source and author. Moreover, in case of an interpolated excerpt the opponent could easily ward off possible criticism pointing out that what is actually being refuted is not his own thesis and the criticism is misdirected. These seem to be Siddharṣigaṇi's motives to leave Dharmakīrti's six faulty illustrations ([S7], [S8], [S9], [V7], [V8], [V9]) in an unmodified form.

Having thus pointed out the target of his criticism, this decision did not compel Siddharṣigaṇi to preserve all the remaining original illustrations of Dharmakīrti intact. Still, he did refrain from introducing any changes to the illustrations taken over from NB in a few other cases, namely in the [B] sub-category of the *sādharmya-dṛṣṭântâbhāsa* (i.e. [S4], [S5], [S6]).

These unmodified categories seem to be of considerably less interest for my purposes, whereas most of the remaining cases when Siddharṣigaṇi interpolates or modifies Dharmakīrti's illustrations form a kind of a puzzle, bringing up the question what purpose he had in mind while taking liberties with the original instances of fallacious examples formulated by Dharmakīrti. A closer look at all remaining illustrations in question, namely the [A] sub-category of [S] and [V] (i.e. [S1], [S2], [S3], [V1], [V2], [V3]) as well as the [B] sub-category of [V] (i.e. [V4], [V5], [V6]), reveals that Siddarṣigaṇi's selection of locutions was deliberate, and his decision was motivated by his sectarian bias, in most part against the Buddhist, the only case of his other than anti-Buddhist prejudice being [V3]. Altogether, one may group illustrations of fallacious example, the original reading of which was modified by Siddharṣigaṇi, under three headings:

1 Anti-Buddhist illustrations provoked by Dharmakīrti's own sectarian anti-Jinistic bias ([V4], [V6]),
2 Anti-Buddhist illustrations not provoked by Dharmakīrti ([S1], [S2], [V1], [V2], [V5]) and
3 Doctrinal illustration without anti-Buddhist bias, endorsing a particular Jaina tenet ([S3]).

Startling as it is, there is not even a single case when Siddharṣigaṇi modified Dharmakīrti's original illustration irrelevantly. There are no 'doctrinally neutral' changes: all alterations are prompted directly by Siddharṣigaṇi's sectarian partiality or doctrinal conviction.

My main concern now will be rather to examine the doctrinal, motivational or sociological background of each of such illustrations, not so much their logical relevance or formal structure.

1 Anti-Buddhist illustrations provoked by Dharmakīrti's own sectarian anti-Jinistic bias. As in the case of Dharmakīrti's original illustrations, these are of insolent nature and do not aspire to establish any doctrinal thesis.

[V4] *sandigdha-sādhya-vyatireka*. Dharmakīrti's illustration of fallacious reasoning based on the fallacious example implicitly puts to doubt the omniscience and authority of Jaina Tīrthaṁkāras. In his illustration science of astronomy–astrology represents the distinguishing quality of cognition that should serve as 'the mark of possessing the status of an omniscient or an authoritative person, [which] is not present' (*avidyamāna-sarva-jñatâptatā-liṅga-°*). Accordingly, Kapila and many other thinkers did not teach astrology, as Jaina Tīrthaṅkāras did, hence they could not aspire to possess omniscience or authority. The doubtful element in this fallacious reasoning is whether teaching astrology necessarily entails omniscience and authority: one may be an expert in astrology without being omniscient or authoritative.[34] Even though both the Buddhist and the Jainas would take the thesis ('Kapila and others are neither omniscient nor authoritative persons') to be true, the whole reasoning is claimed by Dharmakīrti to be fallacious, because the proof formula is faulty, insofar as the negative example – which should adduce a contrary example, that is of someone who is both omniscient and authoritative ('Ṛṣabha, Vardhamāna and other [Jinas]') – is in his opinion fallacious, being doubtful. In this clandestine way Dharmakīrti discredits spiritual or/and intellectual accomplishments of Jaina Tīrthaṅkāras. In retaliation, Siddharṣigaṇi employs the same procedure and questions the Buddha's omniscience and authority, explaining that nothing bars the possibility that a charlatan may likewise teach the Four Noble Truths and deliberately deceive people at the same time, without being omniscient or authoritative.[35] Siddharṣigaṇi's formulation of the doubt indicates that the Buddha was indeed neither omniscient nor authoritative.

[V6] *sandigdha-sādhya-sādhana-vyatireka*. Kapila and the Sāṁkhya school remain the scapegoat of the thesis also in this variety of the fallacious example both in NB and NAV. As in the preceding case, Dharmakīrti chooses the Jainas as the whipping boy in his example. His unpronounced assumption, at least something which is liable to doubt, is whether the Tīrthaṅkāras are dispassionate and free of covetousness and greed. Since in this proof formula both probandum and probans are doubtful, Tīrthaṁkāras' moral status is questioned in two ways. Not only their dispassionateness is disputed by the 'doubtful probandum' (in the correct *vyatireka* example this should be *vīta-rāga*), but also the logical reason imputes that the Tīrthaṁkāras are 'endowed with covetousness and greed' (*parigrahâgraha-yoga*). This is particularly offensive to Jainas, or to Digambaras as Dharmottara specifies, who would refrain even from wearing clothes in order to curb all desire for possessions and to manifest total lack of 'covetousness and greed'. Siddharṣigaṇi is quick to repay him tit for tat, and follows Dharmakīrti's method in every detail. He chooses two doctrinal points regarding Bodhisattvas – a Buddhist parallel of Jaina Tīrthaṅkāras – that are as sensitive to the Buddhists as Tīrthaṅkāras' dispassionateness and lack of possessions for the Jainas. To discredit the Buddhist ideal, he cites Bodhisattvas' compassion as an instance of doubtful probans. As if it were not enough, Siddharṣigaṇi adds a second logical reason (benevolence, *dāna*), which seems doubtful to him: 'Bodhisattvas have offered bits of their own flesh to hungry people who deserved compassion'.[36] Siddharṣigaṇi's charge is repeated explicitly in the concluding part of his argument, where he expresses his doubt through the doubtful probans ('[it is not known] whether the [Bodhisattvas] have offered bits of their own flesh to those deserving sympathy or not'), which follows the repetition of the doubtful probandum ('it is not known whether those [Bodhisattvas] are endowed with passion, etc., or whether they are dispassionate').

Therefore the two virtues of Bodhisattvas put to doubt are therefore compassion (*karuṇā*), the foundation of Buddhist ethics, and benevolence or charity (*dāna*), the first of the Perfections (*paramitā*). Siddharṣigaṇi is accurate to link *karuṇā* to *dāna*, following Buddhist tradition:

> The sons of the Buddha have always renounced even their own life [sacrificing it] for [the sake of anyone] who wishes for what is beneficial. And there is no higher disposition than compassion. There is no fruit [more] welcome [than the one] desired. And precisely thanks to this benevolence [they] have elevated the whole humankind to the triple understanding, and furthermore, by acquiring knowledge, [they] established benevolence in the world, which has not known [it previously].[37]

Clearly, not only is compassion (*karuṇā*) the prime motive for benevolence (*dāna*), but also the proper practice of benevolence connotes absolute lack of passion or attachment (*rāga*): ' "That because of which [something] is given [is] benevolence." Verily [that] is [benevolence]. [However, something] can also be given with passion etc., but this is not meant here.'[38]

> A noble person, who is dispassionate, as well as an ordinary man, who is passionate, can give offering in the temple. If a noble person, who is dispassionate, gives offering to other beings – with the exception of [the case when its results are] to be experienced in the present life – in that case the gift is for the sake of others, because this [offering brings] them benefit.[39]

The three virtues – dispassionateness (*vīta-rāgatva*) as the probandum (*sādhya*), as well as compassion (*karuṇā*) and benevolence (*dāna*, the offering of bits of one's own flesh being the proof of, and motivated by, one's compassion) as the probans (*sādhana*) – are therefore related doctrinally and ethically. However, there is nothing that would compel one to enlist all of them together in an instance of a faulty reasoning. The use of double logical reason (*karunā* and *dāna*) is not enforced by the logical structure of the argument itself. On the contrary, it is rather surprising to find such an elaborate, compounded logical reason in the exposition of the fallacies of the example. Why did then Siddharṣigaṇi avail himself of two logical reasons, both of which express doubts about two virtues of Bodhisattvas?

A possible answer would be to match the double logical reason (*sādhana*) employed by Dharmakīrti (*parigraha* and *āgraha*). Astounding as it may be, the fallacious example of the *sandigdha-sādhya-sādhana-vyatireka* type is the only case when Dharmakīrti avails himself of a double logical reason, without any structural or logical need, and similarly the only case when Siddharṣigaṇi's classification has a double logical reason!

2 Anti-Buddhist illustrations not provoked by Dharmakīrti. In this category of sectarian-biased and doctrinally-bound illustrations, Siddharṣigaṇi attempts to indirectly refute a particular Buddhist thesis.

[S1] *sādhya-vikala*. In view of Jaina theory of multiplexity of reality (*anekânta-vāda*), sound could be said to be both permanent and impermanent, depending on the specific point of reference. However, from this perspective practically every assertoric statement could be problematic for the Jainas, therefore it would be difficult to take Dharmakīrti's instance of the faulty proof formula as something provocative. Nevertheless, in his own illustration of the faulty example, Siddharṣigaṇi indirectly disavows the Buddhist well-known doctrine of erroneousness of inference.[40] It is the thesis (*bhrāntam anumānaṁ*) which conveys the criticism, whereas the example (perception as erroneous knowledge) was as unacceptable to the Buddhist as it was to the Jainas. The background for this faulty proof formula is apparently the discussion (NAV 5) of the idea of cognitive validity (*prāmāṇya*), which by definition entails non-erroneousness of our cognition; hence perception and inference have to be non-erroneous, if they are both cognitive criteria. In fact, the thesis of the defective proof formula in question (NAV 24.2 (p. 409): *bhrāntam anumānaṁ, pramāṇatvāt, pratyakṣavat*) is antithetical to NA 5cd: 'This [inference] is non-erroneous because it is a cognitive criterion, just like perception' (*tad abhrāntaṁ pramāṇatvāt samakṣavat*).

[S2] *sādhana-vikala*. Dharmakīrti's reasoning is almost identical to [S1], with the only exception of the 'infinitesimal atom' (*paramâṇu*) that replaces 'action' (*karman*) in [S1]. Similarly, there is nothing explicitly anti-Jinistic in Dharmakīrti's proof formula. Nevertheless, Siddharṣigaṇi takes this opportunity to criticise another Buddhist theory: the doctrine of illusory character of worldly appearance as the contents of consciousness (*vijñāna-vāda*). What we have here – except for the use of *pramāṇa* in place of the usual *pratyaya* – is one of many formulations of the so-called Dreaming Argument: 'The sensation in the waking state is erroneous, because it is a cognitive criterion, like the sensation in a dream' (*jāgrat-saṁvedanaṁ bhrāntaṁ, pramāṇatvāt, svapna-saṁvedanavat*). This argument is commonly ascribed to the Buddhist and we find references to it also in a number of non-Jinistic sources. In its typical formulation (with '*pratyaya*' or '*khyāti*' as the logical reason), the Dreaming Argument is refuted, for instance, by Kumārila,[41] Uddyotakara,[42] Śaṅkara[43] and by Siddharṣigaṇi himself later on.[44] It is important to note that, as it has been shown by Taber (1994: esp. 28–31), the so-called Dreaming Argument has never been expressed by the Buddhist thinkers in the form as it appears in anti-Buddhist works. In subsequent lines[45] Siddharṣigaṇi employs a series of expressions that describe cognitive states (namely *saṁvedana, pramāṇa, pratyaya*) in the context of Dreaming Argument. It is an open question whether one may be justified to conclude that he saw no qualitative difference between these three expressions in this particular context and therefore used them interchangeably as synonyms. In this particular case he seems to employ the term '*pramāṇa*' (in the place of the logical reason) basically in the sense of *pratyaya*. In any standard formulation of the Dreaming Argument (**mithyā stambhâdi-pratyayaḥ pratyayatvāt, yathā svapnâdi-pratyayaḥ*) the term *pratyaya* is used in the sense of a cognition the contents of which corresponds to the object represented in the cognition.[46] In this manner, being factual and reliable, its meaning comes close to Siddharṣigaṇi's use of '*pramāṇa*'. Accordingly, Siddharṣigaṇi's illustration is a criticism, be it indirect, of the Buddhist idealist standpoint expressed in the Dreaming Argument.

[V1] *sādhyâvyatirekin*. The case is rather analogous, doctrinally speaking, to [S1] in the formulation of Siddharṣigaṇi, apart from '*svapna-jñāna*' used as the negative example.[47]

[V2] *sādhanâvyatirekin*. This illustration of fallacious example immediately invokes the famous Yogācāra-Sautrāntika thesis: 'perception is free from conceptual construction'.[48] Inference (*anumāna*), mentioned as the *dṛṣṭânta* of a conceptual mental event which is not a cognitive criterion, does not fulfil the definition of the proper negative example, being a *pramāṇa* itself, namely lacks negative concomitance with the probans. This particular illustration corroborates the Jaina claim that perception that is free from any conceptual construction could eventually be never experienced by any cogniser. That this illustration is not accidental can be seen from the fact Siddharṣigaṇi refutes the Buddhist thesis at length in NAV 4, cf., for example NAV 4.5 (p. 364): *tan na kadācana kalpanâpoḍhatvaṁ pratyakṣasya pramātur api pratīti-gocara-cāritām anubhavati*. – 'So, [to express it metaphorically], freedom from conceptual construction [in the case] of perception never experiences the phenomenon of [itself] turning into the domain of awareness of the cogniser whatsoever.'

[V5] *sandigdha-sādhana-vyatireka*. The contents of this particular instantiation in Dharmakīrti's formulation is of much interest in itself. In the reasoning, the instantiation of the fallacious example are philosophers or law-makers of the Brahmanic tradition, like Gautama, Manu,[49] etc. The doubtful element in this reasoning is whether these Brahmanic thinkers are reliable teachers:

> Here the exemplification based on dissimilarity [can be formulated in the following manner]: 'Those whose statements can be trusted, are not endowed with passion etc., like Gautama and others, who are promulgators of *Dharma-śāstra*.' It is doubtful [here] whether the property of the probans, namely 'being endowed with passion etc.', does not occur in (is excluded from) Gautama and others.[50]

In this manner, Dharmakīrti casts doubt on their dispassionateness and, thereby, intimates that Brahmanical philosophers or law-makers may be subject to passions. The proof formula has the following structure:

1 *rāgâdimān (H) kaścit vivakṣitaḥ puruṣaḥ (P)*: $P \subset H$,
2 *na trayīvidā brāhmaṇena grāhya-vacanaḥ (S) rāgâdimān (H)*: $H \subset S$,
ergo: *na trayīvidā brāhmaṇena grāhya-vacanaḥ (S) kaścit vivakṣitaḥ puruṣaḥ (P)*: $P \subset S$.

The correct negative example (*D*) should be excluded from the probans/logical reason (*sādhana-vyatireka*: $D \subset H'$) as well as excluded from the probandum/the property to be proved (*sādhya-vyatireka*: $D \subset S'$), namely $(D \subset H') \cap (D \subset S')$. One more condition is that in the negative formulation of the example (*D* exemplifying P') occurs is the contraposition of $P' \subset H \subset S$, viz. $S' \subset H' \subset P'$. Thus, $D \subset S'$ would be the condition for $D \subset H'$: 'if a particular person *d* of the *D*-range ($d \in D$) is trustworthy (S'), then this person is dispassionate (H')'. In other words, to distrust the dispassionateness of Gautama, Manu and other Brahmanic law-givers undermines one's trust in their trustworthiness, and *ipso facto* the veracity and authority of the Brahmanic lore is undermined. This unspoken conclusion is openly expressed by Dharmottara in his commentary:[51] it is unreasonable to rely on words of teachers of Brahmanical tradition, like Gautama, Manu, etc. At the same time, Dharmakīrti is claimed by Dharmottara[52] to question the veracity of statements of other Brahmanic philosophers like Kapila, etc. This criticism has also its social dimension: such is the behaviour of most people who rely on the teaching contained in the works on *dharma* by Gautama, Manu, etc.

Dharmakīrti's thesis refers to 'a Brahmin learned in the three Vedas' (*trayīvidā brāhmaṇena*), who is a follower and/or promulgator of the Brahmanic philosophical and religious tradition in everyday life and a local authority. The Brahmin's scepticism regarding his own Brahmanic tradition, as expressed in *Gautama-dharma-sūtra*, *Manu-smṛti* etc., could undermine the tradition itself. The overall picture of the Brahmanical society relying on tradition would be, therefore, that neither proponents of the social-religious tradition (Gautama, Manu, etc.) nor preceptors of philosophical schools (e.g. Kapila) are a suitable source of reliable teaching for a true Brahmin. Dharmakīrti's approach in the argument is therefore clearly anti-Brahmanical and could be a reflection of Buddhist-Brahmanic strife.

Last but not the least, that the opponents' tradition, which one criticises, was at some point not too well-known is attested by Durveka Miśra, who erroneously identifies the Gautama in Dharmakīrti's example with Gautama Akṣapāda: 'Gautama's other name is Akṣapāda, and he is the thinker who is the author of the *Nyāya-sūtra*.'[53] Dharmakīrti himself was clear enough when he mentioned that Gautama is one of promulgators/authors of Law textbooks (*gautamâdayo dharma-śastrāṇāṁ praṇetāraḥ*), and this could by no means be Akṣapāda!

On his part, Siddharṣigaṇi leaves the basic structure of Dharmakīrti's argument intact and replaces Dharmakīrti's original example *gautamâdayo dharma-śastrā ṇāṁ praṇetāraḥ* with *sugataḥ*, the Buddha. *Mutatis mutandis* the Buddha's dispassionateness becomes subject to doubt, and subsequently the whole Buddhist teaching. What is missing from Siddharṣigaṇi's formulation is 'the Brahmin learned in the three Vedas' (*trayīvidā brāhmaṇena*). This could have been a conscious decision to leave this phrase out: the implication would be that any teacher who is not dispassionate should not be trusted, be he a Hindu or Buddhist; and the truly dispassionate are the Jinas. Moreover, the main opponent for the Buddhist was Brahmanic tradition, whereas the Jainas had to protect their identity and distinctiveness not only against Brahmanic conversions but also against Buddhist influence. To confront this wider picture of the society from Jaina perspective, Siddharṣigaṇi apparently extended it by embracing the proponents of Buddhism and including them into the comprehensive framework of unreliable teachers whose dispassionateness was doubtful.

3 Theses prompted by certain other doctrines that stand in opposition to Jaina tenets.

[S3] *sādhya-sādhana-vikala*. In case of Dharmakīrti, the reasoning is a mere repetition of [S1] and [S2], with a new example ('pot' excluded from both the probans 'imperceptible' and the probandum 'impermanent'). Unlike Dharmakīrti, Siddharṣigaṇi takes this opportunity to corroborate indirectly a crucial dogma of the Jainas, namely the omniscience of the Jinas and the Arhants. From Siddharṣigaṇi's contention that '[this example is fallacious] because, [firstly], a pot is existent and, [secondly], it is comprehended through perception, etc.'[54] one could even venture to infer its antithesis, namely *asti sarva-jñaḥ*. An elaborate discussion of all implications of this reasoning, however, would not be relevant to the subject of the present chapter and would exceed its limits.

As it has been pointed out earlier, Siddharṣigaṇi rejects Dharmakīrti's six subvarieties of the fallacious examples (namely [S7], [S8], [S9], [V7], [V8] and [V9]) as irrelevant and wrongly classified due to two reasons: they are either due to the defects of the logical reason (*hetu*) or due to the incompetence of the speaker.[55] Dharmottara, whose influence on Siddharṣigaṇi is clear,[56] was well aware that some fallacies of the example are in fact due to the ineptness of the speaker to communicate his thoughts properly. Commenting on the [S8] *apradarśitânvaya* category, in which positive concomitance is unindicated, he says:

> Hence, the example has as its objective [the demonstration of] the positive concomitance; its object is not explicated by this [example]. And [the example] that is explicated [here as having as] its objective [the demonstration of] similarity [alone] is of no use, therefore this [alleged example] is – inasmuch as [it is] due to the defect of the speaker – the defect of the example, for the speaker has to demonstrate [his thesis] to the opponent in this [example]. Therefore, even though the circumstances are not defective, nevertheless, they are shown in a defective manner. Hence, [this example] in nothing but defective (*sc.* fallacious).'[57]

Similarly on [S9]:

> Therefore also [S9] [the category] with inverted positive concomitance [is defective] because of the speaker's mistake, not because of circumstances. And in [case of] inference for others one has to consider also the defect of the speaker,[58]

on [V8]:

> In this case [of] inference for others the meaning should be understood [directly] from the opponent's [words]. Even if the [argument] is correct in itself, but is formulated incorrectly by the opponent, it [becomes] such (*sc.* defective): as far as it is expressed, it is not correct, [and] as far as it is correct, it is not expressed. And [what is] expressed is the logical reason. Hence either the logical reason or the example [can be] defective because of the speaker's mistake,[59]

and on [V9]:

> And accordingly, also [the category] with inverted negative concomitance is [is defective] because of the speaker's mistake.[60]

His proof that such varieties as [S8], [S9], [V8] and [V9] are varieties of the fallacious example was rather conversational: although there is a deficiency solely on the part of the speaker, nevertheless, they become fallacies of the example in case of inference for others (*parârthânumāna*). As an ardent commentator, however, Dharmottara accepted Dharmakīrti's typology *en bloc*. Perhaps, it was his candid assertion that all these sub-types are due to various defects of the speaker that inspired Siddharṣigaṇi. A separate question is whether Dharmakīrti himself was aware of the fact that some of his fallacious examples could rather be cases of the speaker's incompetence alone?

What role was actually assigned to the example in the proof formula by both parties? Dharmakīrti admits that *dṛṣṭânta* is not an independent member of the proof formula:

> The triple-formed logical reason has been discussed. This alone [can produce] the cognition of an object. Hence there is no separate member of the proof formula called example. That is why no separate definition of this [example] is given, because its meaning is implied [by definition of the logical reason].[61]

Accordingly, the role of *dṛṣṭânta* is to additionally corroborate what the logical reason expresses.[62] Fallacious examples 'fail to demonstrate with certainty the general characteristic of the logical reason, viz. its presence in the homologue only, and [its] complete absence in the heterologue, and its individual characteristic'.[63]

Dharmottara explains that the example is to demonstrate the sphere of application and validity of invariable concomitance:

> The example is the province of a cognitive criterion that establishes the invariable concomitance. In order to demonstrate it, it is said: 'like some other [object].' It means that the example is some other [object] that is the property-possessor of the probandum.[64]

Indeed, in some cases, for example while offering the illustrations of the fallacious examples [S9] and [V9], Dharmakīrti in the end does not mention any illustration expressly! They have to be supplied from the preceding *sūtra*s. Instead, he merely expresses the invariable concomitance ([S9]: *yad anityaṁ tat kṛtakam*, and [V9]: *yad akṛtakaṁ tan nityaṁ bhavati*). Since, for all practical reasons, the invariable concomitance is employed as intrinsic to the example, this explains both the necessity of the example as an integral member of the proof formula and the fact that the example is not independent of the logical reason: the logical reason relies on the invariable concomitance, which is in turn expressed in the example.

Dharmakīrti's and Dharmottara's view contrasts with Siddhasena Mahāmati's and Siddharṣigaṇi's position, who minimised the role of the example merely to 'the recollection of the relation (*sambandha-smaraṇa*), [i.e. the invariable concomitance].'[65] In their opinion the example was not supposed to prove anything nor to corroborate anything; its role was solely auxiliary, of conversational or instructive dimension.[66] Their standpoint was based on a very intuitive and strongly context-bound assumption that there are three kinds of logical proof conceivable, depending on the conversational context.[67] The most elementary and pragmatic, most context-dependant was a one-membered proof formula consisting of 'a mere demonstration of the logical reason' (*hetu-pratipādana-mātraṁ*), provided both parties knew the thesis and remembered the invariable concomitance. That being the case, the pronouncement of an example was not necessary, because the disputants knew what they were talking about. Moreover, the invariable concomitance became intrinsic to the logical reason: the role to demonstrate the invariable concomitance (*vyāpti*) was assigned to the logical reason alone, not to the example. In this way, the example was no longer supposed to demonstrate anything, but simply to make us aware of the context of the argument.

This easily explains why Siddharṣigaṇi disagrees to accept two of the earlier mentioned varieties ([S7][68] and [V7][69]) as fallacious examples and, in the final result, he classifies them as erroneous cases, or wrongly classified cases of fallacious logical reasons. His opinions contradic that of Dharmottara, namely that the example should either demonstrate – or be, at least, directly related to demonstration of – the invariable concomitance.[70] Four remaining sub-types (namely [S8], [S9], [V8] and [V9]) are taken by Siddharṣigaṇi to be caused by the incompetence of the speaker.[71] In his rebuttal of the Buddhist position, he avails himself of a quotation from Dharmakīrti in order to show inconsistencies in Dharmakīrti's view.[72]

The shift in the importance and role of the example, which justifies Siddharṣigaṇi's motives, was an important change in Indian logic for two reasons. First, we have here a case of 'economical principle', or the tendency to simplify the proof formula and get rid of all unnecessary elements.[73] Second, this is an instance of a tendency to general formalisation, to decontextualise reasoning procedures, namely to make them universally binding. Earlier the example was an integral element of the proof formula with a specific role assigned to it, for example to substitute the universal variable x in a general statement 'wherever there is smoke, there is fire, like in the kitchen etc.' (*yatra yatra dhūmas tatra tatrâgnir, yathā mahānasâdau*) with an individual constant p: 'and there is smoke here' (*tathā câtra dhūmaḥ*). Accordingly, any reasoning needed further empirical justification, and the premises were not enough. Here the reasoning becomes independent of its 'external', empirical exemplification, as long as we have two premises entailed by the logical reason: the explicit contents of the logical reason and the relation of *vyāpti* underlying the logical reason. The traditional proof formula (either three-membered or five-membered) of the general form:

(1) 'there is smoke here': $H(p)$,
(2) 'wherever there is smoke, there is fire': $\forall x\ (H(x) \Rightarrow S(x))$,
(3) 'like in the kitchen': $\exists y\ (H(y) \Rightarrow S(y))$,

ergo: 'there is fire here': $S(p)$
becomes:
either

(1′) 'if there is smoke here, there is fire here'; $H(p) \Rightarrow S(p)$,

ergo: 'there is fire here': $S(p)$.
or

(1″) 'if there were no fire here, there would be no smoke here': $\neg S(p) \Rightarrow \neg H(p)$,

ergo: 'there is fire here': $S(p)$.
Siddharṣigaṇi gives an instance of this reasoning, for example

> If the relation is, however, recollected [then the inference consists of only two members], as follows: '[1] There is fire here, [2] because it is explicable due to [the occurrence of] smoke'; [alternatively,] by [applying an example] based on dissimilarity, [one reasons in a negative way:] '[1] There is fire here, [2] because [the occurrence of] smoke would be otherwise inexplicable.'[74]

The earlier is of course an enthymematical reasoning, with one premise unexpressed, either

(2′) 'wherever there is smoke, there is fire': $\forall x\ (H(x) \Rightarrow S(x))$, or

(2″) 'wherever if there were no fire, there would be no smoke': $\forall x \neg S(x) \Rightarrow \neg H(x)$.

This decrease of necessary members of the proof formula was in fact possible, thanks to the new way of defining the characteristic of the logical reason, namely 'inexplicability otherwise' (*anyathânupapannatva, anyathânupapatti*), which can be either formulated in the positive way (*tathôpapatti*) or (*anyathânupapatti*).[75]

To recapitulate, there can be hardly any doubt that Dharmakīrti immensely contributed to Jaina typology of fallacies of the example (*dṛṣṭântâbhāsa*), at least in case of Siddhasena Mahāmati[76] and his commentator, Siddharṣigaṇi. A closer look at the instances of fallacious examples offered by Dharmakīrti and Siddharṣigaṇi reveals that Dharmakīrti inspired his rivals not only in the realm of strictly logical analysis (in our case: classification of fallacies), but also methodologically: how to attack one's own opponents with arguments clad in harmless illustrations of faulty proof formulas, and to express doubts with regard to fundamental doctrines upheld by rival schools. Neither Dharmakīrti nor Siddharṣigaṇi were negligent when it came to the selection of exemplifications of the fallacious example. On the contrary, their most careful choice reveals considerable amount of prejudice against their rivals. In case of Siddharṣigaṇi, his biased position was provoked to a some degree by Dharmakīrti, whose method was discrediting the antagonist he conscientiously follows.

Furthermore, minor differences in Buddhist and Jaina classification of *dṛṣṭântâbhāsa*s, especially [S7], [S8], [S9], [V7], [V8] and [V9], testifies to a different role assigned to the example and the invariable concomitance in the proof formula. This uncovers also an important tendency among Jaina logicians to simplify the structure of the proof formula and to free it from the need of empirical exemplification.

What is also important, the discussion shows that even such eminent thinkers as Dharmakīrti or Siddharṣigaṇi were not above sectarian prejudice and provocation. Being Human, they did not abstain from expressing such not entirely elevated emotions in a concealed way at every available opportunity.

Having said all this, let me come to my initial question: is there any other disadvantage, apart from occasional 'expense of brevity and facility of communication' mentioned already (p. 118), in having a symbolic and formalised language to describe the way we reason and draw inferences? Obviously, had Indian logicians used symbols and a applied formalised language of logic, decidedly less sources would have been left at our disposal to follow the development of certain ideas or to track down historical dependencies and intellectual influences among philosophers. And Dharmakīrti and Siddharṣigaṇi would not have had an additional tool, of extralogical nature, to censure their opponents.

Notes

* An abridged version of this paper first appeared in Balcerowicz (1999), from which Table 6.1 (p. 122) and Table 6.2 (p. 124) are reproduced with variations.

1 Łukasiewicz (1957: § 4).

2 Aristotle employed symbols only in the form of letters as variables that substituted proper names in a broader sense. The first to employ symbolic expressions – following the method of algebra – that represent logical constants, such as connectives, improper symbols (e.g. parentheses, brackets) etc., was Boole (1847).

3 The opening lines of the 'Introduction' in Boole (1847: 3).

4 Boole (1847: 6).

5 Boole (1847: 7).

6 Russell (1917: 51).

7 Boole (1847: 6).

8 Alex 53.28: ἐπὶ στοιχείων τὴν διδασκαλίαν ποιεῖται ὑπὲρ τοῦ ἐνδείξασθαι ἡμῖν, ὅτι οὐ παρὰ τὴν ὕλην γίνεται τὰ συμπεράσματα ἀλλὰ παρὰ τὸ σχῆμα καὶ τὴν τοιαύτην τῶν προτάσεων συμπλοκὴν καὶ τὸν τρόπον οὐ γὰρ ὅτι ἥδε ἡ ὕλη, συνάγεται συλλογιστικῶς τόδε, ἀλλὰ ὅτι ἡ συζυγία τοιαύτη. τὰ οὖν στοιχεῖα τοῦ καθόλου καὶ ἀεὶ ἐπὶ παντὸς τοῦ ληφθέντος τοιοῦτον ἔσεσθαι τὸ συμπέρασμα δεικτικά ἐστιν.

9 Boole (1847: 9–10).

10 Most of these advantageous characteristics enumerated in the text are concurrent with the recapitulation of Bocheński (1954: 50): 'Der Gebrauch von künstlichen Symbolen ist indessen zugleich mit dem Formalismus aufgekommen. Whitehead und Russell rechtfertigen ihn folgendermaßen. (1) In dem Wissenschaften allgemein, besonders aber in der Logik, braucht man Begriffe, die so abstrakt sind, daß man in der Umgangssprache keine entsprechenden Worte dafür findet. Man ist also zu Symbolbildungen genötigt. (2) Die Syntax der Umgangssprache ist zu wenig exakt, ihre Regeln lassen zu viele Ausnahmen zu, als daß man auf dem Gebiet der strengen Wissenschaft gut damit zu operieren vermöchte. Man könnte sich wohl zu helfen suchen, indem man die Worte der Umgangssprache beibehielte und nur die Regeln änderte, aber dann würden doch die Worte durch Assoziationen immer wieder die lockeren Regeln der Alltagssprache nahebringen, und es entstünde Verwirrung. Deshalb ist es besser, eine künstliche Sprache mit eigenen, streng syntaktischen Regeln aufzustellen. (3) Entscheidet man sich für den Gebrauch einer künstlichen Sprache, dann kann man ganz kurze Symbole wählen, etwa einzelne Buchstaben statt ganzer Worte; so werden die Sätze bedeutend kürzer als in der Umgangssprache und wesentlich leichter verständlich. (4) Schließlich sind die meisten Worte der Umgangssprache sehr vieldeutig; so hat z. B. das Wort «ist» wenigstens ein Duzend verschiedene Bedeutungen, die in der Analyse scharf auseinander gehalten werden müssen. Es ist also zweckmäßig, statt solcher Worte künstliche, aber eindeutige Symbole zu brauchen.'

11 VīVy 51: 'The establishing [of a particular cognitive criterion can] by no means [be accomplished] by [the cognitive criterion] itself or by [cognitive criteria] mutually or by other [cognitive criteria].'

12 Bocheński (1980: § 3 (1)).

13 Church (1956: 2–3).

14 NB 3.9: *tathā svabhāva-hetoḥ prayogaḥ—yat sat tat sarvam anityam, yathā* ghaṭâdir *iti śuddhasya svabhāva-hetoḥ prayogaḥ.*

15 Cf. NBṬ *ad loc*: ***yat sad*** *iti sattvam anūdya* ***tat sarvam anityam*** *iti anityatvaṁ vidhīyate. sarvam-grahaṇaṁ ca niyamârtham. sarvam anityam. na kiñcin nânityam.*

> After existence has been called to mind [as something well known] by [words] 'whatever is existent', impermanence [of everything] is taught as something yet unknown (*sc.* to be proved) with [words] 'that every thing is

impermanent'. And the use of [the word] 'everything' has the purpose of circumscription (reference): 'everything is impermanent', [viz.] 'there is nothing that is not impermanent'.

Cf. PVSV 3.28: *tathā hi yat kṛtakaṁ tad anityam ity ukte 'anarthântara-bhāve vyaktam ayam asya svabhāvas...*

16 NB 3.22: *kārya-hetoḥ prayogaḥ – yatra dhūmas tatrâgniḥ. yathā mahānasâdau. asti cêha dhūma iti.*

17 Cf. NB 2.18: *kāryaṁ yathâgnir atra dhūmad iti*; see also PVSV 3.28: *tathā yatra dhumas tatrâgnir iti ukte kāryaṁ dhūmo dahanasya.*

18 PVSV 3.34: *yeṣām upalambhe tal-lakṣaṇam anupalabdhaṁ yad upalabhyate. tatrâikâbhāve 'pi nôpalabhyate. tat tasya kāryaṁ tac ca dhūmo 'sti.*

19 NP 3.3.1 (=NP (1) 5.19–6.14):
tatra sādharmyeṇa tāvad dṛṣṭântâbhāsaḥ pañca-prakāraḥ, tad yathā: [1] *sādhana-dharmâsiddhaḥ,* [2] *sādhya-dharmâsiddhaḥ,* [3] *ubhaya-dharmâsiddhaḥ,* [4] *ananvayaḥ,* [5] *viparītânvayaś cêti // tatra* [1] <u>*sādhana-dharmâsiddho yathā: nityaḥ śabdo 'mūrtatvāt* ***paramâṇuvat****. yad amūrtaṁ tan nityaṁ dṛṣṭaṁ yathā paramâṇuḥ.*</u> *paramâṇau hi sādhyaṁ nityatvam asti sādhana-dharmo 'mūrtatvaṁ nâsti mūrtatvāt paramâṇūnām iti //...*, NP 3.3.2: *vaidharmyeṇâpi dṛṣṭântâbhāsaḥ pañca-prakāraḥ, tad yathā:* [1] *sādhyâvyāvṛttaḥ,* [2] *sādhanâvyāvṛttaḥ,* [3] *ubhayâvyāvṛttaḥ,* [4] *avyatirekaḥ,* [5] *viparīta-vyatirekaś cêti // tatra* [1] <u>*sādhyâvyāvṛtto yathā: nityaḥ śabdo 'mūrtatvāt* ***paramâṇuvat****. yad anityaṁ tan mūrtaṁ dṛṣṭaṁ yathā paramâṇuḥ.*</u> *paramâṇor hi sādhana-dharmo 'mūrtatvaṁ vyāvṛttaṁ mūrtatvāt paramâṇūnām iti. sādhya-dharmo nityatvaṁ na vyāvṛttaṁ nityatvāt paramâṇūnām iti //*

20 NB 3.124: [S1] *sādhya-vikala – nityaḥ śabdo 'mūrtatvāt, karmavat*, and NB 3.129: [V1] *sādhyâvyatirekin – nityaḥ śabdo 'mūrtatvāt, paramâṇuvat.* For details see the tables below and the respective note 24.

21 Another way of looking at the typology of fallacious example could be the following table, where *x* is a variable (*sādhya, sādhana,* and the relation between them both, that is, *anvaya* and *vyatireka*) and φ is a function of *x*:

	*sādhya-*φ	*sādhana-*φ	*sādhya-sādhana-*φ	φ*-anvaya*	φ*-vyatireka*
x-*vikala*	[S1]	[S2]	[S3]		
x-*avyatirekin*	[V1]	[V2]	[V3]		
*sandigdha-*x*-dharma*	[S4]	[S5]	[S6]		
*sandigdha-*x*-vyatireka*	[V4]	[V5]	[V6]		
*a-*x				[S7]	[V7]
*apradarśita-*x				[S8]	[V8]
*viparīta-*x				[S9]	[V9]

22 This (*rāgâdimān ayaṁ vaktṛtvād*) is how the thesis and the logical reason should be reconstructed, first, in view of the explication of the positive concomitance in NB 3.126 itself (*yathā yo vaktā sa rāgâdimān*), and secondly in view of the NBṬ *ad loc*: ***yo vaktêti*** *vaktṛtvam anūdya* ***sa rāgādimān*** *iti rāgâdimattvaṁ vihitaṁ*, wherein the gerund *anūdya* of *anuṛvad* is used in its conventional meaning of 'having called something to mind [as well known]' and the past passive participle *vihita*, a derivative of the verb *viṛdhā*, occurs in its well attested meaning 'introduced as something new; taught as something yet unknown (*sc.* to be proved)'. Also DhPr *ad loc.* (*vaktṛtvasya heto rāgâdimattve sādhye pratiniyamaḥ pratiniyatatvam uktam iti śeṣaḥ*) expresses plainly the logical reason (*hetu: vaktṛtva*) and the probandum (*sādhya: rāgâdimattva*). The significance of the corresponding section of NAV that offers the formulation of the proof formula *in extenso* and tallies with our reconstructed version, should not be underestimated.

23 The formulation of the thesis and the logical reason (*anityaḥ śabdaḥ, kṛtakatvāt*...) alongside with the example (...*ghaṭavat*) are, obviously, to be supplied from the preceding aphorism NB 3.126. The statement *yad anityaṁ tat kṛtakam* is the formulation of the invariable concomitance (*anvaya*) referring to the proof formula in NB 3.126, which is incomplete, inasmuch as it lacks its explicit statement, being the fallacy of *anavayava* type. Cf. also NBṬ *ad loc*: ***yad anityam*** *ity anityatvam anūdya* ***tat kṛtakam*** *iti kṛtakatvaṁ vihitaṁ*. This proof formula bears resemblance (barring the lack of negation in the thesis of *sādhana-dharmâsiddha* type of fallacious example, which is to be supplied further on in the *viparītânvaya* type) to the one found in NP 3.3.1 (=NP (1) 5.19–6.14): *tatra sādharmyeṇa tāvad dṛṣṭântâbhāsaḥ pañca-prakāraḥ, tad yathā:*... [1] *sādhana-dharmâsiddho yathā: nityaḥ śabdo 'mūrtatvāt paramâṇuvat.*... [5] *viparītânvayo yathā: yat kṛtakaṁ tad anityaṁ dṛṣṭam iti vaktavye yad anityaṁ tad kṛtakaṁ dṛṣṭaṁ iti bravīti* // (cf. n. 19). The reconstruction is independently confirmed by the reading found in the corresponding section of NAṬ.

24 The thesis and the logical reason (*nityaḥ śabdo 'mūrtatvāt*) here as well as in the two following cases are to be supplied from the parallel aphorism of NB 3.124. Besides, the reconstruction is directly confirmed by NBṬ: *nityatve śabdasya sādhye hetāv amūrtatve paramāṇu-vaidharmya-dṛṣṭântaḥ sādhyâvyatirekī.*

25 Cf. n. 24.

26 Cf. n. 24.

27 The formulation of the thesis and the logical reason (*anityaḥ śabdaḥ, kṛtakatvāt*...) alongside with the example (... *ākāśavat*) are, beyond doubt, to be supplied from the preceding aphorism: NB 3.134 states incomplete reasoning lacking the explicit formulation of the negative concomitance which NB 3.135 supplies, though in the reversed order. The proof formula formed correctly would run as follows: *anityaḥ śabdaḥ, kṛtakatvāt, yad akṛtakaṁ tan nityaṁ bhavati, ākāśavat*. This proof formula – with the correct formulation of the negative concomitance – occurs in NP 2.2 (=NP (2) 2.2=NP (1) 1.11 13): *tad yathā: anitye śabde sādhye ghaṭâdir anityaḥ sapakṣaḥ // vipakṣo yatra sādhyaṁ nâsti. yan nityaṁ tad akṛtakaṁ dṛṣṭaṁ yathâkāśam iti.* The reconstruction is independently confirmed by the reading found in the corresponding section of NAṬ. Similarly to [S9], also this proof formula bears certain resemblance (barring the lack of negation in the predicate *anitya*) to the one found in NP 3.3.2 (=NP (1) 6.14 7.8): *vaidharmyeṇâpi dṛṣṭântābhāsaḥ pañca-prakāraḥ, tad yathā:* ... [1] *sādhyâvyāvṛtto yathā: nityaḥ śabdo 'mūrtatvāt paramâṇuvat.* ... [5] *viparīta-vyatireko yathā: yad anityaṁ tan mūrtaṁ dṛṣṭam iti vaktavye yan mūrtaṁ tad anityaṁ dṛṣṭam iti bravīti* // (cf. n. 19).

28 NAV 25.2 (p. 414), vide infra n. 35.

29 On the authorship of NA see Balcerowicz (2001b).

30 NA 25:

> *vaidharmyeṇâtra dṛṣṭânta-doṣā nyāya-vid-īritāḥ /*
> *sādhya-sādhana-yugmānām anivṛtteś ca saṁśayāt //*
>
> Defects of the example, here based on dissimilarity, have been proclaimed by the experts in logic [to arise] from non-exclusion of the probandum, of the probans and of their combination and from the [liability to] suspicion [regarding their presence].

31 One would naturally read *anivṛtteḥ* and *saṁśayāt* as dependent on the compound *sādhya-sādhana-yugmānām*. Theoretically speaking, however, the latter could be taken separately. NA 25 is not the only aphorism that is not conclusive. For instance NA 8:

> *dṛṣṭêṣṭâvyāhatād vākyāt paramârthâbhidhāyinaḥ /*
> *tattva-grāhitayôtpannaṁ mānaṁ śābdaṁ prakīrtitam //*
>
> The cognitive criterion – arisen as grasping reality due to a [momentous] sentence, which is accepted as what is experienced, and which is not

> contradicted [as well as] which communicates the ultimate truth – is declared [to be] the verbal knowledge,

is differently construed by the commentators, for example. (1) NAV 8.1 (p. 380): ***dṛṣṭena*** *pramāṇâvalokitenê****ṣṭaḥ*** *pratipādayiṣito 'vyāhato '****nirākṛtaḥ*** *sāmarthyād artho yasmin vākye tat-tathā* ('in which [momentous] sentence the meaning – due to its efficacy – is "accepted," [i.e.,] desired to be demonstrated, as "what is experienced," [i.e.,] as what is seen by [means of] a cognitive criterion, [and which is] "not contradicted," [i.e.,] which is not revoked; that [momentous sentence] is such.'), and (2) NAṭ *ad loc.* (n. 340, p. 222): ***dṛṣṭenêtyâdi****. ayaṁ bhinnâdhikaraṇas tri-pado bahu-vrīhiḥ yadi vêṣṭo 'vyāhato 'rtho yatra tad iṣṭâvyāhataṁ vākyam, tadanu dṛṣṭena pramāṇa-nirṇītenêṣṭâvyāhatam iti tat-puruṣaḥ* ('This is either a *bahu-vrīhi* compound consisting of three words, which has a substance different [from its constituent elements]: "such a statement in which the meaning is accepted [and] not contradicted"; or it [may be understood as] a *tat-puruṣa* compound: "what is accepted [and] not contradicted by what is experienced, [viz.,] by what is determined through a cognitive criterion".').

32 NAV 24.3 (p. 411): *nanu ca parair anyad api dṛṣṭântâbhāsa-trayam uktam, tad yathânanvayo 'pradarśitânvayo viparītânvayaś cêti.*

33 NAV 25.3 (pp. 415–416): *parair apare 'pi dṛṣṭântâbhāsās trayo 'vimṛśya-bhāṣitayā darśitāḥ. tad yathā–avyatireko, 'pradarśita-vyatireko, viparīta-vyatirekaś cêti. te 'smābhir ayuktatvān na darśayitavyāḥ.*

34 NBṬ *ad loc.*:

> *atra pramāṇe vaidharmyôdāharaṇam. yaḥ sarva-jña āpto vā sa jyotir-jñānâdikaṁ sarva-jñatâptatā-liṅga-bhūtam upadiṣṭatvān. yathā ṛṣabho vardhamānaś ca tāvādī yasya sa ṛṣabha-vardhamānâdi-digambarāṇāṁ śāstā sarva-jñaś ca āptaś cêti. tad iha vaidharmyôdāharaṇād ṛṣabhâder asarva-jñatvasyânāptatāyāś ca vyatireko vyāvṛttiḥ saṁdigdhā. yato jyotir-jñānaṁ côpadiśed asarva-jñāś ca bhaved anāptā vā. ko 'tra virodhaḥ? naimittikam etaj jñānaṁ vyabhicāri na sarva-jñatvam anumāpayet.*

35 NAV 25.2 (p. 414):

> *atra vaidharmya-dṛṣṭânto: yaḥ punaḥ sarva-jña āpto vā 'sāv ārya-satya-catuṣṭayaṁ pratyapīpadat, tad yathā–śauddhôdanir iti. ayaṁ ca sādhyâvyatirekī vârya-satya-catuṣṭayasya duḥkha-samudaya-mārga-nirodha-lakṣaṇasya pramāṇa-bādhitatvena tad-bhāṣakasyâsarvajñatânāptatôpapatteḥ. kevalaṁ tan-nirākāraka-pramāṇa-sāmarthya-paryālocana-vikalānāṁ sandigdha-sādhya-vyatirekatayā pratibhātîti tathôpanyastaḥ. tathā hi: yady apy ārya-satya-catuṣṭayaṁ śauddhôdaniḥ pratipāditavāṁs, tathâpi sarva-jñatâptate tasya na siddhyataḥ, tābhyāṁ sahârya-satya-catuṣṭaya-pratipādanasyânyathânupapatty-asiddher, asarva-jñānāptenâpi para-pratāraṇâbhiprāya-pravṛtta-nipuṇa-buddhi-śaṭha-puruṣeṇa tathā-vidha-pratipādanasya kartuṁ śakyatvāt. tasmāc chauddhôdaneḥ sakāśād asarva-jñatānāptatā-lakṣaṇasya sādhyasya vyāvṛttiḥ sandigdhêti sandigdha-sādhya-vyatirekitvam iti.*
>
> Here the example based on dissimilarity [can be formulated in the following manner]: 'Whoever were either an omniscient or an authoritative person, however, he would teach the four noble truths, for instance: Śuddhodana's son (*sc.* the Buddha).' Or else, [one could say as well that] this is [the first variety of fallacious example] lacking negative concomitance with the probandum, because – inasmuch as the four noble truths characterised by the

suffering, [its] origin, the path [leading to its cessation and its] cessation are subverted by cognitive criteria – an advocate of these [four noble truths] is explicable [only] as a non-omniscient and a non-authoritative person. Simply, [the above fallacious example] has been specified as such [an example in which negative concomitance with the probandum is doubtful] because to [people] lacking the recognition of the efficacy of cognitive criteria that revoke these [four noble truths] it appears as [the fallacious example] in which negative concomitance with the probandum is doubtful. For it is as follows: even though Śuddhodana's son (the Buddha) taught the four noble truths, nevertheless his omniscience and his authority are not proved, because there is no proof that teaching the four noble truths is otherwise inexplicable except together with these two, [i.e., omniscience and authority], inasmuch as it is [equally] possible that a cunning person of an adroit mind, who acts with an intention of cheating others, although he is neither omniscient nor authoritative, can impart teaching of that kind. Therefore, non-occurrence of the probandum characterised by non-omniscience and by lack of authority is doubtful in [the case of] Śuddhodana's son (the Buddha); hence [this instance is called an example] in which negative concomitance with the probandum is doubtful.'

It is worth mentioning that, strangely enough, the typical sequence of the four noble truths is here disturbed: Siddharṣigaṇi interchanges the third and fourth noble truths.

36 NAV 25.2 (p. 415):

na vīta-rāgāḥ kapilâdayaḥ, karuṇâspadeṣv apy akaruṇâparīta-cittatayâ-datta-nijaka-māṁsa-śakalatvād iti. atra vaidharmya-dṛṣṭânto: ye punar vīta-rāgās te karuṇâspadeṣu karuṇā-parīta-cittatayā datta-nija-māṁsa-śakalās, tad yathā–bodhi-sattvā iti. atra sādhya-sādhana-dharmayor bodhi-sattvebhyo vyāvṛttiḥ sandigdhā; tat-pratipādaka-pramāṇa-vaikalyān na jñāyate kiṁ te rāgâdimanta uta vīta-rāgāḥ; tathânukampyeṣu kiṁ sva-piśita-khaṇḍāni dattavanto nêti vā. ataḥ sandigdha-sādhya-sādhana-vyatirekitvam iti.

'Kapila and other [thinkers of his kind] are not dispassionate, because – inasmuch as [their] consciousness is not filled with compassion – they have not offered any bits of their own flesh even to the abodes of compassion (*sc.* to hungry beings who deserved compassion).' Here the example based on dissimilarity [can be formulated in the following manner]: 'Those, however, who are dispassionate, inasmuch as their consciousness is filled with compassion, offered bits of their own flesh to the abodes of compassion (*sc.* to hungry beings who deserved compassion), for instance: Bodhisattvas.' Here the non-occurrence of the properties of both the probandum and the probans in the case of Bodhisattvas is doubtful. Because of lack of any cognitive criterion that [could] demonstrate that (*sc.* that passions, etc., are excluded in the case of Bodhisattvas), it is not known whether those [Bodhisattvas] are endowed with passion, etc., or whether they are dispassionate; similarly, [it is not known] whether they have offered bits of their own flesh to those worthy of sympathy, or not. Hence, [this is the fallacious example] in which negative concomitance with [both] the probandum and the probans is doubtful.

37 MSA 16.36 (p. 105.24–27):

tyaktaṁ buddha-sutaiḥ svajīvitam api prāpyârthinaṁ sarvadā /
kāruṇāt paramo na ca pratikṛtir nêṣṭaṁ phalaṁ prārthitaṁ /
dānenâiva ca tena sarva-janatā bodhi-traye ropitā /
dānaṁ jñāna-parigraheṇa ca punar loke 'jñayaṁ sthāpitam //

38 AK 4.113a and AKBh *ad loc.* (p. 740.10 741.2): ***dīyate yena tad danam***, *bhavati sma. rāgâdibhir api dīyate, na câtra tad iṣṭam.*
39 AKBh *ad* AK 4.113ab (p. 741.14 17): ... *avīta-rāgaḥ āryaḥ pṛthag-jano vā vīta-rāgaś caitye dānaṁ dadāti yadâryo vīta-rāgaḥ para-sattvebhyo dānaṁ dadāti sthāpayitvā dṛṣṭa-dharma-vedanīyaṁ tatra dānaṁ pareṣāṁ arthāya, tena teṣāṁ anugrahāt...*
40 Cf. NBṬ 1.5: *bhrāntaṁ hy anumānaṁ sva-pratibhāse 'narthe 'rthâdhyavasāyena pravṛttatvāt*, and PV in II p. 24.6 7:

de ma yin la der [c] *dzin phyir* /
/ [c]*khrul kyaṅ* [c]*brel phyir tshad ma ñid* //
= (PVin II p. 25:) *atasmiṁs tad-graho* bhrāntir api sambandhataḥ pramā*//
[*Tib. *tad-grahāt*?]

41 MŚV (*Nirālambana-vāda*) 23 (p. 159.7–8):

stambhâdi-pratyayo mithyā pratyayatvāt tathā hi yaḥ /
pratyayaḥ sa mṛṣā dṛṣṭaḥ svapnâdipratyayo yathā //

'The cognition of a column etc. is erroneous, because it is a cognitition, for it is as follows: whatever is a cognition it is false, like the cognition in a dream.'

42 NV on NBh 4.2.34 (p. 489.8 9):

ayam jāgrad-avasthôpalabdhānāṁ viṣayāṇāṁ citta-vyatirekiṇām asattve hetuḥ khyātiḥ svapnavad iti na dṛṣṭāntasya sādhya-samatvāt.

This logical reason [to be provided] for [the thesis that] 'things perceived in the state of wakefulness do not exist as [something] different from consciousness do not exist' is 'cognition', like in a dream. – [This argument] is not [correct], because the example is in the same [predicament as] the probandum,

which is the case of the fallacy of the logical reason (*hetvâbhāsa*): the cited example is in need of proof as much as the thesis it is supposed to prove.
43 BSŚBh 2.2.5.29 (p. 476.2 3):

yad uktaṁ bāhyârthâpalāpinā svapnâdivaj jāgarita-gocarā api stambhâdi-pratyayā vinâiva bāhyenârthena bhaveyuḥ pratyayatvâviśeṣād iti tad prativaktavyam.

What has been said by [the Buddhist idealist] who denies [the existence of] external objects: 'Like in a dream etc., also acts of cognition of a column etc. which have as their domain the waking state are possible solely without external thing, because there is no difference [as regards them being] acts of cognition.' – this is [now] refuted.

44 The argument, in its typical wording, reoccurs later in NAV 29.8 (p. 437):

nirālambanāḥ sarve pratyayāḥ, pratyayatvāt, svapna-pratyayavad.

All acts of cognition are void of the objective substratum, because [they are] acts of cognition, like a cognition in dream.

45 For example NAV 24.2 (p. 410):

svapna-saṁvedanasya pramāṇatā-vaikalyāt tat-pratyanīka-jāgrat-pratyayôpa-nipāta-bādhitatvād iti.

'[This example is fallacious] because the sensation in dream is subverted – inasmuch as it lacks the status of cognitive criterion – by the occurrence of the cognition of a person in the waking state, which is opposite to this [sensation in dream].'

46 Cf., for example NAV 29.1 (p. 425): *iha yad yatra pratibhāti, tad eva tad-gocaratayâbhyupagantavyam.*

47 As far as certain structural nuances are concerned, worth pointing out is the fact that Dharmakīrti employs not more than two different instances of reasoning to represent altogether four types of fallacious reasoning, namely he interchanges them as follows: [S1]=[V2] and [S2] = [V1]. Siddharṣigaṇi uses various intermingled illustrations, in which certain 'semi-variables' overlap as follows: the probandum is – with one exception – the same (i.e. *sādhya* of [S1] = *sādhya* of [S2] = *sādhya* of [V1] = '*bhrāntam*'), the logical reason remains unchanged (i.e. *hetu* of [S1] = *hetu* of [S2] = *hetu* of [V1] = *hetu* of [V2] = '*pramāṇatvāt*'), *pakṣa* of [S1] = *pakṣa* of [V1]; = *dṛṣṭânta* of [V2] (*anumānam*); *pakṣa* of [V2] = *dṛṣṭânta* of [S1] (*pratyakṣam*); *dṛṣṭânta* of [S2] = *dṛṣṭânta* of [V1] (*svapna-saṁvedanam*); *sādhya* of [V2] (= *nirvikalpaka*) has no match.

48 See for example PSV 1.k3c-d: *pratyakṣaṁ kalpanâpoḍhaṁ nāma-jāty-ādy-asaṁyuktam*, and NB 4: *tatra pratyakṣaṁ kalpanâpoḍham abhrāntam.* Comp. also the definition found in NP 4.1 (= NP (1) 7.12-3), bearing striking similarity to the one of Diṅnāga, which fact was initially one of the reasons responsible for the wrong attribution of Śaṅkarasvāmin's manual to Diṅnāga: *tatra pratyakṣaṁ kalpanâpoḍhaṁ. yaj jñānam arthe rūpâdau nāma-jāty-ādi-kalpanā-rahitam tad.* See also NBṬ 1.4 (p. 47.1): *bhrāntam hi anumānam svapratibhāse 'narthe 'rthâdhyavasāyena pravṛttatvāt.*

49 This is an addition to Dharmottara, cf. NBṬ *ad loc.*: *gautama ādir yeṣāṁ te tathôktā manv-ādayo dharma-śāstrāṇi smṛtayas teṣāṁ kartāraḥ*...

50 NB 3.131: *atra vaidharmyôdāharaṇaṁ: ye grāhya-vacanā na te rāgâdimantaḥ, tad yathā gautamâdayo dharma-śastrāṇāṁ praṇetāra iti. gautamâdibhyo rāgâdimattvasya sādhana-dharmasya vyāvṛttiḥ sandigdhā.*

51 NBṬ *ad* NB 3.131:

> *gautamâdibhyo rāgâdimattvasya sādhanasya nivṛttiḥ sandigdhā. yady api te grāhya-vacanās trayīvidā* tathâpi kiṁ sarāgā uta vīta-rāgā iti sandehaḥ.*
>
> Even though those [thinkers like Gautama and others] are [such people] whose statements should be trusted by a [Brahmin] learned in the three Vedas, nevertheless there is a doubt whether [they are] passionate or dispassionate?

[*See the critical apparatus in Dalsukhbhai Malvania's edition and the editor's n. 7: '*vidā tathâpi* A.P.H.E.N.'; the main text reads: *vidas tathâpi.*]

52 NBṬ *ad* NB 3.131: *vivakṣita iti kapilâdi dharmī.*

53 DhPr. *ad* NB 3.131 (p. 247.20-21): *gautamo 'kṣapādâpara-nāmā nyāya-sūtrasyâpi praṇetā muniḥ. manur iti smṛti-kāro muniḥ.*

54 NAV 24.2 (p. 410): *ghaṭasya sattvāt pratyakṣâdibhir upalabdhatvāc ca.*

55 [S7] and [V7] are 'the defects of the logical reason alone' (NAV 24.4: *tadânanvayatva-lakṣaṇo na dṛṣṭântasya doṣaḥ, kiṁ tarhi hetor eva*, and NAV 25.3: *tasmād asiddha-pratibandhasya hetor evâyaṁ doṣo, na dṛṣṭântasyêti*). [S8], [S9], [V8] and [V9] 'rise from the defects of the speaker' (NAV 24.4: *vaktṛ-doṣatvāt*, and NAV 25.4: *vaktṛ-doṣa-samutthau*).

56 Dharmottara (*c.*740–800, see Steinkellner-Much (1995: 67)) preceded Siddharṣigaṇi by at least a 100 years (*c.*900), cf. Shastri (1990: 27: ninth/tenth century). Siddharṣigaṇi finished his work on the *Upamiti-bhava-prapañcā-kathā*, on 1st May 906 CE. (Vikrama Saṁvat 962) according to Vaidya (1928: xxi) and Chatterjee (1978: 287).

57 NBṬ 3.126 (pp. 242.6–243.2): *ato 'nvayârtho dṛṣṭântas tad-arthaś cânena nôpapāttaḥ. sādharmyârthaś côpapātto nirupayoga iti vaktṛ-doṣād ayaṁ dṛṣṭânta-doṣaḥ. vaktrā hy atra paraḥ pratipādayitavyaḥ. tato yadi nāma na duṣṭaṁ vastu tathâpi vaktrā duṣṭaṁ darśitam iti duṣṭam eva.*

58 NBṬ 3.127 (p. 244.3-4): *tasmād viparītânvayo 'pi vaktur aparādhāt, na vastutaḥ. parârthânumāne ca vaktur api doṣaś cintyata iti.*

59 NBṬ 3.134 (p. 250.3-5): *iha parârthânumāne parasmād arthaḥ pratipattavyaḥ. sa śuddho 'pi svato yadi pareṇâśuddhaḥ khyāpyate sa tāvad yathā prakāśitas tathā na yuktaḥ. yathā yuktas tathā na prakāśitaḥ. prakāśitaś ca hetuḥ. ato vaktur aparādhād api parârthânumāne hetur dṛṣṭônto vā duṣṭaḥ syād iti.*

60 NBṬ 3.135 (p. 252.9-10): *tathā ca viparīta-vyatireko 'pi vaktur aparādhād duṣṭam.*

61 NB 3.121 (p. 234.1-2): *tri-rūpo hetur uktaḥ. tāvatā cârtha-pratītir iti na pṛthag dṛṣṭânto nāma sādhanâvayavaḥ kaścit. tena nâsya lakṣaṇaṁ pṛthag ucyate gatârthatvāt.*

62 See NB 3.122 (p. 235).

63 NB 3.122 (p. 235): *na hy ebhir dṛṣṭântâbhāsair hetoḥ sāmānya-lakṣaṇaṁ sapakṣa eva sattvaṁ vipakṣe ca sarvatrâsattvam eva niścayena śakyaṁ darśayituṁ viśeṣa-lakṣaṇaṁ ca. tad arthâpatyâiṣāṁ nirāso draṣṭavyaḥ.*

64 NBṬ 3.8 (p. 188.2-3): *vyāpti-sādhanasya pramāṇasya viṣayo dṛṣṭântaḥ. tam eva darśayitum āha – yathânya iti. sādhya-dharmiṇo 'nyo dṛṣṭânta ity arthaḥ.*

65 NA 18:

> *sādhya-sādhanayor vyāptir yatra niścīyate-tarām /*
> *sādharmyeṇa sa dṛṣṭântaḥ sambandha-smaraṇān mataḥ //*

66 See NAV 18.1 (p. 398):

> *ayaṁ câvismṛta-pratibandhe prativādini na prayoktavya ity āha:* **sambandha-smaraṇād** *iti, lyab-lope pañcamī, prāg-gṛhīta-vismṛta-sambandha-smaraṇam adhikṛtya… gṛhīte ca pratibandhe smaryamāṇe kevalaṁ hetur darśanīyaḥ, tāvatâiva bubhutsitârtha-siddher dṛṣṭânto na vācyo, vaiyarthyāt. yadā tu gṛhīto ''pi vismṛtaḥ kathañcit sambandhas, tadā tat-smaraṇârthaṁ dṛṣṭântaḥ kathyate.*
>
> Subsequently, [having in mind] that this [example] does not have to be pronounced for the disputant who has not forgotten the invariable connection, [the author] says: **'because of the recollection of the relation,'** [wherein] the ablative is used in the place of the gerund, [i.e.,] having taken account of the recollection of the relation, which has been grasped previously and [have been afterwards] forgotten; this [example] **'is known as'**, [i.e.,] intended, by logicians, not in any other case. For when a [person] to be taught does not know the relation characterised by the property [on the part of the probans] of being inseparably connected with the probandum even now, then he should be made grasp the relation by [means of] a cognitive criterion, not merely by an example, for just by seeing [two things] together in some cases it is not proved that one [of them] does not occur without the other one in all cases, because [that would have] too far-reaching consequences. And if the invariable connection, which has been grasped [before], is being recollected, then simply the logical reason has to be shown; since an object which one wants to cognise is proved by that much only, an example does not have to be stated, because it is purposeless. But when the relation – even though it has been grasped [before] – has somehow been forgotten, then an example is mentioned with the purpose of its recollection, [i.e., in order to remind the opponent of the invariable concomitance].

The same remark applies to both kinds (positive and negative) of the example, cf. NAV 19.1 (p. 400): ***yatra*** *kvacid* ***dṛṣṭânte*** *sa* ***vaidharmyeṇa*** *bhavatîti-śabdena sambandha-smaraṇād iti.*

67 NAV 20.1 (p. 401):

tat-siddhau tata eva sādhya-siddher akiñcit-karī dṛṣṭāntôdāhṛtir iti ***nyāya-vido*** *nyāya-vidvāṁso* ***vidur*** *avabudhyanta iti. iha ca prakaraṇe śeṣâvayavānām upanaya-nigamana-śuddhi-pañcaka-lakṣaṇānāṁ saṅkṣipta-ruci-sattvânugraha-paratvād asya, yady api sākṣāl lakṣaṇaṁ nôktaṁ, tathâpy ata eva pratipāditâvayava-trayād buddhimadbhir unneyaṁ; yato 'vayavâpekṣayā jaghanya-madhyamôtkṛṣṭās tisraḥ kathā bhavanti. tatra hetu-pratipādana-mātraṁ jaghanyā. dvy-ādy-avayava-nivedanaṁ madhyamā. sampūrṇa-daśāvayava-kathanam utkṛṣṭā. tatrêha madhyamāyāḥ sākṣāt kathanena jaghanyôtkṛṣṭe arthataḥ sūcayati, tad-sadbhāvasya pramāṇa-siddhatvād iti.*

'**Experts in logic**', [i.e.,] specialists in logic, '**have recognised**' [i.e.,] they know, that when this [invariable connection] has been proved, an exemplification by [adducing] an example is ineffective, inasmuch as the probandum is [already] proved by this [invariable concomitance]. And even though the definition of the remaining members [of a proof formula] characterised by application, conclusion and the five clearances have not been taught directly here in this treatise, inasmuch as this [treatise] aims at the advantage of [human] beings who delight in concise [form], nevertheless [respective definition] can be deduced by the learned from this very triad of the members of the proof formula demonstrated [above], because there are [eventually] three kinds of discourse as regards the [number of] members of the proof formula, viz. lower, intermediate and superior. Out of them, the lower one is a mere demonstration of the logical reason; the intermediate one is a proclamation of two or more [but not all] members of the proof formula; the superior [discourse] is the mention of complete ten members of the proof formula. Regarding these [varieties of the discourse], by the direct mention of the intermediate [discourse] here [in this treatise the author] indicates both the lower and the superior [varieties of the discourse] by implication, because their presence can be proved by cognitive criterion.

68 NAV 24.4 (p. 412):

yadi hi dṛṣṭânta-balena vyāptiḥ sādhya-sādhanayoḥ pratipādyeta, tataḥ syād anavayo dṛṣṭântâbhāsaḥ, sva-kāryâkaraṇād, yadā tu pūrva-pravṛtta-sambandha-grāhi-pramāṇa-gocara-smaraṇa-sampādanârthaṁ dṛṣṭântôdāhṛtir iti sthitaṁ, tadânanvayatva-lakṣaṇo na dṛṣṭântasya doṣaḥ, kiṁ tarhi hetor eva, pratibandhasyâdyâpi pramāṇenâpratiṣṭhitatvāt, pratibandhâbhāve cânvayâsiddheḥ. na ca hetu-doṣo 'pi dṛṣṭânte vācyo, 'tiprasaṅgād iti.

For if the invariable concomitance between the probandum and the probans could be demonstrated by the force of an example, then [the example] without positive concomitance would be [indeed] a fallacy of the example, because it would not produce its effect, [namely it would not demonstrate the invariable concomitance between the probandum and the probans]. But when it is established that an exemplification by [adducing] an example serves the purpose of producing a recollection, whose domain is a cognitive criterion grasping the relation that has occurred before, then the characteristic of being without positive concomitance is not the defect of example, but of the logical reason itself, because the invariable connection has not been determined by cognitive criterion until now; and if there is no invariable connection, then positive concomitance is not proved [either]. And the defect of the logical reason should not be taught in [the case of] (*sc.* should not be blamed on) the example, because that would have too far-reaching consequences.

69 NAV 25.3 (p. 416):

> *ayuktaś câyaṁ vaktum, avyatirekitāyā hetu-doṣatvāt. yadi hi dṛṣṭânta-balenaîva vyatirekaḥ pratipādyeta, tadā tathā-vidha-sāmarthya-vikalasya tad-ābhāsatā yujyeta, na câitad asti, prāk-pravṛtta-sambandha-grahaṇa-pravaṇa-pramāṇa-gocara-smaraṇa-sampādan ārthaṁ dṛṣṭântôpādānāt. na hy ekatra yo yad-abhāve na dṛṣṭaḥ, sa tad-abhāve na bhavatîti pratibandha-grāhi-pramāṇa-vyatirekeṇa sidhyaty, atiprasaṅgāt. tasmād asiddha-pratibandhasya hetor evâyaṁ doṣo, na dṛṣṭântasyêti.*
>
> It is improper to say so, because if there were no negative concomitance, then that would be the defect of the logical reason. For if negative concomitance could be demonstrated by the force of the example alone, then [an example] lacking the efficacy of this kind, [viz. incapable of demonstrating negative concomitance], would be justified as the fallacy of this [example], but that is not the case, because the example is mentioned in order to produce a recollection the domain of which is a cognitive criterion – disposed towards grasping the relation [between the probandum, the probans and the logical reason] – that occurred previously. For [the example] is not established without a cognitive criterion that grasps the invariable connection [in the form]: 'If [at least] in one case, when *y* is absent, *x* is not seen, then *x* does not occur, when *y* is absent,' because that would have too far-reaching consequences. Therefore, that is the defect of the logical reason, alone, whose invariable connection is not proved, not [the defect] of the example.

70 NBṬ 3.8 (p. 188.2): *vyāpti-sādhanasya pramāṇasya viṣayo dṛṣṭântaḥ.*– 'The logical reason is the province of cognitive criterion that establishes the invariable concomitance'. Cf. also NBṬ 3.126 (p. 242.6): *ato 'nvayôrtho dṛṣṭântas.*

71 Re. [S8] and [S9], cf. NAV 24.4 (p. 412):

> *tathâpradarśitânvaya-viparītânvayāv api na dṛṣṭântâbhāsatāḥ svī-kuruto, 'nvayâpradarśanasya viparyastânvaya-pradarśanasya ca vaktṛ-doṣatvāt, tad-doṣa-dvareṇâpi dṛṣṭântâbhāsa-pratipādane tad-iyattā viśīryeta, vaktṛ-doṣāṇām ānantyāt.*
>
> Similarly, both [the example] with unindicated positive concomitance and [the example] with inverted positive concomitance do not secure the status of the fallacy of the logical reason, because not indicating positive concomitance as well as indicating positive concomitance as inverted are the defects [on the part] of the speaker. If the demonstration of fallacies of the logical reason [were carried out] by taking into account the defects of this [speaker] as well, the limited number of those [fallacies] would be shattered, because defects of the speaker [can be] infinite.

Similarly, re. [V8] and [V9], see NAV 25.4 (p. 417): *vyatirekâpradarśanaṁ viparīta-vyatireka-pradarśanaṁ ca na vastuno doṣaḥ, kiṁ tarhi vacana-kuśalatā-vikalasyâb-hidhāyakasya.*

72 PVSV, p. 186.19 (= Gnoli: 18.11) on PV 3.27cd found in NAV 25.4 (p. 417):

> *kiṁ ca, yeṣāṁ bhavatām ado darśanaṁ: yad uta svârthānumāna-kāle svayaṁ hetu-darśana-mātrāt sādhya-pratīteḥ parârthânumânâvasare 'pi hetu-pratipādanam eva kartavyaṁ "viduṣāṁ vācyo hetur eva hi kevala" iti-vacanāt teṣāṁ "kṛtakatvād" itîyatā hetûpanyāsenaîva sisādhayiṣita-sādhya-siddheḥ samasta-dṛṣṭântâbhāsa-varṇanam api pūrvâpara-vyāhata-vacana-racanā-cāturyam āvir-bhāvayati. āsātāṁ tāvad etau, dṛṣṭântasya sādhanâvayavatvenânabhyupagamât.*

Furthermore, yours is that view – namely: inasmuch as, in the time of the inference for oneself, one knows the probandum himself merely by seeing the logical reason, also at the point of the inference for others, only the demonstration of the logical reason should be carried out – on account of the following utterance: '[ ] since for scholars simply the logical reason alone is to be stated' [pronounced by you] whose description of all fallacies of the example, as well – inasmuch as the probandum intended to be proved can be proved by specifying the logical reason alone [in the form of] nothing more than: 'because it is produced' – demonstrates [your] aptitude for formulations in which antecedent and subsequent statements are contradicted [by each other]. Let us leave therefore these two [fallacious examples [V8] and [V9]] alone, because the example is not accepted as a part of the probans.

73 See Balcerowicz (2001a: xx–xxi).

74 NAV 11.1: [*sādharmyeṇa:*] *agnir atra dhūmôpapatter; vaidharmyeṇa: agnir atra, anyathā dhūmânupapatteḥ.*

75 I discuss it at length in Balcerowicz (2003).

76 In Balcerowicz (2001a: esp. xii–xxx), I discuss Dharmakīrti's influence on the NA at length.

Bibliography

AK = Vasubandhu: *Abhidharma-kośa. Abhidharmakośa and Bhāṣya of ācārya Vasubandhu with Sphuṭārthā Commentary of ācārya Yaśomitra.* Critically edited by Svāmī Dvārikādās Śāstri. *Bauddha Bharati Series* 5, 6, 7, 9, Varanasi, 1970: Part I (1 and 2 *Kośasthāna*); 1971: Part II (3 and 4 *Kośasthāna*); 1972: Part III (5 and 6 *Kośasthāna*); 1973: Part IV (7 and 8 *Kośasthāna*) (Reprinted: Vārāṇasī 1987).

AKBh = Vasubandhu: *Abhidharma-kośa-bhāṣya*. See: AK.

Alex = Alexander: *In Aristotelis Analyticorum Priorum Librum I Commentarium*, M. Wallies, Berolini 1883.

Balcerowicz, Piotr 1999 'Taxonomic Approach to *dṛṣṭântâbhāsa in Nyāya-bindu* and in Siddharṣigaṇi's *Nyāyâvatāra vivṛti* – Dharmakīrti's Typology and the Jaina Criticism Thereof.' In: *Dharmakīrti's Thought and its Impact on Indian and Tibetan Philosophy* (Proceedings of the Third International Dharmakīrti Conference – Hiroshima, November 4–6, 1997), ed. by Shoryu Katsura, Verlag der Österreichischen Akademie der Wissenschaften: *Beiträge zur Kultur- und Geistesgeschichte Asiens* Nr. 32, Wien 1999: 1–16.

Balcerowicz, Piotr 2001a *Jaina Epistemology in Historical and Comparative Perspective – A Critical Edition and an Annotated Translation of Siddhasena Divākara's Nyāyâvatāra, Siddharṣigaṇin's Nyāyâvatāra-vivṛti And Devabhadrasūri's Nyāyâvatāra-ṭippana.* Volume I & II. *Alt- und Neu-Indische Studien* 53, 1 and 53, 2. Franz Steiner Verlag, Stuttgart 2001.

Balcerowicz, Piotr 2001b 'Two Siddhasenas and the Authorship of the *Nyāyâvatāra* and the *Saṁmati-tarka-prakaraṇa,' Journal of Indian Philosophy* 29/3 (2001) 351–578.

Balcerowicz, Piotr 2003 'Is "Inexplicability Otherwise" (*anyathānupapatti*) Otherwise Inexplicable?', *Journal of Indian Philosophy* 1–3 (2003) 343–380 (Proceedings of the International Seminar 'Argument and Reason in Indian Logic' 20–24 June, 2001 – Kazimierz Dolny, Poland).

Bocheński, I. M. 1954 *Die Zeitgenössischen Denkmethoden*, Zweite Auflage, Dalp-Taschenbücher Band 304, Lehnen Verlag München, 1959 [First edition: Bern 1954].

Bocheński, I. M. 1980 'The General Sense and Character of Modern Logic' in *Modern Logic – A Survey*; (ed.) by E. Agazzi, D. Reidel Publishing Company, Dordrecht 1980: 3–14.

Boole, George 1847 *The Mathematical Analysis of Logic*; Cambridge – London 1847.

BSŚBh = Śaṅkara: *Brahma-sūtra-śāṅkara-bhāṣya*. Ed. with the commentaries: *Bhāṣya-ratna-prabha* of Govindānanda, *Bhāmatī* of Vācaspatimiśra, *Nyāya-nirṇaya* of Ānandagiri; ed. by J. L. Shastri, Motilal Banarsidass, Delhi 1980 (Reprinted: Delhi 1988).

Chatterjee, Asim Kumar 1978 *A Comprehensive History of Jainism: Up to 1000 A.D.*, Firma KLM Private Limited, Calcutta 1978.

Church, Alonzo 1956 *Introduction to Mathematical Logic*; Vol. 1, Princeton University Press, Princeton, NJ (1956).

DhPr = Durveka Miśra: *Dharmôttara-pradīpa* [being a sub-commentary on Dharmottara's *Nyāyabinduṭīkā*, being a commentary on Dharmakīrti's *Nyāyabindu*], ed. by Pt Dalsukhbhai Malvania, *Tibetan Sanskrit Works Series* 2, Kashi Prasad Jayaswal Research Institute, Patna 1971.

Łukasiewicz, Jan 1957 *Aristotle's Syllogistic from the Standpoint of Modern Formal Logic*, Second Enlarged Edition, Clarendon Press, Oxford 1957 (First edition: 1951).

MSA = Asaṅga (Maitreyanātha?): *Mahāyāna-sūtrâlaṅkāra. Mahāyāna-sūtrâlaṅkāra of Asaṅga*. Ed. by S. Bagchi, *Buddhist Sanskrit Texts* 13, The Mithila Institute of Post-Graduate Studies and Research in Sanskrit Learning, Darbhanga 1970.

MŚV = Kumārila Bhaṭṭa: *Mīmāṁsā-śloka-vārtika*, with the Commentary *Nyāya-ratnâkara*, of Pārthasārathi Miśra, ed by. Rāmaśāstri Tailaṅga, *Chowkhamba Sanskrit Series* 3, Benares 1889–1899.

NA = Siddhasena Mahāmati: *Nyāyâvatāra*. See: Balcerowicz (2001a).

NAV = Siddharṣigaṇi: *Nyāyâvatāra-vivṛti*. See: Balcerowicz (2001a).

NB = Dharmakīrti: *Nyāya-bindu*. See: DhPr.

NBh = Vātsyāyana: *Nyāya-bhāṣya*. See: NV.

NBṬ = Dharmottara: *Nyāya-bindu-ṭīkā*; See: DhPr.

NP = Śaṅkarasvāmin: *Nyāya-praveśa*. Revised critical edition in: Piotr Balcerowicz: 'Śaṅkarasvāmin: *Nyāya-praveśa* – "Introduction to Logic" ("Wprowadzenie w logike")', Part One: *I. Polish Translation, II. Sanskrit Text, III. Notes § I, Abbreviations and Bibliography; Studia Indologiczne* 2 (1995) 39–87: 72–77.

NP (1) = Śaṅkarasvāmin: *Nyāya-praveśa. Part One: The Nyāya-praveśa – Sanskrit Text with Commentaries*, ed. by A. B. Dhruva, *Gaekwad's Oriental Series* 38, Baroda 1930.

NP (2) = Śaṅkarasvāmin: *Nyāya-praveśa*. In: Musashi Tachikawa: 'A Sixth-Century Manual of Indian Logic (A Translation of the Nyāyapraveśa)', *Journal of Indian Philosophy* 1 (1971) 11–45 [Dordrecht].

NV = Bhāradvāja Uddyotakara: *Nyāya-vārttika. Nyāyabhāṣyavārttika of Bhāradvāja Uddyotakara*. Ed. by Anantal Thakur. *Nyāyacaturgranthikā* Vol. I, Indian Council of Philosophical Research, New Delhi 1997.

PSV = Diṅnāga: *Pramāṇa-samuccaya-vṛtti* [Chapter I]. In: Masaaki Hattori: *Dignāga, On Perception, being the Pratyakṣapariccheda of Dignāga's Pramāṇasamuccaya*, from the Sanskrit fragments and Tibetan versions. *Harvard Oriental Series 47*, Harvard University Press, Cambridge, MA 1968.

PV = Dharmakīrti: *Pramāṇa-vārttika*. (1) Ram Chandra Pandeya (ed.): *The Pramāṇa-vārttikam of Ācārya Dharmakīrti with Sub-commentaries: Svôpajña-vṛtti of the Author and Pramāṇa-vārttika-vṛtti of Manorathanandin*. Motilal Banarsidass, Delhi 1989. (2) Tripiṭakāchārya Rāhula Sāṅkṛityāyana (ed.): *Pramāṇavārttikabhāshyam or*

Vārtikālaṅkāraḥ of Prajñākaragupta (being a commentary on Dharmakīrti's Pramāṇavārttika). Kashi Prasad Jayaswal Research Institute, Patna 1953. (3) Raniero Gnoli (ed.): *The Pramāṇavārttikam of Dharmakīrti. The First Chapter with the Autocommentary*. Instituto Italiano per il Medio ed Estremo Oriente. *Serie Orientale Roma* XXIII, Roma 1960.

PVin II = *Dharmakīrti's Pramāṇāviniścayaḥ, 2. Kapitel: Svārthānumānam*. Tib. Text und Sanskrittexte von E. Steinkellner. Veröffentlichungen der Kommission für Sprachen und Kulturen Süd- und Ostasiens 12, Österreichische Akademie der Wissenschaften, Wien 1973.

PVSV = Dharmakīrti: *Pramāṇa-vārttika-svôpajña-vṛtti*. See: PV (1).

Russell, Bertrand 1917 'The Study of Mathematics' in *Mysticism and Logic and other Essays*. Third impression, Unwin Books, London 1970: 48–58. (First edition: 1917).

Shasti, Indra Chandra 1990 *Jaina Epistemology*. P. V. Research Series 50, Vārāṇasī 1990.

Steinkellner, Ernst; Much, Michael Torsten 1995 *Texte der erkenntistheoretischen Schule des Buddhismus (Systematic Survey of Buddhist Sanskrit Literature) II*, Abhandlungen der Akademie der Wissenschaften in Göttingen, Vandenhoeck & Ruprecht in Göttingen 1995.

Taber, A. John 1994 'Kumārila's Refutation of the Dreaming Argument: The *Nirālambanavāda-adhikaraṇa*', in *Studies in Mīmāṁsā – Dr. Mandan Mishra Felicitation Volume*, ed. R. C. Dwivedi, Motilal Banarasidass, Delhi 1994: 27–52.

Vaidya, P. L. 1928 'Introduction' to *Nyāyâvatāra of Siddhasena Divākara with The Vivṛti of Siddharṣigaṇi and with The Ṭippana of Devabhadra*, ed. by, Shri Jain Shwetamber Conference, Bombay 1928: vii–xliii.

Vīvy = Nāgārjuna: *Vigraha-vyāvartanī. The Dialectical Method of Nāgārjuna (Vigraha-vyāvartanṛ)*, Skt. text ed. by E. H. Johnston and Arnold Kunst. Transl. by Kamaleswar Bhattacharya, Motilal Banarsidass, Delhi 1978. (Second edition: 1986).

Part III

ROLE MODELS FOR WOMEN AND FEMALE IDENTITY

7

RESTRICTIONS AND PROTECTION

Female Jain renouncers

Sherry E. Fohr

Once the nun[1] Satī Rājīmatī was caught in the rain and took refuge in a cave. She took off her soaked clothing in order to dry it, not knowing that there was someone else in the cave with her. The monk Rathanemi was also in the cave and had seen her naked. When she realized he was there, she became frightened and tried to hide her body, but he had already succumbed to sensual desire and started to proposition her. She warned him to control himself and to maintain his practice of celibacy. Rathanemi did so and they both eventually achieved *mokṣa* (liberation).[2]

There are many such Jain narratives extolling the chastity of women; they are the *satī*-narratives, narratives about "virtuous women." When I went to India to ascertain why there are more nuns than monks in the Jain religion I found that the value of female chastity was arguably the most important factor involved.[3] I once talked about this ancient story of Satī Rājīmatī with the Gujarati Śvetāmbar Sādhvī (nun) Akṣayānanda Śrī Jī of the Mūrtipūjak Tapā Gacch[4] while I was studying with her and a group of nuns in Ahmedabad, Gujarat. According to her this cave incident, involving Satī Rajīmatī, indicates the need for monks and nuns to be kept separate.

> "Men and women should remain separate because it is people's nature to have lustful thoughts," she said. "You cannot stray from the vow of celibacy. There are times when the other vows may not be followed, but not this vow."
>
> "In your religion (*dharm*), do monks and nuns remain separated?" I asked, knowing that this was common practice.
>
> "Yes, they do not live together in one place, and if they sit in one hall, they sit separately."
>
> "And this is because it is difficult to remain strong in one's practice of celibacy?"
>
> "Yes," she replied.[5]

Although there are differences between the Śvetāmbar and Digambar sects in this regard, the rules that limit and regulate Jain renouncers' interactions with members of the opposite gender are so strict that most Jain monks and nuns live largely separate lives. This is not to claim that monks and nuns never meet with each other, but their contact is minimal, especially in the Śvetāmbar sect.[6]

Digambar monks and nuns have more contact with each other, but this contact is limited. For example, Digambar monks have studied under the nun-scholar Gaṇinī Jñānamatī Mātā Jī. One was living at her *āśram* for this purpose when I was studying with nuns there. Also, Zydenbos (1999: 295, 297) has reported that while Digambar monks and nuns previously followed the rule that they should travel separately, they now sometimes travel and stay in the same area together. Indeed, while I was conducting research I heard of Digambar nuns who traveled with an *ācārya* (male head of a Jain sect or sub-sect/group) in Madhya Pradesh. So while a few monks and nuns may travel together or stay in the same area, it seems that it is more common for Digambars to do so. However, when Digambar monks and nuns do travel together there are still rules by which they should abide and they therefore reside in separate buildings (Zydenbos 1999: 297). But simply traveling together, Zydenbos states, "inevitably draws ridicule from malicious non-Jaina onlookers," which indicates the extent to which such contact is problematic in India in general. Celibacy is difficult and transgressing are considered egregious. Sādhvī Akṣayānanda Śrī Jī, who told me the story of Satī Rajīmatī, once said to me, "If the other vows are broken, they can be fixed, but not the vow of chastity."

Although Jain nuns frequently opined that celibacy is much easier for women, there is still a general acknowledgement that completely abstaining from sex is not easy. This abstention means not having sex, not talking about sex, and not thinking about sex. It requires both internal and external maintenance. In the former case, renouncers must struggle to diminish and contain internal urges that are sometimes very strong (see Goonasekara 1986). In the latter case, rules help renouncers avoid compromising situations, a renouncer's peers help him or her when struggling against such urges, the laity keep careful watch on renouncers, and if a renouncer willingly engages in sexual relations, he or she will face severe punishment and possible expulsion from his or her community of renouncers. Restrictions, watchfulness, and protection serve to separate renouncers from anyone of the opposite gender and therefore serve to guard against sexual transgressions. For women this is especially important considering the value of female chastity in Jainism in particular and in India in general. Jains therefore consider their communities of renouncers suitable for girls and women to join, and there are now four times more Jain nuns than monks.[7]

Hindu and Jain renunciation compared

Although the external factors related to chastity explained above do not in and of themselves account for the preponderance of nuns over monks in Jainism, without these factors this majority could never have existed within the Indian cultural context in which female chastity is both highly valued and suspect. This becomes especially clear when comparing Hindu and Jain renunciation.

There are mainly two types of renunciations available for women in India, Hindu and Jain.[8] While female renouncers predominate in Jainism, they are a marginal and small minority in Hinduism. Various scholars (note 8) have investigated this situation in Hinduism and their studies have focused on social proscriptions against women renouncing, women's duty (*strīdharma*) to marry and have children, women's mandatory dependence on male family members, and women's identification with *saṃsāra* (the world that renouncers want to escape) through giving birth.

However, more important for the purposes of this chapter, according to Young (1994: 73–74) and Clémentin-Ojha (1981: 256) there is a Hindu tendency to identify women as temptresses[9] who would trap men in *saṃsāra* through sensual desires. The conjoining of women with sexuality in Indian culture was shown by community resistance to the Ramakrishna movement's inauguration of an independent *maṭh* (monastic establishment) for women in the 1960s. Wendy Sinclair-Brull (1997: 63) reported that this resistance was based on the idea "that women suffered from the inherent inability to be chaste, and that to allow them independence of action was therefore against the interest of society." Khandalwal (2001: 171–172) also has described this Hindu resistance.

> The idea that young people, especially young girls, should become ascetics in large numbers seemed so wrong as to be sinister. In contemporary Hindu society, female celibacy is a social and conceptual possibility in that women celibates are visible in society, but it seems that they are tolerated, even revered, only as long as they remain exceptions. If women, especially young presexual women, were to begin taking vows of celibacy in large numbers, I believe that the limits of society's tolerance would be reached.

While it is precisely these women in Jainism ("young presexual women") who are renouncing in large numbers, it is difficult for women to renounce in Hinduism because, although female chastity is highly valued in Hinduism, many Hindus also believe that women are overly sexual. There is a fear that the renouncer life, unconstrained by the limits of marriage, would unleash their supposedly overwhelming sexual urges. Jains also value female chastity, but many Jains believe men are more libidinous. Jain nuns sometimes adduced the *satī*-narratives to demonstrate how this is so, such as the story of Satī Rajīmatī at the beginning of this article. Many even claimed that men's difficulty in maintaining celibacy is the reason why there are more Jain nuns than monks. The female Hindu renouncers with whom Khandelwal (2001) talked also opined that women can maintain celibacy more easily, but apparently this is not enough to encourage more Hindu women to renounce. How many Hindus perceive Hindu renunciation and its relative lack of organization is a significant hindrance in this regard.

There is the perception among many people in India that Hindu renouncers can be as notorious as they are respected.[10] Some Jains also assert that Jain renunciation is better than Hindu renunciation because of this. The lack of systematized and extensive rules and/or the organization needed to enforce those rules in many orders of Hindu renouncers are reasons why they are regarded with a wary and suspicious eye. Although there are occasional instances of sexual impropriety among Hindu renouncers, this perception or suspicion is generally unwarranted. Nevertheless, although very strong-minded women can become Hindu renouncers, despite orthodox proscriptions, they do so at a perceived risk because they enter a purportedly uncertain community of peers. More realistically, single women who are not connected to a family group are more likely to be sexually harassed or assaulted. Female Hindu renouncers are more vulnerable because there is less institutional organization to protect them.[11]

There are significant exceptions to this, and notable ones are the highly organized *Śrī Śarada Maṭh*s for female renouncers that originated from the male-run Ramakrishna Mission. Both these male and female *maṭh*s are highly organized, strict, and protected.[12] Furthermore, at the *Śrī Śarada Maṭh* in Calcutta, I was told that they also deemed it important to keep male and female renouncers separate, and that their *maṭh*s are run separately from the men's *maṭh*s. When I talked with *Saṃnyāsini* (renouncer) Vijñanaprāṇa Jī at the *Śri Śarada Maṭh* in Delhi about my research concerning why Jain nuns constitute the majority of Jain renouncers, she told me that the separation of male and female renouncers is the key. "In Buddhism there was no separation and so there were problems," she asserted.[13] In fact, monastic rules in early Indian Buddhism subordinated nuns to monks to such an extent that monks supervised nuns during certain rituals and other circumstances. Buddhist monks and nuns therefore had more contact with each other and arguably more opportunity to stray from their vows of celibacy (see note 34).

Considering the larger Indian milieu, it is somewhat surprising that Jain women and girls would be allowed to or encouraged to renounce as a part of their practice of chastity. Occasionally, I also heard comments from Śvetāmbar laity that some families even persuade their daughters to take initiation or raise them to become nuns, confident that Jain renunciation is a chaste institution. It was said that families did this because they were unable to pay dowries, but in my experience this is probably true of only a small number of Jains.[14]

Although Jains generally perceive Jain renunciation as a chaste institution, there have been cases of sexual impropriety and laxity among Jain renouncers. For example, John Cort (2001: 43–46) has written about a Gujarati Mūrtipūjak reform movement in the nineteenth and twentieth centuries that was created to eliminate Jain *yati*s because they did not conform to the renouncer conduct that is now relatively standard for all Jain sects and sub-sects. The systematized nature of most Jain renouncer organizations today allows for more control, including control in the area of sexual conduct, thereby providing a virtuous alternative to marriage for women. However, even more important are the relationships between renouncers and their peers as well as relationships between renouncers and the scrutinizing and protective Jain laity.[15] This chapter contains discussions translated from Hindi which I had with various Śvetāmbar and Digambar nuns and monks in Bihar, Rajasthan, Uttar Pradesh, and Gujarat about restrictions and protection related to chastity among Jain renouncers.[16]

Field-research

During my research I travelled throughout North India to interview Jain nuns. Most of my interviews were done with Rajasthani and Gujarati Śvetāmbar nuns. Because I interviewed South Indian and Digambar nuns less often, my assertions' relevance for them will have to be verified by further research. I also interviewed a few laypeople and monks. However, I could not talk with laymen or monks often or extensively because to do so would be considered unsuitable for a woman. I was most interested in talking with those women who were responsible for nuns' preponderance in Jainism, those who became nuns themselves. My research methodology was largely that of discussions with these nuns, some of which are reproduced here.

In his 1959 article "Comparative Religion: Whither – and Why?" the Harvard scholar Wilfred Cantwell Smith claimed that it is essential that scholars understand the personal nature of religion.[17] Like Smith, I contend that to understand the external manifestations of religion and culture it is vital to understand what they "mean to those that are involved" (p. 143). The most important part of my research concerned recording Jain nuns' views about the beliefs, ideals, and stories they were explaining to me and recording their interpretations of the events they shared with me from their own life experiences. I was less interested in my perceptions of Jain nuns, and more interested in Jain nuns' perceptions and what their religion *meant* to them. It was in these perceptions that the mystery of Jain nuns' preponderance began to reveal itself to me. I let their opinions about their own majority in the Jain renouncer population guide my research. When a significant number of them emphasized the external regulation of renouncers' celibacy as responsible for their preponderance, this became one of the focuses of my research. I asked the nuns who asserted this for further explanations, and also talked with other nuns about these issues. However, my emphasis on their perceptions does not negate my own. While some nuns thought that external regulations of celibacy were largely responsible for Jain nuns' preponderance, I believe somewhat differently. In so far as this regulation influences Jains' view of renunciation as a safe and chaste institution for girls and women to join, it was and is necessary for female renunciation to occur and is therefore a necessary condition for Jain nuns' preponderance. However, this regulation did not in and of itself produce this preponderance (see Fohr 2001).

This chapter is less about "facts" or "reality" or what may or may not be "accurate" and more about the ideas and ideals held by Jain nuns concerning their own religion, that is, about opinions presented to me during interviews. Without these ideas and ideals supporting female renunciation, it would not be as prevalent. If, similar to Hinduism, large numbers of women renouncing in Jainism were to be considered bad, wrong, "sinister," or, more germane to this chapter, sexually suspicious or dangerous, there would be fewer if any Jain nuns. But on the contrary, during my interviews many of the nuns with whom I talked emphasized their chastity, almost always without my prompting.

Chastity as defined by Jain nuns

At this point I need to clarify what my Śvetāmbar and Digambar interviewees meant by "chastity." Nuns explained that chastity in Jainism ranges from fidelity in marriage to complete celibacy in renunciation, with the former being a less complete form of the latter. Marital fidelity is primarily defined in terms of wives who should marry once and be sexually faithful to their husbands in body, speech, and mind. Male and female renouncers' celibacy also refers to restraint in body, speech, and mind, but it allows for no sexuality whatsoever. Although it is extremely important for all renouncers (male and female) to remain chaste, most nuns claimed that chastity is much more important for laywomen than it is for laymen. For example, traditionally a widower may remarry while a widow should not. Indeed, in India in general, it is much more important for women to remain chaste than men. As nuns are both women and renouncers, it is not surprising that they would emphasize chastity in their lives. Although almost all Jain scholars have argued or assumed that the vow of non-violence is the most important vow that Jain renouncers adopt and that virtually all Jain practices stem from it, Jain nuns asserted the primacy of chastity instead.

The terms nuns used to signify chastity referred both to the chastity of wives and the chastity renouncers. There was no term that referred exclusively to one or the other. These terms included: *satītva* ("virtue" or "chastity"), *śīla* ("morality" or "virtuous nature or conduct"), *cāritra* ("character," "virtue," or "proper conduct"), and *brahmacarya* ("chastity" or "celibacy"). Most of these terms do not refer to chastity exclusively, but also encompass other behaviors or qualities that are considered religious and good.[18] However, nuns used these words when they were specifically talking about chastity, and that is how I interpreted these words in the English translations of the discussions that follow. For my nun-collaborators, these words described their celibacy as the fulcrum of their ascetic identities, practices, and qualities.[19]

Discussions with Śvetāmbar nuns about the rules of celibacy

Many nuns asserted that celibacy was the most important of their vows. Indeed, it has been given much attention in Jainism and was deemed important enough to merit the development of strict monastic rules designed to support celibacy and guard against sexual impropriety, especially in the Śvetāmbar sect.[20] There are many restrictions placed on renouncers in this regard, some are directly related to celibacy and some are indirectly related. Those in the latter category are mainly meant to affect the renunciation of worldly life and the body, but they also curtail renouncers' attractiveness. For example, monks and nuns do not wear jewelry or apply scented oil, and they pull out their hair two to five times a year (*keś-luñcan*).[21] However, Jain nuns emphasized rules that more directly regulate celibacy when they talked with me. These include rules that keep renouncers from meeting too often with the opposite gender, meeting them alone, or touching them.[22] I include these discussions in the following paragraphs, as well as some background information about the groups of nuns with whom I studied.

In Ahmedabad, Gujarat I met with Śvetāmbar Mūrtipūjak Tapā Gacch Pravartinī[23] Lāvaṇya Śrī Jī who had 125 nuns under her care. This Gujarati religious leader was seventy-eight years of age when I interviewed her, had taken initiation when she was fifteen, and was educated up to the fourth standard. When I visited her, there were ten nuns, who were mostly Gujarati, staying with her in Ahmedabad. Their ages ranged between thirty and eighty. The three older nuns (ages sixty-five and above) had taken initiation when they were in their mid-teens and the rest had taken initiation in their late teens and twenties. Only one nun had been married and then decided to renounce, and that was after her husband had become a monk. The older nuns were relatively uneducated before they renounced, while the other nuns were educated until the eleventh standard or had college degrees. This group of renouncers was unusual in two ways. First, none had siblings who had also become initiated. Second, two of the younger nuns told me that they had been very irreligious in their teens, but had been impressed by Jainism after meeting certain nuns in this group.

When I arrived I was directed to talk with Sādhvī Akṣayānanda Śrī Jī because of her erudition on Jain matters. She was forty-six when I interviewed her and had taken initiation when she was twenty-one years of age. She had four brothers and one sister and her family were Gujarati Jains living in Andhra Pradesh. Although she was only educated until the eleventh standard, she was famous for her memory and for being a very learned scholar. Jain renunciation is frequently an avenue for monks and nuns to increase their knowledge and education. She was certainly knowledgeable, but also taciturn and offered me almost no information for which I did not ask directly. She was also very strict in her ascetic conduct. Her erudition and punctiliousness were such that even Pravartinī Lāvaṇya Śrī Jī regarded her as an authority and would consult her on various issues. After Sādhvī Akṣayānanda Śrī Jī talked with me about the story of Satī Rajīmatī, she discussed some of the rules that restrict renouncers' contact with the opposite gender.

"Men [generally] don't come here [to the *upāśray*[24]]" she asserted. "And after sunset and before sunrise, they are not allowed to come." [. . .]

"When you go out for alms (*gocarī*) do women give you food?" I asked.

"Men do also, but they cannot touch us."

"Men cannot touch you?"

"Men cannot touch us or anything that is touching us. And we don't touch any male, whether child or adult. If there is no female doctor available and we need to see a male doctor, if he touches us, then we have to do some type of penance (*paścāt*)."

"Like fasting?" I asked.

"Yes," she replied.[25]

The above restrictions are directly aimed at maintaining renouncers' celibacy. However, when she referred to the proscription of touching between nuns and males, this is not a euphemism referring to sex only. These rules literally mean no physical contact with the opposite gender. Most monks and nuns may not even touch something that is being touched at the same time by someone of the opposite gender. If a man or boy needs to hand something to a nun, he usually hands it to a laywoman (if he is not a monk) to give to her, drops it into her hands, or places it on the floor in front of her. Nuns also do the same if they need to give something to a man or a boy. The same rules apply to monks and women or girls. Adherence to these rules was something I observed consistently throughout my research, with the exception of the Digambars. Bīsapanthī Digambar[26] renouncers allow members of the opposite gender touch their feet to acquire blessings and also to hand something to them directly. However, among Śvetāmbars even small children are taught to abide by these restrictions and carefully observe them. I only witnessed one instance of a child who transgressed in this regard. This boy of three pounced into the lap of a nun and was then corrected by his embarrassed and consternated mother.

The middle-aged Sādhvī Nirañjanā Śrī Jī, from Chennai, talked with me about some other rules that separate monks and nuns when and if they meet. She was also in Ahmedabad with a group of seven other Śvetāmbar Mūrtipūjak Kharatar Gacch nuns under the care of Sādhvī Manohar Śrī Jī. Most were Gujarati and Rajasthani. Some were related to each other, three had taken initiation together in Delhi, four had earned PhD's, and one was a published author. Their ages ranged from the thirties to sixties and most had never been married. This group's good-natured cheerfulness impressed me, and they were one of the groups of Jain nuns who asked if I might join them in renouncing. Sādhvī Nirañjanā Śrī Jī, from Chennai, was in her late thirties when I interviewed her. About rules concerning monks and nuns she told me that,

> We meet during lectures and we also discuss religion. When we go to the temple and if the monks are senior to us then we go to pay our respects.[27]

> We also ask them questions. We do things like this with them, but we don't live with them in one place and we eat separately. We only go for their blessings (*darśan*). And we also go if we should ask them some question. But [not] if there is only one monk there alone . . . or if for some reason there is no other nun to go with us, then we go with a [lay]woman, but we do not go alone, this is a rule.[28]

Śvetāmbar laity also should not meet a renouncer of the opposite gender if that renouncer is alone, and a laywoman should bring at least one other woman with her when meeting with monks. In my experience, these rules are not as strict among Digambars.

Although most Jain nuns with whom I met restricted their interactions with men, Pravartinī Lāvaṇya Śrī Jī's group of Gujarati Śvetāmbar Mūrtipūjak Tapā Gacch nuns was more careful than any other group I visited in India. In her group, the older nuns acted as a sort of a barrier between the younger nuns and the few laymen who might come for blessings, advice, or religious knowledge. One younger and educated nun, Sādhvī Bhāvananditā Śrī Jī, explained this to me in English. Her family was Gujarati and living in Mumbai. She was twenty-four when I interviewed her, and she had become a nun at the age of nineteen. What is remarkable about this nun is that she admitted to being irreligious as an adolescent and to "roaming about and seeing movies and such." Only one other nun I met described her life before initiation in these terms and she was also in this group of nuns. Most of the time nuns described themselves as pious and religious before renouncing.[29] After Sādhvī Bhāvananditā Śrī Jī encountered Sādhvī Akṣayānanda Śrī Jī in Mumbai, she decided to become a nun with Sādhvī Akṣayānanda Śrī Jī as her guru. This once rebellious youngster then sat beside me as a self-possessed nun and explained how the older nuns helped support younger nuns' practice of celibacy.

> If [men] want to come [to the *upāśray*], they first have to ask permission from the head nun. She is very strong, but we youngsters, our minds may become filthy. We may collapse and become attracted to them. Downfall can come from anyone's side. If instead of you, an American man had come here, then only the elder nuns would have talked to him.[30]

The rules and practices enumerated above by Jain nuns are very straightforward in their function to ensure renouncers' practice of celibacy by separating them from the opposite gender and limiting their interactions.[31]

Some nuns compared Jain rules with Hindu renunciation, claiming that these rules make Jain renunciation superior. While I was living in Jamshedpur, Bihar, the Rajasthani Śvetāmbar Sthānakavāsī Sādhvī Prītisudha Śrī Jī was the first nun to argue this with me. This nun's mother had renounced and in turn inspired many of her female relatives (including her daughters, sisters, and nieces) to do so as well. As a result, all but two nuns were related in this group of twelve, headed by Sādhvī Prītisudha Śrī Jī, and most were Rajasthani. These nuns' ages were between twenty and seventy and most had never been married, having been initiated in their early teens, while a few of the older nuns had renounced as widows later in life. Comparing Hinduism and Jainism, Sādhvī Śrī Prītisudhā Jī averred,

> Because there are many restrictions concerning this [the separation of monks and nuns], people think it is all right if their daughters become Jain nuns. Even the highest *ācārya* cannot enter where we stay in the evening. A nun's brother cannot even enter to visit his sister. If one nun has a relationship with a man, then people will think that all nuns are bad. Therefore there need to be restrictions.[32]

According to this nun, parents do not want their daughters to be in a situation where their chastity could be compromised. She added that while communities of Jain renouncers have good reputations in this regard, communities of Hindu renouncers do not. This latter view is arguable, but she was not the only Jain nun to voice it, and this opinion is more or less widely held among Jains.

Conversations about Śvetāmbar and Digambar restrictions for nuns

All the regulations mentioned thus far apply to both monks and nuns, but there are other restrictions that apply only to nuns, especially among Śvetāmbar Mūrtipūjak Tapā Gacch and Digambar renouncers.[33] Some of these rules result in limiting nuns' progress and status within Jain communities, as I will explain later. However, Nalini Balbir (1994: 122–123) has examined extra rules for nuns in the Śvetāmbar *Chedasūtra*s and how they are related to maintaining nuns' chastity; and my collaborators also told me that these rules were not created because of concerns about nuns' status, but because of concerns about nuns' celibacy.

I rarely talked with Jain monks, but the Śvetāmbar Mūrtipūjak Kharatar Gacch nuns under the care of Sādhvī Manohar Śrī Jī informed me that a high *ācārya* was going to arrive at Koba nearby and encouraged me to interview him. He was Śvetāmbar Mūrtipūjak Tapā Gacch Ācārya Śrī Padmasāgarsūri Jī, and when I interviewed him we talked about these rules for nuns.

I approached him with trepidation because there happened to be no other woman around who could go with me while I interviewed him. Instead, a layman showed me into the *upāśray* and I sat down on the floor in front of him although there was no other monk with him. After another monk quickly came into the room to join us, as Jain rules prescribe, we started our short interview. When I asked him why there have been so many female Jain renouncers in comparison to other religions in South Asia, he told me that this is because women are given respect in Jainism, the only difference being that women have more restrictions in order to protect their chastity.

> [. . .] In the Hindu religion women are not respected in the same way they are in Jainism. Women are looked down upon. It is the same in the Vedic and Buddhist traditions. Buddha gave women a place in the [Buddhist] religion only after some time.[34] But since the beginning, Mahāvīr established the four-fold community [of male and female renouncers and laity]. [Women] were given equal rights. There are some differences between male and female renouncers' restrictions, because they are women, to protect their chastity (*śīl rakṣaṇ*). There are some limitations (*maryādā*) for their protection. In everything else, there are no differences.[35]

Although all monks are technically superior to nuns in the Śvetāmbar renouncer hierarchy, most of the Śvetāmbar nuns I met did not consider themselves inferior to monks in status or spiritual abilities. Many asserted that monks and nuns have the same rights, that Jainism is not a male-dominated religion, and because of this Jain nuns have thrived. Furthermore, many Śvetāmbar nuns did not believe that the extra restrictions placed on nuns were related to spiritual inferiority in any way.

But what are these further restrictions that protect nuns' chastity to which Ācārya Śrī Padmasāgarsūri Jī alluded? In one of my many conversations with Śvetāmbar Mūrtipūjak Tapā Gacch Sādhvī Vairāgya Pūrṇā Śrī Jī from Rajasthan, she discussed this issue of special rules for women's protection with me in slightly more detail. This nun was part of a group of three Tapā Gacch Mūrtipūjak nuns with whom I spent most of my time while I was in Delhi. The group was headed by Sādhvī Kusum Prabhā Śrī Jī, who was chronically ill during my research and so, until she was well, they all had to remain in Delhi before resuming their itinerancy. At the time of my research her age was forty-one and she had taken initiation at the age of sixteen, when she had completed the tenth standard. She had never married and was the second child in her family, which lived in the small town Sojat in Rajasthan where they sold silk sarees. She had six sisters and two brothers, and two of her sisters had also taken initiation. Sādhvī Vairāgya Pūrṇā Śrī Jī was one of them. She was twenty-eight at the time of my research and had been eighteen years of age when she took initiation. She had an education similar to her sister's and also had never married. The third nun in this group was Sādhvī Saṃyam Ratnā Śrī Jī who was also from Rajasthan where her parents had a cloth store. She had been married at the age of sixteen and widowed at eighteen. At the time of my research she was forty-two years of age and she had taken initiation when she was thirty-one. Although she was one of the wisest nuns I had encountered, she had little formal education. I visited these three nuns often and our interactions were usually less formal than those with other nuns.

During one of my conversations with Sādhvī Vairāgya Pūrṇā Śrī Jī, we talked about Tapā Gacch Mūrtipūjak nuns' more restricted access to religious education in the past.

> "Monks used to be the scholars because they studied with laymen (*śrāvak*) scholars and professors. They studied with them," she said. "These types of facilities were not available to nuns. This is why there were fewer nuns who were scholars. But it is not the same way now. Today, Guru Mahārāj has made these facilities available [to nuns].[36] We have already obtained every type of facility. [Nuns] have become scholars. They are reading every scripture (*Āgam*). They are catching up in every way concerning their studies."
>
> "So nuns did not have these facilities in the past?" I asked.
>
> "The only reason was to protect our chastity (*caritra*)," she explained. "We did not progress in order to protect our practice of celibacy (*śīl-dharm*)."
>
> "I don't understand (*matalab*?)," I said bluntly.
>
> "They [nuns] remained by themselves. In former times women did not leave their houses, so similarly nuns were also not allowed to go out very much. They were not allowed to meet too many men. This was for their protection, for this reason."[37]

Protecting nuns' chastity is also the reason behind another restriction followed among Tapā Gacch Mūrtipūjak Jains. Nuns are usually active at religious functions in all sects and sub-sects and, except in the Tapā Gacch, nuns frequently give sermons to both men and women. As other scholars have already noted,[38] while nuns of this gacch are allowed to preach to women, they are restricted from preaching to groups of both men and women. This proscription was also designed to regulate nuns' chastity by keeping them separate from men.

There is also a significant restriction applied to nuns and not monks in the Digambar sect. Nuns of this sect may not renounce clothing. Although this restriction limits female renouncers' status in the Digambar sect, Digambar renouncers asserted that this is not its purpose. Furthermore, the Digambar hierarchy of monks and nuns complicates the issue of status. While in Śvetāmbar Jainism, all monks are technically higher in status than nuns, in Digambar Jainism status is more complex. The lowest in the Digambar hierarchy are *brahmacāriṇī*s (female) and *brahmacārin*s (male). Their practices are the least difficult and some remain more or less in householder life despite taking vows of celibacy, but to become one is also often the first step for those who want to progress in the Digambar renouncer hierarchy. Above them are celibates of increasing asceticism including *kṣullikā*s (female), *kṣullak*s (male), and *ailak*s (male); and then *āryikā*s (female) and naked *muni*s (male). Monks have a higher status than nuns within each level of this Digambar hierarchy. So, for example, *kṣullikā*s are lower in status than *kṣullak*s, but *kṣullak*s are lower in status than *āryikā*s. Although I identify all the celibates listed above as renouncers, Digambars consider only a *muni* to be a complete renouncer capable of achieving mokṣa because he renounces his clothing. Virtually all *kṣullikā*s, *kṣullak*s, *ailak*s, *āryikā*s and some *brahmacāriṇī*s and *brahmacārin*s generally function as, and are respected as, renouncers in that they are unmarried and celibate and can still make significant progress towards *mokṣa*, but they are still officially only advanced laypeople. From this point of view, there are also officially no Digambar female renouncers, although certainly most Digambars consider at least *āryikā*s to be nuns. While Śvetāmbar nuns claimed they were at least equal to monks, Digambar nuns did not make similar claims, despite the complexity of their hierarchy of renouncers. Instead, they explained to me that they would have to be reborn as men to become *muni*s before they could attain *mokṣa*.

While in Delhi, I met briefly with Digambar Muni Kamkumarānanda Jī from Karnataka and talked with him about this rule concerning nakedness. He had renounced householder life in 1988, after completing a degree in electrical engineering. He was initiated by Ācārya Śrī Kunthū Sāgar Jī Mahārāj as a naked *muni* in 1989, and he was thirty-three when I interviewed him in 1999. An author, his books included *Universal Message of Jainism* and *Ten Universal Virtues*, both written in English.

> "A nun (*āryikā*) is a woman," he began after I told him about my research. "Women's status is not less then men's status in Jainism. I will show you how this is so. For example, we monks practice religion. We practice self-control (*saṃyam*). We eat and drink water once in twenty-four hours. *Āryikā*s also do what we do. *Āryikā*s also only eat once a day, they also practice self-control, and they do not keep many clothes. They cannot be completely unclothed, this is the Indian tradition and culture, and it is also said that this is their moral restriction (*maryādā*). They cannot break with this moral restriction (*maryādā*). They are not attached [to this clothing], but they cannot give it up. From the point of view of society, they cannot give it up. For this reason she has [some, but] very little, property. She has a few sarees, two sarees, but there is no difference between them and us concerning our practice of austerities (*tapascarya*). [We] both practice the same austerities."
>
> "So the difference between *muni*s and *āryikā*s is that *āryikā*s wear clothing. Does this come from society or because *āryikā*s are women?" I asked hoping for further elaboration.
>
> "This is women's *maryādā*," he replied simply.
>
> "What does *maryādā* mean?"
>
> "*Maryādā*, in other words it is her culture (*saṅskṛti*). It is their morality (*naitiktā*). There is morality[39] in this. For this reason women cannot remain naked. For this reason they have clothing."
>
> "Does this have to do with a woman's body, or society, or women's traditions? Where does this clothing-issue come from?" I asked, still hoping for a more detailed answer.

"They wear clothing because of morality – morality (*naitiktā*). And secondly they cannot remain without clothing, not only among themselves, but also among us. But men can remain without clothing."

"This means that clothes are not necessary for men's morality, but are necessary for women's morality?"

"Yes, this is a fact (*bāt*)." He replied.[40]

In the Digambar Jain religion, the rule that nuns cannot go without clothing, as the most advanced Digambar monks do, theoretically impedes women's achievement of *mokṣa* because Digambars believe that one must renounce clothing in order to reach that state.[41] This restriction also means that women cannot attain the highest status of full Digambar *muni*s. However, this rule is deemed necessary for women's morality. It would be immoral for a woman to travel around India naked. In other words, these rules in both the Śvetāmbar and Digambar sects, which have resulted in keeping nuns from having equal opportunities, were intended to protect women's chastity by working within accepted cultural norms that demanded that women adhere to *pardā* restrictions[42] (especially in Rajasthan) and remain fully clothed. These rules indicate the seriousness with which Jains view nuns' chastity, and the extent to which Jains maintain it. Although no Digambars cited the story of Satī Rajīmatī to indicate what might happen if women renounced clothing, they could have easily done so. If a nun did renounce clothing, she would encounter a great deal of difficulty.

Conversations with Śvetāmbar nuns about protection

When Jain nuns and monks talked about issues concerning renouncers' chastity they often used words such as *rakṣaṇ* or *sūrakṣā*, both meaning protection, to describe how these rules "protect" their chastity. Chastity is considered to be something of great value, and therefore it should be kept safe, safe from one's own urges and safe from the sexual aggression of others. Deo and Shāntā have already described evidence of this latter concern in the past, and this concern still exists today.[43] Although there are misogynist strains of thought in Jain texts, in which women are primarily portrayed as temptresses,[44] I found that most of the nuns with whom I talked believed differently. If anyone is more inclined toward sexual activity or misconduct, according to them, it is men. As stated previously, many nuns cited the popular Jain narratives about *satī*s,[45] such as the story of Satī Rajīmatī, to support this assertion, arguing that the women of these stories must frequently protect their honor from ill-intentioned men. Although nuns acknowledged that all men and women have sexual urges and therefore renouncers must be careful, there is a more pervasive concern about women's safety in Jainism. This includes the safety of nuns' "virtue" against male sexual aggression.

Among Jain renouncers, it is children and women who are the most vulnerable to sexual aggression (or aggression of any sort). Nuns not only explained that their rules protect them from such aggression, but also emphasized that Jain communities provide security as well. Nuns are conscious of this need for protection. For example, one day when I went to visit the Mūrtipūjak nuns of Kusum Prabhā Śrī Jī's group we talked as usual for a little while. I then started to joke about how I liked the natural beauty products available in Delhi such as the Shahnaz Hussian facial packs. My life was such a contrast to theirs in this way and sometimes I joked about this with them. They, according to Jain regulations, pulled out their hair regularly, wore simple white clothing, and did not use beauty products or wear jewelry. So Sādhvī Kusum Prabhā Śrī Jī asked me why I bought these beauty products.

> I continued to joke, "I should be beautiful, shouldn't I?"
>
> With this, the tone of the conversation became serious.
>
> "You shouldn't be too beautiful because some man might try to rape you." Saṃyam Ratnā Śrī Jī asserted soberly.
>
> I tried to keep the conversation light by joking that I always had my umbrella to defend myself. I usually carried a long umbrella with me wherever I went. It helped protect me from the sun, and occasionally from ill-mannered men as well.
>
> But Sādhvī Saṃyam Ratnā Śrī Jī continued, "There was once a girl who went out at night. Two men from a taxi forced her into a car, injected her with drugs, and raped her for two days. She didn't tell anyone until five months later and this was only because she complained about stomach pains. When her parents took her to the doctor, they found out she was pregnant. The police wouldn't do anything unless they were bribed. Now they have gone to court."
>
> She paused and then continued, "Two days ago, two men grabbed a Sthānakavāsī nun when she went out for alms (*gocarī*). She started to scream and was rescued. The men are now in jail."
>
> Again she paused, looking at me with concern, "You shouldn't give anyone your complete address so that you remain safe."[46]

This recent incident concerning the Sthānakavāsī nun had seriously hurt their usual good humor, and all three remained taciturn and morose for the rest of my visit that day.

Protection is also important for monks, especially Digambar *muni*s who are usually protected by Jain laymen because they are occasionally attacked by non-Jains offended by their nakedness (Zydenbos 1999: 296). However, women are more vulnerable to aggression than men and so Jain nuns should never be alone. The most potentially dangerous time for nuns is during *vihār* (itinerancy). When they stay in a town or village, Jain renouncers usually stay in an area densely populated by Jains who protect them. But what happens when they travel across India by foot? Most Jain nuns must travel in groups since there is safety in numbers.

The only exception I heard about during my research was a Digambar *āryikā* who was traveling through Bihar with no other nuns or monks. No doubt Jain laity traveled with her to keep her safe.

Jain laypeople are assiduous in their care of renouncers, including female renouncers. Many lay Jains have near or distant female relatives who have joined orders of nuns, and their responsibility toward protecting nuns is encouraged by this. Furthermore, their care is so diligent that many laity would be offended at the notion that nuns experience any danger at all. It is also probably not a coincidence that the one sub-sect that is most systematically and uniformly concerned with taking care of its renouncers, the Terāpanthī sub-sect, has one of the highest ratios of nuns to monks, five to one.[47] But the laypeople of all sects and sub-sects of Jainism are very watchful. Not only are they concerned that these renouncers practice what they preach, they are also concerned with their safety, sometimes paying bodyguards to travel with them.[48]

While in Delhi I briefly met three Śvetāmbar Sthānakavāsī Sādhvīs: Sādhvī Vimalā Śrī Jī (most senior) who was fifty-nine when I met her and had taken initiation when she was seventeen, Sādhvī Kṛpā Śrī Jī who was thirty-four and had taken initiation at the age of seventeen, and Sādhvī Nidhī Śrī Jī who was thirty-five and had taken initiation when she was nineteen. Sādhvī Nidhī Śrī Jī was from Bangalore and once had aspirations to become a doctor. After she encountered a Jain nun who asked her why she wanted to be a "doctor of the body" when she could be a "doctor of the soul," she gradually decided to pursue the more spiritual of the two options. She was educated, extremely articulate, could speak English, and was an author. When I asked her about the dangers of *vihār*, she explained that there was no danger because Jain laypeople walk with them from village to village, escorting them.

> If there is the least bit of danger, then people take care of so much that they walk with us themselves. They walk with us and take care of us. They don't leave [us] until the people from the next village come. Then those people escort us. This is how Jain people take care of us when we go anywhere where there are no Jain households.[49]

Gujarati Mūrtipūjak Tapā Gacch Sādhvī Nandiyaśā Śrī Jī had a similar answer. She was fifty-two when I interviewed her and had taken initiation when she was twenty-two. Like Sādhvī Akṣayānanda Śrī Jī, she also had a reputation for being extremely learned, but unlike Sādhvī Akṣayānanda Śrī Jī, I only met her briefly while I was in Ahmedabad. When I asked her if they have any problems on *vihār* because they are women, she replied,

> We are in a group, and whenever there is a necessity, the Jain society provides us with a guard. There is no problem. Some people usually

> come with us and carry our extra materials and protect us. There are usually no problems.[50]

While some nuns argued that ascetic restrictions make it safe for women to renounce in Jainism, others argued that it is protection by Jain communities that does so. Gujarati Mūrtipūjak Tapā Gacch Sādhvī Virapiyaśā Śrī Jī was one nun who asserted this. I met her briefly with Sādhvī Nandiyaśā Śrī Jī. She was sixteen years of age when she decided to take initiation after being inspired by the religious preaching of monks and nuns. When she told her family this, her parents sent her to college, saying that if she still did not want to marry afterwards, they would let her become a nun. She was between thirty and forty years of age when I interviewed her.

> "In Jainism, Lord Mahāvīr has made arrangements for women. The Jain society takes care of us. The Jain society takes full responsibility for us. It is the entire Jain society's responsibility to protect us."
>
> "So it is necessary to protect women." I stated inquiringly.
>
> "In other religions there is not as much [protection.]"
>
> "So what you mean is that it is a little dangerous to take initiation in other religions."
>
> "There is no protection. There is no group. There is no education. It seems to me that these occur more in Jainism."[51]

Conclusion

Scholars have already noted that although more widows constituted Jain nuns' populations in the past, this is not the case today. Now it is mostly unmarried girls who decide to become nuns.[52] In either case, chastity is a factor in their initiations. In the past, when more child marriages took place, young widows were encouraged to renounce because they could not remarry (unlike their male counterparts) and they therefore needed to control their sexual feelings. Now that girls are married later in life, they are deciding to become nuns in their late teens and twenties because they must either marry or renounce at this time, otherwise their chastity will be called into question. Renunciation is considered a respectable and suitable institution for these Jain women because of strict rules and community watchfulness.

Some Jain nuns claimed that communities of Jain renouncers tend to be secure, secure in general and also secure from sexual advances and misconduct. Fastidious rules that limit contact with the opposite gender make it difficult to stray from the practice of celibacy. Watchfulness by fellow Jains, especially senior renouncers and laypeople, discourages any fall from grace on the part of renouncers themselves and any potential for sexual violence against nuns.

Some nuns even claimed that strict Jain regulations are responsible for nuns' preponderance in Jainism. This does not seem to be the case as there are many other factors contributing to this, factors I have discussed elsewhere[53] and alluded to earlier. However, if the rules of separation and community watchfulness did not exist in Jainism, there could never have been a female majority among Jain renouncers because it would not have been considered suitable or safe for girls and women to become nuns. In other words, while strict regulations are not a sufficient condition for nuns' preponderance, they are a necessary condition. This includes the extra restrictions for nuns, because without them female renunciation would not have been considered respectable within extant Indian social norms. The fact that these restrictions are not as stringent in the less organized Digambar sect further bolsters this assertion because this is the only Jain group in which there are more monks than nuns.[54] If Jains believed that compromising situations could occur in Jain renunciation, such as the one described in the story of Satī Rajīmatī and the monk Rathanemi at the beginning of this article, there most likely would not have been very many Jain nuns at all.

Acknowledgments

I thank John Cort, Peter Flügel, and Samuel Fohr for their valuable advice during various drafts of this article. My gratitude to the many renouncers with whom I studied including those mentioned in this article: Tapā Gacch Mūrtipūjak Ācārya Śrī Padmasāgarsūri Jī, Digambar Muni Kamkumarānanda Jī, Tapā Gacch Pravartinī Lāvaṇya Śrī Jī, Tapā Gacch Sādhvī Akṣayānanda Śrī Jī, Tapā Gacch Sādhvī Bhāvananditā Śrī Jī, Kharatar Gacch Sādhvī Manohar Śrī Jī, Kharatar Gacch Sādhvī Nirañjanā Śrī Jī, Tapā Gacch Sādhvī Kusum Prabhā Śrī Jī, Tapā Gacch Sādhvī Vairāgya Pūrṇā Śrī Jī, Tapā Gacch Sādhvī Saṃyam Ratnā Śrī Jī, Sthānakavāsī Sādhvī Śrī Prītisudha Jī, Sthānakavāsī Sādhvī Vimalā Śrī Jī, Sthānakavāsī Sādhvī Śrī Kṛpā Jī, Sthānakavāsī Sādhvī Śrī Nidhī Jī, Tapā Gacch Sādhvī Nandiyaśā Śrī Jī, Tapā Gacch Sādhvī Virapiyaśā Śrī Jī and Hindu Saṃnyāsini Vijñānaprāṇa Jī. I also thank my hardworking research assistant, Vandana Vora.

Notes

1 I use the term "nun" to refer to all of the following: *sādhvī*s (contemporary designation for a virtuous or chaste women, usually used in the Śvetāmbar sect to refer to female renouncers), *samaṇī*s (women who make an effort in renunciation, designation for a special type of female renouncer in the Terāpanthī sub-sect who, unlike full renouncers, may use transportation such as motor vehicles, trains, and planes), *āryikā*s (venerable women, of the Digambara sect) (see Shāntā 1985: 56–58), *kṣullikā*s (lesser renouncer women, of the Digambara sect), and *brahmacāriṇī*s (women who practice celibacy, of the Digambara sect).

2 This story is from lecture twenty-two of the Śvetāmbar *Uttarādhyanana Sūtra* and is arguably the oldest existent Jain narrative about the importance of chastity, dating BCE (Alsdorf 1974). It is also a very well-known story in Jain communities.

3 This chapter only describes one way the value of female chastity is involved in Jain nun's larger population, that is, the way restrictions regulating the celibacy of renouncers influence their numbers. Others concern perceptions about women as more naturally chaste, young widows being encouraged to renounce in the past, women's choice of renunciation over marriage now that child marriages are less frequent, the connection between the fidelity of wives and the celibacy of renouncers (and the power they both produce), and the popular stories about "virtuous women" called *satī*s. See Fohr (2001) and Kelting in this volume.

4 The Śvetāmbar sect is divided into three sub-sects, the Sthānakavāsī, Terāpanthī, and Mūrtipūjak. The Mūrtipūjak sub-sect is also divided into smaller groups or sub-groups called *gacch*s. The largest of these are the Tapā Gacch and Kharatar Gacch.

5 Conversation in Ahmedabad on February 2, 1999.

6 During his research among Śvetāmbar Mūrtipūjak Kharatar and Tapā Gacch renouncers in Jaipur, Laidlaw (1995: 56) also found that "groups of monks and nuns operate separately and independently. They hardly ever meet."

7 This estimate is from Flügel's statistics (Chapter 12 this volume) that are largely derived from the *Samagra Jain Cāturmās Sūcī*, edited by Bābūlāl Jain. In 1999 there were 154 monks and 557 nuns in the Śvetāmbar Terāpanthī sub-sect, 533 monks and 2,690 nuns in the Śvetāmbar Sthānakavāsī sub-sect, 1,489 monks and 5,354 nuns in the Śvetāmbar Mūrtipūjak sub-sect (most within the Tapā Gacch), and 610 monks and 350 nuns in the Digambar sect. In 1999 there was a total of 2,786 monks and 8,951 nuns. There seems to have been a very marked and recent increase in the number of Sthānakavāsī and Mūrtipūjak nuns in particular (see Table 12.10: Flügel Chapter 12 this volume).

While most Śvetāmbar renouncers are women, there are twice as many monks than nuns in the Digambar sect, according to these statistics. Nevertheless, the relatively small ratio of Digambar monks to nuns is still unusual within Indian culture. If *ailak*s (male), *kṣullak*s (male), and *kṣullikā*s (female) are taken into account the ratio of male to female renouncers is five to four (see Table 12.8: Flügel Chapter 12 this volume). If *brahmacārin*s (male) and *brahmacāriṇī*s (female) are also factored in, the Digambar ratio of monks to nuns would be even smaller or would demonstrate a majority of Digambar nuns as well, but further research is needed to verify this. For example Flügel (Chapter 12 this volume) points out that in 1999 Digambar Ācārya Vidyāsāgar had 150 *brahmacāriṇi*s and only 50 *brahmacārin*s under his care.

8 For example, Denton 1991; King 1984; Leslie 1983; Clémentin-Ojha 1981; Young 1994. See also Babb 1986: 97–154 for descriptions of different groups of Hindu renouncers, including an exceptional group in which there are more female than male renouncers. See Khandelwal 1997; Olivelle 1995; and Kane 1941–1974: vol. 2, part 1 for textual information about women's position in renunciation.

9 Weinberger-Thomas (1999: 149) notes how Indian notions concerning the danger of women's sexuality resembled the old "Western fantasy of India" in which Indians had an "immoderate appetite for sensual pleasure (most highly pronounced in women)." Apparently, some Westerners also were ready to believe that Indian women were lustful. This raises interesting questions about who believes what about women and why. The colonial stereotype about Indian women, described by Weinberger-Thomas, is now applied to Western women by Indians.

10 See Narayan (1989).

11 See Khandelwal (1997: 88–92). She states on page 90 about renouncers in Haridwar, "Local wisdom has it that women [renouncers] must protect themselves not only from violence perpetrated by strangers but also from the sexual advances of their own gurus and peers." See also Harlan (1992: 216–217) who discusses some related reasons why Hindus do not think renunciation is suitable for women; and Narayan (1989) for suspicion concerning Hindu ascetics.

12 See Sinclair-Brull (1997).
13 Conversation in Delhi on May 11, 1998.
14 As Gutschow (2001: 57) has so elegantly put it, "To treat the monastic vocation as an economic solution to the problem of feeding one's children is to reduce social actors to a Parsonian rationality which neglects affective and irrational aspects of human nature and fortune." This also pertains to dowry issues.
15 See Cort (1999: 47, 53–54). Some sects and sub-sects are more systemized than others.
16 I am grateful to have received a Fulbright-Hays (DDRA) fellowship to conduct research in India from March 1998 to March 1999. I would also like to thank the University of Virginia and its benefactors for supporting my studies, research, and writing with the following grants: Ann Francis Stead Fellowship, Mrs Charles A. Bryant Fellowship, Commonwealth Fellowship, Foreign Language Area Studies (FLAS) Fellowships. I am also grateful to the American Institute of Indian Studies (AIIS) for their Language Fellowship for Hindi language training in India.
17 Smith (originally published in 1959 and published again in 1976: 142), with a quote from Smith (1950: 51).
18 See Khandelwal (2001) about *brahmacarya* as not just celibacy, but also as controlling all passions and living a life of religious restraint on many levels.
19 See Reynell (1987: 340, 1991: 54–65) for the importance of chastity in Jain laywomen's religious identities and practice. See also Fohr (2001).
20 Flügel (Chapter 12 this volume) points out that Digambars are less systematized in this way.
21 This practice of pulling hair out by the roots has various functions in Jainism. First, it detracts from renouncers' attractiveness. Second, it is also a form of austerity (*tapasya*). Third, it is done in emulation of Lord Mahāvīr who pulled his hair out when he decided to renounce householder life.
22 For further recent scholarship about these rules see Vallely (2002: 105) and Flügel (2003).
23 A *pravartinī* functions like the *ācārya* towards the nuns under her care, she is the head of the nuns in her gacch.
24 Temporary place of residence in which traveling groups of Jain renouncers may stay for long or short periods of time.
25 Conversation in Ahmedabad on February 24, 1999.
26 There are three types of Digambars: Bīsapanthī, Terāpanthī, and Tāraṇapanthī. The first two types use statues in worship, while the last use scriptures. Among the Bīsapanthī, there are no restrictions against women touching male gurus' feet or male *Jina*s' (founders of the Jain religion) feet in temples. Women may also perform *abhiṣeka* worship (anointing of Jain images) in temples. There are no restrictions concerning green vegetables. Among the Terāpanthī, women are restricted from touching male gurus' feet and *Jina*s' feet. Women cannot perform *abhiṣeka* and the intake of green vegetables is restricted during certain times of the month. (Conversation with Digambar Āryikā Candanāmatī Mātā Jī in Hastinapur on January 1, 1999.)
27 Note that Sādhvī Nirañjanā Śrī Jī says that "if" the monks are senior, nuns pay respects to them. This indicates that Śvetāmbar rules that prescribe all nuns pay respects to all monks, no matter their seniority, are not always practiced. This may be especially true in the Kharatar Gacch in which there is a shortage of monks.
28 Conversation in Ahmedabad on February 22, 1998.
29 This may be different for monks. As John Cort has pointed out to me, the irreligious and profligate becoming religious is "a standard trope of religious conversion the world around" (personal communication, September 9, 2002). It is not, however, for Jain nuns.
30 Conversation in Ahmedabad on February 27, 1999.
31 Rules separating men and women are also observed in lay life and can be seen during Jain functions and lectures, during which men and women sit separately. James

Laidlaw (1995: 207) describes an interesting instance of rules separating the sexes during a lay gathering for *pratikraman̩* (rite of karmic purification). Usually laywomen and laymen perform this ritual separately and "even in separate buildings." However, Laidlaw observed one family's observance of this ritual together. The men and women of the family sat opposite each other in a circle and married couples sat where a man and a woman had to sit by each other at either end. The older of these couples could be closer together than the younger. The elderly woman who led the rite kept her face covered entirely and the younger women partially during the *pratikraman̩* and almost no eye contact took place between the men and women. When something needed to be handed to someone of the opposite gender, the rules for handing things to the opposite gendered renouncer were observed.

32 Conversation in Jamshedpur April 24, 1998.

33 See also Shāntā (1997: 531, n. 6).

34 Ācārya Śrī Padmasāgarsūri Jī is referring here to a story told in various Buddhist texts including the *Vinayapiṭaka, Cullavagga* (10.1–3), in which Mahāpajāpatī (the Buddha's foster mother and aunt) and 500 women asked the Buddha for ordination. They asked and were refused by him three times. However, they were determined and so shaved their heads and wore monks' robes. After the monk Ānanda finally interceded on their behalf and the Buddha also refused him three times, Ānanda inquired as to whether women are indeed capable of reaching enlightenment. The Buddha answered affirmatively and finally relented to the women's wishes to be initiated, but only upon the condition that they accept eight rules subordinating nuns to monks. The Buddha also warned that the Buddhist religion would now last only 500 years instead of 1,000. The eight rules are as follows:

1 Any nun, no matter how long she has been in the order, must honor all monks, even the rudest of novices.
2 Nuns should not reside in any place during the annual rainy-season retreat where monks are not available to supervise them.
3 Monks determine the dates for biweekly assemblies.
4 At the end of the rainy season retreat when the nuns and monks invite criticism from their own communities, nuns must also invite criticism from the monks.
5 Monks must share in determining and supervising penance for nuns.
6 Monks must share in the ordination of nuns.
7 Nuns must never reprove monks.
8 Nuns must never criticize monks officially.

(Falk 1980: 215, Law 1927: 73–78)

35 Conversation in Koba, outside Ahmedabad on February 23, 1999.

36 Her guru is known for these reforms. For example, in *The Life and Work of Acharya Sri Vijaya Vallabh Suriswarji*, Jhabak states,

> Pujna Acharya laid great stress on girls' education and opened many schools for girls. He also permitted and encouraged the sadhvis (nuns) for delivering discourses. Even today his sishyas (sadhvis) are preaching the teachings of Lord Mahavir in all parts of India.
>
> (Jhabak, *The Life and Work of Acharya Sri Vijaya Vallabh Suriswarji*, 13)

37 Conversation in Delhi on December 10, 1998.

38 For example, Cort (2001: 307–308); Laidlaw (1995: 57); and Shāntā (1985: 418).

39 English words and phrases that my interviewees used are surrounded by asterisks.

40 Conversation in Delhi on January 1, 1999.

41 However, it is believed that no one can reach liberation in this degenerate age. Instead monks and nuns will have to wait in heaven for a better age to come when they will be reincarnated, practice the Jain religion, and achieve liberation. Therefore the prescription

that nuns remain clothed does not really limit their spiritual progress in a significant way in this age. When they reincarnate, just as monks will, they will reincarnate as men.

42 *Pardā* restricts women's behavior as a way to regulate their chastity while living with their in-laws after marriage. These restrictions mean that women cannot leave the home often, cannot travel alone, and must cover their heads when in the presence of men.

43 Not only do nuns protect each other, there is some evidence that

> monks were expected to guard the nuns. A young monk well versed in the act of fighting was allowed to punish an intruder by disguising as a nun. In certain cases even brother-monks had to protect their sister-nuns with the permission of the *ācārya* and the *pravartinīs*.
>
> (N. Shānta 1997: 197, n. 175, citing Deo 1956)

At first glance this situation seems to contradict the rules separating monks and nuns. However, the spirit behind the rules, to keep renouncers chaste, is still being preserved.

44 See Śvetāmbar Sūtras *Sūtrakṛtāṅga* (1.4), *Uttarādhyanana* (32.13–16). See also similar images in Digambar texts in Jaini (1991) and Ryan (1988).

45 For information about *satī*s see Shāntā (1985, 1997); Kelting (2001, Chapter 8 this volume); and Fohr (2001).

46 Conversation in Delhi on October 5, 1999.

47 See Flügel (Chapter 12 this volume) about organization being related to populations of renouncers.

48 Personal communication with Peter Flügel.

49 Conversation in Delhi on October 20, 1998.

50 Conversation in Ahmedabad on February 21, 1999.

51 Conversation in Ahmedabad on February 21, 1999.

52 See Cort (1991: 660); Jaini (1979: 247, n. 8); Jaini (1991); Sangave (1980); Shāntā (1985, 1997); and Cort (2001: 47).

53 See Fohr (2001).

54 However, the other factors mentioned in this article, such as the Digambar belief that women are unable to reach liberation in a female body and their purported spiritual inferiority, probably also discouraged more women from renouncing in the Digambar sect.

Bibliography

Alsdorf, Ludwig. 1974. "Vāntam Āpātum." In *Kleine Schriften*, 178–185. Wiesbaden: Franz Steiner Verlag.

Babb, Lawrence A. 1986. *Redemptive Encounters: Three Modern Styles in the Hindu Tradition*. Berkeley, CA: University of California Press.

Balbir, Nalini. 1994. "Women in Jainism." In *Women and Religion*, ed. Arvind Sharma, 121–138. Albany, NY: State University of New York Press.

Bartholomeusz, Tessa. 1985. "The Female Mendicant in Buddhist Sri Lanka." In *Buddhism Sexuality and Gender*, ed. Jose Ingocia Cabezon, 37–64. Albany, NY: State University of New York Press.

—— 1994. *Women Under the Bo Tree*. Cambridge: Cambridge University Press.

Clémentin-Ojha, Catherine. 1981. "Feminine Asceticism in Hinduism." *Man in India*, 61: 254–288.

Cort, John. 1991. "The Śvetāmbar Mūrtipūjak Jain Mendicant." *Man in India* (N.S.), 26: 651–671.

—— 1999. "Fistfights in the Monastery: Calendars, Conflict, and Karma among the Jains." In *Approaches to Jaina Studies: Philosophy, Logical, Rituals Symbols*, eds N. K. Wagle and O. Qvarnström, 36–59. University of Toronto: Center for South Asian Studies.

—— 2001. *Jains in the World: Religious Values and Ideology in India*. New York: Oxford University Press.

Denton, Lynn Teskey. 1991. "Varieties of Hindu Female Asceticism." In *Roles and Rituals for Hindu Women*, ed. Julia Leslie, 211–231. Rutherford: Fairleigh Dickinson University Press.

Deo, S. B. 1956. *History of Jaina Monachism from Inscriptions and Literature*. Poona: Deccan College dissertation Series: 17.

Falk, Nancy. 1980. "Case of the Vanishing Nuns." In *Unspoken Worlds*, ed. Nancy Falk and Ritam Gross, 207–224. San Francisco, CA: Harper and Row Pub.

Flügel, Peter. 2003. "The Codes of Conduct of the Terāpanth Samaṇ order." *South Asia Research* 23 (1): 7–53.

—— This volume. Demographic Trends in Jain monasticism.

Fohr, Sherry E. 2001. *Gender and Chastity: Female Jain Renouncers*. PhD dissertation, University of Virginia.

Goonasekera, Ratna Sunilsantha Abhayawardana. 1986. *Renunciation and Monasticism Among the Jainas of India*. PhD thesis. San Diego, CA: University of California.

Gutschow, Kim. 2001. "Women Who Refuse to be Exchanged." In *Celibacy, Culture and Society*, ed. Elisa Sobo and Sandra Bell, 47–64. Madison, WI: The University of Wisconsin Press.

Harlan, Lindsey. 1992. *Religion and Rajput Women*. Berkeley, CA: University of California Press.

Jain, Babūlāl, ed. 1999. *Samagra Jain Cāturmās Sūcī*. Mumbai: Jain Ektā Mahāmaṇḍal.

Jaini, Padmanabh S. 1979. *The Jaina Path of Purification*. Berkeley, CA: Universiry of California Press.

—— 1991. *Gender and Salvation: Jaina Debates on the Spiritual Liberation of Women*. New Delhi: Munishiram Manoharlal Publishers Pvt. Ltd.

Jhabak, Kasturchand M. *The Life and Work of Acharya Sri Vijaya Vallabh Suriswarji*. Secunderabad: Shiva Press.

Kamkumarānanda. 1998. *Ten Universal Virtues*. Dehradun: Vikalp Printers.

—— 1998. *Universal Message of Jainism*. Delhi: Vikas Computers.

Kane, P. V. 1941–1974. *History of Dharmaśāstra*. Poona: Bhandarkar Oriental Research Institute.

Kelting, Whitney. 2001. *Singing to the Jinas*. New York: Oxford University Press.

Khandelwal, Meena. 1997. "Ungendered *Atma*, Masculine Virility and Feminine Compassion: Ambiguities in Renunciant Discourses on Gender." *Contributions to Indian Sociology* (N.S.) 31 (1): 79–107.

—— 2001. "Sexual Fluids, Emotions, Morality: Notes on the Gendering of Brahmacharya." In *Celibacy, Culture and Society*, ed. Elisa Sobo and Sandra Bell, 157–179. Madison, WI: The University of Wisconsin Press.

King, Ursula. 1984. "The Effect of Social Change on Religious Self-Understanding: Women Ascetics in Modern Hinduism." In *Changing South Asia: Religion and Society*, ed. K. Ballhatchet and D. Taylor, 41–59. London: School of Oriental and African Studies.

Laidlaw, James. 1995. *Riches and Renunciation*. Oxford: Clarendon Press.

Law, Bimala Churn. 1927. *Women in Buddhist Literature*. Ceylon: W.E. Bastian & Co.

Leslie, Julia. 1983. "Essence and Existence: Women and Religion in Ancient Indian Texts." In *Women's Religious Experience*, ed. Pat Holden, 89–112. Totowa, NJ: Barnes and Noble Books.

Narayan, Kirin. 1989. *Storytellers, Saints, and Scoundrels*. Philadelphia, PA: University of Pennsylvania Press.

Olivelle, Patrick, ed. 1995. *Rules and Regulations of Brahmanical Asceticism*. Albany, NY: State University of New York Press.

Reynell, Josephine. 1987. "Prestige, Honour and the Family: Laywomen's Religiosity Amongst Śvetāmbar Mūrtipūjāk Jains in Jaipur." *Bulletin D'Études Indiennes* 5: 313–359.

—— 1991. "Women and the Reproduction of the Jain Community." In *The Assembly of Listeners*, ed. Michael Carrithers and Caroline Humphrey, 41–68. Cambridge: Cambridge University Press.

Ryan, James. 1988. "Erotic Excess and Sexual Danger in the *Cīvakacintāmaṇi*." In *Open Boundaries*, ed. John E. Cort, 67–83. Albany, NY: State University of New York Press.

Sangave, Vilas A. 1980. *Jaina Community*. Bombay: Popular Prakashan.

Shāntā, N. 1985. *La Voie Jaina*. Paris: O.E.I.L. Translated in English in 1997. *The Unknown Pilgrims, The Voice of the Sādhvīs: The History, Spirituality and Life of Jaina Women Ascetics*. Delhi: Sri Satguru Publications. (An English translation of *La Voie Jaina*.)

Sinclair-Brull, Wendy. 1997. *Female Ascetics*. Richmond: Curzon.

Smith, Wilfred Cantwell. 1950. "The Comparative Study of Religion: Reflections on the Possibility and Purpose of a Religious Science." In *McGill University, Faculty of Divinity, Inaugural Lectures*, 39–60. Montreal: McGill University.

—— 1976. "Comparative Religion: Whither – and Why?" In *Religious Diversity: Essays by Wilfred Cantwell Smith*, ed. Williard G. Oxtoby. New York: Harper and Row, Pub. (reprinted from 1959. *The History of Religions: Essays in Methodology*, ed. Mircea Eliade and Joseph M. Kitagawa. Chicago, IL: University of Chicago Press).

Vallely, Anne. 2002. *Guardians of the Transcendent*. Toronto: University of Toronto Press.

Weinberger-Thomas, Catherine. 1999. *Ashes of Immortality*. Chicago, IL: University of Chicago Press.

Young, Serinity. 1994. "Gendered Politics in Ancient Indian Asceticism." In the *Union Seminary Quarterly Review*, 48 (3–4): 73–92.

Zydenbos, Robert J. 1999. "The Ritual giving of Food to a Digambara Renunciant." In *Approaches to Jaina Studies: Philosophy, Logical, Rituals Symbols*, ed. N. K. Wagle and Olle Qvarnström, 291–303. University of Toronto: Center of South Asian Studies.

8

THINKING COLLECTIVELY ABOUT JAIN *SATĪ*S

The uses of Jain *satī* name lists

M. Whitney Kelting

Jains venerate virtuous women (*satī*s) who are virtuous and who, through their virtue, protect, promote, or merely uphold Jain values and the Jain religion. Jains narrate the lives of *satī*s both individually and in the context of Jain Universal Histories (such as the Śvetāmbar *Triṣaṣṭiśalākāpuruṣacaritra* of Hemacandra and the Digambar *Ādipurāṇa* of Jinasena) and some of these *satī*s are named in early Jain texts like the Śvetāmbar *Kalpa Sūtra*. Śvetāmbar Jains also list *satī*s (often sixteen of the following names: Brāhmī, Sundarī, Candanbālā, Rājīmatī, Draupadī, Kauśalyā, Mṛgāvatī, Sulasā, Sītā, Subhadrā, Śivā, Kuntī, Śīlavatī, Damayantī, Puṣpacūlā, Prabhāvatī, and Padmāvatī) who stand in for the greater totality of *satī*s. They also have more inclusive lists which extend the title *satī* to an unbounded number of women. *Satī* lists, through their fluidity and their inclusivity, serve as representatives of the totality of women's virtue and as such are efficacious primarily by creating auspiciousness but also by reducing karma. While *satī*s are revered in all Jain sects, this discussion is centered on the ways that Śvetāmbar Mūrtipūjak Tapā Gacch Jains have constructed the idea of collectivities of *satī*s.[1] At present there are five *gacchs* (mendicant lineages) of Śvetāmbar Mūrtipūjak Jain mendicants: Tapā, Añcal, Khartar, Paican, and Tristuti. Between 85 and 90 percent of the Śvetāmbar Mūrtipūjak mendicants belong to the Tapā Gacch, which was formed in the thirteenth century CE, when the mendicant Jagaccandrasūri left the mainstream Vaṭa Gacch as a response to mendicant laxity.[2] The Jains with whom I conduct my research in Maharashtra identify themselves with Tapā Gacch mendicants, and when they perform rituals where the liturgies vary from *gacch* to *gacch*, they likewise choose those associated with the Tapā Gacch.[3]

To examine the Tapā Gacch Jain conception of *satī*s, we can look at the ways in which these Jains frame the multiplicity and/or collectivity of *satī*s through their presence in recitations of lists of the names of the *satī*s. Four short texts were chosen for discussion in this chapter because they were the most commonly found *satī* lists and were used in ritual performances. They are the *Brāhmī*

Candanbālikā (BC), the *Soḷ Satī no Chand* (The Verses of the Sixteen *Satī*s; SSC), the *Bharahesara nī Sajjhāy* (The Instruction on Lord Bharat; BS), and the *Satā Satī nī Sajjhāy* (The Instruction on the True and Virtuous Men and Women, SSS). Here it is important to distinguish between ritual texts (those intended for performance) and ritual instructions (those which guide performance) (Bruhn 1981: 21). The four texts discussed hereafter are ritual texts intended for performance. I include short glosses which serve to give an interpretation to these texts as well; these commentarial glosses should be understood as a kind of ritual instruction informing the performer of the efficacy and meaning of the texts.

The texts discussed in this chapter are each linked to laity by practices drawn from mendicant praxis, such as the *pratikramaṇ* (ritual repentance and expiation of sin) and blessings bestowed by the recitation of *māṅgalik* (holy verses). Further, these texts are neither restricted to the monks nor relegated to the laity. The uses and interpretations of these lists of *satī*s matter because they are embedded within texts shared by all members of the four-fold congregation suggesting that these *satī*s names have an efficacy of their own and are significant beyond the standard explanation of *satī*s being merely good role models for laywomen. One can think of the lists of *satī*s as falling into three patterns of use or understanding: (1) the totality of individual narratives as a corpus of ritual texts for lay practices; (2) the unbounded collectivity of women's virtue which permits Jain women's identification with *satī*s as a model for linking them and their practices with *satī*s and the virtues of *satī*s; and (3) name lists as mantras whose recitation is efficacious. The first pattern, which is not central to our discussion here, will be briefly treated in the following lines and the latter two will be addressed in greater detail in their turn. The first pattern in the use of *satī* collectivities manifests in the annual calendar of rituals (holidays, ceremonies, and fasts) in which *satī* narratives are recited; on these occasions women recite or read narratives individually. The idea of a group or the totality of *satī*s is distinctly missing in these ritual texts: There is no sense of interchangeability and the *satī* invoked in narrative is the one whose narrative and name is efficacious in that context.[4] Though I am not focussing on this kind of telling of *satī* narratives here, it is important to note that most of the time among contemporary Tapā Gacch lay Jains *satī*s are invoked as individuals through the telling of particular narratives and not in the form of a group or of the totality of *satī*s. However, one can think of the collection of these individual narratives as forming (with one or two narratives of great men such as Śreyaṃs) a corpus of Jain ritual texts (*kathā*) associated predominantly with fasting.

The bulk of the chapter is divided into four sections. The first examines the discourse of *satī*s and the ways *satī* discourse manifests itself in the Jain tradition. The second addresses the history, context and the text of each of the four lists discussed in this chapter. Third, the lists are analyzed for the ways in which variation in the content of the lists indicates an unbounded totality of virtue and how this unbounded ideal allows for Jains to see Jain laywomen and nuns in connection with *satī*s; in essence, this is the second pattern of use. The fourth analyzes the third pattern of use for *satī* lists as mantric, more generally articulating the ways in which the recitation of the *satī*s names is efficacious in karma reduction (as part of the *pratikramaṇ*) and as *māṅgalik* (auspicious verses especially propitious for the start of any religious practice).

*Satī*s and the Jain tradition

There has been much scholarship dedicated to defining the term "*satī*" and outlining its use in Hindu sociopolitical and religious contexts.[5] There is an important distinction drawn between the Hindu religious use of the term "*satī*" which refers to a virtuous woman and the British use of the term "suttee" to refer to the act of a widow dying on her husband's funeral pyre an act called "going with" (or *sahagaman*) in the Hindu context.[6] The *satī* of the Hindu context is one who fulfills utterly her role as a dedicated wife (*pativratā*) and whose dedication to her husband extends to her own acts of self-sacrifice, though not necessarily through death (Harlan 1992: 118–133, 172–181, Weinberger-Thomas 1999: 28–34). A *satī* in the Hindu context always articulates her virtue through her dedication to her husband and her chastity. However, in the Hindu context the intention to die before or with one's husband is key to attaining the virtue that makes one a *satī*. A *satī* who succeeds in her total self-sacrifice by dying with her husband can reach the highest level of virtue attainable for a Hindu woman, that is, to be a *satīmātā* who serves as a protector deity for her family and others.

Jains likewise participate in the language of the chaste, dedicated, and self-denying wife who protects her husband and her husband's family. Many contemporary Jain women, like their Hindu counterparts, are very concerned with protecting their status as auspiciously married women (*saubhāgyavatī*) and perform fasts and other rituals specifically with the intent of protecting their husband and children.[7] These rituals include the recitation and study of particular *satī* narratives or of texts which have *satī* narratives embedded in them. Jain *satī* narratives often center around the protagonist's chastity and protection of husband, but I found elsewhere that the language of virtue in these narratives can also be linked to the renunciation of family (Kelting 2003). The Jain use of the term always carries with it the language of virtue often articulated through the language of chastity or celibacy but without the idealization or potential of self-sacrifice; rather, Jains see the highest potential for women in renunciation rather than self-sacrifice for husband and family.

Jain *satī* lists share several names and narratives found (with some subtle and some not so subtle variations) in Hindu narratives of virtuous women – an important indicator of the shared discourse of women's virtue between these two traditions. However, the particular status of these narratives in the Jain corpus suggest the ways that Jains articulate the superiority of their models for women's virtue. The narratives of *satī*s who are also found in Hindu narratives are the less commonly told stories (except that of Damayantī) and they are also often (like

Kuntī who lives on after the self-immolation of Madrī who is not a *satī* for Jains) articulated against the Hindu model of the *satī* who dies with her husband (*sahagamanī*). Because so many of the Jain *satī* narratives end with the *satī* taking ordination (*dīkṣā*) as a Jain nun, we can see the more than just implicit juxtaposition of taking *dīkṣā* against the sinful (here, to Jains) path of self-immolation. This balance is particularly problematic because at some point each of these women either has to die without renouncing, renounce her husband, or be a widow who then renounces. These choices illustrate the difficult balance of the competing models – the nun and the dedicated wife – of women's virtue for Jains.[8] Though Somani (1982: 79–80) found inscriptional evidence that in Rajasthan there were Jain women who performed the rite of *sahagaman* as late as the nineteenth century, this is clearly not the norm and there does not seem to be any evidence of this as a contemporary practice. The Jain counter rhetoric is powerful enough that many women I interviewed insisted that I be clear that Jain *satī*s are truly virtuous and therefore would not commit such an act of violence and a disruption of the living out of their karma.

In the Śvetāmbar Jain lay context, where any woman can potentially become a celibate nun, chastity can be understood as fidelity to one's husband and a general limitation on sensual attachments while performing one's duties of taking care of and producing children (usually sons) for one's husband's lineage. I found that laywomen would customarily speak of a *satī*'s virtues in speaking of her as steadfast, dedicated to her husband and her religion, and generally morally good, of which chastity is a part. Though Hindu women, Jain nuns, and Jain laywomen might not agree in their priorities in telling *satī* narratives (stressing self-sacrifice, celibacy and chastity and piety in turn), they all share the definition of a *satī* as a virtuous woman who demonstrates steadfast moral strength in the face of profound challenges, especially to her chastity.

The variations in the content in the corpus of *satī* narratives and in the lists of their names suggest that multiple kinds of virtue can be included (the term "*satī*" is understood to be multivocal and multivalent) and that there is an interchangeability within the lists (in a sense, the narratives behind them do not matter). Although the lists discussed hereafter do not include these narratives (though the SSC has abbreviated narratives), it is useful for our discussion to briefly show how variation in the *satī* narratives is the norm. Here are two encapsulated *satī* narratives:

> Candanbālā was a princess who is sold into slavery to a merchant. The merchant's wife becomes jealous of Candanbālā's beauty so she has Candanbālā's hair shaved off, chains her hands and feet, and leaves her in a hut with no food. Meanwhile Mahāvīr had taken a vow five months and twenty-five days earlier that he would only break his fast if the food were offered by a princess now a slave with her head shaved, in chains, chanting the Navkār mantra, sorting black lentils, and crying. When he sees Candanbālā she fulfills all of the details of his vow but she is not

> crying. When he keeps walking she begins to cry and he comes back and accepts her alms. Once she gives Mahāvīr his alms her chains break and her hair instantly grows back. Candanbālā then vows to become a nun at Mahāvīr's hand and the whole village converts to Jainism. Later after her *dīkṣā* (initiation), Candanbālā leads the community of nuns.
>
> Rājīmatī is engaged to Neminath. On his way to their wedding he hears the sound of crying. He asks what the sound is and when he is told it is the cries of all the animals to be slaughtered for his wedding feast, he decides not to marry but to become a Jain monk instead. Rājīmatī then goes to ask for dīkṣā from Neminath and she becomes a nun. Later when Neminath's brother tries to sexually assault Rājīmatī, she gives him a sermon that convinces him to become a monk.

Even in just these two capsule narratives we can see variations from the bulk of *satī* narratives. Candanbālā's narrative is centered around her miraculous interaction with Mahāvīr while Rājīmatī's includes her *dīkṣā* and events that follow it. Most of the *satī*s marry, have children and later become Jain nuns. Right away, however, significant exceptions surface. Candanbālā never marries, Rājīmatī is nearly married, Damayantī though married has no children, Sulasā never renounces and, in fact, leads the lay community, and Sītā has children and never renounces. Among the *satī*s who take *dīkṣā* (initiation) into Jain mendicancy, there are those *satī*s, such as Rājīmatī, for whom *dīkṣā* is central and whose narratives include significant incidents after their *dīkṣā* and those *satī*s, like Draupadī, for whom *dīkṣā* appears almost like an afterthought or the inevitable conclusion of the "ideal life."[9] These variations suggest most powerfully the idea that perfect virtue can be demonstrated by a variety of women's lives. While being a mendicant is understood to have a higher religious status than a layperson and marriage is assumed for all laity, in the *satī* narratives neither marrying, nor bearing children, nor becoming a nun are the singular templates for female virtue. Similarly, as part of the *Dīvāḷī* festival, most Śvetāmbar Mūrtipūjak Jains write a benediction on the first page of new account books (Cort 2001a; Kelting 2001; Laidlaw 1995). Laidlaw calls this a "shopping list, as it were, of worldly virtues" (1995: 380). This list includes married men who renounce, unmarried men who renounce, married men who do not renounce and a king; the list suggests a totality of men's virtues in a way reminiscent of the *satī* lists. However, the list of virtuous men varies across a good many more paradigms than just marriage and renunciation as they lead public lives in which other forms of virtue (leadership, wealth, donation) also obtain while the *satī*s share virtues centering only on house-holding and renunciation.

The texts

This article looks at four texts listing the names of *satī*s which I am calling *satī* lists. The BC is simply a list of *satī* names and a short comment on their efficacy.

The SSC includes a short verse for each name listed. Two of the texts, the BS and the SSS, are lists of *satī*s alongside lists of great men (*mahāpuruṣa*). All four texts discussed are linked with Tapā Gacch practices and found in popular, larger compilation texts clearly identified with the Tapā Gacch, such as *Bhakti Bhāvanā*, *Śrī Jain Sajjhāy Māḷā*, *Śrī Pañca Pratikramaṇa Sūtra*, *Śrī Sudhāras Stavan Saṅgrah*, and *Śrī Taporatna Mahodadhi*. Two texts, the SSC and the SSS, have named authors who are Tapā Gacch mendicants. The two unsigned texts, the BC and the BS, are found in Tapā Gacch texts but without identifiable authors and there is some difficulty in their dating. At best one can say that all these texts date from at the latest the fifteenth to the early eighteenth century but the BC and the BS may be even older. The history of these texts remains for the most part unstudied because scholarship has not focused on these kinds of devotional and ritual literature in the Jain tradition. Each of the four texts is given in the following pages in full along with information about the history and context of each text. This will establish a foundation for the discussion of the idea of collective virtue and *satī* list efficacy that follow.

Brāhmī, Candanbālikā

The BC (sometimes titled: "*Soḷ Satī nī Stuti*," – Praises of the Sixteen *Satī*s) is little more than a list of names:

> Brāhmī, Candanbālikā, Bhagavatī Rājīmatī, Draupadī,
> Kauśalyā and Mṛgāvatī and Sulasā, Sītā, Subhadrā, Śivā;
> Kuntī, Śīlavatī, Nalaḥ's Damayantī, Cūlā, and Prabhāvatī,
> Padmāvatī and Sundarī. May this auspiciousness be performed everyday.[10]
> (*Jina Śāsananāṃ Śramaṇīratno* 1994: 121)

In *Jina Śāsananāṃ Śramaṇīratno*, the BC is called the "earliest remembrance" (*prātaḥsmaraṇ*) of the sixteen *satī*s, suggesting its place as the root text, at least, for the *idea* of the sixteen *satī*s.[11] If we can take that "*prātaḥsmaraṇ*" as authoritative, then we can establish that the BC predates the SSC which was written by the monk Udayratna and which appears to be based on it. That said, one cannot totally rule out yet earlier unattributed precursors to either text though none have, to my knowledge, been encountered.

Soḷ Satī no Chand

Udayratna who wrote the SSC sometime between 1692 and 1743[12] is credited with writing several devotional pieces, often using the *chand* form. The *chand* form itself is a devotional metrical verse form commonly used by Jain writers.[13] Most ritual manuals include a number of *chand*s as part of their collection of devotional literature for use by the laity and many include Udayratna's better studied work: *Śrī Śankheśvar Pārśvanāth no Chand* (the Verses of the Auspicious

Śankheśvar Pārśvanāth). The SSC and other *chand*s are often memorized by mendicants (and occasionally by lay Jains) as a devotional practice. The SSC is found in hymnbooks, such as the ubiquitous *Śrī Sudhāras Stavan Saṅgrah* (The Collection of Nectar-like Hymns) and popular lay manuals, such as *Bhakti Bhāvanā* (Devotional Sentiments).

The SSC is a seventeen couplet devotional poem which tells in almost cryptic condensation the narratives of the sixteen *satī*s. The first and last couplets frame the *chand* and its power as a *māṅgalik* (auspicious prayer). The middle fifteen tell, in condensed form, the key narratives associated with each of the *satī*s named.

Praises to Ādināth, the first Jina, make our prayers fruitful.
At sunrise, create auspiciousness, and repeat the sixteen *satī*s' names (1).
The young girl beneficial to the whole world, Brāhmī was Bharat's sister.
The soul living in every sound and letter, she is the greatest of the sixteen *satī*s (2).
Bāhubalī's sister, the crown jewel of the *satī*s, Ṛṣabha's daughter is named Sundarī.
Her beauty was matchless in the three worlds and her good qualities, unparalleled (3).
Candanbālā was a chaste and pious laywoman since childhood.
Mahāvīr finally found her winnowing lentils, she who would fulfill his omniscient vow (4).
Ugrasen's daughter, faithful as the North Star, was Rājīmatī, the beloved of Nemināth.
Conquering the lust of youth, she showed a restraint difficult even for the gods (5).
The five great Indian Pāṇḍavas' wife, Draupadī praised god.
She received one hundred and eight lengths of cloth and from this we know the chastity in her heart (6).
King Daśarath's matchless queen, Kauśalyā, that moon flower,
Chaste, excellent mother of Rām, upheld the family's tradition of merit (7).
In Kauśāmbī, there was a king named Śatānik who had a splendid reign.
The housewife of his home was Mṛgāvatī *satī*. Her fame resounded in God's temple (8).
Sulasā was truly chaste and without flaw, charming but without the poison of sensuality,
Seeing her crown, sin vanishes; Saying her name, one is joyful (9).
Thus too was the sweetheart of Rām, Janak's daughter Sītā *satī*.
All the world knows that when she undertook her test, she cooled the fire with her chastity (10).
With a sieve tied to a weak thread, she drew water from the well.
That stain-removing *satī*, Subhadrā, opened the doors of Campā city (11).
Śivapad's village's Śivā is worshiped by men and gods, her virtue unbroken.
Her name makes one pure, which is that name's secret talent (12).

In Hastināpur, Pāṇḍu's sweetheart, was Kuntī.
She was the mother of the Pāṇḍavas, the sister of the ten Daśār's and a lotus-like dedicated wife (13)
Śīlavatī is the name of she who upheld her virtuous vows, offer her praises and benefit in three ways:
Recite her name, receive *darśan*, and destroy sinful acts (14).
In Niṣidhā city, Nalaḥ's wish fulfiller, Damayantī, was his wife.
Troubled, she protected her chastity, illuminating the three worlds (15).
Unconquered by Kamdev, Puṣpacūlā and Prabhāvatī are revered by all the world.
Famous in all the universe, granter of wishes, the sixteenth of the *satī*s is Padmāvatī (16).
Victoriously recite the couplets from the scriptures, Udayratna gives this evidence.
Recited by men at dawn, those who listen gain joy and prosperity (17).[14]
(*Śrī Sudhāras Stavan Saṅgrah*, No date: 87–90)

The BC and the SSC are the most commonly reproduced and named texts focussing on the sixteen *satī*s. In both cases, the names included are the same (in fact, the same seventeen names are included in both which will be discussed in the following lines) suggesting a relationship between the texts.

Bharahesara nī sajjhāy

The BS is a thirteen verse *sajjhāy* (instruction) which is recited as part of the Tapā Gacch morning *Pratikramaṇ* (*Rāïa Pratikramaṇa*).[15] It has no signed author and is as of yet undated.[16] Even if the Tapā Gacch *Pratikramaṇ* texts were to be dated, the individual pieces of the *Pratikramaṇ* could not be clearly determined from the dating of what are compilations. However, the BS must predate its commentary, the *Śrī Bharateśvara Bāhubalī Vṛttiḥ* (The Auspicious Commentary Lord Bharat and Bāhubalī = BBV), which is dated to 1453 CE. The *pratikramaṇ* rite, a ritual repentance and expiation of sins, is ranked as one of the obligatory actions (*āvaśyaka*) of mendicants and also lay Jains.[17] In each of the *pratikramaṇ* rituals (morning, evening, fortnightly, thrice-yearly, and annual) a *sajjhāy* is recited but it is only in the morning *Pratikramaṇ* that the *sajjhāy* text is fixed as a particular *sajjhāy*. The term "*sajjhāy*" means "instruction" or "study." However, the texts called *sajjhāy*s are usually devotional prayers and most are verse-narratives in form. Most of the other *sajjhāy*s in the commonly used *Śrī Jain Sajjhāy Mālā* are dedicated to particular "virtuous individuals" and present narratives in verse form. In this the BS (and the SSS discussed hereafter) are somewhat unusual in their lack of narrative or even imagery. The morning *pratikramaṇ* is performed by all mendicants, by especially pious lay Jains, and as a part of all Jain fasts. The BS is the most widely performed and well known text discussed in this article.

The BS begins with a list of virtuous men (*mahāpuruṣa*), which is followed by a list of women referred to as *satī*s at the close of the text.

> Bharat, Bāhubalī, Abhaykumār, and Ḍanḍaṇakumār;
> Śrīyak, Arṇikāputra. Atimukta, and Nāgdatta (1).
> Metāryamuni, Sthūlabhadra, Vajrarṣi, Nandiṣeṇa, Sinhgirī;
> Kṛtapuṇya and Sukośalmuni, Puṇḍariksvāmī, Keśīkumār, Karakaṇḍu (2).
> Halla, Vihalla, Sudarśana, Sālmuni, Mahāsālmuni, Śālibhadra;
> Bhadrabāhu, Daśārṇbhadra, Prasannacandra and Yaśobhadrasūri (3).
> Jambusvāmī, Vankacūlā, Gajasukumāl, Avantisukumāl;
> Dhannā, Ilācīputra, Cilātīputra and Yugbāhumuni (4).
> Āryamahāgiri, Āryarakṣitsūri, Āryasuhastisūri, Udāyī, Manak;
> Kālikācārya, Śāmba, Pradhyumna, and Muldeva (5).
> Prabhava, Viṣṇukumār, Ārdrakumār, and Dṛḍhaprahārī;
> Śreyaṃs and Kurgaḍu, Śayyaṃbhava and Meghakumār (6).
> And also other noble men with knowledge and a multitude of like virtues.
> Through remembering their names one can destroy the bonds of sin (7).
> Sulasā, Candanbālā, Manoramā, Madanrekhā, Damayantī;
> Narmadasundarī, Sītā, Nandā, Bhadrā, and Subhadrā (8).
> Rājīmatī, Rṣidatta, Padmāvatī, Anjanā, Śrīdevī;
> Jyeṣṭhā, Sujeṣṭhā, Mṛgāvatī, Prabhāvatī, Cellnādevī (9),
> Brāhmī, Sundarī, Rukimaṇī, Revatī, Kuntī, Śivā, and Jayantī;
> Devakī, Draupadī, Dhāraṇī, Kalāvatī and Puṣpacūlā (10),
> Padmāvatī, and Gaurī, Gāndhārī, Lakṣmaṇā and Susīmā;
> Jambuvatī, Rukimaṇī-Kṛṣṇa's queens (11).
> Yakṣā and Yakṣadattā, Bhutā, and, also certainly, Bhutadattā;
> Seṇā, Veṇā, Reṇā-the sisters of Sthūlabhadra (12),
> And all the other important *satī*s who upheld their stainless virtue alongside their victorious acts.
> Still today their fame resounds like a drum throughout the three worlds (13).[18]
>
> (*Śrī Pañca Pratikramaṇa Sūtra*, No date: 20–21)

This text should be understood within the context of the *Pratikramaṇ* texts as a whole which include a number of lists, among them the *Logassa Sūtra* (or *Caturviṃsāti Stava*) – a list of the twenty-four Jinas – the *Sāt Lakh Sūtra* (the *Sūtra* of the Seven Hundred Thousand) – a list of the kinds of beings whose injury one is confessing – and the *Tīrtha Vandanā* (Obeiscances to the Pilgrimage Places) – a list of the main pilgrimage sites for Śvetāmbar Mūrtipūjak Jains. Laidlaw (1995: 211–213) discusses various lists in the Khartar Gacch *pratikramaṇ* and suggests that the *Sāt Lakh Sūtra*, the list of eighteen sins (*aḍhār pāp*), the list of all the ways one might infringe of law vows (*vandittu*), and other lists are an attempt at including all the possibilities which the *pratikramaṇ* should address. The BS has the names listed and an open-ended inclusion of all the other similarly virtuous humans not named. We can see this *sajjhāy* as a totality of human virtues expressed through a list of names of virtuous people.

Satā Satī nī sajjhāy

The relatively common *sajjhāy* collection *Śrī Jain Sajjhāy Mālā* includes another *sajjhāy* very similar to the BS. The SSS, attributed to the Tapā Gacch mendicant Jñānvimalsūri (1645/6–1713/4 CE)[19] includes a list of virtuous men and women in a list that is clearly based on the BS or the BBV. Jñānvimalsūri wrote several commentaries and narratives in Sanskrit and several long *rāso* (verse narrative) texts in Gujarati such as *Āśokcandrarohiṇī Rās*, as well as a number of other *sajjhāys* in Gujarati dedicated to individual virtuous men and women (Koṭhārī and Śāh 1993: 230–235).

> Every morning revere their names, those pillars of Jainism, Bharat, Bāhubalī;
> Abhaykumār and Ḍhaḍhaṇo, Śrīyak and Kṛtapuṇya (1).
> Arṇikāputra and Atimukta, Nāgadatta, Sthūlibhadra;
> Vajrasvāmī, Nandiṣeṇa, Dhannā and Śālibhadra (2).
> Simhagirī, Kīrti, Sukośalmuni, Karakaṇḍu, Puṇḍarīksvāmī;
> Halla, Vihalla, Sudarśan, Śāḷ and Mahāśāḷ (3).
> Gajasukumār, Jambūprabhu, Keśī, Avantīsukumāḷ;
> Daśārṇbhadra, Yaśobhadrajī, Īlācī, Cilātīputra, Sālmuni (4).
> Yugbāhu, Udāī, Manakmuni, Āryarakṣitsūri, Āryamahāgirī;
> Āryasuhastīsūri, Prabhav, and also, Śāmba, Pradhyumna-those munis (5).
> Those munis: Muldev, Kālikācārya, Viṣṇukumār, Śreyaṃs;
> Ārdrakumār, Dṛḍhaprahār and also those munis, Kurgaḍu, Meghakumār (6).
> Sayambhav, Prasannacandrajī, Mahāsāl, Vankacūla;
> Take these true names, as though they were a beautiful lineage (7).
> Sulasā, Candanbālikā, Maṇoramā Madaṇrekhā;
> Kuntī, Narmadāsundarī, Brāhmī, Sundarī-those storehouses of virtue (8).
> Damayantī*satī*, Revatī, Śivā, Jayantī, Nandā;
> Devakī, Draupadī, Dhāriṇī, Śrīdevī, Subhadrā, Bhadrā (9).
> Ṛṣidattā, Rājīmatī, Padmāvatī, Prabhāvatī, say them;
> Anjanā and Kaḷāvatī, Puṣpacūlā, listen with your heart (10).
> Gaurī, Gāndhārī, Lakṣamaṇā, Jambūvatī, Satyābhāmā;
> Padmā, Susīmā, Rūkaminī-these are the eight wives of Kṛṣṇa (11).
> Jyeṣṭhā, Sujyeṣṭhā, Mṛgāvatī, Cellaṇā, Padmā, and Queen Prabhā;
> The seven sisters of Sthūlibhadra, the source of intellectual virtue (12).
> Yakṣā, Yakṣadattā, and also, Bhutā and Bhutadattā;
> Senā, Venā, Renā, these majestic young women are named (13).
> And all those *mahāsatīs*, victorious in the three worlds;
> Today even, their fame still resounds like a drum (14).
> Śīlavantī, Sursundarī, Kauśalyā, and Sumitrā;
> These purest of Jain people, they are known as those given by god (15).

Cooling sin and worldly troubles, indeed, these names make a garland of auspiciousness;
Jñānvimal attained these virtues, recognize their wondrous greatness (16).[20]
(*Śrī Jain Sajjhāy Māḷā* (*Sacitra*) 1968: 18–20)

Here the *satī* list differs from the BS in its ordering of the names, by the inclusion of additional names of *satī*s and exclusion of two men's names.[21] In the section of virtuous women it includes all the women from the BS and then adds four more: Śīlavatī, Sursundarī, Kauśalyā, and Sumitrā. The first two *satī*s, Śīlavatī and Sursundarī, are the heroines of commonly told narratives and Śīlavatī is also often included in the sixteen *satī* lists. Kauśalyā is always included in the list of sixteen *satī*s. Sumitrā does not appear in any other *satī* list I have found leading me to suspect that her narrative had been popular at the time that the SSS was written. The inclusion of these names suggests that the author of the SSS felt that the list in the BS was not complete without the addition of these four names. The SSS may draw its additional *satī* names from the BBV which expands slightly on the list included in the BBV's root text, the BS.

Satī lists as a totality of virtue

The four *satī* lists display both a fluidity and an inclusivity within their collectivities of *satī*s. This combination of fluidity and inclusivity suggests that *satī* lists serve as a representation of the totality of virtue as well as the collectivity of virtuous women. When juxtaposed with collectivities of virtuous men, *satī* lists illuminate the gendered implications of virtue. The linking of *satī*s and great men (*mahāpuruṣa*) in the BS and the SSS represents a totality of human virtue. However, the term *satī* as the only the available term for virtuous women subsumes a wide variety of women by identifying them by their chastity and piety (virtues available to all women) while lists of great men display a wider variety of virtues but a narrower scope of who can have these virtues (designated by bounded categories). This single unbounded term, *satī*, allows a flexibility to extend the designation to other women as they are identified as virtuous.

Fluidity within satī *lists*

The list of the sixteen *satī*s is not stable. This instability may arise partly because both root texts: the BC and the SSC, include the names of seventeen *satī*s in spite of the common titles for these lists referring to sixteen *satī*s. They are: Brāhmī, Sundarī, Candanbālā, Rājīmatī, Draupadī, Kauśalyā, Mṛgāvatī, Sulasā, Sītā, Subhadrā, Śivā, Kuntī, Śīlavatī, Damayantī, Puṣpacūlā, Prabhāvatī, and Padmāvatī. Both lists are identical but for the placement of Sundarī who is in the last position in the BC while the SSC has her name in the second position (where most Jains named her when they attempted to list the sixteen *satī*s for me).[22] In an effort to make the lists conform to the number sixteen, contemporary list makers – published authors, contemporary renouncers and laywomen with whom I spoke – had to decide which of these seventeen names to omit. Most commonly Śīlavatī was omitted, owing probably to the fact that the name can understood to be a generic term (one who is chaste) that might be read as an adjective for another *satī*.[23] However, since Śīlavatī has her own verse in the SSC, there is no question that the author Udayratna, saw Śīlavatī as a name of a *satī* rather than as an adjective. During *Paryuṣaṇ* 2001 in Pune there was a huge parade in the old city of men and women who had performed major fasts during the festival. The parade was designed around a series of sixteen floats bearing the names of the sixteen *satī*s. The list of the sixteen *satī*s for the parade floats varied from the root texts' lists given earlier by omitting Draupadī and Puṣpacūlā. The parade planners retained Śīlavatī and, interestingly, inserted Mayaṇāsundarī, who did not appear in any other lists of the sixteen *satī*s I found.[24] With the exception of the parade floats, whose order may well have reflected the exigencies of Pune traffic,[25] the order of the sixteen *satī*s in other contexts tend to match either the BC or the SSC closely, suggesting a direct connection between these reconstructions of the sixteen *satī*s and the root texts. These choices indicate a degree of familiarity with the root text, but it is clear that the number sixteen has a kind of totemic significance that outweighs a careful reproduction of exactly which sixteen. The fact of variability within the lives of these *satī*s as indicated in our earlier discussion, the significance of the idea of sixteen, and the fluidity of the lists of sixteen suggest that the "sixteen *satī*s" stands in as a collectivity of virtue. In the case of the variations within the sixteen there is a strong sense of interchangeability which becomes even more significant when one compares this idea of the collectivity of the *satī*s with the longer and more inclusive lists.

The BBV, also called the *Kathākoś* (Collection of Stories), composed by Śubhaśīlagaṇi in 1453 is a commentary on the BS and serves presently as an important source for narratives about ideal Jains. It was included in a proposed curriculum at the 1988 Conference of Tapā Gacch monks in Ahmedabad, in which the monks in their third year of a seven-year program would study either this text or the *Pañcatantra* (Cort 2001b: 335). Both collections of edifying narratives can serve as sources for the use of narratives for giving sermons. Further, the BBV is one of only two narrative texts that a Tapā Gacch monk is enjoined to study first in this curriculum (Cort 2001b: 339). It includes the narratives of each of the great men and virtuous women who are listed in the root text, the BS. In addition to the men and women listed in the root text, it has ten more virtuous men[26] and five more *satī*s: Śīlavatī, Nandyantī, Rohiṇī, Ratisundarī, and Śrīmatī. It could be that the narrative collection seemed incomplete to Śubhaśīlagaṇi without the narratives of these very popular *satī*s. Whatever his motives, his departure from the list in the root text may well have set a precedent of fluidity in these lists of virtuous Jains which was subsequently continued by the authors of the SSS and later lists and collections.

Śubhaśīlagaṇi's is not the only commentary of the BS, though it is the most substantial, the *Śrī Pañca Pratikramaṇ Sūtro Vivecan Sahit* (The Five *Pratikramaṇs* with Commentary) is an extended commentary on the *Pañca*

Pratikramaṇ Sūtra. The longest and most detailed section is the gloss on the BS. Here, as in the BBV, a narrative is given for each of the virtuous Jains named in the root text. Owing to its inclusion of the same five *satī* names added in the BBV, the list of *satīs*' narratives in the *Śrī Pañca Pratikramaṇ Sutro Vivecan Sahit* is clearly based on the BBV. In addition to the fifty-three men, there is a second grouping of twelve narratives of men under the heading: "Beyond these, some additional stories."[27] The additional five *satīs* are under a heading: "Because of their popularity, five more *satīs*." It is not impossible that the "popularity" referred to in the heading derives from a widespread, early adoption of the BBV commentary in mendicant instruction or study and the subsequent broadcast – through mendicant sermons and writings – to the greater community of precisely those stories.

Gender and categories of virtue

As alluded to earlier with the *Dīvāḷī* book inscriptions, the collectivity of *satīs* might be profitably compared to the collectivities of virtuous men. The BS begins with a list of fifty-three great men (*mahāpuruṣa*), followed by a list of forty-seven *satīs*. These fifty-three men are great men of whom some became monks. This list, in turn, can be seen in light of another collectivity of great men, the sixty-three illustrious men (*śalākāpuruṣa*) of *Mahāpurāṇa* narrative collections such as the ninth-century Digambar scholar-monk Jinasena's *Ādipurāṇa* and twelfth-century scholar-monk Hemacandra's *Triṣaṣṭiśalākāpuruṣacaritra*.[28] Each of the categories of men included in the sixty-three has its unique relationship to Jain values and to the various life paths which may or may not lead to achieving liberation from rebirth: twenty-four Jinas (Jain teacher-saints responsible for revitalizing the faith in this era who achieve liberation as *arhats*),[29] twelve *cakravartins* (universal rulers who attain liberation as *siddhas*), nine *baladevas* (devout laymen who attain liberation), nine *vāsudevas* (half-*cakravartins* and ideal Jain kings who spend a lifetime in hell for killing enemies before attaining liberation), and nine *prativāsudevas* (powerful Jain leaders who abuse their powers, are killed by the *vāsudevas* and are reborn in hell). Each of these categories is linked to each other by their placement in the narratives of the Jinas themselves, while the category designations themselves serve as a link between great men of different narratives. Here, like the *satīs*, there are both monks and laymen but in contrast to the *satīs*, these categories include the Jinas and *cakravartins* both of whom have a special identity at birth arising out of past karma; and those destined for at least one lifetime in hell.

The fifty-three men in the BS are mostly monks and none are going to hell, which is a closer counterpoint to the *satīs*. After the list of these great men, the BS includes a gloss commenting on men's virtue: "And also other noble men with knowledge and a multitude of like virtues" (BS, 7). This brief is followed by a listing of the names of the forty-seven *satīs* followed by an explanation of their greatness: "And all the other important *satīs* who upheld their stainless virtue alongside their victorious acts" (BS, 13). The BS suggests that the virtues of great

Jains are divided along gender lines; recall, that the list of men ends with a statement of their virtue based on their knowledge and good qualities, while the women's list ends with a separate statement of women's virtue focused on their "stainless virtue" (read chastity) and great acts worthy of remembering.[30]

In the second most common text containing the morning *Pratikramaṇ*, the *Jain Prakāśan Mandir*'s Gujarātī edition of *Śrī Devasīa-Rāīa Pratikramaṇ Sūtro* (The Auspicious *Sūtra* of the Evening and Morning *Pratikramaṇ*s), the gloss following the BS claims: "In this instruction, the names of excellent men and women who are chaste, great patrons (of Jainism) and ascetics are listed. From remembering their names every morning, auspiciousness arises and sorrow is driven away" (*Śrī Devasīa-Rāīa Pratikramaṇ Sūtro*, No date: 76).[31] The qualities of men and women are the same: chastity, religious generosity, and asceticism. The volume *Śrī Pañca pratikramaṇ Sārth* (The True Meaning of the Five *Pratikramaṇ*s; a text which gives both the text of the five *Pratikramaṇ*s and the meaning in Gujarātī of each section) also provides a short gloss on the significance of each section in more general terms. Of the BS it writes: "In this instruction, excellent and truly virtuous men and virtuous women who protected themselves with their virtue and steadfastness, are remembered together with the pronunciation of their names." (*Śrī Pañca pratikramaṇ Sārth*, 1995–1996: 172).[32] These men are virtuous because among other virtues shared with the *satī*s of virtue and steadfastness, they display a kind of virtue (*sattva*) often associated with *satī*s.

The texts discussed earlier (especially the BS) could be seen to include the totality of virtue as expressed by the great man and the *satī*. Every Jain woman and man, nun and monk I spoke to made it clear that there were more *satī*s than those listed in the sixteen *satī* prayers. When I asked whether there were more than the *Pratikramaṇ* list, they once again stressed that there were even more than the longer list. The idea of the totality of *satī*s is necessarily greater than the known list. There are no limits on the number of *satī*s; as there are with the twenty-four Jinas, the twelve *cakravartin*s, and so forth. Of course there are virtuous men who are not in these categories of illustrious men (*śalākāpuruṣa*), such as most of those great men (*mahāpuruṣa*) in the BS. Men's virtues are multiple but not unbounded. For instance both terms – illustrious men (*śalākapuruṣa*) and great men (*mahāpuruṣa*) – represented closed groups. Great monks in recent history are referred to as glorifiers of the faith (*prabhāvaka*) rather than using these other existing terms whereas the term *satī* encompasses mythological women as well as modern and contemporary Jain nuns. Great laymen of known history are called by yet another term, great layman (*mahāśrāvaka*). In other words, this sense of virtue – that is defined by an unbounded list of virtuous women – seems specifically to do with women more than it does with men. Clearly the list of *satī*s is destined to never be finished. Laidlaw (1995: 213) suggests in his discussion of the lists of forbidden foods, that the additions to the lists and the litany of names serves precisely to indicate that the list is unbounded, even endless and that it would be nearly impossible to avoid all these foods. The unbounded lists of *satī*s share the idea of the potential endlessness, but here by their focus on virtue suggest the multiplicity of potential rather than impossibility.

Further virtuous women bear a single taxonomy as *satī*s. Regardless of their narrative, marital status, status as a renouncer, nature of death, or nature of their relationship to Jinas, virtuous women all can be subsumed under the single category of *satī*: in contrast to the multiple categories of virtuous men. There is one significant subcategory within the totality of women – the mothers of the Jinas – which is sometimes marked off in texts as separate and whose narratives are often not given in texts collecting *satī* narratives. Perhaps they are not included as *satī*s because they achieve their status through a divine blessing (as the conception of the Jinas is articulated) whereas the *satī*s gain their status through their own efforts.[33] For our purposes, we see that the idea of women's virtue (rather than status) is framed as relatively uniform. In addition, *satī*s are never consigned to hell as are the *vāsudevas* and *prativāsudevas*; there is, then, no category for women who do not clearly uphold Jain values while upholding social values.[34] Women have the "advantage," one supposes, of never being compromised by the demands of kingship. Of course, a parallel is that neither do they have available widely varying avenues of becoming illustrious, nor does upholding mere social values quite qualify them for inclusion in lists. Women's consolation lies in the unboundedness of the lists; though it is difficult – indeed, close to impossible – to achieve the necessary virtue, the ellipses at the lists' end is perhaps an invitation to make the attempt.

Inclusivity and **satī** *lists*

Śvetāmbar Jain women identify with *satī*s and their narratives in generalized ways, supporting their own religiosity which suggest ways of including yet more women – here, contemporary Jain women – under the rubric of the term, *satī*. Fohr found nuns identifying other nuns as *satī*s and *mahāsatī*s (though she did not attribute this practice to Tapā Gacch nuns). Nuns in the Sthānakavāsī tradition are all called "*Mahāsatī*s," which, on one hand, diminishes the extraordinary claims on virtue of the *satī*s; on the other hand, it simultaneously suggests that these great *satī*s are among us now in the form of all nuns. Fohr (2001: 133–136, 150–156) gives several examples of the use of the term "*satī*" for contemporary known nuns drawn from the Śvetāmbar Terāpanthī and Sthānakavāsī communities. While Tapā Gacch nuns did not explicitly name other nuns as *satī*s, they did see the *satī* narratives as having a direct connection to and effect on their own lives as nuns today (Fohr 2001: 142–143). One popular collection, *Jina Śāsananāṃ Śramaṇīratno* (The Gemlike, Virtuous Women who Protect the Religion of the Jinas), includes a mixture of the mothers of the Jinas, *satī*s, and great Jain nuns (mythological, historical, and contemporary). The narratives are organized by the time (mytho-historically like the *Mahāpurāṇā*s) in which the women lived: those women who lived in the times from Ādināth to Parśvanāth, those who lived in the time of Mahāvīr, then early great nuns, then later great nuns divided by order first, and then within the Tapā Gacch divided by mendicant groupings (*parivār*). This text clearly intends to link the lives of contemporary Tapā Gacch nuns with the lives of the great women in Jain mytho-history by including these contemporary nuns' lives in a list that suggests a lineage devolving from the narratives being told in a *Mahāpurāṇa* format.[35] In *Jina Śāsananāṃ Śramaṇīratno* the extension of the lists to include contemporary Jain nuns suggests that the list of *satī*s can be ever-expanding.

No Tapā Gacch laywomen I knew referred to other laywomen or nuns as *satī*s; laywomen did speak of women as virtuous but without using the term "*satī*." And yet, despite the extreme popularity of narratives of *satī*s who never married and whose *dīkṣā*s are central – Candanbālā and Rājīmatī, – laywomen with whom I spoke understood the *satī* narratives as evidence of the actual existence of heroic wives whose virtue was extraordinary and sometimes even perfect. Laywomen were identified with *satī*s, but in less explicit ways. The fasts associated with the *satī* narratives are generally seen as women's fasts and the public performance of these fasts is clearly connected to the display of the virtues of Jain laywomen (Kelting 2001: 48–53, 2006). Interestingly, great and virtuous men whose narratives center around fasting do not in turn become icons for male fasting behavior in the ways that these *satī*s do for Jain women. When I mentioned that great and virtuous men were not comparable to *satī*s as role models for lay practice in front of an audience of lay Jains, several men named men they considered comparable to these *satī*s, but these were all monks and were not associated with lay praxis. (Interestingly, not one Jain suggested Śreyaṃs – the only really comparable *mahāpuruṣa* – though I suspect in India where the fast associated with Śreyaṃs (*Varṣī Tap*) is more commonly performed his name might have been mentioned.) When Jain laymen are ritually linked to great men of the Jain tradition, they are usually linked to the kings Kumārpāl and Śrīpāl both of whom would be categorized as great laymen, *mahāśrāvak*.

The floats at the 2001 *Paryuṣaṇ* parade are but one example of a displayed identification between contemporary laywomen and the mythological *satī*s. Each float in the parade was the vehicle for a Jain layperson who had completed a substantial fast during the *Paryuṣaṇ* season. In 2001, there were quite a few young unmarried men and women who had chosen to perform the eight-day fast during *Paryuṣaṇ* and who rode in decorated automobiles, trucks, and horse- and ox-pulled carts in the parade with signs proclaiming the length and kind of fast they had completed.[36] However, the sixteen *satī* floats all carried married women[37] who had presumably performed substantial fasts (probably the eight or nine-day *Paryuṣaṇ* full fast). While the floats of all the other fasters listed the specifics of their fasts, the "*satī*s" here were not even identified as fasters and there were no details to justify their position in the parade. In a sense, these married women were assumed to be virtuous (probable fasters), but did not need to display their credentials. The link between these *satī*s and married laywomen was clear in the minds of the parade organizers and was considered an obvious connection by all the women I interviewed at the parade and afterwards. *Satī* lists are fluid and unbounded suggesting a totality of virtue unbounded by the particulars of identities.

Efficacy of *satī* lists

The term *satī* and the *satī* lists serve as an invocation of the power of the *satī*s' collective virtue. Each of these *satī* lists can be understood as mantric because their recitation has purifying powers or creates auspiciousness (*māṅgalik*). The texts themselves and their commentaries suggest that these lists have their own efficacy. This is by no means unique to these texts (it is true of all *mantras*), but it suggests that they should be examined by themselves within their textual and performative contexts. In three texts (the BC, the SSC, and the BS) the names are the sole focus of this efficacy rather than the narratives which may serve to justify the inclusion of each of these names in these lists. Even in the more narrative SSC, the cryptic nature of the narratives makes the text only slightly more than a list. Likewise, in the SSC, the text itself declares that the names themselves have power. In several verses of the SSC, various powers are attributed to saying the names of the *satī*s "Saying her name, one is joyful" (SSC, 9), "Her name makes one pure, which is that name's secret talent" (SSC, 12), and "Recite her name, receive *darśan*, and destroy sinful acts" (SSC, 14). The frame of SSC sets the *satī*s as a group in a context where their names function as a *mantra* whose efficacy can be tapped by merely reciting the prayer:

> Victoriously recite the couplets from the scriptures, Udayratna gives this evidence.
> Recited by men at dawn, those who listen have joy and prosperity (17).
> (*Śrī Sudhāras Stavan Saṅgrah*, No date: 90)

Ultimately even those who merely listen to these names gain "joy and prosperity." These *satī*s names, like the presence of women or women's singing at auspicious events like weddings (Henry 1988), create the necessary auspiciousness and well-being for the event which follows. This link between the recitation of the *satī*s names and the state of well-being may indicate one way these women get linked to the lives of laywomen whose concerns often center around the well-being of their family. These *satī*s names, according to the SSS: "make a garland of auspiciousness" (SSS, 16) and thus encircle the event with the auspiciousness of their collective virtue. These *satī* lists serve in mantric ways to reduce karma (reducing *pāp*) and to create auspiciousness.

Satī *lists and the reduction of karma*

In the SSC, there are several times when particular *satī*s and their names are said to be able to decrease one's sin (*pāp*), purify, or in other ways decrease one's karma. Having *darśan* of the *satī* leads to a decrease in sin: "Seeing her crown, sin vanishes" (SSC, 9) and "Recite her name, receive *darśan*, and destroy sinful acts" (SSC, 14). In other verses, the language is more oblique but the implication is that these *satīs* will also remove sin: "That stain-removing *satī*, Subhadrā" (SSC, 11) and "Her name makes one pure, which is that name's secret talent (SSC, 12). The suggestions that these *satīs* names may decrease sin is claimed in other *satī* lists as well.

After the list of the *satīs*' names, the SSS ends with the following couplet: "Cooling sin and worldly troubles, indeed, these names make a garland of auspiciousness; Jñānvimal attained these virtues, recognize their wondrous greatness" (SSS, 16). The *satī*'s names have several powers here. Their names will cool – a Jain trope for diminishing passion and its ensuing karma – sin and worldly troubles. There are two basic ways that Jains can decrease their karma: one, by blocking the influx (*saṃvara*) of karma through inaction and diminishing the passion which binds karma; and two, by removing karma that has already bound (*nirjarā*) through asceticism and the performance of the *pratikramaṇ*. Jains often use the metaphor of "cooling" to indicate a decrease in the passions that lead to the binding of karma. Thus these names which cool "sin and worldly troubles" lead to decrease in karma by stopping the influx of karma while the presence of these same names in the BS as part of the *pratikramaṇ* suggests that they are also effective in the removal or destruction of one's bound karma. Once again in the SSS, we see the ways in which these lists serve with the karmic effect of decreasing "sin" echoing the ritual use of the BS as part of the morning *pratikramaṇ*.

The fixed position of the BS in the morning *Pratikramaṇ* text contrasts with the other *pratikramaṇ* performances where the *sajjhāy* are chosen according to the date of the performance. For example, there are particular *sajjhāys* enjoined for during the ritual observances of *Paryuṣaṇ, Dīvāḷī*, at the *Saṃvatsarī*, and other significant dates on the Jain calendar. In the evening *pratikramaṇ* ritual, the *sajjhāy* can vary from day to day at the appropriate (for the date) choice of those performing the ritual. These various *sajjhāys* are often recited from *sajjhāy* collections (such as the *Śrī Jain Sajjhāy Mālā*) because particular *sajjhāys* are not included in the other printed *Pratikramaṇ* texts. This allows a certain possibility of variation in choice among multiple contextually acceptable *sajjhāys* for that day. However, the BS is the fixed *sajjhāy* for the morning *pratikramaṇ*; it is printed in the morning *Pratikramaṇ* text and cannot have another *sajjhāy* substituted. This indicates that it is necessary for the efficacy of the *pratikramaṇ* itself.

In the many editions of the *Pratikramaṇ* texts which include the morning *pratikramaṇ*, there are often glosses explaining the significance of each section to the Jain who is performing the *pratikramaṇ* rite. The most commonly owned *Pratikramaṇ* collection among Jains I researched was the Jain Prakāśan Mandir's Gujarātī edition of the *Śrī Pañca Pratikramaṇa Sūtra* (The Auspicious Sūtra of the Five *Pratikramaṇs*). After the BS, this edition includes the gloss: "In this instruction are great men (*mahāpuruṣa*) possessing many good qualities, and from merely taking their names the bonds of sin are broken and one is given true joy" (*Śrī Pañca Pratikramaṇa Sūtra* No date: 20).[38] The benefits here – freeing the reciter from sin and giving true joy – are in addition to the overall benefits of the expiation of sin that one gets by performing the *pratikramaṇ* ritual.

Satī *lists as* māṅgalik

The *māṅgalik* is a blessing, not a petition (Shāntā 1997: 256). It has the effect of creating auspiciousness. According to Jaini (2000: 237), Jain *maṅgala* serve to remove impurities and to bring happiness. One can see the *māṅgalik* texts as holy verses whose recitation both create auspiciousness in this world and celebrate that which is holy – in the Jain context, those things which lead to liberation (Cort 2001a: 194). *Māṅgalik* texts are particularly important for demarcating ritual time and serve to frame ritual actions. They are recited at the start and end of ritual performances – for example, daily worship, congregational liturgies, and mendicant's sermons. On the first day of the Jain New Year at *Dīvāḷī*, the Jains in the congregation where I conduct my primary research went to hear the recitation of what they call the "*Māṅgalik*." Every year that includes the *Navkār Mantra*, the *Bhaktāmar Stotra*, and also the *Gautam Svāmī no Rās*. These were considered particularly good texts to hear at the start of the new year. Cort (2001a: 172) describes Śvetāmbar Mūrtipūjak Jains in Gujarat going to hear the *Navasmaraṇ*[39] (The Nine Remembrances, of which the *Navkār Mantra* is the first and the *Bhaktāmar Stotra* the seventh) on the first day of the new year; one year, Cort notes, the *Gautam Svāmī no Rās* was also recited. These show a clear similarity in the ways that *māṅgalik* texts are categorized in this ritual context to demarcate and make auspicious the start of the new year.

In *Bhakti Bhāvanā*, a popular lay manual, both the BC and the SSC are inserted under the heading: "*māṅgalik kāvyā*" (auspicious poems appropriate for the start of things) with other texts, such as the *Navkār Mantra* and several longer prayers (*chand*). The SSC is located in the ritual manual, *Śrī Sajjan Sanmitra Yane Ekādaś Mahānidhi* with other key *māṅgalik* texts in a section called "*maṅgala praveśakā*" (auspicious beginnings). In the *Śrī Sudhāras Stavan Saṅgrah*, the SSC is located in a short section with four other *māṅgalik* texts including the *Gautam Svāmī nī Chand*. Its proximity to the *Gautam Svāmī nī Chand* and other texts categorized as *māṅgalik* texts highlights the connection of all these texts to those texts more commonly thought of as *māṅgalik*, such as the *Navasmaraṇ*.

This categorization of these texts as *māṅgalik* may arise in part out of the claims they themselves make that they create auspiciousness. In the BC, it admonishes one to recite the *satī*'s names: "May this auspiciousness be performed everyday" (*Jina Śāsananāṃ Śramaṇīratno* 1994: 121). The SSS, likewise, declares itself *māṅgalik* and also suggests that it be recited in the morning: "Every morning revere their names, those pillars of Jainism" (SSS, 1) and "indeed, these names make a garland of auspiciousness" (SSS, 16). The text of the SSC itself suggests its use as a *māṅgalik*: "At sunrise, create auspiciousness, and repeat the sixteen *satīs*' names" (SSC, 1). All three texts include these statements within their own text indicating their potential use, and both the SSS and SSC suggest that they should be recited in the morning which contributes to their identities as *māṅgalik*.

That the BC serves as a *māṅgalik* is furthered by lay manuals in which monks instruct the laity in proper praxis, such as *Sāmāyik* written by the Tapā Gacch monk Hariśbhadrācārya who writes that the sixteen *satīs*' names should be recited by all Jains every morning (*Sāmāyik* No date: 22). Śvetāmbar Mūrtipūjak Jain nuns recite the names of the sixteen *satīs* as part of their early morning devotions (Fohr 2001: 19, Shāntā 1997: 256). Shāntā (1997: 257) also wrote that many lay Jains recite the BC everyday. The use of the BC as a way to start the day and to thereby make the entire day auspicious links this text to other *māṅgalik* texts. Likewise, the SSC is used as a *māṅgalik*. Stevenson (1987: 67), describing Śvetāmbar Jain practice in the early twentieth century, writes that "Sulasā is considered the highest type of the purely domestic woman, the faithful wife or *satī*, and the Gujarātī Jaina women sing the following verse about her in the hymn of praise to the sixteen faithful wives which they chant every morning when they get up." Stevenson proceeds to translate the Sulasā verse from the SSC. Though the SSC does not appear to be a widely recited text at present,[40] according to the Tapā Gacch nun, Divyaprabhāśrījī, the SSC can be recited as a *māṅgalik* to start a sermon (as long as the *Navkār Mantra* is recited first)[41] and would be particularly appropriate if the subject of the sermon were a *satī* narrative. Likewise, the SSC was, not surprisingly, included as a frontispiece of Dhami's *Soḷ Mahasatīo*; here the text both serves as a *māṅgalik* to start the book and also as a frame for understanding the significance of the book itself. The SSC and the BC were clearly connected with the morning while the SSC also creates the necessary auspiciousness for lengthier reflections on the *satīs*. All three texts, the BC, the SSC, and the SSS, claim their status as *māṅgalik* and their performances as morning recitations reifies these claims.

Even the BS clearly has its own powers separate from the karma reduction of the *Pratikramaṇ*. One gloss of the BS claims that: "from merely taking their names the bonds of sin are broken and one is given true joy" (*Śrī Pañca Pratikramaṇa Sūtra* No date: 20) while another claims: "From remembering their names every morning, auspiciousness arises and sorrow is driven away" (*Śrī Devasīa-Rāīa Pratikramaṇ Sūtro*, No date: 76). Not only is this text capable of driving away sorrow (perhaps the other side of the coin of giving true joy) but it also creates auspiciousness. Like the list of the sixteen *satīs* that the mendicants recite each morning, this text serves as a *māṅgalik* – a creator of auspiciousness. In its ritual context, the placement of the list of *satī* names (along with those of the virtuous men) found in the BS in the morning *Pratikramaṇ* text suggests that this text's efficacy may be – at least in part – to serve as a *māṅgalik* blessing to the first ritual of the day and to the day as a whole. This serves as another context of the use of the *satī*'s names – here the larger sense – to frame the entire day as auspicious.

Concluding thoughts

Satī lists are effective as *māṅgalik* and in karma reduction. They are efficacious because the lists serve as a mantric representation of all virtue (especially women's virtue). Drawing on Jain articulations of virtue through the discourse of *satī*s, these texts articulate a totality of virtue. The ideas of the collectivity of *satī*s and the ways in which that collectivity is understood to be unbounded – in a sense infinite – contrasts with the bounded categories of virtuous men especially the strongly numeric lists of the sixty three illustrious men of the Jain *Mahāpurāṇa* literature. The lists then posit the possibility that all kinds of women can attain perfection worthy of veneration. That the *satī* lists are efficacious suggests that women's virtues – here metonymically represented by the *satī*s names – have profound religious power. The rhetorical uses and efficaciousness of personifications of women's virtue makes real the Śvetāmbar women's claims to religious potential in the Jain religious discourse.

Acknowledgments

My thanks to Peter Flügel, who organized the Annual Jain Workshop at sons, for inviting me to present a paper and to all the participants in the workshop for their helpful suggestions and questions about this paper particularly Nalini Balbir, John Cort, Paul Dundas, Peter Flügel, Josephine Reynell, and Kristi Wiley – and also to Steven Runge.

Notes

1 Fohr (2001: 80) writes that the idea of the sixteen *satī*s is found only among the Śvetāmbar Mūrtipūjak and Sthānakavāsī Jains. The Digambar and Śvetāmbar Terāpanthī Jains did not give a number to the totality of *satī*s.

2 The information I give here on the Tapā Gacch and its history and practices is drawn from the work of Cort (2001a: 42–53) and Dundas (2002: 142–147).

3 The Tapā Gacch *samudāy*s – the subdivisions of a *gacch* – share their rituals and texts (*vidhi*). Thus there is but one *pratikramaṇ vidhi* for the Tapā Gacch as a whole. In addition, Tapā Gacch monks can move from one *samudāy* to another. There is also more structural emphasis put on the *parivār* – the group of mendicants under a single monk (John Cort, personal correspondence). A look at the texts of the other Śvetāmbar Mūrtipūjak Gacchs and other Jain sects would be instructive especially in questions of how the efficacy of women's names varies from Jain community to community. The larger project of which this chapter is a piece will include such comparative work.

4 These recitations may either be part of the rituals associated with a particular holiday – such as Rājīmatī's narrative in the Nemināth narrative recitation during the *pratikramaṇ* on the day of Nemināth's liberation (the dark fifth of the Gujarati month *Śrāvaṇ*) – or they may be part of the acts associated with a particular fast – as are the narratives of Candanbālā during the Candanbālā fast (*Śrī Ārādhanā Tathā Tapavidhi* 1984; *Śrī Taporatna Mahodadhi* 1989).

5 For more information on the scholarly discussions about *satī*s in the Hindu context, see for instance Harlan 1992; Hawley 1994; Mani 1998; Rajan 1993; Weinberger-Thomas 1999.

6 I use the term "Hindu" here to refer to Hindus who are in the linguistic ethnic communities who venerate *satī*s. These communities are predominantly in western India (Gujarat and Rajasthan) and among those who have migrated from these regions to other areas of India and the world. These linguistic ethnic groups are the same linguistic ethnic groups which are dominant among Śvetāmbar Jains making this comparison particularly fruitful.

7 I have found this model of the auspicious wife who transfers her merit to male relatives to be widespread in the Jain community. Other scholars have found that the ideals of the auspicious wife performing rituals for her family's wellbeing is common (Cort 2001a: 140–141, 191–192; Reynell 1991: 62–64; and, to a lesser extent, Laidlaw 1995: 355–357).

8 Fohr (2001: 113–116) illustrates the ways that Jain nuns frame the lives of the *satī*s primarily in terms of celibacy (*brahmacarya*) rather than the more domestic but related virtue of chastity (*śīl*) while suggestively showing these virtues on a continuum marked by greater similarity than difference.

9 Draupadī's narrative is virtually identical to the Mahābharata in its basic story but in the end Draupadī becomes a Jain nun. When discussing the BS, Shah (in a text I have chosen to read as a primary source) clearly identifies several *satī*s as laywomen despite their subsequent *dīkṣā*s suggesting that their *dīkṣā*s are not part of (or at least not central to) their common narratives. Shah writes: "Laymen: Karkandu, Sudarsan Sheth, Vankacul, Salibhadra, Dhanyakumar, Abhaykuman, Ilaciputra, Nandisena... Laywomen: Sulasa, Revati Manorma, Damyanti, Sita, Nanda, Bhadra, Risidatta, Padmavati, Anjana, Sridevi, Jyestha, Prabhavati, Celana, Rukhmini, Kunti, Devaki, Dropadi, Dharani, Kalavati" (Shah 1998, Vol. I: 62).

10 *brāhmī candanbālikā bhagavatī rājīmatī draupadī; kauśalyā ca mṛgāvatī ca sulasā sītā subhadrā śivā / kuntī śīlavatī nalasyā dayitā cūlā prabhāvatyapi; padmāvatyapi ca sundarī kurvantu no maṣgalam // Jina Śāsananāṃ Śramaṇīratno* (1994: 121). My translation.

11 Digambar Jains also venerate *satī*s through a recited list including Brāhmī, Sundarī, Rājīmatī, Kuntī, Draupadī, Sītā, Subhadrā, Candanā, and others (Shāntā 1997: 257 refers us to Jñānamatī 1976: 68–74).

12 These dates (vs 1749–1799) refer to a Jain monk Udayratna who wrote several similar genre devotional pieces including *chand*s. For more about Udayratna, see, Jayantvijay 1998; Krause 1999: 299–307; and Patel 1993: 317–324. I am deeply indebted to John Cort for supplying me with these resources and specifics which led me to this provisional date.

13 *Chand*s have a simple poetic meter determined by an even count of syllables without attention to the weight or length of the syllables (Tulpule 1979: 450).

14 *ādināth ādi jinavar vandī, saphaḷ manorath kījīye e; prabhāte uṭhī māṅgalik kāme soḷ satīnāṃ nām līјīe e. 1. bālakumārī jagahitakārī brāhmī bharatnī bahenaḍī e. ghat ghat vyāpak akṣar rūpe, soḷ satīmāṃhe je vaḍī e. 2. bāhubal bhaginī satīy śiromaṇī, sundarī nāme ṛṣabhasutā e, svārūpī tribhuvanmāṃhe jeh anupam guṇajuttā e. 3. candanbālā bālapaṇāthī sīyalavantī śuddh śrāvikā e; aḍadnā bākule vīr pratilābhyā, keval lahī vrat bhāvikā e. 4. ugrasen dhuā dhāriṇī nandinī, rājīmati nemavallabhā e; jobanaveśe kāmne jītyo, saṃyam laī devdullabhā e. 5. pañca bharatārī pāṇḍav nārī, drupadatanayā vakhāṇīye e; ekso āṭhe cīr pūrāṇā, śiyal mahimā tas jaṇīye e. 6. daśarath nṛpanī rāṇī nirūpam, kauśalyā phulacandrikā e; śīyal saluṇī rām janetā, puṇyataṇī paranālikā e. 7. kauśāṃbik ṭhāme śatānik nāme rājya kare rang rājīyo e; tas ghar gṛhiṇī mṛgāvatī satī, sur bhavane jaś gājīyo e. 8. sulasā sācī śiyale na kācī, rācī nahī viṣayārase e; mukhaḍuṃ jotāṃ pāp palāye, nām letāṃ man ullase e. 9. ām raghuvaṃśī tehanī kāminī, janakasutā sītā satī e; jag sahu jaṇe dhīj karantā anal śītal thayo śīyalthī e. 10. kace tāntaṇe cālaṇī bāndhī kuvāthakī jal kāḍhīyuṃ e. kalank utāravā satī*

subhadrāe, campā bār ughāḍīyuṃ e. 11. surnar vandit śiyal akhaṇḍit, śivā śivpadgāminī e. jehane nāme nirmaḷ thaīe, balihārī tas nāmanī e. 12. hastināpure pāṇḍurāyanī kuntā nāme kāminī e; pāṇḍav mātā daśe daśārṇanī, bhen pativratā padmīnī e. 13. śīlavatī nāme śīlavrat-dhāriṇī, trividhe tehane vandiye e, nām japantā pātak jāye, dariśaṇ durit nikandīe e. 14. niṣidhā nagarī nalah narīndanī, damayantī tas gehinīe; sankaṭ paḍatāṃ śiyalaj rākhyuṃ, tribhuvan kīrti jehanīe. 15. anang ajitā jagajanapūjitā puṣpacūlā ne prabhāvatī e; viśvavikhyātā, kāmitdātā, soḷamī satī padmāvatī e. 16. vīre bhākhī śāstre sākhī, "udayaratna" bhākhe mudā e; vahāṇaṃ vātāṃ je nar bhaṇaśe, te laheśe sukh paṃpadā e. 17. (*Śrī Sudhāras Stavan Saṅgrah*, No date: 87–90) My translation.

15 The name of the *Rāīa Pratikramaṇ* indicates that this is the morning repentance and expiation of sins and errors committed during the night.

16 To my knowledge, there have been no systematic studies of Tapā Gacch *Pratikramaṇ* and few about *pratikramaṇ*. Flügel (1994: 510–535) writes of the structure and performance of the Terāpanthī *pratikramaṇ* and Laidlaw (1995) of the performance of the Khartar Gacch *pratikramaṇ*. In terms of early dating, Caillat writes that the independent *pratikramaṇ* was not a part of the earliest texts on Jain mendicant atonement (Caillat 1975: 139). More research on the development of the *pratikramaṇ* text and the history of the ritual would be extremely useful.

17 *Pratikramaṇ* is performed by Śvetāmbar Mūrtipūjak Jains minimally on the *Saṃvatsarī* day (bright fourth (Tapā Gacch) or fifth (other *gacchs*) of the month *Bhādrapad* on the Gujarati calendar). Pious Jains are enjoined to perform *pratikramaṇ* on the three days which divide the year into three seasons (the bright fourteenth days of the months of *Kārtik*, *Fāgun*, and *Āṣāḍh* on the Gujarati calendar), as well as fortnightly on the fourteenth day of each waxing and waning moon. There are also morning and evening *pratikramaṇ* rites, which are performed daily by all mendicants as well as by some of the most devout laywomen; and these are also performed as part of the fasts that most lay Jains occasionally undertake.

18 *bharahesara bāhubalī abhaykumāro a, ḍanḍaṇakumāro sirio aṇiāutto. aīmutto nāgdatto a. // 1 // meajja thulibhadro vayararisī nandiṣeṇa sinhgirī kayavanno a sukosala puṇḍario keśī karakaṇḍu. // 2 // halla vihalla sudaṃsaṇa sāla mahāsāla śālībhadro a bhadro dasanna bhadyo pasannacando a jasabhadro. // 3 // jambupahū vankacūlo gayasukumālo avantisukumālo dhanno īlācīputto cilāīputto a bāhumunī. // 4 // ājjagiri ajjarakkhia ajjasuhatthī udāyago maṇago kālayasūrī sāmbo pajjunno muldevo a. // 5 // pabhavo vinhukumāro ādkumāro a daḍhappahāri a sijjaṃsa kurgaḍu a sijjaṃbhava mehakumāro. // 6 // emāī mahāsattā diṃtu suhaṃ guṇagaṇehiṃ saṃjuttā jesīṃ nāmaggahaṇe pāvappabandhā vilayaṃ jaṃti. // 7 // sulasā candanbālā manoramā mayaṇrehā damayantī namayāsundarī sīyā nandā bhadrā subhadrā ya. // 8 // Rāīamaī risidattā paumāvaī anjaṇā sirīdevī jiṭṭh sujiṭṭha migāvaī pabhāvaī cillaṇādevī. // 9 // bambhī sundarī ruppiṇī revaī kuntī sivā jayanti a devaī dovaī dhāraṇī kalāvaī pupphacūlā ya. // 10 // paumāvaī ya gorī gandhārī lakkhamaṇā susīmā jaṃbuvaī saccabhāmā ruppiṇī kaṇhaṭṭha mahisīo // 11 // jakkha ya jakkhadinnā bhūā taha ceva Bhuadinnā ya seṇā veṇā reṇā bhayaṇīo thulibhadrassa. // 12 // īccāī mahāsaīo jayanti akalaṃk-sīl-kaliāo ajja vi vajjaī jāsiṃ jas paḍaho tihuaṇe sayale // 13 //* (*Śrī Pañca Pratikramaṇa Sūtra* No date: 20–21). My translation.

19 This date, vs 1702–1770, is drawn from Koṭhārī and Śāh (1993: 230–234).

20 *suprabhāt nitya vandiye, bharat bāhubaḷī thambhā re, abhaykumār ne ḍhaḍhaṇo, sirio ne kayavanno re. // 1 // arṇikāputra ne aīmatto, nāgadatta sthulibhadra re; vayarasvāmī nandiṣeṇjī, dhanno ne śālibhadra re. // 2 // simhagirī kīrti sukośalo, karakaṇḍu puṇḍarīko re; halla vihalla sudarśan, śāḷ ane mahāśāḷ re. // 3 // gayasukumār jambū prabhu, keśī vantīsukumāḷo re; daśāraṇabhadra jasabhadrajī, īlātī cilātī putra sālo re. // 4 // bāhu udāī manak muni, āryarakṣit āryagirīśo re; ārya suhastī prabhav vaḷī, sāmb*

pradhyumna munīśo re. // 5 // muldev kālik sūri, viṣṇukumār śreyaṃso re; ārdrak dṛḍha prahār vaḷī, kurgaḍu meh munīśo re. // 6 // sayambhav prasannacandrajī, mahāsāl kankacūlo re; eha satā nām līјiye, jim hoy sundar kulo re. // 7 // sulasā candanbālikā, maṇoramā mayaṇrehā re; kuntī, narmadā sundarī, brāhmī sundarī guṇagehā re. // 8 // damayantī satī revatī, śivā jayantī nandā re; devakī draupadī dhāriṇī, śrīdevī subhadrā bhadrā re. // 9 // ṛṣidattā rājīmatī, padmāvatī prabhāvatī kahīye re; anjanā ne kaḷāvatī, puṣphacūlā man lahiye re. // 10 // gaurī gāndhārī lakhamaṇā, jambūvatī satyābhāmā re; padmā susīmā rūkaminī, e aṣṭa harinī rāmā re. // 11 // jyeṣṭhā sujyeṣṭhā mṛgāvatī, cellaṇā padmāprabhā rāṇī re; bahenī sāt sthūlibhadranī, buddhi mahāguṇ khāṇī re. // 12 // jakṣā jakṣa dinnā vaḷī, bhūyā ne bhūyadinnā re; senā venā renā kahī, e śakaḍālanī kannā re. // 13 // ityādik je mahā satī, tribhuvanamāṃhi viraje re; āj lage paṇ jehano, jas paḍah jag gaje re. // 14 // śīlavantī sur sundarī, kauśalyā ne sumitrā re; devdattādik jāṇīye, savi jinjananī pavitrā re. // 15 // durit upadrav upaśame, hove maṣgaḷamāḷā re; jñānvimal guṇ sampadā, pamīje suviśālā re. // 16 // (Śrī Jain Sajjhāy Māḷā (Sacitra) 1968: 18–20). My translation.

21 This list of men excludes Bhadrabahu and Metāryamuni.

22 Because Brāhmī and Sundarī are narratively linked as the sisters of the heroic brothers Bharat and Bāhubalī, it makes sense that most would link them in their lists.

23 Shāntā (1997: 257) gives a translation of the BC in which she too decides to omit Śīlavatī and does not give it as an adjective either. It is not clear from her text whether the omission arose out of the interpretation of the nuns with whom she spoke or was a decision made during her translation. When Divyaprabhāśrījī listed the sixteen *satī*s for me and a group of Jain laywomen, it was clear she was working from the "Brāhmī Candanbālikā." Her only variation from that list was the placement of the term Bhagavatī (which is never used as a name for a Jain *satī* in any text) in the position normally held by the name Rājīmatī; in that text Rājīmatī's name is proceeded by the word Bhagavatī which again might explain the variation.

24 Mayaṇāsundarī is the heroine of the popular *Śrī Śrīpāl Rājā no Rāso*. She is often given the title of *satī* but she does not appear in any published or recited lists I have found.

25 The floats in the 2001 *Paryuṣaṇ* Parade in Pune: Candanbālā, Rājīmatī, Brāhmī, Kauśalyā, Mayaṇāsundarī, Mṛgāvatī, Sulasā, Śīyalavatī, Sītā, Subhadrā, Prabhāvatī, Śivā, Damayantī, Padmāvatī, Kunta [*sic*], and Sundarī.

26 These ten virtuous men are Skandakumār, Skandasūri, Harikeśabaḷ, Dhanadev, Dhanamitra, Uttamcaritrakumār, Kṣemankarmuni, Kṣullak, Kṛpaṇa, and Āṣāḍhabhuti.

27 These twelve virtuous men are Skandakumār, Skandācārya, Harikeśibaḷ muni, Dhanadev, Dhanamitra, Uttamcaritrakumār, Kṣemankarmuni, Be Kṣullakmuni, Kṣullakmuni and Sulocanā, Kṛpaṇa, and Āṣāḍhabhuti.

28 Bharat and Bāhubalī are the only names included in both the BS list of fifty-three and the sixty-three illustrious men of the Jain *Mahāpurāṇa*s.

29 Jains conceptualize time as a cycle of descending (*avasarpiṇī*) and ascending (*utsarpiṇī*) periods each divided into six sections. Each cycle of time includes the complete dying out of the Jain tradition and is believed to include the lives and teachings of twenty-four Jinas who then reintroduce and revitalize the religion (Dundas 2002: 20).

30 These two groups have a kind of separate but equal status in this text. Of course, the *satī*s are considered equal to great Jain men but not to the list of the sixty-three illustrious men discussed earlier when discussing the Jain *Mahāpurāṇa*s.

31 *bharahesar – ā sajjhāymāṃ brahmacārī, dāneśvarī, ane tapasvī uttam puruṣo ane strīonā nāmo gaṇavyā che. savāre yād karavāthī māṣgalik thāy che ane dukh jatuṃ rahe che* (*Śrī Devasīa-Rāīa Pratikramaṇ Sūtro*, No date: 76). My translation.

32 *ā sajjhāymāṃ śīlavatane dradhatāthī pāḷnār uttam sattvaśālī puruṣo ane satīonuṃ nāmoccārapūrvak maraṇ thāy che* (*Śrī Pañca pratikramaṇ Sārth* 1995–1996: 172). My translation.

33 The mothers of the Jinas are central to the tellings of the Jina narratives (*Jinacaritra*) and yet these women do not get included in the category of *satī*s; similarly the Jina's fathers are also not included in either the lists of the sixty-three illustrious men nor the fifty-three great men. It isn't clear yet why they are not included. There is clear evidence that these women are seen as virtuous and achieve spiritual liberation (*mokṣa*) and that a *satī* can be married and have children. This bears considerable further exploration which I intend to pursue in the future.

34 Thus the queens of great kings must be framed either as *satī*s or are glossed as just so-and-so's wife. There is no category for the great queen who misuses her power or who is linked to violence or other sins through her performance of her duties as queen. One of the few that a woman can be excluded from the *satī* lists is to be one who performed the ritual act of self-immolation on the funeral pyre of one's dead husband – the paradigmatic act of the Hindu *satī*. This specific exclusion raises the question of whether the Jain *satī* lists are designed explicitly to exclude Hindu *satī*s. In addition, Jain philosophical texts argue that women are not capable of going to the lowest hell but they are certainly capable of going to all the other hells in the Jain cosmology (Dundas 2002: 57).

35 Here the stories of the great men are included only insofar as they are necessary to make sense of the women's narratives – a strategy common in the *satī* narrative collections.

36 While we have seen that the model of the forty-seven *satī*s is available to these women and to the parade organizers, it is the sixteen *satī*s which dominates – perhaps the idea of organizing forty-seven floats seemed overly daunting. The young men in the parade are not themselves linked to any of the fifty-three virtuous men listed in the *Pratikramaṇ* text despite the role many of these virtuous men have in modeling laymen's practice and the fact that many of those men listed are known for their fasting. It may be that these young men were unmarried and therefore do not make a nice fit with the predominant image available of the married layman patron of Jainism. When Jain laymen are ritually linked to great men of the Jain tradition, they are usually linked to the kings Kumārpāl and Śrīpāl.

37 All these women were proudly displaying their *maṅgal sutta*s – a gold chain with a pendant and black beads – which in Maharashtra (and increasingly Gujarat and Rajasthan) is a characteristic marker of a woman's status as a married woman whose husband is alive and is therefore particularly auspicious. This necklace is understood to mark the auspicious wife among all the Jain women (and in fact everyone I met Jain or not, male and female) in Maharashtra and increasingly among people I met in Gujarat and Rajasthan.

38 *ā sajjhāymāṃ je mahāpurūṣo anek sadguṇsaṃpanna hatā ane jenā nām mātra levāthī ja pāpbandhan tuṭī jāy che te amne sukh āpo* (*Śrī Pañca Pratikramaṇa Sūtra* No date: 20). My translation.

39 The *Navasmaraṇ* (also called the *Mahāmāṅgalik Navasmaraṇ*) are *Navkār Mantra, Uvasaggaharam Stavanam, Śāntikaram Stavanam, Tijyapahutta Stotram, Namiūṇ Stotram, Śrī Ajitaśānti Stavanam, Bhaktāmar Stotram, Śrī Kalyāṇamandir Stotram*, and *Śrī Bṛhacchānti Stotram (Moṭī Śānti)*.

40 Perhaps recitation of this text has decreased in popularity in recent times or perhaps it is associated with particular communities in Gujarat. Like the BC, I did not in my research find any laywomen who knew this text by heart though most knew it was published in the *Śrī Sudhāras Stavan Saṅgrah*. It may be that hymn singing has superceded the individual daily recitation of these particular texts.

41 In my experience, the *Navkār Mantra* was recited at the start of all *māṅgalik* recitations, sermons, and, in fact, all other rituals.

Bibliography

Primary sources

Ādi Purāṇa. Jinasena. Ed. by Pannalal Jain, Kashi, 1964–1965.

Bhakti Bhāvanā. Ed. by Pannyās Vajrasenavijayjī Gaṇi, Amdāvād: Bhadrankar Prakāśan, No date.

Jina Śāsananāṃ Śramaṇīratno. Vātsalyamūrti. Sārvodayāśrī M., Bhāvnagar: Arihant Prākaśan, 1994.

Kalpa Sūtra. In *Jaina Sūtras, Part I*. Ed. and trans. by Hermann Jacobi, New York: Dover Publications, 1968.

Sāmāyik. Muni Harishbhadra Vijayji, Bombay: Navjivan Granthmala Trust, No date.

Soḷ Mahāsatīo. Vimalkumār Mohanlāl Dhāmī, Rājkot: Navyug Pustak Bhaṇḍār, 1998.

Śrī Ārādhanā Tathā Tapavidhi. Munirājśrī Vivekcandravijayjī, Pālītāṇā: Somcand D. Śāh, 1984.

Śrī Bharateśvar Bāhubalī Vṛttiḥ. Śubhaśīlagaṇi. [vs 1509]. Ed. by Pradyumnavijay, Ahmadābād: Śri Srutajñān Prāsarak Sabhā, Vir Samvat 2510 (1984–1985).

Śrī Devasīa-Rāīa Pratikramaṇ Sūtro (*Gujarātī Bhāvārth Tathā Upayogī Viṣayo Sāthe*), Amadāvād: Jain Prakāśan Mandīr, No date.

Śrī Jain Sajjhāy Māḷā (Sacitra), Amdāvād: Jaśavantlāl Girdharlāl Śāh, Samvat 2025 (1968).

Śrī Pañca Pratikramaṇ Sārth. Ed. by Bābulāl Jesinglāl Mahetā and Maphatlāl Je. Śāh, Mahesāṇā: Śrimad Yaśsovijayjī Jain Saṃskṛt Pāthśālā Ane Śri Jain Śreyaskar Maṇḍaḷ, Vīr Samvat 2521 (1995–1996).

Śrī Pañca Pratikramaṇ Sūtra (Gujarati edition). Amadāvād: Jain Prakāśan Mandir, no date.

Śrī Pañca Pratikramaṇ Sūtro Vivecan Sahit. By Prabhudās Becardās Pārekh, Mahesāṇā: Śri Yaśovijay Jain Sanskṛt Pāṭhśāḷā Tathā Śrī Jain Śreyaskar Maṇḍaḷ, 1997.

Śrī Sajjan Sanmitra yāne Ekādaś Mahānidhi. Ed. by Popaṭlāl Keśavlāl Jhaverī. [Surat?] Śri Pravacan Pujak Sabhā: No Date.

Śrī Srīpāl Rājā no Rās, Amadāvād: Jain Prakāśan Mandir, 1997.

Śrī Sudhāras Stavan Saṅgrah, Amadāvād: Śri Jain Prakāśan Mandir, No date.

Śrī Taporatna Mahodadhi, Śāntipurī (Saurāṣṭra): Śrī Harṣapuṣpāmṛt Jain Granthmālā, 1989.

Triṣaṣṭiśalākāpuruṣacaritra. By Hemacandra, trans. by Helen M. Johnson as *The Deeds of the Sixty-three Illustrious Persons*, Baroda: Oriental Institute, 1931–1962.

Secondary sources

Bruhn, Klaus. (1981) "Āvaśyaka Studies I," in Klaus Bruhn and Albrecht Wezler (eds) *Studien zum Jainismus and Buddhismus*, Wiesbaden: Franz Steiner Verlag.

Caillat, Collette (1975) *Atonements in the Ancient Ritual of the Jaina Monks*, Ahmedabad: L. D. Institute.

Cort, John E. (1993) "An overview of the Jaina Purāṇas," in Wendy Doniger (ed.) *Purāṇa Perennis: Reciprocity and Transformation in Hindu and Jaina Texts*, Albany, NY: State University of New York Press, 185–206.

—— (2001a) *Jains in the World*, New York: Oxford University Press.

—— (2001b) "The Intellectual Formation of a Jain Monk: A Śvetāmbara Monastic Curriculum," *Journal of Indian Philosophy*, 29: 327–349.

Dundas, Paul. (2002) *The Jains*, London: Routledge.

Flügel, Peter. (1994) *Askese und Devotion: Das rituelle System der Terapanth Svetambara Jains*, PhD Dissertation, Johannes, Johnnes Gutenberg-Universität, Mainz.

Fort, Sherry. (2001) *Gender and chastity: female Jain renouncers*, PhD dissertation, University of Virginia.

Harlan, Lindsey. (1992) *Religion and Rajput Women*, Berkeley, CA: University of California Press.

Hawley, John S. (ed.) 1994. *Sati, the Blessing and the Curse*, Oxford: Oxford University Press.

Henry, Edward O. (1988) *Chant the Names of God*, San Diego, CA: San Diego State University Press.

Jaini, Padmanabh S. (2000) "The Pure and the Auspicious in the Jaina tradition," in Padmanabh S. Jaini (ed.) *Collected Papers on Jaina Studies*, Delhi: Motilal Banarsidas, 229–242.

Jayantvijay, Muni V. S. (1998). *Śankheśvar Mahātīrth*, Ujjain: Śrī Vijaydharmasūri Jain Granthmālā: 57.

Kelting, M. Whitney. (2001) *Singing to the Jinas: Jain Laywomen, Maṇḍal Singing, and the Negotiations of Jain Devotion*, New York: Oxford University Press.

—— (2003) "Constructions of femaleness in Jain vernacular devotional literature," in O. Qvarnström (ed.) *Jainism and Early Buddhism: Essays in Honor of Padmanabh S. Jaini*, Berkeley, CA: Asain Humanities Press, 231–248.

—— (2006) "Negotiating Karma, Merit, and Liberation: Vow-Taking in the Jain Tradition," in W. Harman and S. Raj (eds), *Dealing with Deities: The Ritual Vow in South Asia*, Albany, NY: State University of New York Press.

Koṭhārī, Jayant and Śāh, Kāntībhāī Bī. (eds.) (1993) *Madhyakālīn Gujarātī Jain Sāhitya*, Bombay: Mahāvīr Jain Vidyālay.

Krause, Charlotte. (1999) "Kaik Śankheśvar Sāhitya," originally in *Jain Satya Prakāś* 11:3, pp. 73–80, reprinted in Shriprakash Pandey (ed.), *German Jaina Śrāvikā Dr. Charlotte Krause: Her Life and Literature, Vol. I*, Varanasi: Pārśvanātha Vidyāpīṭha, 299–307.

Laidlaw, James. (1995) *Riches and Renunciation*, Oxford: Oxford University Press.

Mani, Lata. (1998) *Contentious Traditions*, New Delhi: Oxford University Press.

Patel, Pramodkumār. (1993) "Udayratnakṛt 'Nemināth Termāsā,'' in Jayant Koṭhārī and Kāntībhāī Bī, Śāh (eds), *Madhyakālīn Gujarātī Jain Sāhitya*, Bombay: Mahāvīr Jain Vidyālay, 317–34.

Rajan, Rajeswari Sunder. (1993) *Real and Imagined Women*, London: Routledge.

Reynell, Josephine. (1991) "Women and the reproduction of the Jain community," in Michael Carrithers and Caroline Humphrey (eds), *The Assembly of Listeners*, Cambridge: Cambridge University Press.

Shāntā, N. (1997 [1985]) *The Unknown Pilgrims: The Voice of the Sādhvīs. The History, Spirituyality, and Life of the Jaina Women Ascetics*, trans. by Mary Rogers, Delhi: Sri Satguru Publications.

Somani, R. V. (1982) *Jain Inscriptions of Rajasthan*, Jaipur: Rawat.

Stevenson, Mrs Sinclair [Margaret]. (1984 [1915]) *The Heart of Jainism*, New Delhi: Munshiram Manoharlal.

Tulpule, Shankar Gopal. (1979) *Classical Marāṭhī Literature*, Wiesbaden: Otto Harrassowitz.

Weinberger-Thomas, Catherine. (1999) *Ashes of Immortality*, trans. J. Mehlman and D. G. White, Chicago, IL: University of Chicago Press.

9

RELIGIOUS PRACTICE AND THE CREATION OF PERSONHOOD AMONG ŚVETĀMBAR MŪRTIPŪJAK JAIN WOMEN IN JAIPUR

Josephine Reynell

Using the fast of *akṣay nidhi* as a case study, this chapter suggests that Jain religious beliefs and practices contribute to the creation of female personhood and strengthens and supports a woman's sense of self, helping her to deal with specific pressures arising from gender and kinship roles within her husband's family.

In his perceptive study of personhood in Tamilnadu, Mattison Mines (1994: 206) asserts that, 'if others have too much control over who a person is, so that person's sense of agency is tightly controlled the person suffers psychologically,' noting earlier that whilst there is a tendency in Indian society for group interests to be put before individual interests, 'Indians too must meet their psychological need for separation' (ibid.: 17).

This observation raises important questions about women whose recognition as persons, amongst both Jain and the encompassing Hindu communities, is intimately bound up with their performance of *sevā* or service to others. Does female personhood among the Jains incorporate a sense of the individual self? And if so, to what extent can women retain a sense of self and agency as separate from others given the constraints on their speech, movement and activities both before but more particularly after marriage?

I would like to make a preliminary exploration of this issue by focusing on religious practice, and re-analysing my previous material (Reynell 1985, 1987a) on Jain women and fasting.[1] This earlier work focused on the way in which female religious practice was an integral part of the social, economic and prestige structure of the Śvetāmbar Mūrtipūjak[2] Jain trading community in the old city of Jaipur. Re-reading my field notes of 20 years, from a more experienced perspective enriched by considerable changes in my own life cycle, encouraged me to explore how religious practice might contribute to the complex creation of female personhood over time. James Laidlaw's observation that Jain doctrine focuses upon the individual human soul (1995: 16–17) is particularly relevant to my argument. To what extent might Jain women's religious belief and practice offer lay women opportunities to imagine, reflect upon and experience a sense of the inner self and individuality? At the same time to what extent does the public enactment of kinship roles within various religious arenas contribute to a woman's reputation as a person worthy of respect, in turn strengthening a woman's conception of herself? This chapter therefore looks at the reciprocal interaction between two aspects of personhood – the inwardly experienced self and the outwardly visible person.

As a cautionary note I should point out that whilst the re-analysis of data is always a fruitful exercise, I did not specifically investigate personhood when doing my fieldwork and so do not have on record emic categories concerning personhood and self amongst the Śvetāmbar Mūrtipūjak Jains in Jaipur. In fact such categories may well vary between different sects and individuals. Thus the chapter is an outsider's analytical perspective and represents an initial attempt to raise some preliminary questions which require further investigation both through textual analysis and ethnographic fieldwork.

My material is drawn from the Śvetāmbar Mūrtipūjak Khartar Gacch Jains living within the Jauhrī Bāzār area of the old city of Jaipur, Rajasthan. So when I refer to 'the Jains' it is specifically to this community.[3] Whilst I hope that my conclusions have general applicability, the rich body of research undertaken on Jains in India in the past 20 years clearly indicates that they are by no means a homogeneous community. There is considerable regional variation both in religious practice as well as in caste membership and more generally in the social and economic structure of the Jain population.

Approaches to personhood within anthropological theory

Anthropological perspectives use the etic category of human personhood to investigate how individual biological humans are conceptualised as, and become, social beings. To this end much anthropological work has focused upon formal and informal roles and institutionalised offices as a way of investigating the various capacities in which the embodied human being is expected to act within a social group, and is given recognition within these groups as a socially defined person, with associated rights, responsibilities and powers *vis à vis* other persons.[4] An important theme in the literature both cross-culturally[5] and in the Indian context[6] is how reciprocal interaction itself within relationships is crucial to the constitution of persons. Such relationships are created through ascribed or achieved membership in both formal and informal groups which range from kin and neighbourhood networks, to groups defined by gender, caste, class, employment, religion, locality, region and nationality.

The self as an aspect of personhood

The emphasis on personhood as externally perceived and awarded by others in the networks to which a human being is a member, is only part of the story. Steven Lukes (1985: 287) wisely cautions against studies of personhood which focus too exclusively on external roles and statuses, thereby neglecting the complex way in which individual selves and social roles are entwined. Crucial to the gradual attainment and constitution of personhood is the actors' self recognition and reflection upon both themselves and the ways in which they as human beings are able to exercise choice in enacting and constituting themselves as persons. In other words, the category of personhood encompasses notions of the self and individuality, and it is worth emphasising that while one ends up defining the self, the individual and the person separately for analytical purposes, it is essential to recognise that these categories are mutually interdependent.

In his perceptive examination of selfhood, Anthony Cohen (1994: 2) defines the self as the universal capacity of the human being 'to reflect on his or her own behaviour – that is to be self-conscious'.[7] Expanding on this, I suggest that the self can be conceptualised as the aspect of mind that recognises and reflects back upon its embodied existence. Self is clearly to do with introspection and a sense of 'I' as a separate being. It is rooted in the psychic processes of cognition and perception and incorporates those intangible aspects of being human, including thoughts, emotions, desires, opinions and beliefs, together with a moral conscience which can also include a notion of the soul. Central to the constitution of the self is an awareness and understanding of the place that the 'I' has *vis à vis* other embodied selves. So that whilst a sense of self is shaped both by social classification and interaction with others it is equally importantly shaped by self-reflection upon such interactions, and can be revealed in self narratives through which human beings reflect upon choices and strategies of self representation and action which serve to distinguish themselves from others and through which they make sense of their actions in respect to others (Mines 1994: 149–186).

The individual and the self

Cohen (1994: 168) argues that the self is inextricably linked to the individual, suggesting that it is the self's perception of society which initiates behaviour distinguishing one human being from another and which therefore defines persons as individuals. He is careful however to qualify his analysis by making the important and often neglected distinction between individual, individuality and individualism. He contrasts individualism or 'a dogmatic posture which privileges the individual over society' to individuality, that is 'the perception of an individual's distinctiveness' which he suggests is a property of selfhood.

Concepts of the self and the individual in Indian anthropology

These distinctions are important because the question as to whether cross-cultural notions of the person incorporate a notion of the individual, and therefore by implication a clear and bounded sense of self, has been a source of debate both in anthropology in general and most particularly in Indian anthropology.[8] Louis Dumont's well-known argument that Indian concepts of the person do not include a notion of the individual, stems from his assertion that Indian values give paramount importance to the interests of the collective group (which can range from the household, extended family to castes or religious communities) rather than to the interests of the respective collectivity's constituent members. In his view 'the perception of ourselves as individuals is not innate but learned' and in societies such as India where humans are valued as part of a collective then the individual as a category is not recognised (Dumont 1980: 8–9). Subsequent theorists have expanded on this idea, most notably McKim Marriott and Ronald Inden (1977), who have emphasised the apparent fluidity of personal boundaries in India whereby people are believed to affect the bodily substance and inner physical and spiritual essence of others through interpersonal transactions such as touching and sharing food. They question whether Indians have a clear notion of the person as an individual bounded entity as compared to north Americans and Europeans,

> single persons are not ultimately individual units; instead persons are "dividuals," or unique composites of diverse subtle and gross substances derived ultimately from one source; they are also divisible into separate particles that may be shared or exchanged with others.
>
> (Ibid.: 232)

McKim Marriott (1989: 17–19) later suggests that whilst the Western social science model posits persons as self-reflexive, self-sufficient and in possession of a clear individual identity, the Indian model presents a picture of persons as non-reflexive, divisible 'dividuals' with no individual identity.

What Marriott and Inden (1977) arguably do is to present a model of the person at the molecular level and indeed suggest their view is an 'indigenous scientific view of flowing substance and striving persons' (ibid.: 233). Certainly they have highlighted an important component of Indian concepts of personhood within the context of inter- and intra-caste relationships, in which, as Louis Dumont has pointed out, the emphasis is placed on how the identity and status of the group is dependent on the carefully regulated interactions of human beings within and between groups. Yet, ethnographic data suggests that this is not the whole picture and that in actual relationships and day to day interactions, people's sense of self and individuality is recognised and plays an important part in people's overall conceptions of themselves as persons. Mattison Mines (1994: 212) suggests, on the basis of his own fieldwork in southern India, that Indian concepts of the person incorporate both 'dividual' and individual identity. Cecilia Busby's

(1997: 274) work, also in south India, questions the notion of 'dividuality', suggesting that whilst people's boundaries may be permeable, Indians perceive themselves as existing as persons in their own right and have a sense of internal wholeness. Similarly, Sarah Lamb's (2000: 39–40) ethnography on gender and ageing in a Bengali village challenges what she sees as an ethnocentric bias in Marriott's perspective, suggesting that whilst personhood is created through shared relationships with others, this does not preclude 'a clear sense of a differentiable self'.

My own fieldwork among Jain women revealed certainly a belief that the qualities of one human being could be affected by close interpersonal transactions with others. But at the same time women were very aware of themselves and those around them as possessing physical and psychological attributes which distinguished them as individual selves with specific interests, preferences and opinions – a perspective supported by Jain doctrines as we shall see shortly.

Jain doctrine and lay belief: notions of the soul, religious activity and the constitution of the self

Religious identity is not always a key factor in a human being's conceptualisation of him or herself and others as persons. But as James Laidlaw (1995: 151, 391–392) observes, Jain religious practice serves to create the individual's religious self and I would say that amongst the majority of Jain families living within the Jauhrī Bāzār area of Jaipur, religious belief and practice was significant in the constitution of both community identity, selfhood and personhood.

Jain doctrine emphasises how central the soul is to all sentient beings and especially to Jain concepts of the human being. What is particularly significant is the belief that when the soul is born within a human body it becomes a part of the self. Walther Schubring's interpretation of Jain doctrine indicates how the canonical texts distinguish between the *jīva* and the *āyā*. Schubring translates *jīva* as the soul which bears life, emphasising its property as the carrier of sentience or the life force (1962: 152). Similarly Paul Dundas (1992: 80) suggests that whilst *jīva* is often translated as soul, a more accurate translation would be 'life monad'. Indeed he points out that *jīva* as a concept is not found in the early texts, such as the *Ācārāṅga Sūtra*, which only mention the *āyā* (ibid.: 38). *Āyā* is the Prakrit equivalent of *ātman* in Sanskrit and has a complex set of meanings. In the Upaniṣads, *ātman* can signify both that element which continues through different rebirths, namely the soul, and those attributes particular to each individual, namely the ego or self. Paul Dundas suggests that *āyā* in the earliest Jain texts takes on this Upaniṣadic meaning (Dundas: personal communication). Schubring points out that often the dividing line between *jīva* and *āyā* is not always clear but suggests that *āyā* refers to 'I' particularly when used in the context of an individual human beings' cognition, passion and activity. What this implies is that when the soul is embodied due to karmic influence it forms a key component of the self. As Schubring (1962: 153) points out, doctrinally it is the *āyā* (*ātman*) which is the carrier of passions, cognitions and intentions initiating actions. These passions and actions in turn shape specific personalities, thereby constituting the self within each human being and making each human being a unique individual in the Jain view (providing a clear counter-example to the views of Dumont and Marriott discussed earlier). In this context Schubring places particular emphasis on the causative role that *karma* plays in creating heterogeneity within human beings. Within Jain doctrine, after the first century BCE *karma* takes on a rather concrete form and is conceived of as particles of matter adhering to the soul, drawn there by passions (*kaṣāya*) which range from anger, pride and greed, to love and enjoyment of comfort (ibid.: 292–293, also Dundas 1994: 83–84). Schubring draws attention to the way in which Jain doctrine actually specifies how individuality is created through a particular kind of karma, namely *nāma* karma. In addition, by influencing the family into which one is born, *karma* is also perceived to be responsible for the more outwardly visible aspects of personhood such as family status and caste identity (ibid.: 176 and 181).

Two key points emerge from this. First, the embodied soul is perceived to lie at the heart of the self and second, *karma* attached to the soul is believed to be responsible for the particular constitution and individuality of the self, which in turn shapes the individuality of each person.

Although the doctrines clearly define the person in terms of the self, individuality and social standing, the overriding emphasis of course is on the cessation of the person through the attainment of *mokṣa* or spiritual liberation, achieved when karmic influx is stopped and the consequences of existing karmic matter played out. At this point the soul is separated from the self or 'I', which is believed to dissolve together with other aspects of personhood such as social ties and statuses.

Conversely, from a lay person's perspective, the constitution of human beings as persons is an essential aspect of each human's ability to negotiate daily life. Both the women and men with whom I worked were familiar with the doctrine that *mokṣa* is not possible in the present age and they placed greater emphasis on trying to live life in such a way that good *karma* is accumulated, ensuring that future rebirths were in an environment conducive to religious practice and gradual worldly disengagement.[9] Nevertheless the purification of the soul was conceived to be a necessary focus of religious activity. Whilst the totality of Jain doctrine is complex, my discussions with, and observations of, practising Jains, and particularly women, indicated that certain doctrines and ritual practices pertaining to the nature of the soul and human life were well understood and profoundly influenced how people behaved and how they perceived themselves and others as persons. In particular, the belief that it is the three jewels (*tri ratna*) of right faith (*samyak darśana*), right knowledge (*samyak jñāna*) and right conduct (*samyak cāritra*) which enable the soul to begin its journey towards liberation, is central to the way in which ordinary people make sense of their place within the universe. This complex philosophy is succinctly embodied in symbolic offerings of rice created during the daily temple worshipping rituals,[10] indicating how these ideas are very much a part of people's worldview. Women repeatedly emphasised that their embodied soul, for which they used the word *ātman*, was the catalyst for intentions and thoughts which then influenced actions. In other words, religious beliefs have a very real influence on Jain women's conception of selfhood and personhood. This conception sees the soul as shaping the self and constituting the source of agency behind behaviour, which in turn defines women as social persons within the family and the wider community.

A young, unmarried Jain woman illustrated this perceived link between religious practice, the self and the socially interactive person with a comment on tricky relationships within her extended family. She explained that she and her parents found it very difficult to get along with her father's brother's wife whom she described as quarrelsome and abrasive. In explanation she suggested that her aunt's difficult character was exacerbated by a lack of interest in religion and religious activity. As James Laidlaw (1995) points out in the conclusion to his rich ethnography on Śvetāmbar Jains in Jaipur,

> Ideas and practices which must have been formed in the context of speculation about the individual soul in a cosmic, natural, and spiritual context, and which continue to be treated as such in explicit philosophical reflection and religious teaching, plainly figure prominently when one looks at what it is for a Jain to be a member of a social collectivity. Thus imagery and practice which looks at first sight – and also is – resolutely world renouncing, plays a central part in living a life in a socially complex, status divided, and in many ways intensely competitive world.
>
> (Ibid.: 393)

Finally one should not underestimate the specifically Śvetāmbar Jain belief that female birth is no bar to the attainment of spiritual liberation or *mokṣa*. This was clearly of profound importance to women's concept of their inner selfhood and encompassing personhood. The way in which women consistently reminded me of this during my fieldwork indicated the central role played by such a belief, not only in building a sense of spiritual authority and thereby their self-confidence, but in offsetting more negative images of women in some of the religious texts.

Gender personhood and the self

Now how might gender as a principle of social organisation interact with religious beliefs in the construction of the self? The importance of developing and shaping the self is expressed within both the Jain and the encompassing Hindu context, by the notion of *saṃskāras*. Jain women explained that *saṃskāras* are the characteristics and dispositions with which a person is born and which are shaped by actions in his or her previous births.[11] These dispositions are believed to affect that individual's behaviour and particular way of interacting in the world. In his analysis of childhood and society in India, Sudhir Kakar (1981: 48–49) suggests that the power of these innate *saṃskāras* can be sufficient to resist attempts by the individual to change. However, the Jain women with whom I talked expressed a different view. They frequently asserted that within a child, whether girl or boy, these *saṃskāras* are not fixed in form but can be moulded and encouraged to develop in a certain way by those people intimately involved in the child's upbringing. They clearly explained that positive dispositions can be supported and negative dispositions with which the child might be born can be encouraged to recede given the right moral guidance, in accordance with Jain principles.

And this is where Jain concepts of gender are important. Although child psychologists and anthropologists would agree that socialisation and personality development is a product of an individual's interaction with all members of a household, the Jain men and women with whom I talked had very clear and gendered models as to the respective responsibilities of family members. Fathers were accorded a more disciplinarian role. They were seen as responsible for overseeing the child's interaction with the world outside the home. This might involve a range of interactions from choice of schools, permission to go shopping or to the cinema and with whom, to teaching their sons' good money management as part of their apprenticeship to the family business, and finally for overseeing marriage negotiations.

In contrast mothers were unanimously accorded responsibility for influencing the development of the self, whereby through example and precept, the child absorbs Jain values and thereby develops a moral conscience, and a sense of internal responsibility and awareness of how to act in the world in accordance with Jain principles. This view immediately highlights the importance of religious values in shaping the self. Equally importantly it emphasises the heavy obligations placed upon women to put the interests of their family members at the centre of their lives, to fulfil their duty of *sevā* or service to others. All Jain women I spoke to were unanimous that *sevā* was an essential aspect of Jain adult womanhood, revealing a source of tension at the heart of women's lives, namely how a woman fulfils the multifarious demands placed upon her without being overwhelmed and losing her own sense of her selfhood and individuality. A closer understanding of the range of obligations is gained by an examination of a Jain woman's place within the kinship system and how her ascribed kinship roles define expectations concerning her behaviour at particular points in her life.

Personhood and kinship

Constitutive of female personhood are the complex range of externally manifest social relationships and roles which individual women are both born into and take on as they progress through the life cycle. Aline Wong's (1992: 163) observations that for Singaporese women 'the family lifecycle is the central axis of their life organisation' holds true of women (and indeed men) in many societies, and is certainly true of women from the conservative, middle-class community of Jains with whom I did my fieldwork during 1982–1984.

The development of selfhood within the female person: the context of caste and patrilineal kinship

A Jain woman's kinship roles as a daughter, and then as daughter-in-law and wife define her as a person and have a crucial impact on her sense of self. Jain kinship and marriage in Rajasthan, and Jaipur in particular, shares most of the features found amongst other high caste Hindu communities in northern India. Inheritance of property and kingroup identity is patrilineal and residence after marriage is patrivirilocal. Within parameters set by caste endogamy, marriage amongst the Osvāl and Śrīmāl Khartar Gacch Jaipur Jains operates within the idiom of hypergamy.[12]

The demands of the patrilineal kinship system weigh particularly heavily on women and there are two important implications. First, in all patrilineal systems paternity is an issue, but it is particularly acute in societies made up of hierarchically ranked endogamous groups.[13] Amongst both the Jains in Jaipur, and other high caste north Indian groups, caste membership is conceptualised in physical terms as passing from father to children through shared blood. The key issue therefore is the control of female sexuality and it is here that externally observable religious practice plays an extremely important role in publicly demonstrating sexual morality and contributing to a woman's reputation as a person worthy of respect. This then has implications for the arrangement of marriages and family social and economic status.[14]

Prior to puberty a girl's social and moral reputation are incorporated within that of her mother. Her approaching adulthood with the onset of puberty marks the gradual separation from her natal family, and particularly her mother, a separation finalised by marriage and which defines her as an adult person in her own right. Thus the post pubertal gradual assumption of visible religious activities serve as symbolic markers of this separation and represent the development of a girl's individual morality and social reputation. In Jaipur, girls are expected to visit the temple regularly, attend preachings in *cāturmās* and undertake short fasts once a month. Similarly, Whitney Kelting (2000: 173) points out that joining a *stavan* singing group marks the approaching adulthood of adolescent girls and is a public expression of piety, marking them out as good potential brides. This pattern of observable piety must continue after marriage, and goes hand in hand with strict *pardā* restrictions.

Indeed such public expressions of morality can refashion and safeguard the reputation of young women whose actions have challenged accepted norms. This was demonstrated by the case of Sushila who came from a well-respected jeweller's family. Their fortunes had declined somewhat and their beautiful *havelī*, located down a narrow alley, was showing signs of dilapidation. Sushila, a vivacious 20-year-old, shared her mother's graceful deportment but did not share her mother's interest in religion. When I first met her she laughingly told me that she was considered a 'very fast girl' due to her love of frequenting the *bāzār* and cinema halls (chaperoned by her brothers of course). Some two years later I was struck by the fact that she was visiting the temple daily and had begun to observe food restrictions. These changes had followed her attendance at a religious camp for young people. Her mother had apparently given instructions to her father not to bring her home until she had completed the camp, lamenting that 'she knows so little about religion'. A year later she was married.

The second implication of the patrilineal kinship system concerns a woman's sense of self, particularly in terms of her emotional development. It is to do with the emotional isolation and the deep division of loyalty a woman experiences after marriage between her natal family (with whom she has enduring roles as a daughter, sister and sister-in-law to her brothers' wives, as well as aunt to her brothers' children), and her affinal family, to whom she moves after marriage, with whom she has to build ties of affection and within which her roles as wife, mother, mother-in-law and grandmother are paramount.

Emotional and social vulnerability after marriage

I had numerous discussions with both Jain mothers and fathers about rearing daughters and from their point of view one of the main consequences of patrilineal kinship, caste linked status and patrivirilocal residence after marriage was female vulnerability.[15] They were not merely referring to her potential vulnerability to male advances prior to and after marriage which might threaten family status, but were concerned with the emotional vulnerability of daughters caused by transferral to a household where they have no close relationships with any member, where they are required to deferentially adjust to the husband's extended family and are the object of intense scrutiny and potential criticism. For instance Jain women frequently pointed out to me that misfortunes in the family were often blamed on new daughters-in-law – a classic illustration of Mary Douglas's (1966: 102) argument that notions of mystical danger adhere to people who are perceived to occupy an ambiguous position within the dominant structure of power. Leela Dube (2001: 229) suggests that socialising a girl for an unknown and unfamiliar setting leads to tentativeness, inhibiting the development of self-confidence and initiative.

I observed that within the safety and emotional security of their natal home, girls in their late teens, who in Jaipur had usually been educated up to degree level, were in fact confident and outspoken. This self-assured demeanour changed after marriage, which is clearly a traumatic transition for a young woman, whereby the relatively relaxed communication between her mother, brothers and father and a certain autonomy as to how she spends her time within the home are replaced by restricted and hierarchical relationships within her new affinal family.

The lesser autonomy of a young daughter-in-law was forcefully brought home to me after returning with a young unmarried friend from a jolly but rather hot and tiring *pūjā*. No sooner had we collapsed exhausted onto the soft cushions within the cool sitting room of the *havelī* when, to my discomfort, my friend sharply ordered her newly married sister-in-law, who was several years her senior, and as exhausted as we were, to go and make tea – a request which was silently and immediately complied with. Indeed Dumont's suggestions that the individual is subsumed by the requirements of the collectivity would seem to be most applicable to women as young daughters-in-law.

The situation is very different for boys and young men as they do not have to leave home on marriage but instead remain within the supportive environment of their parents home. Their efforts to become financially viable, within a competitive business environment, are supported by their father and possibly their brothers and father's brothers. Any stress that accompanies this transition from teenage boy to adult man is alleviated by the fact that a young man remains within an emotionally familiar environment. This is not to say that relationships within the joint family are always harmonious. They are not. But I would argue that potential conflict between brothers, surfaces later on in the male life cycle, often when the influence of the father wanes with age and retirement.[16]

Religious activity and the maturation of the self in the context of marriage

There is clearly a very real question as to what extent a woman's sense of self remains intact after marriage, particularly in the early years when her workload is most onerous and when the pressure to prove her loyalty and respectability are greatest, resulting in significant restrictions on her movement and means of communication both within and outside the home? In this context does religious practice have any significance? Are the religious activities which mothers encourage their daughters to embark upon at the onset of puberty merely a means whereby an adolescent girl begins to creates her separate identity as an adult Jain woman of good reputation? Or are they also a means whereby a young newly married woman, placed in a socially and emotionally vulnerable situation, can strengthen her sense of selfhood, and define herself as a person worthy of respect, which in turn helps her to internally negotiate the pressures, demands and conflicting loyalties which go hand in hand with her roles as wife, daughter-in-law, mother and daughter.

The religious stories with which the women were all conversant certainly suggest that religious activity has a role to play in that it contributes to the gradual maturation of the self in situations of adversity and in so doing offers the means for potential transformation from a self beleaguered by external pressures to a self confident of its own psychic integrity. The story literature is rich and in contradistinction to much of the other religious literature,[17] usually portrays women, in an extremely positive light. Such stories often involve unmarried or young married women, significantly women at a stage in their lives where their sense of self and their status as persons is most undermined. These stories implicitly suggest that such categories of women can seek a solution to their predicament through deep religious beliefs and practices (based upon the Jain principles of right view, right knowledge and right action), which nourish and build clear bounded selves imbued with a sense of moral rectitude and strength which then enables them to successfully face up to and conquer emotional and social adversity. What is of crucial importance is that their success is not merely limited to worldly existence. The strength of their selfhood, which is portrayed as a combination of both emotional maturity and firm spiritual knowledge grounded in Jain principles, enables them to steadfastly follow a religious path, which leads ultimately to spiritual enlightenment. The stories therefore embody a vision of overcoming worldly difficulties at a number of levels. This vision I argue contributes to a gradual development of self confidence and moral authority within those women for whom religious practice is a regular aspect of their lives.

Religious practice and the demarcation of space and time apart from the household

For a young Jain wife the experience of physically and emotionally transcending tensions arising from the myriad ties of daily household and kin obligations, begins in a small way through the daily visits to the temple, which after marriage are expected to become a regular part of a woman's daily routine, if they are not so already. For a newly married woman such visits have particular significance in that they constitute one of the few occasions when she can leave the confines of her affinal home and legitimately turn her attention inwards to herself. The cool space enclosed within temple walls is strikingly different to the hot, noisy bustle of everyday life outside. The white marble walls and dignified statues of the *tīrthaṅkars*, the air heavy with incense and punctuated with sounds of murmured ritual incantations combine to clearly demarcate a sacred and otherworldly space. The focus of temple worship are the *tīrthaṅkars*, clear symbols of the spiritual path to liberation or *mokṣa mārga* and the spiritual journey of each individual soul. Thus the temple visits whilst publicly representing a woman as a good Jain wife, at the same time physically and symbolically separate her from her husband's household and attendant responsibilities where her own needs and interests are low on the list of priorities. Virtually all women told me that these daily temple visits gave them a feeling of peace as well as respite from activity and tensions within their households. Women are able to extend this experience later on in married life by practicing the 48 minute meditation practice of *sāmāyik*, after rising in the morning. The importance of *sāmāyik* within Jain practice as a means whereby lay practitioners can detach their consciousness from the outside world is highlighted by Padmanabh Jaini (1979: 226) who suggests that, 'This sublime experience will sustain him even when he returns to his family and to the bustle of everyday life, drawing him again and again to the inner refuge he has discovered'. After 10 years of marriage, the majority of women I knew practised *sāmāyik* and they echoed Jaini's observations, emphasising how important to them that small period of silence was as a source of peace and reflection. In front of the household shrine, sitting on their 'mat', fingering their *mālās* (rosaries), they created through this ritual an external and internal space for themselves. Many women told me how *sāmāyik* enabled them to 'take their mind off worldly matters' or 'released any mental tension' – a form of detachment which, they felt, gave them greater emotional strength to re-enter and effectively manage the intricate web of emotions and obligations within the household of which they were a part.[18]

Religious practice and the fashioning of personal and family identity

These contemplative ritual practices are an important counterbalance to a woman's other religious duties, which emphasise much more emphatically her responsibilities to her affinal kin group. For a young wife these responsibilities are enacted through food preparation. After marriage the new wife assumes responsibility for cooking food for her affinal family under the watchful tutelage of her mother-in-law. This is perceived as a religious act entailing careful adherence to Jain principles to ensure no violence is committed to microscopic beings.[19] Cooking recreates on a daily basis the identity of a woman as a Jain wife whose inner self has a religious integrity which encourages behaviour enabling her to be viewed as a person worthy of respect. At the same time her food preparation reinforces the identity of household members as Jains – so crucial for the Śvetāmbar Jains of the Jauhrī Bāzār who are essentially a community of jewellery and cloth merchants where Jain religious identity demarcates the boundaries of an economic resources group within which informal credit networks, based on trust, operate.[20] As Marcus Banks (1992) notes, 'Food has an overriding importance to the Jains, being a constant diacritical marker of their otherness and the Jains have an elaborate schema of how, when, where and what to eat' (ibid.: 97). Once children are born, integrating a young woman more fully into her affinal family, food preparation is a potent symbol of her role as mother as it constitutes a central part of the process of socialising children, developing their sense of self by nurturing a moral conscience and an internal understanding as to where they as human beings fit into the social world within and beyond the household. James Laidlaw (1995) notes, the role played by food practices in the constitution of selfhood. 'Dietary practice . . . is actually the way young Jains learn about *ahiṁsā*, the way they come to think about their distinctiveness as Jains, and the most routine medium through which that distinctiveness is made part of the self' (ibid.: 166).

The life cycle and increasing authority: respected behaviour, age and kinship

Clearly, younger wives play an important role in fashioning Jain identity and the symbolic purity of themselves and their close kin through meticulous and time consuming cooking processes. At this stage of a laywoman's life caring for the family on both a physical, spiritual and symbolic level is accomplished through physical activity whose religious aspect gives a sense of personal fulfilment. Careful attention to these duties proves her loyalty to her affinal family, which in turn enables relationships of trust and intimacy to build up between herself and them. The resultant self-confidence is further bolstered by changes in the dynamics of power within the patrilineal family as her children grow older and new sisters-in-law are incorporated into the extended family. Household work can be shared or delegated to other women. Age and a more solid incorporation into her husband's family leads to an increasing relaxation of *pardā* restrictions enabling a woman to go outside the house more often to visit kin or go to the temple. Clearly, therefore, a woman's authority, power and therefore agency as a social person is contingent upon her sense of self, her behaviour, and the constitution and dynamics of the network of social relationships within her husband's household.

As physical tasks of looking after the family become lighter, so a woman assumes greater responsibility for caring for her family on a cosmic level. At the same time this gives her the opportunity to build upon and consolidate her sense of self through more concentrated and individual religious practice, and in Jaipur this is where extended fasting plays an increasingly important role.

In Jaipur, women drew my attention to fasting as an important practice. They were proud to talk about the fasts they had done which they viewed as an important part of their religious year. Whilst recognising that the importance of female group fasting seems to vary between regions, and possibly by sect,[21] and even within Jaipur one cannot assume that fasting is important for all women – as James Laidlaw (1995: 152) points out, religious practices between families and individual practitioners are very varied, I nevertheless suggest that for many of the Jaipur women who have been married for at least 10 years,[22] fasting is one of the ways through which female personhood, and particularly a sense of self, can be further developed. I would now like to explore how this might be the case.

Fasting, *sevā* and selves

Taps or austerities embody one of Jainism's central concepts, namely non-attachment, in two key ways. First, they are intended to detach the performer from some aspect of daily human life and second they are literally believed to produce internal, spiritual heat which literally burns away the particles of karma binding the soul to earthly existence. Fasting is one kind of austerity and it is worth emphasising that fasting within the Jain context does not necessarily involve total denial of food implied by the English gloss of the word *tap*. Rather Jain fasts encourage the practitioner to think about and work to decrease attachment to the material world by challenging patterns of meals and types of food, thereby focusing on the varied ways in which a human being is attached to earthly existence through food. In Jaipur the *āyambil* fasts, which omit the use of oils, spices and salts together with fruit and vegetables, enact detachment to taste. *Ekāsana*, enjoining the practitioner to eat only once a day, separates the practitioner from the usual three meals a day plus snacks which help to structure daily life. It is only the *upavās* fasts which prohibit food altogether, and although there are fasts which involve performing *upavās* for a succession of days, there are equally fasts such as *varṣītap*,[23] whereby one day of *upavās* is alternated with one day of normal eating for the duration of year.

A woman's fasts are ritualised activities carried out within both the home and the sacred spaces outside the home whereby on one level a woman creates and demonstrates her personhood through enacting her roles of wife and mother. First, she represents family morality and creates a good reputation essential in marriage negotiations for daughters. Second, religious activities are believed to attract good *karma*[24] and *puṇya* which bring worldly good fortune to the doer and those who share their lives, as well as positively affecting the inner soul of the doer. Within a patrilineal, patriarchal system a woman's good fortune is intimately connected with that of her husband and children and in this way a wife's and mother's religious activities are believed to benefit her family.[25]

To this extent Jain women are little different from their high caste Hindu counterparts who are subject to the encompassing ideology of *strīdharma* and the *pativrata* or virtuous wife. This portrays married women, and most particularly mothers, as symbols of auspiciousness and purity through whose religious work the health and happiness of the family is assured.[26] Mary McGee (1996: 155) highlights the centrality of the concept of *saubhāgya* as 'the virtue of well-being derived from having a living husband'. Although inherent in women, it nevertheless needs to be nurtured through the conscientious performance of household tasks, service to family members but most particularly to the husband and the performance of religious duties, particularly fasts.

> Married women, as vessels of *saubhāgya*, are constantly dispensing and replenishing their *saubhāgya* through benedictions and observance of *vrats*, bringing good fortune and well being to all with whom they come in contact... Simply put, a married woman who uses her *saubhāgya* in such creative ways is a transformer of destiny... In the Hindu context, she is a virtuous wife, and such deeds are her dharma, no more and no less.
>
> (Ibid.: 165)

Whilst this holds true for Jain women, the doctrinal emphasis on the liberation of the soul, symbolised by the ubiquitous *tīrthaṅkar* images in the temples, encourages Jain women to view fasts in a different way. Thus at another level I suggest the fasts contribute most decidedly to a woman's internal sense of individual selfhood. Jain women made it very clear to me that whilst they celebrated their relationships with their families, and particularly their husband and children, and interpreted their duties as wives and mothers as valid aspects of religious activity, they did not perceive fasts as solely oriented to their family's well-being. The *mokṣa mārga* ideology with its concept of the soul's journey to liberation was a crucial aspect not merely of women's understanding of the social world in which they were embedded but most significantly of their conception of their place within the wider universe. Their discussions about why they fasted and how they benefited always included the sense of inner peace it enabled them to access, the way in which they believed their actions contributed to the purification of their soul and its journey to liberation, however many rebirths that might take. In other words their fasting rituals enabled them legitimately to put themselves in the foreground – not only as selves that were identified with kinship roles but also as selves who had as part of their identity independent souls whose existence and development were not limited by the timeframe of one lifecycle.

Thus the religious Jain laywoman may be less psychically constrained by the demanding expectations linked to her roles than one might expect. Compared to nuns of course, a laywoman's religious practice cannot offer the same degree of transcendence from the obligations inherent in kinship and gender roles. Anne Vallely's (2002) research amongst Terāpanthi female ascetics offers fascinating comparisons and she observes that for such women

> The idiom of renunciation is unequivocally and unabashedly soul-centred, and nuns can avail of it every bit as easily as monks. Female asceticism represents a continuation of female virtues of chastity and restraint but significantly, it also represents a renunciation of *strīdharma* (gender duty).
>
> (Ibid.: 240)

For laywomen, religious practice makes space for a sense of self and individuality within the framework of *strīdharma* rather than beyond it, equipping women with the fortitude to intellectually and emotionally cope with the difficulties thrown up by the structures of power embedded in the relations of gender and kinship encompassing women's worldly life (*saṃsāra*).

The fast of *akṣay nidhi* and the personhood of women

I would like to explore some of these points by looking in detail at *akṣay nidhi tap*, which I witnessed in 1982, 1983 and 1984 in Jaipur.[27] This is a rather unusual fast in that unlike many fasts, it does not seem at first sight to be linked to specifically female interests. The associated story does not incorporate female heroines and the focus appears to be on worldly wealth and Jain identity. A careful analysis, however, reveals a rich web of meanings, intimately connected to the multi-layered personhood of women. The fast not only symbolises women's role in creating Jain identity, but encapsulates women's multiple kinship roles. At the same time it offers women the space and creative means to nurture their sense of self and gain respite from the restrictions imposed through gender and kinship.

Whilst I was in Jaipur, the *akṣay nidhi tap* coincided with *paryuṣaṇ* and was performed eight days prior to and the eight days during *paryuṣaṇ*. It began in 1982 and was repeated for four consecutive years in accordance with instructions laid out in the booklet especially published to accompany the fast, which also claimed that the fast dated back to the time of Mahāvīra and was a fast that he encouraged followers to perform.[28]

Community identity

At its most inclusive the fast is very much concerned with the various levels of Jain segmentary community identity, making its performance by women particularly significant in that they play a crucial role in creating and recreating Jain identity in time and space through their roles as wives, mothers and mothers-in-law. Names of the women who planned to do it were read out in the preachings. The publication of a booklet, the *Akṣay Nidhi Tap Vidhi*, to accompany the fast was paid for by a prominent Jaipur Śvetāmbar Mūrtipūjak jeweller whilst the wife of another prominent jeweller bid Rs. 3001 for the honour of leading the procession – an action which highlighted the role of the jewellery traders in Jaipur in maintaining and continuing Jain religious institutions. The fast was performed only by Khartar Gacch women on the encouragement of the monk, Muni Sāgar jī, resident in the Khartar Gacch *upāśray* for *cāturmās* in 1982.[29] The procession at the end of the fast included all five Mūrtipūjak temples in the old city run both by Khartar Gacch as well as Tapā Gacch.[30] As such it made both a public statement about the piety of Khartar Gacch as compared to other *gacch* communities whilst at the same time transcending *gacch* identity and representing the whole Mūrtipūjak community in Jaipur through the inclusion of these temples.

The story associated with the fast takes the theme of community identity one step further by focusing on the identity of Jains as a religious group within the wider context of caste hierarchy within Rajasthan. It concerns a king, named Puruṣottam, who loses his wealth and kingly position due to unspecified calamities. Whilst working as a servant in another king's palace, he meets a Jain ascetic and is subsequently converted to Jainism. The Jain ascetic advises him to do the fast of *akṣay nidhi* to regain his wealth. This brings immediate results as on completing the fast he is promoted to minister in charge of the king's trade – a clear metaphorical reference to the association of Jains with the trading castes.[31] Subsequently, he embarks on a trading expedition to another kingdom but his ship is caught in a storm and all except him are drowned. Carried to the shore by a crocodile, he finds that the kingdom is facing a dilemma because their ruler had died heirless. To select a new king, the populace decide to let loose an elephant with a young woman riding on its back, the custom being that the man to whom the elephant points his trunk should be made king. As a consequence of performing *akṣay nidhi*, the elephant points its trunk at Puruṣottam and in this way he regains his wealth and kingship – but with one major difference – as a Jain king.

The story I was given[32] is reminiscent of the conversion stories discussed at length by Lawrence Babb (1996), whereby kings convert to Jainism under the influence of Jain ascetics. He points out how such stories are to do with the Jain claims to a particular kind of caste identity, contesting their attributed status as traders or *vaiśyas*, and claiming a status equal or superior to the ruling Rajput community.[33] Such stories claim a non-violent royal identity achieved through conversion by ascetics – contrasting Jain kings with the meat eating and alcohol drinking identity of Rajput rulers – a diet which, according to Jain principles, makes them spiritually inferior (Babb 1996: 161–169). The story may also reflect a competitive demarcation of Jain religious identity *vis à vis* Hindu religious identity in that Puruṣottam is one of the names given to the god Viṣṇu (Gupta 2000: 394).

Unlike many of the stories attached to fasts women do, it did not include women as central characters. Yet the inclusion of a woman riding on the back of the elephant, a pan-Indian symbol of both fertility and royal authority (Kinsley 1997: 225), implicitly indicates that the woman directs the elephant's choice. This suggests that the fast combined with female spiritual wisdom, restores Puruṣottam's fortune, an oblique reference to women's perceived role as guardians of Jain identity, morality and good fortune. The story and procession makes visible women's central role as persons responsible for maintaining community identity. The resultant inner authority and confidence seemed very evident to all who watched their smiling and unveiled faces as they went on a procession through town after the fast. Indeed the fast makes publicly manifest female social power enacted through roles as wives, mothers, grandmothers and aunts, which is otherwise hidden behind the walls of the home, and the invisibility imposed by *pardā* restrictions.

In addition the timing of the fast helped to reinforce the emphasis on a community identity beyond that of individual *gacch* allegiance. I was told that the fast could be performed at other times of the year but the resident monk in 1982 decided to make the fast lead up to and coincide with *paryuṣaṇ* celebrations. This is significant as 8 days of *paryuṣaṇ* are the only time in the year when all the Śvetāmbar Jains in the old city, women, men, young and old make an effort to take on board religious observances in terms of food restrictions, fasting, confession and temple going. The public nature of many of the celebrations, such as the processions, the loud well attended *pūjās*, and the many well dressed Jains on the streets at night visiting the five temples to worship, clearly makes this festival a statement of community identity *vis à vis* the wider society.

Fasting and detachment from the household through the restructuring of time and space: the case of Mrs Bhaṇḍārī

The fast significantly restructured the practitioners' day as the following case of Mrs Bhaṇḍārī shows, encouraging women to turn their attention inwards and away from their home and family. Mrs Bhaṇḍārī was a 38-year-old woman, from the Osvāl caste, whose husband ran a jewellery business. She was typical of many of the women I worked with in that religious belief and practice structured much of her life. She explained to me how she tried to live her life according to the five great vows of Jainism (*pañc mahāvrat*). To illustrate this she related how once she had performed five *upavās* fasts as penance for killing a ladybird whilst cleaning vegetables. On the advice of a nun she had vowed to follow the fourteen principles (*chaudah niyam*) daily and had also taken a vow to give up *rasgūllas*, a particularly delicious sweetmeat, for life. She ate no roots at all and no green vegetables or fruit on the eighth and fourteenth auspicious days (*tithi*) of each lunar fortnight or during *paryuṣaṇ*. She ate before sunset and drank nothing after sunset. She saw her religious practice as a way of life which began in early childhood when she did her first *upavās* at the age of 7. She explained her commitment to religion as due to good *karma* accumulated in a previous birth, implicitly linking soul, self and personhood. She was a confident and outspoken woman and made her own decisions as to how she should put her beliefs in to practice, stating that 'a husband should never interfere in a wife's practice'. Her religious beliefs and practices had clearly contributed to her strong sense of self and individuality, in addition to which she was mistress of her own home as her mother-in-law was dead. Significantly she had frequent contact with her natal family, including her parents and her brothers (also jewellers), who lived close by. In fact she was performing *akṣay nidhi tap* with two of her brother's wives.

She had two sons, one aged 20 years and one aged 11 years, and a daughter of 17 years. She, her husband and children lived as a nuclear family on the second floor of a three storey *havelī*, but her husband's brother (also a jeweller) lived one floor below and her husband's brother's wife helped cook and look after Mrs Bhaṇḍārī's husband and children whilst she performed *akṣay nidhi tap*. This help was absolutely essential as the fast took Mrs Bhaṇḍārī out of the house for most of the day. Prior to embarking on the fast she had received permission from her husband to do it and had taken a vow of celibacy to last for the duration of the fast.

On each day of the fast she took bath after rising and then performed *samāyik* and *pratikramaṇ* before visiting the temple prior to attending the preachings. After the preachings, which included encouragement to those performing the *akṣay nidhi tap*, she would make her way to the shrine in the *upāśray*, along with over one hundred other women doing the fast. In pride of place on the shrine was displayed a silver *Naupad Siddha Cakra Yāntra*, symbolising both essential qualities required to begin the path to spiritual enlightenment as well as the five key categories of renunciant, namely, ascetics, religious teachers, leaders of ascetic orders, liberated souls and *tīrthaṅkars* (*pañc parameṣṭhin*). In front of this shrine a large metal pot was placed (called *a kumbha or kalaśa* in the fasting booklet) and as many smaller pots with coconuts balanced on the top as there were fasting women. Mrs Bhaṇḍārī, along with the other women had her own small table on which she daily made twenty-one rice *svāstikas*[34] and placed offerings of fruit and sweets. She collected her pot from the shrine, removed the coconut which she had covered with an orange cloth, in order to place within the pot additional offerings of money, rice and almonds. She also placed money, rice and almonds within the large metal pot on the central shrine table. By the end of the sixteen days all the pots were full. After making her offerings she joined the other women in hymn singing which lasted until lunch time at which point she accompanied all the women across the road to the *dharma śālā* where everyone partook of a substantial and convivial *ekāsana* meal, specially cooked for them by temple servants. Mrs Bhaṇḍārī then returned home for a short rest before returning to the *dharma śālā* for the scheduled afternoon *pūjās*, which were well attended by the wider community, particularly the women and children. She followed this by evening *pratikramaṇ* and a final visit to the temple for *darśan* before returning home.

Persons of women: kinship as represented through the fast

The symbolism included within the fasting rituals represents both the individual souls and selves of women as well as the kinship roles which constitute their externally perceived personhood. The different layers of meaning encapsulated in the name *akṣay nidhi* indicate how this might be so and well illustrate John Cort's thesis that the values of the *mokṣa marga* ideology, focusing on the soul, and the values of well-being, focusing on life in the world, are intricately interconnected. As one woman carefully explained to me, '*akṣay*' means 'that which can never be destroyed' and '*nidhi*' refers to wealth, fund or treasure. The book given to all the women performing the fast said that practitioners of *akṣay nidhi tap* acquire knowledge and a noble character, thereby implying that the indestructible wealth is that of spiritual qualities gained, as the story implies, through adherence to Jainism. Mrs Bhaṇḍārī supported this view telling me that she believed it contributed to the purification of her soul.

However, other women took the story more literally. For example, Vebhobāī, a woman in her mid-thirties from the Khartar Gacch Śrīmāl caste, who performed the fast, explained to me, 'People do this *tap* so they get wealth in the next birth enabling them to do charitable religious work'.[35] Certainly at one level the symbolism of the fast seems to support the values of worldly well-being and appears to highlight the married woman's perceived role as the cosmic guardian of family health, wealth and happiness. The pot is a particularly interesting focal symbol. Referred to in the fasting booklet as *kumbha*, or sometimes as *kalaśa*, it is significantly one of the eight auspicious symbols (*aṣṭamaṅgal*) in both Jainism and Hinduism and as such is common in both Jain and Hindu ritual. On the afternoon of the first day of the fast in 1982, a *naupad pūjā*, celebrating the soul's path to liberation, was held in the *upāśray*. Included in the shrine were the coconut topped steel pots, which people explained represented the women who were performing the *akṣay nidhi* fast. Indeed, the symbolic linkage of women and pots is suggested by the fact that the water pot is a symbol for the female *tīrthaṅkar* Mallināth. The women who performed the fast clearly identified the pots with woman hood by telling me that the sight of a woman with a pot on her head is a very auspicious sight.[36] They did not elaborate on this but it is relevant to note that in Hinduism the *kumbha* specifically stands for the power of the mother goddess who is the source of fertility and the creative energy of the universe. In addition, it is commonly used to symbolise the household goddesses (Dallapiccola 2002: 120), believed to protect the family and ensure good fortune.[37]

People explained that the pot and coconut together were symbols of pious religious work as they were *śubh ciz* (good things) and *maṅgalik ciz* (auspicious things). John Cort points out that both these terms can refer to the values of worldly well-being and that within a ritual context the coconut specifically is a symbol of fertility and success all over India.[38] The coconut is an important symbol in both Hindu and Jain rituals and the cloth covered coconut in the pot, carried on a woman's head features in a variety of Jain religious contexts. For example I saw these used during a pilgrimage as well as in a statue installation ceremony. In the context of *akṣay nidhi tap* the covering of bright red, orange and yellow cloths, fringed with silver seemed to reinforce the meaning of fertility as such cloths were reminiscent of the *sarīs* worn by women for marriage or other festive occasions – the colour of which represent fertility and auspiciousness. This theme is reinforced by the pots filled to the top with offerings by the end of the fast. The booklet emphasises that by the last day the pots should be full, suggesting a link with the full pot or *pūrṇa kalaśa* in Hinduism as the symbol of good fortune, plenty, fertility and the life force (Saletore 1982: 645, 796 and Dallapiccola 2002: 159).

So there is a strong case for suggesting that at one level the pots signify a woman's procreative and nurturing role within the patrilineal family as wife and mother together with the responsibility she is believed to bear for her family's physical and spiritual well-being through the merit she accumulates as a consequence of her religious work. The fast therefore defines female personhood in terms of their kinship roles and obligations to the wider community:

The focus on selfhood through *akṣay nidhi*

The following narrative, provided by one woman in her late forties, Mrs Nahāta, indicates however that this is far from the whole story and points beautifully to the way in which some women read the pot and coconut as representative of their individual soul and that soul's journey towards enlightenment:

> In the beginning the husk and the coconut are joined together. As time passes the inner part gets separated from the husk. We should be like the coconut fruit – while living in the material world we should not be stuck and attached to material things but must remain separate.

Other women carefully told me that the pot represented the soul and that the inner white fruit of the coconut represented the ideal pure state of the soul when freed from karma. These interpretations support John Cort's (2001: 194) analysis of the pot or *kalaśa* as representing increase and fertility not only at the level of worldly life but also at the level of the soul. He explains that increase in the context of the soul signifies spiritual development whereby detachment is cultivated and freedom from rebirth ultimately achieved. The white rice placed daily into the pots by the women holds similar meanings. Women and men told me that white rice, devoid of its husk, is unable to re-grow, and in this way white rice symbolises the soul devoid of karma and therefore freed from rebirth in this world.

The other items – almonds and money placed inside the pot daily – reinforced such meanings. Almonds as luxury food and money were explained as symbolic of worldly pleasures being renounced. In this way the pot represents the embodied pure and fully spiritual soul to which all religious and renunciatory activity is believed to lead in the end.[39] Similarly, I was informed that the offerings of sweets and fruits symbolise the stage of *vītarāga*, when the soul is free of desires for pleasing things. The timing of the fast during *paryuṣaṇ* – the most important Jain festival of the year when values of renunciation and spiritual liberation are brought to the fore – certainly emphasised the orientation of all religious activity towards the individual soul.

Mrs Jārchur, the woman who led the procession at the end of the fast, reinforced this view. According to her, 'Religious work brings peace to the soul. This fast does not help husbands. To do *akṣay nidhi tap* for your husband is futile. The fast is for the good of your own soul'.

This interpretation was supported by Asha, one of the small number of unmarried young women who performed the fast. Now one could read their performance in terms of action oriented towards good *karma* and attracting a good husband and healthy children. But the example of Asha suggests this is too simplistic. Asha was a 20-year-old girl who had completed her university degree. She was quite a shy, soft-spoken woman who, since leaving university, increasingly made religious activity a central part of her life. Her beliefs linked both her potential kinship roles as an adult woman as well as her conception of herself as embodying an independent soul. Thus she supported her mother's belief that 'through religious activity a woman makes a heaven of her home'. At the same time she emphasised the importance of sincerity behind any religious activity and discussed the way in which she felt religious activity shaped her individual character so that she would have the ability to face any adversity with equanimity. In this way she felt her soul was purified. Significantly, she had participated in a group performance of the three-day Candaṇbālā *upavās*, which re-enacts a fast performed by a woman who became one of the first nuns under the *tīrthaṅkar* Mahāvīra.[40] Her performance of *akṣay nidhi tap* was therefore part of an ongoing process in her shaping of a sincerely felt religious identity which she perceived as the core of her sense of self. Certainly she radiated a calm and quiet self assurance.

Concluding remarks: the pot as a symbol of the self within the person

In pulling all these ideas and interpretations together, I think it is important to emphasise that the fast and its symbolism does not merely represent all these values in the abstract. Each pot is tended by a particular woman, and as I have argued earlier can be seen as representative of that woman. The various interpretations of the symbolism point to the pots as potent representations of women as persons. On one level each pot represents the aspect of a woman's personhood created through interaction with kin and her interpretation of her ascribed roles as mother, wife and nurturer. Through the fast a woman displays the fulfilment of her social responsibilities both within the community and within her household where her spiritual power enables her to mediate between the spiritual and the material realms, safeguarding the health and good fortune of family members. Her moral authority is publicly demonstrated, and through this demonstration she is publicly judged as a good Jain woman who through her fulfilment of *sevā* is judged as worthy of respect. In the process not only is her status as a person elevated but so is that of her affinal family in which she is daughter-in-law, wife, mother and mother-in-law, as well as her natal family which she represents as daughter and sister. So at this level one could argue that women encapsulate Dumont's notion of Indian personhood whereby the individual is subsumed within and works for the interest of the group.

Yet at the same time the structure and symbolism of the fast challenges Dumont's view of personhood as well as Marriott's view of the Indian 'dividual'. The fast detaches the female practitioner from the collectivity of family and community. The husband's permission for his wife to do the fast, legitimately absolves her from conjugal demands and worldly tasks of cooking, cleaning and childcare. The shrine within the *upāśray*, where she spends the morning praying and singing hymns constitutes a sacred space, which further separates her both actually and symbolically from the household. The communal *ekāsana* meal cooked by temple servants and eaten by all the fasting women in the *upāśray* serves further to underline this symbolic separation. In particular the vow of celibacy, undertaken before all fasts, is a particularly potent form of actual and ritualised separation of a woman from her husband. La Fontaine's (1992: 103) observations that gendered activities can temporarily cut across principles which link men and women as husbands and wives are pertinent here. This detachment is most graphically symbolised by the individual pot and coconut which stand in contra-distinction to the large communal pot to which all contribute offerings and which arguably symbolises the community. Each small pot represents in solid form a woman's individual selfhood, self-discipline and independent spiritual existence over which she alone gains increasing autonomy both with age and increased religious activity.

In many ways the fasts are similar to rites of passage. The vow of celibacy and husband's permission constitutes the stage of separation, the fast itself comprises the transitional stage and the procession, formal *parṇā* or fast breaking and celebratory feast symbolically re-emphasises her links with kin, therefore re-incorporating the woman back into daily mundane life. But as with all rituals, the re-incorporated woman is transformed in a subtle way. As Laidlaw and Humphrey (1994: 227–230) point out, participating in rituals is a creative act which not only makes a public statement about the person involved but also works on the emotions. This, as Lawrence Babb (1996: 15) perceptively notes, gives rise to feelings which continue beyond the ritual thereby contributing to the worshipper's personal and social identity.

It is the nature of this identity that is so significant. Religious activity and belief enables participating women to nurture and build upon their sense of individual selfhood in that the ritualised techniques of separation together with the symbolic meanings held by the ritual objects, direct women's attention to what lies at the very heart of Jainsim, namely the journey of the embodied soul or *ātman* towards eventual liberation. In the words of the *Akṣay Niddhi Tap Vidhi* (1982: 1), all forms of *tapasyā* or ascetic practice, including fasting, lead to the purity of the soul (*ātma śuddha*) and self reflection within the soul (*ātma cintan*). Belief in the karmic distinctiveness of each soul, which in turn is believed to fashion each human being's consciousness of self and agency, contributes to a woman's reflexive awareness of individual selfhood separate from her existence as a being linked to others through ties of affection and obligation defined by the framework of kinship and religious community. Contemplative techniques incorporated into the fasting rituals give women the opportunity to reflect on inner selves which incorporate their individual souls engaged in a unique journey to spiritual liberation – a journey not circumscribed by one lifetime. Whilst the widely voiced belief that a woman's morally directed behaviour and religious activity can affect the worldly fortune of close family members supports Marriott's theories of Indians and 'dividual' persons, the belief that the soul of each human being can only be affected by that human being's own actions, defines women as separate selves with their own individuality. Whatever other aspects of her life are influenced or curtailed by kin, she and she alone can influence the progression of her soul – which constitutes the very heart of her sense of self.

The Jain material is thus a clear illustration of Lukes and Cohen's suggestion that notions of the self are inextricable components of the total person. It further highlights how religious beliefs are crucial to understanding the ways in which people conceive of the self within the person cross-culturally. The self consciousness which Cohen emphasises as central to human conceptualisations of the self is particularly developed in Jain belief. This in turn fosters the development of clearly defined concepts of selfhood within both Jain men and women but which has particularly important implications for women given their position within the power structures inherent in the systems of caste and kinship.

In general therefore, the complex of fasting rituals, continue and amplify a process gently initiated in childhood and increasingly consolidated after marriage. Fasting, and particularly the longer more complex fasts, carve out a potent symbolic and sacred space for women, similar to that mentioned earlier as created through *sāmāyik* and temple visiting, a space within which they can reflect and nurture their inner self. As a new wife in a testing and unfamiliar environment the daily contemplative rituals enable a woman to create within her life small areas of sacred space and time. Within this sacred time, carved carefully out of a day filled with household activity, she is enabled to contemplate the rich religious imagery encapsulating complex Jain philosophical ideas.

This in turn allows her to locate herself as a conscious being within the universe – a vision which both enriches her perception of the world and enables her to see beyond and to negotiate her way through the social obligations which frame her life. Undeniably therefore within this particular Jain community, religious belief and practice combine uniquely with kinship roles, age and household developmental cycles, contributing on the one hand to the social construction of female personhood over time, and on the other hand to the construction of the self within the person through nurturing a sense of spiritual fulfilment and self-realisation, enabling a woman to imaginatively orient herself to cosmic as well as social time and space.

Notes

1 This re-analysis was partly inspired by Whitney Kelting's (2001) sensitive ethnography on female religious practice in Maharashtra. Anne Vallely's (2002) ethnography on Terāpanthī Jain nuns provides an important comparison to the material on laywomen.
2 Note on transliteration: I have transliterated most Hindi words which are used in a wide variety of contexts to include the silent inherent 'a'. I have not included the inherent 'a' for words used specifically in a Jain context, such as Śvetāmbar, so as to indicate the specific pronunciation of such words by Jaipur Jains.
3 Subsequent to my own fieldwork, considerable research has been undertaken on the Śvetāmbar Jains residing in the Jauhrī Bāzār, Jaipur. See in particular Laidlaw 1995 and Babb 1996.
4 See for example Mauss 1985, Fortes 1971, Carrithers 1985, La Fontaine 1985 and Strathern 1988.
5 See in particular Strathern 1988.
6 Mines 1994, Lamb 2000.
7 I am in agreement with Cohen's (1994: 5) criticism of social theorists who question whether a concept of self exists cross-culturally.
8 See Lamb 2000: 27–41, for a useful review of these arguments.
9 A lighthearted example of this view was revealed by many Jain womens' attempts to understand how I had got the resources plus permission from my family to travel alone so far from home. They generously concluded that the accumulation of beneficial *karma* had given me the opportunity to learn about the Jain religion, in their view the essential starting point to eventual spiritual liberation.
10 Women shape the offering of dried rice into the four armed *svāstika*, which they explained as symbolic of the four kinds of birth a soul may take, placing above this three dots representing the three jewels, above which a half moon shape is fashioned representing the abode of the *siddhas* or liberated souls.
11 The word *saṃskāras* is also used to denote life cycle rituals which mark changes in social status and which therefore contribute to constituting the externally perceived person.
12 This is not to assume that among other Jain communities hypergamous marriage is always the norm.
13 Amongst the relatively wealthy Jauhrī Bāzār Jains, notions of status and hierarchy played a key role in the organization of arranged marriages. In the absence of sufficient wealth, family reputation represented by female honour was particularly crucial in securing a good match.

14 Reynell 1985: chapters 2 and 4.

15 See Sherry Fohr's article in this volume which deals with the intersection of parental concerns about female sexual vulnerability and nunhood.

16 Men of course face different pressures. They are expected to work hard once they have left school, in joining their father in the family business or initiating a career of their own. Parents looking for potential grooms will pay particular attention to this, taking care not to marry their daughter to a young man whom they consider lazy and therefore who might not be able to provide economic stability for their daughter and future grandchildren. Moreover, a young man's status within the male community will depend on the business connections he makes and his reputation as hard-working and trustworthy. The moral reputation of his family, particularly that of his mother will reflect well on his own reputation, which is further bolstered by a modicum of visible religious activity. Men are not expected, in their young years or prior to retirement, to spend a large amount of time on religious activity – as it is considered that it would detract them from their economic responsibilities. However, daily temple visiting for *darśan* is a minimum requirement to retain a reputation as a man of sound character both in business and as a potential groom in marriage negotiations.

17 As I have argued in a previous paper (Reynell 1987: 33–57), Śvetāmbar Jain ideology has not been immune to the ambiguous attitudes inherent within the encompassing North Indian patrilineal kinship and caste system, whereby control over identity, status and resources is vested in the control of female sexuality. Hence the positive valuations given to women in the religious literature are to some degree offset by contradictory statements associating women with sensual pleasure, lust and deceit (see for example the *Sūtrakṛtāṅga Sūtra*, 271–275 or Hemacandra's *Triṣaṣṭiśalākāpuruṣacaritra, Vol I: 35, Vol VI: 26*). But this is precisely where the story literature is so important. Most of the women I worked with were not familiar with the canonical texts, with the exception of the *Kalpa Sūtra*, which is read out loud during *paryuṣaṇ*. They were far more familiar with the story literature portraying positive images of womanhood. Whitney Kelting (2001: 23–32) also found this to be the case amongst the Śvetāmbar Jain women with whom she worked in Maharashtra, where she highlighted an area of female religious expertise that has received little attention, namely the crucial role of hymn singing and the collection of hymns for performance plays in conveying positive images of women.

18 In a similar vein Sarah Lamb (2000: 141) notes that Bengali villagers view techniques of detachment as a means not to renounce the world but to help deal with the intense emotional attachments which are a part of worldly life.

19 Marie-Claude Mahias' (1985) meticulous ethnography on a community of Digambar Jains in Delhi clearly illustrates the central role food plays as a religious symbol among the Jains.

20 This is not to say that such a resource group is continually activated or that members are always co-operative. As Peter Flügel (1995–1996: 163) points out, economic relationships within the religious community may often be antagonistic and competitive.

21 Whitney Kelting (2001: 44) suggests it is less important among the Śvetāmbar Mūrtipūjak Tapā Gacch Jains in the Maharashtrian town of Pune.

22 Jain women explained that it is not considered appropriate for newly married women to undertake fasts entailing denial of food for long periods and on a regular basis as it would interfere with the heavy housework expected of her within the joint family. Similarly, whilst it was not mentioned explicitly, extended fasting might affect a newly married woman's fertility and ability to breastfeed. In this sense fasting goes against the interests of the joint family and there can be a tension between a woman's desire to engage in religious activity and the interests of her family.

23 This fast celebrates the origins of Jainism and is performed in memory of the first *tīrthaṅkar*, Ṛṣabha. See reference in Hemacandra's *Triṣaṣṭiśalākāpuruṣacaritra*, Vol. I: 177.

24 This chapter does not intend to deal with theories of *karma* in detail. One of the key points is that *karma* affects both the future thought patterns of the mind, future actions enacted through the body inhabited by the soul and the future worldly fortunes of that soul, including its next rebirth. *Karma* is believed to have both spiritual and worldly repercussions. Fruits of good *karma* lead to the purification of the soul and increased worldly good fortune whilst bad *karma* hinders spiritual growth and encourages misfortune. Theories of *karma* are therefore intimately implicated in what John Cort (2001) has identified as the two interwoven sets of beliefs influencing Jain practice, namely the ideology of *mokṣa mārga* and the path of well-being.
25 See Reynell (1985: 126–140), for a more detailed discussion of this.
26 Fuller (1991: 21–22).
27 This is a good example of how specific religious practice can be to one region. Whilst *akṣay nidhi* was important in Jaipur as a group fast, Whitney Kelting (2001: 44) notes that in Pune, Maharashtra, it had nowhere near the same significance.
28 *Akṣay Nidhi Tap Vidhi*, pp. 24–28.
29 Although the accompanying booklet states that men can perform *akṣay nidhi tap*, and the associated story centres on male performance, no men joined in the particular fast that I witnessed.
30 These temples were located within the half square mile of the Jauhrī Bāzār area between Haldiyon kā rāsta and Kundigaron ke Bhairu kā rāsta. One was managed by the Khartar Gacch Osvāl caste and another by the Khartar Gacch Śrīmāl caste. The Tapā Gacch Osvāls ran three more, one of which I was told was privately owned by a family living in Agra.
31 Whilst Jains are popularly associated with trade, and indeed the Śvetāmbar Mūrtipūjak Tapā and Khartar Gacch Jains, with whom I worked, belonging to the Osvāl and Śrīmāl castes, were largely jewellery and cloth merchants, this is not invariably the case. Much of the Digambar community in Jaipur is associated with government administration. To give another example, Marcus Banks (1992: 46–49, 59, 70–74) points out that in Gujarat a proportion of the Jain population are agriculturalists.
32 I am relying on oral versions of the story told to me by women who participated in the fast, together with that given in the accompanying booklet.
33 See also discussion in Maya Unnithan-Kumar's (1997: chapter 2) book on how various caste communities in Rajasthan construct their identity in relation to Rajput dominance.
34 None of the women were able to tell me the significance of the number 21.
35 This statement reflects John Cort's (2001: 201) conclusion that the path of well-being is a valid religious goal for Mūrtipūjak Jains in that without the wealth produced by the Jain laity, Jain institutions and ascetic community would not survive.
36 Indeed, at the 5th Jain workshop held at SOAS on 13th June 2003, I was informed by one Jain participant that men are never allowed to hold the *kalaśa* in religious ceremonies – again clearly identifying pots as a female symbol.
37 Babb notes that the pot can represent the 'physical locus of the deity' (1975: 280). I am told that in *Dūrga pūja* the pot is a focal symbol standing for the self replenishing creative energy of nature (S. Dasgupta, research student, SOAS: personal communication).
38 Cort 2001: 190. See, also, Babb 1996: 32.
39 The story associated with the fast and focusing on Puruṣottam may also suggest this meaning. Thomas Mooren (1997: 18–25) suggests that in Sanskrit *puruṣa* can mean the universal soul and is linked to the concept of *ātman* or self and Brahman or universal consciousness.
40 A version of the Candaṇbālā story can be found in Hemacandra's *Triṣaṣṭiśalākāpuruṣacaritra*, Vol. VI: 112–119.

Bibliography

Primary sources

Akṣay Nidhi Tap Vidhi. (1982) Khartar Gacch Sangh. Jaipur.

Sūtrakṛitāṅga Sūtra. (1895) *The Gaina Sūtras. Part 2. The Sacred Books of the East XVL.* Ed. Max Müller, Oxford: Clarendon Press.

Triṣaṣṭiśalākāpuruṣacaritra of Ācārya Hemacandra. (1931) Translated by H. M. Johnson. *The Lives of 63 Illustrious Persons*. Gaekward Oriental Series: Baroda Oriental Institute. 1931. Vol. I 1962. Vol.VI.

Secondary sources

Ardener, Shirley. (1992) *Persons and Powers of Women in Diverse Cultures*, Oxford: Berg Publishers.

Babb, Lawrence. (1975) *The Divine Hierarchy: Popular Hinduism in Central India*, New York: Columbia University Press.

—— (1996) *Absent Lord: Ascetics and Kings in a Jain Ritual Culture*, Berkley, CA: University of California Press.

Banks, Marcus. (1992) *Organizing Jainism in India and England*, Oxford: Clarendon Press.

Bennett, Lynn. (1983) *Dangerous Wives and Sacred Sisters: Social and Symbolic Roles of High Caste Women in Nepal*, New York: Columbia University Press.

Busby, Cecilia. (1997) 'Permeable and Partible Persons: A Comparative Analysis of Gender and Body in South India and Melanesia', *Journal of the Royal Anthropological Institute*, 3, 2: 261–278.

Carrithers, Michael and Humphrey, Caroline (eds.) (1991) *The Assembly of Listeners: Jains in Society*, Cambridge: Cambridge University Press.

Carrithers, Michael, Collins, Steven and Lukes, Steven (eds.) (1995) *The Category of the Person*, Cambridge: Cambridge University Press.

Cohen, Anthony, P. (1994) *Self Consciousness: An Alternative Anthropology of Identity*, London: Routledge.

Cort, John, E. (2001) *Jains in the World: Religious Values and Ideology in Jainism*, New York: Oxford University Press.

Dallapiccola, Anna, L. (2002) *Dictionary of Hindu Lore and Legend*, London: Thames and Hudson.

Douglas, Mary. (1966) *Purity and Danger: An Analysis of Concepts of Pollution and Taboo*, London: Routledge and Kegan Paul.

Dube, Leela. (2001) *Anthropological Explorations in Gender: Intersecting Fields*, New Delhi: Sage Publications.

Dumont, Louis. (1980) (1st edition 1966) *Homo Hierarchicus: The Caste System and Its Implications*, Chicago, IL: University of Chicago Press.

Dundas, Paul. (1992) *The Jains*, London: Routledge.

Flügel, Peter. (1995–1996) 'The Ritual Circle of the Terāpanth Śvetāmbara Jains', *Bulletin Études Indiennes*, 13–14: 117–176.

Fortes, M. (1971) 'On the Concept of the Person among the Tallensi.' in G. Dieterlen (ed.) *La Notion de Personne en Afrique Noire*, 283–319, Paris: Éditions du Centre National de la Recherche Scientifique.

Fuller, Christopher. (1991) *The Camphor Flame: Popular Hinduism and Society in India*, Princeton, NJ: Princeton University Press.

Gupta, M. G. (2000) *Dictionary of Indian Religions, Saints, Gods, Goddesses, Rituals, Festivals and Yoga Systems*, Agra: M. G. Publishers and Book Distribution Agency.

Humphrey, Caroline and Laidlaw, James. (1994) *The Archetypal Actions of Ritual: A Theory of Ritual Illustrated by the Jain Rite of Worship*, Oxford: Clarendon Press.

Jaini, Padmanabh S. (1979) *The Jaina Path of Purification*, Berkeley, CA: University of California Press.

Kakar, Sudhir. (1981) (1st edition 1978) *The Inner World: A Psycho-analytic Study of Childhood and Society in India*, Delhi: Oxford University Press.

Kelting, Whitney M. (2001) *Singing to the Jinas: Jain Laywomen, Maṇḍal Singing and the Negotiation of Jain Devotion*, Oxford: Oxford University Press.

Kinsley, David (1997) *Tantric Visions of the Divine Feminine*, Berkeley, CA: University of California Press.

La Fontaine, Jean. (1985) 'Person and Individual: Some Anthropological Reflections', in M.Carrithers, S. Collins and S. Lukes (eds.) *The Category of the Person*, 123–140, Cambridge: Cambridge University Press.

—— (1992) 'The Persons of Women' in S. Ardener (ed.) *Persons and Powers of Women in Diverse Cultures*, 89–104, Oxford: Berg Publishers.

Laidlaw, James. (1995) *Riches and Renunciation: Religion, Economy and Society Among the Jains*, Oxford: Clarendon Press.

Lamb, Sarah. (2000) *White Saris and Sweet Mangoes: Aging, Gender and Body in North India*, California: University of California Press.

Lukes, Steven. (1985) 'Conclusion', in M. Carrithers, S. Collins and S. Lukes (eds.) *The Category of the Person*, 282–301, Cambridge: Cambridge University Press.

McGee, Mary. (1996) 'In Quest of *Saubhāgya*: The Roles and Goals of Women as Depicted in Marathi Stories of Votive Devotions', in A. Feldhaus (ed.) *Images of Women in Maharashtran Literature and Religion*, 147–170, Albany, NY: State University of New York Press.

Mahias, Marie-Claude. (1985) *Délivrance et convivialité: Le Système culinaire des Jaina*, Paris: La Maison des Sciences de l'Homme.

Marriott, McKim. (1989) 'Constructing an Indian ethnosociology', *Contributions to Indian Sociology* (n.s), 23,1: 1–39.

Marriott, McKim and Inden, Ronald. (1977) 'Toward an Ethnosociology of South Asian Caste Systems', in D. Kenneth (ed.) *The New Wind: Changing Identities in South Asia* 227–238, The Hague: Mouton Publishers.

Mauss, Marcel. (1985) 'A Category of the Human Mind: The Notion of the Person. The Notion of the Self', in M. Carrithers, S. Collins, S. Lukes, (eds.) *The Category of the Person* 1–25, Cambridge: Cambridge University Press.

Mines, Mattison. (1994) *Public Faces, Private Voices: Community and Individuality in South India*, Berkeley: University of California Press.

Mooren, Thomas. (1997) *Puruṣa: Treading the Razor's Edge Towards Selfhood*, Delhi: Media House.

Reynell, Josephine. (1985) *Honour, Nurture and Festivity: Aspects of Female Religiosity Among Jain Women in Jaipur*, PhD thesis, University of Cambridge.

—— (1987a) 'Prestige, Honour and the Family: Laywomen's Religiosity amongst the Śvetāmbar Mūrtipūjak Jains in Jaipur', *Bulletin d'Études Indiennes*, 5: 313–359.

Reynell, Josephine. (1987b) 'Equality and Inequality: An Examination of the Religious Beliefs associated with Women amongst the Śvetāmbar Jains with Special Reference to the Religious Literature', in N. K. Singhi (ed.) *Ideal, Ideology and Practice: Studies in Jainism*, 33–58, Jaipur: Printwell Publishers.

—— (1991) 'Women and the Reproduction of the Jain Community', in M. Carrithers and C. Humphrey (eds.) *The Assembly of Listeners: Jains in Society*, 41–65, Cambridge: Cambridge University Press.

Saletore, R. N. (1982) *Encyclopaedia of Indian Culture, vol. 2*, New Delhi: Sterling Publishers.

Schubring, Walther. (1962) (1st published 1935) *The Doctrine of the Jainas*, Translated from the original German by W. Beurlen, Delhi: Motilal Banarsidas.

Strathern, Marilyn. (1988) *The Gender of the Gift*, Berkeley, CA: University of California Press.

Unnithan-Kumar, Maya. (1997) *Identity, Gender and Poverty: New Perspectives on Caste and Tribe in Rajasthan*, Oxford: Berghahn Books.

Vallely, Anne. (2002) *Guardians of the Transcendent: An Ethnography of a Jain Ascetic Community*, Toronto: University of Toronto Press.

Wong, Aline. (1992) 'Sex Roles, Lifecycle Stages, Social Networks and Community Development', in S. Ardener (ed.) *Persons and Powers of Women in Diverse Cultures*, Oxford: Berg Publishers.

Part IV

SECTARIAN MOVEMENTS

10

RETHINKING RELIGIOUS AUTHORITY

A perspective on the followers of Śrīmad Rājacandra

Emma Salter

Introduction

Śrīmad Rājacandra (1867–1901 CE) was a Jain saint from Gujarat.[1] He preached that the true path to *mokṣa* (spiritual liberation) begins with experiential knowledge of one's own soul, which he described as self-realisation (*samyak darśana*).[2] In this respect his message is emphatically soteriological. He taught that the most effective way to experience self-realisation is *guru bhakti* (devotion to an authoritative religious preceptor). Śrīmad Rājacandra was also a staunch anti-sectarian.

Today Śrīmad Rājacandra has a dynamic following that extends beyond India into the Jain diaspora communities of East Africa, Europe and North America. The vast majority of his devotees are Jains, although some are Vaiṣṇavas, who originate from Gujarat. A broad range of economic backgrounds is represented in Śrīmad Rājacandra's following, although *baniyā* (business) is the predominant class. The exact number of followers is impossible to determine, but an educated guess would be in the region of 20,000. There is no mendicant presence within Śrīmad Rājacandra's following and almost all its *gurus*, including Śrīmad Rājacandra himself, have been laypeople. It is to these lay preceptors, instead of to mendicants, that Śrīmad Rājacandra's followers turn for authoritative spiritual guidance. It is for these reasons that Śrīmad Rājacandra's following can be described as a lay movement within Jainism.

This chapter discusses the influence of Śrīmad Rājacandra's lay status and his teaching about self-realisation and *guru bhakti* on the development of his following as a lay movement. It also offers some background information about Śrīmad Rājacandra and the organisation of his following.[3] Where possible, the method throughout this essay is phenomenological. This means that I have tried to represent the beliefs and practices of Śrīmad Rājacandra's followers from the perspective of the practitioners themselves. To help orientate the reader the chapter begins with a brief outline of the movement's organisational structure.

The structure of the Śrīmad Rājacandra movement in outline

The organisational structure of the Śrīmad Rājacandra movement is complex.[4] Contrary to Terāpanthī Jainism, for instance, which has a single *ācārya* at its head, the Śrīmad Rājacandra movement has a multifarious organisational structure.[5] It has no central, authoritative spiritual council or administrative body to which all of Śrīmad Rājacandra's followers are accountable. Some followers practice their religion independently, but many are organised into a collection of self-contained communities that are autonomous in terms of their management (usually by a board of trustees), finance and to whom they turn for religious authority. Some communities of followers venerate only Śrīmad Rājacandra, whereas in other communities a living *guru* who teaches in Śrīmad Rājacandra's name is venerated alongside Śrīmad Rājacandra. All Jains who are Śrīmad Rājacandra's followers, regardless of whether or not they are disciples of a living *guru*, also venerate the Jinas to whom they offer appropriate ritual attention. Relations between the different communities of followers are co-operative and representatives from each come together at important events, for example the inauguration of a new temple dedicated to Śrīmad Rājacandra. Even though each community of Śrīmad Rājacandra's followers is separate, they unite to form a discrete movement within modern Jainism because they share the same religious ideology, which is expressed through devotion to Śrīmad Rājacandra and the acceptance of his teachings. This has led to a similarity of religious practice amongst the separate communities, which includes the use of Śrīmad Rājacandra's writings in devotional practices, the veneration of his image and the prominence of *guru bhakti*.

There have been many *gurus* associated with the Śrīmad Rājacandra movement throughout the course of its history. This is one factor that has given rise to its multifaceted organisational structure. Some *guru*s continue spiritual lineages that serve existing communities of followers; others form new, independent communities. In 2002 three communities of Śrīmad Rājacandra's followers looked to the religious authority of a living *guru* or *guru*s. Each of these communities continues to be based at an *āśram* dedicated to Śrīmad Rājacandra, all in Gujarat where most *āśrams* dedicated to Śrīmad Rājacandra are located.

- The *Śrīmad Rājacandra Āśram*, Dharampur in South Gujarat. Established in 2001 by Param Pūjya Śrī Rakeśbhāī Jhaverī (born 1966). In 2002 the site was still under construction, but could accommodate up to a 100 of Śrī Rakeśbhāī's disciples on a temporary basis, visits usually lasting up to two weeks. It is anticipated that in the future many disciples will chose to live permanently at the *āśram*. The majority of Śrī Rakeśbhāī's disciples live in Mumbai where his fortnightly lectures attract an audience in the region of 3,000. His disciples also live in other parts of India (Gujarat, Bangalore Chennai and Calcutta) as well as in Europe (Antwerp and Britain), Nairobi and North America.

- The *Śrīmad Rājacandra Adhyātmik Sādhanā Kendra*, Koba (near Ahmedabad and Gandhinagar). Established in 1975 by Param Pūjya Śrī Ātmanandjī (born 1931). Śrī Ātmānandjī has approximately 1,000 disciples, of whom approximately 60 live permanently at the *āśram*, as does Śrī Ātmānandjī. With the addition of visitors and temporary residents the population at the *āśram* is usually between 80 and 100. This increases to well over 1000 during special festivals and events such as *Dīvālī* and *Paryuṣaṇ* and the *āśram's* annual *śibir* (religious camp). The majority of Śrī Ātmanandjī's disciples live in Gujarat, but like to Śrī Rakeśbhāī, his following also extends to other parts of India and to Britain, East Africa and North America.
- The *Rāj Sanbhāg Satsaṅg Maṇḍal* at Sayla near Rajkot and Ahmedabad. Established in 1976 by Param Pūjya Śrī Lādakcandbhāī Mānekcand Vorā (1903–1977). Since Śrī Lādakcandbhāī's death this community has had two concurrent *guru*s, Param Pūjya Śrī Nalinbhāī Koṭhārī (born 1943) and Adarniya Śrīmatī Sadguṇadben Śāh (born 1928). Śrīmatī Sadguṇadben, who is now elderly, spends most of her time in Mumbai, whilst her counterpart is the more regular spiritual presence at Sayla. These *gurus* have approximately 2,000 disciples, approximately forty of whom live permanently at Sayla. As with Koba, visitors and temporary residents swell the population, which further increases during festivals and special events. Again, although most of these two *guru*'s disciples live in Gujarat they also have a substantial following elsewhere in India, and in Britain, East Africa and North America.

Many thriving *āśram*s dedicated to Śrīmad Rājacandra do not look to a living *guru* for religious authority. The largest *āśram* of this type, and one of the most industrious in the movement, is the *Śrīmad Rājacandra Āśram* at Agas. It was established in 1920 by Śrī Māharāj Lallūjī Svāmī (1854–1936), who was one of Śrīmad Rājacandra's closest disciples. Approximately 300 of Śrīmad Rājacandra's followers live permanently at this *āśram*. Accommodation is available for a further 600 followers to stay temporarily, while during festival times the number increases to 2500.

Each community of Śrīmad Rājacandra's followers that I approached during my field research reported a steady rise in membership. This is reflected in the expansion of some sites. When it is complete, the *āśram* at Dharampur will cover 220 acres. The *āśrams* now situated at Koba and Sayla relocated to their current sites, Koba in 1982 and Sayla in 1985, because they had outgrown their existing locations. A prayer hall that can accommodate 5,000 worshippers has recently been constructed at Agas *āśram*. This *āśram* is also being expanded and its facilities are being improved to meet the needs of its growing population.

As well as *āśram*s, there are independent *mandir*s (temples) dedicated to Śrīmad Rājacandra's veneration, mainly in Gujarat and Mumbai. For example, in February 2002 a third *mandir* in Rajkot dedicated to Śrīmad Rājacandra was

Figure 10.1 Bhakti in the *svādhyāya* hall at Kobā Āśram in 2000. Note portraits of Śrīmad Rājacandra (centre), Kundakundācārya (left) and Śrī Lāllūjī Svāmī (right). Photogrāph by the author.

inaugurated (see figure 10.2). The majority of Śrīmad Rājacandra's devotees also have domestic shrines in their homes.

How Śrīmad Rājacandra's lay status has influenced the development of his following

Śrīmad Rājacandra

Lakṣmīnandan Mehtā (Śrīmad Rājacandra) was born in November 1867 at Vavania, a port town in Saurashtra (also Kathiavad) on the north coastal peninsular of Gujarat.[6] His parents, who were of the *Daśā Śrīmālī* caste, changed his name to Raichand (Rāychand\Rājacandra) when he was four years old. He was attributed the honorific title 'Śrīmad' posthumously by his disciples.

Biographies about Śrīmad Rājacandra describe him as intellectually precocious, and emotionally and spiritually mature beyond his years. In his teens he earned a degree of celebrity by giving public performances of extraordinary feats of memory and concentration, such as attending simultaneously to a 100 different activities. His profound interest in religion began early in his childhood. As a young boy he was initiated as a devotee into the Kṛṣṇa *bhakti* tradition favoured by his father and paternal grandfather, but by the time he turned sixteen he had become fully committed to his mother's religion, Jainism. Śrīmad Rājacandra's mother was a Sthānakvāsī Jain, but as a statement of the anti-sectarian beliefs that Śrīmad Rājacandra held throughout his adult life he never associated himself with a specific Jain denomination. This has caused some confusion amongst scholars. For example, Glasenapp and Titze[7] associate him with Sthānakvāsī Jainism, Banks and Laidlaw[8] refer to him simply as a Jain layman from Gujarat and Dundas[9] associates him with Digambar Jainism.

Śrīmad Rājacandra married when he was twenty and fathered four children, one of whom died in infancy. He claimed that he became a husband and father to satisfy his parents' wishes and that he would have preferred to have remained unmarried. About the same time as his marriage Śrīmad Rājacandra went into business with his uncle-in-law trading precious stones. His biographies describe him as an honest, skilful businessman and the business prospered. Throughout this period he spent whatever time he could in religious retreat. When he was thirty he retired from business altogether, at the same time relinquishing his obligations as a householder. Having left professional and domestic life he headed for remote places, such as Idar in Gujarat, where he could concentrate on his spiritual development without distraction.

By this time Śrīmad Rājacandra was well-known within Saurashtran communities and amongst his business associates as a religious teacher who attracted crowds of interested listeners to his discourses. He had also gathered a number of close disciples, including a core of Sthānakvāsī *munis* (male mendicants) who were based at Khambhat in Gujarat, of whom Lallūjī Svāmī was the most senior. Despite Śrīmad Rājacandra's lay status his disciples were in no doubt of his religious authority, which they believed was proven by the austere and ascetic lifestyle he was now living, by his extensive scriptural knowledge and, most importantly, by what they accepted as the purity of his soul. Nevertheless, his *muni* disciples were keen for him to initiate as a mendicant and so 'legitimise' their relationship with him. Śrīmad Rājacandra too was eager to take *dīkṣā* (mendicant initiation) for which he now believed he was spiritually prepared, but his mother was reluctant to give her son the permission he required to take *dīkṣā* because of her concern for his frail health. Throughout his adult life Śrīmad Rājacandra suffered a chronic digestive complaint. His mother finally gave her permission for his initiation on the condition that he must first recover from his current bout of illness. Śrīmad Rājacandra never did recover. He was under the medical supervision of doctors when he died at Rajkot, in April 1901, aged thirty four.

Śrīmad Rājacandra's current devotees have access to his image and teachings through photographs of him and through an anthology of his writings (in Gujarati). The anthology, which was collated towards the end of Śrīmad Rājacandra's life by one of his close disciples, Ambalālbhāī Lālcand (1869–1904), contains his philosophical and poetic writings, transcriptions of some of his discourses, as well as approximately 800 letters written to his disciples and followers. It is titled *Śrīmad Rājacandra* and is published by the *Śrīmad Rājacandra Āśram* at Agas. Many of

Śrīmad Rājacandra's followers own a copy of *Śrīmad Rājacandra*, which they revere as scripture. Some of Śrīmad Rājacandra's writings have also been published independently, including his most celebrated text, the *Ātma Siddhi* (*AS*), which he composed in 1896.[10] Shortly before his death Śrīmad Rājacandra posed for two studio photographs each of which depict him in a meditative posture (one standing and one sitting). They reveal how tragically emaciated he had become. His skeletal frame and early death have prompted some scholars and devotees to mistakenly assume that he purposefully cultivated his emaciated physique through fasting, ultimately leading to *sallekhanā* (ritual death by fasting).[11] Copies of these photographs are displayed wherever Śrīmad Rājacandra is venerated (see figure 10.1). Images of him fashioned in marble or metal and modelled on these photographs are also displayed at many, but not all, sites dedicated to his veneration.

Śrīmad Rājacandra's lay status, coupled with the criticisms he levied against what he considered to be poor levels of spirituality amongst mendicants, has led to another misconception amongst scholars and opponents of Śrīmad Rājacandra, that he rejected mendicancy outright.[12] Śrīmad Rājacandra was dismayed at institutional Jainism for falling short of its own values, but he did not censure mendicancy in principle. For example, he did not encourage his *muni* disciples to reject their mendicant status (an element of diplomacy may also have been in play here) and his teachings do not deviate from Jain doctrine that states only mendicants can attain *mokṣa*. His followers believe that Śrīmad Rājacandra will take mendicant initiation before his final liberation, although not in this world. As far as his current incarnation is concerned, some followers believe him to be enjoying his penultimate incarnation as a divine-being in the celestial realms of *devlok* before reaching his final incarnation as a mendicant in Mahāvideha, a geographical location in the middle realm of the cosmos from where liberation may be achieved. Others believe he is already experiencing his final incarnation as a mendicant in Mahāvideha.

Religious authority and the spiritual hierarchy in Jainism

Despite his personal aspiration towards mendicancy, the fact that Śrīmad Rājacandra actually remained a layman throughout his life has had a significant influence on his following's development as a lay movement. In most forms of Jainism, mendicants have religious authority over the laity, who regard them not only as religious experts, but also as sacred and worthy of veneration.[13] Babb describes the veneration of ascetics as central to Jain ritual culture.[14] As a layman Śrīmad Rājacandra lacked the authority, according to Jain tradition, to initiate his own disciples and establish a new mendicant lineage. Śrīmad Rājacandra's followers are unofficially barred from aspiring to mendicancy because initiation would place them, technically at least, higher than Śrīmad Rājacandra the spiritual hierarchy of Jainism. Likewise, it is contrary to this spiritual hierarchy for a layman to be the object of a mendicant's veneration. When I asked Śrī Rakeśbhāī why he had not taken *dīkṣā*, despite having attained self-realisation, he made the following comments;

> The problem is they [initiated mendicants] will not let me worship Śrīmad Rājacandra because he was not a *sādhu* [*muni*]. A *sādhu* cannot worship a householder. They are not prepared to believe that Śrīmad was a highly elevated soul. They consider him as a good disciple of Mahāvir, but *sādhus* believe themselves to be higher than him, so if you just wear their dress you are higher than Śrīmad Rājacandra and I am not prepared to believe that. So that [*dīkṣā*] is not possible for us. A *sādhu* cannot bow to a householder and to them he is only a householder because they only see the external.[15]

This *guru* felt mendicant initiation was closed to him because it would conflict with his veneration of Śrīmad Rājacandra. This was unacceptable to him because, just like the other devotees of Śrīmad Rājacandra, he too worships Śrīmad Rājacandra as his divine *guru*. Śrī Rakeśbhāī offered further reasons for not initiating as a mendicant. Not least were the responsibility he felt towards his disciples and the sectarian boundaries that he felt mendicancy may impose upon him.

The restrictions on mendicancy that Śrīmad Rājacandra's lay status places over his followers are linked to the spiritual hierarchy in Jainism that gives mendicants religious authority over the laity. For those Jains who do not accept Śrīmad Rājacandra, his lay status is one criterion that denies him religious authority. Yet according to Śrīmad Rājacandra himself and to his disciples (past and present), his religious authority was in no way diminished by his lay status. This is because he stipulated that religious authority is not an automatic consequence of initiation into mendicancy, but is only verified by self-realisation, a high level of which he claimed to have achieved.

How Śrīmad Rājacandra's interpretation of self-realisation has influenced the development of his following

Śrīmad Rājacandra defines self-realisation as an internal or spiritual state; specifically as the experience of one's own soul as a phenomenon independent from one's physical body or empirical senses.[16] The self-realised aspirant (of liberation) has removed and suppressed sufficient *karma* to experience the soul in its pure state, if even for only a moment. *Karma* are the minute particles of matter that pervade the entire cosmos, which adhere to the soul obscuring it from its true nature. *Karma* is attracted to the soul by *kaṣāya* (passion), which is the stimulus behind any mental, physical or verbal activity. *Kaṣāya* is motivated by *rāga* (attachment by attraction to a person, thing or event) and *dveṣa* (attachment by aversion to a person, thing or event). *Karma* that has adhered to the soul eventually 'ripens' and falls away, having produced its effect. This may be mental, physical or verbal action, usually reflective of the activity by which it was attracted originally. The soul responds to the events produced by *karma* with *rāga* or *dveṣa*, which in turn stimulates *kaṣāya* to attract more *karma* to the soul, and so the cycle continues. Liberation occurs when the soul is freed from all *karma*, enabling it to exist in its pure state. Such a state of ontological perfection is achieved by acquiring the passionless state of *vītarāga* (without *rāga*) through non-attachment to *rāga*, *dveṣa* and, consequently, *kaṣāya*. *Arhats* are souls that have attained *vītarāga* and are free from all deluding *karmas*. Upon the death of the physical body the *arhat* attains *mokṣa* and becomes a *siddha* (a liberated soul). Jinas are *arhats* who are also preceptors.

Śrīmad Rājacandra's followers' religious practice focuses, in part, on reducing the soul's output of *kaṣāya* by psychological non-attachment to *rāga* and *dveṣa*. This is attempted through cultivating a sense of detachment from life's events by understanding them to be no more than the cause and effect of *karma*. One follower explained this in terms of an actor trying to convince an audience of the reality of the character portrayed. No matter how convincing the performance, the actor never forgets her own identity. The actor represents the soul that should always remain aware of its own nature despite having to work through the scenes that *karma* lays before it. Psychological non-attachment is a means of renouncing whilst continuing to live in the world as a householder. It does not, however, relinquish personal responsibility. Jain teachings about *ahiṃsā* (non-violence) mean that an aspirant's responsibility for her or his own salvation includes an ethical responsibility towards others. Non self-realised aspirants aspire to their first

Figure 10.2 A metal image of Śrīmad Rājacandra is processed during the inauguration of a new temple, Rājkoṭ 2002. Photograph by the author.

experience of self-realisation, whilst self-realised aspirants aspire to increase the frequency, duration and intensity of their soul experiences by discharging more *karma* from their soul. By the same token, if an aspirant's religious efforts decline, self-realisation will diminish as more *karma* is allowed to accrue.

The daily programme at Koba is typical of the specific types of religious practice performed by Śrīmad Rājacandra's followers. It begins at 5.30 a.m. with congregational *bhakti* dedicated to Śrīmad Rājacandra, followed at 8.45 a.m. with *pūjā* dedicated in rotation to each of the Jinas. At 10 a.m. Śrī Ātmānandjī, or if he is unavailable a senior disciple, gives *svādhyāya* (religious lecture) for about one hour. Group readings of Jain scripture begin at 4 p.m. followed by meditation at 4.45 p.m. After dinner, at 6 p.m., Śrī Ātmānandjī and his disciples take an evening walk, which allows disciples the opportunity for more informal discussion with their *guru*. *Āratī* (ritual veneration of the Jinas) takes place in the *āśram's* temple at 7.15 p.m. followed by a meditation session. Congregational *bhakti* dedicated to Śrīmad Rājacandra begins at 8.15 p.m. and last for at least one hour, but often much longer. The emphasis given to different types of religious practice vary between different communities of followers. For example followers at Sayla emphasise meditation, whereas at Agas more emphasis is given to congregational *bhakti*.

For Śrīmad Rājacandra's followers self-realisation is a religious experience that results in experiential knowledge. This is part of the reason why, within the ideological framework of the Śrīmad Rājacandra movement, self-realisation is the essential criterion for religious authority. Followers believe experiential knowledge to be immune to misinterpretation and hence superior to intellectual knowledge imbibed by book learning or attendance at lectures. Experiential knowledge is absolute, and therefore universal truth. To express the concept of universal truth followers recite the axiom that one non self-realised person may have a 1,000 different opinions, while a 1,000 self-realised people will all hold the same opinion because that view, arising from self-realisation, is absolute truth. So, an aspirant's theoretical understanding of Jain doctrine gleaned by intellectual study is transformed and confirmed by the unequivocal experiential knowledge of self-realisation.[17] The religious authority of a self-realised person is further secured by the high level of spiritual purity she or he must have attained to have experienced self-realisation. This in turn endorses the efficacy of her or his religious practice. The establishment of self-realisation as the main criterion for religious authority has shaped the development of Śrīmad Rājacandra's following as a lay movement in two main ways. It allows lay *gurus* religious authority without the need for mendicant initiation and it has evoked a profound anti-sectarian ethic amongst Śrīmad Rājacandra's followers.

Self-realisation and **guru** *lineage*

Religious authority is traditionally verified in Jainism, particularly Śvetāmbar Jainism, by a secure lineage passed between the *guru*, who is a mendicant, and the disciple upon initiation into mendicancy.[18] *Guru* lineage in the Śrīmad Rājacandra movement originates with Śrīmad Rājacandra's claim to have been Mahāvīr's disciple during a previous incarnation.[19] Śrīmad Rājacandra's lineal connection with Mahāvīr establishes a *guru*–disciple lineage of the highest quality because it links him with the pure source of a Jina's teachings whilst by-passing the diluting effects of a lineal chain. It is a further indication to his followers of the 'pure', pre-sectarian form of Jainism they believe he preached. A tradition of *guru* lineage is found in some, but not all, communities of Śrīmad Rājacandra's followers. The community at Sayla *āśram* traces its spiritual heritage back to Śrīmad Rājacandra via one of his immediate disciples, Sobhagbhaī of Sayla (1823–1897), through a *guru* lineage that is still active. The *guru* lineage at Agas originated with Śrīmad Rājacandra and passed via Śrī Lallūjī Svāmī to Śrī Brahmacārījī Govardhandās (1889–1954), who was Lallūjī Svāmī's foremost disciple, but then ceased when Śrī Brahmacārījī was unable to locate anyone of sufficient spiritual calibre to continue the lineage.

Guru lineage overcomes the disciple's obvious problem of identifying a self-realised *guru*. Yet despite the tradition of *guru* lineage in some communities, the essential qualification of an authoritative *guru* within the Śrīmad Rājacandra movement always remains self-realisation. This means that an authoritative lineal connection alone is not sufficient to qualify as a *guru* within the movement, moreover as such a connection is not necessary to qualify as a *guru*. For example, devotees do not prioritise Śrīmad Rājacandra's connection with Mahāvīr over his self-realised state; in fact it was barely raised during the course of my various interviews with his followers. Śrīmad Rājacandra's connection with Mahāvīr, and his memory of this past-life, is a further endorsement of his religious authority that is already secured by his self-realised state. The *guru* based at the *āśram* at Koba, Śrī Ātmānandjī, claims no lineal connection to Śrīmad Rājacandra. The acceptance of his religious authority by his disciples is located in their belief that he is self-realised.

The belief that self-realisation is the only legitimate source of religious authority has dispensed with *guru* lineage as the only means of authenticating religious authority. The association of religious authority with self-realisation above *guru* lineage has enabled independent *guru*s who have no lineal connection with Śrīmad Rājacandra or any other authoritative source to emerge spontaneously; their religious authority being verified by their self-realised status of which their disciples are convinced. It is this belief in the absolute authority of self-realisation that has enabled spiritually qualified lay *gurus* to emerge.

Self-realisation and sectarianism

Sectarian difference is an anathema to the absolute truth that self-realisation is thought to represent. Śrīmad Rājacandra's refusal to endorse sectarianism by association with any particular denomination of Jainism or mendicant lineage gave rise to his religious independence. This means that the organisational structure of the Śrīmad Rājacandra movement has not been constrained by conformity to an existing model. Under no circumstances do followers regard themselves as another Jain sect.[20] A practical expression of anti-sectarian values within the movement is seen in followers' freedom to worship in Digambar or Śvetāmbar temples, in the belief that the act of worship is more important than the appearance of the image. In support of Śrīmad Rājacandra's teachings against sectarianism Śrī Lallūjī Svāmī arranged for the construction of a Digambar and a Śvetāmbar temple at the *āśram* at Agas, both of which continue to be used by devotees today. Anti-sectarianism is another obstacle to followers' initiation into mendicancy, as this would inevitably imply sectarian affiliation.

The anti-sectarian value Śrīmad Rājacandra's followers hold so strongly translates into a general attitude of scepticism towards mendicants. This is because mendicants are sometimes perceived as representatives of sectarian Jainism and because sectarianism places mendicants' religious authority under scrutiny. If all mendicants self-realised (according to Śrīmad Rājacandra's interpretation of it) then there would be no sectarian division because all would be like-minded. Sectarianism therefore casts doubt over the mandatory claim to religious authority that most denominations of Jainism attribute to all mendicants. This means that Śrīmad Rājacandra's followers cannot depend on the outward appearance of mendicancy as an indisputable guarantee of religious authority. Śrīmad Rājacandra's concern that 'self-realisation' had become a term coincidental with *dīkṣā*, rather than a genuine spiritual attribute of individual mendicants, is expressed clearly by the distinction he makes between 'false' non self-realised *guru*s and 'true' self-realised *guru*s.[21]

It should be stressed however, that Śrīmad Rājacandra's followers do not impose their anti-sectarian values against individual mendicants, who are shown appropriate respect when encountered. One senior disciple associated with Sayla *āśram* said that just as it cannot be assumed that all mendicants are self-realised, it may also be assumed that some mendicants have attained self-realisation.[22] During my field-study I became aware of a certain amount of interaction between Śrīmad Rājacandra's followers and mendicants. For example, during my visits to Koba and Sayla small groups of *sādhvī*s were spending a few days at these *āśrams*. I was also told that a Digambar mendicant had consecrated the ground at the site of the Dharampur *āśram*. Photographs showed that four or five mendicants (I could not be certain of the exact number) were present at this *āśram's* opening ceremony. A number of mendicants have written commentaries on Śrīmad Rājacandra's literature, including Sādhvī Tārvlatabāī Māhāsatijī, whose book, *I Am Soul*, is translated into English from Gujarati.[23]

Despite these pockets of interaction between mendicants and Śrīmad Rājacandra's following, the association of religious authority with self-realisation, combined with an inherent scepticism of anything sectarian, has firmly established Śrīmad Rājacandra's following as a lay movement in which religious authority is held by spiritually qualified – that is, self-realised – laypeople. This shift in religious authority is made evident by the fact that, with two exceptions, all of the *guru*s throughout the history of the movement have been laypeople, including Śrīmad Rājacandra himself. The two mendicant *guru*s in the history of the movement are Śrī Lallūjī Svāmī and Śrī Sahāj Ānandjī (who died 1970). The latter established an *āśram* dedicated to Śrīmad Rājacandra at Hampi, South India, in 1960. Both initiated as Sthānakvāsī mendicants, Lallūjī Svamī in Gujarat, Sahāj Ānandjī in Rajasthan, before learning about Śrīmad Rājacandra. Neither *muni* actually relinquished his mendicant status when he became Śrīmad Rājacandra's devotee, but both estranged themselves from their respective orders and were effectively ex-communicated from them by their fellow mendicants. Neither *muni* initiated any of his own disciples to establish a mendicant lineage within the Śrīmad Rājacandra tradition. This is particularly significant in the case of Lallūjī Svāmī because he was the only one of Śrīmad Rājacandra's immediate disciples to have survived Śrīmad Rājacandra long enough to gather his own substantial and enduring following of disciples.

Followers' scepticism of mendicant authority is not reflected in their attitude towards mendicancy as an institution. Like most Jains, Śrīmad Rājacandra's followers hold the mendicant ideal as sacrosanct, but to their minds Śrīmad Rājacandra's interpretation of self-realisation has raised – or, more accurately, reinstated – the standard of spirituality expected from mendicants. For example, when I asked Śrī Ātmānandjī why he had not taken *dīkṣā* even though he had attained self-realisation, he responded that he felt his level of spiritual purification was not yet high enough to warrant mendicant initiation and that his physical constitution was not hardy enough to survive the severity of ascetic life. This open and honest response from a *guru* who took lay vows from a Digambar *muni* in 1984, and whose life is dedicated to austerity and religious practice, illustrates the high regard with which he, and consequently his disciples, hold mendicancy.[24] Śrīmad Rājacandra's followers regard self-realisation as an essential prerequisite for initiation into mendicancy because only self-realised people are thought to have the spiritual purity and strength necessary to fulfil the rigours of a mendicant lifestyle, and to qualify for the religious authority with which it is associated. They refuse to devalue mendicancy by attempting to follow the mendicant path before they are spiritually prepared for it and this belief alone prohibits the majority of Śrīmad Rājacandra's followers from taking mendicant initiation.

The shift in religious authority from mendicants to spiritually qualified laypeople that is observed in the Śrīmad Rājacandra movement is an expression of reform motivated by concern about mendicants' ability to uphold the mendicant ideal. A usual response in Jainism to accusations of mendicants straying from the 'true' path is the establishment of a new mendicant lineage that 'properly' reflects (according to the reformer) Mahāvīr's teachings. For example, the Śvetāmbar Khartar Gacch was established by the renowned ascetic, Jineśvarsūri (eleventh century), in protest against the growing trend of Caityavāsī (temple-dwelling) mendicants.[25] Cort describes how, otherwise straight lines of lineal descent, branch when the authority of the *paṭṭadhāras* ('holders (*dhāra*) of the seat (*paṭṭa*) of authority') is successfully challenged by another ascetic.[26] Instead of instigating a 'pure' mendicant lineage, the method of reform adopted by Śrīmad Rājacandra's following has been to protect the mendicant ideal by elevating it to a level of spiritual purity that most souls may only aspire to in the current era. Hence 'true' mendicants become so difficult to locate that the next best alternative is to venerate a lay *guru* whose spiritual purity is assured.

The Śrīmad Rājacandra movement seems to be challenging the identity of a 'genuine' mendicant. For example, some followers were perturbed by my questioning about Śrīmad Rājacandra's lay status. They described him as a true *muni* because, 'he is a *muni* on the *inside*' (a reference to his spiritual purity), irrespective of his lay status. In his study of Jainism in Jaipur, Babb shows that, 'ascetics emerge as the only beings truly worthy of worship' in part because their renounced lifestyles, 'exemplify the path to liberation'.[27] As ascetics they share the same qualities as the Jinas, only not to the same extent. In the Śrīmad Rājacandra movement *gurus* are venerated because they are believed to be self-realised. They have the same quality of knowledge as the Jinas, only not to the same extent. So, whereas in the Jainism of Babb's study the object of veneration is asceticism, in the Śrīmad Rājacandra movement spiritual knowledge is the object of veneration. Asceticism has not been dispensed with entirely, but asceticism alone, without the experiential spiritual knowledge of self-realisation, is not worthy of worship.

Self-realisation and liberation

Scholars and Jains who are not followers of Śrīmad Rājacandra sometimes think that Śrīmad Rājacandra's teachings about self-realisation are actually a reference to liberation.[28] The confusion is most likely due to Śrīmad Rājacandra's particular interpretation of self-realisation as a state of soul purity, knowledge and religious authority, but may also be exacerbated by the fact that the community of Śrīmad Rājacandra's followers based at Agas *āśram* believe he attained the thirteenth *guṇasthāna* (fourteen stages of soul purity leading to *mokṣa*), which is equivalent to an embodied state of omniscience. This community believe Śrīmad Rājacandra is currently incarnated as a mendicant in Mahāvideha, his final incarnation prior to attaining *mokṣa*. To indicate that he is still embodied and yet to attain *mokṣa*, his image is daubed with sandalwood paste on the two big toes and the forehead only during *pūjā* because it does not warrant all thirteen marks on nine parts of the body that is customarily applied on Jina images.[29] The claim that Śrīmad Rājacandra attained omniscience is controversial because it runs counter to traditional Jain doctrine which states that Mahāvīr's disciple, Jambū, was the last omniscient person in this cosmic region. Śrīmad Rājacandra never professed openly that he was omniscient, although he did claim to have attained a high level of self-realisation. Conviction in his omniscience is based, in part, on a brief diary entry discovered after his death in which – followers at Agas interpret – Śrīmad Rājacandra equates himself spiritually with Mahāvīr.[30] This private note was not included in the first published edition of *Śrīmad Rājacandra* because devotees recognised it as controversial. It was Śrī Lallūjī Svāmī who insisted on its inclusion in later editions of the anthology. Not all of Śrīmad Rājacandra's followers believe him to have been omniscient. Most followers with whom I spoke believe he attained somewhere around the sixth or seventh *guṇasthāna*, which they agree is remarkably high for the current era.[31]

Attitudes towards the possibility of achieving self-realisation in current times also differ within Śrīmad Rājacandra's following. Some followers believe that self-realisation is no longer possible in this part of the cosmos and that Śrīmad Rājacandra was the last person to have attained it. Followers holding this belief venerate only Śrīmad Rājacandra and do not turn to any other *guru* who teaches in his name. For this reason they are unlikely to be associated with an *āśram* based community. Followers who are also disciples of a living *guru* believe their own *guru* to be self-realised, so obviously accept self-realisation to be possible in the current era. Of the three communities mentioned who look to a living *guru* for religious authority, followers based at Sayla *āśram* claim to have twelve self-realised people amongst its membership, in addition to their *gurus*.[32] For this group of followers then, self-realisation is very much a realisable goal. When I asked Śrī Rakeśbhāī and Śrī Ātmanandjī if they anticipate that any of their own disciples will attain self-realisation within their lifetimes, they both responded in hopeful terms, but cautioned that nothing was certain. The community based at Agas *āśram* has a different outlook again. Followers here believe that the likelihood of attaining self-realisation has become extremely remote, if not impossible, since the death of Śrī Brahmacārījī. It is not surprising then, that this community regard claims of self-realisation made by some of Śrīmad Rājacandra's other followers with a degree of scepticism.

Self-realisation and soteriology

Within the Śrīmad Rājacandra movement self-realisation is crucial to an aspirant's spiritual progression.[33] It is the vital first step onto the *mokṣa mārga* (the path of liberation) and indicates that *mokṣa* is guaranteed, perhaps within fifteen life spans.[34] The first experience of self-realisation means that the aspirant has achieved a high level of soul purity, but is still a long way from the ultimate purity of liberation. Nevertheless, through self-realisation liberation becomes a relatively imminent goal – no longer so remote as to be virtually impossible, but now achievable within a discernible number of life-spans following self-realisation. Followers who consider self-realisation unlikely in their current lifetimes anticipate that veneration of Śrīmad Rājacandra will soon result in their reincarnation in a cosmic region more favourable to its attainment. So, even for these followers the relative imminence of self-realisation leading to liberation is not precluded. Śrīmad Rājacandra's interpretation of self-realisation, and his emphasis on it in his teachings, has therefore dispensed with the need for mendicant supervision, whilst at the same time it has prioritised soteriology sharply within the minds of his followers. For this reason self-realisation is at the heart of their religious beliefs and its attainment is the primary motivating factor in their religious practices.[35]

Many followers spoke of their conviction in the soteriological efficacy of their religious beliefs and practices inspired by Śrīmad Rājacandra's teachings. Some followers spoke of 'physically sensing' the increase in their soul purity, which they described in terms of decreasing worldly attachment and increase in *bhāv* (sentiment) during their devotional practices. Followers also expressed an intellectual satisfaction in the soteriological justification for their religious efforts. The comments of one devotee were typical. This gentleman, in his early sixties, resides in North America, but for the past few years he and his wife have been staying at Koba *āśram* for about six months annually. He explained that he was brought up in India in a traditional Śvetāmbar Jain family that was meticulous in its observance of Jain rituals and customs. Much to his family's dismay, as an adult he turned to follow Śrīmad Rājacandra. He felt that his study of Śrīmad Rājacandra's teachings awakened him fully, for the first time, to the soteriological purpose of Jain religious practice. This not only encouraged him in his veneration of Śrīmad Rājacandra and of his living *guru*, but also revitalised his general commitment to religious practice. For example, he now performed *pūjā* to the Jinas daily instead of occasionally as he had before following Śrīmad Rājacandra, and he now adhered fastidiously to Jain dietary restrictions such as avoiding root vegetables and not eating after sunset or until forty-eight minutes after sunrise. In his comments this devotee made a distinction between religious practice based on an intellectual understanding of its meaning and effect, and 'empty' religious practice that may help to perpetuate a community's religious identity, but that does not assist the practitioner towards liberation.[36]

Guru bhakti

Different types of guru

In the *Ātma Siddhi* Śrīmad Rājacandra explains that the most certain means of achieving self-realisation in the current age is *guru bhakti*.[37] This emphasis on *guru bhakti* in Śrīmad Rājacandra's teachings has encouraged and sustained the emergence of *gurus* throughout the history of the movement. In its broadest sense '*bhakti*' means 'devotion'. As almost any act of a pious disciple can be interpreted as an expression of devotion, the meanings and applications of *bhakti* are far-reaching. Śrīmad Rājacandra stresses that only a 'true' (self-realised) *guru* has the spiritual purity, knowledge and experience necessary to guide his or her disciples successfully towards their own goal of self-realisation. Misguided devotion to a 'false' *guru* can only result in spiritual devastation.[38]

Śrīmad Rājacandra is venerated by all his devotees as a true *guru* of the highest order, so the necessity of further *gurus* within the movement is brought into question. Devotees who choose to venerate a living *guru* alongside Śrīmad Rājacandra (e.g. the communities based at Dharampur, Koba and Sayla) justify their decision by reference to his teaching that a *pratyakṣa* (directly perceptible) *guru* is of greater benefit to an aspirant's spiritual progression than a *parokṣa* (not directly perceptible) *guru*.[39] These devotees regard Śrīmad Rājacandra and the Jinas as *parokṣa gurus*. Whilst this does not lessen their devotion to them, they also believe in the benefits of venerating a living *guru*. Devotees who do not accept the authority of current *gurus*, and who choose to venerate only Śrīmad Rājacandra (e.g. the community based at Agas), heed Śrīmad Rājacandra's warning against the veneration of false *gurus* and emphasise the difficulty a non self-realised aspirant has in discerning a 'true' from a 'false' *guru*. In practice a devotee's decision about whether or not to submit to a living *guru* may be influenced by a number of factors, including familial or other connections with a particular *āśram* or *guru*, or by an informed decision based on a personal study of Śrīmad Rājacandra's teachings.

Advantages of a lay guru

When the major objective of religious practice is soteriological, as it is for Śrīmad Rājacandra's followers, and the principal event of religious practice is devotion to a 'true' *guru*, it is essential for a disciple to be utterly convinced of her or his *guru*'s self-realised status and hence religious authority. To benefit fully from a *guru*'s religious guidance a disciple must submit utterly to her or his *guru*, this can only occur when a disciple is convinced that the *guru* is self-realised. Followers' belief in Śrīmad Rājacandra's self-realised status, and therefore the authority of his teachings, is an obvious condition of their commitment to him as an authentic *guru* and saviour. Śrīmad Rājacandra's followers who are disciples of a living *guru* also have to be assured of this *guru*'s self-realised status. Some disciples with whom I spoke described their commitment to their *guru* as instantaneous. Others observed their *guru*'s demeanour, religious knowledge and religious instructions over a sustained period of contact until they were satisfied that the *guru* was truly self-realised. This could take anything from a few weeks to several years.

The opportunity to assess a *guru*'s spiritual credentials gives preference to the lay *guru* in an age when, as Śrīmad Rājacandra's followers believe, religious authority cannot be assured by mendicancy alone. This is because the peripatetic lifestyle of mendicants means their contact with individual lay disciples is sporadic, even though mendicant contact with the laity in general is constant because mendicants depend on lay Jains for all of their material needs.[40] During the four months of the rainy season (July/August to November/December) mendicants are required to remain in one place because to travel would risk causing *hiṃsā* (violence) to insects and water-bodies prevalent during the season. Babb describes this period as an opportunity to reinforce lay and mendicant bonds. Indeed, it is during this season that many Jain festivals occur, including *Paryuṣaṇ*, the most important festival in the Jain year, which requires participation by mendicant and lay Jains. However, Babb also observes that popular mendicants may be 'booked' by different lay communities years in advance, so there is no guarantee that a particular mendicant will return to the same town the following year.[41] So, although mendicants have continual interaction with lay communities in general, their peripatetic lifestyles are a barrier to the type of sustained, personal contact a disciple may have with a lay *guru*. Outside of the Śrīmad Rājacandra movement, mendicants' peripatetic lifestyles do not deter lay Jains venerating a particularly beloved mendicant.[42] Laidlaw gives the example of a senior Sthānakvāsī *ācārya* Hastīmal-jī Mahārāj Sāhab (died 1991), who attracted a vast lay following.[43]

Within the Śrīmad Rājacandra movement, a disciple's submission to their chosen *guru* is a matter of personal conviction. At Dharampur and Koba it is not marked by a formal ceremony, at Sayla disciples undergo a brief exchange with their *guru* (the precise details of which should not be revealed to the uninitiated). Once a disciple has submitted to a *guru*, the *guru* becomes the disciple's constant and personal religious preceptor who is always available and willing to resolve any spiritual difficulties. The *guru* provides religious instructions tailored to each individual disciple's specific spiritual requirements and monitors each disciple's spiritual progress. This is achieved primarily by the disciple maintaining contact with her or his *guru* through personal meetings, letters, e-mail and telephone conversations. Some communities also have more structured monitoring procedures in place. For example, disciples of Śrī Rakeśbhāī keep diaries of their personal spiritual progress, based on their feelings of worldly attachment and non-attachment, which their *guru* may ask to see at any time. Every fortnight these disciples attend groups, arranged by geographic location and age and facilitated by senior disciples, to study scripture prescribed by their *guru*, on which they are tested regularly and their progress reported back to their *guru*.[44]

Cort and Laidlaw both point out that, although there are many instances in Jainism of mendicants performing roles similar to that of a personal preceptor, the implication of personal attachment inferred by *guru*–disciple relationships means that they cannot be overtly recognised.[45] Lay Jains are supposed to venerate all mendicants equally as embodiments of the religious ideal. Cort writes that the layperson's performance of *guru-vandan* to a mendicant (any mendicant) 'is not a personalized ritual in which the specific personality of either worshiper or worshiped has any significance'.[46] Vows undertaken by mendicants to renounce ownership and attachment restrict a *guru*–disciple relationship not only in terms of the physical distance imposed between the mendicant and the disciple, but also in terms of the psychological distance that the disciple and the mendicant *guru* are supposed to maintain. Śrīmad Rājacandra's teaching about *guru bhakti* encourages his followers' attachment to a *guru*, indeed a disciple should be devoted to only one *guru* (Sayla is an exception to this). Part of the soteriological rational for this is that a disciple's devotional attachment to her or his *guru* focuses the disciple's mind on the *guru*'s spiritual purity, which the disciple attempts to emulate, and distracts the disciple from reacting to worldly situations with *rāga* and *dveṣa*. Psychological renunciation of one's *guru* occurs only when a disciple has attained a high level of spiritual purity.[47] A mendicant's liberty to communicate with disciples regularly or to manage large groups of disciples are also theoretically restricted by their vows of renunciation. By placing religious authority with lay *guru*s Śrīmad Rājacandra's followers experience purposeful guidance towards liberation that is monitored by a *guru* whose religious authority is believed to be indisputable, with whom disciples can have a sustained, interactive relationship and who is a permanent source of religious instruction and inspiration.

The benefits of a *guru* unencumbered by mendicant vows are especially significant to Jains living outside India. Mendicants are only allowed to travel by foot, which prohibits them from visiting diaspora Jain communities. Banks describes how Jains in Leicester, UK during the 1980s began to re-negotiate patterns of social order and religious authority in the absence of mendicant supervision. He comments how some of the Jains he met lamented that the lack of mendicant presence meant that 'proper' Jainism could not be practised outside India.[48] As a Jain movement whose authoritative *guru*s are not governed by the same travel restrictions as mendicants, the Śrīmad Rājacandra movement is particularly successful amongst diaspora Jain communities. This essay has already shown that there are groups of Śrīmad Rājacandra's followers in East Africa, Europe and North America, and the movement may well be even more widespread.

The three *gurus* referred to in this chapter make regular visits to their communities of disciples who live abroad. Foreign visits help to maintain the buoyancy of *guru*–disciple relationships and so fulfil an important spiritual need for Śrīmad Rājacandra's growing following outside of India. Visits also raise the profile of Śrīmad Rājacandra's teachings, and of Jainism in general, amongst the broader diaspora Jain community. Another effect has been to re-establish the links second and third generation diaspora Jains have with their Gujarati origins. The fact that lay *gurus* are not peripatetic like mendicants makes it convenient for disciples to travel to India to spend time with their *guru*. Very many disciples who live outside of India visit their *guru*'s *āśram* annually, often spending anything up to six months of the year there. For the rest of the time, the lay *guru* is more easily contacted by letter, phone or email than the wandering mendicant. It was not Śrīmad Rājacandra's intention to promulgate Jainism outside of India. In fact, as a young man he refused an invitation to visit London on the grounds that it may hinder his spiritual progression. Nevertheless, the particular qualities the Śrīmad Rājacandra movement has to offer as a lay movement means that it has transferred well to diaspora communities and represents a form of Jainism that has adapted to address the changing needs of Jains in the modern world.

Some concluding observations

The refusal of the Śrīmad Rājacandra movement to accept mendicant authority is not representative of contemporary Jainism. In fact it is this that sets it apart from most other forms of Jainism and is one of the principal criticisms levied against it by Śrīmad Rājacandra's opponents. Nevertheless, Śrīmad Rājacandra's following is just one of a number of modern Jain movements to have either rejected mendicancy or to have moderated mendicant regulations, particularly with respect to travel restrictions. For example, the Terāpanthi leader Ācārya Mahāprajña (born 1920) introduced an interim mendicant level to the Terāpanthi branch of Jainism, during which 'semi-mendicants' (*samaṇ*, male mendicants and *samaṇī*, female mendicants) are permitted to travel abroad to spread the message of Jainism.[49] Kānjī Svāmī (1898–1980), who is the spiritual figurehead of the Kānjī Svāmī Panth, and Srī Citrabhānu (born 1922), who has an extensive following in North America, were both initiated mendicants who came to reject their mendicant status, yet each continued to gather a substantial and enduring following of disciples.[50] The Akram Vijñān movement, inspired by a householder and businessman from Gujarat, Ambalāl Mūljībhāī Paṭel (1908–1988), dispenses with the need for asceticism and mendicancy by claiming to offer followers direct access to enlightenment through the grace of the Jina Sīmandhar. Those Jains who subscribe to the Akram Vijñān movement believe that Sīmandhar's grace was channelled through the mediumship of Ambalāl Mūljībhāī Paṭel and, following his death, through the mediumship of two nominated disciples, Kanu Paṭel and Nīrubahen Amīn.[51]

This chapter has shown that Śrīmad Rājacandra's following developed as a lay movement in response to Śrīmad Rājacandra's own lay status, his interpretation of self-realisation and his teachings about *guru bhakti* as a means of attaining it. Śrīmad Rājacandra's interpretation of self-realisation as a religious experience and the essential criterion for religious authority endorses the religious authority of lay *gurus*, while mendicant religious authority is put into dispute by the shadow of sectarianism. Religious authority validated by self-realisation, rather than through an authoritative lineal connection, has allowed for a random pattern of *gurus* to emerge. The soteriological implications of self-realisation has refocused the soteriological objective of Jainism as a lay concern, rather than the exclusive concern of mendicants, and is a principal motivator for lay religious practice in the Śrīmad Rājacandra movement.

The continued increase in Śrīmad Rājacandra's following, a century after his death, suggests that his teachings address particular needs amongst those Jains who choose to accept them. A point emphasised by the fact that, because Śrīmad Rājacandra was not associated with an existing Jain sect, his followers, particularly the first generation, must have taken a deliberate turn towards him. From an ethical viewpoint the attraction seems to be the stand that Śrīmad Rājacandra's teachings take against sectarianism and what is perceived to be an inadequate level of mendicant spiritual purity. From a practical viewpoint followers seem to be satisfied spiritually by the soteriological emphasis in Śrīmad Rājacandra's teachings and, for some, the intimate and interactive relationship that can be struck with a lay *guru*.

Notes

1 All the dates given in this chapter are CE. Information about the values, beliefs and practices of Śrīmad Rājacandra's followers presented in this essay is drawn from the

findings of field research in Gujarat, Mumbai and London conducted as part of my doctoral research during 1998–2002.

2 Śrīmad Rājacandra's followers always used the term 'self-realisation' when discussing their religious beliefs with me, and with each other, in English.

3 Some of the themes discussed in this chapter are presented in Salter 2001.

4 For a discussion about the organisational structure of the Śrīmad Rājacandra movement see Salter 2001.

5 For an excellent account of Terāpanthī Jainism see Vallely 2003.

6 Details of Śrīmad Rājacandra's life are taken from a number of short, devotional biographies (Desai 2000, Govardhandās 1991, Mehta 1999, and Mehta and Sheth 1971).

7 Glasenapp 1999: 86, Titze 1998: 165.

8 Banks 1992: 208, Laidlaw 1995: 235.

9 Dundas 2002: 266.

10 The *Ātma Siddhi* [AS] has been translated into various Indian languages and into English. The most useful English translation to date, cited throughout this chapter, is by D. C. Mehta (1978), which is available online at www.atmasiddhi.com.

11 Banks 1997: 216–239, Banks 1999: 311–323, Laidlaw 1995: 233.

12 Banks 1992: 208, Dundas 2002: 264, Laidlaw 1995: 235.

13 See Cort 2001, chapter four, for a comprehensive account of mendicants' daily routine and their interaction with the laity.

14 Babb 1996, especially chapters one and three.

15 Mumbai, January 2000.

16 Śrīmad Rājacandra's teachings about self-realisation echo the teachings of the highly influential Digambar *ācārya* and mystic Kundakunda. Some recent scholarship dates Kundakundācārya after 750 CE (Dundas 2002: 107). For further discussion on Kundakundācārya see Dundas 2000: 107–110 and Johnson 1995.

17 Śrīmad Rājacandra did not negate scriptural study or intellectual learning. For most followers this is an integral aspect of their religious practice because intellectual understanding is an essential precursor to the attainment of self-realisation.

18 For example see Cort 1995: 480–481.

19 Govardhandās 1991: 15, 150, 157. Śrīmad Rājacandra is not the only figure in Jainism to claim a lineal connection with a Tīrthaṅkar during a previous life. Kānjī Svāmī's followers believe that, in a prior incarnation as a prince, Kānjī Svāmī (1898–1980) was present at the *samavasaraṇ* (holy assembly) of the Jina Sīmandhar, one of twenty Tīrthaṅkars who is currently preaching in Mahāvideha. Dundas 2002: 265–271.

20 I use the term 'movement' to describe Śrīmad Rājacandra's following collectively. Some followers who I encountered found this term offensive because they felt it had sectarian connotations, although most followers accepted my intended use of the term as a passive literary device.

21 'Knowledge of self, equanimity (i.e. equanimous feeling at pairs, such as friend or foe, pain or pleasure), worldly living due to the operation of past karmas, unique speech (i.e. speech full of theories never heard before and marked with truth and inner conviction), knowledge of true scriptures – these are the qualities worthy of a true guru'*AS* 10.

22 Sayla, December 2001.

23 *I am the Soul*. Śrī Gujarātī Śvetāmbar Sthānakvāsī Jain Association. 2000, Chennai.

24 Koba, January 2002.

25 Babb 1996: 114–115.

26 Cort 1995: 481.

27 Babb 1996: 62 and 174.

28 For example, Laidlaw 1995: 235.

29 There is no consensus on the appropriate treatment of Śrīmad Rājacandra's image within the Śrīmad Rājacandra movement. Not all sites advocate *dravya pūjā* (*pūjā* with substances) towards it.
30 *Śrīmad Rājacandra*, eighth edition, 1998: 499, item 680.
31 Jains believe this part of the cosmos is currently in the *Kali Yuga*, an era of corruption during which spiritual progression is difficult to achieve.
32 January 2002.
33 'Without knowing the real nature of self, I suffered infinite misery. I bow to the adored holy true Guru, who disclosed that self to me' *AS* 1.
34 Similar claims were made to Babb during his research on Śvetāmbar Jainism. He was told, 'if you possess right belief for as little time as a grain of rice can be balanced on the tip of a horn of a cow, you will obtain liberation sooner or later' (Babb 1996: 36).
35 Ethnographic research indicates that a preoccupation with liberation is not commonplace amongst Jain laity. See, for example, Babb 1996: 24.
36 Koba, January 2002.
37 'He who serves the feet of the true *Guru* giving up his own wrong beliefs, achieves the highest ideal and attains the real nature of self.' *AS* 9.
38 'If the untrue Guru takes any disadvantage of such reverence, he sinks into the ocean of embodied existence by being bound with the intense deluding Karmas.' *AS* 21.
39 'The obligation of the present true Guru [*pratyakṣa sadguru*] is greater than that of the non-present Jina. Unless one becomes aware of this, self-contemplation does not start.' *AS* 11.
40 Babb describes mendicants as public figures who are, 'in the centre of a more or less constant hubbub' (Babb 1996: 52).
41 Ibid. 1996: 57.
42 Cort 2001: 114–117.
43 Laidlaw 1995: 63–64.
44 At the time of my visit during October 2001 the prescribed reading was Śrī Rakeśbhāī's commentary on Śrīmad Rājacandra's the *Ātma Siddhi*, for which he was awarded a doctorate by Mumbai University.
45 Laidlaw 1995: 63–64, Cort 2001: 117.
46 Ibid. 2001: 112.
47 *Gurus* experience no feelings of attachment towards their disciples, but maintain a state of equanimity which is a condition of their self-realised status.
48 Banks 1992: 202.
49 Vallely 2003: 72 and 101.
50 See Dundas 2002: 265–271 for a discussion about Śrī Kānjī Svāmī. See www.jainmeditation.org for information about Śrī Citrabhānu.
51 See Flügel 2003. He explains that a schism occurred in the movement soon after Ambalāl Mūljībhāī Paṭel's death because followers tended to accept the authority of either Kanu Paṭel or Nīrubahen Amīn to the exclusion of the other.

Bibliography

Primary sources

Rājacandra, Śrīmad. 1998. *Śrīmad Rājacandra*. 8th edition. Agas: Śrīmad Rājacandra Āśram.

Secondary sources

Babb, Lawrence A. 1996. *Absent Lord. Ascetics and Kings in a Jain Ritual Culture*. Berkeley, University of California Press.

Banks, Marcus. 1992. *Organising Jainism in India and England*. Oxford: Clarendon Press.

——. 1997. 'Representing the Bodies of the Jains'. *Rethinking Visual Anthropology*. Eds. Marcus Banks and Howard Morphy, 216–239. New Haven and London: Yale University Press.

——. 1999. 'The Body in Jain Art'. *Approaches to Jaina Studies: Philosophy, Logic, Rituals and Symbols*. Eds. N. K. Wagle and Olle Qvarnström, 311–323. Toronto: Centre for South Asian Studies, University of Toronto.

Cort, John E. 1995. 'Genres of Jain History'. *Journal of Indian Philosophy* 23: 469–506.

——. 2001. *Jains in the World. Religious Values and Ideology in India*. Oxford: Oxford University Press.

Desai, Kumarpal. 2000. *A Pinnacle of Spirituality*. Translated from Gujarati into English by Ashik Shah and Jaysukh Mehta. San Francisco: Sri Raj Saubhag Satsang Mandal, Sayla, and Asthawala Sri Manharbhai V. Patel (Sri Chhitubhai).

Dundas, Paul. 2002. *The Jains*. 2nd Revised Edition. London and New York: Routledge.

Flügel, Peter. 2005. 'Absent Lord: Simandhar Svami and the Akram Vijnan Movement'. *The Intimate Other Love: Divine in Indic Religions*. Eds. John E. Brockington and Anna King, 194–243. Delhi: Permanent Black.

Glasenapp, Helmuth von. 1925\1999. *Jainism. An Indian Religion of Salvation*. Translated from German into English by Shridhar B. Shrotri. Delhi: Motilal Banarsidas.

Govardhandās, Brahmacārī. 1938\1991. *Jeevan Kala*. Translated from Gujarati into English by D. M. Patel. Agas: Śrīmad Rājacandra Āśram.

Johnson, W. J. 1995. *Harmless Souls. Karmic Bondage and Religious Change in Early Jainism with Special Reference to Umāsvāti and Kundakunda*. Delhi: Motilal Banarsidas Publishers.

Laidlaw, James. 1995. *Riches and Renunciation. Religion, Economy, and Society among the Jains*. Oxford: Clarendon Press.

Mehta, D. C. 1978. *The Self-Realisation*. A translation from Gujarati into English of Śrīmad Rājacandra's *Ātma Siddhi*. Bombay: Bharatiya Vidya Bhavan. Available online at www.atmasiddhi.com.

Mehta, Digish. 1999. *Shrimad Rajchandra: A Life*. Agas: Śrīmad Rājacandra Āśram.

Mehta, Saryuben, R. and Bhogilal G. Sheth. 1971. *Srimad Rajchandra A Great Seer*. Agas: Śrīmad Rājacandra Āśram.

Pungaliya, U. K. 1996. *Philosophy and Spirituality of Srimad Rajchandra*. Jaipur: Prakrit Bharati Academy; Pune: Sanmati Teerth.

Salter, Emma. 2001. 'Unity and Diversity Amongst the Followers of Śrīmad Rājacandra'. *Jinamañjari* 23, 1: 32–51.

——. 2002. *Rāj Bhakta Mārg. The Path of Devotion to Śrīmad Rājacandra. A Jain Community in the Twenty First Century*. Doctoral thesis. University of Wales, Cardiff.

Shah, D. M. and U. K. Pungaliya. 2001. 'Śrīmad Rājacandra on the Role of the Sadguru for Self-Realization'. *JinamañJari* 23, 1: 1–31.

Titze, K. 1997. *Jainism. A Pictorial Guide to the Religion of Non-Violence*. Delhi: Motilal Banarsidas.

Vallely, Anne. 2003. *Guardians of the Transcendent: An Ethnography of a Jain Ascetic Community*. Toronto: University of Toronto Press.

11

A FIFTEENTH-CENTURY DIGAMBAR JAIN MYSTIC AND HIS FOLLOWERS*

Tāraṇ Taraṇ Svāmī and the Tāraṇ Svāmī Panth

John E. Cort

For many years, scholarship on the Jains paid too little attention to the historical, social and geographical contexts within which "Jainism" has always been embedded. At best one might find a general discussion of the philosophical differences between the broad groupings of Śvetāmbar and Digambar. These two "sects," however, have never been unified social groups, and one looked in vain for substantial discussion of the actual sectarian divisions that defined Jain society.[1] In recent years there has been a sea change in this situation, as detailed studies have been published on sectarian groups among the Śvetāmbars such as the Kharatara Gaccha, Tapā Gaccha, Añcala (Acala) Gaccha, Kaḍuā Gaccha, Loṅkā Gaccha, Sthānakavāsīs, and Terāpanthīs. But to date there has been little attention to the sectarian divisions among the Digambars. There are two areas in which such studies are needed. One involves a clearer understanding of the cultural and ritual differences between the northern Digambar communities of Rajasthan, Uttar Pradesh, Madhya Pradesh, and northern Maharashtra on the one hand, and the southern Digambar communities of Karnataka, Tamil Nadu, and southern Maharashtra on the other.[2] The other area involves a clearer understanding of the history, and differences of ideology, ritual, and social organization among the three older sectarian divisions in northern and central India, the Bīs Panth, Terā Panth, and Tāraṇ Svāmī Panth, as well as the twentieth and twenty-first century followers of Kānjī Svāmī and Śrīmad Rājcandra.[3] In this chapter I essay a beginning at addressing a part of the second lacuna, with an outline of some of the features of the Tāraṇ Svāmī Panth (also called the Tāraṇ Panth and Tāraṇ Samāj) of Bundelkhand in central India.

The Tāraṇ Svāmī Panth and its founder Tāraṇ Svāmī are among the least-studied aspects of Jainism. Padmanabh S. Jaini (1979: 310, n. 59) had to relegate them to a brief footnote in *The Jaina Path of Purification*, and Paul Dundas had to leave them out altogether in the first edition of his otherwise inclusive *The Jains*.

The situation in Indian-language surveys of the Jains is hardly better. Little is found aside from brief references to Tāraṇ Svāmī's living in the fifteenth and sixteenth centuries, the eschewing of image-worship by his followers, and the inclusion among his immediate followers of both Muslims and people from low castes.

In December of 1999 I undertook fieldwork among the Tāraṇ Svāmī Panth in Madhya Pradesh as part of a larger on-going research project on Jain attitudes, practices, and discourses concerning images. This fieldwork has been complemented by subsequent textual research on some of the fourteen texts attributed to Tāraṇ Svāmī and also twentieth century literature by members of the Panth.[4] In this essay I present an introductory survey of (1) what is known of Tāraṇ Svāmī himself, as well as five different frames for understanding him found in the community; (2) the fourteen texts attributed to him; (3) the community of his followers; (4) the ritual culture of the contemporary Tāraṇ Svāmī Panth; and (5) the most famous person born in the Panth, Rajneesh.

Sources for the life of Tāraṇ Svāmī

For information on Tāraṇ Svāmī we are indebted to the Digambar Terā Panth scholar Paṇḍit Phūlcandra Siddhānta Śāstrī (1985b), whose 1933 study has not been surpassed as a judicious and scholarly biography. Phūlcandra (ibid.: 96) argued that his full name, as used in the texts attributed to him, was Jin Tāraṇ Taraṇ, meaning "Jina Deliverer Deliverance." Phūlcandra speculated that this name, indicative of an understanding of the man as both liberated himself and capable of aiding others in their liberation, was given by later redactors of the texts. The *Ṭhikānesāra* texts (see below) refer to him simply as Svāmījī, "Reverend Master." He has always been more commonly referred to as Tāraṇ Svāmī. We have no record of his birth name.

Only one of the compositions attributed to Tāraṇ Svāmī contains any information about his life. The *Chadmastha Vāṇī* records that his death was on a Saturday, the seventh day of the dark half of the month of Jeṭha (May–June) in the year Vikram 1572, which corresponds to May 5, 1515 CE.[5] Other information comes from two texts. One is a set of overlapping manuscripts known as *Ṭhikānesāra* ("The essence of what is authentic") found in various Tāraṇ Panth collections in central India. Phūlcandra had access to three of these, copied in the late-nineteenth and early-twentieth centuries. The other is a short text known as the *Nirvāṇa Huṇḍī* ("The promissory note of liberation"). Neither of these has yet been published, although I was informed that there are plans to do so. From these texts Phūlcandra calculated that Tāraṇ Svāmī was born on Thursday, the seventh day of the bright half of the month of Agahan (November–December) in the year Vikram 1505, which corresponds to December 2, 1448.[6] We learn that his mother's name was Vīrasirī or Vīra Śrī, and his father's Gaṛhā Sāha.[7] He was born into the Parvār caste, in the Vāsalla *gotra* (clan) and Gāhā *mūr* (lineage). Further, we learn that he was born in a village called Puṣpāvatī. Most authors, as well as the community itself, have taken this to be the contemporary village Bilharī near Kaṭnī in Jabalpur district.

The only other textual information comes from another passage in the *Chadmastha Vāṇī*, which Phūlcandra (1985b: 401) rightly termed abstruse (*gūṛh*), and for the meaning of which Nāthūrām Premī (1912–1913: 294) wrote that we depend on what the Tāraṇ Panth infers it to mean. The standard interpretation of the passage is that Tāraṇ Svāmī began his studies at age eleven, and continued for ten years. He then spent nine years in various spiritual exercises before taking the lay vows (*vrata*) and becoming a celibate (*brahmacārī*) at age thirty. At age sixty he became a monk (*muni*), and then he died six-and-a-half years later.[8]

Phūlcandra (1985b: 399–401) then extrapolated from this thin foundation, using scholarly sources on the history of the medieval central Indian Digambar community and the oral tradition of the Tāraṇ Panth to reconstruct a biography for Tāraṇ Svāmī. Phūlcandra speculated that when Tāraṇ Svāmī was five years old, his father took him to Tāraṇ's mother's brother's village of Gaṛaulā (also spelled Gaṛhaulā). There he was given to Bhaṭṭārak Devendrakīrti, who occupied the Canderī seat, and was caste guru of the Parvār caste.[9] Devendrakīrti was favorably impressed by certain bodily signs of the boy. Tāraṇ Svāmī began his studies under Devendrakīrti. His fellow student was Śrutakīrti, author of a *Harivaṃśa Purāṇa* in 1495 CE.[10] Tāraṇ Svāmī left his studies at the age of twenty-one, and went to Semarkheṛī, near Siroñj in Vidisha (Vidiśā) district, where his mother's brother lived. He spent nine years in the area, often meditating in the caves in the nearby hills. At the age of thirty, having overcome the three spiritual obstacles of spiritual ignorance (*mithyātva*), illusion (*māyā*), and seeking worldly gain through spiritual practices (*nidāna*),[11] he took the vows (*vrata*) of a celibate (*brahmacārī*) and thereby became a formal renouncer.

The Digambar practice of becoming a renouncer through the formal taking of the vow of celibacy has been little remarked in scholarship on the Jains. While such a person is still technically a layperson, since Digambars hold that only the naked *muni* is a true monk, the *brahmacārī*, like the more advanced *kṣullaka* and *ailaka*, is functionally removed from the lay estate, and follows the practice of observing the rainy-season retreat (*cāturmāsa*). Full-fledged *muni*s were rare if not nonexistent for many centuries, especially in the Digambar communities of central India, and so these non-monastic renouncers played an important role in maintaining the ideals of renunciation. Phūlcandra (1992: 216–234) has listed forty-nine *brahmacāris* from the Parvār caste in central India in the twentieth century. The importance of the *brahmacārī* institution is clearly seen in an article by Johrāpurkar (1964b), in which he discussed the sixteenth-century *Saṅghāṣṭaka* of Brahma Jñānasāgara. In contrast to the usual depiction of the Jain community (*saṅgha*) as being fourfold (monks, nuns, laymen, laywomen), Jñānasāgara describes the Jain community as being sixfold: *śrāvaka* (laymen), *śrāvikā* (laywomen), *paṇḍita* (lay male intellectuals and ritualists, also known as *pāṇḍe*), *vratī* (male celibates), *āryikā* (female celibates), and *bhaṭṭāraka* (male pontiffs). The absence of naked monks (*muni*) from this list is striking; they have been replaced by lay celibates.[12]

Tāraṇ Svāmī remained a *brahmacārī* for thirty years, and continued his spiritual and ascetic practices. At the age of sixty he went to the next stage by becoming a full-fledged *muni*. Unlike the Śvetāmbar tradition, in which it is essential to be initiated into monkhood by another monk, the custom in the medieval Digambar tradition was for a spiritually-inclined man toward the end of his life on his own to renounce all clothing and undertake monastic practice. Tāraṇ Svāmī remained a monk for the final six-and-a-half years of his life.

Phūlcandra was not the only author to sketch a biography of Tāraṇ Svāmī. The first extensive notice of Tāraṇ Svāmī and the Tāraṇ Panth was in a multi-part article published by the Digambar scholar Nāthūrām Premī in 1912 and 1913 in *Jain Hitaiṣī*, an important Hindi journal published from Bombay.[13] Premī based his study on what he learned from his acquaintances in the Tāraṇ Panth, and his study of the very few texts and publications available to him. Premī (1912–1913: 295–297) gave one version of Tāraṇ Svāmī's life based upon oral tradition (*kiṃvadantī*) of other Digambar Jains in Bundelkhand, and another based upon the story contained in an unnamed "old book" given to him by a member of the Tāraṇ Panth (ibid.: 200–206). The first version presented much of Tāraṇ Svāmī's life, especially his opposition to image-worship, his practice of magic (*jādūgarī*), and his Muslim followers, in an unfavorable light. This version, given in the first installment of Premī's article, upset some of its Tāraṇ Panth readers so much that at the end of the second installment Premī said that he had been criticized and even threatened by some members of the Tāraṇ Panth, and he asked them not to criticize his essay until it was published in its entirety (ibid.: 557–558). The second version also appears to be based largely on oral tradition. It presents Tāraṇ Svāmī within Jain cosmology as a Jina-to-be who overcame attempts to assassinate him due to his opposition to image-worship. This second version places his birth at Pohapāvatī (Puṣpāvatī), a village near Delhi, where his father was in the court of an unnamed Muslim king (*bādśāh*). Premī pointed out that the historical lack of Parvārs in the Delhi area and the absence of a name for the king make this version unlikely, but otherwise did not attempt a more scholarly reconstruction of Tāraṇ Svāmī's life.

A third biographical study was essayed by the Digambar scholar Brahmacārī Sītalprasād (also spelled Śītalprasād) in the introduction to his 1932 rendition of Tāraṇ Svāmī's *Śrāvakācāra* into modern Hindi. Sītalprasād's brief biography was based on Premī's article and oral traditions he gathered among members of the Tāraṇ Panth in Sāgar. According to Sītalprasād (1992: 12–14), Tāraṇ Svāmī's birth village of Puṣpāvatī is also known as Peśāvar, a village near Delhi. His father was a wealthy merchant who was in the service of the Lodhī kings. For some unknown reason his father moved to Gaṛaulā, a village in Sagar (Sāgar) district. There a Digambar *muni* saw the boy, and said that from his bodily signs it was clear that he should study the scriptures. His father shifted the family yet again, this time to Semarkheṛī, where he went into business, and the boy began his studies. From a young age he was motivated by worldly aversion (*vairāgya*), and so never married. He remained at home for many years, observing the lay vows and spending time meditating in nearby forests. He eventually left home, and either remained a *brahmacārī* or became a *muni*. He settled in the village of

Malhārgaṛh (in present-day Guna [Gunā] district), whence he travelled and preached, and converted 553,319 people to Jainism. His chief disciples came from a wide range of caste and religious backgrounds.[14]

Biographical frames

Any biography is a historical narrative, and as such is framed as much by the contemporary concerns of the author as it is by the concerns of the subject's time. This is clearly the case with the biographies of Tāraṇ Svāmī. In particular, we can discern five frames within which the biography of Tāraṇ Svāmī has been contextualized: as Digambar mystic, as Digambar ritual reformer, as trans-sectarian iconoclastic *sant* poet, as miracle-worker, and as Jina-to-be.

Tāraṇ Svāmī as Digambar mystic

In his study of the *Śrāvakācāra*, Brahmacārī Sītalprasād (1992: 11–12) wrote that Tāraṇ Svāmī's texts show a familiarity with the earlier writings of Umāsvāti and especially Kundakunda. Sītalprasād proceeded here, and in the discussions of other texts of Tāraṇ Svāmī he translated into Hindi, to read Tāraṇ Svāmī through the interpretive lens of Kundakunda's dialectic of *niścaya naya* and *vyavahāra naya*, or absolute and relative perspectives on reality, and the broader Digambar mystical tradition. In brief, this tradition emphasizes inward spiritual experience over outer ritual form, while never outright rejecting the latter. Kundakunda argued that from the absolute perspective (*niścaya naya*), only soul (*jīva*) exists, and the spiritual goal therefore is direct knowledge (*jñāna*) of the soul through meditation.[15]

It is this tradition that provided Sītalprasād a framework for understanding the oftentimes abstruse writings of Tāraṇ Svāmī. For example, Sītalprasād wrote of the *Jñāna Samuccaya Sāra*, "In [this text] there is much useful discussion of the primacy of the *niścaya naya* or spiritual knowledge (*adhyātma jñān*)" (p. 7). In his introduction to the *Tribhaṅgī Sāra* he wrote, "In [this text] are given the means of the *niścaya* path to liberation (*mokṣamārg*), which is very beneficial.... Everything that Śrī Tāraṇ Svāmī says is in accordance with the ancient Jain teachings.... Svāmī was a renouncer, and the spiritual intellectual of the Jain teachings of his time" (p. 9). Of the *Mamala Pāhuḍa* he wrote, "The author of the *Mamala Pāhuḍa*, Śrī Jin Tāraṇ Taraṇ Svāmī, had a deep knowledge of the Jain teachings, and was a great soul who loved the essence of spirituality (*adhyātma-ras ke premī*)" (p. 9).

Sītalprasād's framing of Tāraṇ Svāmī within the Digambar *adhyātma* or mystical tradition is not at all surprising, since all of Sītalprasād's other writings evince a deep and abiding interest in this subject. Sītalprasād was born in an Agravāl family in Lucknow in 1879. After his education in Sanskrit, English, and Jain doctrine, he worked as a jeweller in Calcutta and then as a government bureaucrat in Lucknow. He received a great spiritual shock when his wife, mother and younger brother all died within an eight day span in a virulent outbreak of the plague in 1909. He devoted the remainder of his life to Jain social work and to the study of the Digambar mystical tradition. He suffered another shock when his young fellow student Lālā Anantlāl also died, and so he went to Solāpur and there took the *brahmacārya* vow from Ailak Pannālāl in 1910. Over the next several decades he produced Hindi paraphrases (*ṭīkā*) on the *Niyamasāra*, *Pañcāstikāyasāra*, *Pravacanasāra*, and *Samayasāra* of Kundakunda, the *Samayasāra Kalaśa* of Amṛtacandra, the *Yogasāra* of Yogīndu, and the *Svayambhū Stotra* of Samantabhadra. He also wrote a study of Paṇḍit Ṭoḍarmal's *Mokṣamārga Prakāśaka*, and independent works with titles such as *Adhyātmik Nivedan*, *Adhyātma Jñān*, *Adhyātmik Sopān*, and *Niścay Dharm kā Manan*. He died in Lucknow in 1942.[16]

When Sītalprasād came to work on the texts of Tāraṇ Svāmī in the late 1920s, after two decades of study and writing on the Digambar mystical tradition, it was only natural that he located Tāraṇ Svāmī within that tradition. Mathurāprasād Samaiyā of the Tāraṇ Panth requested Sītalprasād to come to Sāgar for his rainy-season retreat in 1932 to work on the texts. Mathurāprasād had first taken manuscripts of some of Tāraṇ Svāmī's texts to Gaṇeśprasād Varṇī (1874–1961). Varṇī was one of the great Digambar intellectuals of the first half of the twentieth century, and the man largely responsible for the current Digambar *paṇḍit* tradition of central India.[17] He was unable to make sense of the manuscripts. At this time there were also voices in the Terā Panth community of Bundelkhand that argued that since the texts were unintelligible, and the Tāraṇ Panth did not worship Jina images, the Panth in fact was not Jain at all. Mathurāprasād then turned to Sītalprasād, interested him in the manuscripts, and promised full support for his studies of them. That first year he worked from several manuscripts of the *Śrāvakācāra* to compile an edition and Hindi commentary. He devoted every rainy-season retreat for the next six years to continuing this work, and in the end prepared editions and Hindi versions of nine of Tāraṇ Svāmī's fourteen texts.[18] It is in the context of Terā Panth skepticism of the authenticity of the Tāraṇ Svāmī tradition that we must understand Sītalprasād's repeated assertions that Tāraṇ Svāmī's writings are in full accord with the orthodox Jain doctrine (*siddhānt*). Sītalprasād's editions and translations were published by the office of the Digambar magazine *Jain Mitra* (of which Sītalprasād was editor from 1909 to 1929) in Surat, with the publication costs met by a Tāraṇ Panth patron from Āgāsaud. Sītalprasād did not see some of the oldest extant manuscripts, nor did he use more than two or three manuscripts for any one text, so the editions he prepared are by no means fully critical editions; but they remain the most scholarly editions to date. It was on the basis of these versions that subsequent Tāraṇ Panth authors such as Kavi Amṛtlāl Cañcal, Brahmacārī Jaysāgar, and Paṇḍit Campālāl produced their works. The other five texts remained unedited until 1990–1991, when Brahmacārī Jaysāgar spent two rainy-season retreats in Sāgar to prepare editions of them, although these are by no means as careful or scholarly as those prepared by Sītalprasād.[19]

In addition to recruiting Sītalprasād, the Tāraṇ Svāmī community also enlisted the Terā Panth scholar Paṇḍit Phūlcandra Siddhānta Śastrī to write an introduction to the second of Tāraṇ Svāmī's texts edited by Sītalprasād, the *Jñāna Samuccaya Sāra*, published in 1933. Phūlcandra (1901–1991) was from a village near Lalitpur, a district of current Uttar Pradesh within the Bundelkhand cultural area. He was a protege of Gaṇeśprasād Varṇī, and for four years in the early thirties taught in a Digambar religious school in Bīnā. He was also a social activist in both the Digambar community and the Indian National Congress. He later edited a number of important Digambar philosophical texts. Like Sītalprasād, Phūlcandra was also attracted to the Digambar mystical tradition, and later to the teachings of the neo-Digambar Kānjī Svāmī, who was one of the main propagators of the teachings of Kundakunda in the twentieth century. At the request of leaders of the Tāraṇ Svāmī community, he also edited a collection of Tāraṇ Svāmī's writings entitled *Tāraṇ Taraṇ Jinvāṇī Saṅgrah*.[20] Phūlcandra's positive evaluation of Tāraṇ Svāmī as being firmly within the mainstream Digambar tradition was also of great importance in the acceptance of the Tāraṇ Svāmī Panth by other Digambars, as was Phūlcandra's social work to reduce tensions between the Samaiyā caste, whose members were in the Tāraṇ Svāmī Panth, and his own Parvār caste, whose members were in the Terā Panth.[21]

Sītalprasād's location of Tāraṇ Svāmī within the Digambar mystical tradition was quickly picked up by Tāraṇ Panth intellectuals, and continues to be a dominant interpretation among many members of the Panth today. For example, in the course of a debate with members of the Terā Panth on image worship, the Tāraṇ Panth intellectual Campālāl Jain explicitly equated Kundakunda and Tāraṇ Svāmī, saying, "The Tāraṇ Panth is confirmed by every single word of Kundakunda" (C. Jain 1941: 14–15).

The Surat editions of Tāraṇ Svāmī's works came to the attention of Kānjī Svāmī (1889–1980), the neo-Digambar ex-monk who tirelessly propogated a radically *niścaya* interpretation of Kundakunda's teachings. On three separate occasions in the mid-1960s he delivered eight-day series of lectures on Tāraṇ Svāmī's works, first in Sāgar in 1964, and later at his center in Songaḍh in Gujarat. These were published in three volumes, each entitled *Aṣṭ Pravacan* ("Eight Lectures").[22] In 1964 he delivered a sermon on Tāraṇ Svāmī's *Śrāvakācāra* at Songaḍh on the occasion of the dedication of a building there that was donated by an important member of the Tāraṇ Panth from Sāgar (Kānjī Svāmī 1965). He then came to the annual fair at the main Tāraṇ Panth pilgrimage center of Nisaījī early in 1965. Kānjī Svāmī's confirmation of Tāraṇ Svāmī's place in the Digambar mystical tradition has been repeated by many subsequent Tāraṇ Panth authors. It has also been repeated by the intellectual leader of the Jaipur branch of the Kānjī Svāmī Panth, Hukamcand Bhārill (1985). He was invited to come to Sāgar in the early 1980s to deliver a week of lectures, and he chose as his theme to interpret four verses from Tāraṇ Svāmī's *Jñāna Samuccaya Sāra* as expressions of Kundakunda's focus on the soul from the *niścaya* perspective.

The framing of Tāraṇ Svāmī within the Digambar mystical tradition also fits with the influence of Terā Panth scholars on the interpretation of Tāraṇ Svāmī.

The Terā Panth in its disputes with the Bīs Panth has claimed to represent the original Digambar (and therefore Jain) teachings as found in the writings of Kundakunda and then later brought into Hindi by Banārsīdās and Ṭoḍarmal. It is important to remember that Sītalprasād was a Terā Panth intellectual. Phūlcandra was also a staunch Terā Panth scholar, who in one essay argued at length that the Terā Panth, far from being a creation of seventeenth- and eighteenth-century north India, was the original Digambar tradition (Phūlcandra 1985d). Contemporary Jains in Bundelkhand who are not of the Tāraṇ Panth are exclusively of the Terā Panth, and so there has been extensive influence of the latter on the former. Furthermore, in recent years Terā Panth intellectuals have in various ways included the Tāraṇ Panth within their vision of the Digambar tradition. For example, an *adhyātma*-oriented Terā Panth monthly magazine entitled *Adhyātma Parv Patrikā*, published from Jhāṅsī, in a portion of Uttar Pradesh within the Bundelkhand cultural area, published a special issue devoted to Tāraṇ Svāmī as an *adhyātma-yogī* in June–July 1999, with articles with titles such as "Tāraṇ Svāmī, the expert on Adhyātma" (N. K. Jain 1999).

Tāraṇ Svāmī as Digambar ritual reformer

A second framework for understanding Tāraṇ Svāmī is as a ritual reformer (*sudhārak*). This comes in large part from the Terā Panth intellectual ethos. The Terā Panth developed in conscious opposition to the ecclesiastical and ritual authority of the domesticated pontiffs known as *bhaṭṭārak*s. Even though Phūlcandra posited that Tāraṇ Svāmī studied under a *bhaṭṭārak* for ten years, most contemporary members of the Tāraṇ Panth aver that Tāraṇ Svāmī was staunchly opposed to the *bhaṭṭārak*s. For example, Kapūrcand Samaiyā, one of the leading contemporary Tāraṇ Panth intellectuals, has written of Tāraṇ Svāmī's time,

> The *bhaṭṭārak* institution had spread in Digambar Jain society. This area was under the authority of the Canderī seat. The *bhaṭṭārak*s had assumed king-like powers, and so they had great authority over society. Due to their position and power, their conduct became lax. They began to consecrate and worship images of gods and goddesses such as Padmāvatī and Kṣetrapāl along with the images of the Tīrthaṅkaras. They began to do incantations with *jantra-tantra-mantra*. Due to them much false belief came into Jain philosophy. The chief foundation of Jain philosophy in true knowledge and conduct was replaced by an emphasis on external rituals, and conduct was aimed at worldly prestige. But it was a time of religious revolution, and Jin Tāraṇ Taraṇ lived in this revolutionary time.
>
> (K. Samaiyā 1977: 1–2)

A little further on, Samaiyā wrote, "The Jain society of that time emphasized external ritualism, ostentation and obedience to convention instead of Jain principles. The people had fallen into the clutches of the common *bhaṭṭāraks*" (ibid.: 3). Tāraṇ Svāmī is said to have rejected this emphasis on rituals and the authority of the *bhaṭṭārak*s, and instead to have emphasized the study of the mystical texts of Kundakunda and Yogīndu. He wrote his own texts based on the teachings of these mystical authors, and engaged in meditation and other spiritual exercises for the purposes of strengthening his right faith and purifying his soul. In addition, he toured central India preaching to Jains and non-Jains alike, awakening them to the spiritual truths of the Jain tradition.

Tāraṇ Svāmī as iconoclastic sant

This portrayal of Tāraṇ Svāmī as a reformer blends into a third frame for understanding him, that of Tāraṇ Svāmī as a Jain representative of the iconoclastic *sant* tradition. This is based upon a broader interpretation, found in the writings of many twentieth-century Indian authors, of the medieval *sant* poets as engaged in criticism of both the social hierarchies and elaborate rituals of established religions. Thus the Tāraṇ Panth poet Amṛtlāl wrote,

> The sixteenth century was a century of revolution, not just in India, but the whole world. The party of *sant*s, consisting of men such as Dādū, Kabīr, Nānak, Raidās, Malūkdās, Phalṭūdās, Lokā Śāh, and Martin Luther,[23] came onto the stage of the confusion of the world of the time. They cut away at the disorders that had gradually grown up in religion. Sant Tāraṇ was one of these *sant*s.
>
> (Amṛtlāl 1957: n.p.)

Later in the same pamphlet, Amṛtlāl added Svāmī Dayānand Sarasvatī, the founder of the Ārya Samāj, to this list. Another author writing in a similar vein added the Sufi saints (Gulābcandra 1940 [1974: 8]). In particular, these reforming *sant*s are all understood to have emphasized spiritual practices that aimed at inner mystical realization, and to have criticized elaborate outer rituals, especially those involving the worship of images.

This portrait of Tāraṇ Svāmī as opposed to the worship of images of even the Jinas has become the most widely known in scholarship on the Jains. To cite just four examples, all of them from standard treatments of the Jains, Helmuth von Glasenapp (1925: 357) wrote of the iconoclasm of the Panth ("*sie sind bilderfeindlich*"), Vilas A. Sangave (1980: 53) mentioned its "hatred of idol-worship," Kailāścandra Śāstrī (1985: 316) wrote that the Panth opposes image-worship ("*yah panth mūrtipūjā kā virodhī hai*"), and Hīrālāl Jain (1962: 46) wrote that Tāraṇ Svāmī composed texts that forbad image-worship ("*tāraṇ svāmī dvārā mūrti pūjā niṣedhak granth kī sthāpnā huī*").

Sangave went so far as to suggest that Tāraṇ Svāmī might have been influenced in his iconoclasm directly either by the teachings of Loṅkā Śāh or Islam. His argument concerning Loṅkā Śāh appears to have come from Nāthūrām Premī, who wrote,

> When we see that the Tāran Svāmī Panth was founded some fifty or sixty years after the Ḍhūṇḍhiyā Panth, and in both there was the condemnation of image-worship, then it is not baseless to infer that Tāran Svāmī was influenced by Loṅkā Śāh in the founding of his own Panth. The sad state of the lax conduct of the Digambar *bhaṭṭārak*s was just like that of the Śvetāmbar *yati*s [domesticated monks], and he must have considered how to free the laity from their clutches. He must have seen the example of the new contemporaneous tradition of Loṅkā Śāh, and from the success of its teachings have decided to start on a similar path.
>
> (Premī 1912–1913: 555)

I find the argument that Tāraṇ Svāmī was influenced by Loṅkā Śāh highly unlikely. The two figures were more or less contemporaneous (Loṅkā's dates are not all that much earlier than Tāraṇ Svāmī's; see Dundas 2002: 246–251, Flügel 2000: 46–50), and it is difficult to see how the highly controversial teachings against the cult of images could have spread so quickly from the small Śvetāmbar circle around Loṅkā in Ahmedabad to an equally small circle on the margins of Digambar society in Bundelkhand. Further, Premī has mistakenly conflated the teachings of Loṅkā Śāh and his immediate successors with the later Ḍhūṇḍhiyā or Sthānakvāsī tradition, which emerged from the Loṅkā Gacch only in the mid-seventeenth century, well after Tāraṇ Svāmī (Dundas 2002: 251–254, Flügel 2000: 58–79).

The argument for Muslim influence is also weak. While it is true that there were Muslims among Tāraṇ Svāmī's immediate followers, the suggestion of direct Muslim influences on Tāraṇ Svāmī – a claim similar to that made by many authors about Loṅkā as well – remains highly speculative at best. Premī (1912–1913: 33–34) advanced a slightly different argument. He said that rather than directly incorporating Muslim practices and theologies, Tāraṇ Svāmī (as well as the other *sant* reformers of Hinduism) changed earlier traditions to emphasize spiritual teachings instead of ritual and social practices, as a means of combatting Muslim influence. In other words, we see the influence of Islam posited to account for changes both in imitation of and opposition to Muslim practices. But neither argument is based on anything more concrete than a common de-emphasis on image-worship and privileging of interior spiritual practice.

I find a much more likely explanation of Tāraṇ Svāmī's indifference to image-worship – and it was indifference more than opposition, aniconism more than iconoclasm – to be his reading of Kundakunda and other authors in the Digambar mystical tradition. There is scant reference to image-worship in these earlier texts, and none at all in most of them. It is easy for an independent-minded reader of these texts to come away with the conclusion that they do not lend any support to the cult of images. Tāraṇ Svāmī would not be alone in such a reading, as the initial exposure to Kundakunda's *Samayasāra* had precisely this effect upon Banārsīdās in Agra a little over a century later. Such aniconic responses to the reading of Kundakunda and the Digambar mystical tradition have continued to surface periodically in the Digambar tradition, especially within the Terā Panth which eschews the worship of unliberated Jain deities such as Kṣetrapāl and Padmāvāti, and critiques the use of flowers and liquids in the worship of the Jinas.[24] I think this is a much more plausible explanation for Tāraṇ Svāmī's indifference to image-worship.[25]

These biographical narratives, of Tāraṇ Svāmī as traditional Digambar mystic, as anti-*bhaṭṭārak* reformer, and as a Jain representative of the broader *sant* tradition, all appear to have developed in the twentieth century. On the one hand they are intended to establish the orthodoxy of Tāraṇ Svāmī, and therefore the Jainness of the Tāraṇ Panth. In this the narratives have been successful, as Tāraṇ Panth Jains today are represented at the highest level of local Bundelkhand Terā Panth organizations and regional north Indian Digambar organizations. I have never heard any contemporary Jain argue that Tāraṇ Svāmī and the Tāraṇ Panth are not Jain. On the other hand, these narratives give evidence of modernizing tendencies within the larger Jain tradition, as Jain history is tied to larger, global narratives of religious reform, inner spirituality, and rationality.

Tāraṇ Svāmī as miracle worker

These narratives have displaced an earlier understanding of Tāraṇ Svāmī as a charismatic wonder-working holy man, who was worshiped by his followers. The best known of these stories concerns the efforts of his opponents to drown him in the Betwa (Betvā) River at Malhārgaṛh.

I was told a brief version of this story when I visited Malhārgaṛh, and was taken by my hosts to see the three stone platforms in the river that are the tangible reminders of the story. In the words of K. Samaiyā (1977: 4), "Egoistic people were opposed to Tāraṇ Svāmī. It is said... that one time he was thrown in the Betwa River in an attempt to kill him, but that his lifespan was not yet complete, and so he was saved in a miraculous (*camatkārik*) manner. As a result of this incident he developed a sense of alienation from the world (*virakti*), and began to engage in spiritual practices in the forests on the banks of the Betwa."

A fuller version is found in a 1948 article by Jñāncandra Jain:

> His teachings were not looked upon favorably by his narrow-minded contemporaries. They tried to dissuade him in various ways, and also put pressure on him to stop his preaching. When he refused to cease, they tried to kill him. There was dense forest on the banks of the Betwa River around Malhārgaṛh. Tāraṇ Svāmī was living in this forest, because it was a good place to perform meditation (*sāmāyik* and *dhyān*). There was a boatman there named Cidānand Caudhrī. It is said that he sat Tāraṇ Svāmī in his boat, took him to the deepest part of the river, and threw

> him in. He did this three times, but each time at that very spot Tāraṇ Svāmī was able to sit on a stone platform. When he saw this miracle, Cidānanda realized that Tāraṇ Svāmī must be a holy man (*mahātmā*). He came to regret what he had done, and became a disciple of Tāraṇ Svāmī. These stone platforms are still in the Betwa River, and members of the Tāraṇ Panth believe them to be holy (*pavitra*). Every year thousands of pilgrims come for *darśan* of the platforms, and they bow to Tāraṇ Svāmī.
>
> (J. Jain 1948: 34)

A third telling (R. Samaiyā 1989: 8–9) says that the person who requested the boatman to kill Tāraṇ Svāmī was none other than his own mother's brother, who was angered at Tāraṇ Svāmī's rejection of image-worship.[26] The story of the attempted drowning is tied to an earlier attempt by his maternal uncle to poison him that also failed (Jaysāgar 1990: 55, R. Samaiyā 1977: 8).[27]

Two sources that dwell on Tāraṇ Svāmī as miracle-working holyman refer to the powers he had derived from his practice of *mantra*s (Jaysāgar 1990: 56, R. Samaiyā 1989: 8). From this practice he had obtained extraordinary powers (*siddhi*), such as the ability to travel from Malhārgaṛh to Semarkheṛī in a matter of minutes. He used these powers to rescue a Digambar monk in Gaṛaulā from unspecified harassment (*saṅkaṭ*). He went to fairs and used his magic (*camatkār*) to convert people to his teachings. In particular, he used his magical powers to suspend his texts in the air, and then would bring them back down to earth at fairs.

This latter story is an old one, for it is at the center of the only brief nineteenth-century account of Tāraṇ Svāmī in English.[28] Writing in the *Transactions of the Royal Asiatic Society of Great Britain and Ireland* in 1827, Major James Delamaine says of Tāraṇ Svāmī (or Tāranī Paṇḍit, as he calls him), "He was acquainted with the art of *Indrajála* (juggling), by which he sent up papers to the sky. He then collected the multitude, and a book appeared to descend to him from heaven in their presence. He then read and explained it to them, teaching that they should worship no images at all" (Delamaine 1827: 415).[29]

This association of Tāraṇ Svāmī with jugglers (*naṭ*) emerges elsewhere in the literature. Nāthūrām Premī, for example, wrote that one of Tāraṇ Svāmī's chief disciples was a juggler (*naṭ*), and that Tāraṇ Svāmī successfully competed with jugglers and magicians (*jādūgar*) for the patronage of a local king (Premī 1912–1913: 295). In discussing Tāraṇ Svāmī's death, Premī wrote that one of the three death rites performed for him was the "keeping of a plate" (*thālī rakhnā*) in accordance with the tradition of the jugglers (*naṭ*) (ibid.: 296–297).

Another miracle story concerns Tāraṇ Svāmī as a young child, when his father was in the employment of the king. His father had brought some paper records home with him. They were destroyed in a fire, and he was understandably worried about the king's response. The young Tāraṇ Svāmī saw his father's anxiety, and magically restored the papers (K. Jain 1941: 3–4, Premī 1912–1913: 200, R. Samaiyā 1989: 7).

Yet another miracle accounts for the shrine at Semarkheṛī, where he is said to have spent many years engaged in spiritual practices. At that time he was living in a cave. The area was also infested with thieves (*piṇḍārā*, *ṭhag*). Tāraṇ Svāmī happened to meet a caravan of gypsies (*bañjārā*), who were leading camels loaded with sugar to sell in a nearby city. He asked them what they were carrying, but they took him for a thief dressed in *sādhu*'s clothes, and so they said that the bags contained only salt. Later, when they came to a river and were crossing it, one of the bags broke, and they saw that it did indeed contain salt. They opened the other bags, and found that all the sugar had turned to less valuable salt. The gypsies returned to Tāraṇ Svāmī and asked his forgiveness for lying to him. In return, he turned the salt back into sugar, which they took to the city and sold. When they returned they built a temple at Semarkheṛī, where a pillar erected by them is still standing (R. Samaiyā 1989: 9).

Among Tāraṇ Svāmī's disciples are said to have been a number of Muslims, and a miracle story about his death involves them (Jaysāgar 1990: 55–56). Lukmān Śāh and 500 fellow Muslims were with Tāraṇ Svāmī at the time of his death. They wanted to perform the death rites in the Muslim manner and bury the corpse, but the Jain followers of Tāraṇ Svāmī did not give permission, as they wanted to perform the Jain death rites and cremate the corpse. As a result, the rites were performed according to both the Muslim and Jain traditions, although it not clear to me exactly how this could be done.[30]

Brahmacārī Jaysāgar said that he heard this story from two Muslim watchmen at Nisaījī, Pīr Khāṃ and his father, indicating that there might well have been a local Muslim tradition of veneration of Tāraṇ Svāmī's memorial as that of a Muslim holy man. Jaysāgar reported that Lukmān Śāh also died at Nisaījī, where there is a memorial shrine to him, near the memorial of another Muslim disciple, Ruiyā Rama. Jaysāgar added that there used to be many more memorials to disciples of Tāraṇ Svāmī in the area around Nisaījī, but they have been destroyed by Jains who believe that such memorials are counter to correct Jain faith. This conscious distancing of the cult of Tāraṇ Svāmī from Muslim influences is nothing new. Jaysāgar (1990: 59) wrote that the worship at the memorial of Ruiyā Rama was an integral part of the annual fair at Nisaījī, but that it was discontinued sometime after 1816.

In addition to gypsies and Muslims, Tāraṇ Svāmī has also been worshiped by local Hindus in a wonder-working context. Outside the old gate to the shrine at Nisaījī stands a large platform with two small memorial stones. When I visited Nisaījī they were both smeared with red paste, indicating their active worship as local protector deities. There was also evidence that they had been worshipped with incense, lamps, and coconuts. I was told that these are the memorials of two Bundelā Rājpūt brothers. They were local lords (*ṭhākur*) who were disciples of Tāraṇ Svāmī and had protected him during the time of his oppression. My informants denied that they were worshiped by members of the Tāraṇ Panth, saying that only local Hindus worshiped them. But the *ṭhākur*s used to be more integrally connected with the worship of Tāraṇ Svāmī. Jaysāgar (1990: 57) reported that fifty years earlier he had heard the belief expressed that the two brothers had become *vyantar dev*s,[31] who would occasionally come and perform *āratī* and sing *bhajan*s at a small shrine near the banks of the Betwa where Tāraṇ Svāmī is said to have sat in meditation.

This understanding of Tāraṇ Svāmī as a miracle-working holyman, whose charisma extended both to his own memorial shrine after his death, and to the memorial shrines of many of his immediate disciples, is in little evidence today. The story of his miraculous rescue from drowning is still well known, as it is physically maintained by the presence of the three platforms in the river. But the physical presence of the shrine of the two Bundelā Rājpūts has not prevented their cult becoming somewhat separate from that of Tāraṇ Svāmī, and Jaysāgar said that the memorial shrines of many other disciples have been destroyed. Writing in 1990, Jaysāgar indicated his partial disapproval of the understanding of Tāraṇ Svāmī as a miracle-worker by relegating it to oral tradition (*kiṃvadantī*). But the clearest evidence of the contemporary rejection of this understanding of Tāraṇ Svāmī is found in my copy of Rādhelāl Samaiyā's book, my other principal source for these stories. I was given this book, from among a large collection of books in the temple in Sāgar, by a man who felt that it would be valuable in my research. But he didn't look in this particular copy before he gave it to me. The portion of the book in which the author relates the miracle stories, and which is entitled "Sant Tāraṇ Taraṇ and His Miracles [*camatkār*]," has been heavily crossed out by pen, and someone has written across the top of each page, "This is not a proven account" (*yah pramāṇit vivaraṇ nahī* [*sic*] *hai*).

Tāraṇ Svāmī as future Jina

There is a fifth understanding of Tāraṇ Svāmī that I have encountered only in written works. Nāthūrām Premī gave an extensive summary of a biography of Tāraṇ Svāmī found in an old book given to him by a member of the Tāraṇ Panth, which he said represented the contemporary beliefs (*māntā*) of the Panth. According to this biography, the soul that became Tāraṇ Svāmī was a tribal (Bhīl) king in a previous life. He came under the spiritual influence of a Jain monk, and took a vow not to eat meat. The fruition of this vow was that he was reborn during the time of Mahāvīra as King Śreṇika. According to all the Digambar traditions, Śreṇika's soul is currently residing in a hell, but is destined eventually to be born as Padmanābha, the first Jina of the coming era, because of his earlier connection with Mahāvīra. The Tāraṇ Panth version of the story, however, greatly shortens Śreṇika's stay in hell to only 1,750 years, whereas standard Digambar cosmology avers that the minimum lifespan of a hell-being is 10,000 years (Premī 1912–1913: 535). The soul was reborn as Ācārya Bhadrabāhu, one of the leaders of the Jain monastic community in the early years after Mahāvīra, and lived for 99 years. The soul was again reborn as the great philosopher and mystic Kundakunda, as whom he lived for another 84 years before being reborn as Tāraṇ Svāmī. The soul currently resides in the heaven known as Sarvārthasiddhi; after living there as a god for 84 million years, it will be born as Padmanābha (ibid.: 198–199).[32]

This framework for understanding Tāraṇ Svāmī clearly gives him an almost Jina-like status, while at the same time avoiding the heresy of declaring him actually to be a Jina by locating his attainment of enlightenment in an orthodox future. The inclusion of Kundakunda into this narrative is also noteworthy. Kundakunda is almost universally considered to be the intellectual lodestar of the Digambar tradition, and the Mūla Saṅgha, the monastic lineage that considers itself to be the "original" and "true" lineage, also calls itself the "lineage of Kundakunda" (Kundakunda Anvaya). Claiming that Tāraṇ Svāmī is indeed none other than Kundakunda reborn is to claim total orthodoxy for him.[33]

Premī described another way in which Tāraṇ Svāmī is considered to be even greater than the Jinas:

> The members of the Tāran Panth also believe that there have been other reformers just like Tāran Svāmī, and that there will be more in the future. In between religion becomes extinct, because Tāran or Tārakal is absent. After there have been 149 sets of twenty-four Jinas comes the time of separation (*virahiyā kāl*), also known as the time of shortcomings (*huṇḍā kāl*). Then a Tārakal or Tāran is born, and all the forgetful beings find the way.
>
> (Ibid.: 299)

I have not encountered this cosmic understanding of Tāraṇ Svāmī as a sort of "super-Jina" anywhere other than this one Tāraṇ Panth source paraphrased by Premī. Nor did my informants present an understanding of Tāraṇ Svāmī as a miracle worker. I should add that all of my informants among the Tāraṇ Panth were recommended to me as knowledgeable intellectuals, and so there is an inevitable intellectualist bias in their portrayal of Tāraṇ Svāmī and his teachings. But it is also clearly evident that the interpretive frames for understanding Tāraṇ Svāmī have changed over the past century.

Tāraṇ Svāmī's writings

Tāraṇ Svāmī is credited with authoring fourteen texts. Some scholars have expressed doubts about his authorship of two of them, the *Chadmastha Vāṇī* and the *Nāma Mālā*, the former because it includes a reference to his death, and the latter because it includes the names of many of his disciples. In discussions of his writings one frequently sees a division of them into five systems (*mata*, *mati*). Phūlcandra (1985b: 387) wrote that this categorization is found in a manuscript of the *Ṭhikānesāra* now in the collection of the Tāraṇ Panth temple in Khuraī, which was copied in the late nineteenth-century by one Ṭīkārām of Kuṇḍā, although it is evidently not found in another manuscript of this text copied by the same man and now in the collection at Nisaījī. The five categories of texts are as follows:

Vicāra mata (Reflections)
  Mālārohaṇa ("Garland offering")
  Paṇḍita Pūjā ("Wise worship")
  Kamala Battīsī ("Lotus thirty-two [verses]")
Ācāra mata (Conduct)
  Śrāvakācāra ("Lay conduct")
Sāra mata (Essential teachings)
  Jñāna Samuccaya Sāra ("Collected essence of knowledge")
  Tribhaṅgī Sāra ("Essence in triads")
  Upadeśa Śuddha Sāra ("Pure essence of the teachings")
Mamala mata (Spiritual purity)
  Mamala Pāhuḍa ("Handbook on purity")
  Caubīsa Ṭhāṇa ("Twenty-four topics")
Kevala mata (Enlightenment)
  Chadmastha Vāṇī ("Sayings of the unliberated")
  Nāma Mālā ("Garland of names")
  Khātikā Viśeṣa ("Special uprooter")
  Siddha Subhāva ("Nature of the perfected soul")
  Sunna Subhāva ("Nature of emptiness")

The three texts in the *vicāra mata* are thirty-two verse compositions that have been translated into Hindi more than any other of Tāraṇ Svāmī's texts, and are the best-known to members of the Tāraṇ Panth. K. Samaiyā (1977: 18) said that right faith (*samyag-darśana*) is emphasized in the *Mālārohaṇa*, right knowledge (*samyag-jñāna*) in the *Paṇḍita Pūjā*, and right conduct (*samyak-caritra*) in the *Kamala Battīsī*. According to tradition, Tāraṇ Svāmī composed the *Mālārohaṇa* for the wedding of one of his followers, either a Rājpūt or the daughter of one Padmakamal (Phulcandra 1985b: 386). It is read at weddings in the Tāraṇ Panth. Premī (1912–1913: 301–302) says that during the autumnal observance of Daśalakṣaṇ, people gather in the temple to recite the *Paṇḍita Pūjā* and *Mamalapahuḍa* during the day and the *Mālārohaṇa* and *Kamala Battīsi* during the evening. Some members of the Panth recite one or more of these texts daily.

The other texts are less well-known, although they are the subject of study by contemporary Tāraṇ Panth intellectuals. The *Śrāvakācāra* in 462 verses lays out the basics of Jain lay conduct. It was most likely collated from earlier Digambar *śrāvakācāra* texts, as it does not differ from them to any significant degree.[34]

The *Jñāna Samuccaya Sāra* consists of 908 verses, and the *Upadeśa Śuddha Sāra* of 588 verses. Between them they cover much of the basics of Digambar philosophy and metaphysics. The *Jñāna Samuccaya Sāra* discusses correct knowledge, faith, conduct, and scripture; the stages of lay spirituality (*pratimā*) and the lay vows (*aṇuvrata*); the virtues (*guṇa*) and vows (*vrata*) of a true monk; the seven verities of

Jain philosophy; the six substances (*dravya*); and the four types of meditation (*dhyāna*). The *Upadeśa Śuddha Sāra* covers various aspects of the correct path to liberation and faults that lead one astray from that path. The *Tribhaṅgī Sāra* is a text of seventy-one verses that discusses various topics in groups of three, detailing which triads to follow and which to renounce. All three of these texts, along with the *Śrāvakācāra*, are very close to the mainstream Digambar philosophical tradition.

The *Mamala Pāhuḍa* is a large collection of songs, consisting of over 3,200 verses. The *Caubīsa Ṭhāṇā* in roughly twenty pages of mixed verse and prose provides twenty-four spiritual topics on which the person desiring liberation should meditate.

The *Chadmastha Vāṇī* and *Nāma Mālā* are short prose texts, each about nine pages long in their printed versions, that provide cryptic information about Tāraṇ Svāmī and his disciples, as well as a range of other subjects. Premī (1912–1913: 302) said that the *Chadmastha Vāṇī* is recited for five days after Divālī. The *Khātikā Viśeṣa* is a short text of mixed prose and verse that discusses the process of wearing away karma in the context of the upward and downward cycles of time. The *Siddha Subhāva* and *Sunna Subhāva* are very short prose works, the first describing purification of the soul, and the latter the different ways in which one should be empty of false senses of self.[35]

Tāraṇ Svāmī's teachings

These texts, like much mystical literature the world over, are difficult to understand, and so are open to much interpretation. In general, Tāraṇ Svāmī affirms that by means of insight (*darśana*), purity (*śuddhatā*), knowledge (*jñāna*), and the cultivation of the correct inner spiritual orientation (*bhāva*), one will realize that one's soul (*ātmā*) in fact is the liberated supreme soul (*paramātmā*), and thus overcome the bonds of karma. His writings are full of terms quite commonly found in other Jain writings, such as knowledge (*jñāna*), verity (*tattva*), pure (*śuddha*), faith (*darśana*), intention or sentiment (*bhāva*), innate character (*svabhāva*), and wrong faith (*mithyātva*), but in the absence of good grammar the relationships among concepts are often unclear.

The most widely-known facet of the Tāraṇ Panth is its eschewing of the worship of images of the Jinas. But, as I will discuss further, there is no explicit mention of this in any of the texts attributed to Tāraṇ Svāmī.

The fact that Gaṇeśprasād Varṇā, one of the foundational figures of the modern north Indian Digambar intellectual tradition, is said to have been unable to make sense of Tāraṇ Svāmī's writings is significant. Tāraṇ Svāmī did not write in any one language, but mixed Sanskrit, Prakrit, Apabhramsa and Bundelkhandi Hindi together, often in the same verse or sentence. It is quite clear that he was not trained in grammar (and for this reason I doubt the story that he studied for ten years under a *bhaṭṭārak*). He evidently had read texts by Kundakunda, Yogīndu, Umāsvāti, Samantabhadra, and other orthodox Digambar authors, for in many places his texts read like paraphrases of these authors, except they are paraphrases by someone who did not understand the grammatical details of the languages he had read. Those who are more favorably inclined toward his writings term his use of language "unique" (*svatantra*). This estimation is perhaps best expressed by Phūlcandra (1985b: 401), who wrote, "The language is unique. He never composed according to the limitations of any single language and grammar. He expressed himself in whichever language a spiritual experience arose in his heart." Premī (1912–1913: 7) described Tāraṇ Svāmī's prose as undeclined (*asambaddh*), unclear (*aspaṣṭ*), and unusual (*alaukik*). Those less favorably inclined toward his writings use harsher language to characterize them, such as the Śvetāmbar monk Buddhisāgarsūri (1917: 341), who said that Tāraṇ Svāmī's texts "are in a strange (*adbhūt*) language." The most negative evaluation comes from Lāl Bahādur Śāstrī, a professional Digambar disputant with the Ambālā-based Śāstrārth Saṅgh who engaged several Tāraṇ Panth authors in a written debate on the appropriateness of image-worship in the early 1940s. Lāl Bahādur (1941: *ka*) said simply, "He was not especially learned, as is clear from reading his fourteen texts." Published versions of the texts show wide variation in spellings, and as Phūlcandra (1978: 72) notes, it is obvious that many changes have been introduced into the manuscripts by both the copists and their patrons, and so there is a need for a thorough study of the extant manuscripts. This work has not been undertaken to date.[36] Nor has the Tāraṇ Panth produced any notable intellectuals in the intervening five centuries since Tāraṇ Svāmī, so there are no known commentaries on any of the texts to aid one in interpreting the difficult language.[37]

The Tāraṇ Svāmī Panth

As a result of this lack of a Tāraṇ Panth literary tradition, the history between the death of Tāraṇ Svāmī and the early twentieth century is largely a blank. The *Nāma Mālā* contains some 2,000 names, but the significance of these is not fully clear. In his edition and Hindi version of this text Jaysāgar constructed an elaborate spiritual genealogy, but does not indicate on what basis he did so. Certainly both oral tradition and the cultic memory enshrined in the tombs at Nisaījī have intersected with the *Nāma Mālā*.

According to the community's own tradition, Tāraṇ Svāmī had disciples from a wide range of social backgrounds. Some of them were Jains, including some female renouncers (*āryikā*, *ārjikā*), among whom Kamalāśrī Ārjikā was the most prominent.[38] Many sources have said that his other chief disciple was a Muslim named Ruiyā Jin or Ruiyā Ramaṇ, who is mentioned at the beginning of the *Nāma Mālā*.[39] A. H. Nizami (1980: 309) wrote that Ruiyā Jin was a cotton-carder by trade. Premī (1912–1913: 205) mentioned another cotton-carder named Behanā. He also mentions a juggler (*naṭ*), whose tomb is at Nisaījī (ibid.: 6). Sītalprasād (1992: 13) listed five chief disciples. Lakṣmaṇ Pāṇḍe by his title was possibly a disciple of a regional *bhaṭṭārak*. Cidānand Caudhrī was the boatman mentioned earlier. The third was Paramānand Vilāsī. The last two clearly have Muslim names: Sulpa Sāh Telī (an oil-presser by trade) and Lukmān Sāh Musalmān. There is a local tradition in Cauṅraī or Cānd, a village in Chhindwara (Chindvāṛā) district, of veneration of one Himāū Pāṇḍe (also spelled Himāṅyu and Humāyūṃ), who was an influential disciple of Tāraṇ Svāmī. His followers built a memorial to him on the banks of the Kulbahara (Kulbaharā) River. But the worship of Himāū has been criticized by many other members of the Panth.[40] Earlier I mentioned the two local Bundelā Rājpūts at Nisaījī who protected him from his iconophilic opponents. Earlier I had also discussed the story of the gypsies who built a shrine to Tāraṇ Svāmī at Semarkheṛī in response to one of his miracles. What is clear from this scanty evidence is that he was a charismatic spiritual teacher, who attracted disciples from a wide range of contemporary society, and perhaps had more followers from non-Jain backgrounds than from Jain backgrounds. This could also help account for the stories of opposition to him on the part of the local Jains.

None of these followers wrote anything that we know of (although it is possible that the *Chadmastha Vāṇī* and *Nāma Mālā* were composed by one or more of them), nor have there been any texts composed from within the Tāraṇ Panth in the intervening centuries. We do know that his manuscripts were copied in various places, evincing some degree of on-going intellectual activity. There is also the material evidence embedded in the many temples (*caityālay*) throughout Bundelkhand, as well as at the principal pilgrimage places of the Panth, but with the exception of Nisaījī, which I will discuss further, there has been no research on them. Nor has there been an adequate survey of manuscripts in the temple collections. It might be possible to reconstruct a partial history of the Panth in the centuries between the death of Tāraṇ Svāmī and the emergence of modern records in the first half of the twentieth century, but to date no one has attempted this.

What we do know is that members of the Tāraṇ Panth today are found in six merchant castes in Bundelkhand.[41] According to informants, three of these – Samaiyā, Dosakhe and Gulālāre – were converts from image-worshiping Jain communities, and the other three – Aseṭhi, Ayodhyāvāsī and Cārnagar – were converts from Vaiṣṇav Hindu communities. All of these castes are distinctly Bundelkhandi in language and custom, indicating that the Tāraṇ Panth has long (if not always) been restricted to Bundelkhand.

The Samaiyā and Dosakhe both appear to have formerly been part of the Parvār caste, one of the largest merchant castes of Bundelkhand.[42] Many members of the Gulālāre have migrated to northwestern Maharashtra.[43]

The Aseṭhi caste is still predominantly Vaiṣṇav, with a small number in the Tāraṇ Panth.[44] The Ayodhyāvāsī, as its name indicates, is a caste that claims its origin to have been the area around Ayodhyā in eastern Uttar Pradesh.[45] It is also predominantly Vaiṣṇav, with a small percentage in the Tāraṇ Panth. According to Jaysāgar (1990: 37), members of the Tāraṇ Panth from this caste view the Tāraṇ Svāmī temple in the village of Naṭeran in Vidisha (Vidiśā) district to be a special pilgrimage shrine. The Cārnagar caste also consists mostly of Vaiṣṇavs, with a smaller number of members of the Tāraṇ Panth.[46]

These castes practiced religious rituals together, but exchanged neither daughters nor cooked food until a decision was taken at the annual fair at Nisaījī in 1927 to begin such exchanges (S. Jain 1984: 32). Nowadays there is also fairly extensive intermarriage with Terā Panth Digambars in similar castes.

I was told estimates of the total population of the Tāraṇ Svāmī Panth that ranged between 20,000 and 100,000. One author (R. Samaiyā 1989: 39–62) has presented a district-by-district chart of where there are Tāraṇ Panth households and temples. He lists 131 temples and a little under 20,000 people, located mostly in the areas of Madhya Pradesh, southern Uttar Pradesh and northwest Maharashtra that comprise the area of Bundelkhand. The center of the Tāraṇ Panth area comprises the districts of Vidisha (Vidiśā), Damoh, Sagar (Sāgar), Jabalpur, Raisen (Rāysen), and Hoshangabad (Hośaṅgābād) in Madhya Pradesh.

There is little information about the organization of religious professionals within the Panth before modern times. Informants told me that formerly resident ritual functionaries known as *bhāījī* ("respected brother") or *pāṇḍe* (equivalent to *paṇḍit*, and referring to any learned person) were connected with each temple. They delivered sermons and ritualized readings of Tāraṇ Svāmī's texts. I surmise that some of them also functioned as manuscript copists and maintained the Tāraṇ Panth intellectual culture. Leadership of the Panth was under wealthy and respected lay merchants, who were also responsible for funding the annual pilgrimages to Nisaījī (see later). Rādhelāl Samaiyā (1989: 17–26) gives brief biographical details of seven twentieth-century *brahmacārī*s (m) and four *brahmacāriṇī*s (f) in the Panth. It is unclear to me whether this is a relatively recent tradition of semi-renouncers, or if within the Panth, in common with the broader Digambar ritual culture of central India, there have always been a few men and women who took the vows of lay celibates, and we simply have no records of them. Samaiyā also includes one *muni* and one *kṣullak* who were born in the Tāraṇ Svāmī Panth; informants told me that they are now simply part of the common Digambar mendicant community, which has intentionally eschewed any formal affiliation with the lay division into different *panth*s. They are not Tāraṇ Panth monks. Finally, Samaiyā lists forty *paṇḍit*s from the past century. But this title is often applied to anyone with a literary or intellectual bent, and does not indicate either any formal educational qualifications or any formal ritual role.

Pilgrimage shrines

There are four pilgrimage shrines for the Tāraṇ Panth, although only three of them are the sites of annual fairs, and only one of them has any great antiquity.[47] The most important is on the banks of the Betwa River near the village of Malhārgaṛh in Guna district. It is known simply as Nisaījī, "Honored memorial." It was here that Tāraṇ Svāmī spent his final years with his disciples, and where his last rites were performed. There are also memorials (*samādhi*) of many of his disciples. I will return to it later.

Semarkheṛī, near Siroñj in Vidisha District, is where Tāraṇ Svāmī is said to have engaged in various spiritual practices and formally to have renounced the world. It is also where the Bañjārās erected a shrine to him. The annual fair (*melā*) is held there on Vasant Bright Fifth, a day widely celebrated throughout north India as

Spring Fifth. In addition to a temple and various buildings for pilgrims at the shrine itself, nearby are also some caves in which Tāraṇ Svāmī is said to have meditated. This is the oldest pilgrimage shrine in the Panth after Nisaījī, and there are records of the patrons of the annual fairs going back to 1881 (R. Samaiyā 1989: 12).

Sūkhā, near Pathariyā village in Damoh District, is where he preached. The annual fair here is known as Tāraṇ Jayantī; the use of this name, which has come to be used by the Indian government for the birth days of the "founders" of all religious communities, indicates that the fair is of fairly recent origin. That the fair is a recent development is also indicated by Sītalprasād (1992: 17), for, writing in 1932, he described annual fairs only at Semarkheṛī and Nisaījī. A decade later, Kālūrām Jain (1941: 18–19) also described just Semarkheṛī and Nisaījī as pilgrimage shrines in the Panth. He added that he had heard of a dilapidated memorial in Damoh District; obviously this was the site of at most a local Tāraṇ Panth fair in his time. The fair at Sukhā is on Agahan Bright Seventh, in November–December. This site was relatively neglected by the community for many years, but extensive constructions began in 1938, after a leading layman from Sāgar bought the land from a local Muslim.

The fourth pilgrimage site is in the village of Bilharī, near Kaṭnī in Jabalpur district. According to the tradition of the Tāraṇ Svāmī Panth, this is the village formerly known as Puṣpāvatī where Tāraṇ Svāmī was born. This has only recently become a pilgrimage goal for the community, after the site was purchased from its non-Jain owners. The construction there has all been undertaken in the past few decades, largely under the direction of important laymen from Sāgar and Jabalpur. There is as of yet no annual fair at Bilharī.

Before turning to Nisaījī, I should mention two other sites that are important to some members of the Panth but are not dedicated to Tāraṇ Svāmī himself. The village of Cānd in Chhindwara district is the site of the memorial (*samādhi*) of Himāū Pāṇḍe, one of Tāraṇ Svāmī's chief disciples. It was also neglected for many years, but recently local members of the Panth have begun to develop the site, and there is an annual fair on Jeṭh Dark Sixth, known as Samādhi Sixth, the anniversary of Himāū Pāṇḍe's death. There was just a simple platform here, but a larger temple has recently been built. At Gaṛaulā (or Gaṛhaulā), near Tinduā in Damoh district, where Tāraṇ Svāmī is said to have lived for a few years as a child in his mother's brother's home, there is also a large platform.

By far the most important pilgrimage shrine is Nisaījī.[48] The annual fair here is held for three days from Phāg Bright Fifth in February–March, and is known as Phāg Phūlnā ("Phāg flowering"). Jaysāgar (1990: 59) records that until the early nineteenth century there was an annual fair at Nisaījī in honor of one of Tāraṇ Svāmī's disciples, the Muslim Ruiyā Ramaṇ or Ruiyā Jin, but that the fair was discontinued. This has also been where many members of the Tāraṇ Panth come to have the first tonsure (*muṇḍan*) of their children performed.

The main building is a three-storied structure of stone windows and arched canopies, in a style K. D. Bajpai (1975: 354) has termed "late medieval Rajput." (Figure 11.1) In conception it is a grandiose funerary monument, in which

Figure 11.1 Central shrine at Nisaījī. Photograph by the author, December 11, 1999.

the normally smaller style of a memorial canopy has been expanded into a tall tower. The shrine itself is very simple. There is a small canopied marble altar, on which is a pile of printed books. Behind this altar, inside a small walled enclosure, is an older stone altar, which is said to be the original one.

Phūlcandra (1985c) has traced the history of the site in an important essay.[49] At first there was just a simple *chattrī*, a canopied memorial platform at the site of Tāraṇ Svāmī's *samādhi*, where he was cremated. This served as an altar. About 350 years ago a devotee, whose descendants subsequently lived in Sirpur in Khandesh (modern Dhule District, Maharashtra), arranged for a more ornate *chattrī* with four pillars. In 1817 the annual fair was sponsored by a merchant from Nāgpur named Tārācand Mallūsāv. Among those who accompanied him to Nisaījī was a woman named Kesarīdāū. As part of her devotions she circumambulated the main shrine, and then prostrated herself on the ground. She died when her forehead touched the ground. In commemoration of this holy death her family built the current twelve-doored pavilion that obscures the older altar. The current six-pillared altar presumably dates from that renovation. Also around this time Mallūsāv built the current tall superstructure, as well the eastern gate to the complex. This superstructure has become emblematic of Nisaījī, and is the model for some Tāraṇ Panth temples elsewhere. The last third of the nineteenth century saw extensive construction of additional buildings at Nisaījī by pilgrims from throughout central India. On February 22, 1903 Mahārāo Mādhorāo Siṅghiyā, the king of Gwalior, in which princely state Nisaījī was located, visited the shrine, accompanied by an important Tāraṇ Panth layman from Khuraī. In commemoration of the visit the king donated the land surrounding the shrine to the Tāraṇ Panth. Subsequent construction of buildings on the site has been done with stones quarried from this land.

The archives at the shrine also list the names of those who sponsored the annual fairs, starting with Mallūsāv from Nāgpur in 1817. Other patrons have come from Bāndā, Sāgar, Hośaṅgābād, Āgāsaud, and Ṭimarnī, all towns in the Bundelkhand heartland of the Tāraṇ Samāj. After 1933 the organization of the annual fair has become a community undertaking.

For such an important Tāraṇ Svāmī pilgrimage site, there is very little to see, since the Panth resists the installation of any images, the veneration of any of Tāraṇ Svāmī's disciples, and even the painting of imaginative reconstructions of Tāraṇ Svāmī's life. The tall gateway is relatively recent, built after people started arriving at Nisaījī mostly by car and bus, via the round-about road from Bīnā and the nearby town of Āgāsaud. There is an older, simpler gateway facing the Betwa River about a mile away, dating from when pilgrims travelled from Bīnā and Āgāsaud by the direct route on bullock carts and crossed the river by ferry. By the Betwa are a set of recently built stone steps leading down the bank to the river. A small building built in 1945 covers a canopied stone seat on which Tāraṇ Svāmī sat in meditation. In the middle of the Betwa are the three small stone platforms that arose spontaneously in response to the attempts to drown him.[50]

Temples

The temples of the Panth are all called by the elevated Sanskritic term *caityālay*. From the outside they are not readily distinguishable from Terā Panth Digambar temples of Bundelkhand. This should not surprise us, for temples in India are often identifiable more by regional style than sectarian orientation.

The layout of a *caityālay* is fairly simple. The importance of sermons is indicated by the large open spaces within the temple. The emphasis on a more intellectual, less sensory style of religiosity is also indicated by the lack of much visual ornamentation in the temple. What ornamentation there is tends to be found on the altars, which are often of gilt marble, in a style reminiscent of a royal cenotaph (Figure 11.2). The symbolism in the ornamentation on the altars, however, is indicative of a generalized auspiciousness, and in no way betokens any specifically Tāraṇ Svāmī message. Thus one finds representations of figures such as guards, flywhisk-bearers, *svastika*s, full pots, elephants, and divine musicians. Many temples have three altars, symbolizing the three-fold focus in Digambar ritual on god, teacher, and religion (*dev*, *guru*, and *dharm*).

The most striking aspect of a Tāraṇ Panth *caityālay* is the obvious absence of any images. One story (R. Samaiyā 1989: 8) recounts that Tāraṇ Svāmī's father regularly performed image-worship in the temple, and asked the 11 year-old boy to perform it in his stead when he left town on a business trip. The boy took food to the temple to offer it to the image, and asked the image to eat it. Later, when he returned to the temple and saw that the food was uneaten, he assumed that the image wanted to bathe before eating, and so took the image to a nearby river and immersed it. The boy implored the image to re-emerge from the water, but it did not. He therefore decided that the image was not god, but just inert stone, and so left it in the river. From then on he engaged in meditation rather than image-worship.

This story is also told by Premī (1912–1913: 201–202); but in that version it led directly to his father, another merchant in the village, and a *kṣullak* plotting to kill the boy for his insult of the image.[51] Elsewhere Premī (ibid.: 295) tells a third version derived from the oral tradition of Bundelkhand opponents of the Tāraṇ Panth. When the father had the son perform worship in his stead, the boy ate the food that had been offered to the image. In Jain ritual ideology such food is *nirmālya*, "not to be eaten," and to do so is a karmically wrong action. The father expelled his son from his home. The boy replied that he saw no fault in eating such food, and as a result started his own religious path.

The story of Tāraṇ Svāmī's opponents attempting to drown him in the Betwa River is in some accounts also tied to his reputed iconoclasm. According to this telling, it was specifically his teaching that the worship of images was unnecessary, and even a sign of ignorance, that led to their attempts to kill him.

A reading of the texts credited to Tāraṇ Svāmī, however, does not find any clear denunciation of image-worship. The closest to this comes in his *Śrāvakācārā*, "Manual of Lay Conduct," verses 307–311. In the context of discussing the six standard lay rituals (*karma*),[52] Tāraṇ Svāmī says that only a person who has wrong faith worships a god in the temple. Such a person wanders in the suffering

Figure 11.2 Altar in the *caityālaya* in Sagar. Photograph by the author, December 10, 1999.

of infinite rebirth, and calls as "god" that which is not god:

> The layman (*śrāvaka*) who does not maintain the lay vows (*vrata*s) should practice the six rituals (*karma*s). The six rituals are twofold; they are seen as pure (*śuddha*) and impure (*aśuddha*).

> The faithful soul knows and always practices the pure six rituals. The unfaithful soul practices the impure six rituals. Of this there is no doubt.
>
> That which is impure (*aśuddha*) is called impure (*aśuci*). The impure leads to that which is impermanent. The pure [leads one] on the path to liberation, [whereas] the impure leads to a bad rebirth.
>
> He is called impure (*aśuddha*) who knows the god in the temple. He wanders in infinite places, and calls what is not god as "god."
>
> There is wrong faith (*mithyā*), illusion (*māyā*), and foolishness (*mūḍha dṛṣṭi*) in the person who worships as god that which is not god. Such a person is wholly involved in worldly affairs and worships with wrong faith.[53]

This is certainly not a sweeping critique of image worship. While this passage is understood to criticize image worship, it can equally well refer to other forms of spiritually ignorant religious practice. The *Śrāvakācāra* passage is no more explicitly iconoclastic than any of a number of passages in texts of the Digambar mystical tradition that emphasize the centrality of meditation and other mental practices over external rituals. For example, the Digambar poet Yogīndu writes in his *Yogasāra* (a text that has never, to the best of my knowledge, been interpreted as advocating iconoclasm), "O fool! God is not in the temple, nor in stone nor in plaster nor in pictures!"[54] Furthermore, there is a description in one of the *Ṭhikānesār* manuscripts of the fifty-two temples containing eternal bejewelled Jina images on the continent of Nandīśvara Dvīpa, where the gods come to worship the images during three annual eight-day festivals, a description that would appear to discount any ideological rejection of image worship.[55]

Rituals

The orthodox order of service (*paddhati*) in a Tāraṇ Panth temple was organized in the mid-twentieth century by Jaysāgar; informants told me that he compiled it from his study of earlier, otherwise unspecified texts. The basic temple rite itself is very simple. The person enters the temple, and first bows to the altar (*vedī*) as a form of homage to the scripture. On the altar rest copies of Tāraṇ Svāmī's texts, as well as other standard Digambar philosophical and mystical texts. Some people circumambulate the altar three times, and/or prostrate to it.

Standing in front of the altar, the person then recites three of Tāraṇ Svāmī's verses, known as *Tatva Pāṭh*, "Recitation of the Principles," or *Tatva Maṅgal*, "The Auspicious Principles." They are recited as a blessing (*maṅgalācaraṇ*), and consist of veneration of the true god, teacher, and religion (*dev, guru*, and *dharm*). The verses are taken from his *Mamala Pāhuḍa*, verses 1, 28, and 63. These are the first verses of three hymns in this collection, known as *Deva Dipta* ("Light of God"), *Guru Dipta* ("Light of the Teacher"), and *Dharma Dipta* ("Light of Dharma").[56]

> It is the verity consisting of joy and bliss,
> its innate nature is consciousness.

The supreme verity has attained the unchanging state
so I bow to that which has perfection as its innate nature.

The guru teaches about the hidden form (soul),
along with the hidden knowledge.
The monk is capable of saving (others) and saving (himself),
he wards off the world of rebirth.

The dharma enunciated by the Jina
is the meaning of the three meanings conjoined.[57]
Mind it, for it destroys the fears of faithful souls.
This is the pure knowledge of liberation.

This is followed by the signing of one or more hymns (*bhajan, stuti*).

If there is a sermon (*dharmopdeś*), then the assembled worshipers sit to listen to it. In many cases the sermon might be delivered by a local intellectual who is connected with the temple, known as *bhāījī* or *pāṇḍe*. On some occasions the temple managing committee will pay a *paṇḍit* from elsewhere to come and deliver a series of sermons. Such a visiting *paṇḍit* need not be a follower of Tāraṇ Svāmī himself, and the subject matter of the sermon is often drawn from the broader Digambar tradition. When I visited Sāgar, a visiting Terā Panth *paṇḍit* was delivering a series of sermons based on Tāraṇ Svāmī's *Paṇḍita Pūjā* and a standard textbook on Digambar philosophy edited by Kailāścandra Śāstrī entitled *Jain Siddhānt Praveśikā* ("Introduction to Jain Doctrine").

At the conclusion of the sermon, everyone stands and recites a hymn known as *Abalabalī* ("The Power of the Weak").[58] Some ritual manuals also recommend that the worshiper here recite the three *āśīrvād*s, "blessings," which I give later. The *Abalabalī* is also recited as a *maṅgalācaraṇ*. Jaysāgar wrote that the verses were recited everywhere in the Tāraṇ Panth at the end of sermons (*śāstra sabhā*), but that they were recited incorrectly because their meaning was obscure, and so he edited and translated the text (Jaysen 1939a: 19–20). The first five verses are attributed to Tāraṇ Svāmī, but, to the best of my knowledge, are not found in any of the fourteen texts. The next six verses are drawn from the *Darśana Pāhuḍa*, *Cāritra Pāhuḍa*, *Bodha Pāhuḍa*, and *Mokṣa Pāhuḍa*, texts attributed by the tradition to Kundakunda.[59] The twelfth verse is, according to Jaysāgar, verse 31 of the *Mamala Pāhuḍa*, but does not appear in Sītalprasād's edition. The final verse is from the *Rayaṇasāra*, another text attributed to Kundakunda.[60] The thirteen verses describe the nature of liberation.[61]

Hail to you Jina. Through your firm lotus-like speech you give power to the weak.
My mind is consciousness delighting in the happiness of pure pleasure.

Hail savior (of others) and saver (of oneself). Praise to your saving doctrine, knowledge and meditation.
The teacher whose conduct and actions are pure becomes the omniscient god.

Hail (to the one who has) pleasure, bliss, mental bliss, innate bliss, and supreme bliss.
Praise and homage to the Tīrthaṅkara who himself is pure as evidenced by his meditation.
Hail to the delighting lord, delighting in happiness, in whose lotus(-heart) is pure meditation.

Hail god who shines on your own, lord delighting in shining liberation.
Hail to you, Jina-god, savior, lord, who (experiences) infinite bliss from meditation.

Happiness, delight, pleasure arise. Hail to the god who gives liberation.

I will do homage to the excellent Jinas Ṛṣabha and Vardhamāna (Mahāvīra)
and concisely to the others in succession, and then I will speak the path of faith.

After venerating the supreme lords who are omniscient, all-seeing, undeluded, and have conquered all passions,
the faithful souls in the three worlds venerate the Arhats.

The stage on the path of the Jinas, who are unbound and have conquered passions,
is that of those whose conduct is pure due to its faith and knowledge, and are unshaken by their own or others' teachings.

In the context of human births he has five-senses, and in the context of the spiritual ladder he is on the fourteenth rung.
When he is conjoined with all these virtues, and is absorbed in the virtues, called an Arhat.

Homage homage to that god who has abandoned external matter
by whom karma has been worn away, and who has realized his own soul that consists of knowledge.

The form of the Jina consists of knowledge, is pure due to equanimity, and has thoroughly conquered passions.
He gives pure initiation and instruction because he has eliminated all karma.

The path to liberation, to salvation from rebirth,
consists of shedding the karma of rebirth, knowledge and discrimination of the essence of the triple world, and a yearning for the purity of one's innate nature.

The layman proclaims the virtues, vows, asceticism, equanimity, the stages, gifting,
filtering water, (avoiding) pointless actions,
faith, knowledge, conduct, and the fifty-three rites.

The ritual then concludes with the performance of *āratī*, or offering of a flame in honor of the scriptures. Those who wave the platters holding the candles[62] don a white cap. In some temples this is performed only by men, and in other temples by both men and women. There are two parts to the *āratī*, one that praises god, teacher, and scripture (*dev*, *guru*, and *śāstra*), and the other known as the *Tāraṇ*

Svāmī Āratī that praises Tāraṇ Svāmī himself. This latter hymn is in more or less standard modern Hindi, and so must be a fairly recent composition; the reference to Sūkhā also points to it being recent.[63]

> The lamp of Tāraṇ Svāmī,
> that does victory victory of the Jina's speech. (refrain)
>
> Hold the garland of right faith around the throat,
> and knowledge of the difference (between soul and body) in the heart.
> Fortunate is he who is on the path to liberation,
> who is going to that glorious auspiciousness.
>
> At Nisaī, Sūkhā and Semarkheṛī
> blow the sweet horn of god.
> Listen today o Lord to my petition
> that I bow to the Lordly Guru.
>
> These karmas surround me
> so remove my faults.
> Lord, now don't load me like a porter,
> listen to the petition of your creature.
>
> The lamp of the fourteen scriptures,
> that does victory victory victory of the liberated ones.
> Prince, shout "victory" of the saints,
> I bow to the one on the banks of the Betwa.
>
> I do your lamp, o Lord,
> that my soul become successful.
> The lamp of the five supreme lords,
> that does victory victory victory of the Jina's speech.
>
> Experience the essence of your own soul,
> the essence of victory in a human birth, o prince.
> Here I hold fast to the auspicious path,
> I bow to the feet of the Lordly Guru.

The basic elements of these rituals – ritual purity, *maṅgalācaraṇ*, hymns, sermons, *āratī*, circumambulation, sandalwood forehead marks – are common to most of the indigenous ritual cultures of South Asia. What distinguishes them from other Jain temple rituals is that the objects of worship are scriptures, and in particular the texts authored by Tāraṇ Svāmī, rather than Jina images. While some of the hymns are shared with the broader Digambar society, most of the hymns sung are specific to the Tāraṇ Svāmī community, and would be unknown to other Jains.

There is one other ritual that is unique to the Tāraṇ Svāmī Panth, and that is the marriage rite. According to most sources, this rite was devised by Tāraṇ Svāmī himself for the marriage of a devotee's daughter. Jaysāgar (1990: 45) said that this tradition, "of performing the ideal marriage rite," began in the household of a particular leading family of the community in Sāgar, and so it may be that the tradition was revived in the 1940s on the basis of a textual reconstruction of the rite, perhaps by Jaysāgar himself.[64] I was given a detailed description of the rite by a recently married couple, and there are several written descriptions of it.[65] All of these show some variation, so it is evident that the rite differs according to regional and family custom. My description here is based on what I was told by the informants.

The rite is held in a hall, not in the main shrine room of a temple. One or more lamps are established on a table, on which copies of Tāraṇ Svāmī texts are also ceremoniously displayed. The couple, dressed as a prince and princess,[66] take *darśan* of the texts, and then sit facing each other. Everyone present reads the *Tatva Pāṭha*. Then a *paṇḍit* recites the entirety of the thirty-two-verse *Mālārohaṇa*, the text Tāraṇ Svāmī is said to have composed for his devotee's daughter's wedding. After each verse those present shout "*jay namostu*" and throw yellow rice on the couple as a blessing, while a gong or drum is beaten. After the recitation, the couple marks each others' hands with turmeric paste. The *paṇḍit* then reads the first of three blessings (*āśīrvāda*). The bride stands and applies a turmeric mark on the forehead of the seated groom. The *paṇḍit* reads the second blessing. The groom stands and applies a turmeric mark on the forehead of the seated bride. After the *paṇḍit* reads the third blessing the groom puts a flower garland around the bride's neck to signify the completion of the rite, which takes about thirty minutes in total.[67]

The three blessings are also verses by Tāraṇ Svāmī. While they are not found in any of the fourteen texts, they overlap extensively many of the verses in the *Mamala Pāhuḍa*.[68]

> Oṃ once it has arisen, enjoy that shining one made of faith.
> Enjoy that beneficial sun, it is the efficacious word.
> It arises both endlessly enjoyable and pure, it is firm.
> God's speech has arisen, so hail hail to it, hail to the arising of liberation.
>
> The two are separate. In an instant the unequalled rays lift it up. Hail to the good teaching.
> For just a mere moment, for one hour, and then two hours,
> three hours and then four hours the rays shine, the essence of the Jina for a year.
> The dirt of time is dispatched for a year, for a life. Hail to the Jina shining in liberation.
>
> Don't desire either of the two; make the mind firm in *kāyotsarga*.
> See the Enlightened One's truth in the world, and see the harm done to five-sensed beings.
> The Jina's righteous path shines and saves. Let the lord save and give excellent liberation.
> God's speech from the beginning of the era arises and saves. Let it save the blessed congregation. Hail.

Rajneesh

Let me end this overview of Tāraṇ Svāmī and the contemporary path with a brief discussion of someone who is probably the most famous person ever born in the Tāraṇ Panth, the Indian and later international holy man known in his early career as Rajneesh (Rajnīś), and later as Osho (1931–1990). Most studies of him ignore his early years, or at best make a passing mention of his having been born a Jain. With the exception of one book on his talks, he intentionally refrained from discussing his early years (Devageet, in Rajneesh 1985b: n.p.). The "official biography" written by Vasant Joshi (1982: 9) made just a single reference that his family was Digambar Jain, and only in an endnote do we find a paragraph discussing that his family in fact belonged to the Tāraṇ Panth. There the author wrote,

> Taran Swami opposed the idol worship widely prevalent among Digambar Jains and preached the worship of the formless. He criticized the emphasis the Digambar Jains placed on materialism and exhorted them to turn toward the spirituality taught by Mahavir. Taran Swami was put to a lot of trouble and harrassment by the society for his views.
>
> (Ibid.: 189–190, n. 1)

Rajneesh was raised and schooled in the small town of Gadarwara (Gāḍarvāṛā) in Narsimhapur district in Bundelkhand.[69] He went to Jabalpur for college, studying for two years at Hitkarini College before having to transfer to D. N. Jain College, from which he received his B.A. in philosophy. He then went to Sāgar, where he received an M.A. in philosophy in 1957 from Saugar University (now Dr Harisingh Gaur University). His first teaching position was at the Sanskrit College in Raipur, and from 1960 until he resigned in 1966 he was professor of philosophy at Jabalpur University.

His intellectual interests took him far afield from Jainism at a young age, but in his early years as a professional holy man he still retained a tenuous connection to the tradition.[70] He led his first meditation camp June 4–8, 1964, at the remote Śvetāmbar Jain pilgrimage shrine of Muchālā Mahāvīr near Ghanerao (Ghāṇerāv) in southern Rajasthan.[71] But how far he had already moved from traditional Jainism is seen in that at this camp he taught Buddhist Vipassana meditation, Hindu Nadabrahma meditation, and Muslim Sufi Dervish whirling, and in the published version of his discourses at this camp he is as likely to cite Chuang Tzu and Meister Eckhart as Mahāvīra (Rajneesh 1966). In September 1969 at a camp in Kashmir he delivered a series of sermons on Jainism, which were then edited into a volume by Dayānand Bhārgava, the distinguished scholar of Jainism, with the title *Mahāvīra: Mere Dṛṣṭi Meṃ* ("My Vision of Mahāvīra"). The book was published by the respected Indological publishing house of Motilal

Banarsidass. Here again we see how far Rajneesh had come from traditional Jainism, as Bhārgava in his editor's introduction wrote,

> [Among the] three central points in Rajneesh's teachings . . . is that his teachings are not moral (*naitik*), but are trans-moral (*atinaitik*). This is the essential teaching of the Jain scriptures, in which bad (*pāp*) and good (*puṇya*) are understood to be merely chains of iron and gold.
>
> (Rajnīś 1971: 9)

While it is standard Jain teaching that both *puṇya* and *pāpa*, good karma and bad karma, must be overcome to attain liberation, it is not the case that the distinction between the two is to be ignored by all Jains. Jainism is not antinomian. A key difference between the laity and mendicants lies precisely in the fact that the latter strive to overcome all forms of karmic bondage, while lay ethics are built upon the careful discrimination between the two kinds of karma.

To the best of my knowledge, the last time Rajneesh operated within a traditional Jain orbit was in 1973, when from August 25 through September 11 he delivered a series of lectures in Bombay on the occasion of Paryuṣaṇ. These were published in 1976 as Volume 3 of *Mahāvīra Vāṇī* (the earlier two volumes were also based on Paryuṣaṇ lectures in Bombay). By then he was using Jainism as a prop for his own eclectic teachings, much of which went against fundamental Jain spiritual and ethical principles. Sometime thereafter he broke more completely with his Jain roots, so that by 1985 he wrote of a childhood encounter with a Digambar monk whom he termed an "imbecile" and "just a dirty puddle, not an ocean of bliss or peace" (1985b: 94, 102). Later in this same collection he characterized Jainism as "very stupid" and Jains as "idiots" (ibid.: 610, 611).

He began one collection of his lectures on Mahāvīra by stating explicitly, "I am not a follower (*anuyāyī*) of Mahāvīra, I am a supporter (*premī*) of him, just as I am of Christ, Krishna, Buddha, and Lao Tzu; and in my opinion, a follower never develops the understanding that an imitator does" (Rajnīś 1974: 1). The editor of this same volume stated boldly concerning Rajneesh's unique interpretation of Mahāvīra,

> This is the first time in world history that he has presented the full weight of the meaning of Mahāvīra's message that was Mahāvīra's own intention. By his yogic power and the merit earned by asceticism and spiritual practice in birth after birth Bhagvān Śrī Rajnīś has been able to visit Mahāvīra himself, to reveal his meaning, and having become just like Mahāvīra to publicize the preachings of Mahāvīra.
>
> (Svāmī Ānand Vītrāg [Dr Rāmcandra Prasād] at Rajnīś 1974: i)

This claim was confirmed by one Jain who heard Rajneesh preach on Mahāvīra in late 1960s. He told me that he had asked Rajneesh the basis for the novel ideas he was attributing to Mahāvīra, ideas not found in any Jain text. Rajneesh told him that he met Mahāvīra in his meditations, and heard these teachings directly from him.

In the mid-1950s, when he was studying for his M.A. at Saugar University, Rajneesh had fairly extensive contacts with the Tāraṇ Panth in Sāgar. Two small Hindi pamphlets by Rajneesh on Tāraṇ Svāmī were published, one by a Tāraṇ Panth woman of Sāgar (Rajnīś n.d.), the other by the Tāraṇ Panth itself (Rajnīś 1956). In them we can see very clearly the beginnings of Rajneesh's own eclectic spiritual teachings. The teachings in these essays are very much those of Rajneesh, and very little those of Tāraṇ Svāmī (although one can probably say that about all interpretations of the oftentimes obscure and cryptic writings of this medieval mystic).

Joshi (1982: 190, n. 1) wrote of Rajneesh's Tāraṇ Panth background, "It is said that Bhagwan [Rajneesh] read his works as a child and may have been inspired by his teachings." A cursory reading of the mystical emphasis of Tāraṇ Svāmī on the realization of the innate purity of one's own soul in comparison to Rajneesh's iconoclastic and eclectic spirituality might at first seem to lend credence to such a suggestion, but I think that it is an interpretation that does not hold up under closer scrutiny. Certainly Rajneesh makes no mention of Tāraṇ Svāmī in any of his discourses on Jainism that I have seen, even in his 1985 volume of reminiscences of his childhood. His only extended discussions of Tāraṇ Svāmī are in the two small pamphlets published in Sāgar early in his spiritual career.

Rajneesh wrote of Tāraṇ Svāmī that he taught an inner spirituality. Tāraṇ Svāmī taught "the rule of god is within you" and "the real worship of god is the worship of the soul" (ibid.: 8). He wrote that Tāraṇ Svāmī was opposed to external rituals, and instead taught that true religion is the realization of the soul within. Rajneesh wrote that there were three phrases that were central to Tāraṇ Svāmī's teachings: *ātmā-jñān* (knowledge of the soul), *ātmā-jñān*, and *ātmā-jñān* (ibid.: 10).

Rajneesh placed Tāraṇ Svāmī squarely within the Sant tradition of medieval Indian religion, equating him explicitly with the Sants and the Bauls of Bengal (ibid.: 4), and specific medieval figures including Kabīr, Raidās, Senānāī, Rāmdās, Pīpājī, Ramādās, Dhannā, Nānak, Dādū, and Amardās (ibid.: 2). In a catholicism typical of Rajneesh, he added to this catalogue of saints the Sufis of Iran (ibid.: 4) and Śekh Farīd (ibid.: 2). He further described Tāraṇ Svāmī as a "revolutionary," who strove to wake up the contemporary sleeping society to the spiritual truth (ibid.: 2). In this interpretation Rajneesh was following in the footsteps of other interpreters, as we saw above. But in Rajneesh's case this was part of a larger agenda of advocating a "perennial philosophy" approach to religion,[72] for he also compared Tāraṇ Svāmī to Jesus Christ (ibid.: 8, quoting Jesus, "The kingdom of God is within you"), Saint Augustine (ibid.: 8, quoting him as saying, "Wander throughout the world, but if you want to find the truth, then you have to return to yourself"), and Socrates (1956: 11, quoting him as saying as he drank the hemlock, "I will live on in all of you"). He stated this explicitly when he wrote

> [Tāraṇ Svāmī] was asked time and again, "What is religion (*dharm*)? Where is it? What is the essence of religion? What is God, and what is

> the path to attain him?" In his answer he repeated those words that the saints have always repeated in age after age and place after place. One is amazed to see that the message of the saints is the same. It is obvious that the realization of religion is independent of time or place. It is clear that if there is religion, it is one and eternal. Its expression may differ according to language, but whoever meditates on this will see at once that the meaning is the same. Sant Tāraṇ Taraṇ explained the essence of religion that is expressed in the doctrines at the root of all religions. He said, "Religion is the attainment of your innate self."
>
> (Ibid.: 6)

Just before this passage, Rajneesh (ibid.: 6) explained that as part of this focus on inner spiritual realization, Tāraṇ Svāmī rejected all traditional forms of religion, and even said that religion (*dharm*) and tradition (*sampradāy*) do not provide any valid guidance. The message of Tāraṇ Svāmī was intended to liberate religion from tradition. When one sees the later teachings of Rajneesh, one can see why he wanted to interpret Tāraṇ Svāmī in this way. But it is not in my opinion a defensible interpretation of Tāraṇ Svāmī. A reading of his texts, especially the *Jñāna Samuccaya Sāra*, *Tribhaṅgī Sāra*, *Upadeśa Śuddha Sāra*, and *Śrāvakācāra* – the texts that together constitute Tāraṇ Svāmī's "essential teachings" (*sāra mata*) and his "teachings on conduct" (*ācāra mata*) – shows that Tāraṇ Svāmī remained very much within the mainstream of Digambar doctrine. He downplayed certain ritual forms, especially the cult of temples and images, but in this he is not significantly different from many other orthodox Digambar authors. To claim that he tried to free the Digambar community from its tradition cannot be supported by these texts.

It is not clear that Rajneesh actually read much of Tāraṇ Svāmī's texts. The only ones to which he referred in his two early pamphlets are *Paṇḍita Pūjā* and *Kamala Battīsī*. But he did not engage in any detailed exposition of these texts, and his references were all rather unspecific ones to "Tāraṇ Svāmī's teachings." He seems to have started with the person of Tāraṇ Svāmī and his reputation as a mystic who eschewed exterior image-directed rituals in favor of inner spiritual realization, and then, as Rajneesh was later to do with texts and figures from nearly all the world's religious traditions, interpreted Tāraṇ Svāmī as supporting his own unique and syncretic new religion.

This is confirmed by his brief reference to Tāraṇ Svāmī's *Sunna Svabhāva* and *Siddha Svabhāva* in discourses at his ashram in Kacch in the early 1970s. Of the former he said, "It is just a few pages, but of tremendous significance. Each sentence contains scriptures, but very difficult to understand" (Rajneesh 1985a: 206). He went on to explain that he understood the text due to his upbringing in a Tāraṇ Panth family, as a result of which he understood Tāraṇ Svāmī "not intellectually but existentially" (ibid.: 207). The *Sunna Svabhāva*, he said, had just a single message: "Awake!" (ibid.: 209). The message of the *Siddha Svabhāva*, he averred, is equally simple: "Be empty!" (ibid.). These two texts, Rajneesh concluded, contain the whole message of Tāraṇ Svāmī: "One shows you who you are – pure emptiness; the second, how you can reach it: by becoming aware" (ibid.).

We can see in his two very early pamphlets, as well as his later comments in public talks, the distinctive traits that would later help make Rajneesh one of the most famous religious figures of the late twentieth century. But we do not find in them much if anything that is helpful in understanding either Tāraṇ Svāmī or the community that has followed him for five centuries.

The study of Jains in history and society

At the outset of this essay I said that one of the most important aspects of the recent renaissance in Jain studies has been the close attention paid to historical, social and geographical differences among Jain communities. This is part of a broader shift in emphasis from the study of "Jainism" as a decontextualized and timeless doctrine, to the study of the Jains – people who have lived concrete lives in dialogue with their inherited cumulative traditions, dialogues informed deeply by the specifics of place, time and people.[73]

A focus on "Jainism" tends to emphasize the doctrinal continuities across time and place, and views differences – usually characterized as "schisms" – as problematic eruptions into the otherwise pacific flow of Jain history. A focus on "Jains" reveals that the Jains have expressed themselves religiously (as well as in other fields) in countless ways. It reveals "Jainism" to be a historically rich and variegated family of traditions that have been engaged in internal and external dialogues for over two millennia.

This essay on Tāraṇ Svāmī and the Tāraṇ Svāmī Panth serves as an introduction – and it is only that, an introduction – to a distinctive voice and a distinctive social expression within the broader Jain tradition. We see in Tāraṇ Svāmī himself a unique mystic and charismatic teacher, who synthesized the Digambar traditions available to him in fifteenth- and sixteenth-century Bundelkhand, and presented them in a way that earned him an extensive following. His followers included both Jains and non-Jains, and shows us how porous boundaries of religious identity were in medieval India. His followers included members of merchant castes, the traditional followers of Jainism in medieval times, but also members of other castes, alerting us to the need to see those instances when the teachings and practice of Jainism have drawn into the Jain fold people from the full array of social backgrounds. In the life and community of Tāraṇ Svāmī we see much that is familiar from other studies of the Jains; but we also find Muslims, boatmen, and jugglers. Many of his teachings enunciate themes found in all Jain writings; but these are then socially and ritually expressed in distinctive ways. The Jain presence almost everywhere has been physically marked by numerous temples; only in the Tāraṇ Svāmī Panth do we find Jain temples devoid of images, and instead having scriptures as the focus of worship on the altars.

This essay has raised as many questions about the life of Tāraṇ Svāmī, and the history and practices of his Panth, as it has answered. We are in need of more thorough studies of the texts attributed to Tāraṇ Svāmī. Documentation of both the extant manuscript collections and the architectural history of the Tāraṇ Panth *caityālay*s would tell us much that we do not know about the history and practices of the Panth (and in this we are hampered by the broader absence of historical and anthropological studies of the Jains of central India). This essay, therefore, serves as both an introduction to Tāraṇ Svāmī and his followers, and an invitation to much needed further scholarship. It is also presented as a model of the sort of studies of Jains that are needed to advance our understanding of the Jains – and therefore of "Jainism" – as people located in specific times and places.

Acknowledgments

An earlier version of this paper was delivered as the Third Annual Jain Lecture at the School of Oriental and African Studies, University of London, on March 14, 2002. I thank Peter Flügel for inviting me to deliver the lecture. Research in Bundelkhand was conducted under the auspices of a Senior Short-Term Fellowship from the American Institute of Indian Studies. I thank Seth Dalchandji Jain for his generous hospitality in Sagar. In addition to Dalchandji, the following were all most helpful in aiding my understanding of Tāraṇ Svāmī and the Tāraṇ Panth: Kapoorchand Samaiya "Bhayji," Dinesh K. Jain, Sudhir Jain "Sahayogi," Singhai Jnanchand Jain, Brahmacharini Usha Jain, and Sushil Jain. Any faults in interpretation are mine, of course. I thank Paul Dundas, and the audience of the 2002 SOAS talk, for their comments and questions; Manish Modi for obtaining for me a copy of his grandfather Nāthūrām Premī's 1912–1913 article; and Peter Flügel for obtaining copies of several books in the collection of the India Office Library.

Notes

* I usually give the Hindi transliteration of Indic terms, unless the word is directly from the Sanskrit, as this more accurately conveys the vernacular Hindi nature of Tāraṇ Svāmī and the Tāraṇ Panth. I give full transliterations of towns and villages in Bundelkhand, but give standard English spellings for districts, states, and rivers. All translations from Sanskrit, Prakrit, Hindi, Gujarati, and Tāraṇ Svāmī's idiosyncratic language are mine, unless otherwise noted.

1 This same point was made forcefully in a 1978 paper by the late Kendall W. Folkert, "The *Gaccha* and Jain History" (Folkert 1993: 153–166).

2 A beginning is found in Cort (2001b). Also needed is a clearer understanding of the cultural, social, and ritual differences among the Digambars within each of these regions.

3 On the Bīs Panth and the Terā Panth see Cort (2002). On Kānjī Svāmī see Dundas (2002: 265–271) and R. K. Jain (1999: 100–117). On Rājcandra see Dundas (2002: 262–265), and Salter (2001) and (2003).

4 I have also discussed Tāraṇ Svāmī and the Panth in Cort (2001a) and (2001c).

5 *saṃvata pandraha sau bahattara varṣa jeṭha vadī chaṭhakī rātri sātaē̃ śanivāra dina jina tāraṇa taraṇa śarīra chūṭo. Chadmastha Vāṇī* 10.18. I have used the reading by

Phūlcandra (1985b: 397) in preference to that of Jaysāgar, *Chadmastha Vāṇī*, p. 36. Some authors are of the opinion that this reference to his death means that the *Chadmastha Vāṇī* is not by Tāraṇ Svāmī; see Āyurvedācārya (1978: 5), S. Jain (1984: 101–102). K. Samaiyā (1977: 25–26) reports that this was also the opinion of Sītalprasād and Kānjī Svāmī.

6 The correspondence between the two dates for his death works out if the calendar in use in Bundelkhand at that time used the *pūrṇimānta* system, in which the months start and end with the full moon. The dates for his birth do not quite correspond, as Agahan bright seventh was Tuesday, December 3, 1448, whereas Phūlcandra says his birth occurred on Thursday. For these equivalences I have used Michio Yano's on-line *panchanga* site, which uses the Sūryasiddhānta calendrical system: http://www.kyoto-su.ac.jp/~yanom. I thank Gary Tubb for referring me to this site.

7 Premī (1912–1913: 293) gives his father's name as Guḍhā Sāhu.

8 *Chadmastha Vāṇī* 1.15–28 (p. 2): *unaīsa sai taitīsa varṣa dina rayana sai tīna utpanna sahajādi mukti bheṣa utpanna. mithyā vilī varṣa gyāraha. samaya mithyā vilī varṣa daśa. prakṛti mithyā vilī varṣa nau. māyā vilī varṣa sāta. mithyā vilī varṣa sāta. nidāna vilā varṣa sāta. ājñā utpanna varṣa do. vedaka utpanna varṣa do. uvaśama utpanna varṣa tīna. kṣāyika utpanna varṣa do. evaṃ utpanna varṣa nau. utpanna bheṣa uvasagga sahanam. saṃvata pandrahasau bahattara gatatilakaṃ.*

Phūlcandra (1985b: 398) gives a variant reading of the last two sayings, joined into one: *utpanna meṣa uvasagga sahana varṣa chaha māsa pañca dasa pandraha sau bahattara gata tilaka.*

9 See Phūlcandra (1992: 83–92) on the Canderī *bhaṭṭārak* seat and its connection with the Parvār caste.

10 Some sources say that Śrutakīrti was his teacher; see S. Jain (1984: 29).

11 The importance of this third obstacle that he overcame becomes clear when one considers the many oral tales mentioned further, from both inside and outside the Tāraṇ Panth, of Tāraṇ Svāmī gaining most of his converts through a variety of magical acts.

12 There are also female lay celibates (*brahmacāriṇī*); I do not know how old this institution is.

13 Premī spelled his name "Tāran," as did Sītalprasād in his early editions of texts; all other sources have spelled it "Tāraṇ."

14 There have also been more imaginative reconstructions of Tāraṇ Svāmī's life. Jaysāgar (1990: 6–7) wrote that since about 300 *maṇḍala*s or circles of followers are mentioned in Tāraṇ Svāmī's *Nāma Mālā*, of which 121 were large *maṇdala*s, Tāraṇ Svāmī must have been a *maṇḍalācārya*. This title was used for *bhaṭṭāraka*s, and so it is highly unlikely that it was used for Tāraṇ Svāmī. Jaysāgar also wrote that he had 1,100,000 direct followers, and that a further 4,200,000 had accepted his teachings.

The contemporary Tāraṇ Panth renouncer Brahmacārī Jñānānand has been working on a biography of Tāraṇ Svāmī entitled *Tāraṇ Jīvan Jyoti* ("Light on the Life of Tāraṇ"). There was a public dispute concerning Jñānanānd's narrative, which his critics said came largely from his own imagination, and so was not in accord with tradition (or, in the words of one critic, it was "99% wrong"). Due to this public pressure, the publication of the book was stopped as of 1999. Jñānānand has also been criticized for using the title "Svāmī" for himself in his publications, since this is seen as denoting the status of a monk, whereas he is still technically a householder according to orthodox Digambar understanding.

Brahmacārī Basant, who is a collaborator of Jñānānand, wrote that Tāraṇ Svāmī was a *maṇḍalācārya* who controlled 151 *maṇḍala*s. In addition, under Tāraṇ Svāmī there were 7 *sādhu*s (Hemanandi, Candragupta, Samantabhadra, Citragupta, Samādhigupta, Jayakīrti, and Bhuvananda), 35 *āryikā*s, 231 *brahmacāriṇī*s, 60 *brahmacārī*s, and hundreds of thousands of laity, for a total of 4,345,331 followers (Basant 1999b: 5–6).

Another mid-twentieth century biography, published in 1941 by Kālūrām Jain of Semarkheṛī, is based on Premī's article, contemporary oral tradition, and an anonymous hand-written manuscript. (It is unclear if this is the same manuscript which Premī used.) Kālūrām is refreshing for his frank recognition of the lack of adequate prior research, and he concludes his brief biography with an extended discussion of those aspects of Tāraṇ Svāmī's life and the subsequent development of the Panth that were (and sixty years later still are) in need of further research.

15 Dundas (2002: 107–110), Johnson (2000: 30–45). Scholars have estimated the dates of Kundakunda to have been as early as the second century CE and as late as the eight century (Dundas 2002: 107).

16 Information on Sītalprasād comes from his own brief biographical statement written in 1915, as well as Agravāl (1972), R. Samaiyā (1989: 16–17), and S. Jain (1984: 39–40).

17 On Varṇī, see R. Jain (1999: 50–82), as well as his own very engaging 1949 autobiography.

18 I heard the story of Sītalprasād's work on Tāraṇ Svāmī's texts from several informants in Sāgar; more specific details are found in J. Jain (1948: 35), K. Samaiyā (1977: 5), Gulābcand (1978), R. Samaiyā (1989: 16–17), R. Samaiyā (1993), and Ḍ. Jain (1992).

19 Jaysāgar (1901–1992) was one of the most important Tāraṇ Panth authors and activists of the twentieth century. He was born as Kisanlāl, son of Jhanaklāl, in 1901 in Seoni (Sivnī). He studied in Sāgar, where leaders of the Tāraṇ Samāj honored him with the title (*tilak*) of *paṇḍit* at the age of fifteen. He married at age twenty-one. He became active in the community from 1931 as Paṇḍit Jaykumār, starting magazines and propagating the observance of Tāraṇ Jayantī. In 1938, at the annual fair at Nisaījī, he initiated himself as a *kṣullak* with the name of Jaysen. Three or four years later he became Brahmacārī Jaysāgar. In 1940 and 1941 he was at the center of a dispute concerning the appropriateness of image-worship, in which he debated both with local members of the Terā Panth in Gañj Bāsaudā, and in print with Paṇḍit Lāl Bahādur Śāstrī of the Ambālā-based Śāstrārth Saṅgh; he claimed he was totally victorious in this dispute. He wrote many books and pamphlets, and was responsible for organizing the present form of the regular Tāraṇ Panth temple ritual. He died in Sāgar in 1992. Information on him comes from R. Samaiyā (1989: 19), Jaysāgar (1990: 42–46), Jaysāgar (1991: 5–9), and Jaysāgar (2000: 13).

20 My only reference for this volume is B. Jain (1985: 92).

21 Information on Phūlcandra is from N. Jain (1985).

22 I have seen only volume 3 of the series, published in 1989.

23 Amṛtlāl is not unique in invoking Martin Luther as a predecessor for social reform – although he obviously knew few details about Luther, since he described him as living in England. Various Sthānakvāsī authors have also invoked Luther as an iconoclastic reformer against a corrupt and ritualistic religious hierarchy, much as Mahatma Gandhi credited Luther with Germany's freedom (Wolpert 2001: 68).

24 For example, the scholar Vidyādhar Johrāpurkar (1964a) wrote a short essay in which he critiqued image worship as contravening the teachings of Mahāvīra on *ahiṃsā*. A local Jaipur organization called the Jain Culture Protection Committee (Jain Saṃskṛti Saṃrakṣak Samiti) in the 1980s published several pamphlets (one of them by the Tāraṇ Svāmī poet Amṛtlāl "Cañcal") that strongly criticized most of the cult of images, with titles such as "The Distortions that Pervade Jain Image Worship" (Seṭhī 1981) and "Distortions in the Six Essential Duties and the Making of Images" (Polyākā 1982). These are by no means unique within contemporary Terā Panth discourse on images.

25 There is another possible explanation for the de-emphasis of image-worhip in the Panth, although the evidence here is also slender. We know from the sparse sources on Tāraṇ Svāmī's life that he attracted many followers from lower non-Jain castes. Nāthūrām Premī has hypothesized that the Tāraṇ Panth castes were considered as *vaiśya* or merchant castes when they became followers of Tāraṇ Svāmī and therefore

Jain, on the cultural logic that all Jains in north and central India are automatically *vaiśya*. But, he notes, the Tāraṇ Panth castes were in many ways ranked socially lower than the Parvārs, the dominant Digambar caste of Bundelkhand. Up until the mid-twentieth century many lower Digambar castes, termed *dassā* ("ten") in distinction to the higher *bīsā* ("twenty") castes, were denied full access to Digambar temples (Mukhtār 1963, Nyāytīrth 1935, Sangave 1980: 325). The lack of images in Tāraṇ Panth temples may simply be a result of a lower caste status. I should hasten to add, however, that I have not heard this argument advanced by any Jains, either of the Tāraṇ Panth or other sects.

26 A version related by Premī (1912–1913: 201–203), on the basis of a Tāraṇ Panth book, says that the culprits were Tāraṇ Svāmī's own father and a local semi-renouncer (*kṣullak*). Kālūrām Jain (1941: 8–9) combines versions, and attributes blame for the attempted drowning and later attempted poisoning to a cabal of Tāraṇ Svāmī's father, his maternal uncle, and a semi-renouncer (*yati*).

27 Singh (1998: 879) reports that one caste among Tāraṇ Svāmī's followers practiced cross-cousin marriage until 1930. Since Tāraṇ Svāmī had taken a vow of celibacy, it is possible that the story of the antagonism on the part of his mother's brother – the man whose daughter he could be expected to marry under a cross-cousin marriage system – reflects a social tension over the marriage system.

28 It is also related by Premī 1912–1913: 96.

29 Delamaine then goes on to say that Tāraṇ Svāmī evidently derived his critique of images from Islam.

30 This story bears obvious comparison with that of the death of Kabīr; see Vaudeville (1993: 39–65). Premī (1912–1913: 296–297) also tells this story.

31 *Vyantar dev*s are unliberated Jain deities who are usually connected with specific locations of which they are guardians.

32 A variant of this narrative is also found at Basant (1999c: 153). According to the account given by Premī (1912–1913: 205), Tāraṇ Svāmī's chief disciples, including the Muslim Ruiyā Ramaṇ, will be reborn as Padmanābha's chief disciples (*gaṇadhara*).

33 See Dundas (2002: 269–270) for a discussion of the traditional hagiography of Kundakunda, according to which he gained his knowledge by attending the preaching assembly of the contemporary Jina Sīmandhara, who resides on the continent of Mahāvideha. Dundas also discusses the use of Kundakunda by the controversial twentieth-century neo-Digambar Kānjī Svāmī. We thus see that Kundakunda becomes a complex symbol employed in various ways in Digambar contexts to assert a near-omniscient orthodoxy.

34 On Digambar *śrāvakācāra* teachings, see Hīrālāl (1976–1979) and Williams (1963).

35 Fuller discussions of these texts are found at K. Samaiyā (1977: 17–27), Sītalprasād (1992: 15–16), and S. Jain (1984: 53–103). Phūlcandra (1985b: 387–396) also gives a detailed discussion of the three thirty-two-verse texts.

36 Other discussions of the language of Tāraṇ Svāmī's texts are Sītalprasād (1992: 11), and S. Jain (1984: 210–237). The latter author gives a lengthy discussion of Sanskrit, Prakrit, Apabhramsa, and vernacular (*deśī*) words, cases and verb forms found in his writings.

37 Premī, writing in the early twentieth century, was even harsher in his estimation of the Tāraṇ Panth intellectual tradition. He said,

> There is very little learning (*vidyā*) among the followers of the Tāran Panth. You won't find even a single Tāran Panthī who knows logic, grammar, or *dharma-śāstra*! There is not a single *paṇḍit* among them. There are some who can say what the essence of their teachings (*mat*) is and what is written in their texts. The same condition of religious learning is found in their secular learning. It is lacking. You won't find a single B.A. or M.A. in this Panth. Thus one can see that learning has been banished from the Tāraṇ Panth.
>
> (Premī 1912–1913: 303)

This is obviously one of the points in his essay to which members of the Panth strenuously objected, and from my experience is no longer an accurate assessment.

38 S. Jain (1984: 32–33); Jaysāgar introduction to *Nāma Mālā*, p. 4.

39 "Tāran Taran was born. He had five male disciples. Praiseworthy Ruiyā Jin; three female disciples." *utpannapada tāranatarana. tasya utpanna suva pāñca. anmoya ruiyājina suvanī tīna. Nāma Mālā*, pp. 6–7. In his Hindi expansion on these three sayings, Jaysāgar lists Ruiyā Jin – whose name is found in the third saying – as one of the five disciples referred to in the second saying.

40 R. Samaiyā (1989: 13); Jaysāgar (1991: 14).

41 Most scholarship on the intersection between Jainism and caste has looked at the various *baniyā* and *vāṇiyā* castes of Rajasthan and Gujarat that claim their origins in present-day Rajasthan. There has been almost no research on the merchant castes of central India.

42 On the Samaiyā see Russell and Hira Lal 1916:I: 142–143, 158; and Singh 1998: 3116–3117. One informant, who is himself a learned student of Kundakunda, had a novel etymology for the name of this caste: people in it were fond of reading Kundakunda's texts, especially his *Samayasāra*, and so were known for their constant talking of *samaya* ("doctrine"), as a result of which others applied the name "Samaiyā" to them.

On the Dosakhe, see Singh (1998: 878–879). The name indicates that traditionally marriage alliances were avoided with only two branches (*sakhā*), those of the father and mother's brother. Other groups within the Parvār caste avoided either four (Causakhe) or eight (Aṭhsakhe) branches. This would seem to indicate a hierarchical ranking in terms of purity of marriage practice, with the Dosakhe being at the bottom of the hierarchy. Singh (1998: 879) also says that until 1930 the caste practiced cross-cousin marriage, a form common in southern India but considered impure in the north.

The Parvārs are Terā Panth Digambars. On this caste, see Russell and Hira Lal (1916:I: 157–601); Singh 1998: 2792–2794; Phūlcandra *et al.* (1992) and Porvāl (1991: 234–238).

43 On the Gulālāre see Singh (1998: 1041–1043). This caste is also known as the Golapūrab, Golapūrva, Golahre, and Gollālāre; see Singh (1998: 1030–1031, 1041–1043). The majority of the caste is Terā Panth Digambar.

44 On the Aseṭhi (also spelled Asahaṭhī, Asāti, Asāthi) see Russell and Hira Lal (1916:I: 142) and Singh (1998: 131–132). Singh (1998: 131) writes that this caste was originally from a village near Ayodhyā, and later shifted to the area around Ṭīkamgaṛh, from which it subsequently migrated throughout Bundelkhand. Some members of this caste have been followers of Tāraṇ Svāmī since at least the early seventeenth century. Sītalprasād in his introduction to his edition of the *Mamala Pāhuḍa* (p. 9) said that one of the manuscripts he used was copied in 1624 in an Asahaṭī temple.

45 On the Ayodhyāvāsī (also spelled Ajudhiabāsī, Audhiā) caste, see Russell and Hira Lal (1916:I: 140–142).

46 On the Cārnagars, see Russell and Hira Lal (1916:I: 142–143) and Singh (1998: 646–647). According to Singh (1998: 646), members of the caste derive its name from *cāritra* ("conduct") plus *nagar* ("ahead"). It also seems to have been in a hierarchically inferior position in relation to the Parvār caste, as Russell and Hira Lal (1916:I: 143, 158) say that the Parvārs accepted daughters from the Cārṇagars, but the reverse did not hold true. Russell and Hira Lal write that the Cārṇagars also were originally Parvārs. Phūlcandra (1985a: 355, 1992: 72) is also of this opinion, based on the fact that the *gotra*s (clans) of the two castes are identical. Jaysāgar (1991: 34), on the other hand, writes that this caste was converted from the Vaiṣṇav Gahoī caste. On the latter, see Russell and Hira Lal (1916:I: 145–146).

47 Information on these sites comes from Jaysāgar (1990: 19–22) and (1991: 13–14), and R. Samaiyā (1989: 10–13).

48 The word *nisaī* is found only in Jain contexts. According to A. N. Upadhye (1982: 393) it comes from the Prakrit *ṇisīhiyā* or *ṇisīdhiyā*, from which a false Sanskritization of *niṣidhikā* or *niṣiddhikā* was derived. It originally referred to a place outside a city where a monk practiced austerities. The term then was extended to refer to other platforms in such a place, and finally to a memorial shrine at the site of the death of a monk where carved stone footprints (*padukā*) were consecrated. It is related to the word *nasiyāṃ*, which also refers to a memorial shrine for a monk. See also Hīrālāl Śāstrī (1967) and Polyākā (1990).

49 See also Jaysāgar (1990: 20–22).

50 K. Jain (1941: 9) wrote that the tallest of the three platforms held an old memorial structure (*smārak cabūtrā*), which is often renovated. I did not get close enough to any of the platforms to see if there is still such a structure.

51 K. Jain (1941: 8–9) follows Premī, but adds that the other merchant was Tāraṇ Svāmī's mother's brother.

52 See Williams (1963: 185) on the six *karma*s.

53
avrataṃ śrāvakaṃ yena ṣaṭakarmaṃ pratipālae
ṣaṭakarmaṃ duvidhaścaiva śuddha aśuddha paśyate.
śuddha ṣaṭkarma jānīte bhavyajīva rato sadā
aśuddhaṃ ṣaṭakarmaṃ rata abhavya jīva na saṃśayaḥ.
aśuddhaṃ aśucim proktaṃ aśuddhaṃ aśāśvataṃ kṛtaṃ
śuddhaṃ muktimārgasya aśuddhaṃ durgati bhājanaṃ.
aśuddhaṃ proktaścaiva devali devaṃpi jānate
kṣetra ananta hiṇḍante adevaṃ devȧ ucyate.
mithyā māyā mūḍhadṛṣṭī ca adevaṃ deva mānate
prapañcaṃ yena kṛtaṃ sārddhaṃ mānyate mithyādṛṣṭitaṃ.
Śrāvakācāra 307–311

54 Yogīndu, *Yogasāra* 44, as translated by Hardy (1995: 534). Dates for Yogīndu range from the sixth to the ninth centuries CE (Johnson 2000: 38 n. 28).

55 S. Jain (1984: 186), citing Jaysāgar (1980); I have not seen this latter source.

56 The original text, as given in Jaysen (1939a: 15–17) and Sītalprasād's edition of the *Mamala Pāhuḍa*, reads as follows. Other printings of the three verses are K. Samaiyā (1998: 8), *Ārādhnā* (1995: 10), and Basant (1999a: 11); I have not indicated variant readings from these.
Jaysen:

tatvaṃ ca nanda ānanda maü ceyānanda sahāva
parama tatva pada vindamaya namiyo siddha sahāva.

guru uvaesiu gupta rui gupata nyāna sahakāra
tāraṇa taraṇa samartha munī bhava saṃsāra nivāra.

dharma ju oto jinavarahiṃ artha ti artha saṃjoya
bhaya vināsa bhavya ju muṇahu mamala nyāna paraloya.

Sītalprasād:

tattvaṃ nanda ānanda maü ceyānanda sahāü
parama tattva pada vinda paü namiyo siddha sahāü.

guru uvaesiu gupata rui gupata jñāna sahakāra
tārana tarana samartha muni bhava saṃsāra nivāra.

dhamma ju utto jina varaha arthati athaha joya
bhaya vināsa bhava jū munahu mamala jñāna paraloya.

57 Sītalprasād translates this line as "The dharma which the Jina enunciates after seeing the aims in their actual form through the absolute perspective" (*jinendra bhagvānne niścay se yathārth rūp meṃ padārthoṃ ko dekhkar jo dharm kahā hai*), while Jaysen translates it as "The three conjoined ends – right faith, knowledge and conduct – enunciated by the Jina after he has seen them" (*jo jinendra dev ke dvārā prayojan bhūt samyakdarśan, jñān, cāritra, in tīn arth saṃyukt kahā gayā hai*).

58 Premī (1912–1913: 302) refers to this as *Avalavānī*. In its present form it appears to have been drawn from Tāraṇ Svāmī's writings by Jaysāgar.

59 Walther Schubring (1957) has adjudged these texts to have been composed by a later author.

60 According to Baṅsīdhar Śāstrī (1977), this is also by a later author.

61 Text from Jaysen (1939a: 1–11), with alternate readings from Campālāl (1951: 56) indicated in parentheses. Campālāl gives only the first five verses, so it is quite possible that the recitation of the final eight verses was an innovation by Jaysāgar. Other printings are K. Samaiyā (1998: 16–17) and *Ārādhnā* (1995: 64–65).

> *jaya abalabalī uvana kamala vayana jina dhuva* (C: *dhruva) tere*
> *anmoya śuddhaṃ rañja ramaṇa ceta re maṇa mere.*
>
> *jaya tara taraṇa samaya tāraṇa nyāna dhyāna vivande*
> *āyaraṇa caraṇa śuddhaṃ sarvanya deva guru pāye.*
> (C: *jaya taraṇa tāraṇa samaya jñāna dhyāna'bhi vande*
> *āyaraṇa jñānācaraṇa śuddhaṃ sarvanya deva guru pāye.*)
>
> *jaya nandā ānanda ceyānanda sahaja paramānande*
> *paramāṇa* (C: *pramāṇa) dhyāna svayaṃ vimala tīrthaṅkara nāma vande.*
>
> *jaya kalana kamala uvana ramaṇa rañja ramaṇa rāye*
> *jaya deva dīpati svayaṃ dīpati mukati ramaṇi rāye.*
> (C: *jaya deva dīpti svayaṃ dīpti mukti ramaṇa pāye.*)
>
> *jaya* (C: *guru) tohi dhyāvata sukha ananta svāmī tāraṇa jinadevā*
> *utpanna rañja ramaṇa nanda jaya mukati* (C: *mukti*) *dāyaka devā.*
> *kāūṇa ṇamukkāraṃ jiṇavaravasahassa vaḍḍhamāṇassa*
> *daṃsaṇamaggaṃ vocchāmi jahākamaṃ samāseṇa.*
> *(Darśana Pāhuḍa 1)*
>
> *savvaṇhū savvadaṃsī ṇimmohā vīyarāya parameṭṭhī*
> *vandittu tijagavaṇdā arahantā bhavvajīvehiṃ.*
> *(Cāritra Pāhuḍa 1)*
>
> *saparā jaṅgamadehā daṃsaṇaṇāṇeṇa suddhacaraṇāṇaṃ*
> *ṇiggāntha vīyarāyā jiṇamagge erisā paḍimā.*
> *(Bodha Pāhuḍa 10)*
>
> *maṇuyabhave pañcindiya jīvaṭṭhāṇesu hoi caüdasse*
> *ede guṇagaṇajutto guṇamārūḍho havaha araho.*
> *(Bodha Pāhuḍa 36)*
>
> *ṇāṇamayaṃ appāṇaṃ uvaladdhaṃ jeṇa jhaḍiyakammeṇa*
> *caiuṇa ya paradavvaṃ ṇamo ṇamo tassa devassa.*
> *(Mokṣa Pāhuḍa 1)*
>
> *jiṇavimbaṃ ṇāṇamayaṃ sañjamasuddhaṃ suvīyarāyaṃ ca*
> *jaṃ dei dikkhasikkhā kammakkhayakāraṇesuddhā.*
> *(Bodha Pāhuḍa 16)*

saṃsagga kamma khipaṇaṃ sāraṃ tīloya nyāna vinyānaṃ
ruciyaṃ mamalasahāvaṃ saṃsāre taraṇa muttigamaṇaṃ ca.
(Mamala Pāhuḍa 31)

guṇa vaya tava sama paḍimā dāṇaṃ jalagālaṇaṃ aṇatthamiyaṃ
daṃsaṇa ṇāṇa carittaṃ kiriyā tevaṇṇa sāvayā bhaṇiyaṃ.
(Rayaṇasāra 149)

62 In every performance of *āratī* I observed candles were used, rather than the wicks in clarified butter one usually finds in Jain and Hindu temples.

63 I give only the *Tāraṇ Svāmī Āratī* here. Text in Samaiyā (1998: 19–20), and *Ārādhnā* (1996: 66).

āratī tāraṇ svāmī kī ki jay jay jinvāṇī kī (refrain).

gale meṃ samakit kī mālā hṛday meṃ bhed-jñān pālā
dhanya vah mokṣ-panth vālā ki mahimāmay śivgāmī kī.

nisaī sūkhā semarkheṛī bajāveṃ dev madhur bherī
suno prabhu vinay āj merī ki śrī gurudev namāmī kī.

mujhe in karmoṃ ne gherā asātā dūr karo merā
lagānā ab na prabhu berā vinay sun apne prāṇī kī.

āratī caudah granthoṃ kī ki jay jay jay nirgranthoṃ kī
kuṅvar jay bolo santoṃ kī betvā tīr namāmī kī.

āratī karhūṃ nāth tumhārī ātmā saphal hoy hamarī
āratī pañc parameṣṭhī kī ki jay jay jay jinvāṇī kī.

sār nij ātam anubhav kā sār jay kuṅvar so narbhav kā
yahī partīt dharuṃ śubh rīt caraṇ guru dev namāmī kī.

64 On the other hand, Premī's (1912–1913: 302) description of the wedding rite, which he said he had not actually seen, but was on the basis of what members of the Tāraṇ Panth told him, is very similar to what I was told. This would indicate that the rite predates Jaysāgar. Premī said that in place of the seven circumambulations of a fire as performed by Parvārs in Bundelkhand, the groom places a garland around the bride's throat while the *Mālārohaṇa* is recited.

65 R. Samaiyā (1989: 33); Jaysagar (1991: 15–16); *Ārādhnā* (1995: 166–167); K. Samaiyā (1998: 130–131).

66 My informant said that as part of the royal costume, there are cardamom pods on each spike of the crowns. Two of the written sources describe the couple exchanging cardamoms at a later part of the rite. The significance of cardamoms eludes me.

67 Several sources, both interviewees and pamphlets, say that the couple exchange garlands.

68 The text is as given in *Ārādhnā* (1995: 62) and K. Samaiyā (1998: 105–106). See also Jaysen (1939b) and Campālāl (1951: 104–106). While the translation of any of Tāraṇ Svāmī's writings is frought with difficulty, my translation of these three verses is even more tentative.

oṃ uvana uva su ramaṇaṃ dīptam ca dṛṣṭī mayam
hiyayāraṃ taṃ arka vinda ramaṇaṃ śabdaṃ ca prāyojitam
sahayāraṃ sahi nanta ramaṇa mamalaṃ uvavanna sāhaṃ dhruvam
suyaṃ deva uvavanna jaya jayaṃ ca jayanaṃ uvavannaṃ mukte jayam.

jugayaṃ khaṇḍa sudhāra rayaṇa anuvaṃ nimiṣaṃ su samayaṃ jayam
ghaṭayaṃ tujja muhūrta pahara paharaṃ dutiya paharaṃ trīya paharam
catru paharaṃ dipta rayaṇī varṣa svabhāvaṃ jinam

varṣa khipati su āyu kāla kalano jina dipte mukte jayam.

ve do chaṇḍa virakta citta diḍhiyo kāyotsargāmino
kevalino nṛta loya loya pekha pikhaṇaṃ dalayaṃ ca pañcendriṇo
dharmo mārga prakāśino jina tāraṇa taro muktaivaraṃ svāmino
suyaṃ deva juga ādi tāraṇa taro uvavannaṃ śrī saṅgha jayam.

The written sources all follow these three verses with the following standard Jain blessing, although none of my sources indicate that it is recited in the wedding rite:

sarvamaṅgalamāṅgalyaṃ sarvakalyāṇakārakam
pradhānaṃ sarvadharmāṇāṃ jainaṃ jayatu śāsanam.

It is the holiness of all holies, the cause of all welfare,
the foremost of all religions: may Jainism be victorious.

69 All biographical information is from Joshi (1982). See also Urban (1996) for a more recent scholarly study of Rajneesh and his movement.

70 That his early publications were in Hindi, as were the lectures on which they were based, indicates that this was also before Rajneesh had become firmly entrenched in the English-language guru circuit.

71 These lectures were published in Rajneesh (1966). On this Śvetāmbar shrine, which since about 1960 has been under the control of the Āṇandjī Kalyāṇjī trust of Ahmedabad, see *Tīrth Darśan* (1980: 209) and Desāī (1986: 199–200).

72 This is also the title of a 1981 collection of his discourses on the Greek philosopher Pythagoras.

73 My use of the term "cumulative tradition" is obviously a nod to Wilfred Cantwell Smith (1964), and his argument for deconstructing "religion" as an overly reified concept in the study of religion.

Bibliography

Primary sources

Ārādhnā. Itarsi: Śrī Digambar Jain Tāraṇ Samāj Saṅgaṭhan Sabhā, 1995. First published 1972.

Aṣṭapāhuḍa of Kundakunda. With *Ṭīkā* of Śrutasāgara. Hindi translation by Pt. Pannālāl Sāhityācārya. Sonagiri: Bhāratvarṣīya Anekānt Vidvat Pariṣad, 1989.

Bṛhad Tīn Battīsī of Jina Tāraṇa Taraṇa. [*Paṇḍita Pūjā, Mālārohaṇa, Kamala Battīsī*]. Edited with Hindi *Ṭīkā* by Brahmacārī Śītalprasād. Sagar: Śrī Tāraṇ Taraṇ Caityālay Ṭrasṭ Kameṭī, 1978.

Chadmastha Vāṇī of Tāraṇa Tāraṇa. Edited with Hindī *Ṭīkā* by Brahmacārī Jaysāgar. Co-edited by Rājendra Suman. Sagar: Bhagvāndās Śobhālāl Pāramārthik Ṭrasṭ, 1991.

Grantha Ratna Traya of Tāraṇa Taraṇa. [*Khātikā Viśeṣa, Siddha Subhāva, Sunna Subhāva*]. Edited and translated by Brahmacārī Jaysāgar. Sagar: Pāramārthik Ṭrasṭ, 1991.

Jñāna Samuccaya Sāra of Tāraṇa Svāmī. Edited by Brahmacārī Gulābcand, with Hindi translation by Amṛtlāl "Cañcal." Two volumes. Sagar: Śrī Indrānī Bahū Bhogābāī Kastūrbāī Samaiyā Ṭrasṭ, 1974.

——. *Nyāna Samuccaya Sāra* of Jina Tāraṇa Tāraṇa Svāmī. Edited with Hindi translation by Brahmacārī Sītalprasād. 1933. Reprint Sagar: Śrī Digambar Jain Tāraṇ Taraṇ Caityūlay Ṭrasṭ Kameṭī, 1996.

Kamala Battīsī of Jina Tāraṇa Taraṇa Svāmī. With Hindi *Adhyātma Kamal Ṭīkā* by Svāmī Jñānānand. Edited by Brahmacārī Basant. Bina: Tāraṇ Taraṇ Jain Dhārmik Ṭrasṭ, 1999.

Mālārohaṇa of Tāraṇa Taraṇa. Edited by Brahmacārī Sītalprasād, with Hindi *Vistār* by Buddhilāl Śrāvak and Hīrālāl Negī. Sagar: Śrīmān Mathurāprasād Samaiyā Bajāj, and Surat: Jain Vijay Printing Press, 1930.

Mamala Pāhuḍa of Tāraṇa Taraṇa Svāmī. Edited with Hindi *Ṭīkā* by Brahmacārī Śītalprasād. Three volumes. 1937–1939. Reprint in one volume, Nisaiji: Śrī Tāraṇ Taraṇ Jain Tirth Kṣetra Nisaījī Ṭrasṭ, 1993.

Nāma Mālā of Tāraṇa Taraṇa. Edited by Brahmacārī Jaysāgar. Co-edited by Rājendra Suman. Sagar: Bhagvāndās Śobhālāl Pāramārthik Ṭrasṭ, 1991.

Paṇḍita Pūjā of Tāraṇa Taraṇa. Edited by Brahmacārī Śītalprasād, with Hindi *Vistār* by Buddhilāl Śrāvak and Hīrālāl Negī. Sagar: Śrīmān Mathurāprasād Samaiyā Bajāj, and Surat: Jain Vijay Printing Press, 1930.

Tāraṇa Taraṇa Śrāvakācāra of Tāraṇa Svāmī. Edited with Hindi *Ṭīkā* by Brahmacārī Sītalprasād. 1932. Reprint Sagar: Śrī Dev Tāraṇ Taraṇ Digambar Jain Caityālay Ṭrasṭ Kameṭī, 1992.

Tāraṇa Trivenī of Tāraṇa Taraṇa Svāmī. [*Paṇḍita Pūjā, Mālārohaṇa, Kamala Battīsī*]. Hindi translation by Amṛtlāl "Cañcal." 1940. Reprint Malhargarh: Śrī Tāraṇ Taraṇ Jain Tīrth Kṣetra Nisaījī Ṭrasṭ, 1974 (third printing).

Tribhaṅgī Sāra and *Cauvīsa Ṭhāṇā Ṭīkā* of Tāraṇa Taraṇa Svāmī. Edited with Hindi *Ṭīkā* by Brahmacārī Śītalprasād. 1937. Reprint Sagar: Śrī Digambar Jain Anāthīlay Ṭrasṭ, 1993.

Upadeśa Śuddha Sāra of Tāraṇa Taraṇa Svāmī. Edited with Hindi *Ṭīkā* by Brahmacārī Sītalprasād. 1936. Reprint Sagar: Śrī Indrānī Bahū Bhogābāī Kastūrbāī Samaiyā Ṭrasṭ, 1991 (second printing).

Secondary sources

Agravāl, Pannālāl Jain. 1972. "Bra. Śītalprasād aur unkī Sāhitya Sādhnā." *Anekānt* 25, 22: 83–87.

Amṛtlāl "Cancal." 1957. *Sant Tāraṇ: Ek Paricay*. Sagar: Tāraṇ Jayantī Samāroh Samiti.

Āyurvedācārya, Dr Kapūrcand. 1978. "Āmukh" to *Bṛhad Tīn Battīsī* of Jina Tāraṇa Taraṇa, 1–8. Sagar: Śrī Tāraṇ Taraṇ Caityālay Ṭrasṭ Kameṭī.

Bajpai, K. D. 1975. "Monuments and sculptures AD 1300 to 1800: Central India." *Jaina Art and Architecture*, Volume II. Ed. A. Ghosh, 349–354. New Delhi: Bharatiya Jnanpith.

Baṅsīdhar, Śāstrī. 1977. "Rayaṇasāra ke Racayitā Kaun?" *Anekānt* 30, 2: 54–60.

Basant, Brahmacārī. 1999a. *Adhyātma Ārādhnā: Dev Guru Śāstra Pūjā*. Bhopal: Tāraṇ Taraṇ Śrī Saṅgh, 1990 (fifth printing).

——. 1999b. "Bhārat Bhramaṇ Samīkṣā." In *Kamala Battīsī* of Jina Tāraṇa Taraṇa Svāmī, 145–157. Bina: Tāraṇ Taraṇ Jain Dhārmik Ṭrasṭ.

——. 1999c. "Sampādakīya," in *Kamala Battīsī* of Jina Tāraṇa Taraṇa Svāmī, 5–12. Bina: Tāraṇ Taraṇ Jain Dhārmik Ṭrasṭ.

Bhārgava, Dayānand. 1971. "Sampādakīya" to Rajnīś, *Mahāvīra: Merī Dṛṣṭi Meṃ*, 7–12. Delhi: Motīlāl Banārsīdās.

Bhārill, Hukamcand. 1985. *Gāgar meṃ Sāgar*. Sagar: Śrī Digambar Jain Tāraṇ Taraṇ Samāj.

Buddhisāgarsūri, Ācārya. 1917. *Gacchmat Prabandh, Saṅgh Pragati, tathā Jain Gitā*. Bombay: Śrī Adhyātma Jñān Prasārak Maṇḍal.

Campālāl, Pt. (ed.). 1951. *Tāraṇ Taraṇ Nitya Pāṭh*. Sagar: Śrīmān Samāj Bhūṣaṇ Seṭh Bhagvāndās Śobhālājī.

Cort, John E. 2001a. "The Hardest-To-See Image Is No Image At All: The Digambar Aniconism of the Taraṇ Swami Panth." Paper presented at American Council for Southern Asian Art Symposium X, Baltimore, MD.

——. 2001b. "The Jina as King." *Vasantagauravam: Essays in Honour of Professor M. D. Vasantha Raj of Mysore, on the Occasion of his Seventy-fifth Birthday*. Ed. Jayandra Soni, 27–50. Bombay: Vakils, Feffer and Simons.

——. 2001c. "Pilgrimage to Nisaiji: Vande Shri Guru Taranam: researching the Jains in Central India." *Dak: The Newsletter of the American Institute of Indian Studies* 5: 4–10.

——. 2002. "A Tale of Two Cities: On The Origins of Digambar Sectarianism in North India." *Multiple Histories: Culture and Society in the Study of Rajasthan*. Eds Lawrence A. Babb, Varsha Joshi, and Michael W. Meister, 39–83. Jaipur: Rawat.

Delamaine, Major James. 1827. "On the Sráwacs or Jains." *Transactions of the Royal Asiatic Society of Great Britain and Ireland* 1, 413–438.

Desāī, Ratilāl Dīpcand. 1986. *Śeṭh Āṇandjī Kalyāṇjīnī Peḍhīno Itihās*, Vol. 2. Ahmedabad: Śeṭh Āṇandjī Kalyāṇjī.

Dundas, Paul. 2002. *The Jains*. London: Routledge (second revised edition).

Flügel, Peter. 2000. "Protestantische und Post-Protestantische Jaina-Reformbewegungen. Zur Geschichte und Organisation der Sthānakavāsī I." *Berliner Indologische Studien* 13/14, 37–103.

Folkert, Kendall W. 1993. *Scripture and Community: Collected Essays on the Jains*. Ed. John E. Cort. Atlanta: Scholars Press.

Glasenapp, Helmuth von. 1925. *Der Jainismus: Eine indische Erlösungsreligion*. Berlin: Alf Hägar.

Gulābcand, Brahmacārī. 1940. "Śrī Tāraṇ Svāmī kā Jīvan Darśan." *Tāraṇa Trivenī* of Tāraṇa Taraṇa Svāmī, 6–15. Reprint Malhargarh: Śrī Tāraṇ Taraṇ Jain Tīrth Kṣetra Nisaījī Ṭrasṭ, 1974 (third printing).

——. 1978. "Dharmdivākar Śrī Śitalprasādjī ke Prati Ābhar Pradarśan." *Bṛhad Tīn Battīsī* of Jina Tāraṇa Taraṇa, 30–31. Sagar: Śrī Tāraṇ Taraṇ Caityālay Ṭrasṭ Kameṭī.

Hardy, Friedhelm. 1995. *The Religious Culture of India: Power, Love and Wisdom*. Cambridge: Cambridge University Press.

Hīrālāl, Śāstrī. 1967. "Nisīhiyā yā Naśiyāṃ." *Bābū Choṭelāl Jain Smṛti Granth*. Eds Pt. Cainsukhdās Nyāytīrth *et al.*, Hindi section, 393–399. Calcutta: Bābū Choṭelāl Jain Abhinandan Samiti.

Hīrālāl Siddhāntālaṅkar, Nyāytīrth (ed.). 1976–1979. *Śrāvakācāra Saṅgraha*. Five volumes. Sholapur: Jain Saṃskṛti Saṃrakṣak Saṅgh.

Jain, Bhagvāndās. 1985. "Samāj ke Gaurav." *Siddhāntācārya Paṇḍit Phūlcandra Śāstrī Abhinandan Granth*. Chief ed. Bābūlāl Jain Phāgull, 92–93. Varanasi: Siddhāntācārya Paṇḍit Phūlcandra Śāstrī Abhinandan Granth Prakāśan Samiti.

Jain, Campālāl. 1941. *Tāraṇ Panth Samarthan*, Vol. 1. Sohagpur: The author.

Jain, Ḍālcand. 1992. "Śubhkāmnā." *Tāraṇa Taraṇa Śrāvakācāra* of Tāraṇa Svāmī, n.p. Reprint Sagar: Śrī Dev Tāraṇ Taraṇ Digambar Jain Caityālay Ṭrasṭ Kameṭī.

Jain, Hīrālāl. 1962. *Bhāratīya Saṃskṛti meṃ Jain Dharm kā Yogdān*. Second printing 1975. Bhopal: Madhya Pradeś Śāsan Sāhitya Pariṣad.

Jaini, P. S. 1979. *The Jaina Path of Purification*. Berkeley, CA: University of California Press, 1979.

Jaini, Sāvitrī. 1984. "*Śrī Tāraṇ Svāmī: Vyaktitva evaṃ Kṛtitva.*" PhD thesis, Dr Harisingh Gaur University (Sagar).

Jain, Jñāncandra. 1948. "Tāraṇ Svāmī aur un ke Updeś." *Jain Siddhānt Bhāskar* 14, 2: 33–36.

Jain, Kālūrām. 1941. *Dharmprāṇ Tāraṇ Taraṇ, yā, Śrī Tāraṇ Taraṇ Maṇḍalācārya Mahārāj kā Saṅkṣipt Jīvan Caritra*. Ganj Basoda: Śrī Tāraṇ Taraṇ Sāhitya Pracārak Kāryālay.

Jain, Narendra Kumār. 1999. "Adhyātmavettā Śrī Tāraṇsvāmī." *Adhyātma Parv Patrikā* vol. 6, 6–7: 8–10.

Jain, Nīrjā. 1985. "Mere Pitājī." *Siddhāntācārya Paṇḍit Phūlcandra Śāstrī Abhinandan Granth*. Chief ed. Bābūlāl Jain Phāgull, 45–64. Varanasi: Siddhāntācārya Paṇḍit Phūlcandra Śāstrī Abhinandan Granth Prakāśan Samiti.

Jain, Ravindra K. 1999. *The Universe as Audience: Metaphor and Community Among the Jains of North India*. Shimla: Indian Institute of Advanced Study.

Jaysāgar, Brahmacārī. 1980. "Tāraṇ Sāhitya meṃ Akṛtrim Caityālayoṃ kā Varṇan." *Tāraṇ Jyoti* 3, 5: 5.

——. 1990. *Maṇḍalācārya*. Sagar: Sant Tāraṇ Taraṇ Samādhān Samiti.

——. 1991. *Tāraṇ Taraṇ Āmnāy kā Saṅkṣipt Paricay*. Sagar: Pāramārthik Ṭrasṭ.

——. 2000. *Śrī Tāraṇ Taraṇ Śabd Koṣ*. Ed. Rājendra Suman. Sagar: Akhil Bhāratīya Tāraṇ Samāj Tīrthkṣetra Mahāsabhā.

Jaysen, Kṣullak [= Brahmacārī Jaysāgar]. 1939a. *Abalabalī Jinendra Stavan aur Tatva kā Arth*. Hoshangabad: Śrī Digambar Jain Tāraṇ Samāj.

——. 1939b. *Tāraṇa Taraṇa Āśīravāda*. Rahatgarh: Śrīmān Dharmpremī Cunnīlāljī Pannālāljī Asahaṭhī.

——. 1939c. *Tāraṇa Taraṇa Dharmopadeś*. Hoshangabad: Śrī Digambar Jain Tāraṇ Samāj.

——. 1940. *Tāraṇ Śabd Koṣ*. Haidargarh Basoda: Śrīmān Seṭh Kundanlāl Hajārīlāljī.

Johnson, William J. 2000. "Knowledge and practice in the Jaina religious tradition." *Jain Doctrine and Practice: Academic Perspectives*. Ed. Joseph T. O'Connell, 18–49. Toronto: University of Toronto, Centre for South Asian Studies.

Johrāpurkar, Vidyādhar. 1964a. "Jain Dharm meṃ Mūrtipūjā." *Anekānt* 17, 4: 155–157.

——. 1964b. "Jain Saṅgh ke Chah Aṅg." *Anekānt* 17, 5: 231–232.

Joshi, Vasant. 1982. *The Awakened One: The Life and Work of Bhagwan Shree Rajneesh*. San Francisco: Harper & Row.

Kailāścandra, Śāstrī. 1948. *Jain Dharm*. Mathura: Bhāratvarṣīya Digamsarh. Jain Saṅgh, 1985 (eighth printing).

Kānjī Svāmī. 1965. *Dharmī Śrāvak kī Divyadṛṣṭi*. Ed. Brahmacārī Harilāl Jain. Sagar: Seṭh Bhagvāndās Śobhālāl Jain.

——. 1989. *Aṣṭ Pravacan*, Vol. 3. Collected by Brahmacārī Harilāl Jain. Hindi translation by Tārācand Samaiyā. Sagar: Bhagvāndās Śobhālāl Jain Pāramārthik Saṅsthān.

Lāl Bahādur, Śāstrī. 1941. *Mūrti Pūjā kī Upyogitā tathā Tāraṇ Samājiyoṃ ke Praśnoṃ kā Uttar*. Mathura: Bhāratvarṣīya Digambar Jain Saṅgh.

Mukhtār, Jugal Kiśor. 1963. "Jin Pūjā Mīmāṃsā." *Yugvīr Nibandhāvalī*, Vol. 1, 47–106. Delhi: Vīr Sevā Mandir.

Nizami, A. H. 1980. "Chanderī under Malwā Sultāns." *Siddhantacharya Pandit Kailashchandra Shastri Felicitation Volume*. Eds. Vaggesh Shastri *et al.*, 304–310. Rewa: Siddhantacharya Pandit Kailashchandra Shastri Felicitation Committee.

Nyāytīrth, Pt. Parameṣṭhīdās Jain. 1935. *Dassāoṃ kā Pūjādhikār*. Delhi: Lā. Jauhrīmal Jain Sarāf.

Phūlcandra, Śāstrī, Pt. 1978. "Upodghāt." *Bṛhad Tīn Battīsī* of Jina Tāraṇa Taraṇa, 65–95. Sagar: Śrī Tāraṇ Taraṇ Caityālay Ṭrasṭ Kameṭī, 1978.

——. 1985a. "Paurpāṭ (Parvār) Anvay." *Siddhāntācārya Paṇḍit Phūlcandra Śāstrī Abhinandan Granth*. Chief ed. Bābūlāl Jain Phāgull, 338–369. Varanasi: Siddhāntācārya Paṇḍit Phūlcandra Śāstrī Abhinandan Granth Prakāśan Samiti.

Phūlcandra, Śāstrī, Pt. 1985b. "Śrī Jin-Tāraṇ-Tāraṇ Svāmī aur unkī Kṛtiyāṃ" *Siddhāntācārya Paṇḍit Phūlcandra Śāstrī Abhinandan Granth*, 385–408. Originally "Prastāvnā" to Brahmacārī Sītalprasād (ed.), Tāraṇ Svāmī, Nyāna *Samuccaya Sāra*, 1933.

——. 1985c. "Atiśay Kṣetra Nisaījī." *Siddhāntācārya Paṇḍit Phūlcandra Śāstrī Abhinandan Granth*, 409–414.

——. 1985d. "Mūlsaṅgh Śuddhāmnāy kā Dūsrā Nām Terāpanth Hai." *Siddhāntācārya Paṇḍit Phūlcandra Śāstrī Abhinandan Granth*, 535–540.

—— (author and editor). 1992. *Parvār Jain Samāj kā Itihās*. Assisted by Devendrakumār Śāstrī and Kamleśkumār Jain. Jabalpur: Śrī Bhāratvarṣīya Digambar Jain Parvār Sabhā.

Polyākā, Pt. Bhaṅvarlāl. 1982. *Ṣaḍāvaśyakoṃ evaṃ Mūrti Nirmāṇ meṃ Vikṛtiyāṃ*. Jaipur: Jain Saṃskṛti Saṃrakṣak Samiti.

——. 1990. "Naśiyā: Ek Vivecan." *Jaypur Digambar Jain Mandir Paricay*. Chief ed. Anūpcand Nyāytīrth, 29–31. Jaipur: Śrī Digambar Jain Mandir Mahāsaṅgh.

Porvāl, Manoharlāl. 1991. *Porvāl Samāj kā Itihās*. Second edition. Javra: Porvāl Itihās Śodh Samiti.

Premī, Nāthūrām. 1912–1913. "Tāranpanth." *Jain Hitaiṣī* 8: 291–303, 549–558; 9: 33–38, 198–206, 532–539.

Rajnīś (Rajneesh). N.d. *Sant Tāraṇ Taraṇ: Jīvan aur Darśan*. Sagar: Sau. Śāntībāī Śobhālāl Jain.

——. 1956. *Sant Tāraṇ Taraṇ*. Sagar: Tāraṇ Taraṇ Samāj.

——. 1966. *Path of Self-Realization*. Delhi: Motilal Banarsidass. [Translation of *Sādhnā Path*.]

——. 1968. *Philosophy of Non-Violence*. Trans. Dayanand Bhargava. Delhi: Motilal Banarsidass.

——. 1971. *Mahāvīra: Merī Dṛṣṭi Meṃ*. Eds. Dayānand Bhārgava. Delhi: Motīlāl Banārsīdās.

——. 1972. *Mahāvīra Vāṇī*. Collected Mā Yog Lakmṣī. Eds Svāmī Kṛṣṇa Kabīr and Svāmī Yog Cinmay. Bombay: Jīvan Jāgṛti Āndolan Prakāśan.

——. 1974. *Mahāvīra: Paricay aur Vāṇī*. Ed. Svāmī Ānand Vītrāg. Delhi: Motīlāl Banārsīdās. Ācārya Rajnīś Pravacan Mālā 2.

——. 1976. *Mahāvīra Vāṇī*, Vol. 3. Collected Mā Dharmā Jyotī. Ed. Svāmī Ānand Harīś. Pune: Rajnīś Phauṇḍeśan.

——. 1981. *Philosophia Perennis*. Two volumes. Antelope: Rajneesh Foundation International.

——. 1985a. *Books I Have Loved*. Eds Sambuddha Swami Devaraj and Mahasattva Swami Devageet. Rajneeshpuram: Rajneesh Foundation International.

——. 1985b. *Glimpses of a Golden Childhood*. Eds. Sambuddha Swami Devaraj and Mahasattva Swami Devageet. Rajneesphuram: Rajneesh Foundation International.

Russell, R. V. and Rai Bahadur Hīra Lāl. 1916. *The Tribes and Castes of the Central Provinces of India*. Four volumes. London: Macmillan.

Salter, Emma. 2001. "Unity and Diversity amongst the Followers of Śrīmad Rājacandra." *Jinamañjari* 23, 1: 32–51.

——. 2003. "Raj Bhakta Marg: The Path of Devotion to Srimad Rajacandra, a Jain Community in the Twenty-First Century." PhD thesis, University of Cardiff.

Samaiyā, Kapūrcand, "Bhāyjī." 1977. *Solahvīṃ Śatābdī ke Jain Ādhyātmik Sant Śrī Jin Tāraṇ Taraṇ Svāmī: Vyaktitva aur Kṛtatva (San 1448–1515 Ī.)*. Sagar: Śrī Digambar Jain Tāraṇ Taraṇ Samāj.

——. 1990. *Dainik Pūjā evaṃ Mandir Vidhi*. Sagar: Sakal Tāraṇ Taraṇ Samāj, 1998 (third printing).

Samaiyā, Rādhelāl, "Tanmay." 1989. *Tāraṇ Panth Pradarśikā*. Sagar: The author.

——. 1993. "Āp kī Apnī Bāt." *Tribhaṅgī Sāra* and *Cauvīsa Ṭhāṇā Ṭīkā* of Tāraṇa Taraṇa Svāmī, 4–5. Sagar: Śrī Digambar Jain Anāthālay Ṭrasṭ, 1993.

Sangave, Vilas Adinath. 1980. *Jaina Community: A Social Survey*. Second revised edition Bombay: Popular Prakashan.

Schubring, Walther. 1957. "Kundakunda echt und unecht." *Zeitschrift der Deutschen Morgenländischen Gesellschaft* 107: 557–574.

Seṭhī, Birdhīlāl. 1981. *Jain Mūrti Pūjā meṃ Vyāpt Vikṛtiyāṃ*. Jaipur: Jain Saṃskṛti Saṃrakṣak Samiti.

Singh, K. S. (ed.) 1998. *India's Communities*. Three volumes. Delhi: Anthropological Survey of India and Oxford University Press.

Sītalprasād, Brahmacārī. 1915. "Hindī Ṭīkākār kā Paricay." *Samayasāra Ṭīkā*, 326. Reprint New Delhi: Śrīmatī Godāvarī Devī Jain Cairiṭebal Ṭrasṭ, 1998.

——. 1992. "Bhūmikā" to *Tāraṇ Taraṇ Śrāvakācāra* of Tāraṇa Svāmī, 11–18. Sagar: Śrī Dev Tāraṇ Taraṇ Digambar Jain Caityālay Ṭrasṭ Kameṭī, 1992.

Smith, Wilfred Cantwell. 1964. *The Meaning and End of Religion*. New York: Mentor.

Tīrth Darśan. 1980. Madras: Śrī Mahāvīr Jain Kalyāṇ Saṅgh.

Upadhye, A. N. 1982. "Nisidhi – it's [*sic*] meaning." *Memorial Stones: A Study of Their Origin, Significance and Variety*. Eds. S. Settar and Gunther D. Sontheimer, 45–46. Dharwad: Institute of Indian Art History, Karnataka University; and Heidelberg: South Asia Institute.

Urban, Hugh B. 1996. "Zorba the Buddha: capitalism, Charisma and the Cult of Bhagwan Shree Rajneesh." *Religion* 26, 161–182.

Varṇī, Kṣullak Gaṇeśprasād. 1949. *Merī Jīvan Gāthā*. Varanasi: Śrī Gaṇeś Varṇī Di. Jain Saṅsthān.

Vaudeville, Charlotte. 1993. *A Weaver Named Kabir: Selected Verses with a Detailed Biography and Historical Introduction*. Delhi: Oxford University Press.

Williams, R. 1963. *Jaina Yoga: A Survey of the Medieval Śrāvakācāras*. Oxford: Oxford University Press. Reprint Delhi: Motilal Banarsidass, 1983.

Wolpert, Stanley. 2001. *Gandhi's Passion: The Life and Legacy of Mahatma Gandhi*. New York: Oxford University Press.

12

DEMOGRAPHIC TRENDS IN JAINA MONASTICISM

Peter Flügel

The study of Jainism as a living religion is still hampered by a lack of reliable sociological and demographic information both on the Jain laity and Jain mendicants.[1] Most empirical studies to date have been thematically oriented or were of an exploratory nature. They were based on the methods advanced by the classical anthropological village studies or on small surveys of a non-representative nature.[2] In both cases, the units of investigation were defined in terms of observer categories[3] which were often created *ad hoc* in the field due to the advantages of snowball sampling under conditions of limited resources. In a paper read at the American Oriental Society Meeting in 1978, at a time when comprehensive field studies had yet to be conducted, the late Kendall Folkert (1993: 156) suggested avoiding the inevitable abstractions of 'general accounts of the Jains' by concentrating on 'the smaller divisions within the tradition' which 'have actually been the basic units of the tradition'. What Folkert had in mind was to study the individual 'schools, sects or orders' (*gaccha*) of the Jain mendicant tradition,[4] rather than 'Jain religious culture' in general.[5] Certainly, not all Jains coalesce around monastic groups, but the majority does so in one way or another.

The investigation of categories which are recognised by the Jains themselves promises indeed to yield testable results of greater accuracy and relevance for the Jain community itself. However, the research programme envisaged by Folkert has yet to be implemented.[6] Despite the pioneering studies of Vilas Sangave (1959/1980) on the social divisions of the Jain lay community and of Muni Uttam Kamal Jain (1975) on the pre-modern history of the religious divisions of the Jain mendicants, most students of Jainism, and indeed most Jains, have still no way of knowing how many independent mendicant orders exist today and how they are organised.[7] The aim of this chapter is to fill this gap and to provide a brief overview of the present schools, orders and sects[8] within both the Śvetāmbara- and the Digambara-denomination[9] and to bring together the available demographic data on the current Jain monastic traditions.

A comprehensive description of the Jain lay movements is beyond the scope of this chapter.

Jain laity

Although no studies of the demographic trends in Jain monasticism are currently available, general surveys of the Jain lay community have been produced on the basis of the available census data by Sangave (1959/1980), Sharma (1976) and M. K. Jain (1986). The inclusion of the category 'Jain'[10] into the questionnaire for the Census of India 1881[11] is widely regarded as one of the defining moments for the modern construction of Jainism as an independent 'religion'.[12] It was introduced by the colonial government after Jacobi (1879) proved the historical independence of Jainism from Buddhism, and a number of high court judgements in favour of westernised Jains such Paṇḍit Padmarāja (1886), J. L. Jaini (1916) and C. R. Jain (1926) who were interested in securing a privileged legal status for their community. However, notwithstanding the desire of the educated Jain elite to establish a clear-cut boundary between 'Jainism' and 'Hinduism', in the census itself many Jains continued to return themselves as 'Hindu'.

A number of explanations have been put forward for this. Amongst them 'enumerators' error' figures most prominently, since local volunteers frequently filled in the census forms themselves on the basis of their own local knowledge.[13] Another interpretation suggests that many respondents were either unable or unwilling to make a distinction between the categories. They may have followed the example of their ancestors who often, in the fear of persecution, maintained an outward conformity with Hinduism (cf. Williams 1983: xix). In other words, they were not so much confronted with the question of 'who they were' (Cohn 1992: 248), but rather how they preferred to be perceived.[14]

Reform orientated Jain intellectuals were highly conscious of the problem of communal self-objectification already by the 1870s, and in response to the low turnout of Jains in 1881 actively embraced the census as a medium of communal self-representation. At the turn of the twentieth century, the leaders of the newly founded Jain Conferences even designed petitions which actively encouraged community members to return themselves as 'Jain' and not as 'Hindu'. They also volunteered to carry out the census in their own communities in an attempt to boost the numbers and hence the importance of the Jain community in the eyes of the colonial government.[15] Demographic growth was generally depicted as a sign of communal progress and used as an argument in contexts of 'democratic' politics of representation.[16] This sentiment is still echoed today in the work of Vilas Sangave (1980) and other Jain intellectuals who lament the fact that, even after a century of communal revival, many Jains keep on regarding themselves and are regarded as Hindus,[17] which 'necessarily vitiates the census figures and obscures the increase or decrease of the Jaina population from census to census' (ibid.: 3).[18]

The debate on whether Jains are culturally 'Hindus' or a 'minority community' wages unabated within the community. Thus far, Jain communalists have failed to establish the Jains 'as a separate social group' (ibid.: 411) against the opposition of many Śvetāmbara *ācārya*s. The majority of the Jain laity retains an ambiguous social identity midway between the Jain mendicant communities and the wider 'Hindu' society. It is therefore not surprising that still no reliable demographic data is available for the Jain laity. Certainly, the Jain community is very small. The official figure generated by the Census of India 1991 was 3,352,706, that is, 0.4 per cent of the Indian population (Vijayanunni 1991: x–xi). The Census of 2001 produced the figure of 4,225,053, also 0.4 per cent of the Indian population (www. censusindia.net). In addition, about 150,000 Jains live outside India, but no mendicants. No data is available on the number of lay followers of particular Jain schools and sects, although some of these may be estimated on the basis of caste directories, in cases where caste and sect membership widely overlap.

Jain mendicants

The rhetoric of numbers, adopted by the Jain lay Conferences, also had a significant influence on the monastic orders, which were put under pressure to compete with each other not only in terms of behavioural purity and education, but also in terms of sheer numbers – in the name of democracy and modernisation.[19] The rhetoric of numbers is not necessarily new, but no documents containing information on the actual number of Jain monks and nuns are known before the early-modern period.

There are two exceptions. The Jinacaritra in the so-called Paryuṣaṇa Kalpa Sūtra, which was traditionally attributed to Bhadrabāhu I who is said to have lived *c.*170 or 162 years after Mahāvīra although the Jinacaritra is certainly much younger, tells us that Mahāvīra's four-fold community comprised of

> fourteen thousand Śramaṇas with Indrabhūti at their head; thirty-six thousand nuns with Candanā at their head; one hundred and fifty-nine thousand lay votaries with Saṅkhaṣataka at their head; three hundred and eighteen thousand female lay votaries with Sulasā and Revatī at their head.
>
> (Jinacaritra 136f., in Jacobi 1884: 267f.)

The Sthavirāvalī, or List of the Elders, which is generally attributed to Devarddhi Gaṇi, the fifth century CE redactor of the Śvetāmbara canon, mentions not 14,000, but merely 4,411 monks and gives no total figures for nuns and laity (Sthavirāvalī 1, in Jacobi 1884: 286f.). Both of these accounts, colltected in the same compilation, are somewhat mythical, but they clearly depict relatively small communities.[20] The first text pictures a very high proportion of mendicants (1–9.54 laity) and an overwhelming numerical dominance of female ascetics and lay supporters. The prevalence of nuns is all the more remarkable, because, until very recently, neither Buddhist nor Hindu monastic orders had significant, if any, numbers of female ascetics. Even today, Theravāda Buddhist orders in Sri Lanka, Thailand, Burma and Laos do not have fully initiated *bhikkunis*.[21] The second account contains a list of the succession after Mahāvīra, which is corroborated by epigraphical evidence.[22] It mentions only the names of 7 nuns amongst a total of 19 disciples of Nandanabhadra, the seventh elder (*thera*) after Mahāvīra.[23] The corresponding inscription of the first or second century CE, mentions 9 nuns, which Bühler (1890: 321) accepted as 'clear proof that in the first century of our own era the order of female ascetics was well established'.

At the beginning of the twentieth century most lay communities began to publish sporadic demographic information on the numbers of their monks and nuns in community newsletters. However, these newsletters had only a limited circulation. Readily available information on individual monastic communities remained largely inaccessible until the last two decades of the twentieth century, which saw a significant improvement. The person responsible for this is the Sthānakavāsī layman Bābūlāl 'Ujjavala' Jain of Mumbaī. Once an active member of the Akhil Bhāratīya Jain Mahāmaṇḍal, the principal ecumenical forum of the Jain communalists[24] founded in 1899 under the name Jain Young Men's Association but renamed in 1929, he began to compile and publish charts of the *cāturmāsa* residences of all the mendicants of the reformist Sthānakavāsī Śramaṇa Saṅgha from 1979 onwards. The rational was to generate a sense of unity and coordination amongst the followers of the Śramaṇa Saṅgha, which, although nominally governed by only one *ācārya*, is internally subdivided into many local mendicant traditions. The documentation proved to be useful in keeping track of the movements of the almost 1,000 mendicants, which from the time of the foundation of the Śramaṇa Saṅgha in 1952 began to extend their *vihāras* from their traditional strongholds in western and northern India to the entire territory of the new independent state of India.

In 1984, B. U. Jain produced an extended version of the *cāturmās* list, now covering not only the Śramaṇa Saṇgha, but all Sthānakavāsī ascetic and lay communities. In this he was supported by the Śramaṇa Saṅgha *muni* Kanhaiyālāl, the Mūrtipūjaka *paṅnyās* Haraṣ Sāgar, and the Akhil Bhāratiyā Samagra Jain Cāturmās Sūcī Prakāśan Pariṣad Bambaī. Finally, in 1986, the first annual Samagra Jain Cāturmāsi Sūcī was published with the intention of providing information on the *cāturmās* residencies of all Jain mendicants.[25] This project was officially endorsed by the great assembly of the Śramaṇa Saṅgha ascetics in Pune in 1987 (AISJC 1987: 19f., B. U. Jain 1987: 71). From this time onwards, the available demographic data of all Jain mendicant communities were published annually, first by the Cāturmās Sūcī Prakāśan Pariṣad 1986–1992, then by the Jain Ektā Mahāmaṇḍal, and last by B. U. Jain himself (SJCS 1987: 67f.).

The following overview of the current divisions of the Jain mendicants, their numbers and main demographic shifts between 1987 and 2002 is to a significant extent based on the data compiled in B. U. Jain's Cāturmās Sūcī publications of 1987, 1990, 1996, 1999 and 2002. For want of reliable information, I was not always able to shed light on earlier demographic developments. To my knowledge, only the Śvetāmbara Terā Panth has published complete demographic and biodata going back to the time of its foundation in 1760 (Navratnamal 1981ff.). I was able to locate some useful material on the numbers of Sthānakavāsī mendicants in the early twentieth century, but little on the Mūrtipūjaka and Digambara ascetics. In these instances I had to rely on sporadic information scattered in the secondary literature.

I have rearranged B. U. Jain's data on the Śvetāmbara mendicant orders into a number of tables summarising figures from 1987, 1990, and 1996, with additional information from 1999 and 2002 provided either in the text or in supplementary tables or footnotes. Initially, the figures published by B. U. Jain were not reliable for non-Sthānakavāsī orders, but this has changed with regard to the Śvetambara orders. An important lacuna in B. U. Jain's publications is the lack of reliable information on the Digambara ascetics, on which no sound data existed until recently. I have nevertheless cited some of B. U. Jain's fragmentary and inconsistent figures on the Digambaras between 1986 and 2000, because they contribute significantly to our generally meagre knowledge on the Digambara mendicants, whose organisational history is reviewed in greater detail in this chapter. From the year 2000 onwards, reliable information on the Digambara mendicants and *cāturmāsa* places is published annually by A. Jain (2000a, 2000b, 2001) of Indore in form of a brochure which together with D. Śāstrī's (1985) Digambara Jain Sādhu Paricay is the main source on the demography of the Digambara ascetics.

The figures in the available Jain publications rely on credible self-reporting by the different Jain orders. The quality of this data, especially from the Mūrtipūjaka traditions, varies from year to year. In order to compensate for this, B. U. Jain included personal estimates in his summary tables to account for those ascetics for whom no detailed information was supplied to him (B. U. Jain 1996: 37, 27f., n. 1–2, 1999: 382, n. 1–7). By contrast, I only counted those ascetics which were listed individually and not B. U. Jain's considerably higher estimates, which may nevertheless represent a more accurate picture. Another difference concerns the classification of mendicant orders into broader categories. From 1990, B. U. Jain re-classified certain reformist movements, such as Amar Muni's Vīrāyatan, Muni Suśīl Kumār's Arhat Saṅgha and the Nava Terā Panth, under the new category 'independently roaming progressive thinkers who use vehicles' (*pragatiśīl vicārak vāhan vihārī svatantra vicaraṇ karne vāle*). But I continued listing them together with their traditions of origin. A major deficit of the publications of B. U. Jain and A. Jain is the lack of statistical data on the social background of the ascetics, especially on caste, class and region, their initiation age and level of formal education. They also offer no overview of the history and organisation of the mendicant groups. As far as possible, I have supplemented this information from other sources.

In the following tables, the *ācārya*s are also included in the total numbers of *sādhu*s. A hyphen indicates that no information is available or means zero. The data is neither complete nor entirely consistent. But, in general, it is reliable and provides the most accurate available information to date.

Mūrtipūjaka

The Mūrtipūjaka mendicants are currently divided into six independent traditions, which emerged between the eleventh and the sixteenth century CE from the *caityavāsin*, or temple-dwelling, Śvetāmbara tradition:[26] (1) the Kharatara Gaccha (1023), (2) the A(ñ)cala Gaccha or Vidhi Pakṣa (1156), (3) the Āgamika- or Tristuti Gaccha (1193) and (4) the Tapā Gaccha (1228), from which (5) the Vimala Gaccha (1495), and (6) the Pārśvacandra Gaccha (1515) separated.[27] The two main reasons for these so-called *gaccha*-reforms were (a) the laxity of the *caityavāsin*s, and (b) minor doctrinal differences. Similar reforms within the *gaccha*s in the seventeenth century led to the division between *yati*s and *saṁvegī sādhu*s. The term *saṁvegī*, upright, was introduced by Upādhyāya Yaśo Vijay (1624–1688) for his own reformist mendicant group, whose tradition was revived in the nineteenth and early twentieth centuries, at a time when most of the previously dominant white-clad *yati*s were replaced by yellow-clad *saṁvegī sādhu*s. Today, almost all Mūrtipūjaka mendicant groups are *saṁvegī* orders. With the exception of the Vallabhasūri Samudāya of the Tapā Gaccha, all reverted to wearing white dresses. The orders are independently organised and form the institutional core of distinct sects and schools. At present, no detailed sociological or demographic information is available for most of these monastic traditions, especially for the period before the twentieth century. Two notable exceptions are the studies of the recent history and organisation of the Tapā Gaccha by Cort (1989: 93–112) and of the A(ñ)cala Gaccha by Balbir (2003), both of which are supplemented by the studies of the *paṭṭāvalī*s of both traditions by Śivprasād (2000, 2001). Of the Kharatara Gaccha only the *paṭṭāvalī* of its monastic order and contemporary religious practices of the laity have been studied (Laidlaw 1995, Babb 1996).

The Kharatara Gaccha and the A(ñ)cala Gaccha are the only Mūrtipūjaka traditions which still have a dual system of succession (*paramparā*) of *yati*s and *saṁvegī sādhus*;[28] although there is only one *yati* left in the A(ñ)cala Gaccha (see Figures 12.1 and 12.2).[29] The *sādhu*s and *sādhvī*s of the A(ñ)cala Gaccha are nowadays centrally organised under the supervision of only one *ācārya* (*gacchādhipati*) and still[30] constitute one of the largest mendicant orders of the Mūrtipūjaka tradition.[31] By far the largest of the six Mūrtipūjaka *gaccha*s is the Tapā Gaccha. According to Darśanavijaya (1933: 67, fn.), it had only 428 members at the end of the fifteenth century. By 2002 this figure had risen to 6,696.[32] Today, the Tapā Gaccha is divided into two branches (*śākhā*), the Vijaya Śākhā and the Sāgara Śākhā. The śākhas are further subdivided into a number of lineages which

Figure 12.1 Yati Motī Sāgar of the A(ñ)cala Gaccha in Mumbaī. Photograph by the author, December 2004.

are currently divided in twenty separate groups, or *samudāya*s, which are named after prominent *ācārya*s of their root lineage, with the *sādhvī*s defined through the male members of the traditions (Cort 1991: 661f.). The origins of the Sāgara Śākhā are opaque. Kañcansāgarsūri *et al.* (1977: 311–76) attribute its beginnings to Hīra Vijaya Sūri (1527–1569), though Śāh (1987: 14, 65, 168) points to the year 1630 in which Ācārya Rāj Sūri (formerly Muni Mukti Sāgar) seceded from the main line of the Tapā Gaccha with the help of the first *nagarśeṭh*

Figure 12.2 Paraphernalia of Yati Motī Sāgar. Photograph by the author in Mumbaī, December 2004.

of Ahmedabad, Śāntidās Jhaverī (1585/1590–1659);[33] who in 1660 also sponsored the Ānandjī Kalyāṇjī Trust.[34] According to Dundas (1996: 101, n. 108), this tradition was disrupted in the eighteenth and nineteenth centuries.[35] It was revived in the mid-nineteenth century by Mayā Sāgar with the help of Hemābhāī, another *nagarśeṭh* of Ahmedabad, and of Śeṭh Haṭhīsiṁha Keśarībhāī (died 1845).[36] After Mayā Sāgar, the tradition split into two *samudāya*s, the two most famous *ācārya*s of which were Buddhi Sāgar Sūri (1874–1925) and the 'Āgamoddhāraka' Sāgar Ānand Sūri (1875–1950) respectively. The Vijaya Śākhā emerged apparently in 1657, a date which roughly corresponds to Śāh's (1987) version of the origin of the Sāgar Śākhā, following a succession dispute after the death of Vijay Deva Sūri (1577–1656).[37] In 1999, it was internally subdivided into twenty *samudāya*s.

Cort (1989) observed momentous changes within the Vijaya Śākhā over the last one and a half centuries, as narrated in the histories of the Tapā Gaccha orders by Ratna Prabha Vijay (1948) and others. First of all, the *yati*s, that is, sedentary ascetics who fulfil ritual and administrative tasks and who do not pledge themselves fully to the observance of the *mahāvrata*s, became almost extinct in the twentieth century[38] and were replaced by the reformed *saṁvegī* *sādhus*, of which apparently only two dozen or so existed in the early nineteenth century:[39]

> In the mid-19th century, several activist *sādhus* reinvigorated the institution of the *saṃvegī sādhu*. Over two-thirds of the over 1,000 *sādhus* in the Tapā Gacch today trace their lineage back to Paññyās Maṇi Vijay Gaṇī (1796–1879), known as Dādā (Grandfather). One of his disciples was the former Sthānakvāsī *sādhu* Muni Buddhi Vijay (1807–1882), known by his Sthānakvāsī name of Buṭerāyjī. He was very active in the Panjab among both mendicants and laity, convincing Sthānakvāsīs of the correctness of the Mūrtipūjak teachings. Among his disciples was the charismatic Ātmārāmjī (1837–1896), who in 1876 in Ahmedabad took a second *dīkṣā* (initiation) as the Mūrtipūjak *saṃvegī sādhu* Ānand Vijay, along with eighteen other Sthānakvāsī *sādhus*, under the leadership of Ātmārāmjī and other similar minded *sādhus*, and later under the umbrella of the Śvetāmbar Mūrtipūjak Conference, a wide-ranging campaign was waged to reform both mendicant and lay practices. As the result of this reform the institution of the *yati* has virtually disappeared from the Mūrtipūjak society.
>
> (Cort 1989: 99f.)

Cort showed that after the disintegration of the *gaddī*-centred *yati*-orders, new decentred patterns emerged, based on demographics, geography and charisma rather than on organisational power and property. It is worthwhile quoting him again at length:

> As the Tapā Gacch has grown, it has subdivided in new ways which shed light on earlier processes of subdivision and *gacch* formation. The former subdivisions, which were based primarily on affiliation with the *gāḍīs* (seats, thrones) of specific *śrīpūjyas*, have disappeared, with the exception of the Vijay-Sāgar *śākhā* distinction, and been replaced by about 15 *samudāys* (literally 'co-arising', i.e. descendants of the same *sādhu*; here synonymous with *sampradāy*). In general, three interrelated principles accounted for the development of the various *samudāys*: geography, demographics, and charisma. As the number of *sādhus* increased, it became increasingly difficult for one *ācārya* to oversee the large number of *sādhus* under him. Smaller groups of *sādhus* were placed under the direction of other senior *sādhus*, and the sharp increase in the number of the *ācāryas* within the Tapā Gacch in the past several years is directly related to this need for additional supervisory personnel. As the *sādhus* increasingly interacted solely with the lesser *ācārya* rather than the seniormost *ācārya*, a new *samudāy* might evolve.
>
> (Cort 1989: 103f.)

According to Jacobi (in Glasenapp 1925: 342, 352–354), the Tapā Gaccha was in 1913–1914 still ruled by 'a number' of *śrīpūjya*s and, as a whole, comprised 1,200 *sādhu*s and *sādhvī*s.[40] Guérinot (1926: 56) reported the existence of '30 subdivisions' of the Tapā Gaccha at the beginning of the twentieth century, without mentioning any figures, while B. U. Jain (1986) and Cort (1989: 100–105) found only two *śākhā*s and altogether 15–17 autonomous groups (*samudāya*). Table 12.1 shows that by 1999 this figure had grown to twenty due to further splits in the dominant Vijaya Śākhā tradition of Prem Sūri, the latest being the separation of Kamal Ratna Sūri from the Rāmacandrasūri Samudāya in 1998. Prem Sūri was one of the chief disciples of Buddhi Vijay, the reformer of the *saṁvegī sādhu*s, together with Ātmā Rām, Dharma Vijay (1868–1922) and Nīti Sūri (whose lineage further split into the Bhaktisūri- and the Siddhīsūri Samudāya) (Ratna Prabha Viyay 5, 2 1948: 218). At present, four *samudāya*s trace themselves back to Prem Sūri: the Rāmacandrasūri Samudāya, the Kamalaratnasūri Samudāya, the Bhuvanabhānusūri Samudāya and the Amṛtasūri Samudāya. Four *samudāya*s descend directly from Ātmā Rām (Vijay Ānand), the most famous disciple of Buddhi Vijay: the Vallabhasūri Samudāya, the Mohanalāla Samudāya, the Dharmasūri Samudāya and the Śānticandrasūri Samudāya. The Rāmacandrasūri Samudāya is the only group which advocates the *be tithi* interpretation of the religious calendar,[41] and has therefore been excluded from many Tapā Gaccha *upāśraya*s. Table 12.1 does not include detailed figures for 1986 (cf. Cort 1989: 491f.), 1999 and 2002, which are appended in the endnotes. But it reflects the group structure of 1999 and shows that at the time the Mūrtipūjaka tradition was divided into some twenty-seven independent monastic groups.

In 1999, the Mūrtipūjaka *gaccha*s comprised altogether 6,843 mendicants, 1,489 *sādhu*s and 5,354 *sādhvī*s. Amongst them, the Tapā Gaccha was the largest tradition, with 6,027 mendicants, 1,349 *sādhu*s and 4,678 *sādhvī*s.[42] The table shows a massive increase in numbers particularly of female ascetics within little more than a decade.[43] It also illustrates the fact, emphasised by Cort (1989: 494, 1991: 661), that occasionally significant population shifts occur within and between *samudāya*s, which – in the absence of centralised *gaddī*-structures – seem to divide and unite like segmentary lineages, under the influence of circumstantial factors. Similar changes cannot be observed at the level of the *gaccha* categories.[44] Commensality between ascetics of different *gaccha*s is, for instance, prohibited.[45] Schubring (2000: § 139, p. 252) already noted that *gaccha*s are not necessarily actual groups. Mūrtipūjaka *gaccha*s are in the first place doctrinal schools and at the same time social categories which may or may not be congruent with organised monastic groups, such as the *samudāya*s. However, doctrinal disputes are also significant for processes of group-formation at the *samudāya* level. A good example is the *ek tithi/be tithi* dispute between Rām Candra Sūri and Bhuvan Bhānu Sūri, which split the Premsūri Samudāya into two main sections in 1986 (Cort 1999: 50f.).

Another important factor influencing processes of fission and fusion are the ways in which *gaccha*s and *samudāya*s are organised. Shāntā (1985: 329–331) and

Table 12.1 Mūrtipūjaka *sādhus and sādhvīs* 1987, 1990 and 1996[46]

Gaccha Samudāya	*Gacchādhipati*[47] *1996*	*Ācārya*			*Cāturmāsa-places*			*Sādhu*			*Sādhvī*			*Total*		
		1987	*1990*	*1996*	*1987*	*1990*	*1996*	*1987*	*1990*	*1996*	*1987*	*1990*	*1996*	*1987*	*1990*	*1996*
1 Tapā Gaccha																
A. Vijaya Śākhā																
Rāmcandrasūri	Mahodaysūri[48]	27	17	28	144	124	131	423	238	265	443	463	520	866	701	785
Kamalratnasūri[49]	—	—	—	—	—	—	—	—	—	—	—	—	—	—	—	—
Bhuvanbhānusūri	Jayghoṣsūri[50]	—	12	9	—	78	80	—	225	232	—	225	210	—	450	442
Amṛtsūri	Jinendrasūri[51]	—	—	1	—	—	6	—	—	5	—	—	21	—	—	26
Nītisūri	Arihantsiddhasūri[52]	4	4	3	94	82	70	61	42	40	312	329	385	373	371	425
Bhaktisūri (Samīvalā)	Premsūri[53]	7	7	6	55	44	36	65	59	48	193	163	195	258	222	243
Siddhisūri (Bāpjī)	Bhadraṅkarsūri[54]	2	4	3	13	54	13	24	28	26	80	373	99	104	401	125
Dharmavijay (Ḍehlāvālā)	Rāmsūri[55]	6	6	6	58	62	67	35	33	29	196	214	220	231	247	249
Nemīsūri	Devsūri[56]	19	18	27	102	93	112	180	189	195	340	362	396	520	551	591
Vallabhsūri	Indradinnsūri[57]	2	2	6	69	57	57	57	60	52	195	210	205	252	270	257
Labdhisūri (Navinsūri)	Jinbhadrasūri[58]	13	12	9	36	39	35	57	56	52	163	177	181	220	233	233
Mohanlālsūri	Cidānandsūri[59]	1	1	1	20	19	17	13	17	19	46	34	23	59	51	42
Dharmasūri (Mohansūri)	Yaśodevsūri[60]	3	4	7	62	50	65	36	34	30	189	200	186	225	234	216

Keśarsūri	Hemprabhasūri[61]	1	3	2	44	41	45	28	26	25	157	162	173	185	188	198
Kanaksūri (Vāgaḍvālā)	Kalāpūrṇsūri[62]	1	1	1	73	72	84	22	24	26	455	379	421	477	403	447
Himācalsūri	Panyās Ratnākar[63]	1	1	—	28	23	27	17	16	20	81	75	121	98	91	141
Śanticandrasūri																
Bhāg 1	Bhuvanśekharsūri[64]	2	6	4	21	19	26	41	25	25	62	120	160	103	145	185
Bhāg 2	Jincandrasūri[65]	—	—	2	—	—	21	—	—	12	—	—	109	—	—	121
B. Sāgara Śākhā																
Ānandsāgarsūri	Sūryodaysāgarsūri[66]	3	6	14	116	111	141	114	122	127	583	640	564	697	762	691
Buddhisāgarsūri	Subodhsāgarsūri[67]	6	6	6	34	38	30	58	52	50	95	100	101	153	152	151
Tapā Gaccha altogether		98	110	135	969	1006	1063	1231	1246	1278	3590	4226	4290	4821	5472	5568
2 Vimala Gaccha	Cidānandsūri[68]	1	1	1	8	2	17	9	6	19	20	—	23	29	6	42
3 Añcala Gaccha	Guṇodaysāgarsūri[69]	2	2	2	85	81	84	42	37	39	181	194	213	223	231	252
4 Kharatara Gaccha	Jin Mahodaysāgar[70]	2	1	1	65	64	58	19	22	19	188	192	205	207	214	224
5 Tristuti Gaccha																
Bhāg 1	Jayantsenasūri[71]	2	1	1	22	23	22	32	27	25	57	68	80	89	95	105
Bhāg 2	Hemendrasūri[72]	—	1	1	—	12	14	—	14	16	—	41	48	—	55	64
Bhāg 3	Up.Praśanncandra[73]	—	1	—	—	1	2	—	3	6	—	—	—	—	3	6
6 Pārśvacandra Gaccha[74]	Muni Bhuvancandra	—	—	—	24	29	30	12	12	8	64	68	64	76	80	72
7 Other[75]	Ānanddhansūri etc.	4	1	7	9	2	19	30	6	40	—	—	—	30	6	40
Total		109	118	148	1182	1220	1309	1375	1373	1450	4100	4789	4923	5475	6162	6373

Source: B. U. Jain 1987: 85–165, 1990: 113–184, 1996: 165–304.

Cort (1991) explain population shifts and processes of group segmentation amongst the Tapā Gaccha *samudāya*s mainly with reference to charismatic leadership. Cort emphasises, for instance, the effect of the unusually high numbers of *ācārya*s on the processes of segmentation and the size of Tapā Gaccha *samudāya*s. He explains this effect both with 'internal organisational pressures for the growth of the number of Tapā Gacch *ācārya*s – a growth which has been criticised by many *sādhu*s and laity' and with 'the desire of influential laity to have the *sādhu* of whom they are a personal devotee be an *ācārya*' (ibid.: 668, n. 16). But he also notes that a distinction between 'charismatic' *saṁvegī sādhu*s and 'domesticated' *yati*s is not exactly applicable, since even the *saṁvegī sādhu*s have a succession of leaders and thus are not 'purely charismatic figures in the Weberian sense' (ibid.: 669, n. 22). Weber (1978) himself categorised Jain monastic orders not as charismatic movements but primarily as 'hierocratic organisations'.[76]

Although some *samudāya*s share the same customary law (*maryādā*),[77] Tapā Gaccha *samudāya*s are generally organised independently, and compete with one another, even within their *śākhā*s. As a rule, members of one *samudāya* do not share food with those of another (personal invitations notwithstanding).[78] Each *samudāya* is governed by a *gacchādhipati* or *pramukhā ācārya*, head teacher, who is generally determined according to monastic age (*dīkṣā paryāya*) or by consenus, except in the Rāmacandrasūri Samudāya, where the *gacchādhipati* ideally selects his own successor.[79] The *gacchādhipati* presides over a varying number of monastic functionaries, including subordinate *ācārya*s with or without administrative duties, who received their title solely because of their academic achievements.[80]

I suspect that the maximum size of Jain monastic groups is primarily a function of their rules and regulations, which mediate between the categories of descent and the imperatives of group integration (Flügel 2003b: 191ff.).[81] Circumstantial factors such as the socio-economic resources of a particular religio-geographic field (*kṣetra*) or charismatic leadership are important in specific cases, particularly on the level of gatherings. But generally, the degree of organisation determines its chances of reproduction over time, the maximum group size and thus the potential geographic influence of a particular monastic order. To put it simply, the better the organisation of a group, the greater its potential size and the greater its size, the greater its potential influence. The three principal dimensions of Śvetāmbara monastic orders are descent, succession and seniority. They can be combined in various ways to produce different types of organisation.

In theory, it should be possible to develop a formula for calculating the ability of different types of organisation to compensate for demographic pressure. Practically, there is an upper limit for the size of groups without formal organisation based solely on the principle of recurrent personal interaction. As a first approximation, the breaking point leading to group fission within the orders of the Vijaya Śākhā can be estimated through simple averages. In 1996, the average group size of the smallest organised units of the Tapā Gaccha *samudāya*s, the itinerant groups or *saṅghaḍā*s, gatherings, was 5.24 at *cāturmāsa*. This figure is not unusual for Śvetāmbara orders. It reflects both religious rules on minimal group sizes as well as socio-economic factors, such as the number and wealth of lay-supporters. Evidently, a large group of alms-collecting ascetics can only stay together at one particular place if provisions are available and if their procurement is carefully organised (with the help of the laity).

Within the Mūrtipūjaka tradition, as a rule, the *saṅghaḍā*s have a fluctuating membership. They comprise the members of one or more categories of ascetics who belong to the lineage of one particular *ācārya*. These are called *parivāra*s, or families, and are composed of both *sādhu*s and *sādhvī*s. The *parivāra*s are co-ordinated by one *pramukha ācārya*, who is the leader of a *gaccha* or a *samudāya*. The majority of the *ācārya*s have no administrative duties, although this varies from group to group, but they possess the qualification for the transformation of their *parivāra*s into independent groups. In 1996, the actual average size of a Tapā Gaccha *samudāya* was 278.4 ascetics, distributed, on average, among 53.13 itinerant groups. However, the number of Tapā Gaccha ascetics divided among the total number of *ācārya*s is 41.24, which represented theoretically the lowest average limit of potential group fission between Tapā Gaccha *ācārya*s in 1996. The difference between average actual group sizes and potentially lowest average group size demonstrates the importance of other organisational factors determining group size. But in order to understand, for instance, how the 447 ascetics under the sole leadership of Ācārya Kalāpūrṇ Sūri of the Kanakasūri Samudāya operate as an integral monastic order, further historical and ethnographic research is required. Segmentary lineages can temporarily form very large groups. Nevertheless, it seems that *samudāya*s of such a size are not merely segmentary lineages, but internally highly organised, and divided into subgroups whose membership is not based on descent alone.[82] That the Tapā Gaccha *samudāya*s form distinct monastic orders, whose members share specific rules and regulations (*maryādā*), is evident for instance in the explicit prohibition of sharing meals with members of other *samudāya*s.[83] In fact, most Jain mendicant groups operate on the basis of an internal administrative hierarchy and a rudimentary division of labour. However, further statistical investigation of the correlation of group size and group structure becomes only meaningful if more information on organisational structures and other important variables is available. Complete data and careful theoretical modelling might, in future, lead to reliable predictions of expected group sizes under specified conditions.

Sthānakavāsī

The Sthānakavāsī mendicants are presently divided into twenty six monastic orders. These can be classified according to regional affiliation, doctrinal schools and the lineages descending from one of the five founders of the contemporary traditions, the so-called *pañcmuni*.[84] Three of these founders separated themselves from the now virtually extinct Loṅkā Gaccha *yati* traditions to set up reformed ascetic orders within the aniconic, or non-image worshipping, Jain tradition which originated between 1473 and 1476 after the 'protestant' reforms of the Jain layman Loṅkā (*c.*1415–1489) in Gujarāt:[85] (1) Jīv Rāj (seceded 1551, 1609 or 1629), who apparently canonised the thirty two Śvetāmbara scriptures that are acceptable to the Sthānakavāsīs, established the permanent use of a mouthmask (*muhapattī*), and other principal features shared by all modern-day Sthānakavāsī traditions; (2) Dharma Siṅha (seceded 1628, 1635 or 1644) and (3) Lava (seceded 1637, 1648, 1653–1655 or 1657). Dharma Siṅha was the founder of the Āṭh Koṭi (eighth grade) traditions,[86] and Lava the founder of the Ḍhūṇḍiyā traditions, which are also known under the name Ṛṣi Sampradāya. (4) The founder of the Bāīs Tolā traditions, Dharma Dāsa (seceded 1659, 1560, 1564 or 1665), was originally a member of the lay order of the Ekala Pātriyā Panth and maybe a follower of Jīv Rāj shortly before Jīv Rāj's death; and (5) Hara (seceded 1668 or 1728), the ancestor of the Sādhu Mārgī traditions, divorced himself either from the Lahaurī Loṅkā Gaccha or from the Ṛṣi Sampradāya.

Doctrinally, Dharma Siṅha's Āṭh Koṭi tradition differs significantly from the other four schools, which disagree only on minor points of interpretation. It is today represented by the Dariyāpūri tradition in Gujarāt and by the two Āṭh Koṭi traditions in Kacch, one of which – the Nānā Pakṣ – is very orthodox. The other Sthānakavāsī traditions are divided along regional lines between the Gujarātī and the non-Gujarātī (North Indian) traditions. The non-Gujarātī traditions are further subdivided into those who joined the reformist Śramaṇa Saṅgha, which was founded in 1952 in a merely partially successful attempt to unite all Sthānakavāsī groups, and those who remained outside or left the Śramaṇa Saṅgha. Both the centralised Śramaṇa Saṅgha and the independent traditions include ascetics from four of the five main Sthānakavāsī traditions which were split into thirty three different organised groups at the beginning of the twentieth century (excluding only the Āṭh Koṭi traditions).

I have written elsewhere on the history and organisation of the aniconic Loṅkā, Sthānakavāsī- and Terā Panth Śvetāmbara traditions.[87] Therefore, I confine myself here to the description of their principal demographic features. Like the Jain Śvetāmbara conference of the Mūrtipūjaka laity, the second All India Sthānakavāsī Jain Conference in Ajmer in 1909 resolved to increase the educational standard and the total number of Sthānakavāsī *ācārya*s in order to raise the competitiveness of the Sthānakavāsīs *vis-à-vis* other Jain traditions (AISJC 1988 II: 8–32). In 1933 in Ajmer, the first assembly of representatives of all the Sthānakavāsī monastic orders decided to unify all traditions under the leadership of one *ācārya*. Finally, the Śramaṇa Saṅgha was created by 22 out of the 30 traditions present at the assembly in 1952 in Sādaṛī in Rājasthān. Table 12.2 shows the regional distribution and the number of ascetics of the Śramaṇa Saṅgha, which is now the largest organised group amongst the Sthānakavāsī mendicants, from 1987–1996.

Although they are nominally under the command of one single *ācārya* (at present: Dr Śiv Muni), the remaining founding traditions continue to operate within the Śramaṇa Saṅgha more or less independently. The official statistics therefore do not tell the whole story. Some mendicant orders never joined the Śramaṇa Saṅgha: for instance, the Jñāna Gaccha. And because of perpetual discord

Table 12.2 Regional distribution of the Śramaṇa Saṅgha *sādhus and sādhvīs* 1987, 1990 and 1996[a]

States (prānta)	*Ācārya 1996*	*Cāturmāsa-places*			*Sādhu*			*Sādhvī*			*Total*		
		1987	*1990*	*1996*	*1987*	*1990*	*1996*	*1987*	*1990*	*1996*	*1987*	*1990*	*1996*
1 Rājasthān	—	40	42	51	21	42	48	140	164	173	161	206	221
2 Dillī	1	24	22	33	21	12	25	93	105	170	114	117	195
3 Mahārāṣṭra	—	70	55	37	111	42	34	202	184	115	313	22	149
4 Hariyāṇā	—	11	16	25	4	19	12	52	56	107	56	75	119
5 Madhya Pradeś	—	17	32	28	7	21	24	76	63	77	83	84	101
6 Pañjāb	—	26	18	14	38	23	26	49	38	22	87	61	48
8 Uttar Pradeś	—	4	6	8	2	7	13	18	17	30	20	24	43
9 Karṇāṭak	—	2	7	10	—	7	2	7	11	37	7	18	39
10 Āndrah Pradeś	—	2	3	4	2	8	2	4	8	15	6	16	17
11 Tamil Nāḍu	—	5	11	4	—	20	2	21	29	14	21	49	16
12 Paścim Baṅgāl	—	1	—	1	2	—	10	—	—	—	2	—	10
13 Himācal Pradeś	—	—	1	2	—	—	4	—	5	5	—	5	9
14 Gujarāt	—	—	—	3	—	—	2	—	—	6	—	—	8
15 Caṇḍīgaṛh	—	1	2	1	2	3	3	—	4	—	2	7	3
16 Bihār	—	3	2	1	7	3	1	—	—	—	7	3	1
17 Uṛīsā	—	1	—	—	3	—	—	—	—	—	3	—	—
Other	—	—	16	—	—	11	—	—	6	—	—	17	—
Total	1	207	224	222	221	220	208	662	690	771	883	910	979

Source: B. U. Jain 1987: 73f., 1990: 59–60, 1996: 3–38.

Note

a The table is based on the group-by-group accounts listed in B. U. Jain 1996. B. U. Jain did not have accurate information on 'other' Śramaṇa Saṅgha mendicants in 1996, but cited the total figure of 1,017 mendicants and 230 *cāturmāsa* places. For 1996, he quotes the figure of 208 *muni*s (identical figure) and the much higher figure of 809 *sādhvī*s, based on estimates (see ibid.: 37f.).

Table 12.3 *Sādhu*s and *sādhvī*s of the Independent Sthānakavāsī-Traditions outside Gujarāt 1987, 1990 and 1996

Sampradāya	*Ācārya/ Gacchādhipati*	*Cāturmāsa-places*			*Sādhu*			*Sādhvī*			*Total*		
		1987	*1990*	*1996*	*1987*	*1990*	*1996*	*1987*	*1990*	*1996*	*1987*	*1990*	*1996*
1 Dharmadās	Mānmuni	8	7	8	6	6	6	19	21	23	25	27	29
2 Jñāngacch I	Campālāl	53	61	72	40	42	47	240	255	306	280	297	353
3 Jaymalgacch	Ācārya Śubhcand	8	9	8	6	5	5	32	31	26	38	36	31
4 Ratnavaṃś	Ācārya Hīrācand	10	9	9	18	16	9	34	35	40	52	51	49
5 Vardhamān V.	Śītalrāj	—	1	1	—	3	2	—	—	—	—	3	2
6 Amarmuni I[a]	Ācārya Sādhvī Candanā	7	9	1	15	13	—	8	9	10	23	22	10
7 Amarmuni II	Ācārya Vimalmuni[b]	—	—	3	—	—	7	—	—	—	—	—	7
8 Māyārām I	Sudarśanlāl	6	6	7	26	25	30	—	—	—	26	25	30
9 Māyārām II	Rāmkṛṣṇa	1	1	1	5	6	9	—	—	—	5	6	9
10 Sādhumārgī	Ācārya Nānālāl	49	51	51	46	41	31	211	233	254	257	274	285
11 Śāntikrānti	Śāntimuni[c]	—	—	3	—	—	11	—	—	—	—	—	11
12 Nānakgacch	Ācārya Sohanlāl	4	2	4	4	6	5	15	11	12	19	17	17
13 Hagāmīlāl	Ācārya Abhaykumār	3	3	1	2	2	3	3	3	—	5	5	3
14 Arhat Saṅgh I	Saubhāgyamuni[d]	2	—	2	2	—	6	—	—	—	2	—	6
15 Arhat Saṅgh II	Sādhvī Dr Sādhanā[e]	2	—	3	—	—	—	6	—	8	6	—	8
Other[f]		21	13	15	16	12	15	18	5	18	34	17	33
Total	6	175	172	189	186	177	186	586	603	697	772	780	883

Source: B. U. Jain 1987 II: 23–42, 73f.; 1990 II: 27–53; 1996 II: 39–86, 305f.

Notes

a Today: Vīrāyatan.

b The group had only two ascetics in 1999 (B. U. Jain 1999: 365).

c The information for 1996 is incomplete.

d The Arhat Saṅgha was founded by Muni Suśīl Kumār. In 1999 it was lead by Yuvācārya Amarandra.

e There is no information for the year 1990.

f This category also comprises mendicants who 'walk alone' (*ekala vihārī*).

Table 12.4 Sādhus and *sādhvīs* of the Gujarātī Sthānakavāsī-Traditions 1987, 1990 and 1996

Sampradāya	*Ācārya/ Gacchādhipati*	*Cāturmāsa-places*			*Sādhu*			*Sādhvī*			*Total*		
		1987	*1990*	*1996*	*1987*	*1990*	*1996*	*1987*	*1990*	*1996*	*1987*	*1990*	*1996*
1 Dariyāpurī Āṭh Koṭi	Ācārya Śāntilāl	26	27	33	14	13	14	107	115	118	121	128	132
2 Kacch Āṭh Koṭi Moṭā Pakṣ	Gādīpati Prāṇalāl	22	25	27	17	17	14	72	72	73	89	89	87
3 Kacch Āṭh Koṭi Nānā Pakṣ	Ācārya Rāghva	14	14	14	23	23	21	32	34	37	55	57	57
4 Khambhāt	Ācārya Kantīṛṣi	9	9	11	12	11	9	34	34	37	46	45	46
5 Līmbḍī Cha Koṭi Moṭā Pakṣ	Gādīpati Narsiṅha	56	55	64	18	21	19	216	232	266	234	253	285
6 Līmbḍī Cha Koṭi Nānā Pakṣ	Tapasvī Rāmmuni	17	22	27	9	12	11	98	105	128	107	117	139
7 Goṇḍal Moṭā Pakṣ	Tapasvī Ratilāl	64	68	69	18	19	18	246	231	249	264	250	267
8 Goṇḍal Saṅghāṇī	Narendramuni	5	7	6	1	1	1	29	32	33	30	33	34
9 Barvāḍā	Sardārmuni	6	6	8	6	5	7	11	12	12	17	17	19
10 Boṭād	Navīnmuni	8	10	12	4	4	4	36	36	48	40	40	52
11 Sāyalā	Balbhadramuni	1	1	1	1	2	1	—	—	—	1	2	1
12 Hālārī	Keśabmuni	—	—	2	—	—	2	—	—	4	—	—	6
13 Vardhamān	Nirmalmuni	—	—	2	—	—	1	—	—	6	—	—	7
Other		8	8	3	10	7	3	8	10	4	18	17	7
Total	3	236	252	279	133	135	125	889	913	1014	1022	1048	1139

Source: B. U. Jain 1987: 73f., 1990: 59–60, 1996: 87–140.

Table 12.5 Sthānakavāsī *sādhus* and *sādhvīs* 1987, 1990, 1996 and 1999

Sampradāya	*Ācārya*			*Cāturmāsa-places*			*Sādhu*			*Sādhvī*			*Total*		
	1987	*1996*	*1999*	*1987*	*1996*	*1999*	*1987*	*1996*	*1999*	*1987*	*1996*	*1999*	*1987*	*1996*	*1999*
Śramaṇsaṅgh	1	1	1	207	222	264	221	208	227	662	771	869	883	979	1096
Independent	5	6	5	181	188	208	186	182	183	586	694	784	772	876	967
Gujarātī	3	3	3	236	279	296	133	125	123	889	1014	1037	1022	1139	1160
Total	9	10	9	624	689	768	540	515	533	2137	2479	2690	2677	2994	3223

Note
Compare B. U. Jain 1987: 73–82, 1996: 143–64, 306f., 1999: 101.

between the founding traditions, many disappointed ascetics, such as Upācārya Gaṇeśīlāl (1890–1963) of the Sādhu Mārgī or Upādhyāya Amar Muni (1901–1992) of the Manoharadāsa Dharmadāsa tradition, subsequently left the Śramaṇa Saṅgha and re-established their own independent groups. Moreover, in May 2003 the Śramaṇa Saṅgha split into two groups, one of which is nominally presided over by the orthodox Pravartaka Umeś Muni, who has however not officially accepted the *ācārya* title in order to avoid further conflict. Table 12.3 shows the independent Sthānakavāsī groups outside Gujarāt (for details see Flügel 2003b).

The majority of the Sthānakavāsī traditions in Gujarāt, listed in Table 12.4, descend from Dharma Dāsa and separated themselves in the years after 1788 from the Līmbḍī Dharmadāsa Sampradāya (Chah Koṭi Moṭā Pakṣa). The only surviving Ṛṣi Sampradāya in Gujarāt, the Khambhāt Sampradāya, and the Āṭh Koṭi traditions restrict their activities to Gujarāt and Mumbaī. None of these Gujarātī groups joined the Śramaṇa Saṅgha, which is a Hindī-speaking order or association. They are usually not lead by a selected head, like the independent traditions outside Gujarāt, but by the monk with the highest monastic age, or *dīkṣā paryāya*, who may or may not be called *ācārya*.

The overall number of Sthānakavāsī mendicants is much higher than generally assumed.[88] At the time of the first All India Sthānakavāsī Śramaṇa Sammelan in Ajmer, the total number of mendicants of the then 30 Sthānakavāsī traditions was 1,595, 463 *sādhus* and 1,132 *sādhvīs* (Maṇilāl 1934: 263). This figure had more than doubled by 1999 to altogether 3,223 mendicants, 533 *sādhus* and 2,690 *sādhvīs*, and by the year 2002 had increased further to altogether 3,331 mendicants, 559 *sādhus* and 2,772 *sādhvīs*.[89] In the sixty-six years between 1933 and 1999 the total number of Sthānakavāsī ascetics grew by 102.07%. However, the number of *sādhus* increased merely by 15.19%, while the number of *sādhvīs* expanded by a staggering 137.63%, increasing their share by 12.48% from 70.97% to 83.46%. Table 12.5 shows that the total number of Sthānakavāsī mendicants grew from 1987–1999 by 20.40%. All this growth was generated by an accelerated increase in the number of Sthānakavāsī *sādhvīs* during the last 12 years. At the same time, the absolute number of *sādhus* slightly declined.

The overall growth rate in 1987–1999 was almost twice as high in the Śramaṇa Saṅgha and the independent orders than in Gujarāt (Śramaṇa Saṅgha 24.12%, Independent 25.26%, Gujarātī 13.5%). This can partly be explained by the fact that in 1987 the percentage of *sādhvīs* was already particularly high in Gujarāt (1999: Gujarāt 89.39%, Śramaṇa Saṅgha 79.29%, Independent 81.08%). While the overall share of the *sādhvīs* increased by 3.63%, their growth was higher outside Gujarāt (Śramaṇa Saṅgha 4.32%, Independent 5.17%, Gujarātī 2.4%). It is difficult to say why Gujarātī traditions have a larger percentage of *sādhvīs* in the absence of detailed historical studies. It is not inconceivable that initiations were artificially increased in Gujarāt; since already in 1933, at the Ajmer *sammelan*, an inconclusive debate was held amongst leading monks of the Sthānakavāsīs about a proposal to deliberately increase the number of disciples (Devendramuni 2000: 20).

B. U. Jain does not supply any information on the biodata and on the social background of the mendicants. According to Bordiyā (in Shāntā 1985: 336f.), 30% of the Sthānakavāsī *sādhvī*s were widows in 1975, 16% married and 53% unmarried. The average age of initiation was 10–20 years. Most of the Sthānakavāsī ascetics stem from the Osvāl and Śrīmālī castes in Gujarāt, Rājasthān, Madhya Pradéś, Mahārāṣṭra and Pañjāb, but also from southern India (Shāntā 1985: 333). In contrast to many other Sthānakavāsī traditions, the Śramaṇa Saṅgha comprises a large number of mendicants recruited from non-Jain castes such as Rājputs, Brāhmaṇas, or Jats particularly in the Pañjāb, while the lay following is almost entirely composed of members of the Osvāl castes, who are almost all Jain by religion. However, by convention, only an Osvāl can become *ācārya*.[90] Like most orders, the Śramaṇa Saṅgha has banned the initiation of children below the age of 8 (*bāla dīkṣā*) and of old people (*vṛddha*) (AISJC 1987: 52).[91] However, the Jñāna Gaccha[92] and the Dariyāpurī Sampradāy set a minumum age of 15 years.[93]

The two largest schools amongst the five principal Sthānakavāsī traditions are at the moment the Bāīs Tolā (Dharmadāsa) and the Lavjīṛṣi tradition. Maṇilāl (1934: 211, 233) mentions that before its internal division in 1788, the Mūlacandra Dharmadāsa tradition in Gujarāt comprised about 300 mendicants. In 1933 it had not much more than 334 mendicants. If the figure for 1788 is correct, then little growth occurred in the 150 years between 1788 and 1933.[94]

Groups of more than 100 mendicants are rarely reported before the twentieth century. This may be due to the fact that no reliable figures are available before the nineteenth century, which had generally lower numbers of Jain ascetics than the twentieth century. In 1933, the six largest organised mendicant orders (*saṅghāṛā* or *saṅghāḍā*) were the Amarasiṁha Lavjīṛṣi Sampradāya in the Pañjāb (133 mendicants: 73 *sādhu*s and 60 *sādhvī*s), the Amolakaṛṣi Lavjīṛṣi Sampradāya in Mālvā (105 mendicants: 24 *sādhu*s and 81 *sādhvī*s), the orthodox Rāmaratna Dharmadāsa Jñāna Gaccha in Rājasthān (118 mendicants: 13 *sādhu*s and 105 *sādhvī*s), the Jayamala Gaccha of the Bāīs Tolā tradition in Rājasthān (103 mendicants: 13 *sādhu*s and 99 *sādhvī*s), the Līmbḍī Moṭā Pakṣa of the Bāīs Tolā tradition in Gujarāt (94 mendicants: 28 *sādhu*s and 66 *sādhvī*s), and the Goṇḍal Moṭā Pakṣa of the Bāīs Tolā tradition in Gujarāt (86 mendicants: 20 *sādhu*s and 66 *sādhvī*s) (Maṇilāl 1934: 211–262).

A closer look at the gender composition of the mendicant groups in 1933 shows that, with the remarkable exception of the Amarasiṁha tradition and certain subgroups within the Śramaṇa Saṅgha, all traditions with more than ten mendicants tended to have many more *sādhvī*s than *sādhu*s (generally at the rate of 3:1). It also becomes clear that small groups, such as the Manoharadāsa tradition (7 *sādhu*s)[95] or the Boṭād and Sāyalā traditions (6 *sādhus* each), were and often are homogeneous male groups.[96]

The principal factor for the emergence of exclusively male groups is schisms. Generally, divisions are only instigated by *sādhu*s who initially form small single sex groups which, after a while, may or may not accrete an entourage of *sādhvī*s.

The severance of the Terā Panth from the Ragunātha Sampradāya in 1760 is one example. In some cases breakaway groups are formed by both *sādhu*s and *sādhvī*s. But even then, *sādhu*s are generally the majority.

Larger groups of up to 100 mendicants seem to have emerged more frequently at the end of the nineteenth century with the general revival of Jainism. In response, some groups, such as the influential Amarasiṁha Lavjīṛṣi tradition, re-introduced rudimentary hierocratic structures to prevent the breakup of their communities. Organisation is necessary for the integration of nuns and for the reproduction of a monastic order over time. The need for organisation arises in times of expansion, when the mendicant orders grow and attempt to exert their influence on society as a whole. Organisation is also a major factor determining group size, as indicated earlier. It is symptomatic for an increase in power, not necessarily purity, because it counteracts the segmentary pressures that are systematically generated by the observation of the canonical rules for mendicant-lay interaction. These rules prescribe the itinerary of the ascetics and unmediated face-to-face interaction between guru and disciple, thus impeding the permanent aggregation of large assemblies of ascetics in small towns and villages. Even sizable and well-organised groups are split into smaller itinerant groups of 2–15 and, rarely, up to 70 mendicants, called *saṅghāḍā* or *parivāra* among the Sthanakavāsīs, to make the observation of the canonical rules of non-violent conduct easier.

Another approach to the processes of group segmentation amongst Jain mendicants follows from network theory. I have outlined this approach in an earlier, yet to be published, paper (Flügel 1991) and restrict myself here to general remarks. As mentioned earlier, the size of sustainable groups depends partly on the number of followers in a given region. Studies in network size have shown that informal personal networks rarely exceed thirty individuals in a modern urban environment: 'In general it appears that there is probably a limit to the number of people with whom an individual might be in direct and regular contact, but as yet there does not seem to be enough empirical evidence available to provide an estimate of what it might be' (Mitchell 1969: 19f.).[97]

By observing the canonical codes of conduct for their itinerary, or *vihāra*, and the collection of alms, or *gocarī*, Jain mendicants are both forced and able to sustain much larger networks of personal, if formal, contacts. In practice, this often requires the keeping of lists of addresses and various other organisational techniques which cannot be detailed here.[98] In other words, while the monastic code of conduct limits the size of mendicant groups, it simultaneously contributes to the widening of the circle of lay contacts. However, even if one accepts that the formalisation of mendicant-lay interactions through the Jain monastic code results in a larger personal network, there seems to be an upper limit of sustainable contacts (a figure which awaits to be calculated). Beyond this limit, both the mendicant order and the mendicant-lay network can only be enlarged with the help of hierocratic organisation. The permutations of this general postulate still await thorough sociological analysis.[99] However, given that schisms privilege male ascetics, it seems that the sustenance of large numbers of female mendicants is predicated on the existence of large and formally organised monastic groups with the capacity of weaving partial individual or *parivāra* networks into aggregate group networks. Historically, the emergence of organised monastic orders amongst the Śvetāmbaras seems to be related to the problem of integrating the principally bilateral structure of descent of nuns and the unilateral structure of descent of monks within a single tradition.[100]

Śvetāmbara Terā Panth

Systematic research in the history of the Terā Panth began in 1946 under the supervision of Ācārya Tulsī, who commissioned Muni Navratnamal (1921–2004) to collect the biographies of all Terā Panth mendicants and asked his lay followers to submit all family records and personal notes on the movements of the mendicants, since little reliable data can be found in the writings of the early Terā Panth monks. It is due to Muni Navratnamal's meticulous study of these sources, spanning more than five decades, that the Terā Panth offers now almost complete published demographic data on the monastic order and on the individual life-histories of its ascetics from its inception in 1760. During the last four decades an annual census was conducted and published under the title Terāpanth Digdarśan. The demographic statistics extracted from these materials differentiate between region of origin (*deś*), caste (*jāti*), age (*vay*), marital status before initiation: unmarried (*avivāhit*), married (*patnī/patī ko choṛkar*), or widowed (*patnī/patī-viyog ke bād*), age at the time of initiation (*navalīg/bālig*), initiation with or without spouse (*sapatnī/patī sahit*), initiation of one spouse after the other (*prāg dīkṣit patnī/patī*), death (*svargavās*), departure (*gaṇ bāhar*), and the name of the initiating *ācārya*. Most of the available data was compiled by Muni Navratnamal (1981 ff.) and published in 26 volumes under the title *Śāsana Samudra*. Slightly different figures are quoted by Muni Budhmal (1995) and in other Terā Panth publications. The statistics of different Terā Panth publications do not always match, but are reliable enough to support general conclusions.

The Terā Panth is governed autocratically by a single *ācārya* who is invested with the constitutional power to select his successor, to initiate all mendicants, to annually rotate the personnel of the itinerant groups, and to determine the number and size of the groups. This administrative technique is unique amongst Jain orders, although the *ācārya* of the Sthānakavāsī Jñāna Gaccha – always the monk with the highest monastic age – also rotates the personnel of the itinerant groups, while most other Sthānakavāsī orders similarly operate with only one *ācārya*. It was devised deliberately to counteract segmentary pressures resulting from the fact that traditionally the members of a *saṅghāḍā* stayed together for life and automatically developed a distinct group identity and clientele. The centralised system of administration was introduced by Ācārya Bhikṣu (1726–1803) and refined by Ācārya Jītmal (1803–1881). It allowed the Terā Panth to grow both numerically and geographically well beyond the size of an average *samudāya* in the twentieth century. In 1955 the Terā Panth comprised of

Table 12.6 Terā Panth *sādhus* and *sādhvīs* 1987, 1990, 1996 and 1999

Sampradāya	*Ācārya 1996*	*Cāturmāsa-places*				*Sādhu*				*Sādhvī*				*Total*			
		1987	*1990*	*1996*	*1999*	*1987*	*1990*	*1996*	*1999*	*1987*	*1990*	*1996*	*1999*	*1987*	*1990*	*1996*	*1999*
Terā Panth	Ācārya Tulsī	135	128	123	121	148	149	142	145	559	553	538	543	707	702	681	688
Nava Terā Panth 1[a]	Muni Candanmal	—	—	4	4	—	—	3	3	—	—	7	7	—	—	10	10
Nava Terā Panth 2	Muni Rūpcandra		6	3	2		8	2	2		9	7	7		17	9	9
Nagrāj	Muni Dr Nagrāj			17	1			22	4			32	—			54	4
Total		135	134	147	128	148	157	169	157	559	562	584	557	707	719	754	711

Source: B. U. Jain 1987: 73–82, 1990: 97–106, 1996: 143–64, 306f., 1999: 169, 365f.

Note

a The Nava Terā Panth was already split in two sections in 1990, but B. U. Jain 1990: 106 did not have any figures. Therefore, numbers for both groups are listed under Rūp Candra's section for 1990.

Table 12.7 Initiations, deaths, departures and total numbers of Terā Panth *sādhus* and *sādhvīs* 1764–1997[a]

Ācārya (period of reign)	*Entry*			*Death*			*Exit*			*Total*		
	Sādhu	*Sādhvī*	*Total*	*Sādhu*	*Sādhvī*	*Total*	*Sādhu*	*Sādhvī*	*Total*	*Sādhu*	*Sādhvī*	*All*
1 Bhikṣu (1760–1803)	49	56	105	10	12	22	18	17	35	21	27	48
2 Bhārīmāl (1803–1821)	38	44	82	16	26	42	8	3	11	35	42	77
3 Rāycand (1821–1851)	77	168	245	29	65	94	16	2	18	67	143	210
4 Jītmal (1851–1881)	105	224	329	68	151	219	33	11	44	71	205	276
5 Maghrāj (1881–1892)	36	83	119	25	89	114	9	6	15	71	193	264
6 Māṇaklāl (1892–1897)	16	42	58	10	22	32	5	2	7	72	194	266
7 Ḍālcand (1897–1909)	36	125	161	31	87	118	9	1	10	68	231	299
8 Kālūrām (1909–1936)	155	255	410	49	132	181	35	1	36	139	333	472
9 Tulsī (1936–1997)	257	619	876	143	396	539	119	39	158	144	541	685
Total	769	1616	2385	381	980	1361	252	82	334	688	1909	2597

Note

a These figures stem from Budhmal 1995: 237, 292, 328, 532 and Navratnamal (personal correspondance 30 April 2000). They refer to the day of death of the *ācāryas*.

altogether 660 mendicants (180 *sādhu*s and 480 *sādhvī*s), in 1975 of 657 mendicants (151 *sādhu*s and 506 *sādhvī*s) and in 1981 of 695 mendicants (164 *sādhu*s and 531 *sādhvī*s).[101]

The 1981 figures would have been higher had they not been compiled shortly after the secession of the groups of the Muni Nag Rāj and the Nava Terā Panth, lead by Muni Candan Māl and Muni Rup Candra. The main reason for the constitution of breakaway groups was the controversial introduction of a new intermediary category of novices, called *samaṇa śreṇī*, by Ācārry Tulsī in 1981. The dispute leading to the division focused on the decision to allow these novices to travel abroad and to use modern means of transportation and even money. In this respect, Terā Panth *samaṇa*s resemble the *bhaṭṭāraka*s of the Digambara and the *yati*s of the Śvetāmbara, which form similar categories midway between the laity and fully initiated mendicants.[102] While orthodox ascetics rejected the innovation, reformist ascetics were disappointed that the reforms did not go far enough.

Initially, the *samaṇa śreṇī* proved to be extremely popular, at least among young females, who were interested in religious education and travel. But the expansion has periodically slowed down. In 1992 the order comprised of 4 *samaṇa*s and 51 *samaṇī*s, in 1996 of 4 *samaṇa*s and 81 *samaṇī*s, and in 1999 of 4 *samaṇa*s and 80 *samaṇī*s.[103] However, in the meantime the recruitment has been accelerated. Altogether 89 *samaṇī*s existed by 2001, and more than 100 in 2003. The periodical reduction in numbers is a result of the progression of many *samaṇī*s into the order of the *sādhvī*s.

In 1992 the main branch of the Terā Panth had altogether 827 ascetics and novices and apparently more than 300,000 lay followers. At that time, it was one of the largest corporate Jain mendicant groups. If ascetics and novices are taken together, the Terā Panth had also the highest rate of growth of all Śvetāmbara Jain orders between 1987–1999. However, if only the numbers of fully initiated ascetics are taken into account, the growth rate seems to be stagnating. Table 12.6 shows that the main group had 688 members in 1999, 145 *sādhu*s and 543 *sādhvī*s, that is, much more than in 1955, particularly if the 23 ascetics of the splinter groups of Muni Dr Nag Rāj and the Nava Terā Panth are taken into account. But the figures confirm the stagnation of the number of fully initiated ascetics between 1987 and 1999. This general trend is underlined by the low recruitment of male novices (*samaṇa*), whose growth has stagnated.

The main expansion of the Terā Panth occurred under Ācārya Kālū Rām (1877–1936) and Ācārya Tulsī (1914–1997) in the first half of the twentieth century, that is, during the Indian struggle for independence and the first decade after independence. Table 12.7 shows that under Kālū Rām's reign both the absolute number of initiations of mendicants and the ratio of female mendicants increased dramatically. Simultaneously, caste exclusivity also increased. Terā Panth mendicants were increasingly recruited only from the Osvāl *jāti*s. By contrast, many of the ascetics that were initiated by the first four Terā Panth *ācārya*s between 1760 and 1881 were Agravālas (sometimes Sarāvagīs) and Porvālas, and Maheśvarīs, though Bhikṣu himself was also a Bīsa Osvāl.[104] The recruitment patterns also reflect regional changes. Initially, most of the Terā Panth mendicants came from Mārvāṛ and Mevāṛ. However, after a series of *cāturmāsa* sojourns by Ācārya Jītmal in Lāḍnūṁ and Bīdāsar between 1872 and 1877, the focus of activities shifted towards the Thalī region. From Ācārya Kālū Rām onwards the great majority of Terā Panth ascetics were recruited from the area of the old principality of Bīkāner.[105] Table 12.7 shows the pattern of growth of the Terā Panth, whose *ācārya*s initiated altogether 2597 mendicants between 1760 and 1997.[106]

The table shows that one of the factors contributing to the low number of *sādhu*s are secessions or excommunications, which occur much more frequently amongst *sādhu*s than amongst *sādhvī*s (cf. Navratnamal 1981 II: 311, 322, III: 273, 291, X: 309, 325). This confirms Balbir's (1983: 42) observation that the disposition to rebel against the autocratic regime of the Terā Panth *ācārya*s is greater amongst male ascetics. The figures show that the number of exclusions was much higher under the regimes of the reformist disciplinarians Jītmal, Kālūrām and Tulsī.

Goonasekere's (1986: 87ff.) analysis of the recruitment patterns between 1760–1944 shows that, with the exception of the first years after the foundation of the Terā Panth during which the *sādhu*s were in the majority, at all times significantly more *sādhvī*s were initiated than *sādhu*s (on average 65.97% *sādhvī*s and 34.03% *sādhu*s), and that the percentage of female ascetics continually increased. His investigations of the marital status at the time of initiation give further insights into the historical changes taking place within the monastic community. He shows that until 1944 the two dominant categories were 'unmarried men' and 'widows': 49.83% of all *sādhus* were unmarried between 1760–1944, 37.28% widowed, 12.89% married, and altogether 67.77% of the *sādhvī*s – 44.77% of all Terā Panth mendicants – were widows (ibid.: 100f.). Goonasekere explains the different ratio of widows and widowers by the fact that, in contrast to women, men were always permitted to remarry (due to Ācārya Tulsī's reforms widow remarriage is today officially accepted by the Terā Panthīs though it is still despised by the Osvāls). From this he infers the prevailing motives for renunciation: widowhood for women, and impossibility or fear of marriage for men. But he also mentions other socially induced reasons for renunciation, such as infertility, bankruptcy, unhappy marriage, and death of a family member (ibid.: 114f.) – in my experience a very, if not the most, significant external factor, particularly for women, apart from the influence of the monks and nuns, and the alternative to marriage that is offered to women by a well-organised monastic order.[107]

Cort's (1991: 660) re-analysis of Goonasekere's data reveals important changes in the marital status of the Terā Panth ascetics. Under Ācārya Bhikṣu (1760–1803) less than 10% of all mendicants were unmarried. However, between 1909 and 1944 all mendicants under Ācārya Kālū Rām and Ācārya Tulsī were unmarried (women: 72.7%, men: 56 %). Similar increases in the share of unmarried women amongst the *sādhvī*s had already been observed by Shāntā (1985: 320, 336f., following Bordiyā 1975) for the Sthānakavāsīs and the Kharatara Gaccha, and by Cort (1989b) amongst the Tapā Gaccha *samudāya*s. Cort (1991: 660) rightly concludes that 'P. S. Jaini's (1979: 247, n. 8) statement that most Jain *sādhvī*s are widows needs to be qualified'.

The average age at the time of the initiation has also increased. It is today 18–19 years, compared to 15–16 years some sixty years ago. The significant increase of the age of initiation can be explained by Ācārya Tulsī's reversal of Ācārya Kālū Rām's preference for child initiations (*bāla dīkṣā*). Kālū Rām favoured child initiations in order to reduce the prevalence of widows in the order and to boost the overall number of mendicants.[108] Tulsī, by contrast, was primarily interested in increasing the standard of education. The rising age of initiation is mainly a consequence of his decision to initiate only educated female candidates, given the overall trend towards the initiation of young unmarried women, who seem to prefer the relative independence of monastic life to marriage. One of the reasons for the creation of the *samaṇa* category was to give young women the opportunity to study and thus to qualify themselves for full mendicancy, which nowadays can only be entered by young females after some years as a novice. Usually, girls are not initiated before the age of 20. But there is no such arrangement for boys, who are generally less inclined to join mendicancy. They are trained after initiation.

Initiations of children from the age of 8 and initiations of 45–60 year olds are exceptions today, although they still take place.[109]

Digambara

With the exception of very small traditions, such as the Tāraṇa Svāmī Panth, the Gumāna Panth and the Totā Panth,[110] the overwhelming majority of the Digambaras follow either the Terah Panth, the 'path of thirteen', or the Bīsa Panth, the 'path of twenty' or both traditions in a non-discriminate manner. In contrast to the aniconic Śvetāmbara Terah Panth, the image-worshipping Digambara Terah Panth – both are also called Terā Panth – was originally not a tradition led by mendicants but a lay movement. It emerged in the sixteenth and seventeenth centuries in North India in protest against the lax and ostentatious conduct of contemporary orange-clad 'Bīsa Panthī' ascetics, the so-called *bhaṭṭāraka*s, whose 'modern'[111] monastic lineages evolved from those of the naked *muni*s and increasingly replaced them from the thirteenth century onwards.

The precise significance of the distinction between Terah Panthīs and Bīsa Panthīs is not known anymore. Nor do we know much about the history and organisation of the contemporary Digambara ascetics.[112] Most writers associate the beginning of the Terah Panth movement either with Paṇḍit Ṭoḍarmal (1719–1766), an influential Digambara layman of Jaypur, or with Banārsīdās (1586–1643), a merchant and co-founder (*ādiguru*) of the Adhyātma circle in Āgrā which drew on the mystical philosophy of Ācārya Kunda Kunda to inspire its own version of a non-ascetic lay religiosity that is oriented towards self-realisation through the direct meditative experience of the soul. Yet, the fundamental ideas of both the Adhyātma circle and the Terah Panth movement clearly antedated both Banārsīdās and Ṭoḍarmal.[113] Lath (1981: xxxvi–vii), for instance, points to the influence of the revenue minister of

King Akbar, Rājā Ṭoḍarmal (died 1589) in Vārāṇasī and to his younger associate Bāsū Sāh, who introduced Banārsīdās to Digambara mysticism. Cort (2002: 63f.) emphasised the fact that 'we cannot conclude that an interest in Digambar mysticism equates automatically with the Terah Panth emphasis on reforming the Digambar ritual culture' (p. 66). It appears rather that in the sixteenth and seventeenth centuries the trans-sectarian Adhyātma circle in Āgrā and the more ritualistically oriented and more radically *anti-bhaṭṭārak* Digambara Terah Panth movement around Jaypur constituted distinct though related lay movements, which became indistinguishable only with the waning of the influence of the Adhyātma movement in the eighteenth century and the institutional consolidation of the Terah Panth through the construction of numerous temples in North India.

According to M. U. K. Jain (1975: 137f.), the radical *anti-bhaṭṭāraka* movement was started either in 1528[114] or in the early seventeenth century by Amar Cand, a resident of Sāṅganer near modern Jaypur. The movement first called itself Vidhi Mārga, though its opponents mocked it 'Terah Panth', the path of (only) thirteen. The second account is corroborated by Lath (1981: xxxix), who points to Amar Siṅgh as the founder of the 'Terah Panth' movement in 1626. The most detailed investigation of the origin of the Terah Panth/Bīsa Panth distinction was undertaken by Nāthurām Premī (1912, 1957), one of the main sources for M. U. K. Jain and Lath, who identified the oldest confirmed record of the word Terah Panth and of the year 1626 as its date of origin in Paṇḍit Bakhat Rām's eighteenth century work Buddhivilās v. 631.[115] He concluded, therefore, that the origin of the Terah Panth must be located in the early seventeenth century. In Premī's (1912/n.d.: 22f.) assessment, the passage refers to the ritualistic Terah Panth and not to the Adhyātma movement, as Cort (2002: 67) argues.[116] Premī (1957) later recorded three versions of the origin of the Terah Panth in the literature of its opponents.[117] All of these point to the pivotal role of the family of Amrā Bhauṁsā Godīkā of Sāṅganer: One version can be found in Bakhat Rām's work Mithyātva Khaṇḍan Nāṭak of 1764, which describes how Amrā Bhauṁsā Godīkā was expelled from the congregation of the *brahmacārī* Amar Cand [*sic*!] because of his ostentatious display of wealth. In turn, he founded his own group which initially had only thirteen (*terah*) members and was therefore mocked as the 'Terah Panth'. The group built a temple apparently with the help of a minister of the king of Amer. A second version is given in a poem called Kavitt Terāpanthkau by Cand Kavi. The poem describes how Jodhrāj Godīkā, the son of Amrā Bhauṁsā Godīkā, in 1618 – a date which Premī regards as fifty years too early[118] – repeatedly interrupted the sermon of the visiting *bhaṭṭāraka* Narendrakīrti of the Balātkāra Gaṇa Dillī-Jaypur Śākhā of Amer. He was then expelled and founded his own group on the basis of thirteen unreported principles. The third and oldest version goes back to Jodhrāj Godīkā himself who, in his 1667/1669 Hindī translation of Kunda Kunda's Pravacanasāra, exploited the homonym of *terah* and *terā* by interpreting *terah panth*, 'path of thirteen', as *terā panth*, 'your path', that is, as another term for the 'Jina's path' or the 'right path'.[119] Hence, the Śvetāmbara Terā Panthī ascetics must have borrowed their own identical explanation of the three possible meanings of their name from existing Digambara Terā Panth sources;[120] though M. U. K. Jain (1975: 138) reports that N. Premī elsewhere expressed the view that the name *terā panth* only became current amongst the Digambaras after the founding of the Śvetāmbara 'Terā Panth' in 1760 – a view which may merely reflect the fact that Bakhat Rām's works Mithyātva Khaṇḍan Nāṭak and Buddhivilās were composed in the year 1764 and 1770.

None of the sources cited by Premī give a clear answer to the question of the significance of the numbers thirteen and twenty in *terah panth* and *bīsa panth*, which may indeed just reflect a superficial claim of superiority by the self-declared 'Bīsa Panthīs' 'since the number 20 exceeds 13 by 7' (Nathmal 1968: 7). The influential twentieth century Terā Panth *paṇḍit* Phūlcand Śāstrī (1985b: 538), a born Parvār, could therefore take the liberty to identify the Terā Panth with the 'orthodox Mūla Saṅgha of Kunda Kunda' and the Bīsa Panth with the 'heterodox Kāṣṭhā Saṅgha';[121] and also to associate the 'pure line' (*śuddhāmnāya*) of the Parvār caste with the tradition of Kunda Kunda (ibid.: 536).[122] Śāstrī could, of course, only identify the entire *bhaṭṭāraka* tradition with the Kāṣṭhā Saṅgha by disregarding the known history of the *muni* and *bhaṭṭāraka* traditions. However, many Terā Panthīs nowadays claim descent from the 'orthodox' Mūla Saṅgha and interpret the words *terā panth* as a designation of the 'right path' shown by the Jinas and Kunda Kunda.[123] The words *bīsa panth*, 'path of twenty', is in turn polemically depicted as a corruption of *viṣam panth*, 'irregular-' or 'poisonous path' (Śāstrī 1985b: 538),[124] or as a corruption of *viśva panth*, 'universal path' (Glasenapp 1925: 357 for both versions).

Digambara Terā Panth

The Digambara Terā Panthīs are today guided by *paṇḍit*s, or lay intellectuals, who are associated with predominantly local religious trusts and temples. There is no unifying organisational framework. About 500–600 Terā Panth *paṇḍit*s exist in North India today with strongholds in Jaypur, Āgrā and Vārāṇasī. Most of them teach Jainism only part-time. Although they do respect 'true' Jain mendicants,[125] the Terā Panthīs represent largely a temple-centred form of lay asceticism, whose main doctrinal inspirations derive more from the mystical writings of Ācārya Padmanandin, known as Kunda Kunda (Pkt. Koṇḍa Kunda), than from Bhūtabāli and Puṣpadanta for instance. Their following has recently split between those who accept Kānjī Svāmī's (1889–1980) deterministic interpretation of Kunda Kunda's teachings and those who do not.[126]

Two-thirds of today's Digambaras[127] are said to be Terā Panthīs,[128] who are the predominant Digambara tradition in Rājasthān, Madhya Pradeś and Uttar Pradeś, while the Bīsa Panthīs dominate in Mahārāṣtra, Karṇāṭaka and Keralā, as well as in Tamil Nāḍu and Gujarāt where only few Digambaras are left[129] apart from the followers of Kānjī Svāmī. The reasons for the differential distribution of Terā Panthīs and Bīsa Panthīs have not yet been studied, but there seems to be a clear correlation between caste membership and sectarian affiliation in North India, where, today, most Agravāls and Parvārs are Terā Panthīs and most Khaṇḍelvāls

Bīsa Panthīs.[130] However, the majority of the Digambara laity does not consciously differentiate between Terā Panthīs and Bīsa Panthīs *qua* sectarian membership or following, and merely practises local Jain rituals and caste customs.[131] The absence of deep-seated sectarian awareness amongst the Digambara laity in North India[132] – apart from the divide between the followers and the opponents of Kānjī Svāmī[133] – can be attributed to a number of factors: the extinction of the last North Indian *bhaṭṭāraka* seats in the early twentieth century, the revival of the doctrinally amorphous *muni* traditions, and the lack of organisation not only of the Terā Panth,[134] but of the Digambaras in general whose dearth of inspirational religious leaders in the nineteenth century resulted in the dominance of caste (*jāti*) identities amongst the local Digambara communities (*samāj*) in both North- and South India.[135] Another factor may have been the long-standing cultural influence of Terā Panth practices on the Bīsa Panthīs in North India, whose rituals are less elaborate than those of the Bīsa Panthīs in the South.[136]

Bīsa Panth

In contrast to the Terā Panthīs, who practise a dry *pūjā* and reject the *bhaṭṭāraka*s, the Bīsa Panthīs practise *pūjā* with flowers and fruits and support the *bhaṭṭāraka*s, who continued the ascetic tradition after the decline of the *muni*s in the late medieval period. The reconstruction of the organisational history of the Digambara ascetics is a difficult and not yet fully accomplished task.[137] Carrithers (1990: 154) suspects that the current use of specific designations for monastic lineages or groups is largely fictitious since from the medieval period onwards no independently organised *muni saṅgha*s existed besides the *bhaṭṭāraka*s. One of the problems is the unclear contextual meaning of the lineage and group categories used by the Digambaras. Muni U. K. Jain (1975: 132) writes that 'Units like Āmnāya, Anvaya, Bali, Samudāya, Saṁgha and Vaṁśa appear to be peculiar to the Digambara section'; though he does not fail to mention the common use of the terms *gaṇa, gaccha, kula* and *śākhā* in both the Digambara and the Śvetāmbara traditions.[138] The difficulty in connecting the influence of the classical Digambara teachings of Umāsvāmī, Guṇadhara, Puṣpadanta and Bhūtabalī, on the one hand, and the mystical tradition of Kunda Kunda, on the other, with specific lines of succession is, at least in part, connected to the problem of clearly identifying enduring organisational units within the relatively unorganised Digambara ascetic lineages. It has only sporadically been observed that the doctrine of Kunda Kunda, who in old inscriptions is generally associated with the Nandi Saṅgha, was more prominent in the Māthura Gaccha and in certain factions of the Sena Gaṇa.[139]

The nineteenth century *paṭṭāvalī*s of the Sarasvatī Gaccha (Balātkāra Gaṇa Uttara Śākhā), which were translated by Hoernle (1891, 1892), trace the origin of the lineages of the contemporary Digambara *bhaṭṭāraka*s to a disciple of Ācārya Bhadrabāhu II, Guptigupta, who is also known under the names of Ardhabalin and Viśākhācārya.[140] Ardhabalin is presented as the last pontiff who was able to keep the monks (*muni*) of the originally undivided Mūla Saṅgha, or root community, together. When he was succeeded, apparently in the year 21 BCE, each of his four chief disciples – Māghanandin, Vṛṣabha called Jinasena, Siṁha and Deva – took over one of the four sub-groups which subsequently developed into independent traditions: the Nandi, the Vṛṣabha- (Sena-), the Siṁha- and the Deva Saṅgha.[141] The oldest sources for this narrative are two inscriptions in Śravaṇabeḷagoḷā dated 1398 and 1432.[142] The later inscription dates the group formation within the Mūla Saṅgha to the latter half of the eight century.[143] Schubring (2000: § 30, p. 63) pointed out the discrepancy between this account and references to a Mūla Saṅgha of a different internal composition of the twelfth to thirteenth centuries, and Dundas (2002: 122) concludes 'that the Mūla Saṅgha gradually became little more than a prestigious but artificial designation, redolent of a long unattainable orthodoxy'.[144]

For the early medieval periods four 'heterodox' Digambara traditions are attested to by Deva Sena's tenth century polemical work Daṃsanasāra (Darśanasāra):[145] the Drāviḍa-, Kāṣṭhā-, Māthura- and the Yāpanīya- or Gopya Saṅgha. The four traditions are described as 'heterodox', because they differed on specific points of doctrine and practice from the 'orthodox' Mūla Saṅgha,[146] which is not mentioned in the text because it was represented by Deva Sena himself (Schubring 2000: § 30, p. 63).[147] The reported dates of origin of these traditions vary in the surviving manuscripts of the Darśanasāra. Hence, the Drāviḍa Saṅgha may have been founded either in 479 CE,[148] 469 CE,[149] or in 583 CE[150] by Pūjya Pāda's disciple Vajra Nandin in Madurā (Madurai) in South India. The reported reason was a disagreement within the Mūla Saṅgha over the eating of particular plants, bathing in cold water, practising agriculture and trade.[151] The origins of the Kāṣṭhā Saṅgha[152] seem to go back to the seventh or eighth century CE. By the tenth century it was divided into four divisions:[153] the Māthura Gaccha,[154] Lāḍa Bāgaḍa/Lāṭa Vargaṭa Gaccha,[155] Bāgaḍa Gaccha[156] and Nandī Taṭa Gaccha.[157] The Yāpanīya Saṅgha – the only one of the four 'heterodox' traditions which is depicted as a non-Digambara tradition in the academic literature[158] – originated apparently in 648 CE,[159] in 159 CE,[160] or in 148 CE.[161]

In North India the most influential traditions[162] were the Sena Gaṇa[163] and the Balātkāra Gaṇa (Sarasvatī Gaccha)[164] with its ten sub-divisions which were internally further sub-divided: Kārañjā Śākhā,[165] Lātūra Śākhā,[166] Uttara Śākhā,[167] Īḍara Śākhā,[168] Bhānapura Śākhā,[169] Surat Śākhā,[170] Jerahaṭa Śākhā,[171] Dillī-Jaypur Śākhā,[172] Nāgaura Śākhā,[173] and Aṭera Śākhā.[174] Both the Sena Gaṇa and the Balātkāra Gaṇa presented themselves as branches of the 'orthodox' Mūla Saṅgha in a direct line from Kunda Kunda (Padmanandin). However, the link appears to be a later construction.[175] The currently available sources point to Ācārya Śrī Candra (r. 1013–1030) as the founder of the Balātkāra Gaṇa.[176]

After the demise of the Yāpanīya- and the Drāviḍa Saṅgha in the late medieval period, merely a few branches of the Kāṣṭhā Saṅgha – especially the Māthura Gaccha – and of the Sena Gaṇa, the Balātkāra Gaṇa and the Deśiya Gaṇa of the Mūla Saṅgha remained, and only some sections of the Sena Gaṇa and the Balātkāra Gaṇa survived until today. In the late medieval period the members of most sub-branches of these traditions transformed themselves from naked *munis* to orange-clad *bhaṭṭāraka*s with a relaxed code of conduct. These domesticated *bhaṭṭāraka*s had only very few disciples, amongst them occasionally nuns (*āryā*),[177] which may be the reason why the term *yati* is rarely used in the Digambara tradition. There is no reliable demographic information available on the *bhaṭṭāraka* traditions, but one can safely assume that the absolute number of both Digambara *muni*s and *yati*s was very small during this period. In the first of his planned two volumes on the early *bhaṭṭāraka* traditions, Joharāpurkara (1958: 23) identified the names of only 400 *bhaṭṭārakas* and 165 disciples who were associated with 31 *jātis* and 200 place names in North India between the thirteenth and nineteenth centuries.

Bhaṭṭāraka traditions

The honorific title *bhaṭṭāraka*, 'great lord' or 'learned man', was given to prominent *ācārya*s and *muni*s in the early medieval period (Premī 1912/n.d.: 3ff.). From the late medieval period onwards, the term came to designate the celibate heads of monasteries (*maṭha*)[178] who observe a relaxed set of ascetic vows, which entitles them to wear clothes, to administer monastic property in the name of the *saṅgha* (private property is not permitted), to live permanently in one or more monastery, to use vehicles, to act as heads of the Jain communities and later of Jain castes, etc. To distinguish the two types of *bhaṭṭāraka*s, the term *paṭṭācārya* is also used for the latter.[179] Domesticated *bhaṭṭārakas* are not fully initiated mendicants, but occupy an intermediary status between the naked *muni*s and the common laity.[180] Technically, they are defined as *kṣullaka*s and classified together with the ordinary *kṣullaka*s and *ailaka*s as 'superior laymen' (*utkṛṣṭa śrāvaka*) who accept to observe the eleventh *śrāvaka pratimā*, to different degrees, in contrast to the 'basic' (*jaghanya*) and the 'intermediate' (*madhyam*) laity, who must only observe the *pratimā*s 1–6 and 1–9 respectively.[181] In practice, *jaghanya śrāvaka*s observe at best the first or *darśana pratimā*, that is the stage of 'right views' combined with vegetarianism. The *barah vratas* or 'twelve vows' of the second or *vrata pratimā* are rarely formally accepted (in toto) by lay Jains, who are reluctant to impose lifelong (*ājīvana*) vows upon themselves, except sometimes in old age.[182] Similarly, the intermediate status is regarded as almost synonymous with the seventh or *brahmacarya pratimā*, the vow of sexual continence which is outwardly marked by wearing a white dress. The eleventh or *uddiṣṭa tyāga pratimā*, which should be practiced by *bhaṭṭāraka*s, demands world-renunciation and the observance of a monastic lifestyle, including the begging of food. The *uddiṣṭa tyāga pratimā* is today sub-divided in the stages of the *kṣullaka* and the *ailaka*.[183] The *kṣullaka* (f. *kṣullikā*) or 'junior' (monk) gives up all but two (or three) pieces of cloth of orange colour, while the *ailaka* keeps only a loincloth (*kaupīna*).[184] Both the *kṣullaka*s and *ailaka*s are consecrated by a personal guru. At their *dīkṣā* they are both given the three possessions of a Digambara ascetic: peacock feather broom (*piñchī*), scripture (*śāstra*) and water pot (*kamaṇḍalu*).[185] In contrast to the *kṣullaka*s, who may reside with householders, the *ailaka*s always stay with the *muni*s, and should eat their food, like the *muni*s, with 'one hand', that is the two hands folded into one, but in a seated position. They also have to practice *keśa luñcana*, or the ritual plucking of hair and beard, and silence at night, and are not permitted to use vehicles.[186] For this reason *ailaka*s are considered to be superior to *bhaṭṭāraka*s although this is disputed some *bhaṭṭāraka*s who as the descendants of the original *muni* tradition claim predominance even over the modern *munis* and perform a modified *muni* dikṣā.

The procedures of selection and the inauguration or *paṭṭābhiṣeka* ceremony of a *bhaṭṭāraka* are different from an ordinary *kṣullaka dīkṣā* which usually precedes it. Nowadays, a *bhaṭṭāraka* is often not chosen by his predecessor, but by a *pañcāyat* or by prominent members of the community, who judge the available candidates according to their attitude, conduct and knowledge. If no suitable successor, a *laghunandana* or 'small son' such as a *brahmacārī* or *yati* under training[187] with a good horoscope, is available, the *ācārya*s of the *muni saṅgha*s are approached to recommend one of their *kṣullaka*s or *ailaka*s who could be persuaded to fill the position.[188] If a candidate is accepted by consensus, the *paṭṭābhiṣeka* is organised, in which a Digambara *muni* plays the role of the *dīkṣā-dātā* or giver of initiation. The candidate first renounces his old clothes and his personal name[189] in public and is then given a single orange dress and the traditional title of the occupier of the seat. After taking his vows (at least a lifelong *brahmacārya vrata*), he is blessed with *mantra*s and by sprinkled water on his head and then presented with the principal insignia of a *bhaṭṭāraka* – a *piñchī* with a handle made out of silver or gold, an insignia ring, and a metal *kamaṇḍalu*. A *bhaṭṭāraka* also commands ceremonial elephants, litters (*meṇā*), and other symbols of worldly status. Generally, he does not keep money on his own nowadays, but leaves the financial assets of the *maṭha* in the hands of the lay trustees, who will cover all his expenses.[190]

The tradition of domesticated *bhaṭṭāraka*s evolved at the beginning of the thirteenth century under Muslim rule from the existing traditions of the naked *muni*s who they replaced almost entirely until the revival of the *muni* tradition in the twentieth century. There are three accounts of its origin, all of which emphasise the pioneering role of the Balātkāra Gaṇa: The first account attributes the introduction of the custom of wearing clothes – symbolic of possessions in general – to Ācārya Vasant Kīrti (1174–1207) of the Uttara Śākhā of the Balātkāra Gaṇa, who died only one year after his accession to the seat in Ajmer. According to Śruta Sāgar Sūri, he took the decision to cover himself with a sheet of cotton (*taṭṭī-sādara*) when going for alms in the village of Maṇḍapadurga (Māṇḍalagaṛh) in Rājasthān in reaction to the Muslim rulers' criticism of the custom of walking naked in public.[191] Other accounts locate the beginning of the practice in the time of Phīroz Śāh (1350–1387), the sultan of Delhi, who desired to meet the guru of the Digambaras.[192] A *paṭṭāvalī* names the seventh *ācārya* of the Uttara Śākhā of the Balātkāra Gaṇa, the miracle working Padma Nandin (born 1318, r. 1328–1393),[193] as the first *bhaṭṭāraka* who put on a loin cloth. It is said that the title of a *bhaṭṭāraka* was conferred on him by a Gujarātī *śrāvaka* who wanted him to consecrate a statue and in this way to transmit to it his miraculous powers (Hoernle 1891: 354). According to an oral tradition, the reason for putting on clothes was Padma Nandin's acceptance of the request by

King Muhammad Ghôrî to present himself in a decent manner to his wife who desired to meet him (ibid.: 361).[194]

Under the impact of the Terā Panth reform movement in the sixteenth and seventeenth centuries, most of the *bhaṭṭāraka* seats in North India collapsed. The two last remaining seats in Rājasthān, Mahāvīrjī and Prātapgaṛh, were discontinued in the first and second half of the twentieth century respectively, due to the increasing influence of the 'modern' lay reform movements which criticised the *bhaṭṭāraka*s with arguments similar to those of the 'protestant'[195] Digambara reform movements of the sixteenth and seventeenth centuries.[196] Only the southern *bhaṭṭāraka* traditions of the 'Mūla Saṅgha' in Mahārāṣṭra (Sena Gaṇa: Kolhāpura, Nāndaṇī), Karṇāṭaka (Balātkāra Gaṇa: Hūmachā; Deśiya Gaṇa: Kambadahalli/Nagamaṅgala, Kanakagiri/Maleyur, Kārkala, Mūḍabidrī, Śravaṇabeḷagoḷā; Sena Gaṇa: Narasiṅharājapura) and Tamil Nāḍu (Sena Gaṇa: Melasittamūra (Arahatasugiri); Deśiya Gaṇa: Tiruvannamalai) survived. The institutional pillars of the present-day Bīsa Panth traditions, the twelve[197] surviving *bhaṭṭāraka* seats in Hūmachā,[198] Kambadahalli, Kanakagiri, Kārkala,[199] Kolhāpura,[200] Melasittamūra,[201] Mūḍabidrī,[202] Nāndaṇī,[203] Narasiṅharājapura,[204] Śravaṇabeḷagoḷā,[205] Sondā/Svādī and Tiruvannamalai are all located in the south, and closely connected with individual local castes.[206] The cultivation of exclusive links with the members of specific Jain castes in South India was facilitated by the fact that many of them were founded by *bhaṭṭāraka*s,[207] who protected and dominated them for centuries as their religious rulers, or *rājāgurus*, who exercised penitential powers. The *bhaṭṭāraka*s still initiate and excommunicate their followers and in some cases select their own successor, who is then installed by the members of the respective caste and cannot be removed during his lifetime.[208] In the past, the *bhaṭṭāraka*s accumulated large assets in land and artwork and maintained an exclusive monopoly over the surviving manuscripts of the principal sacred scriptures of the Digambaras, the Kaṣāyapāhuḍa of Guṇadharācārya and the Ṣaṭkhaṇḍāgama of Puṣpadanta and Bhūtabalī, until copies were produced and smuggled out of the *maṭha* of Mūḍabidrī in the early twentieth century.

The exclusivist orientation of the *bhāṭṭāraka*s towards the castes which they dominated and to the property of their *saṅgha* proved to be a major obstacle to the ambitions of Jain communalists to unify the Jain community on a national platform during the years of the freedom struggle in the nineteenth and twentieth centuries. *Saṅgha* reforms were imposed on the *bhaṭṭāraka*s by the laity, who also increasingly took control of the monastic property from the latter half of the nineteenth century onwards. Much of the landed property was recovered by the state governments through Land Reform Acts.[209] As a consequence, the legal powers which the *bhaṭṭārakas* once held over their followers have now completely disappeared. With the re-establishment of separately organised *saṅgha*s of itinerant naked *muni*s in the 1920s,[210] who were predominantly recruited from the relatively impoverished agricultural Digambara castes of the Bogāras, Caturthas, Pañcamas and Saitavālas in northern Karṇāṭaka and southern Mahārāṣṭra, even the southern *bhaṭṭāraka*s lost much of their worldly and religious influence. They have no disciples amongst the newly established lineages of *muni*s and *āryikā*s, who are independent and considered to be of a higher religious status.[211] However, they are still consulted as arbiters for conflict resolution, and supervise the conduct of the *upādhyāya*s who conduct the temple rituals in southern India. It is due to the continuing influence of the *bhaṭṭāraka*s on the social life of South Indian Jains that their castes tend to be homogenously 'Jain' and that the feeling of 'Jain' social identity, is more prevalent than in mixed Jain-Hindu castes.

The lack of credible mendicant leaders with a national reputation may explain why the desire for social and religious reform was at the time particularly strongly expressed by the Digambara laity in North India. Another factor was the aspiration of some community leaders to bridge the caste divisions, and the economic divide between the poor Digambara agriculturists in the South and the wealthy Digambara (and Śvetāmbara) merchants in the North. The revival of the *muni*s came therefore just in time. The *muni*s were promoted by the laity as symbols of Digambara unity on a national platform.[212] Particularly the leading members of the Akhil Bhāratvarṣīya Digambara Jain Mahāsabhā and the Khaṇḍelvāla Mahāsabhā[213] associated themselves closely with the new *muni saṅgha*.[214] The reformist Akhil Bhāratvarṣīya Digambara Jain Pariṣad also supported the revival of the *muni*s and the unity of all Digambaras, but advocated for social reforms in addition to the religious reforms which were promoted by the *muni*s.[215] The association was founded on the 22 January 1923 in Delhi by Champat Rāy Jain (1867–1942), Brahmacārī Sītal Prasād Jain (1879–1942) and other reformers from North India who had left the conservative Bhāratvarṣīya Digambara Jain Mahāsabhā, which was established in 1892 in Mathurā under Rājā Lakṣmaṇdās and supported by traditional *bhaṭṭāraka*s and *paṇḍit*s, who resisted both the publication of the scriptures,[216] and socio-religious reform movements amongst the Digambaras, such as the Dasa Pūjādhikāra Āndolan, the Dasa's Right to Worship Movement.[217] Reportedly, some members of the Mahāsabhā even opposed the independence of the *muni*s from the *bhaṭṭāraka*s.[218]

History of the modern *muni saṅgha*

The Digambara *muni* tradition never entirely disappeared, though for the nineteenth century the names of only a handful of *muni*s are reported whose precise relationship, if any, with the *bhaṭṭāraka*s is still not entirely clear.[219] A Muni Nara Siṅha is reported to have visited the town of Ḍhākā with his disciple Muni Vinay Sāgar in 1870, and another *muni* is reported to have visited Jaypur.[220] In South India, several *muni*s lived away from larger settlements on hillsides and in caves, though reliable information on them is difficult to obtain. Amongst them was 'Tapasvī' Muni Candra Kīrti, who was probably born in Guramaṇḍayā, but no detailed information on him is available. At the time, the only *muni* in North India was Candra Sāgar, who was born into the Padmasī family of the Hūmaḍ caste in Phalaṭan (Satārā). He took the *kṣullaka* vow in 1912 in Jinappāsvāmī (Śolāpur) and a few months later the *mahāvrata*s in Jhālarāpāṭan and started to wander as a naked *muni* as far as Āgrā.[221] Muni Anant Kīrti was born in 1883 in Nellīkār (Kārakal) and died untimely on 16 February 1918 in Gvāliyar where, in his memory, an eternal light (*akhaṇḍa jyoti*) is still maintained by his followers.[222] In South India, three additional *munis* existed: Candra Sāgar 'Maṇihalī', Sana Kumār, and Siddha Sāgar 'Tervāl' (1828–1903),[223] who reportedly self-initiated himself in front of a statue at Sammet Śikhar. In 1921, one Muni Ānand Sāgar lived in Udaypur. It has been reported that he often visited the nearby shrine of Ṛṣabhdeva Keśariyā.[224]

Although the Digambara mendicants are not organised, most, but not all present-day *munis* trace their lines of descent to 'Cāritra Cakravartī' Śānti Sāgar 'Dakṣiṇ' (1872–1955) – not to be confused with his namesake from North India: Muni Śānti Sāgar 'Chāṇī' (1888–1944) – who is 'regarded as having revived the institution of *munis* single-handedly from nearly complete eclipse' (Carrithers 1989: 232). Śānti Sāgar was born on the 26 July 1872 (1929 Āṣāḍh Kṛṣṇa 6) in the village Aināpur-Bhoj in the Belgāṁv District of Karṇāṭaka. His original name was Gauḍā Pāṭīl, and he belonged to a family of farmers of the Caturtha caste. When he was nine years old, he was married to a five year old bride, who died only seven months after the wedding. In 1890, he took the *brahmacarya* vow 'in the presence of a *muni*'[225] on 25 June 1915 (1972 Jyeṣṭh Śuklā 13), the *kṣullaka* vow from the Digambara '*muni*' Devendra Kīrt;[226] in Uttaragrām, and in 1916 the *ailaka* vow from Muni Akalīk Svāmī (? = Ādi Sāgar 'Aṅkalīkar'), who lived on the Bāhubalī hill near Kumbhoj. He was finally initiated as a *muni* from another '*nirgrantha muni*' on 4 March 1920 in Yarnāl (Yeranāl) in Karṇaṭaka[227] and recognised as an *ācārya* after the initiation of his first disciple, Muni Vīr Sāgar, on 9 October 1924 (1981 Āśvin Śuklā 11) in Sāṅglī. He initiated altogether 18 *munis*, *kṣullakas*, *āryikās* and *kṣullikās*, most of whom accompanied him on his barefoot journeys throughout India.

At the time, roaming naked in the streets of large cities was prohibited (*berok-ṭok*) by the Colonial Government (K. P. Jain 1938: 161f.). In British India and in the Indian princely states (*riyāsat*) wandering naked was an arrestable offence. The *munis* were therefore more numerous in southern India. In 1926, the Commissioner of Kāṭhiyāvāḍ gave permission for Muni Munīdra Sāgar to move lawfully, if he was surrounded by a circle of his devotees, though this restriction was opposed by the Akhil Bhāratīya Jaina Samāj, and a committee was formed to repell it with the argument that according to both British and a Indian law, neither the government nor any other ruler or *sampradāya* should interfere in the religious affairs of a particular tradition.[228] When Ācārya Śānti Sāgar entered Bombay in 1927, the case was still pending. He therefore had to transgress the rule of wandering naked (*nagna muni vihāra*) and to cover his body during his visit to the city (Kāsalīvāl 1992: 35). On the request of the local Seṭh Ghāsīrām Pūnamcand Jauharī, he then lead a communal pilgrimage to the sacred sites of the Digambaras throughout India, to re-establish for the Digambara *munis* the right to roam naked and uninhibited by provincial boundaries, and to revive the 'true' Digambara religion.[229] On his tour, he was welcomed by the provincial kings of Mahārāṣṭra. In the year 1927–1928, he led the pilgrimage from Bhopāl to the *mahā sammelan* of Digambara *munis* at Mount Śikhar in Bihār,[230] and on to Jabalpur, Lakhnaū, Kānpur, Jhāṁsī, Āgrā, Dhaulapur, Mathurā,

Phirozābād, Eṭā, Hātharas, Alīgaṛh, Hāstīnapūr, Muzapharnagar, etc. to Delhi, where he spent *cāturmāsa*. He was famously stopped by the police in Delhi for breaking the law by walking naked, but was pardoned because he refused to move from the spot where he was stopped, asking: 'how can I walk back?' After *cāturmāsa*, he went on to Alavar for a *sammelan* of all existing *sādhu gaṇa*s, that is, the groups of ascetics which performed mainly *jñāna-dhyāna* and *tapas* rather than the rituals promoted by the *bhaṭṭāraka*s, though rituals were not rejected per se. The following six Digambara mendicant groups (*saṅgha*) were present (K. P. Jain 1932: 161f.):

1 Ācārya Śānti Sāgar 'Dakṣiṇ', with the *muni*s Candra Sāgar, Śrut Sāgar, Vīr Sāgar, Nami Sāgar and Jñān Sāgar (6 *muni*s altogether).

2 Muni [Ācārya] Śānti Sāgar 'Chāṇī', with Muni Malli Sāgar, Brahmacārī Phatah Sāgar, and Brahmacārī Lakṣmī Cand (2 *muni*s altogether). Śānti Sāgar 'Chāṇī' was born as Kevaldās Jain into a family of the Dasa Humaḍ caste in the village Chāṇī, some 15 km from Ṛṣabhdev Keśariyā in the state of Udaypur. He took the *brahmacarya vrata* on 1 January 1919 at Sammet Śikhara, and a few months later, with permission of the lay community of Gaṛhī in Rājasthān, initiated himself as *kṣullaka* under the name Śānti Sāgar in front of the image of 'Bhagavān Jinendradeva' (due to the absence of *muni*s in North India). On 5 September 1922 (*anant caturdāśī*) in the Ādināth temple of Sāgavāṛa he started 'to wear the dress of a Digambara *muni*' (*Digambara veṣa dhāraṇa*). In 1926, he was installed as an *ācārya* by the Digambara community of Giriḍīha. He converted Ṭhākur Krūrasiṁha of Bhukhiyā (Bāṁsavāṛā) to Jainism, but had fewer disciples than his counterpart in the south.[231]

3 Muni Sūrya Sāgar (9 November 1883 to 14 September 1952), with Ajit Sāgar, Dharma Sāgar and Brahmacārī Bhagavān Dās (3 *muni*s altogether). Sūrya Sāgar's birthname was Hajārīmāl and he belonged to the Porvāḍ caste of Jhālarāpāṭan. In 1916 his wife died. He was initiated by Śānti Sāgar 'Chāṇī' first as a *kṣullaka* on the 19 October 1924 in Indore and a few weeks later as a *muni* on the 22 December 1924. In 1928 he was given the *ācārya* title from the *samāj*. He initiated at least four male ascetics: Ācārya Vijay Sāgar, Muni Ānand Sāgar, Muni Padma Sāgar, and Kṣullaka Cidānand.[232]

4 'Muni'[Ācārya] Ādi Sāgar, (13 September 1866 to 21 October 1944) with Muni Malli Sāgar and Kṣullaka Sūri Siṅha. 'Mahātapasvī' Ādi Sāgar 'Aṅkalīkar'was born in the village Aṅkali in southern Mahārāṣṭra. He belonged to the Caturtha caste and was named Śiv Gauṛā by his parents. In 1909 he took the *kṣullaka* vow, and in 1913 initiated himself in front of the Jinendra image at Kunthalgiri. He died in 1944 in the village Ūd (Kāsalīvāl 1992: 35, Suśīlā Bāī, in Brahmacāriṇī Mainābāi Jain 1996: iv–x). In the year 1926, his group stayed at Udgāṁv (3 *muni*s altogether).

5 Muni Munīdra Sāgar, with the *muni*s Devendra Sāgar and Vijay Sāgar. Munīdra Sāgar was born in Lalitpur into the Parvār caste. He was very young in 1927 and spent his previous *cāturmāsa* in Māṁdvī (Surat) (3 *muni*s altogether).

6 Muni Pāy Sāgar, who restricted his movements to South India (1 *muni*).

In addition, Muni Jñān Sāgar of Khairābād and Muni Ānand Sāgar (and possibly others for which no record is available at the moment) belonged to the Digambara *sādhu gaṇa*. These 21 mendicants were the only naked *muni*s who performed *vihāra* at the time.

It seems, though this is a question for further research, that of these six groups only the lineages of Śānti Sāgar 'Dakṣiṇ', Śānti Sāgar 'Chāṇī', and of Muni Ādi Sāgar 'Aṅkalīkar' survived. In accordance with the general tendency amongst modern Jains to present a homogenous image of the Jaina community to the outside world, it is often said that doctrinal disagreements are not significant within the tradition of the modern *muni*s, only minor differences in lineage and succession. There is, indeed, no clear doctrinal division between the *ācārya saṅgha*s with regard to the Terā Panth/Bīsa Panth distinction concerning the latter's use of green vegetables, fruit, worship with lamps (*dīpa pūjā*) or incense (*dhupa*), etc. Effectively, each ascetic follows his own interpretation. However, Ācārya Śānti Sāgar 'Chāṇī' was known for his rejection of the *pañca abhiṣeka* ritual because it is conducted with milk. Instead he advocated for the use of 'pure' water in *abhiṣeka* rituals. He spent one *cāturmāsa* together with Śānti Sāgar 'Dakṣiṇ' in Byāvar, where differences of opinion emerged, since Śānti Sāgar 'Dakṣiṇ' insisted on the Bīsa Panthī view. Śānti Sāgar 'Chāṇī's main line of succession is represented by the *ācārya*s Sūrya Sāgar (1883–1952), Vijay Sāgar, Vimal Sāgar (Bhiṇḍa) (1891–1973), Sumati Sāgar (1917–1994), and Upādhyāya Jñān Sāgar (b. 1957).[233] However, a number of splits occurred due to succession disputes, and several *guru-śiṣya paramparā*s exist today.[234]

Doctrinal disagreements were also instrumental for the schisms between the successors of Śānti Sāgar 'Dakṣiṇ', who after his death on the 20 August 1955 (2012 Bhādrapad Śuklā 2) in Kunthalgiri split into five independent lineages. Four lines were started by Śānti Sāgar's disciples Ācārya Nami Sāgar (1888–1956), Ācārya Pāy Sāgar (1890–1956), Ācārya Sudharma Sāgar (1885–1938) and Ācārya Kunthu Sāgar (1894–1945). However, the dominant line of his successors (*paṭṭadhāra* or *paṭṭādhīśa*) is represented by the *ācārya*s Vīr Sāgar (born 7 June 1876, *kṣullaka* 13 March 1924, *muni* 9 October 1924, *ācārya* 9 September 1955, died 23 September 1957), Śiv Sāgar (born 1901, *dīkṣā* 7 July 1949, *ācārya* 3 November 1957, died 18 March 1969), Dharma Sāgar (born 11 January 1914, *dīkṣā* 13 December 1951, *ācārya* 24 June 1969, died 22 April 1987),[235] Ajit Sāgar (died 1988),[236] and the present *ācārya* Vardhamān Sāgar (*dīkṣā* 24 February 1969), who was chosen by Ajit Sāgar, though the older and much more popular monk Abhinandan Sāgar (*dīkṣā* 29 October 1968) was favoured by the majority of the lay followers.[237] After Ajit Sāgar's death, Abhinandan Sāgar and his teacher Śreyāṁs Sāgar therefore separated themselves from Vardhamān Sāgar and founded their own group which is now headed by Ācārya Abhinandan Sāgar.

A third influential line was started by Ācārya Vīr Sāgar's disciple Muni Jñān Sāgar (*c.*1891–1 June 1973), a Khaṇḍelvāla (Chābṛā) Jain from Sīkar, previously known as the Terā Panth Paṇḍit Bhūrāmal Śāstrī and from 1955 as Kṣullaka Jñānbhūṣaṇ (*dīkṣā dātā: Ācārya Vīr Sāgar*). He was intiated as a *muni* in 1959 in Jaypur by Ācārya Śiv Sāgar but seceded on doctrinal grounds from Śiv Sāgar and his dedicated successor Dharma Sāgar, in 1961 and – though not being recognised as an *ācārya* – initiated Vidyā Sāgar (*dīkṣā* 30 June 1968) in the same Saṃvat year in Ajmer. In turn, he was installed as an *ācārya* by his disciple with the consent of his lay followers on the 7 February 1969 in Nasīrābād and immediately afterwards initiated Muni Vivek Sāgar (*dīkṣā* 7 February 1969 or 8 March 1969). Vidyā Sāgar was born on the 10 October 1946 into a middle-class Aṣṭage family of the Caturtha caste in the village Cikkoḍī-Sadlagā in Belgāṁv.[238] He took the *brahmacarya* vow from Ācārya Deś Bhūṣaṇ in 1967, and *muni dīkṣā* from Ācārya Jñān Sāgar, who appointed him as the new *ācārya* on the 22 November 1972 in Nasīrābād, and immediately afterwards resigned and asked Vidyā Sāgar to bestow upon him the *sallekhanā* vow (M. Jain 2001: 23–26, 494, K. R. Jain 2003: 23–52). After Jñān Sāgar's death in 1973, Vivek Sāgar parted company from Vidyā Sāgar, apparently because the charismatic Vidyā Sāgar was junior to him in physical age, although slightly older in monastic age. But the main reason may have been doctrinal differences. In the group of Vidyā Sāgar, *āryikā*s cannot initiate *ailaka*s, on behalf of the *ācārya*, on the grounds that the *ailaka*s wear only one piece of cloth and therefore deserve a higher status than the *āryikā*s, who cover their entire body.[239] This reversal of the traditional hierarchy – *muni*, *āryikā*, *ailaka*, *kṣullaka*, *kṣullikā* – was a main point of contention between Jñān Sāgar and Ācārya Śiv Sāgar.[240] Other disputes concerned the consumption of 'green' vegetables such as tomatoes, and Jñān Sāgar's refusal to condemn the use of the sacred thread, which is common among the Digambara laity in South India but not practiced north of Karṇāṭaka, which prevented him to become installed as an *ācārya* by Śiv Sāgar. Vidyā Sāgar additionally resolved that *āryikā*s should not wear the *piñchī*, the principal status symbol of a Digambara ascetic, during their menses, and that only 'born Jainas' should be able to become *muni*s. The highest status for renouncers from non-Jain families amongst his followers is thus the position of an *ailaka* in his group.[241]

A fourth line was started by Ādi Sāgar 'Aṅkalīkar', who was a contemporary of Śānti Sāgar 'Dakṣiṇ', and is often presented as his disciple, despite the fact that he was not initiated by him.[242] He was succeeded by Mahāvīr Kīrti (born 1 June 1910, *dīkṣā* 1937, died 6 Febuary 1972) and Vimal Sāgar (born 30 October 1915, *dīkṣā* 19 July 1950, *ācārya* 24 December 1961), who apparently gained the *ācārya* title not through succession but by acclamation of the lay community, especially by the *paṇḍit*s Lālā Rām Śāstrī and Māṇik Candra Śāstrī.[243] Both Mahāvīr Kīrti and Vimal Sāgar[244] were succeeded by a great number of *ācārya*s who created numerous small groups.[245] Vimal Sāgar's successors were Ācārya Sanmati Sāgar (born 26 January 1939, *dīkṣā* 9 November 1962, *ācārya* 5 March 1972), and the current *ācārya*s Bharat Sāgar (born 7 April 1949, *dīkṣā* 23 November 1972)[246] (who was Vimal Sāgar's *upādhyāya*),[247] Puṣpadanta Sāgar (born 1 January 1952, *dīkṣā* 31 January 1980) (who shifted from Vidyā Sāgar to Vimal Sāgar and teaches an idiosyncratic mixture of Terā Panth and Bīsa Panth views), Nirmal Sāgar (born 10 December 1946, *dīkṣā* 12 July 1967), Sanmati Sāgar

'Tapasvī Samrāṭ', Vāsu Pūjya Sāgar, Virāg Sāgar, as well as Muni Nirañjan Sāgar, Gaṇinī Vijay Matī, the *kṣullaka*s Dhaval Sāgar, Ratna Kīrti, and the *kṣullikā* Siddhānta Matī (A. Jain 2001: 1–34). Amongst Mahāvīr Kīrti's successors were the present *ācārya* Sambhav Sāgar and the present '*gaṇadharācārya*' Kunthu Sāgar, who initiated many disciples under new names ending in the suffix *-nandī*. Some of his disciples parted from him in order to establish themselves as *ācārya*s, *ācāryakalpa*s, *upādhyāya*s and *muni*s in their own right – to name only the present *ācārya*s Deva Nandī, Guṇadhara Nandī, Guṇa Nandī, Gupti Nandī, Kanak Nandī, Karma Vijay Nandī (? = self-initiated), Karuṇā Sāgar, and Kumud Nandī, Kuśāgra Nandī, Padma Nandī, Śānti Sāgar 'Korasār Vāle', the *ācāryakalpa*s Karuṇā Nandī and Śruta Nandī, the *ailācārya* Niścay Sāgar, and the *upādhyāya*s Kāma Kumār Nandī Śruta Sāgar. Ācārya Deś Bhūṣaṇ (1908–1987), the politically most influential Digambara *muni* after Śānti Sāgar, was a disciple of Ācārya Jay Kīrti, who may have been associated with Mahāvīr Kīrti, though the link is not clear.[248] He is succeeded by the presently influential *ācārya* Vidyānand 'Rāṣṭrasant' (born 22 April 1925), who also comes from Belgāṁv but has few disciples and resides predominantly in New Delhi, by Ācārya Bāhubalī Sāgar, who separed himself from Vidyānand and by Ācārya Subāhu Sāgar, Ācārya Subal Sāgar, Muni Guṇ Bhūṣaṇ, Kṣullaka Vṛṣabh Sena, and Kṣullikā Anant Matī (ibid.).

In 1981, 151 mendicants and representatives of the national Digambara lay associations gathered in Śravaṇabeḷagoḷā in order to witness the *mahāmastakābhiṣeka* ceremony and to overcome the differences between the growing number of Digambara ascetics and lineages by establishing a common institutional framework for the mendicants – the Digambara Jain Muni Pariṣad. Several rules were drafted with the intention of preventing the practice of wandering alone (*ekala vihāra*) and a decline in the standards of conduct (*śithilācāra*). But these resolutions were not implemented and had no effect (Kāsalīvāl 1992: 24).

Though there are no clear-cut divisions among the *muni*s with regard to political-ideological and doctrinal orientations, conservative Bīsa Panthī *muni*s tend to support the Mahāsabhā, while modern monks such as Ācārya Vidyānand and Ācārya Vidyā Sāgar associate themselves with the Mahāsamiti whose wealthy leadership has a wider support base in North India and tends to support Terā Panth views. The main catalyst for the recent trend towards a conscious doctrinal self-demarcation of Bīsa Panthī and Terā Panthī mendicant groups was the debate on Kānjī Svāmī's idiosyncratic 'Terā Panth' interpretation of Kunda Kunda's philosophy from the early 1960s onwards, which split the Digambaras into two clearly distinguished factions.[249] Beyond the specific context of this dispute, the picture is less clear. There is no exclusive link between Kunda Kunda and the Terā Panth tradition. In the late twentieth century, the Terā Panth *paṇḍit* Phūlcand Śāstrī (1985b: 244, 1992: 146) came to the conclusion that the Terā Panth is identical with the *śuddhāmnaya*, the 'pure tradition' of the Mūla Saṅgha Kundakundāmnaya Balātkāra Gaṇa Sarasvatī Gaccha,[250] which propagates the *mokṣa mārga* and not – like the Bīsa Panthī *bhaṭṭāraka*s ('= Kāṣṭhā Saṅgha') – the ways of living a religious life in the world (*saṃsāra*). The same claim had already been made at the beginning of the century by the Bīsa Panthī *ācārya* Śānti Sāgar 'Dakṣiṇ'[251] who, somewhat imaginatively, attributed himself to the line of the 'Mūla Saṅgha' Kundakundāmnaya Nandi Saṅgha Balātkāra Gaṇa Sarasvatī Gaccha (Jñān Matī 1980: 249) – which may have inspired Phūlcand Śāstrī's view. Although few details about his life are known, Ācārya Kunda Kunda (*c.*1–8 CCE)[252] is currently regarded by all contemporary Digambara *muni*s as their ancestor.[253] According to Anupam Jain,[254] all *muni*s derive their descent from the lineage of Kunda Kunda and Ācārya Śānti Sāgar.[255] However, although the majority belongs to the lineage of Śānti Sāgar 'Dakṣiṇ' and propagates southern, that is Bīsa Panthī, practices, a minority descends from Śānti Sāgar 'Chāṇī', who rejected the Bīsa Panthī *pañca abhiṣeka* and *devī pūjā* rituals, and from Ādi Sāgar 'Aṅkalīkar'.

After the recent death of the influential Ācārya Vimal Sāgar (born 1915), the most prominent *ācārya*s of today are Vidyānand (born 1925), who took the twelve year long *sallekhanā* vow in 1999, and the charismatic Vidyā Sāgar. Vidyā Sāgar is renowned and respected for his strict observance of the rules of the Digambara Āgamas, and for his emphasis on Jain philosophy rather than on rituals and imposed vows; especially for his single-handed revival of the study of the Ṣaṭkhaṇḍāgama. He explicitly favours the Terā Panth view on rituals and speaks out both against the *bhaṭṭāraka*s (first on 8 November 1998),[256] and against the followers of the Kānjī Panth. Like his *guru*, Jñān Sāgar, who did not express any objections to the *bhaṭṭāraka*s, he also favours the mystical teachings of Kunda Kunda. In contrast to his late rival, the ritualistically oriented Ācārya Vimal Sāgar, who was from a Khaṇḍelvāl business class background and supported the Mahāsabhā, Vidyā Sāgar comes from a South Indian merchant family of modest income and favours the 'liberal' Digambara Mahāsamiti and the Digambara Pariṣad which promote both ritual and social reforms.[257] He explicity propagates the recognition of the Jains as a 'minority' community, which is now supported by most Digambaras, particularly in the South, where they form homogenous Jain castes. The North Indian Śvetāmbaras and Digambaras, especially those from Gujarāt and Rājāsthan, are traditionally self-employed merchants and wealthier than the sourthern Digambara agriculturalists and petty traders whose preferred route of social advancement tends to be government service. They form predominately mixed Jain–Hindu castes and tend to oppose the minority status for Jains.[258] Vidyā Sāgar is also a strong supporter of the cow protection movement and inspired the formation of a lay organisation called Ahiṁsā Army which is based in Delhi and works for a total ban on the slaughter of cows in India.[259] It is possible that the North Indian cultural environment has influenced Vidyā Sāgar's change of attitude towards the *bhaṭṭāraka*s and the Bīsā Panthī tradition in general. He was born in Karṇāṭaka, but recruited most of his disciples in the North, particularly in Madhya Pradeś, where he spends most of his time.

With the notable exception of the strictly anti-monastic Kānjī Panth, the revived *muni* traditions are today respected both by the Terā Panth *paṇḍits*[260] and by the Bīsa Panth *bhaṭṭāraka*s, though the contact of the *muni*s with either of them is irregular.[261] In fact, the majority of the present-day mendicants attach themselves neither to the Bīsa Panth- nor the Terā Panth Digambara tradition, but act independently and are free to articulate their individual doctrinal interpretations. The widely held view that Digambara ascetics always preferred to impress people 'more by their behaviour than by their church organisation' and 'seemed to favour solitary life' (Deo 1956: 360f.) indirectly supports the claims of the modern *muni*s that they are the revivers of the authentic form of Jain monasticism that was introduced by Mahāvīra himself. However, although the Digambaras did not, like the Śvetāmbaras, create elaborate monastic codes of conduct, their *ācārya*s and later their *bhaṭṭāraka*s presided over *maṭha*s, or monasteries, which were highly organised manifestations of monastic landlordism.[262] It was monastic property rather than a code of conduct which stabilised the tradition. The long-standing organisational and numerical weakness of the Digambara mendicants from the beginning of Muslim rule may thus be related to the relative success of the *bhaṭṭāraka*s as well as the educated laity, whose influence within the Digambara community is reflected in the extensive post-canonical Digambara *Śrāvakācāra* literature, which is partly written by lay intellectuals: 'Digambars seem to have felt more keenly than the Śvetāmbars the need to concretize and systematize the lay doctrine' (Williams 1983: xviii). The strength of the Digambara laity over the last 500 years also explains the leading role of Digambara intellectuals within the twentieth century Jain reform movement. Yet, the increasing influence of the scholars amongst the modern *muni*s seems to displace the communal role of the lay intellectual for the time being.

Organisation of the *muni saṅgha*

Since the demise of the Drāvīḍa Saṅgha and other regional traditions, and with the ascendancy of the *bhaṭṭāraka*s who profess to continue some of these traditions even today, Digambara mendicants are not split into distinct schools and sects anymore. Amongst modern *muni*s the popular suffix *-nandī* or *-sāgar* does not indicate sectarian affiliation, only lineage affiliation. Not much is known about the doctrinal and organisational differences between the lineages. Maybe by using these suffixes some modern *muni*s attempt to recapture the symbolic identities (and properties) of old *bhaṭṭāraka* lineages which are now extinct. But our empirical knowledge of Digambara history and sociology is presently not sufficient to answer this question.[263] The lack of a reliable demographic survey of the contemporary Digambara ascetics was lamented by Carrithers (1989), who encountered great difficulties in his attempt to piece together a reasonably accurate ethnographic picture of the Digambara mendicants: 'The *munis* as I met them are significantly different from their predecessors, especially those in the nineteenth century. *Munis* are few. They have no central organisation and it is difficult to gather even the most elementary census data concerning them. Jaini (1979: 247, n. 8) estimated that there were only sixty-five *munis* when he was writing, and another sixty novices. An unattributable Hindi newspaper cutting shown to me by the *muni* Vidyānandajī Mahārāj in 1984 estimated the number of *munis* at 100. These numbers have to be understood in relation to the number of Digambar laity. The 1981 Census of India returned about three and a quarter million Jains of

Table 12.8 Digambara ascetics in 2000 and 2001

Position	*Total number*		*Number of groups*		*Male members*		*Female members*		*All members*	
	2000	*2001*	*2000*	*2001*	*2000*	*2001*	*2000*	*2001*	*2000*	*2001*
Ācārya	51	51	51	51	237	213	122	128	359	341
Ācāryakalpa	4	4	3	4	3	4	1	0	4	4
Ailācārya	3	4	2	2	4	3	0	0	4	3
Bālācārya	1	1	1	1	5	3	8	6	13	9
Upādhyāya	16	20	13	18	22	25	1	0	23	25
Muni	269	305	81	133	147	208	33	23	180	231
Gaṇinī Āryikā	10	8	5	5	2	2	31	31	33	33
Āryikā	312	325	41	67	0	0	162	194	162	194
Ailaka	26	29	10	13	13	15	0	0	13	15
Kṣullaka	80	94	19	35	20	35	0	0	20	35
Kṣullikā	46	63	6	12	0	0	7	12	7	12
Total	818	902	232	341	453	508	365	394	818	902

Source: A. Jain 2000: 1–27, 2001: 1–34.

whom Jaini estimates a third to be Digambar. On that estimate there is one *muni* for every 11 or 12 thousand Digambars' (ibid.: 221).[264]

According to the information on individual ascetics made available by B. U. Jain, the Digambara mendicants were 1987–1996 split into some 175 independent groups, including ascetics who wander alone. But B. U. Jain's figures on the Digambara ascetics are, in his own judgement, unreliable and inconsistent, due to insufficient self-reporting by the Digambara monks.[265] Often, for instance, only the leader of an itinerant group is mentioned and not the total number of group members, which was simply estimated by B. U. Jain (1999: 382, n. 1–7) in his summary figures. However, his lists give some idea of the structure of the Digambara mendicant groups in the decade before the turn of the millennium and a rough estimate of the overall number of ascetics.[266]

A more precise annual *cāturmāsa* list, the Digambara Jain Sādhu-Sādhvīyoṁ ke Varṣayoga kī Sūcī, was compiled for the first time for the year 2000 by A. Jain of the Tīrthaṅkara Ṛṣabhadeva Jaina Vidvanta Mahāsaṅgha in order to provide information for the laity 'who want to contact different *saṅgha*s' (Letter 25 September 2002). The categories he used to compile complete alphabetical[267] lists of groups (*saṅgha*),[268] names (*sādhu/sādhvī*, etc.), initiating monks (*dīkṣā guru*), and addresses of the monsoon retreats (*cāturmās sthāl evaṃ sampark sūtra*) of the Digambara mendicants in the years 2000 and 2001, confirm that the Digambaras effectively treat both nuns (*āryikā*) and novices who observe the eleventh *śrāvaka pratimā*[269] – the *ailaka*s,[270] *kṣullaka*s, and *kṣullikā*s – as members of the ascetic community. The change of status is indicated by the changes of the name at the *kṣullaka/kṣullikā dīkṣā* and the *muni dīkṣā*. *Brahmacārī*s and *brahmacāriṇī*s are not listed in the almanacs of A. Jain and B. U. Jain, because they are considered to be lay ascetics, although they sometimes accompany the wandering ascetics like novices. According to B. U. Jain (2002: 312), there are more than 100 *brahmacārī*s and 300 *brahmacāriṇī*s today amongst the disciples of Vidyā Sāgar alone, and some, though very few, are still under the command of the *bhaṭṭāraka*s.

Table 12.8 summarises the data published by A. Jain in 2000–2001. The ranking of the monastic positions (*pada*) adopted by A. Jain indicates that the status of *āryikā*s is generally considered to be higher than the status of *ailaka*s and *kṣullaka*s. The status categories *ācāryakalpa*, *ailācārya*[271] and *bālācārya*[272] designate the most disciplined and learned *muni*s and the chosen successor of an *ācārya*, whom he will consult in all important matters regarding the *saṅgha*. With or without the official permission of an *ācārya*, members of all categories can form their own groups (*saṅgha*), which may comprise members from all lower status categories.[273]

There is only one *ācārya* in every *saṅgha*. A Digambara *ācārya* acts independently. He either wanders alone or forms his own ascetic group (*saṅgha*), which usually includes *muni*s, *āryikā*s, *kṣullaka*s, *kṣullikā*s and sometimes one or two *ailaka*s. In 2001, of altogether 51 *ācārya*s,[274] 14 *ācārya*s wandered alone and 37 lead small groups of 2–25 ascetics. Of the 37 group leaders, 5 wandered with only one other *muni*, 2 with one *āryikā*, 18 led small groups of up to 9 male and/or female ascetics, and only 12 formed groups with 10 or more members (A. Jain 2001: 1–11).

For practical reasons, larger groups are usually sub-divided into smaller units of itinerant ascetics. Even if they belong to the *saṅgha* of one and the same *ācārya*, most *muni*s roam alone or in small bands of 2–5 male mendicants who spend their *cāturmāsa* together in one place. *Āryikā*s, however, should never wander alone and travel always in company of laity. Sometimes they can be found in pairs, or they form larger groups of 4–20 nuns who wander together independently of the monks. However, in most *saṅgha*s the members of the central group surrounding the *ācārya* are of mixed gender, and the male and female sub-groups travel and assemble together in public. They also stay at the same location for *cāturmāsa*, but reside in different buildings.[275] In the year 2001, for instance, only 13 of the 37 groups that were led by *ācārya*s were composed entirely of men – notably the groups of the popular *ācārya*s Kunthu Sāgar and Vidyā Sāgar (A. Jain 2001: 1–11).

The large and centrally organised group of Ācārya Vidyā Sāgar is exceptional amongst the contemporary Digambara *saṅgha*s because of its size and influence.[276] In the year 2001, 20.8% of all Digambara mendicants were under the control of Vidyā Sāgar. Uniquely, the structure and demographic composition of Vidyā Sāgar's group in the years 2000–2002 can be precisely reconstructed from the accounts of A. Jain (2000b, 2001) and of B. U. Jain (2002: 309–12), who received comprehensive information for this particular Digambara *saṅgha* in the year 2002. Despite its exceptional status, the Vidyāsāgara Saṅgha can serve as a paradigmatic example for the organisation of contemporary Digambara mendicant groups in general. From the year 1999 onwards, B. U. Jain's demographic figures for this *saṅgha* are said to be reliable (B. U. Jain 1996: 323, 1999: 372, n. 2). They show that in 1999 Vidyā Sāgar had 190 disciples and more than 50 *brahmacārīs* and 150 *brahmacāriṇīs* (commonly called *dīdīs*: elder sisters) under his personal command, although the figures do not exactly correspond to the self-reported number of 195 members in 1999 (62 *munis*, 10 *ailakas*, 114 *āryikās*, 9 *kṣullakas*) (Ṭoṅgyā 1999: 8). For 2001, the figure of 188 members (63 *munis*, 10 *ailakas*, 113 *āryikās* and 2 *kṣullakas*) is reported by A. Jain (2001: 9–34). Because of the rapidly increasing membership of this group, the mendicants were distributed into 26 different sub-groups in 1996, 34 in 1999, and 44 in 2001, as reflected in the number of *cāturmāsa* residencies.

In the year 2002, the group had 183 members which were divided into 42 groups: 64 *munis*, 109 *āryikās*, 8 *ailakas* and 2 *kṣullakas* (there are presently no *kṣullikās* in Vidyā Sāgar's *saṅgha*).[277] The *munis* were divided in seventeen units.[278] The majority (37) stayed together with Ācārya Vidyā Sāgar, 9 *munis* formed groups of three, 10 *munis* groups of two and 7 wandered alone. The 3 *kṣullakas* and 6 of the 8 *ailakas* – which are considered to be superior to the *āryikās* in Vidyā Sāgar's order – wandered alone.[279] The *āryikās* were divided into 16 groups of 2–17 members, who roamed independently from the male mendicants. Male and female mendicants never wander together or spend *cāturmāsa* at the same location in order to maintain the reputation of this *saṅgha* for strict standards of conduct (B. U. Jain 2002: 312).[280]

Due to the large number of sub-units, the *saṅgha* commanded a vast geographical sphere of influence, covering Madhya Pradeś (20 sub-divisions), Mahārāṣṭra (5), Rājasthān (4), Hariyāṇā (2), Uttar Pradeś (1) and Karṇāṭaka (1). At the same time, almost half of all *munis* and half of all *āryikās* spent *cāturmāsa* together in one single location in Madhya Pradeś and Mahārāṣṭra respectively.[281] These states are the two main recruitment areas for the Vidyā Sāgar Saṅgha. With few exceptions, all disciples of Ācārya Vidyā Sāgar come from Mahārāṣṭra, Madhya Pradeś and Uttar Pradeś, although he himself was born in Karṇātaka. Similar patterns of a nationwide mission starting from a regional base can be observed amongst the Śvetāmbara Terā Panthīs and amongst other contemporary Jain orders.

As a rule, all Digambara ascetics associated with the *muni saṅgha* are initiated by an *ācārya* or with his permission.[282] Indeed, all members of the Vidyāsāgara Saṅgha today have been initiated by Vidyā Sāgar himself. *Āryikās* are also by rule always initiated by an *ācārya* and should never constitute entirely autonomous orders, although they do not always move around with the *munis*.[283] Within a *saṅgha* led by an *ācārya* the *munis* and *āryikās* remain under the control of the *ācārya* who initiated them. However, though a *gaṇinī* has a lower status than a *muni*, under certain circumstances an *ācārya* will appoint a qualified nun as the leader of all the *āryikās* in his *saṅgha*, while the *munis* remain always under the direct control of the *ācārya*. As amongst most Śvetāmbara orders, in the absence of an *ācārya*, the head of the *āryikā gaṇa*, the *gaṇinī*, will act like an *ācārya* for the *āryikās*.

Sometimes, *gaṇinīs* or *āryikās* are given permission by the *ācārya* to initiate their own female disciples.[284] The lists of A. Jain for the year 2001 show that 4 *gaṇinīs* had initiated altogether 16 *āryikās* and 4 *kṣullikās*, and 4 *āryikās* initiated altogether 8 *āryikās*. There are evidently also male ascetics who performed initiations independently. In 2001, 1 *upādhyāya* and 2 *muni*s initiated altogether 6 *āryikā*s. One *ailaka*, 7 *kṣullaka*s, and one *kṣullikā* were also initiated by various *ācāryakalpa*s, *ailācārya*s and *muni*s – with or without the permission of an *ācārya*.[285] Occasionally, even self-initiations of *muni*s are reported.[286]

The monastic names of the *āryikā*s always have the double suffix *-matī mātā* at the end. The *gaṇinī*s are called *gaṇinī āryikā śrī* ____ [name] *matī mātā jī*. The *gaṇinī pramukha* Āryikā Jñān Matī and her namesake Āryikā Jñān Matī (Gujarāt), have each one *kṣullaka* amongst their disciples. However, the *kṣullaka*s were not initiated by the *āryikā*s themselves but by Ācārya Vimal Sāgar and by Ācārya Ajit Sāgar respectively.[287] According to Shāntā (1985: 514f.) and Balbir (1990: 182f.), the prominent Āryikā Jñān Matī (born 19 October 1933) was initiated by the late Ācārya Deś Bhūṣaṇ. However, D. Śāstrī (1985: 150) points out that only her *kṣullikā dīkṣā* was performed by Deś Bhūṣaṇ in 1953, but her *āryikā dīkṣā* by Ācārya Vīr Sāgar in 1956. After his death, Jñān Matī was associated with the late Ācārya Sumati Sāgar. She now commands her own separate group, which is largely composed of family members but includes also celibate male lay followers (*brahmacārī*) who were personally initiated by her in 1987 – the first event of its kind. Due to health reasons, she stays more or less permanently in her abode in Hastināpur, where her followers have built a giant cosmographic model of the continent Jambūdvīpa in concrete.[288] She is closely associated with the Mahāsabhā and with the opponents of the cosmological interpretations of the Kānjī Panth.[289]

Even the largest Digambara *saṅgha*s have a flat administrative structure, which confirms that formal organisation does not play a prominent role in Digambara monasticism. The *guru-śiṣya* link alone constitutes the institututional core of the Digambara mendicant traditions. This is reflected in publications such as D. Śāstrī's (1985) Digambara Jain Sādhu Paricay, which lists only the immediate disciples of a *muni*, but does not depict any lineages. Of the 37 groups led by *ācārya*s, only 5 comprise another office-holder apart from the *ācārya* himself. The majority of these 5 groups are not even particularly large, which suggests that the titles (2x *upādhyāya*, 2x *ailācārya*, 1 x *gaṇinī*) designate honorary rather than administrative roles. The dedicated successors of an *ācārya*, the *ācāryakalpa*s, *ailācārya*s or *yuvācārya*s,[290] *bālācarya*s and *upādhyāya*s, are usually permitted to form their own groups and to initiate their own disciples, while continuing to respect the moral authority of their *dīkṣā guru*. Because of his limited powers, an *ācārya* cannot prevent his disciples leaving, if they are supported by members of the lay communities.[291] Although, in principle, only an *ācārya* can convey the titles of *ācāryakalpa*, *ailācārya*, *bālācarya*, or *upādhyāya* or *gaṇinī* on highly respected monks or nuns,[292] there are several recognised methods for becoming an *ācārya*: either by the choice of the acting *ācārya*, or – if the *ācārya* dies without having determined a successor – by the choice of the *muni saṅgha*[293] and/or the *samāj*, or by the acclamation of a self-selected successor (e.g. the oldest disciple). In practice, the laity always interfere in the decision making process. Often, individual monks sever themselves from their *ācārya*s and simply declare themselves to be *ācārya*s in their own right. However, most *ācārya*s, even those who command their own disciples, remain nominally part of the lineage of their teacher, although 'there is no formal recognition of a line of pupillary succession' (Carrithers 1990: 153). In the absence of clear organisational and disciplinary rules (*maryādā*) – there are no established criteria for initiation and excommunication (which is never practised) – the group structure and the personnel of the peripatetic groups of a Digambara *muni saṅgha* is in perpetual flux. Changes occur not only through temporary visits in other groups for purposes of study, but also through the inflow and outflow of new mendicants from one *saṅgha* to another, and through the deliberate division of a large group into smaller groups for convenience by the *ācārya*s. It is therefore doubtful whether descent constructs are of practical importance beyond the purpose of legitimisation qua tradition. However, the doctrinal differences between the group of Vidyā Sāgar, who promotes idiosyncratic Terā Panth teachings, and the majority of the other Digambara *ācārya*s, sometimes causes the rejection of the *muni*s of one lineage by another.

Demographic trends

According to the data collected by A. Jain, the total number of Digambara ascetics increased between 2000 to 2001 by 10.3% or 84 mendicants, within a single year. The category with the greatest increase is the one of the *muni*s, who are responsible for the higher growth rate of male rather than female ascetics. In the year 2000, the 450 male ascetics represented 55% of all Digambara ascetics, the 368 female ascetics 45%, and in the year 2001 the 508 male ascetics represented 56.42% and the 394 female ascetics 43.7%. In 2001, the totally 902 ascetics were distributed over 341 groups. The average group size was only 2.65 (*āryikā*: 2.9). However, the average size of the groups (*saṅgha*) of the *ācārya*s was 6.9, which reflects their importance for the organisation of the Digambara ascetics. The fissiparous tendencies of the Digambara ascetics are illustrated by the fact that the groups led by *ācārya*s lost 18 members altogether within one year, whereas the groups led my *muni*s and *āryikā*s gained 51 and 32 members respectively.

The data published by B. U. Jain (1999: 382) show that the Digambara as a whole have by far the highest growth rate of all Jain mendicant traditions, even if we take into account that the nominal statistical growth largely reflects underreporting in earlier years.[294] Within 12 years, the reported numbers have almost tripled from a total of 363 in 1987 to a total of 960 in 1999. The overall trend has been confirmed by the reliable information of A. Jain for the years 2000–2001. This growth is all the more astonishing considering the fact that one of the first modern *muni*s, Ādi Sāgar, who died in 1943, initiated himself as late as 1913. The accelerated increase in numbers started even later, after Śānti Sāgar's death in 1955, when the Digambara laity began to actively encourage the initiation of *muni*s (Kāsalīvāl 1992: 35). Two explanations for the revival of the *muni saṅgha* are generally offered by the Digambaras: The abolition of the limitations imposed by both the colonial government and local kings on the free movement of the naked ascetics after Indian Independence, and the lack of any examination of the qualifications of the candidates because of the absence of organisational rules. Critics noted that the artificial increase of numbers due to the unchecked intake resulted in diminishing standards of conduct amongst the *muni*s, many of whom joined the mendicant life 'mainly to gain influence and to enrich themselves' and to leave again as they please.[295] This argument is rejected by others, who point out that, if this would be true, then even more initiations would take place. Instead, the inspirational role of family members who became *muni*s is highlighted, and the effects of the renaissance of Jain religious education in the last 100 years. Economic factors are generally discredited with reference to the fact that the main recruiting grounds for *muni*s in northern Karṇāṭaka and southern Mahārāṣṭra, and elsewhere, have experienced considerable economic growth over the last decades.

The most interesting result of this preliminary demographic analysis of the Digambara mendicants is that the Digambaras are the only contemporary Jain tradition which has more monks than nuns (monks 1986: 86.89%, 1990: 63.38%, 1995: 54.13%, 1998: 54.25% and 1999: 63.54%).[296] Part of the explanation for this must be sought in the Digambara doctrine of the spiritual inferiority of women, which is naturally unappealing for unmarried girls who may perceive monastic life as an alternative to marriage (Jaini 1991: 26). Yet, for all practical purposes, Digambara *āryikā*s have more personal freedom than Mūrtipūjaka *sādhvī*s, and their numbers are currently increasing. Another factor may be the lack of institutional structures, which offer protection to nuns.[297]

Jaina mendicants 1987–1999

The total number of Jain mendicants for the period between 1987 and 1999, and the relative size of the four principal mendicant traditions are summarised in Table 12.9 and Table 12.10. According to the figures published by B. U. Jain, 11,737 Jain *sādhu*s, *ailaka*s, *kṣullaka*s, *sādhvī*s and *āryikā*s have been counted in 1999. This total is based on confirmed figures only, excluding the personal estimates by B. U. Jain. The real number of mendicants was certainly higher, maybe between 100–300, disregarding *yati*s, *bhaṭṭāraka*s, *brahmacārī*s and *brahmacāriṇī*s.

The figures illustrate the continuing numerical dominance of the Mūrtipūjaka ascetics and particularly of the Tapā Gaccha mendicants, who retained more than 50% of the overall share. A look at the summary figures for 1999 and a comparison with those of 1987 shows that the ratios of the main sectarian schools remain relatively stable, considering the significant underreporting of the number of Digambara ascetics before 1996. In 1987, 59.37% of all mendicants were Mūrtipūjakas and 52.28% belonged to the Tapā Gaccha, and in 1999, 58.30% were Mūrtipūjakas and 51.51% belonged to the Tapā Gaccha. The percentages of the Sthānakavāsīs and the Terā Panthīs – whose rapidly increasing number of *samaṇīs* was not taken into account in the statistics – fell slightly; in the case of the Sthānakavāsīs, from 29.03% in 1987 to 27.46% in 1999, and in the case of the Terā Panthīs, from 7.66% in 1987 to 6.06% in 1999. By contrast, the share of the

Table 12.9 Total number of Jaina *sādhus* and *sādhvīs* 1987, 1990 and 1996

Sampradāya	*Ācārya*			*Cāturmāsa-places*			*Sādhu/Muni*			*Sādhvī/Āryikā*			*Total*		
	1987	*1990*	*1996*	*1987*	*1990*	*1996*	*1987*	*1990*	*1996*	*1987*	*1990*	*1996*	*1987*	*1990*	*1996*
Mūrtipūjaka	109	118	148	1182	1220	1309	1375	1373	1450	4100	4789	4923	5475	6162	6373
Sthānakavāsī	9	9	10	624	647	689	540	532	515	2137	2206	2479	2677	2738	2994
Terā Panth	1	1	1	135	134	147	148	157	169	559	562	584	707	719	754
Śvetāmbara	119	128	159	1941	2001	2145	2062	2062	2134	6796	7557	7986	8859	9619	10121
Digambara	19	32	36	52	103	125	227	225	326	136	130	213	363	355	539
Total	138	160	195	1993	2104	2270	2289	2287	2460	6932	7687	8199	9222	9974	10660

Note
Compare B. U. Jain 1987: 77, 1990: 59–63.

Table 12.10 Total number of Jaina *sādhus* and *sādhvīs* 1999[a]

Sampradāya	*Ācārya*	*Cāturmāsa-places*	*Sādhu/Muni*	*Sādhvī/Āryikā*	*Total*	*%*
Mūrtipūjaka	164	1485	1489	5354	6843	58.30
Sthānakavāsī	9	768	533	2690	3223	27.46
Terā Panth	1	128	154	557	711	6.06
Digambara	40	190	610	350	960	8.18
Total	214	2571	2786	8951	11737	100

Note

a These figures do not include the three recent splinter groups of the Terā Panth, nor the Sthānakavāsī traditions of Vīrāyatan and the Arhat Saṅgha.

Digambaras rose sharply from 3.94% in 1987 to 8.18% in 1999 for the reasons given earlier.

A comparison of the data from 1987 and 1999 shows that the total number of Jain mendicants has increased from 9,222 in 1987 to 11,737 in 1999.[298] The overall growth rate for the twelve year period 1987–1999 was an astonishing 26.75%: Mūrtipūjaka 24.99%, Sthānakavāsī 20.40%, Terā Panth 0.57% (1987–1996: 6.65%) and Digambara 164.46%. The growth rate would have been even higher if the sharply rising number of novices and lay ascetics had been taken into account.[299]

The accelerated increase in the number of Jain ascetics in recent years contrasts with the slow growth of the Jain population as a whole, which rose between 1981 and 1991 by 4.98%, from 3.193 million to 3.352 million. Apart from the Zoroastrians, the Jains had by far the lowest relative growth rate of all Indian religions (4.42% between 1981 and 1991, 26% between 1991 and 2001), which reduces their share of the total population from 0.48% in 1981 to 0.40% both in 1991 and 2001 (cf. M. K. Jain 1986: 33f., Vijayanunni 1991: x–xi, www.censusindia.net). The divergent growth rates of the mendicants and the lay population indicate an increasing popularity of monastic life for the period under investigation.[300] This is a puzzling fact, especially if one assumes that secularisation and religious decline are two sides of the same coin. Cort (1989: 100, n. 16) remarked that the continuing rise of the numbers of Jain mendicants is a 'quite striking phenomenon . . . given the economic and social status and the degree of Westernisation of Jain society'. If the data is correct, our pre-conceptions need to be revised. Apparently, westernisation and modernisation have not contributed to a decline, but to an increase in the popularity of renunciation amongst Jains.

Reasons for renunciation

How can we explain this? There is no easy answer. One explanation would be to argue that renunciation became more popular as a consequence of the monastic reforms at the beginning of the twentieth century, which improved the standards and therefore the appeal of monastic life. A social psychological perspective, on the other hand, would focus on the function of the institution of renunciation as a socio-cultural defense-mechanism which compensates for the disruptive effects of modernisation and socio-economic change.[301] We can, for instance, observe a strong rise in the number of male mendicants during the struggle for national independence and in the first years after Indian independence, when Gāndhī's influence reached its zenith. During these years, male mendicants in particular were attracted both by the political utility of the cultural symbolism of renunciation for the purpose of social integration and by the social activism of reform-orientated Jain *ācārya*s. But this interpretation does not account for the unprecedented popularity of renunciation in the last two decades.

Another argument points to the recent economic success of the Jain community, which enables it to lose some male workforce and to sustain larger mendicant communities. This point is sometimes raised within the Śvetāmbara Jain community. The absolute number of Jain mendicants is very small, compared to Buddhism which has at least 300,000 fully initiated *bhikkhus* worldwide[302] or Christianity which still has more than 1,000,000 monks and nuns.[303] However, the proportion of mendicants relative to the Jain population as a whole is higher than amongst Buddhists or Christians, and probably always was. In 1990 the ratio was 1 mendicant for every 336 laity (9,974 mendicants: 3,352,706 laity). This extraordinary high ratio of mendicants may indeed be explained in terms of the wealth of the Jain population, which can easily afford to feed such a big mendicant community.

Another explanation is given by Goonasekere (1986: 118f.), who interprets Jain renunciation as an institutionalised protest movement against specific social constraints within the status-conscious *baniyā* castes in Western India. Yet, this variant of the deprivation theory which explains the higher proportion of mendicants from families with a relatively lower income from a rural or small town background[304] with reference to economic difficulties and the resulting psychological tensions[305] does not account for the motivation of the monks in his own sample, who cited charismatic attraction to a monk or nun as the main factor. As we have seen, the recent accelerated increase of Digambara *munis* is sometimes explained by members of the Digambara community itself by the lack of disciplinary procedures within the Digambara mendicant orders and by the opportunity for young men from the relatively poor Digambara agricultural castes in South India to increase their status and power by joining one of the *saṅgha*s. However, if these were the only reasons, then even more young men would renounce.[306]

The main reason for the rapidly growing popularity of monastic life must be sought amongst the population of male Digambara and female Śvetāmbara renouncers. One of the most interesting findings is the continuing predominance of the male ascetics amongst the Digambara, which reflects the different status of nuns in this tradition. Amongst the Śvetāmbaras, only the Tapā Gaccha Bhuvanabhānusūri Samudāya has – for the said reasons – also more *sādhu*s than *sādhvīs*. Śvetāmbara Jainism is unique, because of the institutionalised option of

Table 12.11 Percentage of *sādhvīs* 1987–1999

Year	*Mūrtipūjaka*	*Sthānakavāsī*	*Terā Panth*	*Digambara*	*Total*
1987	74.88	79.83	79.07	37.46	75.17
1990	77.72	80.57	78.16	36.61	77.07
1996	77.25	82.80	77.45	39.52	76.91
1999	78.24	83.55	78.92	36.46	76.30

full ordination for women, which is neither offered by Hinduism nor Theravāda Buddhism.[307] Why is the percentage of female Jain mendicants presently rising? A comparison of the percentages of the *sādhvīs* between 1987 and 1999 shows a significant (>3%) increase in the number of female ascetics amongst the Mūrtipūjakas and Sthānakavāsīs, while the ratios of the Terā Panthīs and the Digambaras remained stable for the reasons cited earlier (Table 12.11). Sthānakavāsīs have the highest percentage of female mendicants, most certainly because they allow the greatest degree of freedom for *sādhvīs*, who are permitted to read all scriptures, to preach, and to roam separately. However, the overall ratios between *sādhu*s and *sādhvīs* remained not only relatively stable between 75% and 77%, they also roughly corresponded to the percentage of 72% *sādhvīs* quoted in the Kalpa Sūtra.

Social reasons, such as widowhood, unmarritability, high dowry claims amongst higher castes,[308] and other experiences of institutionalised social constraints have been cited already by Bühler and others,[309] in order to account for the consistent popularity of renunciation amongst Jain women. But this does not explain either the absence of female renunciation in similar social groups or recent developments. Reynell (1985: 269) pointed to the rising age of marriage in the Jain communities. Following on from Goonasekera (1986), Cort (1991) diagnosed 'drastic changes in the demographics of Śvetāmbar mendicancy' (ibid.: 659), from 'a situation not unlike the traditional Brāhmaṇical prescription for the *vanaprastha* and *saṁnyāsa āśrama*s, the stages of gradual withdrawal and renunciation after the householder (*gṛhastha*) stage of life', to a pattern in which 'the vast majority of contemporary ascetics are unmarried and take *dīkṣā* before the age of thirty' (ibid.: 660). He sees the improvements in the social world of women as the reason for the declining number of widow mendicants during the twentieth century. He argues that because nowadays most widows are likely to have had children – due to the rise in the age of marriage and rising health standards – they are less inclined to renounce than child widows in the nineteenth century: 'Having to raise the children means that becoming a *sādhvī* is less of a realistic option for a widow. Changing social attitudes towards widows also make it less likely that a Jain widow feels that she has little choice but to become a *sādhvī*' (Cort 1989: 111f.). Therefore, 'becoming a *sādhvī* is now seen as an alternative vocation to that of a housewife' (ibid.).[310]

This theory certainly explains the declining number of widows within the mendicant orders, but not the increasing number of unmarried women. Why should more and more young Jain women become disillusioned with family life under conditions of increasing prosperity and personal freedom? An important factor, which has not been considered thus far, is the significant change in the standard of education of Jain women. One hundred years ago, most Jain women were illiterate. Yet, the last Census of India in 2001 recorded a female literacy rate of 90.6 per cent amongst the Jains – the second highest after the Parsis – while in India as a whole it was only 47 per cent. Contemporary Śvetāmbara women are often born into privileged social groups and increasingly able to enjoy higher education, to choose their husbands within given limits but rarely to give up housework for an independent professional career, unimpaired by customary constraints. Formal education and the experience of an extended period of pre-marital independence often raise expectations which make it difficult for young educated women to re-adjust to the lifestyle of a traditional Jain housewife.

The experience of small freedoms generally increases the desire for more. Yet, monastic life does not offer more individual freedom, but an even more disciplined and restrained way of life. Socio-economic reasons for renunciation are recognised as a matter of fact but not condoned by the Jain scriptures (Ṭhāṇā 712a, 335a, Schubring 2000, § 137) and can only offer a partial explanation to a difficult question. A more complete answer must take into account multiple factors, in particular the motivating role of the Śvetāmbara doctrine of salvation and the opportunity of an alternative lifestyle offered by the existing *sādhvī* traditions themselves, as well as the elevated individual status of a nun in the Jain community. I think the most likely candidate for further exploration is the romantic image of freely roaming female ascetics, who enjoy enhanced conditions of living in reformed and materially well supported mendicant orders which offer opportunities for education and self-development that are still unavailable in traditional family life, which currently catches the imagination of young Jain women,[311] in the same way as men were attracted by the political symbolism of renunciation during the independence struggle.[312]

Concluding remarks

The most interesting result of this study, however preliminary it may be, is the emerging, nearly complete, pattern of the group structure of the current Jain mendicant traditions. The Digambara *muni* tradition is currently divided into some 341 itinerant groups and individuals, who belong to three lineages and maybe a dozen sub-lineages which have a flat administrative structure. However, more than half of all Digambara mendicants were initiated and are supervised by only a handful of *ācārya*s.[313] Although the Digambara tradition has currently no monastic orders, nor clearly identifiable schools and sects, it shows significant organisational and doctrinal faultlines which deserve further investigation. In total, the Śvetāmbara tradition is composed of some 57 independently organised groups: 27 Mūrtipūjaka, 26 Sthānakavāsī and 4 Terā Panth. These independently organised 'orders', together with their lay followers can be designated as sociological 'sects', in contrast to doctrinal 'schools', although some overlap and fluid transitions between the three categories occur. There are, of course, fewer doctrinal schools than orders and sects. The principal schools of the Mūrtipūjakas are the six *gaccha*s. The situation amongst the Sthānakavāsīs is more diffuse, since not all of the 5 founding fathers had major doctrinal differences. However, there are at least two broad schools within the Sthānakavāsī movement. On the one hand, those who follow the teachings of Dharma Siṅha, who may have had a significant, though never acknowledged, influence on the Terā Panth *ācārya* Bhikṣu and his idiosyncratic teachings, and, on the other hand, those who follow the teachings of Lava and Dharma Dāsa, who had only minor disagreements. The few globalising mendicant groups on the fringe of the Sthānakavāsī movement, which allow their ascetics to use modern means of transport and travel abroad, represent a new development, and share many attributes with Jain lay movements with the *yati* traditions, and with the disdained mendicants 'who wander alone' (Pkt. *egalla vihārī*), who can always be found on the fringes of the organised Jain ascetic traditions.[314] The use of modern means of transport might in future significantly modify the relationship between group size and size of lay following. However, the use of modern means of communication which, in contrast to the modern means of transport, are now endorsed by most, but not all, mendicant groups, has presently no significant influence on the pattern of recruitment of devotees, which continues to be predicated on regular personal contact between guru and devotee.

Acknowledgement

I am very grateful to Professor Padmanabh S. Jaini for his comments on an earlier version of this study.

Notes

1 Throughout the text, the colloquial 'Jain' rather than 'Jaina' is used, and with the exception of the Sanskritic names of sects and schools and technical Jain terms, proper names are not sanskritised.

2 See the volume *Village India* edited by McKim Marriott in 1955. Survey techniques were first used in Jaina Studies by Sangave 1959/1980, whose literature review on the social divisions of the Jains is still the standard reference source. The first book length field studies were the monographs by Mahias 1985 and Shāntā 1985. Regional, subaltern, media, etc. studies have yet to be applied on a larger scale in the emerging field of Jaina Studies.

3 'Jains', 'lay Jains in a particular location', 'Mūrtipūjaka/ Digambara Jain laity', 'Jain mendicants', 'Jain merchants', 'Jain women', 'Jain nuns', etc.

4 Following Schubring 2000: §139, 252, Folkert 1993: 153, 163 translates the ambivalent terms *gaccha* and its Digambara equivalent *saṅgha* variably as 'school', 'sect' and 'order'. He defines schools as 'doctrinally' demarcated units, sects as 'modern', and monastic orders as primarily concerned with issues of 'praxis'. Balbir 2003: 48 focuses only on 'orders' or 'lineages' – the terms are used as synonyms – and dismisses the doctrinal dimension as insignificant with regard to *gaccha*s. However,

many orders are doctrinally demarcated, as Balbir's study of doctrinal controversies concerning proper praxis shows; and even in the pre-modern period sects existed with and without core monastic orders. For alternative definitions of the terms school, order and sect see Flügel 2000: 77f. and note 8.

5 For a similar research strategy see Banks 1986: 458 and Flügel 1994: 4, 1995–96: 119, n. 4.

6 See also Cort in this volume, p. 261.

7 Sangave's 1959/1980 attempt at conducting a representative survey did not meet sufficient response from the Jain community.

8 It is neither possible nor methodologically desirable to find for every Jain (Indian) term an equivalent analytical term and *vice versa*. I would propose to define Jain schools, orders and sects in the following way (cf. Flügel 2000: 42, n. 9). Doctrinal 'schools' may inform both individuals or (un-) organised religious 'movements' of various types; organised monastic 'orders' contrast with unorganised ascetic groups and ascetics who 'wander alone' (*ekala vihārī*); 'sects' are exclusive groups which either (a) encompass both ascetics and laity, that is the classical four-fold community (*caturvidha saṅgha*) and variations created by added intermediary categories such as the *pañcavidha saṅgha* etc. or by the deliberate exclusion or factual absence of one or more of the four categories, or (b) represent self-conscious lay movements. Corresponding to the distinction between orders and sects is the distinction between the casual 'supporter' of the ascetics, the initiated (through the vow of allegiance) or simply dedicated lay 'follower', and the born and/or paying 'member' of a sect-specific Jain caste- or community organisation. See Flügel 1994: 404; and Dundas' 2003: 129 for the differentiation between 'affiliation' and 'conversion'. For the distinction between Indian monastic 'orders' and 'sects' which encompass both ascetics and laity see Vallée-Poussin 1918: 716. The peculiar dual organisation of the majority of the contemporary Jain (and other Indian) 'sects', with monastic orders as a core supported by amorphous lay communities under the spiritual command of the monks, was also highlighted by Max Weber 1920/1978: 207. See Dumont's 1980: 284 distinction between the doctrinal exclusivity of an Indian 'sect' and its social inclusivity. Generally, social categories, organised groups and gatherings need to be distinguished..

9 It seems advisable to distinguish the level of more or less exclusive 'schools', organised 'sects' and 'movements' from the level of the two principal religious 'denominations' in Jainism which Leumann 1934: 1 called '*Confessionen*'.

10 The use of the word 'Jaina' as a self-designation for both the monastic community and the lay community is a relatively recent one (Böhtlingk and Roth 1861: 132, Flügel 2005: 3f.). In the ancient texts, the words *niggaṃtha* and *niggaṃthī* referred only to Jain monks and nuns, but not to their followers, or *upāsakas* (Jacobi 1879: 5), who were classified as part of the four-fold *saṅgha* only from the late-canonical period onwards by both the Śvetāmbaras (Viyāhapannatti 792b, Ṭhāṇa 281b) and by the early Digambaras (Mūlācāra, Chappāhuḍa, etc.) (Schubring 2000, § 30, § 137).

11 Between 1871 and 1891, the Census of India gradually substituted the initial classification of the Indian population in terms of religion with a dual religion/caste classification: 1871: 'Hindu', 'Muslim', 'Other', 1881: 'religion (caste)', 1891: 'religion (sect)', 'caste (sub-caste)' (Baines 1893: 186f.). 'The…change was made in order to get rid of the notion that caste, or social distinction, was not required for Musalmans, Sikhs, Jains, and so on, or was held to be subordinate in any way to sect or religion' (ibid.: 187).

12 Brekke 2002: 129–132, cf. Dundas 2002: 4–6, Flügel 1994: 11–15.

13 'Many Jains have…undoubtedly given their religion as Hindoo, and in some cases, though these are not many, I am inclined to think the enumerators have returned as Hindoos persons who really stated their religion to be Jain. As the followers of the

Jain creed are generally held and themselves generally claim, to be Hindoos, this is not surprising: nor is this error of importance, for the domestic and social economy of the Jains differ little from the orthodox Hindoo' (Plowden 1883: 23, cf. Kitts, in Plowden 1883: 19f., Baines, in Plowden 1883, III: cvii). See Cohn 1992: 248, Sangave 1980: 3, Dundas 2002: 4–6, Carrithers 2000: 833f.

14 The main reason for the ambiguous self-identification of many Jains is the equivocal nature of the concept 'Hindu' itself.

15 For example, Keshroy 1924, Maṇilāl 1934: 270f., Natarajan 1971 I: 39. The preface of Singh's 1894: 1 report on the census of 1891 in Marwar states that in addition to the questionnaire of the census supervisors and inspectors 'a good many facts were investigated through personal enquieries from trustworthy representatives of various communities'.

16 There is no evidence for the inflated estimates that are frequently quoted in popular Jain publications. Kalidas Nag wrote in his speech to a Jain audience, 'Jainism – A World Religion', in the *Jaina Gazette* 57, 2–3 (1951): 'You should prepare a census of your own, regardless of the government census, to arrive at a correct conclusion' (ibid.: 35). Earlier attempts to produce community censuses, such as the Jain Śvetāmbara Directory (Gujarāt) written in Gujarātī (Jain Śvetāmbara Conference 1909, 1915, 1916), were lacking an integral 'Jain' communal or communitarian perspective. The first Jain Śvetāmbara Directory was produced between 1906 and 1907 in accordance with resolution No. 8 of the Jain Śvetāmbara Conference in 1904 which called for the collection of information on the followers of the different Mūrtipūjaka and 'Loṅkāgaccha' Śvetāmbara *gaccha*s and *samudāya*s in all districts (*jillā*), sub-districts (*tāluka*) and villages (*gāma*) in India. The book was intended in particular as a travel guide, for instance for pilgrimages (*yātrā*). With the help of local volunteers a questionnaire was distributed by the main coordinators Śobhacand Mohanlāl Śāh and Ḍāhyācand Trībhovan Gāndhī, who listed the following categories: the number of family houses (*kula ghara*), women (*strī*), men (*purūṣa*), caste (*jñāti*), sect (*gaccha*), literacy; and the local temples (*jina-mandīra*), images (*jina-pratimā*), monasteries (*upāśraya*), libraries (*jñāna-bhaṇḍāra*), schools (*pāṭhśālā*), old books (*pūrvācārya praṇīta grantha*), Jain societies (*sabhā*) and associations (*maṇḍala*). The interesting resulting statistics suffer from imprecise lists of *jñāti*s and *gaccha*s and problems of inaccurate self-reporting and counting, as the compilers of the first report emphasise (Jain Śvetāmbara Conference 1909: ii–iii). It was probably in response to the Śvetāmbara efforts that the eleventh meeting of the Digambara Jain Mahāsabhā inspired Māṇikcand Hīrācand Jauharī of Bombay to produce between 1907 and 1914 the Shri Bharatvarshiya Digambara Jain Directory (Jhaveri 1914) 'for the good of all Digambara Jain brothers'. The ensuing publication contains lists of towns, leading community members, caste, professions, etc. Cf. Sangave 1980: 119–121, 124–130. I am grateful to Yashvant Malaiya, who has pointed this source out to me. Nowadays, excellent self-produced national statistics are available for certain castes, such as the Khaṇḍelvālas, which have a high proportion of Jain members.

17 A Digambara Jain layman told me that the results of the Census of India of 1981 and 1991 in North Indian states were manipulated by 'Hindutva' inspired enumerators who wrote 'Hindu (Jain)' into the forms, even if the answer given was 'Jain'. During the Census of 2001, Jain community leaders started awareness rising campaigns to prevent a recurrence of these practices.

18 The introduction of a question on religious affiliation into the UK-census of 2001 stirred similar sentiments amongst leading members of the Jain community in Britain. For a Hindutva inspired variation of demographic *angst* regarding the outgrowth of the Hindus by the Muslims in India see A. P. Joshi *et al.* 2003.

19 B. U. Jain 1999, for instance, lists the Mūrtipūjaka *samudāya*s according to their size. See Appadurai 1993: 117 on the role of numbers for the colonial 'illusion of

bureaucratic control'. The role of numbers (regarding fasts etc.) is even greater in traditional Jainism.

20 Jacobi 1884: 267, n. 1, Schubring 2000 § 22: 44. Sharma 1999: 78f. noted that Ācārya Hemacandra's 12th C. Triṣaṣṭiśalākāpuruṣacaritra associates varying numbers of monks, nuns and laity with different Jinas.

21 Cf. Jaini 1991: 25.

22 Plates 13–15 in A. Cunningham's Archaeological Survey Report 20.3, in Bühler 1887: 169.

23 Sthavirāvalī 5, in Jacobi 1884: 289.

24 Sangave now seems to prefer the less charged term 'communitarianism' (personal communication, 2 January 2005).

25 Cort 1989: 491–94 summarised B. U. Jain's demographic data of the Mūrtipūjaka *sādhus* and *sādhvīs* in 1986 in an appendix, but noted their incompleteness, which was partly rectified by B. U. Jain's subsequent publications.

26 These are the conventional dates. Except in the case of the 'panths', I have represented the names of monastic orders in their sanskritised form, but proper names in their spoken form.

27 The primary source of information on the origins of these groups is the Pravacanaparīkṣā of the sixteenth century Tapā Gaccha *upādhyāya* Dharma Sāgara. For an overview of their history, doctrines and practices see M. U. K. Jain 1975.

28 The *paṭṭāvalīs* of the Kharatara Gaccha and of the A(ñ)cala Gaccha were published in many Sanskrit and vernacular editions. They were studied by Klatt 1894 and by Śivprasād 2001. See also Pārśva 1968: 9–21.

29 The Gacchādhipati of the A(ñ)cala Gaccha is presently Śrīpūja Moti Sāgar Sūri (born 1944). See Photographs. The Śvetāmbara Loṅkāgaccha still has one *yati* but no *sādhus*. A notable feature of the *yati* traditions is that they do not have any female members.

30 The surprisingly high figure of more than 3,517 ascetics and a higher proportion of monks than nuns is reported in the A(ñ)cala Gaccha Paṭṭāvalī for the A(ñ)cala Gaccha in the year 1180. It is said that Ācārya Āryarakṣita Sūri (1080–1180) initiated '2100 sâdhus and 1130 sâdhvîs, the âcârya-padam to 12 sâdhus, the upâdhyâya-padam to 20, the paṇḍita-padam to 70, the mahattarâ-padam to 103 sâdhvîs (Samayaśrî and others), the pravartinî-padam to 82 sâdhvîs, the total number of sâdhus and sâdhvîs being 3517' (Klatt 1894: 175). If the figures are true, then a huge number of Jain mendicants must have existed during the heydays of Jainism in the medieval period.

31 The equally centralised Rāmacandrasūri Samudāya of the Tapā Gaccha is the largest order. Balbir 2003: 48f. provides much information on the doctrinal foundation of the A(ñ)cala Gaccha, but not on initiation procedures.

32 According to Ācārya Jay Sundar Sūri of the Bhuvanabhānu Samudāya, the last *saṅghācārya* of the Vijaya Śākhā was Ācārya Vijay Prabhā, who commanded. *c.*200–300 ascetics. After him the number of *saṁvegī sādhus* decreased to 20–25 under Buṭerāy in the early nineteenth century (plus 10–15 in the Sāgara Śākhā, and 40–50 in the Vimala Gaccha), while the Tapā Gaccha *yati* orders had more than 1,500 members. Personal communication, Mumbaī 23 October, 2005.

33 Cf. Kañcansāgarsūri *et al.* 1977: 355–61.

34 Desāī 1983 I: 106ff., M. Śāh 1987. The precise origins of the trust are not known, but Śāntidās Jhaverī was instrumental in institutionalising this influential organisation.

35 Probably only the *saṃvegī sādhu* tradition was interrupted.

36 Kañcansāgarsūri *et al.* 1977.

37 See Paul Dundas' forthcoming book.

38 Only the Kharatara Gaccha and the A(ñ)cala Gaccha still have some *yatis*.

39 'In his biography of Nemīsūri, one of the great reformist *ācāryas* of the early twentieth century, Śīlcandravijay 1973: 6 has estimated the number of *saṃvegī sādhus*

in the period 1845–1865 to be no more than 25 to 30. While it is not clear if he means only within the Tapā Gacch, or in all the Mūrtipūjak *gaccha*s, the number is still very small. He further comments on the low level of scholarly knowledge among these *sādhu*s. Thus, the position of the Śvetāmbar *saṃvegī sādhu* in the early nineteenth century was not all that different from the position of the full-fledged *muni*, or *nirvāṇ svāmī*, among the South Indian Digambaras (see Carrithers...)' (Cort 1989: 99, n. 14). Unfortunately, the only information we have on the numbers of *yati*s in the nineteenth century are a number of *kṣetrādeśapaṭṭakas* and sporadic evidence in the reports of British colonial officials. A *cāturmāsa* list of 1867 issued by the successor of Ācārya Vijay Devendra Sūri, Ācārya Vijay Dharaṇendra Sūri, for instance, lists 212 monks (figures for nuns are not given) organised into 74 groups of 2 and 14 groups of 4 (Sandesara 1974: 229–233). For the year 1891, Singh 1894: 82 cites the number of 834 '*jati*s' in Marwar (Jodhpura) alone, but gives no figures for the *saṃvegī*s, who 'owe their origin to one Anand Bimal Suri' (ibid.: 95). The Jain mendicants in Mārvāṛ were classified as 'devotees' of the 'priests' (*yati*s, *brāhmaṇ*s, etc.) and all counted under the label 'Samegi, Dhundia etc.' (ibid.: 85). Their total figure of 2,314 comprises 725 male and 1,589 female mendicants.

40 The Jain Śvetāmbara Directory published in 1916 by the reformist Jain Association of India lists some 228 monks, divided into 79 groups, and 203 nuns, divided into 40 groups, apparently belonging to reformed segments of the Tapā Gaccha, including the groups of the *ācārya*s Vijay Kamal Sūri, Vijay Nemī Sūri and Buddhi Sāgar Sūri which were mainly active in Kacch and Mārvāṛ (Jain Śvetāmbara Conference 1916: 18–22).

41 See Cort 1999.

42 In 2002, the total number had increased to 7,541 mendicants, 1,585 *muni*s and 5,947 *sādhvī*s. The Tapā Gaccha had 6,696 mendicants, 1,445 *sādhus* and 5,242 *sādhvī*s (cf. ibid.: 70, 305).

43 Jaini 1991: 26 explains the attractiveness of the Tapā Gaccha for women with the 'spiritual equality' offered to Śvetāmbara *sādhvī*s. However, Mūrtipūjaka *sādhvī*s are still not allowed to read certain *āgama*-texts nor to deliver public sermons, a fact which Shāntā 1985: 315, 321f., n. 5, 456 explains by pointing at the high number of *ācārya*s, which limits speaking opportunities.

44 'The *samudāy* is not as formal a grouping as the *gacch*. Mendicants in one *samudāy* will, for a variety of reasons, sometimes travel with mendicants of another *samudāy*. But mendicants do not travel with mendicants of another *gacch*, as that would involve changing some of the details of their daily practices' (Cort 1991: 663). In his later publications, Cort 1999: 44, 2001: 46 supplies enough material for the conjecture that many *samudāya*s have a distinct doctrinal and organisational identity with separate *pañcāṅga*s, rituals and lay support.

45 Shāntā 1985: 329.

46 The use of the sign '-' in the columns indicates cases of separation (cf. Tristuti Gaccha).

47 The names of all *ācārya*s of the Vijaya Śākhā are preceded by the title 'Vijaya'. Some *gacchādhipati*s are not *ācārya*s (*sūri*).

48 After his death, Prem Sūri's line split into two *samudāya*s, led by Rām Candra Sūri and Bhuvan Bhānu Sūri respectively. Following Rām Candra Sūri's (1896–1991) death, this *samudāya* was named after him by his successor Mahoday Sūri (died 2002), who was in turn succeeded by Ācārya Hem Bhūṣaṇ Sūri (B. U. Jain 1996: 165–177). Rām Candra Sūri was one of the most influential and orthodox *ācārya*s of the Vijaya Śākhā. He nearly became the leader (*śāsanasamrāṭa* or *adhipati*) of the entire Tapā Gaccha. Cort 1989: 103, n. 18 quotes demographic data which show that the Dān-Prem Samudāya has grown from 36 *sādhu*s in 1944 to 219 *sādhus* in 1975

(Cort had no information on the numbers of *sādhvīs*). By 1999, this tradition had split into four sections, including Śānti Candra Sūri's group, and Vibuddha Prabhā Sūri's group. However, after 1996 the Amṛtasūri Samudāya, lead by Jinendra Sūri, was re-integrated into the Rāmacandrasūri Samudāya, which had in all 905 members in 1999, 290 *sādhus* and 615 *sādhvīs*, and 1,138 members in 2002, 310 *munis* and 828 *sādhvīs* (B. U. Jain 1999: 197, 2002: 169). Important particularities, in addition to the *be tithi* doctrine, are the performance of *guru pūjā* in the manner of the *aṣṭaprakārī pūjā* to the body of the *ācārya* Rām Candra Sūri and his statues, and the permission for lay followers to mount Śatruñjāya Hill even during *cāturmāsa* (personal communication).

49 This group separated in 1998 from the Rāmacandrasūri Samudāya. It operates mainly in Rājasthān. In 1999 it had 45 mendicants, 23 *sādhus* and 22 *sādhvīs* (B. U. Jain 1999: 325f.).

50 This *samudāya* also derives from Prem Sūri, but was renamed after Bhuvan Bhānu Sūri (1911–1993) who broke with Rām Candra Sūri in 1986 after a dispute on calendrical issues (*ek tithi-be tithi*). See Cort 1999, B. U. Jain 1996: 179–87. Originally, the group was active in Hālār, but its main sphere of activity is now Gujarāt and Mahārāṣṭra. In 1999 it had 560 members, 285 *sādhus* and 275 *sādhvīs* (B. U. Jain 1999: 230), in 2002 712 members, 361 *sādhus* and 351 *sādhvīs* (B. U. Jain 2002: 186). It is one of the few contemporary Jain orders which has more monks than nuns, because Ācārya Prem Sūri objected to the initiation of *sādhvīs*, since their presence would inevitably cause the development of relationships between monks and nuns. One of Prem Sūri's disciples, Ācārya Jaśodev Sūri, successfully criticised this rule, by pointing to the unnecessary problems it creates when entire families want to renounce. Prem Sūri allowed him to start an order of nuns within his tradition, on the condition that he and his successors would be responsible for the supervision of the nuns, of which the main line of *gacchādhipatis* should remain aloof. After the death of Jaśodev Sūri, his successor Rajendra Sūri is now responsible for the *sādhvī* section.

51 This group separated itself in 1995 under Prem Sūri from the tradition of Rām Candra Sūri (whose *guru* was Prem Sūri). In 1999, it was nominally reincorporated into the Rāmacandrasūri Sampradāya, but still maintains a separate existence. It is mainly active in Hālār, near Jāmnagar. In 2002 it had 26 mendicants, 4 *sādhus* and 22 *sādhvīs* (B. U. Jain 2002: 170, cf. 273).

52 Nīti Sūri was a pupil of Buddhi Vijay and the teacher of Bhakti Sūri and Siddhi Sūri (Ratna Prabha Vijay 5, 2 1948–1950: 217f.). In 1999, this group had 465 mendicants, 50 *sādhus* and 415 *sādhvīs* (B. U. Jain 1999: 254), in 2002, 426 mendicants, 40 *sādhus* and 386 *sādhvīs* (B. U. Jain 2002: 211).

53 In 1999, this group had 245 mendicants, 49 *sādhus* and 196 *sādhvīs* (B. U. Jain 1999: 295), the figures for 2002 – 128 mendicants, 46 *sādhus* and 82 *sādhvīs* – are incomplete (B. U. Jain 2002: 250).

54 Figures for the period between 1987 and 1996 are incomplete. In 1999, this group had 384 mendicants, 27 *sādhus* and 357 *sādhvīs* (B. U. Jain 1999: 271), in 2002, 311 mendicants, 31 *sādhus* and 280 *sādhvīs* (B. U. Jain 2002: 227). Today, Ācārya Vijay Arihant Sūri is the head of the order. Apparently, 150 *sādhvīs* joined the Rāmacandrasūri Sampradāya (ibid.: 231).

55 Siddhi Sūri (1895–1959) was succeeded by Megh Śrī. One of his pupils was Bhuvan Vijay, the father and *dīkṣā guru* of the influential scholar Muni Jambū Vijay. In 1999, it had 250 mendicants, 30 *sādhus* and 220 *sādhvīs* (B. U. Jain 1999: 289), in 2002, 260 mendicants, 29 *sādhus* and 231 *sādhvīs* (B. U. Jain 2002: 240). The present *gacchādhipati* Rām Sūri has been selected, because he is the *ācārya* with the highest monastic age (ibid.: 246).

56 Dev Sūri's (1911–2002) predecessor was Merū Prabhā Sūri. The present head of the order is Ācārya Suśīl Sūri. In 1999 this group had 543 mendicants, 138 *sādhus* and

405 *sādhvī*s (ibid.: 242), and in 2002, 567 mendicants, 146 *sādhu*s and 421 *sādhvī*s (B. U. Jain 1999: 230). It is mainly active in Gujarāt and Rājasthān, and has produced many scholarly monks.

57 Vijay Vallabh Sūri (1870–1954) was one of the most influential reformers of the Tapā Gaccha in the twentieth century and an important promotor of modern education and social reform. He was initiated in 1886 by Vijay Ānand Sūri (Ātmā Rām). The ascetics of this tradition wear yellow garments, originally to distinguish themselves from the *yati*s who were clad in white. They permit nuns to give public lectures, and use microphones and in big cities flush toilets (in other *samudāyas* the excretions of the mendicants are collected and then flushed away by the laity). They share food with the mendicants of the Keśarasūri and Dharmasūri Samudāyas, who descend from the same lineage. In 1999, this group had 274 mendicants, 54 *sādhu*s and 220 *sādhvī*s (B. U. Jain 1999: 277), and in 2002, 295 mendicants, 60 *sādhu*s and 235 *sādhvī*s (B. U. Jain 2002: 232). After the death of Vijay Indradinn Sūri (1923–2002), who originated from a tribal group in Gujarāt, Ācārya Vijay Ratnākar Sūri became the head of the order.

58 In 1999, it had 259 mendicants, 57 *sādhu*s and 202 *sādhvī*s (B. U. Jain 1999: 284), in 2002, 250 mendicants, 55 *sādhu*s and 195 *sādhvī*s (B. U. Jain 2002: 235). Jin Bhadra Sūri died in 1999. His predecessor was Kīrti Candra Sūri, his successor as *gacchādhipati* is Aśok Ratna Sūri (B. U. Jain 1999: 288f.).

59 Mohan Lāl was a pupil of Khānti Viyay, who was a disciple of Buddhi Vijay. He was particularly active in Bombay. In 1999, this group had 44 mendicants, 22 *sādhu*s and 22 *sādhvī*s (B. U. Jain 1999: 323), in 2002, 57 mendicants, 26 *sādhu*s and 31 *sādhvī*s (B. U. Jain 2002: 272).

60 Vijay Dharma Sūri (1868–1922) was an influential moderniser. He was initiated in 1887 by Vṛddhi Candra Vijay (died 1893), a pupil of Buddhi Vijay, and was succeeded by Vijay Indra Sūri (born 1881). In 1999, this group had 236 mendicants, 33 *sādhu*s and 203 *sādhvī*s (B. U. Jain 1999: 302), in 2002, 229 mendicants, 33 *sādhu*s and 196 *sādhvī*s (B. U. Jain 2002: 251).

61 Hem Prabhā Sūri's predecessor was Svayam Prabhā Sūri. The figures for 1987–1996 are based partly on estimates. In 1999, this group had 188 mendicants, 14 *sādhu*s and 174 *sādhvī*s (B. U. Jain 1999: 309), in 2002, 217 mendicants, 22 *sādhu*s and 195 *sādhvī*s (B. U. Jain 2002: 258).

62 Kanak Sūri was the teacher of Catur Vijay, the teacher of Puṇya Vijay (1895–1971), who inspired the creation of the L. D. Institute in Ahmedabad in 1957. In 1999, this group had 451 mendicants, 29 *sādhu*s and 422 *sādhvī*s (B. U. Jain 1999: 262), in 2002, 533 mendicants, 35 *sādhu*s and 498 *sādhvī*s (B. U. Jain 2002: 217). After the death of Kalāpūrṇ Sūri in 2002, Ācārya Vijay Kalā Prabhā Sūri became head of the order (*gacchādhipati*), which is also called Kaccha-Bāgaṛa Samudāya, because of the regional base of Kanaka Sūri (ibid.: 226).

63 Ratnākar's predecessor was Lakṣmī Sūri. This *samudāya* is predominantly active in Mevāṛ. In 1999, this group had 148 mendicants, 20 *sādhu*s and 128 *sādhvī*s (B. U. Jain 1999: 313), in 2002, 153 mendicants, 22 *sādhu*s and 131 *sādhvī*s (B. U. Jain 2002: 261).

64 Śānti Candra Sūri was a pupil of Vijay Ānand Sūri (Ātmā Rām). In 1999, this group had approximately 75 mendicants, 25 *sādhu*s and 50 *sādhvī*s (B. U. Jain 1999: 322), and in 2002, 165 mendicants, 19 *sādhu*s and 146 *sādhvī*s (B. U. Jain 2002: 270). In 2002, Bhuvan Śekhar Sūri died and was succeeded by Ācārya Rājendra Sūri (ibid.: 271).

65 Both the present *ācārya* Som Sundar Sūri and Jin Candra Sūri were initiated by Bhuvan Śekhar Sūri. In 1999, this group reported the figure of 80 mendicants, 8 *sādhu*s and 72 *sādhvī*s (B. U. Jain 1999: 320), in 2002, 151 mendicants, 19 *sādhu*s and 132 *sādhvī*s (B. U. Jain 2002: 268), but the figures are incomplete.

66 This group was started by Ānand Sāgar Sūri, a bitter opponent of Rām Candra Sūri, the leading monk of the Vijaya Śākhā in the twentieth century (cf. Cort 1999: 43): 'Rāmcandra Sūri (1895–1991) has argued that the scriptures should not be published at all, a view which found many partisans, while the other party followed the view that of Sāgarānanda Sūri (1875–1950), celebrated as the "uplifter of the scriptural tradition" (*āgamoddhāraka*), who advocated the publication of the scriptures but along with the old *niryukti* and *vṛtti* commentaries' (Dundas 1996: 90, cf. Banks 1992: 110). The group experienced frequent changes of leadership in the 1980s. In 1986, the leader was Devendra Sāgar, 1987 Cidānand Sāgar, 1990 Darśan Sāgar, who was succeeded by Sūryoday Sāgar, and Aśok Sāgar in 2004–2005. The former *sādhu* Citra Bhānu (Candra Prabhā Sāgar), who continues to inspire diaspora Jains in the US and the UK, was a member of this lineage from 1942 to 1970. In 1999, this group had 740 members, 150 *sādhu*s and 590 *sādhvī*s (B. U. Jain 1999: 215), in 2002, 956 members, 136 *sādhu*s and 820 *sādhvī*s (B. U. Jain 2002: 171). Its main agenda is currently the defence of the scientific accuracy of the canonical Jaina cosmography.

67 Buddhi Sāgar Sūri (1874–1925), a disciple of Ravi Sāgar and one of only four *saṃvegī sādhu ācārya*s in 1913 (Cort 1997: 125), popularised the worship of the protector god Ghaṇṭākarṇa amongst Gujarātī Jains, particularly in Mahudi near Vījāpur (Cort 1989: 406–407, 428–433, 2001: 91, 164–168). He was succeeded by Monogam Sāgar (?), Rudhi Sāgar, and Subodh Sāgar Sūri, who inspired the construction of the *tīrtha*s Vījāpur and Mahesāṇā, where the *tīrthaṅkara* Sīmandhara Svāmī is venerated. Ācārya Padma Sāgar Sūri (born 1934), who inspired the construction of the Jain centre at Kobā near Ahmedabad, also belongs to this order. In 1999, this *samudāya* had 135 mendicants, 45 *sādhu*s and 90 *sādhvī*s (B. U. Jain 1999: 316); for 2002 the figures are incomplete: 115 mendicants, 45 *sādhu*s and 70 *sādhvī*s (B. U. Jain 2002: 264).

68 Cidānand Sūri's predecessor was Ravi Vimal Sūri. He is now succeeded by Pradyumna Vimal Sūri. Figures are based on estimates. In 1999, it had about 51 mendicants, 6 *sādhu*s and 45 *sādhvī*s (B. U. Jain 1999: 360), in 2002 approximately 49 mendicants, 4 *sādhu*s and 45 *sādhvī*s (B. U. Jain 2002: 304).

69 This *sampradāya*, which is also called Vidhi Pakṣa, is mainly active in Kacch, Hālār and Mumbaī (Jain 1996: 274). In 1999, it had 250 members, 29 *sādhu*s and 221 *sādhvī*s (B. U. Jain 1999: 327), in 2002 249 members, 29 *sādhu*s and 220 *sādhvī*s (B. U. Jain 2002: 274). For its history see Śivprasād 2001, Balbir 2003.

70 Jin Mahoday Sāgar Sūri's predecessor was Jin Uday Sāgar (died 1996). The current *gacchādhipati* is Upādhyāya Kailāś Sāgar. This *sampradāya* is mainly active in Rājasthān, Mahārāṣṭra, Gujarāt, M.P., Dillī and Mumbaī. In 1999, it had 229 mendicants, 20 *sādhu*s and 209 *sādhvī*s (B. U. Jain 1999: 340), in 2002 258 mendicants, 28 *sādhu*s and 230 *sādhvī*s (B. U. Jain 2002: 286).

71 Figures are incomplete. In 1999, this group had 118 mendicants, 28 *sādhu*s and 90 *sādhvīs* (B. U. Jain 1999: 340), in 2002, 127 mendicants, 27 *sādhu*s and 100 *sādhvī*s (B. U. Jain 2002: 293). The *ācārya* position is the only administrative post of this group (B. U. Jain 1999: 252, n.4). In the year 2000, a group of three *sādhu*s led by Muni Jay Ānand split off and founded a fourth Tristuti tradition (B. U. Jain 2002: 293). The most famous monk of the Tristuti Gaccha was Rājendra Sūri (1827–1906), who is renown as the composer of the Abhidhānarājendra Kośa.

72 In 1999, this group comprised approximately 70 mendicants, 19 *sādhu*s and 51 *sādhvī*s (B. U. Jain 1999: 353); in 2002, 73 mendicants, 22 *sādhu*s and 51 *sādhvī*s (B. U. Jain 2002: 297).

73 Praśam Candra's predecessor was Labdhi Sūri (1884–1961). In 1999 and 2002, this group consisted of 2 *sādhu*s only (B. U. Jain 1999: 361, 2002: 299).

74 Because of a dispute on proper ascetic conduct, this order split from the Tapā Gaccha in 1515 under Sādhu Ratna Sūri (Ratna Prabha Vijay 5, 2 1948–1950: 134). Although this group is sometimes considered to be part of the Tapā Gaccha, its *sādhu*s do not use

'*vijaya*' or '*sāgara*' as a suffix or prefix. The group does not have administrative posts and is the only order that is led by two monks: Muni Bhuvan Candra is currently responsible for the region of Kacch and Saurāṣṭra, and Muni Vijay Candra for the region of Mumbaī. Bhuvan Candra's predecessor was Muni Rām Candra. In 1999, this group had 74 mendicants, 9 *sādhus* and 64 *sādhvīs*, though numbers are incomplete (B. U. Jain 1999: 356), in 2002, 68 mendicants, 9 *sādhus* and 59 *sādhvīs* (B. U. Jain 2002: 301).

75 Figures are incomplete. B. U. Jain 1999: 362 estimates a total of 28 *sādhus* for the year 1999, and 16 for the year 2002 (B. U. Jain 2002: 305).

76 Cort's observations are inversely mirrored by R. K. Jain's 1999: 32 distinction between the charismatic 'individualistic, prophet-derived and sect-like character of the Digambara religious field as contrasted with the group-bound, "priest"-derived and church-like ambience of the Shvetambara religious field'; a distinction which deliberately ignores the institutions of the *bhaṭṭāraka* traditions.

77 Cort 2001: 46 observed that subtle liturgical differences do not exist 'between samudāys'. However, according to Muni Mukti Vallab Vijay of the Bhuvanabhānu Samudāya, four different lists of *maryādās* exist within the Tapā Gaccha. A leading monk of the Ramacandrasūri Samudāya mentioned the figure of 64 differences in the rules and regulations of the *samudāyas*. A number of monks and nuns of other *samudāyas* confirmed these statements (personal communications, December 2004–January 2005). But more research is necessary to map out the details.

78 Only if their *samudāyas* derive from the same lineage food is sometimes shared; for instance between the members of the Vallabhasūri, the Keśarasūri and the Dharmasūri Samudāyas.

79 Personal communication of monks and nuns of the Vallabhasūri Samudāya and of the Rāmacandrasūri Samudāya in January 2005. In his will, Rām Candra Sūri determined Mahodaya Sūri as his successor. But according to A. Luithle (personal communication, July 2005) the present *gacchādhipati* Hem Bhūṣaṇ Sūri was elected in an assembly of *ācāryas* in 2003 after one year of dispute.

80 Cf. Jacobi 1915: 270, Cort 1991: 669, n. 19.

81 As evidence, the cases of the centralised orders of the A(ñ)cala Gaccha, the Ramacandrasūri Samudāya, and the Śvetāmbara Terā Panth may be cited, all of which have a large number of members.

82 The contrast between the principles of pupillary descent and group organisation in Jain monastic traditions has been analysed in Flügel 2003b: 182–193.

83 Personal communication, Ācārya Jay Sundar Sūri, Mumbaī 23 October 2003.

84 The term *sthānakavāsī* in its present meaning became only current in the context of the early twentieth century unification movement of the traditions of the *pañcmuni*.

85 The dates given in the available sources are not matching up. See Flügel 2000: 46–48, in press.

86 See Flügel 2000: 61–68 on the grades of the *sāmāyika* vow.

87 Flügel 1995–1996, 2000, 2003a, 2003b, in press.

88 Jaini 1979: 246f., n. 8 quotes the figure of 847 mendicants for the year 1977. Goonasekere 1986: 27 speaks of about *c.*900 for the year 1983. Cort 1989: 491, 96 calculates altogether 553 ascetics – probably for the year 1986. Shāntā 1985: 332, 341, 489 cites Terā Panth sources for the much higher figure of 1,757 ascetics for the year 1981, which broadly corresponds to Sangave's 1980: 323f. plausible figure of 1,900 Sthānakavāsī mendicants in the year 1946.

89 B. U. Jain 2002: 65f.

90 This is seen as a potential cause of conflict. Personal communication, Ratan Jain, Delhi 16 October 2004.

91 This is in accordance with the scriptures. See Ṭhāṇa 164b, Vav 10.15–17 and the Nisīha Bhāsa. On the issue of child initiation see also Balbir 2001.

92 See Flügel forthcoming.

93 The resolution was taken on the 5–6 December 1932. See Jauharī 1946: 197.

94 Another source informs us that, at the time of Loṅkā's death, the Loṅkā Gaccha had 400 disciples and 800,000 lay followers (Prakāścandra 1998: 32).

95 Manohar Dās was a disciple of Dharma Dās. The two Amarmuni traditions continue his line today.

96 The following figures were given by Maṇilāl (1934) for selected smaller traditions in 1933: Khambhāt Sampradāya (15 mendicants: 6 *sādhus* and 9 *sādhvīs*), Cauthamala (Raghunātha Dharmadāsa) Sampradāya (18 mendicants: 3 *sādhus* and 15 *sādhvīs*), Ratnavaṃśa (Dharmadāsa Sampradāya) (47 mendicants: 9 *sādhus* and 38 *sādhvīs*), Nānā Pṛthvīrāja (Mevāṛa Dharmadāsa Sampradāya) (43 mendicants: 8 *sādhus* and 35 *sādhvīs*), Kaccha Āṭh Koṭi Moṭā Pakṣa (53 mendicants: 22 *sādhus* and 31 *sādhvīs*), Kaccha Āṭh Koṭi Nānā Pakṣa (39 mendicants: 14 *sādhus* and 25 *sādhvīs*), Līmbaḍī Gopāla Sampradāya (26 mendicants: 7 *sādhus* and 19 *sādhvīs*), Goṇḍala Nānā Pakṣa (no *sādhus* and 'some' *sādhvīs*), Barvāḍā Sampradāya (24 mendicants: 4 *sādhus* and 20 *sādhvīs*).

97 The latest findings have been summarised by Degenne and Forsé (1999: 21): 'Acquaintances form the largest, a virtual network that includes everyone the respondent has ever met. The average for this outermost circle is about 5,000 people. The circle of immediate contacts is far smaller. The average respondent has only 100–200 people he can contact to link himself up to a target stranger. She has regular talks with fewer than twenty people per week, subject to variation with age, sex, education and other sociodemographic criteria. Again, real confidants average only three'.

98 It is regarded as a sign of the laxity though if Jain mendicants deliberately maintain contacts, because this contradicts their vow to renounce the world.

99 For a comparable study in the context of Christian monasticism see Sampson 1969. I have collected data for an analysis of a Jain monastic network in the year 2001. See Flügel forthcoming.

100 This argument is outlined in Flügel 2003b: 183.

101 Nair 1970: 6–7 quotes Muni Dhana Rājā's data for 1955 and 1969. Balbir 1983: 40f gives figures for 1975 and 1981. Shāntā 1985: 332, 341, 489 cites a Terā Panth census by Nāhaṭā for 1982. The total number of ascetics in 1983 can be found in Goonasekere 1986: 27, who reproduced historical data from 'a Jain Śvetāmbara Mahāsabhā Publication' (ibid.: 88f.). His tables do not contain information on the composition of the monastic community after 1944, which can be extracted from the volumes edited by Navratnamal 1981ff. and the tables of Balbir 1983: 41, B. U. Jain 1987: 77, 1990: 62–63 and in the annual almanacs of the Terā Panth (e.g. Navratnamal 1991: 28).

102 See Flügel 2003a.

103 Cf. B. U. Jain 1999: 193. New intermediary categories of female novices, or *samaṇera*, are also characteristic for the reformist 'protestant Buddhism'. See Bloss 1987: 13, Kawanami 1990: 20.

104 The change affected the *sādhvīs* first. Under Ācārya Rāy Cand (1821–1851) and Ācārya Jītmal (1851–1881) only 58.44% and 57.1% of all newly initiated *sādhus* were Osvāls, but already 73.8% and 89.3% of all new *sādhvīs*. Under Kālū Rām, 89.7% of newly initiated *sādhus* and 95.3% of *sādhvīs* were Osvāls (Navratnamal 1981 II: 311, 322, III: 273, 291, X: 309, 325). This pattern still prevails. In 1985, 96.98% of the Terā Panth *sādhus* and 94.46% of the *sādhvīs* were Osvāls (Navratnamal XII 1985: 522f.).

105 A percentage of 58.6 of Ācārya Jītmal's ascetics came from Mārvāṛ and Mevāṛ and only 24.9% from the Thalī region. By contrast, only 29.7% of Ācārya Kālū Rām's ascetics were recruited in Mārvāṛ and Mevāṛ, but 60.97% in Thalī. This pattern was perpetuated under Ācārya Tulsī. In 1985, 23.5% of his mendicants came from Mārvāṛ and Mevāṛ and 63.3% from Thalī (*sādhus*: 58.62%, *sādhvīs*: 65.35%)

(cf. Navratnamal 1981 II: 311, 322, III: 273, 291, VI: 486, 495, VIII: 348, 356, X: 309, 325, 1985 XII: 522).

106 The average number of initiated ascetics is one of the determinants of the status of an *ācārya*. On average, Bhikṣu initiated 1.13 *sādhus* and 1.3 *sādhvīs* per year, Kālū Rām 5.63 *sādhus* and 9.44 *sādhvīs*, and Tulsī 4.84 *sādhus* and 11.13 *sādhvīs* between 1936 and 1981.

107 For a statistical analysis of the demographic structure of the Terā Panth order and the motives of renunciation in the year 2001 see Flügel forthcoming.

108 While his predecessors initiated on average *c.*20% of minors, Kālū Rām initiated 45.8% under age *sādhus* and 41.5% under age *sādhvīs* (Navratnamal 1981: 309, 325). The Terā Panth has not yet followed the example of the Sthānakavāsī Śramaṇa Saṅgha, which has officially raised the minimum age for initiation for both girls and boys from eight to fourteen.

109 Cf. Balbir 1983: 42, 2001.

110 On the Tāraṇa Svāmī Panth see Cort (in this volume). The Totā Panth and the Gumāna Panth, an eighteenth century splinter group of the Terā Panth, have not yet been studied systematically. For an overview see Sangave 1980: 51–54.

111 M. U. K. Jain 1975: 94f.

112 The following historical reconstruction is therefore necessary.

113 P. Śāstrī 1985b: 537.

114 No source is given.

115 '*Inhī gach meṁ nīkasau, nūtan terahpanth / solah sai terāsie, so sab jab jānant //631//*' (Bakhatrām, in Premī 1912/n.d.: 22).

116 Cort 2002: 67 lists a reference to Megha Vijaya, who located the origin of the Adhyātma movement in 1623, in an appendix.

117 No original sources of the tradition itself on its origins have been found so far. I follow John Cort's 2002: 52f., 67–69 summary here.

118 Narendra Kīrti of Amer was *bhaṭṭāraka* between 1634 and 1665 (Premī, cited by Cort 2002: 52).

119 P. Śāstrī 1985b: 536, cf. p. 538 found the expression '*terā – bhagavan āp kā panth*' not only in Joghrām (Joghrāj) Godīkā's work, but also in Jñān Cand's work Śrāvakācāra and in the Jaypur Paṇḍit Pannālāl's Terā Panth Khaṇḍan, where also thirteen practices are listed which the tradition rejected – opposing the use of fruits in *pūjā*, the worship of Padmāvatī and other gods and goddesses, etc. (ibid.: 539). For more references see P. Śāstrī 1992: 146–149.

120 Like the Śvetāmbara Terā Panthīs, the Digambara Terā Panth *paṇḍits* exploit the ambiguity of the word *terā panth*. The two words *terā* and *terah* are homonyms: *terā* means 'your' and *terah* means 'thirteen'. However, it seems the Śvetāmbara Terā Panthīs prefer to interpret 'your' (*terā*) more in the sense of 'the people' rather than 'God'. Cf. Budhmal 1995: 69–76, Flügel 1994–1995: 123, n. 12, cf. p. 122, n. 9. It is likely that this wordplay is a religio-poetic topos that can be found in other traditions as well.

121 He refers to a newly found inscription from 950 CE which identifies the Balātkāra Gaṇa with the Sarasvatī Gaccha and the Mūla Saṅgha: '*vi. saṃvat 1007 māsottamamāse phālgunamāse śuklapakṣe tithau caturthāṃ budhavāre śrīmūlasaṅgha sarasvatīgaccha balātkāragaṇa ṭhākurasī dās pratiṣṭhaṃ*' (in P. Śāstrī 1985b: 535), and – because the word *śuddāmnāya* is used in different contexts both for the Terā Panth and the Balātkāra Gaṇa – concludes elsewhere that they are one: '*terāpanth śuddhāmnāya tathā mūlasaṅgha kundakundāmnāya balātkāragaṇa sarasvatīgaccha ye donoṁ ek haiṁ*' (P. Śāstrī 1992: 146).

122 On the presumed special relationship with the Parvār caste see particularly P. Śāstrī 1992: 114–149.

123 '*kahe jodh aho jin! terāpanth terā hai*' (Joghrām Godīkā, in P. Śāstrī 1985b: 538). See also Paṇḍit Pannālāl cited ibid., and P. Śāstrī 1985b: 536: '*terā – bhagavan āp kā panth*'.

124 '*bīsapanth arthāt viṣampanth – ṭeṛhāpanth jinmat meṁ mānya nahīṁ*' (Jaina Nibandha Ratnāvalī, in P. Śāstrī 1985b: 538). The word was apparently coined by Jinendra in his Jñānānand Śrāvakācāra which is cited by P. Śāstrī with approval (ibid.: 244).

125 Like the Terā Panthīs, the Tāraṇa Panthīs also venerate 'true' ascetics. See Tāraṇa Taraṇa Svāmī 1933, P. Śāstrī 1985c, and J. E. Cort (in this volume).

126 For the two debates between 20 August 1963 and 1 October 1963 in Jaypur on Kānjī Svāmī's theory of *krama-baddha-paryāya*, or sequence-bound-modification, see P. Śāstri 1967, 1985a, Jaini 1977, Bharill 1980, P. H. Śāstrī 1985. On the divisive disputes amongst the Digambaras after Kānjī Svāmī's death, see R. K. Jain 1999: 101–117.

127 Jhaveri's 1914: 1418–1424 community census counted altogether 450, 584 Digambaras in 1914. For detailed numerical data on Jain castes from this census and the Śvetāmbara Directory of 1909 as well as the Colonial Indian Census see Sangave 1980: 119–121, 124–130.

128 Sangave 1980: 52. This estimate may be too high. According to P. S. Jaini (personal communication), the distinction was totally unknown in South India and is even now rejected by most.

129 Glasenapp 1925: 357, Sangave 1980: 52.

130 Cf. Cort 2002: 62. Earlier, the now extinct 'heterodox' Kāṣṭhā Saṅgha was associated with the Agravāls in Rājasthān (K. C. Jain 1963: 72), and the Mūla Saṅgha, which was dominant in Western India between the fourteenth and the nineteenth century, primarily with the Khaṇḍelvālas (and Parvārs) (ibid.: 73, 103). Both in South India and in North India, close relationships developed between Digambara *gaccha*s and certain *jāti*s or *gotra*s. An important factor for the success of the Terā Panth amongst specific Digambara caste communities seems to have been the long term absence of the institution of the *bhaṭṭāraka* as a caste guru. Sangave 1980: 318 notes that in the 1950s 'the Hummaḍa Mevāḍā, Narasiṅgapurā, Khaṇḍelvāla, Saitavāla, Chaturtha, Pañchama, Bogāra, Upādhyāya, Vaiśya and Kshatriya castes have their separate *Bhaṭṭārakas* while the Kaṭhanerā, Buḍhelā, Agravāla, Golāpūrva, Jaisavāla, Nevi and Hummaḍa (from Mahārāshṭra) castes have no *Bhaṭṭāraka* system at all. Besides in some castes like Paravāra, Bannore, Dhākaḍa and Bagheravāla the *Bhaṭṭāraka* system was prevalent formerly but now it is extinct'.

131 Glasenapp 1925: 357 reported that the contrast was so big that the followers of one 'sect' do not visit the temples of the other. However, through an unrepresentative survey amongst the Jain laity Sangave 1980: 299 found that 'among the persons who do not know about their divisions the Digambaras form a larger proportion than the Śvetāmbaras. Besides, it has been stated that there are no such divisions among the Digambaras at present'.

132 'The Bīspanth-Terāpanth division is not found in Karnataka, Tamil Nadu or southern Maharashtra' (Cort 2002: 70, n. 3).

133 R. K. Jain 1999: 89f., 101–117.

134 Cort 2002: 65 contrasts the lack of organisation of the Adhyātma movement with the 'organisational foundation' of the Terā Panth which is still influential. However, the organisational capacity of the local temple- and library trusts of the Terā Panthīs is insignificant compared to the old institutions of the *bhaṭṭāraka* traditions and in particular the (trans-) regionally organised Śvetāmbara sects.

135 Cf. Jhaveri 1914, Sangave 1980: 119ff.

136 Cort 2002: 62.

137 See Deo 1956: 360ff. for a beginning.

138 We have seen that the Sthānakavāsīs also use the terms *samudāya, saṅgha* and *vaṃśa*. According to Hoernle 1891: 342 *āmnāya* – 'succession' – is a synonym of *kula*, as is the term *santāna. Anvaya* – 'line' – can also be used as a synonym. Sangave 1980: 299 presents a less convincing picture of the organisational levels of the Digambara *bhaṭṭāraka* traditions (*saṅgha, gaṇa, gaccha, śākhā*) than Joharāpuraka 1958, whose book is still the most detailed study to date.

139 Joharāpurkara 1958: 19 noted that the writings of Kunda Kunda were 'certainly some cause of unease' between some of the late medieval *bhaṭṭārakas* of the Sena Gaṇa. Allegedly, the 52 *paṭṭa* Bhaṭṭāraka Vīr Sena (died 1938) had a great belief in Kunda Kunda's Samayasāra (ibid.: 35, n. 20). Many *paṭṭāvalī*s of the *bhaṭṭāraka* traditions present Kunda Kunda conventionally as their ancestor, for instance the Balātkāra Gaṇa (ibid.: 44, 71, n. 24).

140 Translated by Hoernle 1891: 350f., cf. Hoernle 1892: 59.

141 The third leader of the Nandi Saṅgha was apparently Kunda Kunda (Padma Nandin), who is cited as the ancestor of today's Sarasvatī Gaccha of the Nandi line (*anvaya*) which identifies itself with the Balātkāra Gaṇa of the Mūla Saṅgha and calls itself Kundakundānvaya (Hoernle 1891: 342, 350f.). The early dates for Kunda Kunda have been questioned by Dhaky 1991: 190, and the artificial link to Kunda Kunda by Dundas 2002: 122.

142 Epigraphia Carnatica 2, 77, 82, in Schubring 2000: § 30, p. 63.

143 Schubring 2000: § 30, p. 63 cites in this respect also Indra Nandin's sixteenth century work Nītisāra and the nineteenth century *paṭṭāvalī*s translated by Hoernle 1891, 1892.

144 See M. U. K. Jain 1975: 126–128 for the complex (putative) internal divisions of the Mūla Saṅgha, whose history in South India has not been analysed.

145 Apart from the available inscriptions, *praśasti*s and nineteenth century *paṭṭāvalī*s, the two main sources on the history of the Digambara traditions are Deva Sena's Darśanasāra of 933 CE and the Śvetāmbara monk Guṇa Ratna's fifteenth century commentary to Haribhadra's Ṣaḍdarśanasamuccaya. See the summaries by Glasenapp 1925: 355f., Schubring 2000: § 30, pp. 61–63, Varṇī 1997 I: 317 and Joharāpurkara 1958. A source cited by Delamaine 1827: 414 is the Buddhavilāsa.

146 Rāja Śekhara writes in his Ṣaḍdarśanasamuccaya 21–25 (*c.*1350): 'In the Kāṣṭhāsaṅgha, the broom is ordained to be made of the yak's tail. In the Mūlasaṅgha, the brush is made of peacock feathers. The broom has never been an issue in the Māthura Saṅgha. The Gopyas sweep with peacock feathers; their greeting is "*dharma labhā*". The rest greet with "*dharma vṛddhi*". The Gopyas declare release for women. The three Saṅghas other than the Gopya declare that women cannot attain it. Neither the other three nor the Gopyas hold that an omniscient takes food; There is no release for one wearing a monk's garb, though he keep the vow well' (tr. by Folkert 1993: 363). Schubring 1964: 224 mentions that both the Yāpanīya and the Kāṣṭhā Saṅgha taught that women can reach salvation.

147 The view that the North Indian Kāṣṭhā Saṅgha is 'heterodox' and the Mūla Saṅgha 'orthodox' is nowadays – after the disappearance of the Kāṣṭhā Saṅgha – expressed by Bīsa Panthīs and Terā Panthīs alike, which both claim descent from the Mūla Saṅgha. See P. Śāstrī 1985b.

148 Premī 1912/n.d.: 4, M. U. K. Jain 1975: 130.

149 Schubring 2000: § 30, p. 62.

150 Glasenapp 1925: 355.

151 Cf. Folkert 1993: 161, and Dundas 2002: 122.

152 The tradition was first mentioned in Deva Sena's Darśanasāra. There are two versions of its origins. According to the prevalent version it was founded in the year 753 CE (? Vikram Saṃvat: 696 CE) in the village Nāndeḍ (Nandiyaḍ) in the region of modern Bombay by Ācārya Kumār Sena I of the Pañcastūpa Saṅgha (Kumārasena II lived around 955). Kumār Sena was a reformer who insisted on the observation of the 'sixth

aṇuvrata', that is, no consumption of food and drink after dark, and on the performance of atonements in accordance with the Digambara Āgamas. A later and less popular (and convincing) version relates that Ācārya Loha I from the Nandi Saṅgha Balātkāra Gaṇa founded this tradition some 515 years after Mahāvīra. He converted 125,000 members of the Agravāla caste in Agrohā near Hisār, and used wooden (*kāṣṭhā*) images for the *pūjā* ritual (this story contradicts other legends narrating the origins of this caste). The use of wooden images was strongly opposed by the older Digambara traditions, because it begins to rot after being bathed with milk and water during the traditional *pañca kalyāṇaka pūjā*s. The tradition was also known under the name Gopuccha Saṅgha, because the *muni*s used whisks made of the hair of cow tails rather than peacock feathers (Glasenapp 1925: 356, Varṇī 1998 I: 320f.). According to Joharāpurkara (1958: 211), the name Kāṣṭhā Saṅgha derives from the name of a village near Dillī. From the fourteenth century internal divisions are reported, and at the end of the seventeenth century four distinct branches, such as the older Māthura Gaccha, were established, with important seats in Ārā (Bihār), Hisār (Hariyāṇā), Surat (Gujarāt), Gvāliyar (Madhya Pradeś) and Kārañjā (Mahārāṣṭra) (ibid.: 6f., 210–212). The *ācārya*s and *bhaṭṭāraka*s of this tradition produced important literary works (cf. ibid.: 238–247). The Kāṣṭhā Saṅgha seems to have continued at least till the early nineteenth century and maybe into the twentieth century (cf. Glasenapp 1925: 356, Dundas 2002: 124 citing Col. Tod).

153 This is again mentioned in Surendra Kīrti's work Dānavīra Maṇikcandra of 1690. See M. U. K. Jain's (1975: 112–126) extensive description of the sub-divisions of this tradition.

154 According to both the Darśanasāra (Glasenapp 1925: 356), and the Subhāṣita Ratnasaṃdoha of Ācārya Amitagati II (993–1026 CE), the founder of the Māthura Gaccha was Muni Rām Sena, who became *ācārya* in 896 CE; but he is not mentioned in the *paṭṭāvalī* of the tradition (Varṇī 1998: 321f.). He originally belonged to the Kāṣṭhā Saṅgha and rejected both the use of peacock feather and cow hair whisks (*picchī* or *piñchī*). His tradition was therefore called Niṣpacchaka Saṅgha. He demanded from his disciples the explicit rejection of other *guru*s, and argued that salvation can only be reached through meditation on the true self (*ātmā dhyāna*) following the teaching of Kunda Kunda rather that Bhūtabali and Puṣpadanta's Ṣaṭkhaṇḍāgama (Darśanapāhuḍa and Darśanasāra, ibid., Schubring 2000: § 30, p. 62). Until its demise sometime in the nineteenth or twentieth century, the main seats of this *gaccha* were in Hisār (Rājasthān), Gvāliyar, and Senāgiri (Madhya Pradeś) (Joharāpurkara 1958: 6f., 238–247). Its followers belonged mainly to the North Indian Agravāla caste (ibid.: 13).

155 Bāgaḍa is a region near Chittor (M. U. K. Jain 1975: 118). Certain branches of the tradition may have predated the formation of the Kāṣṭhā Saṅgha (cf. ibid.: 118–120). It was also called Punnāṭa Gaccha, with reference to its place of origin in Karṇāṭaka, or Lāḍabāgaḍa Gaccha, with reference to its centre in Gujarāt. It is mentioned in inscriptions between the seventh century and fifteenth century and maintained important seats in Masāṛh (East India) and Kārañjā (Mahārāṣṭra) (Joharāpurkara 1958: 6f., 257–262). Its followers belonged mainly to the Baghervāl caste (ibid.: 13).

156 This tradition is mentioned only in two sources of the tenth and fifteenth century (Joharāpurkara 1958: 6f., 263). It apparently re-joined the Lāḍa-Bāgaḍa Gaccha (M. U. K. Jain 1975: 120).

157 This tradition (also: Vidyā Gaṇa and Rāmasena-Anvaya) was founded in the fifteenth century in the village Nandītaṭ – the modern Nāndeḍ/Mumbaī. It came to an end in the early ninteenth century. One of its main seats was Sojitrā in Gujarāt (Joharāpurkara 1958: 6f, 293–299). Its followers belonged mainly to the Hūmaḍa caste (ibid.: 13). The founder of this tradition appears to have been Ratna Kīrti (M. U. K. Jain 1975: 125).

158 See in particular A. N. Upadhye 1933, 1970, 1974. For the subdivisions of the Yāpanīya tradition see M. U. K. Jain 1975: 136.

159 Premī 1912, n.d.: 4, Glasenapp 1925: 356.

160 Upadhye 1933: 225.

161 Schubring 2000: § 30, p. 62, n. 2.

162 The details of the lineage histories in South India have yet to be investigated.

163 The tradition is first mentioned in the *praśasti* of the Uttarapurāṇa of Guṇa Bhadra's disciple Loka Sena (898 CE) and in inscriptions of the ninth century and of the sixteenth century. It started with Candra Sena, Ārya Nandin and the famous scholastic Vīra Sena (816 CE), the author of the Dhavalā Ṭīkā of the Ṣaṭkhaṇḍāgama, and is famous for the many important Digambara philosophers such as Samanta Bhadra and Siddha Sena Divākara in its ranks. It had/has seats in Kārañjā (Akola, Berara) and Kolhāpura (still existing) in Mahārāṣṭra. The tradition was occasionally called Sūrasthagaṇa and may have been popular in Saurāṣṭra during a certain period. The last *bhaṭṭāraka* of this tradition was apparently Vīra Sena, a great believer in Kunda Kunda's Samayasāra, who died sometime between 1850 and 1938 (Joharāpurkar 1958: 6f., 26–38, cf. Upadhye 1948, M. U. K. Jain 1975: 84–88).

164 The tradition is first mentioned in inscriptions of the tenth century, most of them in Karṇāṭaka. Its branches had seats in Ajmer, Bhānpur, Cittauṛ, Jaypur, Jehrahaṭ, Nāgaur (Rājasthān), Aṭer, Gvāliyar, Senāgiri (Mālvā), Īḍar, Surat (Gujarāt), Bhānapur, Jherahaṭ, Malakheḍ and its sub-branches Kārañjā and Lātūr (Mahārāṣṭra). See Joharāpurkara 1958: 6f., 44–47, and the lineage diagram p. 209. The seats had special links to particular local castes, such as the Hūmaḍ caste in Surat, the Lamecū caste in Aṭer, the Parvār caste in Jerahaṭ and the Khaṇḍelvāla caste in Dillī and Jaypur (ibid.: 12). From the tenth (Śāstrī 1985b: 535) or the fourteenth century (Joharāpurkara 1958: 44) the tradition was known under the names Sarasvatī Gaccha, Vāgeśvāri Gaccha, Bhāratī Gaccha, Śāradā Gaccha. The original name seems to have been Balagāra Gaṇa (ibid.: 44. cf. M. U. K. Jain 1975: 88ff.) and Nandi Saṅgha (Hoernle 1891: 350, 1892: 73). In Kananda Balagāra (*baḷegāra*) means bangle-maker (a caste name) which was transformed into Skt. *balatkāra* or 'force' according to A. N. Upadhye. I am grateful to P. S. Jaini for this information.

165 Joharāpurkara 1958: 71–78. The tradition was established in the late fourteenth/early fifteenth century. The nineteenth and last *paṭṭa* of this branch was Devendra Kīrti, who died in 1916 (ibid.: 76f., n. 29). The Lātūra Śākhā split off this line in 1675 (ibid.: 77). Two *samādhis* have been built for *bhaṭṭāraka*s of this tradition (M. U. K. Jain 1975: 90, n. 80).

166 Joharāpurkara 1958: 86–90. See the picture of Bhaṭṭāraka Viśāl Kīrti (died 1891) and of his successor who was also called Viśāl Kīrti and enthroned in 1914 (ibid.: 89f.). The seat in Lātūra is revered by the Saitavāla Jains (M. U. K. Jain 1975: 94, n. 92). According to Tuschen (1995: 23), it became defunct only recently.

167 This tradition started the *bhaṭṭāraka* tradition by introducing the custom of wearing clothes in public. The main seats of this now defunct line, which was first closely connected with the Baghervāla caste and later with the 'Hūṃbad' and Brāhmaṇ castes were Surat etc. in Gujarāt, Ajmer, Dillī and Jaypur. After the death of Padma Nandin in 1493, the Uttara Śākhā branched out into the Īḍar, Surat and Dillī-Jaypur Śākhās (Joharāpurkara 1958: 93–96, cf. M. U. K. Jain 1975: 94–96).

168 This tradition was started by Sakal Kīrti. It possesses a famous library in Īḍar. See Joharāpurkara 1958: 153–158, cf. M. U. K. Jain 1975: 102–105.

169 In 1477 the Bhānapura Śākhā split off the Īḍara Śākhā. The last *bhaṭṭāraka* was apparently Devacandra (1730–1748). See Joharāpurkara 1958: 166–168. According to M. U. K. Jain 1975: 105 a splinter group of the tradition still prevailed in South India in 1975 (?).

170 This branch, founded in 1436 by Devendra Kīrti, was closely associated with the Hūmaḍa caste. In 1495 Tribhuvan Kīrti split off and founded the Jerahaṭa Śākhā. See Joharāpurkar 1958: 194–201, 207, cf. M. U. K. Jain 1975: 107–111.

171 This branch, which became defunct early in the seventeenth century, was closely associated with the Parvār caste (Joharāpurkar 1958: 202–209, cf. Varṇī 1998 I: 320f.)

172 After 1514 the tradition split into three branches, two of which are the Nāgaura- and the Aṭera Śākhā. The last *bhaṭṭāraka* of the Dillī-Jaypur line was apparently Candra Kīrti who either died or was installed in 1918 (Joharāpurkara 1958: 109–113). Cort (2002: 62) writes that the last *bhaṭṭāraka*, a Candra Kīrti, died in 1969 and was deliberately not replaced. The Dillī-Jaypur Śākhā was closely related to the Khaṇḍelvāla caste and established special links to the Kachavāhā kings of Amer, where the *bhaṭṭāraka* seat was shifted in the sixteenth century (ibid.: 51, cf. Clémentin-Ojha, forthcoming).

173 In 1524, Ratna Kīrti was appointed as the first head. The last *bhaṭṭāraka* was apparently Devendra Kīrti in the mid-twentieth century (Joharāpurkara 1958: 121–125). Many *bhaṭṭāraka*s belonged to the Chābaḍā and Seṭhī sub-castes (M. U. K. Jain 1975: 98–101).

174 This branch splitt off the Uttara Śākhā in 1493 and was closely associated with the Lamecū caste (Joharāpurkara 1958: 132–135, cf. M. U. K. Jain 1975: 101f.).

175 The inscriptions artificially incorporate the names of all famous Digambara *ācārya*s of the past in one lineage.

176 Joharāpurkara 1958: 44.

177 Shāntā 1985: 137f.

178 Until the nineteenth century, the term *bhaṭṭāraka* was used both by Bīsa Panthī Digambaras and Mūrtipūjaka Śvetāmbara *yati*s. Today, it is only used by Bīsa Panthī Digambaras.

179 Personal communication of Bhaṭṭārak Lakṣmī Sena, Kolhāpura 4 January 2005.

180 Sangave 1980: 317–322.

181 The Śvetāmbaras list the *abhrama-varjana pratimā* already on the sixth position, before the *sacitta-tyāga pratimā*, and call the eleventh stage *śramaṇa-bhūta pratimā* (Williams 1963: 173).

182 Williams 1963: 172 notes that the *pratimā*s were originally conceived as a progressive sequence rather than as alternative options. Jaini 1979: 185 suggests that originally each *pratimā* may have been practiced only of a limited period of time.

183 Williams 1963: 179 found the first mentioning of this distinction in the eleventh century text Śrāvakadharmadohaka by an unknown Digambara author.

184 Hiralāl Jain's view that the word *ailaka* derives from Skt. *acelaka*, 'unclothed' or 'partially clothed', was rejected by Williams 1963: 179, n. 5 who pointed out that the *ailaka* is characterised explicitly as *cela-khaṇḍa-dhara* in the twelfth century Vasunandi-Śrāvakacāra edited by H. Jain.

185 If the sources of Williams 1963/1983: 180 are still of influence, then full access to the 'mysteries' of the scriptures is not granted to lay ascetics. The initiation rituals of the (Vimala Saṅgha) Digambara *muni*s are detailed in Syādvādmatī 2000: 442–452. Their key ritual elements apart from the acceptance of the respective vows (*vratāropaṇa*) are: the shaving and pulling out of some of the hair (*keśa-luñcana*), change of dress/nakedness (*nāgnya-pradāna*), change of name (*nāma-karaṇa*), ritual giving of the peacock feather broom (*piccha-pradāna*), of the scriptures (*śāstra-pradāna*), and of the water pot (*kamaṇḍalu-pradāna*) (ibid.: 442). The *muni*s receive a large broom (*picchi*), and all other (lay) ascetics only a small broom (*picchikā*). For a commented compilation of other textual sources for the Digambara *muni dīkṣā* see Kanakanandī 1994: 214–226. On the basis of incomplete information, Carrithers 1990: 153 suspects that there is little evidence for the existence of a *saṅgha* in the Digambara *dīkṣā* rituals: 'there is not even an explicit vow to live in obedience to a guru' and 'no formal recognition of a line of pupillary succession', nor the passing on of a mantra

(ibid.: 155). He argues that the orientation towards the 'aesthetic standard of self-restraint' is the main element in the transmission of tradition (ibid.: 157). Although his general observation is shared by all modern scholars, mantras of a general nature, oriented toward the veneration of the guru, are prescribed in the *dīkṣā vidhi* texts. For instance: '*ṇamo arahaṃtāṇaṃ... atha gurvāvalīṃ paṭhitvā, amukasya amukanāmā tvaṃ śiṣya iti kathayitvā saṃyamādyupakaraṇāni dadyāt*' (Syādvādmatī 2000: 447). One of the mantras used for the inauguration of an *ācārya* is: '*oṃ hṛīṃ śrīṃ arhaṃ saḥ ācāryāya namaḥ. ācāryamantra*' (p. 482).

186 Varṇī 1997 I: 468f., II: 188f. Personal communication of Āryikā Muktimatī of the Vimal Sāgar Saṅgha, 22.10.2004, and of the *bhaṭṭāraka*s Jina Sena and Lakṣmī Sena, 2–4 January 2005. The rules and regulations cannot be discussed here in detail.

187 *Bhaṭṭāraka*s do not have many *śiṣya*s and often ask dedicated followers to send their young sons to take boarding and lodging in their *maṭhas* to receive religious training in addition to their secular school education.

188 This happened in the case of Jina Sena of the Nāndaṇī *maṭha*.

189 Since the generic name is apparently associated with the *bhaṭṭāraka* lineage there are at least three Lakṣmī Senas, of the *maṭha*s in Kolhāpura, Jinākāñcī and Siṅhanagadde (Penagoṇḍa in Andrah Prades̒), amongst the contemporary *bhaṭṭāraka*s.

190 According to Premī 1912, n.d.: 27, the *bhaṭṭāraka dīkṣā* is – in principle – similar to a *muni dīkṣā*. The *bhaṭṭāraka* can therefore not be categorised as a layman. The ritual, he writes, is prescribed in an ancient book in the Bhaṇḍār of Īḍar. There it is stated that a layman can only be installed as a *bhaṭṭāraka* when the search for a worthy *muni* has failed. The initiation requires the nakedness of the candidate and the ritual plucking of the hair (*keśa luñcana*). After receiving the *sūri mantra*, the candidate is attributed with the qualities of an *ācārya*, and continues to practise nakedness when he eats his meals and during certain ceremonies: '*is se sāph mālūm hotā hai ki, bhaṭṭārak vāstav meṁ gṛhastha nahīṁ hai, muni tathā ācārya haiṁ*' (ibid.: 28). Joharāpurkar, interviewed by Shāntā 1985: 186, n. 99, emphasised that even today's *bhaṭṭāraka*s continue to accept five '*mahāvrata*s' (effectively *aṇuvrata*s), not only four as often mentioned in the literature, for instance in Flügel 2003a: 8. According to Carrithers 1990: 151, 'the method of succession was derived not from any Jain prescriptions but from the usages of local polity'. This impression is echoed by the views of the *bhaṭṭāraka*s Jina Sena and Lakṣmī Sena (personal communication 2–4 January 2004).

191 Śruta Sāgara Sūri's sixteenth century commentary of the Ṣaṭprābhṛta, the Ṣaṭprābhṛtādisaṃgraha 1.24. See Glasenapp 1925: 72, Joharāpurkar 1958: 89 (original passage reproduced), 91, M. U. K. Jain 1975: 94f., Cort 2002: 41.

192 Cort 2002: 41 quotes Bakhatrām Sāh's Buddhi Vilās of 1770 as the source of the information that 'Bhaṭṭārak Prabhācandra of Delhi' [(r. 1253–1327) the predecessor of Padma Nandin (M. U. K. Jain 1975: 95f.)] 'took to wearing a loincloth during the reign of Feroz Śāh Tughluq (1351–1380) at the request of the king'. Cort (ibid.) also cites a discussion of an inscription suggesting the date of 1333. Premī 1912/n.d.: 1f. refers to oral accounts of the events in Delhi. See also Sangave 1980: 269–271, 317–322 and Tuschen 1995: 20f.

193 Dates according to M. U. K. Jain 1975: 95f.

194 According to Bhaṭṭāraka Lakṣmī Sena of Kolhāpura, the name of the first *bhaṭṭāraka* of the Sena Gaṇa was Vidyā Sāgar and the first *maṭha*s were established in Dillī, Kolhāpura, Jinākāñcī (Tamil Nāḍu) and Penagoṇḍa (Andrah Prades̒) – the *maṭha*s of his associates. Personal communication, Kolhāpura 4 January 2005. V. Śāstrī 1932: 5–7 gives the line of succession of Vidyā Sāgar, whose *samādhi* is in Akīvāṭ/Zilā Cikoḍī. It comprises some *muni*s, but ends with Bhaṭṭāraka Vidyā Mān (r. 1904 ff.), whose conduct is unfavourably contrasted with Muni Śānti Sāgar's.

195 Lath 1981: lvi.

196 See Sangave 2001: 136. In 1875–1876, Bühler 1878: 28 visited a *bhaṭṭāraka* in Delhi, who was accompanied by 'ascetics (who are called paṇḍits)'. Bühler described the *bhaṭṭāraka*s he had met during his travels as 'very ignorant'. This statement was still echoed by Sangave 1980: 321f. 100 years later. See Cort (in this volume p. 299 n.9) on the Canderī seat of Bhaṭṭāraka Devendrakīrti.

197 Personal communication by the Jain Bhavan in Bangalore 31 December 2005 and by Bhaṭṭāraka Jina Sena, Nāndaṇī 2 February 2005, who seems to be the only *bhaṭṭāraka* who currently has a disciple, Brahmacārī Vṛṣabha Sena. According to Tuschen 1997: 23, the seats of Bhaṭṭāraka Viśālakīrti in Lātūr in Mahārāṣṭra (traditionally associated with the Saitavāla caste) and Bhaṭṭāraka Yaśakīrti in Pratāpgaṛh in Rājasthān (traditionally associated with the Narasiṁhapura caste), which are mentioned by Sangave 2001: 135, are now defunct. This would leave only nine *bhaṭṭāraka*s. For the names of more than thirty-six old *bhaṭṭāraka* seats see Joharāpurkara 1958: 6f., M. U. K. Jain 1975: 131, Sangave 2001: 134. In addition to the seats that can be linked to specific traditions, Joharāpurkara 1958: 6f. mentions a number of other, now equally defunct, seats in Eastern India (Ārā), Gujarāt (Navasārī, Bhaḍaurī, Khambhāt, Jāmbūsar, Ghoghā), Mālvā (Devgaṛh, Dhārā Nagarī, Lalitpur, Mahuā, Ḍūṅgarpūr, Indaur, Sāgavāḍā, Aṭer) and Mahārāṣṭra (branches in Riddhipur, Bālāpur, Rāmaṭek, Nāndeḍ, Devagiri, Paiṭhan, Śiraḍ, Vaṇṭ, Vairāṭ, Vaphād, Malayakheḍ, Kāryarañjakpur, etc.). There is currently no information on the old seats in the Pañjāb, only on various seats in Dillī. Apart from Meraṭh and Hastināpur, there are no *bhaṭṭāraka* seats reported from Uttar Pradeś. Sangave 2001: 134 mentions the additional seats of Jehrahaṭ, Keśarīyajī, Mahāvīrjī (Rājasthān), Sonāgiri (Mālvā), Bhanpur, Sojitrā, Kalol (Gujarāt), Nāgpur, Nāndaṇī (Mahārāṣṭra), Narasiṁharājapura (Karṇāṭaka), Svādī in Sondā (Karṇāṭaka) and Melasittamūra, that is Jinakāñcī (Tamil Nāḍu).

198 The seat was established in the eighth century and belongs to the Mūla Saṅgha Kundakundānvaya Nandi Saṅgha Sarasvatī Gaccha Balātkāra Gaṇa (Tuschen 1997: 28). It is associated with the Bogāra caste (Sangave 1980: 318, 2001: 137) and governed by Bhaṭṭāraka Devendrakīrti.

199 Associated with the Kṣatriya caste (ibid.), and governed by Bhaṭṭāraka Lalitkīrti.

200 Associated with the Pañcama caste (ibid.), and governed by Bhaṭṭāraka Lakṣmī Sena I (I add Roman numbers to distinguish *bhaṭṭāraka*s with the same title). The seat has two other *maṭha*s under its administration, in Hosūr-Belgāṁv and Rāybāg, and is associated with the Sena Gaṇa *maṭha*s in Dillī, Jinakāñcī and Penagoṇḍa (Siṁhanagaddī in Narasiṁharājapura). For Lakṣmī Sena's works see for instance Sangave 2003.

201 Also called Jinakāñcī. Associated with the Kṣatriya and Vaiśya castes and governed by Bhaṭṭāraka Lakṣmī Sena III of the Sena Gaṇa (Sangave 2001: 137).

202 Traditionally associated with the Upādhyāya caste (ibid.). According to P. S. Jaini (personal communication), the last two, including the current Bhaṭṭāraka Cārukīrti II, who is a non-Shetty (Śreṣṭhi) Jain, were not of that caste. There is a Trust comprising members of all three local castes (Shetty, non-Shetty, Upādhyāya) who selected the current *bhaṭṭāraka* (on suggestion of Bhaṭṭāraka Cārukīrti of Śravaṇabeḷagoḷā).

203 The seat is associated with the Caturtha caste (ibid.), 'the only caste among the Jainas which follows agriculture as the main occupation' (Sangave 1980: 96), and is governed by Bhaṭṭāraka Jina Sena. The seat has three other *maṭha*s under its administration, in Kolhāpura, Tesdāl and Belgāṁv – and in the past also in Dillī.

204 Associated with the Bogāra (and Kṣatriya and Vaiśya) caste and governed by Bhaṭṭāraka Lakṣmī Sena II of the Sena Gaṇa (Sangave 2001: 137).

205 The current seat was established in the tenth century and derives its descent from the Mūla Saṅgha Deśiya Gaṇa Pustaka Gaccha. It is associated with the Vaiśya caste (ibid.) and occupied by Bhaṭṭāraka Cārukīrti I.

206 A summary table of the relationship between specific castes and their principal *bhaṭṭāraka* seats can be found in Sangave 1980: 318. There were only nine *bhaṭṭāraka*

seats left until the head of the Deśiya Gaṇa, Bhaṭṭāraka Cārukīrti of Śravaṇabeḷagoḷā, created three more *bhaṭṭāraka* seats: in Karṇāṭaka Kambadahalli/Nagamaṅgala (Bhaṭṭāraka Bhānukīrti), and Kanakagiri Maṭha in Maleyur (Bhaṭṭāraka Bhuvanakīrti), and in Tamil Nāḍu Tiruvannamalai (Bhaṭṭāraka Dhavālakīrti). Apart from the Hūmachā Maṭha, and the Svādī Maṭha in Sondā which is governed by Bhaṭṭāraka Bhaṭṭākalaṅka, all *bhaṭṭāraka* seats are presently under the authority of Lakṣmī Sena of Kolhāpura for the Sena Gaṇa, and of Cārukīrti of Śravaṇabeḷagoḷā for the Deśiya Gaṇa.

207 Many castes of the Jains were founded by *ācāryas* and/or *bhaṭṭārakas*. The most important Śvetāmbara castes are the Osvāls and the Śrīmālīs. Of the Digambara Kāṣṭhā Saṅgha, the Nandītaṭ Gacch leader Rām Sena founded the Narasiṁhapura caste, his pupil Nemi Sena the Bhaṭṭāpurā caste, and the Ratnākar caste was apparently founded by Devendra Kīrti I. Of some Digambara castes the exogamous subgroups (*gotra*) or/and their *dasa* and *bīsa* sub-categories are associated with different branches of the main *bhaṭṭāraka* traditions. The Baghervāla caste was partly founded by the Mūla Saṅgha *ācārya* Rām Sena (25 *gotras*) and partly by the Kāṣṭhā Saṅgha *ācārya* Loha (27 *gotras*). The Nāgaur branch of the Balātkāra Gaṇa commanded the following of several *gotras* of the Khaṇḍelvāla caste etc. (Joharāpurkara 1958: 13).

208 The *bhaṭṭārakas* of the Humaḍa, Narasiṁhapura and Khaṇḍelvāla castes until recently selected their own successor (? Kalol, Narasiṁhapura), while the *bhaṭṭāraka* of the Saitavāla, Caturtha, Pañcama, Upādhyāya, Bogāra, Vaiśya and Kṣatriya castes were chosen by the representatives (*pañca*) of these castes (Sangave 1980: 319f.). The only exception is the influential seat of Śravaṇabeḷagoḷā, whose *bhaṭṭāraka* is since 1931 chosen by a committee of lay followers which is selected by the Government of Karṇāṭaka (ibid., Tuschen 1997: 33). Sangave 1980: 319–321 found that only the *bhaṭṭārakas* of the Humaḍa caste could be removed by their followers in the past. Although they preside over a particular caste, the *bhaṭṭārakas* do not need to be member of the caste and ideally represent all Jains. Lakṣmī Sena of Kolhāpura, for instance, was born in Tamil Nāḍu into the Saitavāla caste, but presides over the Pañcama caste.

209 In 1945, the Land Sealing Act of Karṇāṭaka led to the aquisition of most landholdings of the *bhaṭṭārakas* by the government in exchange for monetary compensation, whose ownership is in many cases still disputed in the courts between the Digambara laity and the *bhaṭṭārakas*.

210 According to Shāntā 1985: 134f., the *munis* apparently entirely disappeared in the seventeenth century.

211 Shāntā 1985: 134f. A modest revival of the institution of the *bhaṭṭāraka* was triggered recently because of the desire to spread Jainism across the borders of India and because of a renewed interest in community education. In response to modern demands, the *bhaṭṭārakas* made themselves accessible to members of other castes than their own and created – without much success – a common institutional platform in 1969 and arranged the first *bhaṭṭāraka sammelan* (Sangave 2001: 143), which was followed by several others.

212 Carrithers 1989: 150. In 1926–7, Rāvjī Sakhārām Dośī, in G. P. Jauharī, in V. Śāstrī 1932: 7f., and G. P. Jauharī of the Akhil Bhāratvarṣīya Digambara Jain Mahāsabhā (ibid.: 56f.,) emphasised the need to re-introduce the *munis* to North India to propagate true religion (‘*jain dharma kī yathārtha tathā utkṛṣṭa prabhāvanā*’), and unity amongst all Digambara societies in India (ibid.: 84–86).

213 Most Khaṇḍelvālas live in North India, where no *bhaṭṭāraka* seats exist anymore.

214 Some of the first disciples of Śānti Sāgar, such as Vīr Sāgar and Candra Sāgar, were Khaṇḍelvāls. See D. Śāstrī 1985.

215 S. C. Jain 1940: 3f. In the twentieth century, after an earlier failure of transregional sect-caste associations, a number of Digambara Jain caste associations were established with the intention of reforming the Digambara community and creating

transregional solidarities amongst geographically dispersed North Indian castes with a dominant Digambara Jain membership. The Jain Khaṇḍelvāla Mahāsabhā, for instance, which was founded in 1920, is today organised into 15 *prānta*s, or regions. Other examples are the Baghervāl Jain Mahāsabhā and the Jain Padmāvatī Porvāl Mahāsabhā. Similar organisations which strive to establish independent sect-castes are relatively rare among Śvetāmbara Jains, whose transregional organisations are usually founded exclusively on religious criteria (Kāsalīvāl 1992: 14f.). Cf. R. K. Jain 1999: 67.

216 The anti-printing movement called itself Śāstra-Mudraṇa Virodhī Āndolana: 'Murder threads were made against those involved in printing, and printing shops were blown up' (Sangave 1981/2001: 62).

217 At the time, Jain castes were generally divided in at least two ranked sections: the lower *dasa* and the higher *bīsa* sub-castes. The following social reforms were advocated by the Pariṣad: 1. child widow remarriage (*bāla-vidhvā vivāha*); 2. marriage across caste boundaries; 3. allowing members of *dasa* families to participate in the *pūjā pāṭha*, etc., within a society where mixed *dasa-bīsa* marriages were practised; 4. abolition of death feasts (*maraṇa bhojana*); 5. abolition of excessive feasts and gift-giving at *pratiṣṭhā* ceremonies (new *pratiṣṭhā pāṭha*: as a rule only old images should be consecrated); 6. raising the status of women through the foundation of womens' institutions (S. C. Jain 1940: 3f.).

218 Kāsalīvāl 1992: 11f. In 1902, the influential Bhāratvarṣīya Digambara Jain Tīrtha Kṣetra Kameṭī (BDJTKK) was founded by Maṇikcand Hirācand Jauharī (1851–1913) in Bombay as a sub-committee of the Mahāsabhā. It became independent on 24 November 1930 and still has its office in the Hīrābāg Dharmaśālā compound in Mumbāī, owned by the Jauharī family trust. For administrative reasons, it divided India into six zones. Another national association, the Digambara Jain Mahāsamiti, was set up in 1974 by Sāhū Śānti Prasād in New Delhi for the promotion of Digambara unity during the year celebrating Mahāvīra's 2500th death day. In contrast to the Mahāsabhā, which is composed of individuals, it is organised in the form of a 'Jain *saṃsad*', or parliament, that is, on the basis of regional representatives (Kāsalīvāl 1992: 12f.). However, after the death of its founder, the organisation failed to deliver and is now defunct. In 1983, the Kundakunda-Kahnā Tīrtha Rakṣā Trust was founded in order to promote the worship of Kānjī Svāmī (who declared himself to be a Digambara Terā Panthī) in his putative reincarnation as the *tīrthaṅkara* Sūrya Kīrti. This was in 1985 vigorously opposed both by the Mahāsabhā, whose patron saints were Muni Dharma Sāgar and Āryikā Jñān Mātā in Hastīnapur, and by the Mahāsamiti, whose patron saint was Muni Vidyānand in 1985. However, the main representatives of the Mahāsamiti, the Sāhū Jain family (Times of India) and Premcand Jain (Jayna Watch Co.) in Delhi, had once supported Kānjī Svāmī and failed to join the united front against the Kanjī Panth supporters at Soṅgaḍh (R. K. Jain 1999: 114–117). The Meerut Court decided on the 6 December 2000 that Kānjī Panthīs are not Digambara Jains (case no. 9/91, quoted by N. K. Jain, jain friends@yahoogroups.com, 21 June 2001). Both the Mahāsabhā and the Mahāsamiti are dominated by Khaṇḍelvāls. A rival organisation to the Tīrtha Kṣetra Kamaṭī, the Jaina Saṃrakṣaṇ Māñca, was recently set up in Jaypur, in order to protect old temples from partial demolition and reconstruction under instructions of modern *muṇi*s.

219 V. Śāstrī 1932: 5 lists a number of '*nigrantha bhaṭṭāraka*s' for the beginning of the nineteenth century. See Carrithers 1990: 148f. and Cort 2002: 71, n. 8 for further references on the so-called *nirvāṇ svāmī*s, who did not travel much and seemed to have dressed themselves in public.

220 K. P. Jain 1932: 158, n. 2: '*Mainapurī Digambara Jain Baḍā Mandir kā ek Guṭkā*'.

221 Ibid., citing Digambara Jain 9, 1: 18–23, ed. Mūlcand Kiśandās Kāpaḍiyā, Surat.

222 Eternal lights in the form of oil-lamps can be found at a variety of *samādhi mandiras* for Digambara *munis*; for instance at the Vimal Sāgar Samādhi Mandira in Madhuban.
223 ibid.: 159, citing Digambara Jain, Special Issue, 1916.
224 Carrithers 1990: 155.
225 K. P. Jain 1932: 159, citing Digambara Jain 14, 5–6: 7; cf. Mahias forthcoming, p. 3.
226 Ibid. His name was Vardhamān Sāgar according to D. Śāstrī 1985: 54.
227 K. P. Jain 1932: 159. His name was Devappā Svāmī according to D. Śāstrī 1985: 55. Carrithers 1990: 155 identifies Devendra Kīrti as a *bhaṭṭāraka*.
228 K. P. Jain 1932: 159. Akkole 1987: 43 writes that the *kṣullaka dīkṣā* took place in 1916 and the *muni dīkṣā* in 1976 Phālguṇ Śuklā 14 (Śaka 1841). All initiations were given by Devendra Kīrti (Ibid.: 51–53, D. Śāstrī 1985: 56).
229 Cf. C. R. Jain 1931, Ghoshal 1932.
230 The original announcement of G. P. Jauharī was published in 1926 in the journal Jaina Bodhaka. It was reprinted by V. Śāstrī 1932: 46–48, whose book gives a detailed account of this momentous pilgrimage.
231 One should assume that the visit to Mount Śikhar would have helped the pending court cases between Digambara, Śvetāmbaras, and the Government concerning the control of the site.
232 K. P. Jain 1932: 161, Kāsalīvāl 1992: 35, Kāsalīvāl 1998, Kāsalīvāl 2001: 36ff., Śruta Saṃvarddhana Saṃsthān 2002: 3.
233 Ibid.
234 Ibid.: 3–5, Kāsalīvāl 2001: 26–29. Sūrya Sāgar's main disciples were Vijay Sāgar, Ānand Sāgar, Padma Sāgar and Kṣullaka Cidānand. Vimal Sāgar's main disciples were Nirmal Sāgar, Sumati Sāgar, Kunthu Sāgar and Kṣullaka Dharma Sāgar.
235 For one view of the resulting structure, see Kāsalīvāl 1998: n.p.
236 D. Śāstrī 1985, Rājkul Jain 2003: 213–221. Dates were converted with the computer program of M. Yano and M. Fushimi: http://ccnic15.kyoto-su.ac.jp/yanom/pancanga
237 See Varṇī 1998 I: 334, Kāsalīvāl 1992: 30, 34. Personal communication Nīraj Jain, 12 June 2003, D. K. Jain 25 October 2003.
238 P. Śāstrī 1992: 212, cf. Varṇī 1998: 211–216. His childhood name Vidyādhar was derived from the famous 'miracle working' *samādhi* of Bhaṭṭāraka Vidyādhar in Karṇāṭaka (M. Jain 2001: 3). Both his father (Muni Malli Sāgar 1975) and his mother (Āryikā Samay Matī 1975) took *dīkṣā* from Ācārya Dharma Sāgar, and his three brothers (Muni Samay Sāgar 7 March 1980, Muni Yoga Sāgar, Muni Niyam Sāgar 15 April 1980) took *dīkṣā* from him (ibid.: 29–31). In 2003, his birthhouse has been converted into a temple.
239 *Āryikā*s never receive foods in their hands nor in a standing posture, and apparently do not perform *keśa luñcana*.
240 The *ailaka*s, *kṣullaka*s and *kṣullikā*s are also called *tyāgī*s. See R. K. Jain 1999: 80. Similar debates on the status of women are known from early on (Jaini 1991). According to some early medieval Digambara scriptures, at least some medieval Digambara or Yāpanīya traditions also formed a four-fold *saṅgha*, with nuns being recognised as mendicants rather than as laypeople (Schubring 2000: § 30, p. 61).
241 Personal communications by different Digambara *śrāvakas*.
242 This is emphasised in a proclamation by Ācārya Vimal Sāgar 23 October 1993, reprinted in Brahmacāriṇī Mainābāī Jain 1996: xv, which requests the laity to mediate the 'foolish' disputes between the two lineages with reference to the common Āgamas: '*samāj kā kartavya hai ki kisī kā vivād na karke donoṁ ācārya paramparā ko āgam sammat mānakar vātsalya se dharma prabhāvanā kareṁ*.' The writings of Ādi Sāgar were published by B. M. Jain 1996.
243 D. Śāstrī 1985: 344, 450–452.
244 His death memorial is in Madhuban at Sammet Śikhara.

245 The desire to became an *ācārya* and the abolishment of the once prevalent practice that an *ācārya* can be enthroned only after the death of his predecessor have contributed to the creation of many splits and independently roaming *ācārya*s (personal communication by Nīraj Jain, 12 June 2003).
246 According to Kāsalīvāl 2001: 35 he was a disciple of Mahāvīr Kīrti.
247 Kāṣalīvāl 1992: 36–38.
248 D. Śāstrī 1985: 411–413. According to Ācārya Puṣpadanta, he was a disciple of Śānti Sāgar 'Dakṣiṇ' (personal communication, Mumbaī 24 October 2003). He was born in Kothalpur iṇ Belgāṁv in Karṇāṭaka and died on the 22 May 1987.
249 Vīr Sāgar 'Śolapur' is said to have been close to Kānjī Svāmī's views, though his interpretation of the texts was slightly different.
250 This line is also claimed by the *bhaṭṭāraka* of Hūmachā today.
251 Copaḍe 1936.
252 On the dating of Kunda Kunda, see the divergent views of Upadhye 1935: 21 and Dhaky 1991: 193.
253 According to Dhaky (1991), this is because of 'the profound reverence and a very false notion as regards the antiquity of Kundakundācārya' (ibid.: 203, n. 30).
254 Personal correspondance, 25 September 2002.
255 This is also documented by M. U. K. Jain 1975: 126–128, Shāntā 1985: 489, and Carrithers 1989: 232.
256 Personal communication of Nīraj Jain, 16.6.2003.
257 Including, occasionally, demolishing old temples in order to replace them with new ones.
258 The Agravāla Digambaras, who are dominant in the Pañjāb and in U.P., belong also to mixed Hindu-Jain caste.
259 Critics ask: 'Why only cows?'
260 '*vītarāg sādhu kā koī panth nahīṁ hotā*' (P. Śāstrī 1985b: 540).
261 Tuschen 1995: 50.
262 Saletore 1940: 124.
263 For information on the contemporary Digambara ascetics I wish to thank in particular Dr A. Jain, Dr N. L. Jain, Nīraj Jain and Manish Modi.
264 Jaini 1979: 246f., n. 8 reported the number of 175 ascetics in 1979 (65 *muni*s, 60 *kṣullaka*s and *ailaka*s and 50 *āryikā*s and *kṣullikā*s) and 150–200 in 1991 (Jaini 1991: 24–26). Goonasekere 1986: 27 calculated the figure of 170 *muni*s and altogether 400 mendicants (p. 116). Shāntā 1985: 489 mentioned 62 *āryikā*s and 23 *kṣullikā*s. Zydenbos 1999: 291 heard that there were only 120 *muni*s in 1999 and emphasises their 'decline in numbers'. For 1990, Kāsalīvāl 1992: 35 quotes the figure of 32 *ācārya*s, 11 *upādhyāya*s, 130 *muni*s, 154 *āryikās*, 22 *ailaka*s, 80 *kṣullaka*s and 45 *kṣullikā*s. In 1992, Upādhyāya Kanak Nandī cited to me the figure of about 418 Digambara ascetics: 14–15 *ācārya*s, 2–3 *upādhyāya*s, 125 *muni*s, 20–25 *ailaka*s, 40–50 *kṣullaka*s and about 200 *āryikā*s and *kṣullikā*s.
265 In 2002, only Ācārya Vidyā Sāgar provided complete data to B. U. Jain 2002: 324.
266 For 1996, B. U. Jain 1996: 326 gives the following sums, which differ from the detailed information on individual ascetic groups in his own text: 36 *ācārya*s, 143 *cāturmāsa* places, 352 *muni*s, 305 *āryikā*s and a total of 657 mendicants. For want of additional information, I was unable to check the extent of the inaccuracy of the figures. I met Muni Ānand Sāgar, who is now an *upādhyāya*, in 1981. He was then alone and apparently still is. In 1992, I observed that the group of Kunthu Sāgar had in all 34 ascetics, 18 *muni*s, 3 *kṣullaka*s, 2 *ailaka*s and 11 *āryikā*s, a figure which seems to corroborate B. U. Jain's numbers for 1987. The subsequent decrease in numbers can be explained by Ācārya Kanak Nandī's separation from Kunthu Sāgar in the early 1990s. My third example shows that the true number of ascetics must be much higher. Ācārya Rayaṇ Sāgar who is not included in the table, is listed by B. U. Jain as a single individual

without mentioning the number of ascetics accompanying him. In 1999, his group had 8 members: 1 *ācārya*, 1 *upādhyāya*, 4 *muni*s, 1 *ailaka* and 1 *kṣullaka*.

267 Roman alphabet.

268 The word *saṅgha* is used for groups of two and more ascetics.

269 On the definition of these categories as 'novices' see Carrithers 1990: 153, Flügel 2001: 76f.

270 There is no equivalent female category because *ailaka*s (*elaka*) can wear only one loin cloth, which is not considered to be proper for women.

271 The *ailācārya* corresponds to the *upādhyāya* amongst the Śvetāmbaras. The Digambara word *elācārya* is an ancient designation for 'a pontiff of the highest learning and for a qualified teacher of Jain doctrines, a position more or less equivalent of *vācaka, vācanācārya*, or *kṣamāśramaṇa* or *mahattara* in the ancient Northern Nirgrantha of which the Śvetāmbara Church is the off-shoot. Once a pontiff received the ecclesiastical title of *elācārya* his original monastic appelation apparently went into the background' (Dhaky 1991: 191).

272 The chosen successor, who is called *yuvācārya* among the Śvetāmbaras.

273 The titles have been given to only nine monks by the *ācārya*s Sanmati Sāgar (*ācāryakalpa* and *bālācārya*), Kunthu Sāgar (*ācāryakalpa* 2x, and *ailācārya*), Ajit Sāgar (*ācāryakalpa*), and Sumati Sāgar (*ailācārya*) (A. Jain 2001: 11).

274 For their names, see B. U. Jain's and A. Jain's publications.

275 This is evident in the mixed composition of the *ācārya*s' groups documented by A. Jain 2001: 1–11. See also Zydenbos 1999: 296f.; who cites questionable estimates that no more than 10–15 Digambara *saṅgha*s, headed by an *ācārya*, exist.

276 The other bigger *saṅgha*s are those of Ācārya Dharma Sāgar's successors Abhinandan Sāgar and Vardhaman Sāgar, Deś Bhūṣān's successors Bāhubalī Sāgar and Subal Sāgar, and Vimal Sāgar's successor Virāg Sāgar. Cf. A. Jain 2001: 1–11.

277 The accuracy of the data is confirmed by the identical names in A. Jain's lists. Through the comparison with the names listed by B. U. Jain (2002) the independently roaming groups of *muni*s and *āryikā*s under the command of Vidyā Sāgar can be clearly identified. In 2001 the *saṅgha* had 188 members: 63 *muni*s, 10 *ailaka*s, 113 *āryikā*s and 2 *kṣullaka*s. The changes between 2001 and 2002 are minimal: in 2002 the group had 3 more divisions of altogether 2 more independently roaming *muni*s, but 2 members less in the *ācārya*'s group, 4 *āryikā*s less, and 2 *kṣullaka*s less (A. Jain 2001). The *muni*s were divided into 17 divisions: the *ācārya*'s group, with 39 members (38 *muni*s including the *ācārya* and 1 *ailaka*), and 16 other groups of altogether 25 *muni*s. In addition, 1 unit of 2 *ailaka*s roaming together, and 7 *ailaka*s and 2 *kṣullaka*s wandering alone. The 113 *āryikā*s were divided in 17 divisions, which altogether represented 23.6% of all 72 divisions of Digambara nuns.

278 The word 'group' is not really applicable.

279 R. K. Jain 1999: 80 describes these '*tyāgī*s', or renouncers, as regionally oriented 'priests' which can be compared to the *bhaṭṭāraka*s, a hypothesis which still needs to be tested.

280 According to B. U. Jain 1999: 372f., Vidyā Sāgar's order is the only mendicant group where the *āryikā*s do not spend *cāturmāsa* at the same location as the *muni*s.

281 Six groups of altogether forty seven *āryikā*s spent *cāturmāsa* Kārañjā in Mahārāṣṭra (B. U. Jain 2002: 310).

282 According to M. Jain 2001: 494, cf. 539f., Vidyā Sāgar had initiated 195 disciples between 1972 and 2001: 62 *muni*s, 114 *āryikā*s, 10 *ailaka*s, and 9 *kṣullaka*s.

283 Shāntā 1985: 136.

284 Zydenbos 1999: 295. Svarṇa Matī (1), Viśuddha Matī (1), and Ananta Matī (1) are listed by D. Śāstrī 1985: 555, 567.

285 It happens that individuals, though initiated by other *muni*s, are counted under the name of their new '*dīkṣā guru*' after changing to a new *saṅgha*. Personal communication by Nīraj Jain, June 2003.

286 D. Śāstrī 1985: 569.
287 A. Jain 2001: 23.
288 Cf. B. U. Jain 1999: 187, n. 107, cf. 320, 513f.
289 R. K. Jain 1999: 90.
290 Kāsalīvāl 1992: 38.
291 This is one of the biggest difference between Digambara *ācāryas* and *bhaṭṭārakas* as well as Śvetāmbara *ācāryas*.
292 See also Zydenbos 1999: 297.
293 This is the oldest method amongst the modern *muni saṅghas* according to Ācārya Puṣpadanta (personal communication Mumbaī 24 October 2003).
294 B. U. Jain 1996: 326, n. 4 notes an increase of about 100–125 mendicants between 1995 and 1996 and cites details of many new initiations.
295 An estimated figure of 10% was cited to me, which may be exaggerated.
296 The data are too unreliable to attach much significance to specific changes, such as the diminishing percentage of male mendicants.
297 See Fohr's article in this volume.
298 B U. Jain 2002: 70 gives the summary figure of 12,469 Jain mendicants for the year 2002: Mūrtipūjaka 7,553, Sthānakavāsī 3,331, Terā Panth 691, Digambara 894. In 2005, the figure had risen to 13,307: Mūrtipūjaka 8,061, Sthānakavāsī 3,546, Terāpanthī 692, Digambara 1008 (B. U. Jain 2005: 25).
299 These percentages do not reflect a similar share of the Jain laity, for which no reliable data are available. Many Digambaras are affiliated to reformist lay traditions without separate ascetic orders. The regional, caste and class background of the ascetics also varies. Most of the ascetics of the Śramaṇa Saṅgha and the independent Sthānakavāsī traditions stem from the Osvāl and Śrīmālī castes in Rājasthān, Madhya Pradeś, Mahārāṣtra and the Pañjāb, but also from southern India (Shāntā 1985: 333). The Gujarātī Sthānakavāsī traditions and the Tapā Gaccha groups recruit their ascetics almost exclusively in Gujarāt and amongst the Gujarātī population in Mumbaī, the Kharatara Gaccha and the Śvetāmbara Terā Panth in Rājasthān, and the Digambara groups mainly in Karṇāṭaka and Madhya Pradeś, to name only the most important mendicant traditions. The average size of the itinerant groups in 1999 was 4–5 in all four traditions (Mūrtipūjaka 4.6, Sthānakavāsī 4.2, Terā Panth 5.69, Digambara 5.05).
300 The comparison is only meaningful because of the 'improvement in reporting of religion' in the censuses after 1971 (M. K. Jain 1986: 35). The doubling of the absolute number of Jains recorded in the censuses of 1951–1971 (which is not matched by the mendicant population) is generally interpreted as an effect of under-reporting during the colonial period. If this is true, then it must be concluded that – relative to the total population of India – the number of Jains is continually declining.
301 A variant of this approach is M. Spiro's theory of renunciation as a psychological defense-mechanism, which has been applied to the Jain case by Goonasekere 1986: 179f.
302 This figure more than doubles, if nuns and novices are included. See Bechert 1973: 580f.
303 The 2000 edition of the Vatican's Annuario Pontificio, gives for 1998 the figure of 57,813 monks and 814,779 nuns (ratio 1: 14). The monastic population as a whole represented 0.086% of all Roman Catholics. Overall numbers are declining, especially the population of nuns, which was 990,768 in 1978: http://www.sspxasia.com/Countires/World/NewsArchive.htm
304 For data confirming this for the Terāpanthīs see Flügel forthcoming.
305 'Socioeconomically troubled families, especially those of the middle classes, often seek relief from their frustrations and insecurities by becoming religious' (Goonasekere 1986: 123).
306 Vallely 2002: 197 tried to solve the problem through re-definition: 'Within the order, desire to belong to the group, or attraction to a charismatic leader, is not treated as a

"social" motivation, stemming from worldliness. Instead, it too is seen as evidence of a spiritual purity'.

307 Cf. Bloss 1987: 18, Kawanami 1990: 26.

308 'field investigations have revealed that this is more an accusation and a speculation than reality' (Goonasekere 1986: 179f.).

309 E.g. Bordiyā 1975: 265–80. Reasons which are rarely cited in the literature are (a) recruitment drives to satisfy the formal requirement of Mūrtipūjaka monks to have disciples in order to be able to advance in the monastic hierarchy, (b) family pressure informed by material considerations.

310 'In the decades since Independence, with the rise in the age of marriage and the increase in health standards, this [widows becoming *sādhvīs*, P.F.] has changed. Most Jain women are now married when they are in their early or mid 20s, and so even if they become widows they most likely have had children. Having to raise the children means that becoming a *sādhvī* is less of a realistic option for a widow. Changing social attitudes toward widows also makes it less likely that a Jain widow feels that she has little choice but to become a *sādhvī*... Today the vast majority of *sādhvīs* have never been married; becoming a *sādhvī* is now seen as an alternative vocation to that of a housewife' (Cort 1989: 111f.).

311 Most but not all *sādhvī*s come from Jain families, while an increasing number of *sādhu*s are recruited from non-Jain tribal communities who seek material improvements through the association with the Jains. An unresolved difficulty for this interpretation is that, for reasons of tradition, educational opportunities are limited for Mūrtipūjaka *sādhvī*s.

312 In a personal conversation, the Tapā Gaccha *ācārya* Jay Sundar Sūri stated that men believe in 'heroism', while women are 'more impressionable, more spiritual' (Mumbaī 23 October 2003). An investigation of the self-reported motives of Terā Panth mendicants showed, however, that 'religious' reasons were more prevalent amongst *sādhu*s rather than *sādhvī*s (Flügel, forthcoming). Jay Sundar Sūri's disciples Prem Sundar Vijay and Harṣad Vijay explained the increasing number of (male) mendicants with the increasing wealth of the Jain community, which now can afford to lose valuable workforce and to feed a growing community of materially dependent mendicants. Apparently, nowadays families of renouncers are more supportive than in the past (Mumbaī 1 November 2003).

313 By 1982, nine *ācārya*s alone had initiated some 300 ascetics (*muni*s, *ailaka*s, *kṣullakas, āryikās, kṣullikās*): Śānti Sāgar (20), Vīr Sāgar (23), Śiv Sāgar (28), Dharma Sāgar (61), Vidyā Sāgar (18), Deś Bhūṣaṇ (33), Mahāvīr Kīrti (24), Sanmati Sāgar (26), Vimal Sāgar (65) (D. Śāstrī 1985).

314 At the moment, the increased mobility of the laity compensates only for the migration from rural to urban locations and abroad.

Bibliography

AISJC = Akhil Bhāratīya Sthānakavāsī Jain Kānfrens (ed.). *Akhil Bhāratvarṣīya Vardhamaṇ Sthānakavāsī Jain Śramaṇ Saṅghīya Samācārī*. Comp. Saubhāgyamuni 'Kumud'. Dillī: Akhil Bhāratīya Vardhamān Sthānakavāsī Jaina Kānfrens, 1987.

——. *Amṛt-Mahotsav Gaurav Granth*. Naī Dillī: Akhil Bhāratvarṣīya Śvetāmbara Sthānakavāsī Jain Kānfrens, 1988.

Akkole, Subhāṣcandra. *Śantśreṣṭha Parampūjya 108 Cāritracakravartī Ācāryaśrī Śāntisāgar Caritra*. Śolāpūr: Jain Saṃskṛti Saṃrakṣak Saṅgh, 1987.

Appadurai, Arjun. 'Number in the colonial imagination'. *Orientalism and the Postcolonial Predicament*. Eds C. A. Breckenridge and P. van der Veer, 314–339. Philadelphia: University of Pennsylvania Press, 1993.

Baines, Jervoise Athelstane *Census of India 1891. General report.* London: Eyre & Spottiswoode, 1893.

Balbir, Nalini. 'Observations sur la secte jaina des Terapanthi'. *Bulletin D'Études Indiennes* 1 (1983) 39–45.

——. 'Recent Developments in a Jaina Tīrtha: Hastinapur (U.P.) – A Preliminary Report'. *The History of the Sacred Places in India as Reflected in Traditional Literature.* Panels of the VIIth World Sanskrit Conference Vol. II. Ed. H. Bakker. General Editor: Johannes Bronkhorst, 177–191. Leiden: E. J. Brill, 1990.

——. 'La question de l'ordination des enfants en milieu jaina'. *Les âges de la vie dans le monde Indien.* Ed. Christine Chojnacki, 153–182. Paris: Diffusion de Boccard, 2001.

——. 'The A(ñ)calagaccha Viewed from Inside and from Outside'. *Jainism and Early Buddhism. Essays in Honor of Padmanabh S. Jaini.* Ed. Olle Qvarnström, 47–77. Fremont: Asian Humanities Press, 2003.

Banks, Marcus. 'Defining Division: An Historical Overview of Jain Social Organization'. *Modern Asian Studies* 20, 3 (1986) 447–460.

——. *Organizing Jainism in India and England.* Oxford: Clarendon Press, 1992.

Bechert, Heinz. *Buddhismus, Staat und Gesellschaft in den Ländern des Theravāda Buddhismus.* Bd. III. Bibliographie, Dokumente, Index. Wiesbaden: Otto Harrassowitz, 1973.

Bharill, Hukam Chand. *Kramabaddha Paryaya (Sequence Bound Modifications).* Tr. M. Jain. Jaipur: Pandit Todarmal Smarak Trust, 1980/1987.

Bloss, Lowell W. 'The Female Renunciants of Sri Lanka: The *Dasasilmattawa*'. *Journal of the International Association for Buddhist Studies* 10, 1 (1987) 7–31.

Böhtlingk, Otto and Rudolph Roth. *Sanskrit Wörterbuch. Dritter Theil.* St. Petersburg: Kaiserliche Akademie der Wissenschaften, 1861.

Brekke, Torkel. *Makers of Modern Indian Religion in the Late Nineteenth Century.* Oxford: Oxford University Press, 2002.

Budhmal, Muni. *Terāpanth kā Itihās. Pratham Khaṇḍ: Terāpanth ke Pratham Cār Ācārya.* 4th Revised Edition. Calcutta: Jain Śvetāmbar Terāpanth Mahāsabhā Prakāśan, 1964/1995.

Bühler, Georg. 'The Digambara Jainas'. *The Indian Antiquary* 7 (1878) 28f.

——. 'On the Authenticity of the Jaina Tradition'. *Vienna Oriental Journal* 1 (1887) 165–180.

——. 'Further Proofs of the Authenticity of the Jaina Tradition'. *Vienna Oriental Journal* 4 (1890) 313–331.

Carrithers, Michael. 'Naked Ascetics in Southern Digambar Jainism'. *Man (N.S.)* 24 (1989) 219–235.

——.'Jainism and Buddhism as Enduring Historical Streams'. *Journal of the Anthropological Society of Oxford* 21, 2 (1990) 141–163.

——. 'On Polytropy: Or the Natural Condition of Spiritual Cosmopolitanism in India: The Digambar Jain Case'. *Modern Asian Studies* 34, 4 (2000) 831–861.

Clémentin-Ojha, Catherine. 'Ascetics' Rights in Early 19th Century Jaipur (Rajasthan)'. *Asceticism and power in South- and Southeast Asia.* Eds P. Flügel and G. Houtmann. London: Routledge, forthcoming.

Cohn, Bernard S. (ed.). 'The Census and Objectification in South Asia'. *An Anthropologist among the Historians and Other Essays*, 224–254. Delhi: Oxford University Press, 1987/1992.

Copaḍe, Tātyā Keśav. *Kīrtanopayogī Dharmadivākar Śrī 1008 Ācārya Śāntisāgar Caritra.* Bhoj: Rāygauḍā Devagaḍsā Pāṭīl, 1936.

Cort, John E. *Liberation and Wellbeing: A Study of the Mūrtipūjak Jains of North Gujarat.* PhD dissertation, Harvard University, 1989.

Cort, John E. 'The Śvetāmbar Mūrtipūjak Jain Mendicant'. *Man (N.S.)* 26 (1991) 651–671.

——. 'Fistfights in the Monastery: Calendars, Conflict and Karma among the Jains'. *Approaches to Jain Studies: Philosophy, Logic, Rituals and Symbols.* Eds N. K. Wagle and O. Qvarnström, 36–59. University of Toronto: Center for South Asian Studies, 1999.

——. *Jains in the World: Religious Values and Ideology in India.* New York: Oxford University Press, 2001.

——. 'A Tale of Two Cities: On the Origins of Digambara Sectarianism in North India'. *Multiple Histories: Culture and Society in the Study of Rajasthan.* Eds L. A. Babb, V. Joshi and M. Meister, 39–83. Jaipur: Rawat Publications, 2002.

——. 'A Fifteenth Century Digambara Mystic and his Contemporary Followers: Tāraṇ Taraṇ Svāmī and the Tāraṇ Svāmī Panth'. (in this volume).

Darśanavijaya, Muni (comp.). *Paṭṭāvalī-Samuccaya.* Pratham Bhāg. Vīramgām (Gujarāt): Cāritra-Smārak-Granthamālā, 1933.

Degenne, Alain and Michel Forsé. *Introducing Social Networks.* Tr. by A. Borges. London: Sage, 1994/1999.

Delamaine, Major James. 'On the Sra'waks or Jains'. *Transactions of the Royal Asiatic Society of Great Britain and Ireland* 1 (1827) 413–438.

Deo, Shantaram Balchandra. *History of Jaina Monasticism from Inscriptions and Literature.* Poona: Deccan College, 1956.

Desāī, Ratilāl Dīpcand. *Seṭh Ānandjī Kalyāṇjī nī Peḍhī no Itihās.* Bhag 1–2. Amadāvād: Seṭh Ānandjī Kalyāṇjī, 1983–1986.

Devendramuni, Ācārya. "Sant Sammelan: Ek Cintan (Śramaṇ Saṅgh)." *Jain Prakāś (Ānandṛṣi Janma Śatābdī Viśeṣāṅk)* 87, 73 (2000) 16–22.

Dhaky, Madhusudan A. 'The Date of Kundakundācārya'. *Paṇḍit Dalsukhbhāī Mālvaṇiyā Abhinandana Grantha I.* Sampādak: Madhusūdan Ḍhākī & Sāgarmal Jain, 187–206 (English Section). Vārāṇasī: Pārśvanāth Vidyāśrama Śodha Saṃsthān, 1991.

Dullā, Pāsvīr Vīrjī 'Pārśva Śrī' (Prayojak). *Añcalgaccha Digdarśaṇ.* Muluṁḍ/Mumbaī: Muluṁḍ Añcalagaccha Jain Samāj, 1968.

Dumont, Louis. *Homo Hierarchicus: The Caste System and its Implications.* Complete Revised English Edition. Chicago and London: The University of Chicago Press, 1966/1980.

Dundas, Paul. 'Somnolent Sūtras: Scriptural Commentary in Śvetāmbara Jainism'. *Journal of Indian Philosophy* 24 (1996) 73–101.

——. *The Jains.* Second revised edition. London: Routledge, 1992/2002.

——. 'Conversion to Jainism: Historical Perspectives'. *Religious Conversion in India: Modes, Motivations, and Meanings.* Eds Rowena Robinson and Sathianathan Clarke, 125–148. Oxford: Oxford University Press, 2003.

Flügel, Peter. 'Jain Transactions: Food Restrictions as Interactive Matrices'. *DGV-Symposium Überbrücker von Unüberbrückbarem*, München, 17 October 1991.

——. *Askese und Devotion: Das rituelle System der Terapanth Svetambara Jains.* Doctoral dissertation, Johannes Gutenberg-Universität Mainz, 1994.

——. 'The Ritual Circle of the Terāpanth Śvetāmbara Jains'. *Bulletin D'Études Indiennes* 13 (1995–1996) 117–176.

——. 'Protestantische und Post-Protestantische Jaina-Reformbewegungen: Zur Geschichte und Organisation der Sthānakavāsī I'. *Berliner Indologische Studien* 13–14 (2000) 37–103.

——. 'R. K. Jain. 1999. The Universe as Audience: Metaphor and Community among the Jains of North India [review]'. *Jinamañjari* 23, 1 (2001) 70–77.

——. "The Codes of Conduct of the Terāpanth Samaṇ Order." *South Asia Research* 23, 1 (2003a) 7–53.

——. 'Protestantische und Post-Protestantische Jaina-Reformbewegungen: Zur Geschichte und Organisation der Sthānakavāsī II'. *Berliner Indologische Studien* 15–17 (2003b) 149–240.

——. 'The Invention of Jainism: A Short History of Jaina Studies'. *Journal of Jaina Studies* (Kyoto) 11 (2005) 1–19 (also: *International Journal of Jain Studies* 1, 1 (2005) http://www.soas.ac.uk/ijjs).

——. 'The Unknown Loṅkā: Tradition and the Cultural Unconscious'. Eds C. Caillat and N. Balbir. *Proceedings of the Jaina Panel of the World Sanskrit Conference in Helsinki*. Delhi: Motilal Banarsidas (in press).

——. 'A Socio-Demographic Analysis of the Terāpanth Jain Monastic Order in Rājasthān'. *Paper delivered at the School of Social Sciences Research Seminar*, University of East London, 10 December 2003 (forthcoming).

Folkert, Kendall W. *Scripture and Community: Collected Essays on the Jains*. Ed. J. E. Cort. Atlanta: Scholars Press, 1993.

Ghoshal, Sarat Chandra. *The Digambara Saints of India*. Cooch/Behar: Digambar Jain Muni Raksha Committee, 1932.

Glasenapp, Helmuth von. *Der Jainismus: Eine indische Erlösungsreligion*. Berlin: Alf Häger Verlag, 1925 (English translation: Delhi: Motilal Banarsidas, 1998).

Goonasekere, Ratna Sunilsantha Abhayawardana. *Renunciation and Monasticism among the Jainas of India*. PhD dissertation. San Diego, CA: University of California, 1986.

Guérinot, A.-A. *La Religion Djaina: histoire, doctrine, culte, coutumes, institutions*. Paris: Librairie Orientaliste P. Geuthner, 1926.

Hoernle, Rudolph A. F. 'Two Pattavalis of the Sarasvati Gachcha of the Digambara Jains'. *Indian Antiquary* 20 (1891) 341–361.

——. 'Three Further pattavalis of the Digambaras'. *Indian Antiquary* 21 (1892) 57–84.

Jacobi, Hermann. 'Kalpasūtra of Bhadrabāhu'. *Abhandlungen für die Kunde des Morgenlandes* 7, 1 (1879).

——. *Jaina Sūtras Part I*. Sacred Books of the East. Ed. M. Müller. Vol. 22. Oxford: Clarendon Press, 1884.

——. 'Jainismus'. *Zeitschrift für Religionswissenschaft* 18 (1915) 268–286.

Jain, Anupam (col.). *Sampark*. Hastināpur: Tīrthaṅkara Ṛṣabhdev Jain Vidvat Mahāsaṅgh, 2000a.

——. *Digambara Jaina Sādhu-Sādhvīyoṁ ke Varṣāyoga – 2001 kī Sūcī*. Indaur: Akhil Bhāratīya Digambara Jaina Mahilā Saṅghaṭhan, 2000b.

—— (col.). *Digambara Jaina Sādhu-Sādhvīyoṁ ke Varṣāyoga – 2001 kī Sūcī*. Indaur: Akhil Bhāratīya Digambara Jaina Mahilā Saṅghaṭhan, 2001.

Jain, Bābūlāl 'Ujjavala' (col.). *Samagra Jain Cāturmās Sūcī*. Bombay: Akhil Bhāratvarṣīya Samagra Jaina Cāturmās Sūcī Prakāśan Pariṣad, 1987.

—— (col.). *Samagra Jain Cāturmās Sūcī*. Bombay: Akhil Bhāratvarṣīya Samagra Jaina Cāturmāsi Sūcī Prakāśan Pariṣad, 1990.

—— (col.). *Samagra Jain Cāturmās Sūcī*. Mumbaī: Jaina Ektā Mahāmaṇḍal, 1996.

—— (col.). *Samagra Jain Cāturmās Sūcī*. Mumbaī: Ujjavala Prakāśan, 1999.

—— (col.). *Samagra Jain Cāturmās Sūcī*. Mumbaī: Ujjavala Prakāśan, 2002.

—— (col.). *Samagra Jain Cāturmās Sūcī*. Mumbaī: Ujjavala Prakāśan, 2005.

Jain, Brahmacāriṇī Mainābāī (comp.). *Ācārya Śrī Ādisāgar (Aṅkalīkar) kī Jhalak*. Dillī Ācārya Śrī Sanmati Sāgar jī Saṅgh, 1996.

Jain, Champat Rāy. *The Jain Law*. Madras, 1926.

——. *The Nudity of Jain Saints*. Delhi: The Jain Mitra Mandal, 1931.

Jaini, Jugmandir Lāl. *Jaina Law: 'Bhadrabāhu Saṃhitā'*. text with translation and appendix containing full text of an important judgement in a jaini case by the original side of the High Court of Judicature, Indore. The Library of Jaini Literature Vol. IV. Arrah: The Central Jaina Publishing House, 1916.

Jaini, Padmanabh S. 'Bhavyatva and Abhavyatva: A Jaina Doctrine of "Predestination" '. *Mahāvīra and his Teachings*. Eds A. N. Upadhye, N. Tatia, D. Malvania, M. Mehta, N. Shastri and K. Shastri, 95–111. Bombay: Mahāvīra Nirvāṇa Mahotsava Samiti, 1977.

——. *The Jaina Path of Purification*. Berkeley: University of California Press, 1979.

——. *Gender & Salvation: Jaina Debates on the Spiritual Liberation of Women*. With a Foreword by Robert P. Goldman. Berkeley, CA: University of California Press, 1991.

Jain, Kailash C. *Jainism in Rajasthan*. Sholapur: Jaina Samskrti Samrakshaka Sangha, 1963.

Jain, Kāmtā Prasād. *Digambaratva aur Digambar Muni*. Baṛaut: Digambar Jain Yuvā Samiti, 1932/1992.

Jain, K. Rājul. *Ācārya Jñānsāgar ke Hindī Sāhitya kā Samīkṣātmak Adhyayan*. Sāṅgāner: Bhagavān Ṛṣabhdev Granthamālā, 2003.

Jain, M. K. 'A Demographic Analysis on Jains in India'. *Jain Journal* 21, 2 (1986) 33–51.

Jain, Miśrīlāl. *Ātmaśilpī Ācārya Śrī Vidyāsāgar (Jīvan Darśan)*. Amadāvād: Ahiṁsā-Ārmī Mānav Kalyāṇ Jīvdayā Ceriṭebal Ṭrasṭ 2001.

Jain, Muni Uttam Kamal. *Jaina Sects and Schools*. Delhi: Concept Publishing, 1975.

Jain, Rākeś (comp.). *Bīsvīṁ Sadī ke Divaṁgat Jaina Manīṣī*. Naī Dillī: Digambara Jaina Sāhitya-Saṃskṛti Saṃrakṣaṇ Samiti, 2002.

Jain, Ravindra K. *The Universe as Audience: Metaphor and Community among the Jains of North India*. Shimla: Indian Institute of Advanced Study, 1999.

Jain, Sureś Candra. *Jain Dharma-Bhūṣaṇ, Dharma-Divāraka Brahmacārī Śītalprasād jī (kī 61 vīṁ Jayantī ke Avsar Par Prakāśit)*. Lakhnaū: Jaina Dharma Pravarddhanī Sabhā, 1940.

Jain Śvetāmbara Conference. *Jain Śvetāmbara Directory (Gujarāt)*. Mumbaī: Jain Śvetāmbara Conference Office, Pāydhunī, 1909.

——. *Jain Śvetāmbara Directory*. Compiled by Ratancand Bhāstar and Dalsukhbhāī Vāḍīlāl. Mumbaī: Jain Association of India, 1915.

——. *Jain Śvetāmbara Directory*. Compiled by Ratancand Bhāstar and Dalsukhbhāī Vāḍīlāl. Mumbaī: Jain Association of India, 1916.

Jauharī, Durlabhbhāī. *Sādhu-Sammelan kā Itihās*. Sampādak: Cimmanasiṅha Loḍhā. Saṃśodhak: Paṇḍit Śobhācandra Bhārill. Byāvar: Cimmanasiṅha Loḍhā (Mainejar, Śrī Mahāvīr Priṇṭiṅg Pres), 1946.

Jhaveri, Thakurdas Bhagavandas (comp.). *Shri Bharatvarshiya Digambara Jain Directory*. Bombay, 1914.

Jñān Matī, Āryikā. *Digambara Muni*. 2nd edition. Hastināpur: Digambara Jaina Trilok Śodha Saṃsthān, 1980.

Joharāpurkara, V. P. *Bhaṭṭāraka Sampradāya*. Śolāpura: Jaina Saṃskṛti Saṃrakṣaka Saṃgha, 1958.

Joshi, A. P., M. D. Srinivas and J. K. Bajaj. *Religious Demography of India*. Chennai: Centre for Policy Studies, 2003.

Kanakanandī, Upādhyāya. *Śramaṇ Saṅgha Saṃhitā*. Jaypur: Dharmadarśan Vijñān Śodha Saṃsthān, 1994.

Kañcansāgarsūri, Sūryodaysāgar, Abhaysāgar (eds). 1977, 1983. *Āgama Jyotirdhara*. Vibhāg I-II. Āgamoddhārak Granthamālā Puṣpa 18–19. Kapaḍvañj (Kheḍā): Ramaṇlāl Jecandbhāī.

Kāsalīvāl, Kastūrcand. *Jaina Samāj kā Bṛhat Itihās*. Vol. 1. Jaypur: Jaina Itihās Prakāśan Sansthān, 1992.

—— (ed.) *Praśamamūrti Ācārya Śāntisāgar Chāṇī Smṛti Granth*. Meraṭh: Ācārya Śāntisāgar Chāṇī Granthamālā, 1998.

Kaṭariyā, Milāpbhand. 'Terā Panth aur Bīsa Panth'. *Jaina Nibandha Ratnāvalī*. Bhāg 1, 383–385. (xerox copy).

Kawanami, Hiroko. 'The Religious Standing of Burmese Nuns (*thila shin*): The Ten Precepts and Religious Respect Words'. *Journal of the International Association of Buddhist Studies* 13, 1 (1990) 17–39.

Keshory, Seth Kesree Chand. 'Account of the Terapanthi Sect of Swetambar Jains'. *Census of India 1921*, Vol. I. India, Part I. Report. Ed. J. T. Marten. Appendix IV, xiii–xiv. Calcutta: Superintendent Government Printing, 1924.

Klatt, Johannes. 'The Samachari-Satakam of Samayasundara and Pattavalis of the Anchala-Gachcha and other Gachchas (Revised with Additions by Ernst Leumann)'. *Indian Antiquary* 23 (1894) 169–183.

Lath, Mukund. *Half a Tale: A Study in the Interrelationship between Autobiography and History. The Adhakathānaka. Translated, introduced and annotated.* Jaipur: Rajasthan Prakrit Bharati Sansthan, 1981.

Leumann, Ernst. *Die Āvaśyaka-Erzählungen*. (Abhandlungen für die Kunde des Morgenlandes herausgegeben von der Deutschen Morgenländischen Gesellschaft. X. Band, No. 2). Leipzig: F. A. Brockhaus, 1934.

——. *Übersicht über die Āvaśyaka Literatur*. Aus dem Nachlass herausgegeben von Walther Schubring Alt-und Neuindische Studien. Hamburg: De Gruyter, 1934.

Mahias, Marie-Claude. *Délivrance et convivialité: Le système culinaire des Jaina*. Paris: Éditions de la Maison des Sciences de l'Homme, 1985.

——. '*Āhāra dāna*, the Gift of Food to Digambara Ascetics (*muni*)'. *Purushartha* (forthcoming).

Maṇilāl, Muni. *Śrī Jainadharmano Prācīn Saṅkṣipt Itihās ane Prabhu Vīr Paṭṭāvalī*. Amadāvād: Jīvaṇlāl Chaganlāl Saṅghvī, 1934.

Marriott, McKim (ed.). *Village India: Studies in the Little Community*. Chicago: University of Chicago Press, 1955.

Mehta, Rama. *Inside the Haveli*. London: Penguin, 1977/1996.

Mitchell, Clyde. 'The Concept and Use of Social Networks'. *Social Networks in Urban Situations: Analyses of Personal Relationships in Central African Towns*. Ed. J. C. Mitchell, 1–50. Manchester: Manchester University Press, 1969.

Nair, V. G. *Jainism and Terehpanthism*. Bangalore: Shri Adinath Jain Svetambar Temple, 1970.

Natarajan, B. *Indian Census through a Hundred Years*. Part I. Census Centenary Monograph No. 2. Census of India 1971. New Delhi: Office of the Registrar General. Ministry of Home Affairs, 1971.

Nathmal, Muni [now: Ācārya Mahāprajña]. *Acharya Bhiksu: The Man and his Philosophy*. Translation of *Bhikṣu Vicār Darśan* by N. Sahal. Cūrū: Ādarś Sāhitya Saṅgha Prakāśan, 1959/1968.

Navratnamal, Muni. *Śāsana Samudra*. Vol. 1–25. Published by Uttamcand Sethia. Calcutta: Śrī Jain Śvetāmbara Terāpanthī Mahāsabhā Prakāśan & Lāḍnūṁ, Jain Viśva Bhāratī, 1981ff.

——. *Terāpanth Pāvas Pravās*. Lāḍnūṁ: Śrī Jain Śvetāmbar Terāpanthī Sabhā, 1991.

Padmarāja, Paṇḍit. A Treatise on Jain Law and Usages. Bombay: Karnatak Press, 1886.

Plowden, W. Chichele *Report on the Census of British India taken on the 17th February 1881*. Vol. I–III. London: Eyre & Spottiswoode, 1883.

Prakāśacandra, Muni. *Ā Che Aṇagāra Amārā*. Mumbaī: Śrī Naval Śāhitya Prakāśan Maṇḍal, 1989/1998.

Premī, Nāthūrām. "Bhaṭṭāraka." *Jaina Hitaiṣī* 7 (1912) 59–69, 9: 13–24, 10–11: 1–9; 8, 2 (1913) 57–70 [cited from a reprint of unspecified selections, no date].

——. (ed.). *Kavivar Banārsīdās viracit Ardha Kathānaka*. Bombay: Hindī Granth Ratnākar, 1957.

Ratna Prabha Vijay, Muni. *Śramaṇa Bhagavān Mahāvīra*. Vol. 5.2. Ahmedabad: Śrī Jaina Siddhānta Society, 1948.

Reynell, Josephine. *Honour, Nurture and Festivity: Aspects of Female Religiosity amongst Jain Women in Jaipur*. PhD dissertation, University of Cambridge, 1985.

Śāh, Mālti. *Nagarśeṭh Śāntidās Jhaverī*. Amadāvād: Gūrjar Grantharatna Kāryālay, 1987.

Saletore, R. N. 'Monastic Life in Śravaṇa Beḷagoḷa." *Jaina Antiquary* 5, 4 (1940) 123–132.

Sandesara, Bhogilal, J. 'Kṣetrādeśapaṭṭaka issued by Ācārya Vijayadharaṇendrasūri of Tapā Gaccha.' *Journal of the Oriental Institute* 24 (1974) 228–233.

Sangave, Vilas A. *Jaina Community*. 2nd revised edition. Bombay: Popular Prakashan, 1959/ 1980.

——. *Facets of Jainology: Selected Research Papers on Jain Society, Religion and Culture*. Mumbai: Popular Prakashan, 2001.

——. 'Karavīravaibhav Śrī Lakṣmīsena Bhaṭṭārak Pīṭh: Paramparā va Kārya'. *Paṭṭācārya Bhaṭṭārak Ratna Svastiśrī Lakṣmīsena Mahāsvāmī Ṣaṣṭyabdipūrtī Gaurav Aṅk*. Sampādak: Prācārya Śrīdhar Heravāḍe, 1–4. Kolhāpura, 3 August 2003.

Śāstrī, Dharmacandra. *Digambara Jain Sādhu Paricay*. Sanghastha: Ācārya Dharmasāgara. Dillī: Lālā Śyāmlāl Ṭhekedār, 1985.

Śāstrī, Nāthūlāl. 'Bīs Panth Terah Panth Carcā'. *Jain Pracārak* (2002) 10f., 17.

Śāstrī, Phūlcand 'Siddhāntācārya' (ed.). *Khāniyā Tattva-Carcā*. 2 Vols. Jaypur: Ācāryakalpa Paṇḍit Ṭoḍarmal Granthamālā, 1967.

——. 'Songaḍh aur Jainatattvamīmāṃsā'. *Siddhāntācārya Paṇḍit Phūlcand Śāstrī Abhinandan-Granth*. Ed. Bābūlāl Jain Phāgull, 527–532. Vārāṇasī: Siddhāntācārya Paṇḍit Phūlcand Śāstrī Abhinandan Granth Prakāśan Samiti, 1985a.

——. 'Mūlasaṅgh Śuddhāmnāyakā Dūsrā Nām hī Terāpanth hai'. Ibid., 535–540, 1985b.

——. 'Śrī Jin Tāraṇataraṇa aur unkī Kṛtiyāṁ'. Ibid., 385–408, 1985c.

——. *Parvār Jain Samāj kā Itihās*. Jabalpur: Bhāratvarṣīya Digambar Jain Parvār Sabhā, 1992.

Śāstrī, Prakāś Hitaiṣī. 'Jaypur Khāniyā Tattva-Carcā: Ek Samīkṣā'. *Siddhāntācārya Paṇḍit Phūlcand Śāstrī Abhinandan-Granth*. Ed. Bābūlāl Jain Phāgull, 643–661. Vārāṇasī: Siddhāntācārya Paṇḍit Phūlcand Śāstrī Abhinandan Granth Prakāśan Samiti, 1985.

Śāstrī, Vaṃśīdhar. *Ācārya Śrī Śāntīsāgar Mahāmuni kā Caritra*. Solāpur: Rāvjī Sakhārām Dośī, 1932 (2nd edition, Mumbaī: Guṇamālāben Javherī, 1995).

Schubring, Walther. *Die Lehre der Jainas. Nach den alten Quellen dargestellt*. Berlin: Walter De Gruyter & Co., 1935.

——. *The Doctrine of the Jainas. Described after the Old Sources*. Tr. Wolfgang Beurlen. 2nd English edition. Delhi: Motilal Banarsidas, 1962/2000.

——. 'Jinismus'. *Die Religionen Indiens III*. Hg. v. A. Bareau, Walther Schubring, Christoph von Führer-Haimendorf, 217–242. Stuttgart: Kohlhammer, 1964.

Sen, Amulyachandra. *Schools and Sects in Jaina Literature*. Calcutta: Visva-Bharati Boos Shop, 1931.

Shāntā, N. *La Voie Jaina: Histoire, Spiritualité, Vie des ascètes pèlerines de l'Inde*. Paris: OEIL, 1985.

Sharma, Jagdish P. 'Jainas as a Minority in Indian Society and History'. *Jain Journal* 10, 4 (1976) 137–148.

——. 'The *Jinasattvas*: Class and Gender in the Social Origins of Jaina Heroes'. *Approaches to Jain Studies: Philosophy, Logic, Rituals and Symbols*. Eds N. K. Wagle and O. Qvarnström, 72–85. University of Toronto: Center for South Asian Studies, 1999.

Śīlcandra Vijay, Muni. *Śāsan Samrāṭ*. Ahmedabad: Tapāgacchīya Śeṭhśrī Jinadās Dharmadās Dhārmik Trust, Kadambagiri Vāṭī, 1973.

Singh, Munshi Hardyal. *Report on the Census of 1891. Vol. II. The Castes of Marwar. Illustrated*. Jodhpur: Published by the Order of the Marwar Darbar, 1894.

Śivprasād. *Tapāgacch kā Itihās*. Bhāg 1, Khaṇḍ 1. Vārāṇasī: Pārśvanāth Vidyāpīṭh, 2000.

——. *Añcalgacch kā Itihās*. Vārāṇasī: Pārśvanāth Vidyāpīṭh, 2001.

SJCS = Samagra Jain Cāturmās Sūcī Prakāśan Pariṣad Bambaī. 'Pariṣad ke Baṛhte Kadam'. *Samagra Jain Cāturmāsi Sūcī*. Ed. B. U. Jain, 67f. Bombay: Akhil Bhāratīya Samagra Jaina Cāturmās Sūcī Prakāśan Pariṣad, 1987.

Śrut Saṃvarddhan Saṃsthān (Ed.). *Śrut Saṃvarddhan Saṃsthān dvārā Pravartit Pāñc Śrut Saṃvarddhan Vārṣik Puraskāroṁ evaṃ Sarāk Puraskār Varṣ – 2002: Paricay Pustikā*. Preraṇāstrot Upādhyāy Muni Jñānsāgar. Meraṭh: Śrut Saṃvarddhan Saṃsthān, 2002.

Syādvādmatī, Āryikā (comp.). *Vimal Bhakti Saṃgraha*. Vārāṇāsī: Bhāratvarṣīya Anekānt Vidvat Pariṣad, 2000.

Tāraṇataraṇasvāmī. *Śrāvakācāra*. Anuvādak: Brahmacārī Sītalprasād. Sūrat: Śrī Tāraṇataraṇa Samāj ke Jain Caityālay – Sāgar Kī Or Se, Mathurāprasād Bajāj, Baṛā Bājār, 1933.

Ṭhāṇa = *Ṭhāṇa (Sthānāṅga Sūtra)*. Vācanā Pramukha: Ācārya Tulsī. Sampādaka Vivecaka: Muni Nathamala. Lāḍnūṁ: Jaina Viśva Bhāratī, 1976.

Tomgia, V. G. 'Changing Patterns of the Status of Women in the Jain Community. Traditional and Modern Trends in their Status'. *Indian Journal of Social Research* 32 (1991) 283–288.

Ṭoṅgyā, Rameś, Amit Ṭoṅgyā and Atul Pāṭedī (comp.). *Ācārya Śrī 108 Vidyāsāgarjī Mahārāj Sasaṅgh. Gommaṭagiri – Indaur Cāturmās 1999. Saṅgh Paricay evaṃ Āhārdān Vidhi*. Indaur: Sugan Grāphiks & Ṭoṅkyā Ṭelīkamyūnikeśans, 1999.

Tuschen, Stefanie. *Das Bhaṭṭāraka-Amt bei den Digambara-Jainas in Karṇāṭaka*. Magisterarbeit, Philipps-Universität Marburg, 1997.

Upadhye, Adinath Neminath. 'Introduction'. *Śrī Kundakundācārya's Pravacanasāra (Pavayanasāra). A Pro-Canonical Text of the Jainas* (2nd edition), i-cxxvi. Bombay: Sheth Manilal Revashankar Jhaveri (Rāyacandra-Jaina-Śāstra-Mālā 9), (1930) 1935.

——. 'Yāpanīya Sangha: A Jaina Sect'. *Journal of the University of Bombay* 1, 4 (1933) 224–231.

——. 'A Paṭṭāvalī of the Senagaṇa'. *Jaina Antiquary* 13, 2 (1948) 1–9.

——. 'On the meaning of Yāpanīya'. *S. Srikantha Sastri Felicitation Volume*, 197–198. Mysore, 1973.

Upadhye, Adinath Neminath. 'More Light on the Yāpanīya Saṅgha'. *Annals of the Bhandarkar Oriental Research Institute* 55, 1–4 (1974) 9–22.

Vallée-Poussin, Charles Louis Joseph, de la. 'Religious Orders (Indian)'. *Encyclopaedia of Religion and Ethics* Vol. 10. Ed. Hastings, 715–718. Edinburgh: T. & T. Clark, 1918.

Vallely, Anne. *Guardians of the Transcendent: An Ethnography of a Jain Ascetic Community*. Toronto: University of Toronto Press, 2002.

Varṇī, Kṣullaka Jinendra. *Jainendra Siddhānta Kośa*. Bhāg I-V. Chaṭhā Saṃskaraṇ. Naī Dillī: Bhāratīya Jñānpīṭh, 1970/1998.

Vidvatratna, Sumerucandra Divākara. *Cāritra Cakravartī. Śramaṇ Śiromaṇa Suvargīya Ācārya Śāntīsāgar Mahārāja kā Puṇya-Cāritra*. Vārāṇasī: Mahāvīra Press, 1972.

Vijayanunni, M. *Religion*. Census of India 1991. Series 1. India. Paper 1 of 1995. New Delhi.

Weber, Max. *Gesammelte Aufsätze zur Religionssoziologie*. Bd. II. Tübingen: J.C.B. Mohr (Paul Siebeck), 1920/1978.

——. *Wirtschaft und Gesellschaft: Grundriß der Verstehenden Soziologie*. Studienausgabe. Ed. Winckelmann. Tübingen: J.C.B. Mohr (Paul Siebeck), 1920/1978.

Williams, Robert H. B. *Jaina Yoga*. Delhi: Motilal Banarsidas, 1963/1983.

Zydenbos, Robert J. 'The Ritual Giving of Food to a Digambara Renunciant'. *Approaches to Jain Studies: Philosophy, Logic, Rituals and Symbols*. Eds N. K. Wagle and O. Qvarnström, 291–303. University of Toronto: Center for South Asian Studies, 1999.

Part V

PROPERTY, LAW AND ETHICS

13

ARCHITECTURAL, SCULPTURAL AND RELIGIOUS CHANGE

A new interpretation of the Jaina temples at Khajuraho

Julia A. B. Hegewald

Introduction: the continuity of religious sites

It is a common feature of sacred architecture throughout the world that at times of political conflict, of changes in population or of religious belief in an area, sites sanctified by one religious sect have frequently been appropriated by the followers of other faiths. Well-known examples of this are the Dome of the Rock in Jerusalem[1] and the Hagia Sophia in Istanbul. In some cases changes in the denomination of religious buildings have happened peacefully, by the adoption of deserted and decaying religious buildings and their conversion to the requirements of a new faith. Sometimes, however, the destruction and forceful re-appropriation of active places of worship have also been used as potent symbols of victory and proof of superiority by different peoples asserting their power. Ancient sacred sites are, however, not only potent places in political but also in religious geography. The latter derives its significance from the fact that holy sites are generally regarded to be qualitatively different from ordinary space. They are places where a break between the different hierarchical levels and spheres of the religious cosmos enables contact and communication with the divine.[2]

In South Asia, there are ample examples of the forcible expropriation of religious sites during the period of Muslim invasion and domination. Well-known examples are the Quwwat al-Islām Mosque (1197 CE) in Delhi (Dillī) and the Arhāī-din-kā-jhonprā Mosque (1199 CE) in Ajmer (Ajmīr). In Delhi, a large number of Hindu and Jaina temples and at Ajmer, a Jaina theological college (erected in 1153 CE), were destroyed and completely dismantled. The old building material was reused to build new edifices of the Islamic faith on the sacred sites. Although the mosques were constructed from the ruins of Hindu and Jaina edifices, and therefore display decorative elements associated with those religions, in layout and design the mosques do not resemble the former religious edifices.

Robert Hillenbrand argues that such a 'naked assertion of power' is typical of the early period of the Islamic conquest and is followed by a more subtle and persuasive approach.[3] There are, however, also examples from later periods in the history of Islam in India where religious sites were forcibly islamicized: for instance, the Bina-Niv-ki-Masjid at Anantpeth in Ujjain (Ujjaynī), constructed out of the remains of a Jaina temple in about 1400 CE, and the Bīja Maṇḍal Mosque at Vidisha (Vidiśā), originally a Hindu temple from the eleventh or twelfth century, destroyed and converted by Aurangzeb (Ālamgīr) in the seventeenth century.

The Muslims were, however, not the first to annex and convert ancient local places of worship, and there is a long tradition of the continuity of religious sites in South Asia. Sacred locations which were used for Vedic sacrifices were appropriated and converted by later forms of Brahmanism, Buddhist sites were reconfigured for Hindu worship and there was much mutual appropriation between Hindu and Jaina religious buildings. In these cases, the temples were usually not completely dismantled. The main religious images were replaced and the edifices were altered to a certain extent to adapt them to the distinct ritual of the new religion. Examples where Jaina temples were adopted and converted into Śaivite temples are the Śvetāmbara Jaina temple at Bijolia (Bijauliyā) in Rajasthan, now called the Undeśvara Temple, and the Digambara Jaina temple in the village of Hallur near Bagalkot (Bāgalkoṭh) in northern Karnataka. In both cases, prominent Jaina figures still adorn the temple exterior although their shrines (*garbha-gṛha*) now house *śiva liṅgas*.

Because of the powerful position of Hinduism in India today, it is much rarer to find examples where Hindu temples have been adapted to Jaina worship. I would like to propose in this chapter that two examples illustrating this point, which show how Hindu temples were appropriated and altered by the Jaina community, are the Pārśvanātha and Ādinātha Temples at Khajuraho (Khajurāho) in Madhya Pradesh. The discussion of these two temples, with particular attention to the larger and more elaborate Pārśvanātha Temple, will form the focus of this chapter.

The Jaina temples at Khajuraho

The temples at Khajuraho were constructed between the late ninth and the early twelfth centuries. The city was one of the capitals of the Chandellas who ruled the area of Jekābhukti, known today as Bundelkhand. Whilst the Hindu temples of the so-called Western Group have been well researched and documented in detail, the temple structures to the east of the village, today comprising mainly Jaina edifices, have received much less scholarly attention. The Eastern Group consists of four large Digambara Jaina temples: the ruined Ghaṇṭai Temple, the Pārśvanātha Temple (Figure 13.1), the Ādinātha Temple (Figure 13.2) and the Śāntinātha Temple. It also includes several smaller Jaina shrines, many of them constructed either on the foundations of earlier structures, or out of the reused building material of previous temples.[4] A large number of Jaina images, the earliest bearing

Figure 13.1 The small shrine attached to the rear of the Pārśvanātha Temple.

inscriptions from the beginning of the eleventh century, were uncovered in the area and are now housed in the small Government Museum next to the complex of Jaina temples. It is noteworthy that although several art historians have drawn attention to the prominent Hindu imagery on the walls of the Pārśvanātha and the Ādinātha Jaina Temples, few have even begun to question the belief that these edifices were originally built as Jaina shrines. It appears that so far no research has analysed the structure of the buildings in sufficient detail to suggest that they were initially designed for Hindu worship.

The present chapter will examine the architectural design and certain aspects of the sculptural format[5] of the Pārśvanātha and the smaller Ādinātha Temples,

Figure 13.2 The Ādinātha Temple adorned with Hindu sculptures.

and argue that the two religious edifices were originally constructed as Hindu temples. The original shrines seem to have been deserted during the Islamic destructions of Khajuraho between the eleventh and the thirteenth centuries,[6] and then taken over by the local Jaina community during the thirteenth century. As will be shown here, the buildings continued to change over the centuries and as some parts were closed, new elements were added to distinguish them from their Hindu neighbours and to suit the ritual requirements of the Jaina faith. Both temples seem to have changed their name and main sacred image, once again within the Jaina religious framework. The fact that the conversion process from Hindu to Jaina worship has largely remained unnoticed shows how well and with how much sensitivity the reconstructions and conversions of the temples were carried out. The results are convincing specimens of Jaina architecture.

The Jaina temples and shrines of the Eastern Group are located in a walled enclosure, typical of Jaina temple complexes not only in this region, but all over India.[7] Only the remains of the dilapidated Ghaṇṭai Temple are located outside this walled temple area, about a quarter of a mile (*c*.500 metres) to the north-west. Today, the Śāntinātha Temple is the largest edifice within the temple compound and represents the principal place for Jaina worship at Khajuraho. It is a multi-shrined construction, consisting of several smaller temples (*devakulikā*), dating from the early eleventh and later centuries, which were linked and arranged around a central courtyard. Although the main sanctuary houses a large standing image of Śāntinātha, dated to VS 1085, or 1028 CE,[8] the temple as a whole is largely a modern architectural arrangement. Amongst the older temples on the site, the Pārśvanātha Temple is the largest and most elaborate. It is the best preserved of the religious edifices in this group, and one of the finest at Khajuraho. In the entrance pavilion, placed on the left doorjamb, is a Sanskrit inscription dating the temple to VS 1011, corresponding to 954 CE. It has been unanimously accepted that this inscription, which is written in the Nāgarī script, is a copy of an earlier record re-engraved during the thirteenth century. The re-writing of ancient inscriptions is relatively common at Khajuraho.[9] Although the inscription is a copy, the structure is so close in style and sculptural treatment to the Lakṣmaṇa Temple, constructed between 930–950 CE, that a dating of the Pārśvanātha Temple to 950–970 CE has generally been accepted.[10] This dating makes the temple one of the earliest edifices on the site.

The Pārśvanātha Temple was constructed of fine-grained buff sandstone and is raised on a large but relatively low platform (*jagatī*),[11] providing the temple with an open ambulatory for the performance of the rite of circumambulation (*pradakṣiṇā*). The temple measures about eighteen metres in length and nine metres in width (about 60 by 30 feet). It was planned along an east – west axis with the entrance facing east. It consists of a small, beautifully decorated porch (*mukha-maṇḍapa*) with a profusely ornamented doorframe,[12] a closed hall (*gūḍha-maṇḍapa*) with a four pillared nave (*śālā*) in its centre, leading to a vestibule (*antarāla*). The latter leads to the sanctum enshrining a modern black marble sculpture of Pārśvanātha from Rajasthan. The image is placed on a sandstone pedestal which bears the bull *lāñchana* of Ṛṣabhanātha or Ādinātha, and indicates that even during the time of the Jaina occupation of this temple, its dedication has changed.[13] Alternatively, the pedestal could have come from a damaged Jaina temple nearby, but since the statue of Pārśvanātha is dated and appears to have been installed as late as 1860 CE, there must have been an earlier image in its place.[14] The *garbha-gṛha* is surrounded by an internal ambulation path, a *pradakṣiṇā-patha* (*sāndhāra-prāsāda*) with small latticed windows on the north and south sides admitting a limited amount of light and air. At the west end of the temple, a small additional shrine, with access from the outside, has been constructed and attached to the rear of the Pārśvanātha Temple (Figure 13.1). This subsidiary structure houses a figure of Ādinātha and might possibly represent the image originally housed in the main sanctum of the temple.[15] Beautifully carved statues adorn both the inside and outside of this large religious building. Numerous rows of mouldings, and three diminishing bands of sculptures run around the temple exterior as well as the outside of the inner sanctum inside the *pradakṣiṇā-patha*. The well-preserved large temple tower (*śikhara*) above the sanctum goes over into the roof of the closed *maṇḍapa*. In front are two smaller roof structures which are clearly later reconstructions.

Although scholars such as Alexander Cunningham, Krishna Deva and George Michell drew attention to the prominent Hindu imagery adorning the walls of the Pārśvanātha Temple,[16] and Eliky Zannas pointed to the striking absence of figures of Jaina Tīrthaṅkaras (Zannas 1960: 151), specialists in Indian art history have not attempted to explain these unusual features. One reason for this neglect could have been the presence of the inscription identifying the temple as a place of Jaina worship.[17] In this respect it is, however, important to bear in mind that the text was re-engraved about three centuries after the event which it is recording, and that there is no proof that the epigraphic record was originally associated with the present temple. A further justification for the lack of inquiries into this matter might have been the well-documented fact that the craftsmen who worked for the followers of one faith at a sacred site were frequently also employed to build temples for other religious groups. Such cross-fertilization is especially common in a Jaina context, where many Hindu motifs and divinities were integrated and re-interpreted to fit the Jaina creed. Later, Islamic decorative features also entered the Jaina vocabulary of architecture. It is worthy to note that James Fergusson was troubled by the layout of the Jaina temples at Khajuraho which appeared so untypical to him (Fergusson 1967: 49). Only rarely, however, have art historians suggested explanations for the presence of such an unusually large number of Hindu images on the walls of these Jaina structures. Klaus Bruhn, in his detailed analysis of the sculptures adorning the Pārśvanātha Temple, argued that the images are not Hindu as such but strongly Brahmanized in style. He questioned, however, why not at least a few strong markers of correct Jaina iconography, such as Jaina *yakṣas* or *yakṣiṇīs*, were placed in prominent positions on the temple wall. Based on his iconographic study of the temple, Bruhn thought it unlikely that the temple might have changed over from Hindu to Jaina ownership, but he is one of the few to mention this possibility at all and to aim at finding an explanation for the unusual phenomenon (Bruhn 1956: 31–34). Shobita Punja proposed that long after its construction as a Hindu shrine, the Pārśvanātha Temple might have been presented as a gift to the local Jaina community (Punja 1992: 146), but there are no inscriptions recording this event. It is worth mentioning that Fergusson, as early as 1876, believed that the neighbouring but smaller Ādinātha Temple was built as a Vaiṣṇava temple and only later appropriated by the Jainas.

There are a number of strong indications in the actual fabric of the Pārśvanātha and the Ādinātha Temples which show that they were originally constructed as Hindu temples and later adopted by the Jaina community. A careful examination of the external walls of the Pārśvanātha Temple reveals that it used to have two lateral transepts with fenestrations (*vātāyana*). Such decorated balconies are typical of the Hindu temples at Khajuraho, creating the ubiquitous Latin cross with two principal arms on the temple ground plans. In the Pārśvanātha Temple these large projecting windows were later enclosed.[18] On the outside, the openings were carefully filled with sculptures taken from dilapidated temples in the surrounding area.[19] Today, only two small projections on both the north and the south sides of the temple indicate their former existence and create pronounced *bhadra* projections in the centre of the sanctum and the *maṇḍapa* walls. The presence of plastered brick sections in these protuberances, which are made to look like sandstone, further support the fact that changes were undertaken to the original fabric of the building.[20] The central portion of the temple wall (*jaṅghā*) is enlivened by further shallow protrusions (*ratha*) and recesses (*salilāntara*). Nevertheless, the effect of a play of light and shade is here much less pronounced than in the developed Hindu temples at Khajuraho, which are furnished with large protruding open balconies creating clear interruptions and voids in the temple facades. At the Pārśvanātha Temple small fenestrations are present below the *śikhara*, but these are too small to create pronounced breaks in the long and continuous sculptural bands. Consequently, the whole appearance of the structure is somewhat more solid. On the inside, the enclosed balconies are even more obvious, because only on the north side has the infill been covered with sculptural decorations.[21]

Several reasons might explain why the Jaina community decided to fill in the balconied openings when restoring and converting the temple. First, by enclosing the large windows, wall space was gained inside the building to accommodate further religious images for the Jaina ritual of venerating a large number of statues. Today only one large and two middle sized freestanding Tīrthaṅkara sculptures are housed in the temple hall, in addition to the two Jinas located in the shrines. Deva's detailed description of the temple interior from the early 1970s, however, still mentions ten statues of the venerated fordmakers, placed on elaborate pedestals along the walls of the closed hall (Deva 1975a: 259).[22] Another motive for enclosing the large open windows might have been to prevent people from looking into the sacred space of the temple interior. Cunningham, on his second visit to Khajuraho in 1864–1865, was not allowed to enter the religious edifice and could only glance into the inside from the small porch. It is a common feature of Jaina temple architecture in general to create secluded internal spaces which are frequently protected by rings of high walls. A third reason for the infill of the typical Khajuraho balconies, which is not derived from ritual requirements, might have been the wish to differentiate themselves visually from the Hindu shrines in the Western Group.

Further structural changes were undertaken on the doorframes of the original temple. The entrance to the *gūḍha-maṇḍapa* is framed by a double doorway of posts and beams (*śākhā*). Its lintel is adorned with representations of the nine planetary deities, the *navagrahas*, with a central image of the ten armed *yakśī*

Cakreśvarī seated on Garuḍa, the whole flanked by two figures of four armed seated Sarasvatīs. It is worthy to note that there are wide cement grooves between the two sets of doorframes and also where the outer frame was connected to the temple wall. From this, it appears that the lintels and beams were not originally carved for this edifice, as they are too small to fill the available space. In tenth-century India, buildings were constructed of interlocking stones and even during the thirteenth century when the temple appears to have been converted to Jaina worship for the first time, cement was not used for masonry construction.[23] Consequently, the alterations carried out on the doorframes must have been conducted at a later stage, possibly in the mid-nineteenth century, when the main image of the temple was changed to Pārśvanātha and the Jaina character of the edifice was consciously emphasised. It is worth noting that although most of the Hindu temples at Khajuraho were damaged and extensively reconstructed, none of them have such cement grooves. The explanation here seems to be that in those cases the original temple constituents found within the collapsed buildings, were re-inserted into their initial location and thus fitted exactly. The beams and lintels of the Pārśvanātha Temple must be reused parts from destroyed Jaina temples on the site,[24] such as the dilapidated Ghanṭai Temple nearby.[25] The re-employment of old temple material for the repair of damaged edifices and the construction of new Jaina shrines was still continuing when Cunningham stayed at the site in February 1865 (*A. S. I.* II: 435). The entrance to the *garbha-gṛha* is surrounded by a further double doorframe. As in the example discussed earlier, it was cemented in at a later stage and does not appear to be the original frame belonging to the temple (Figure 13.3). As such, the presence of Jinas on the door lintels of the temple cannot, as many scholars have argued,[26] be taken as lasting proof of the original dedication of the shrine. The doorway leading to the *garbha-gṛha* has two superimposed lintels. Whilst the lower example again exhibits depictions of the *navagrahas*, a seated Jina, and two flanking images of standing Tīrthaṅkaras, the upper architrave is adorned with alternate images of five seated and six standing Jaina figures. The availability of additional doorframes at the site is supported by the fact that additional parts of such frames have been positioned on the north wall inside the closed *maṇḍapa*. They frame a seated and two standing Tīrthaṅkara figures and cover the blind wall where the former open balcony has been filled in. According to R. Nath a similar frame was also loosely positioned against the inside wall on the south side of the *gūḍha-maṇḍapa* (Nath 1980: 41).[27] The fact that the high threshold leading to the inner sanctum of the Pārśvanātha Temple depicts a small *liṅga* in its centre points to the original dedication of the temple as Śaivite.[28] This is further supported by Shobita Punja's interpretation of the imagery on the outside walls of the temple as a depiction of the story of Śiva's wedding on Mahā-Śivarātri as narrated in the *Śiva Purāṇa* (Punja 1992: 145–146).

The small additional shrine constructed at the rear of the Pārśvanātha Temple, facing west, represents another alteration to the original temple building. It was constructed after Cunningham's visit in 1884, probably during the later part of the nineteenth or early in the twentieth century.[29] Whilst some of the local Hindu

Figure 13.3 Wide cement grooves are visible between the two doorframes leading to the shrine.

temples have further shrines and *maṇḍapas*, these are all freestanding edifices, located either in front or in the four corners surrounding the main temple (*pañcāyatana*). Nowhere else at Khajuraho have subsidiary shrines either been connected to a main temple building or placed at its rear. Whilst J. C. Harle argued that this kind of additional shrine '...is not repeated elsewhere, and it cannot be said that it is a function of the temple's being Jain',[30] additional inter-connected shrines and small temples located behind a central religious edifice are very common in a Jaina context. The small shrine attached to the rear of the Pārśvanātha Temple provides space for an additional image and is adapted to the

Jaina ritual of venerating multiple Jinas.[31] From an aesthetic point of view, the external shrine also helps to balance the large temple structure. It creates a second axial projection and seems to counterbalance or mirror the front porch projecting from the opposite shorter side.

Changes were, however, not only done to the architectural structure of the temple but also to the sculptural configuration. The main sacred image in the sanctum of the original Hindu temple was probably destroyed during the Muslim assaults on Khajuraho. When Cunningham returned to the site in 1852, the main sanctum of the temple, which he calls the Jinanātha Temple, was empty and deserted although he reported that the shrine had been repaired by a Jaina banker five years earlier (*A. S. I.* II: 432). In 1865 he was no longer permitted to enter the building which at that time had been restored, internally painted and become an active place of Jaina worship. The first Jaina image to be enshrined in the sanctum seems to have been a statue of Ādinātha. This was replaced by a figure of Pārśvanātha, bearing a date of 1860 CE, which seems to indicate the date of the latest change. A statue of Ādinātha was placed in the additional shrine attached to the rear of the temple.

Sculptural changes were also undertaken on the temple exterior. It is striking that there are fewer erotic scenes and depictions of *mithuna* couples on the Pārśvanātha Temple than on most other temples at Khajuraho. Because most of the surviving erotic sculptures are found high up on the temple wall, where they can hardly be seen, one might question if others were not consciously removed and carefully replaced by different kinds of representations during the temple conversion.[32] This is not to say that *mithuna* couples or erotic scenes are not to be found on Jaina temples. The Pārśvanātha Temple at Ranakpur (Rāṇakpur) in Rajasthan, for example, has small erotic scenes carved onto its external walls. At Khajuraho, however, the removal of large erotic scenes might have served to differentiate the Jaina temples from the Hindu structures nearby.

Whilst a small number of Jina images adorn the outer walls of the Pārśvanātha Temple, there are none at all on the Ādinātha Temple. It is striking that the few sculptures of Jaina Tīrthaṅkaras are either placed close to the porch of the Pārśvanātha Temple on the eastern side, which was entirely rebuilt during the reconstruction process, or they are located on the walls of the western shrine, which is a later addition. Most other figures adorning the *jaṇghā* of the temple, are either clearly identifiable Hindu gods, such as the *dikpālas*, Śiva and Kṛṣṇa, or they are lesser known goddesses, which could either be derived from the Hindu or the Jaina pantheon. There are also representations of various composite mythical animals, the *vyālas* or *śārdūlas*.[33] Through the positioning of clear Jaina imagery at the entrances to the two shrines of the Pārśvanātha Temple, the Jaina character of the edifice was reinforced, and the otherwise Hindu-looking shrine could not be mistaken for a Brahmanical place of worship.

The most interesting changes to the sculptural repertoire were undertaken on the inside of this complex religious edifice. The outer walls of the sanctum, inside the *pradakṣiṇā-patha*, are adorned with standing sculptures of playful female figures such as *apsaras*, nymphs and dryads (*vṛkṣikā*). These images show a very high standard of workmanship and are amongst the most beautiful at Khajuraho. The exquisitely carved female statues of *devāṅganās* are interspersed with representations of sitting Jaina Tīrthaṅkaras. These Jinas are clearly replacements of earlier Hindu sculptures which were carefully chiselled out of their niches and replaced with religious icons from the Jaina faith. These changes were carried out with such sensitivity that they are not at all obvious at first glance. Clear evidence for these alterations is, however, to be found in the positioning of the parasols on top of the Jinas. The umbrellas are not placed exactly above the heads of the straight sitting and centrally located Jaina images. Whenever they are found in association with figures of the Tīrthaṅkaras, the parasols are positioned further to the side within the niches, indicating that they either belonged to images in a bent position, such as *ābhaṅga* or *tribhaṅga*,[34] commonly associated with Hindu imagery of this period,[35] or that they originally framed representations of divine Hindu couples, such as Śiva and Pārvatī (Figure 13.4). It is interesting to observe, that such replacements of Hindu with Jaina images are much more common on the inside than on the outside of the temple. On the exterior, Hindu sculptures seem even to have been inserted into the wall spaces to enclose the balconied openings. Those statues, however, are largely images of goddesses, female figures or of divine couples where the religious denomination is generally more difficult to determine. Perhaps not enough scattered Jaina figures were available from destroyed temples at the site to be used for such major structural changes. We assume that the majority of temples at Khajuraho were Hindu and that only a much smaller number was constructed by the Jaina community. The increase in the number of figures on the temple, the reuse of sculptures from other buildings, as well as the combination of Hindu and Jaina imagery, might also explain why it is so difficult to define a clear iconographic pattern for the location of individual figures on the structure (Bruhn 1956: 32). The emphasis on the temple interior shows that the inner ambulation around the *garbha-gṛha* was given more importance than that on the outside of the temple, and that the ritual life of the shrine was concentrated on the interior. It is typical of Jaina architecture throughout India to have a comparatively plain exterior, often with high protective walls, but a very ornate interior sheltered from outside gaze and intrusion.

The Ādinātha Temple, slightly to the north of the Pārśvanātha Temple, is a much smaller structure. When Cunningham documented the temple in the mid nineteenth century, it consisted only of the *prāsāda*, raised on a *jagatī* and crowned by a tall *śikhara* (*A. S. I.* II: 432). The porch, made of plastered brick, was added later, either at the end of the nineteenth or early in the twentieth century. A noteworthy feature which further supports the argument that the two major Jaina temples at Khajuraho were initially constructed as Hindu religious edifices, is the presence of an image of Garuḍa, carved onto the pedestal in the *garbha-gṛha* (Fergusson 1967: 51). During Cunningham's first visit to the temple, in 1852 CE, the seat carried an image of Pārśvanātha (*A. S. I.* II: 432), whilst these days a sculpture of Ādinātha is found in its place. Consequently, this temple also changed its dedication once again within the period of Jaina ritual use. The outside of the

Figure 13.4 Seated Tīrthaṅkara image with misplaced parasol inside the *pradakṣiṇā-patha*.

Ādinātha Temple is also adorned with Hindu images. This, together with the presence of Viṣṇu's *vāhana* Garuḍa, led Fergusson to argue that the temple was built as a Vaiṣṇava shrine and later appropriated by the Jainas of Khajuraho (Fergusson 1967: 51).

Conclusion: from Hindu to Jaina worship

The earlier discussion has shown that the Pārśvanātha and the Ādinātha Jaina Temples at Khajuraho are highly complex structures with a long history of architectural, sculptural and religious change. Without new discoveries of local textual sources or inscriptions, precisely recording and dating events in the history of these temples, it will be difficult to ascertain at what stage which alterations were carried out. A detailed examination of the edifices, however, indicates very strongly that they were not designed as Jaina temples from the outset, as has generally been believed. The two shrines are profusely adorned with Hindu imagery and Jaina figures are only to be found on those parts of the buildings which were added at a later stage, or to the temple interior, where it is obvious from their positioning that the Jaina sculptures were inserted into already available niches.

The presence of a large number of dated Jaina figures from as early as the beginning of the eleventh century, which were excavated at Khajuraho, shows that there were Jaina temples at the site during the Chandella period. The Ghaṇṭai Temple, which survives only in a very reduced form, seems to be one of them. A large concentration of Tīrthaṅkara images with dated inscriptions from the reign of Madanavarmā, who ruled the area from the early to the mid-twelfth century, points to a pronounced Jaina presence during that period.[36] From the available architectural material, it does, however, seem questionable that the Pārśvanātha and the Ādinātha Temples were initially conceived as Jaina structures. The inscription on the left doorjamb of the Pārśvanātha Temple, dating it to 954 CE, is a re-engraving carved in the thirteenth century, and there is no proof that the epigraphic record was originally associated with this edifice. Either the entire doorjamb or the text for the inscription might well have come from another destroyed local Jaina shrine. During the restoration process, the Jaina community clearly aimed at making the temples more Jaina by adding Tīrthaṅkara images and doorframes removed from ruined Jaina structures in the area. There is no reason why in the course of the complete reconstruction of the porch, they should not, in order to add substance to their claim to the temple, also have engraved the copy of a local Jaina inscription on the doorjamb.

Based on the epigraphic and architectural evidence available to us at present, and on the reports by Cunningham and Fergusson who paid several visits to the site during the course of the nineteenth century, a possible historical sequence for the evolution of the Pārśvanātha Temple may have been that it was constructed as a Hindu temple under King Dhaṅga in the mid or late tenth century. The edifice was probably destroyed and desecrated during the Muslim attacks on Khajuraho in 1022 and 1182 CE. Because the Jaina inscription was re-engraved during the thirteenth century it seems that the shrine must have been appropriated and rebuilt by local Jainas during this period. The *caturviṃśati-paṭṭa* of Ādinātha might also have been placed inside the sanctum at this stage. The temple must then have been damaged again during the Islamic invasion of 1202/3 CE, because the shrine room was empty when Cunningham surveyed the structure in 1852. He found the dated inscription in place in the porch but no shrine had yet been added to the rear of the main temple. On the basis of the inscription of the Pārśvanātha image, nowadays housed inside the main shrine, this statue was inaugurated in 1860, around the time of Cunningham's second survey of the site. The sequence of events as described earlier is supported by Fergusson's view that the temple was reoccupied by the Jainas in 1860 but that it had been restored and altered at a much earlier date (Fergusson 1967: 50). In 1865, when Cunningham returned to Khajuraho, the Pārśvanātha Temple was completely restored and had become an active place of Jaina worship.

Although certain details in the history of the Jaina temples at Khajuraho might never come to light, the present paper proposes a new interpretation for the Ādinātha and Pārśvanātha Temples, which for several decades have troubled art historians working at the site. Another perspective on the new theory proposed earlier is given by the fact that at the end of my research stay in Khajuraho, I came to hear about a fierce and longstanding argument between the local Hindus and Jainas. Their dispute is over the rightful ownership of these two sacred Jaina edifices which the local Śaivite community claims are Hindu in origin.

Acknowledgements

I would like to thank University College Oxford, the Society for South Asian Studies, the Wingate Foundation and the Deutsche Forschungsgemeinschaft without whose generous financial support this research could not have been undertaken.

All photographs are by the author.

Notes

1 The Dome of the Rock (Quabbat al-Ṣakhara) was constructed on the site of a pagan temple which was first reclaimed as a place of worship by the Jews and then converted by the Muslims into a mosque.

2 Mircea Eliade has written about this phenomenon at great length, see for example his *The Sacred and the Profane: The Nature of Religion*, originally published in 1957 and reprinted in 1987.

3 Hillenbrand 1988: 105–115. See especially p. 112.

4 Hindu temples belonging to the Eastern Group are the Brahmā Temple (early tenth century), the Vāmana Temple (eleventh century), and the Javārī Temple (late eleventh century). These Hindu edifices are located outside the compound wall of the Jaina temple complex, close to the Ghaṇṭai Temple.

5 A detailed iconographical study of the sculptures adorning the Pārśvanātha Temple has been conducted by Klaus Bruhn (1956).

6 The first attack on the temples at Khajuraho was carried out under Mahmud of Ghazni in 1022 CE. In the twelfth century, the last official Chandella Rājā, Paramardi Deva, also known as Parmāl (*c.*1165–1202), was defeated by Prithīrāj (III) Chauhān in 1182 CE, and in 1202–1203 CE, Qutubu-d dīn Aibak invaded the area again and took Kalinjar (Kālanjara). See Alexander Cunningham's reports in *Archaeological Survey of India* (*A. S. I.*) II: 412 and XXI: 59, Smith 1981: 203 and Mehta 1979 I: 70.

7 Although most art historians have described the Jaina temples at Khajuraho as lacking a surrounding wall, such an enclosing structure is present today, and is already marked on the plan drawn by Cunningham for his report of the years 1864–1865 (*A. S. I.* II: plate XCV).

8 On his first visit to the site, in January 1852, Cunningham recorded an inscription dating the image to VS 1085, 1028 CE, which was later covered with plaster and whitewash (*A. S. I.* II: 434 and XXI: 61).

9 A further example of the re-engraving of an ancient record at Khajuraho is King Dhaṅga's stone inscription from 1059 CE which was renewed by Jayavarmādeva in 1173 CE. In this case, both dates are engraved on the same stone (Kielhorn 1892: 137–147).

10 See for example Deva 1997: 59, or his long discussion of the issue in 1998: 61, 68–70. The Pārśvanātha Temple seems to have been constructed during the early part of the reign of King Yaśōvarmā's son, King Dhaṅga (*c.*950–1002).

11 The platform is just over one metre (about 4 feet) high and its original mouldings are now lost. The sandstone for the construction of the temple is believed to have come from the quarries of Panna (Pannā) on the Ken River.

12 The porch has a highly decorated ceiling (*vitāna*) with an unusually elaborate pendant consisting of an intertwined pair of figures, probably *vidyādharas*, carved in the round. The construction of the *mukha-maṇḍapa* is of one *catuṣkī* (*mukha-catuṣkī*).

13 The plinth also retains its original image frame (*parikara*) and halo (*prabhāvalī*). From this it can be derived that the pedestal supported a *caturviṃśati-paṭṭa* with Ādinātha as the main image (Deva 1975a: 259; Deva 1975b: 287; Deva 1998: 71).

14 For the dated inscription see Deva 1975a: 259. Eliky Zannas read the date on the inscription as 1865 (Zannas 1960: 147).

15 Deva suggested that the shrine at the rear might once have been larger and more elaborate (Deva 1975a: 259; Deva 1975b: 287). According to Nath (1980: 42), the additional shrine on the west side houses another image of Pārśvanātha and not of Ādinātha. It is worthy of note that an image of Garuḍa is carved on the front of the pedestal supporting the image in the rear shrine.

16 See for example Cunningham (*A. S. I.* II: 432) and Michell (1990: 170). Although the sculptures adorning the outer walls of the temple are predominantly Vaiṣṇava, including some rare images of Paraśurāma, Balarāma with Rēvatī and others (Deva 1997: 59; Deva 1998: 69), Shobita Punja argues that the external decorations depict the congregation of the gods at Śiva's wedding (Punja 1992: 146) and that consequently the temple must have been Śaivite.

17 Kielhorn translated the first lines of the inscription as 'He who bears the auspicious name Pāhilla,... is pleased by good people [and] held in honour by king Dhaṅga, he bows down here to the lord of the Jinas' (1892: 136).

18 Because of the absence of projecting window openings, the Pārśvanātha Temple also has no stone seats (*āsanapaṭṭikā*) or backrests (*kakṣāsana*), typically found within the ornate balconies of the Hindu temples of the Western Group.

19 Out of the originally eighty or so temples at Khajuraho, only about twenty five survive today, and sculptures and debris from the ruined temples are still being unearthed.

20 It is noteworthy that the *bhadras* adorning the *maṇḍapa* walls are not centrally aligned. On the north side, the projection is much closer to the porch. This is also the area where the repair works in brick and plaster are most obvious. Also the additional shrine at the rear of the temple has pronounced *bhadra* protrusions.

21 This is not a feature of the Hindu architecture at the site.

22 It is slightly confusing that later on in his article he states that almost half of the pedestals are empty. It is not quite clear if there were still ten images and another ten empty pedestals in the hall, or if a total of ten pedestals carried five sculptures when he visited the site (Deva 1975a: 260). The figures described by Deva were mostly Jinas, a four-armed standing Yakṣī with a lion, and a representation of the parents of the Jina, probably the one now housed in the complex of the Śāntinātha Temple.

23 During this period, cement seems only to have been used to cover and seal roof spaces.

24 Fergusson drew attention to the reuse of old building materials in the restoration of temples and for the construction of other edifices (Fergusson 1967: 49).

25 The Ghaṇṭai Temple is named after the chain-and-bell motifs (*ghaṇṭa*) adorning its pillars. Only the *ardha-maṇḍapa* and the *gūdha-maṇḍapa* of this structure survive, which is believed to have been similar in design but larger than the Pārśvanātha Temple (some believe it was almost twice as large; see e.g. Deva 1975b: 280). On the basis of its plan and design as well as the presence of pilgrims' records carved onto its walls, the Ghaṇṭai Temple appears to be very close in date to the Pārśvanātha Temple. It probably dates from the late tenth century CE (Deva 1975a: 261; Deva 1998: 72). Cunningham argued initially that the temple was a sixth to seventh century CE Buddhist structure and suggested that it might have been converted to Jaina use during the eleventh century (*A. S. I.* II: 431). After extensive excavations at the site, the discovery of a large number of Digambara Jaina figures inside and around the temple, and the re-examination of the door lintels, Cunningham revised his interpretation and concluded that the temple must have been Jaina from the outset (*A. S. I.* X: 16). Nowadays, this identification has been accepted unanimously.

26 See for instance Michell 1990: 170.

27 A further example of a Jaina door lintel excavated at the site is exhibited in the Jaina museum at Khajuraho. This lintel, too, shows representations of the Navagrahas and Cakreśvarī, as well as images of Ambikā and Padmāvatī.

28 Other scholars have interpreted the relief carvings on the threshold as a depiction of the churning of the cosmic ocean (*A. S. I.* II: 433).

29 Whilst Zannas considers the western projection to be a later addition, Deva believed that it was part of the initial layout. A closer examination of the stonework, the grooves and the sculptural representations, however, shows that the projecting shrine on the rear must have been added at a later stage. Cunningham, in his minute descriptions of the temple on his visits to Khajuraho in 1852, 1865 and 1884, never mentioned the existence of the western shrine, which further supports the fact that it must have been constructed after his last reported visit to the site.

30 Harle 1986: 234 and footnote no. 51 (p. 513).

31 For a discussion of the veneration of large numbers of images, and issues of multiplication in Jaina architecture, see my 'Multi-shrined Complexes: The Ordering of Space in Jaina Temple Architecture' (2001).

32 A small number of *mithuna* sculptures also survive in the friezes of the *gūḍha-maṇḍapa* and the plinth of the entrance portico.

33 For an iconographic analysis of the sculptures adorning the Pārśvanātha Temple and a map exactly marking the location of the few Jina images on the temple structure, see the detailed study by Klaus Bruhn (1956).

34 There is some controversy about the origin and validity of the term '*tribhaṅga*'. I am using it here in the art historical sense summarised by Gösta Liebert (1986: 301).

35 Images in *ābhaṅga* or *tribhaṅga* are also associated with representations of Jaina patrons and donors, and with Hindu divinities which were integrated into the Jaina religion during the middle ages, but not with the sculptures of Tīrthaṅkaras.

36 Punja (1992: 222) suggests that a Jaina community must have settled in the area of Khajuraho after the invasions of the Islamic rulers of Delhi.

Bibliography

Beglar, J. D. 1878. 'Report of a Tour in Bundelkhand and Malwa, 1871–72 and in the Central Provinces, 1873–74'. *Archaeological Survey of India* VII Calcutta: Office of the Superintendent of Government Printing.

Bruhn, Klaus. 1956. 'The Figures of the Lower Reliefs on the Pārśvanātha Temple at Khajurāho'. *Ācārya Vijayavallabha Sūri Commemoration Volume*. 7–35. Bombay: Shri Mahavira Jaina Vidyalaya.

Chakravarty, Kalyan Kumar. 1985. *The Art of India: Khajuraho*. New Delhi: Arnold–Heinemann Publishers.

Cunningham, Alexander. 1871. 'Four Reports Made During the Year 1862–63–64–65'. *Archaeological Survey of India* II.

—— 1880. 'Report of Tours in Bundelkhand and Malwa in 1874–75 and 1876–77'. *Archaeological Survey of India* X.

—— 1885. 'Reports of a Tour in Bundelkhand and Rewa in 1883–84; A Tour in Rewa, Bundelkhand, Malwa, and Gwalior, in 1884–85'. *Archaeological Survey of India* XXI.

Deva, Krishna. 1975a. 'Jaina Art and Architecture under the Candella-s'. *Aspects of Jaina Art and Architecture*. Eds U. P. Shah and M. A. Dhaky, 257–268 plus plates. Ahmedabad: L. D. Institute of Indology.

—— 1975b. 'Central India'. *Jaina Art and Architecture*. Ed. A. Gosh II: 277–299. New Delhi: Bharatiya Jnanpith.

—— 1987. *Khajuraho*. (first edn. 1966) New Delhi: Archaeological Survey of India.

—— 1990. *Temples of Khajuraho*. 2 vols. Archaeological Survey of Temples No. 5. New Delhi: Archaeological Survey of India.

—— 1997. *Temples of North India*. (first edn. 1969) New Delhi: National Book Trust.

—— 1998. 'Beginnings of Medieval Idiom: Jējākabhukti style, phase 2, c. A.D. 950–1000'. *Encyclopaedia of Indian Temple Architecture: North India – Beginnings of Medieval Idiom (c. A. D. 900–1000)*. Ed. M. A. Dhaky, 57–81 plus plates. New Delhi and Mumbai American Institute of Indian Studies & Indira Gandhi National Centre for the Arts.

Dikshit, R. K. 1977. *The Chandellas of Jejākabhukti*. New Delhi: Abhinav Publications.

Eliade, Mircea. 1987. *The Sacred & the Profane: The Nature of Religion*. (first edn. 1957) San Diego, CA, New York and London: Harcourt Brace Javanovich Publishers.

Fergusson, James. 1967. *History of Indian and Eastern Architecture*. Vol. 2 (first edn. 1876) Delhi: Munshiram Manoharlal.

Harle, J. C. 1986. *The Art and Architecture of the Indian Subcontinent*. The Pelican History of Art. Harmondsworth: Penguin Books.

Hegewald, Julia A. B. 2001. 'Multi-shrined Complexes: The Ordering of Space in Jaina Temple Architecture'. *South Asian Studies* 17: 77–96.

Hillenbrand, Robert. 1988. 'Political Symbolism in Early Indo-Islamic Mosque Architecture: The Case of Ajmīr'. *Iran* 26: 105–115.

Jain, Niraj and Dashrath Jain. 1999. *Jain Monuments at Khajuraho*. (2nd edn.), Khajuraho: Shri Digambar Jain Atishay Chhetra Khajuraho.

Kielhorn, F. 1887. 'Three Chandella Copper-Plate Grants'. *Indian Antiquary* XVI: 201–210.

—— 1892. 'Inscriptions from Khajuraho'. *Epigraphia Indica*. Vol. I. Ed. J. A. S. Burgess, 121–153. Calcutta: Superintendent of Government Printing.

Kulke, Herman and Dietmar Rothermund. 1991. *A History of India*. (first edn. 1986) Calcutta, Allahabad, Bombay and Delhi: Rupa & Co.

Liebert, Gösta. 1986. *Iconographic Dictionary of the Indian Religions*. (first edn. 1976) Asian Arts and Archaeology Series No. 5. Delhi: Sri Satguru Publications.

Mehta, J. L. 1979. *Advanced Study in the History of Medieval India*. Vol. 1 (1000–1526). New Delhi, Bangalore and Jullundur: Sterling Publishers.

Michell, George. 1990. *Monuments of India: Buddhist, Jain, Hindu*. Vol. 1. London, New York, Victoria, Ontario and Auckland: Penguin Books.

Mitra, Sisir Kumar. 1954. 'Darbat Śāntinātha Image Inscription of the Time of Candella Kīrttivarman V. S. 1132'. *The Indian Historical Quarterly* XXX, 1: 182–192.

Mitra, Sisir Kumar. 1958. *The Early Rulers of Khajurāho*. Calcutta: Firma K. L. Mukhopadhyay.

Nath, R. 1980. *The Art of Khajuraho*. New Delhi: Abhinav Publications.

Punja, Shobita. 1992. *Divine Ecstasy: The Story of Khajuraho*. New Delhi: Viking Penguin India.

Smith, Vincent A. 1981. *The Oxford History of India*. (first edn. 1958) Delhi, Oxford, London and New York: Oxford University Press.

Smith, Vincent A. and F. C. Black. 1879. 'Observations on some Chandel Antiquities'. *Journal of the Asiatic Society of Bengal* XLIII, I: 285–296.

Zannas, Eliky. 1960. *Khajuraho*. The Hague: Mouton & Co. Publishers.

14

JAINA LAW AS AN UNOFFICIAL LEGAL SYSTEM

Werner Menski

Against a background of comparative jurisprudential analysis, this chapter demonstrates that despite its formal amalgamation into Hindu law in India during 1955–1956, Jaina law continues to manifest itself in various unofficial and semi-official forms. Thus, it is not productive to dispute *whether* Jaina law existed or exists. The need is rather to research what culture-specific manifestations Jaina law has been taking, and what role it continues to play in maintaining a separate Jaina identity.

The chapter suggests that two major factors have affected the visibility of Jaina law. While the official legal recognition of local customs under Hindu law could potentially act as a protective umbrella for Jaina law, strict evidence requirements have restricted the scope for official legal recognition and inclusion of Jaina religio-cultural elements. Further, strengthening this process of keeping Jaina law within the unofficial realm appears to be a deliberate traditional strategy, by Jainas as individuals and as a community, to keep a cautious distance from the processes of official law and the law courts. Much of Jaina law is therefore found in unreported cases from lower courts, and in unrecorded private agreements within the context of 'family arrangements'.

The problem of understanding law

On a global level, legal debates now acknowledge more widely that the dominant approach of Western legal positivism or 'model jurisprudence' (Chiba 1986), which simplistically assumes that all law comes from the state and appears in more or less codified form, remains deeply problematic, academically incoherent and socially unrealistic. A conceptual analysis of traditional and modern non-Western legal systems inevitably shows that this eurocentric methodology and perspective of certain legal models fails to record many culture-specific forms of law (Menski 2000). Since, somehow, comparative jurisprudence still stops at the Bosporus (Örücü 1999: 31), it is no surprise that Jaina law has been treated as an exotic specialist subject with little practical relevance. As a result, there is hardly any writing on Jaina law.

Within this wider context, the question whether there is something worth studying which we might call Jaina law turns out to be quite complex. Common sense would suggest that if Jainas and Jainism exist, there must also be something like Jaina law. However, such a theoretical acceptance of the existence of Jaina law relies on common sense and on a broad, non-technical definition of 'law' as a culture-specific human phenomenon, rather than the technical, positivist view of 'law' as a body of rules made by some ruler or a state. An interdisciplinary analysis of this problem requires explicit recognition of the fact that lawyers as practising professionals and as academics operate without a universally agreed definition of 'law' (Menski 2000). Still, many lawyers and social scientists follow only the dominant Western legal methodology of positivism and try to define away non-state law by labelling it 'custom', 'convention' or 'culture'. Such forms of law then become more or less unofficial. It is important to be aware that Indian jurisprudence has been deeply influenced by such dominant theories of positivism.

Thus it would appear that modern India has abolished Jaina law and that, at any rate since the introduction of the *Hindu Marriage Act* of 1955 and other Hindu law legislation of 1956, Jaina law no longer exists as a separate personal law.[1] For 'black letter lawyers', that would be the end of the story – Jaina law has now ceased to exist, and there is nothing to study. However, from a variety of perspectives Jaina law continues to exist, albeit now at an unofficial level.[2]

In view of the multiple challenge of conflicting perspectives, relating to law and – no less relevant – concerning the identity of Jainas themselves as a religious community, it becomes difficult to ascertain to what extent Jaina law exists. Even if we find that many people (including numerous Jainas themselves) perceive Jainas as Hindus, or as part of Hinduism in some form, the problems of identifying distinct Jaina social and legal identities remain. There will be specific situations in which Jaina families and individuals will want to follow particular rules as an expression of their very own Jaina identity and way of life. In the present article, rather than focusing on the distinction between Jainas and Hindus, I shall argue, from a socio-legal perspective, that wherever there are Jainas, there will also be some manifestation of Jaina law, if not official, then unofficial.

The diasporic and transnational dimension

Before turning to the law, it may be useful to consider Jainas briefly as forming a transnational community with its own complex identity.[3] If, in India itself, Jainas have been rendered more or less officially invisible, nothing stops the globally dispersed Jainas in diaspora, if they wish to do so, from reconstructing and re-asserting their separate identity and ethnicity, including elements of their own personal law.[4] Jainas have been making notable public statements about their presence in diaspora and about the contributions that Jainism can make to the well-being of mankind and all creations. In Britain, one may think of the impressive Jain Centre (or Jaina Mandir) in Leicester and its aims, community facilities like the Oshwal Centre in rural Hertfordshire, or the Jaina Studies Programmes at De Montfort University and now at SOAS. There are many more manifestations of the private and public face of Jaina life all over the world.

Jainas tend to be gentle, soft people, not aggressive lobbyists and violent demonstrators for their cause. Such relatively quiet and unobtrusive modes of asserting Jaina identity may not be sufficiently loud to remind lawyers, and others who claim to make or influence law, that there is indeed something like Jaina law. Perhaps, therefore, a task of the future is to assert Jaina legal identity more effectively than has been done so far, not through violence, but in a targeted, strategically planned fashion which overcomes the current purposeful silence. Even in Britain, it is not too late: The legal reconstruction process of multi-ethnic Britain is only just beginning to move into a more public arena, as evidenced by a recent Runnymede Report (Parekh 2000). Relevant academic writing is beginning to cover general legal issues (Jones and Welhengama 2000), and one finds more specifically anthropological assessments which are relevant also to Jainas (generally Ballard 1994: 1–34, specifically Banks 1994), and evidence of specific strategies of Jainas in planning law (Gale and Naylor 2002). However, as we shall see, there are several factors impeding Jaina activism in giving a higher profile to aspects and manifestations of Jaina law.

The legal evidence

As soon as one opens one of the leading law books from India which many practitioners use, doubts about the existence of Jaina law resurface. The 17th edition of Mulla's *Hindu Law* (Desai 1998: 825–826), states under the heading 'Law applicable to Jains':

> It is too late in the day to contend that Jains are not included in the term 'Hindus'. The Jains are governed by all the incidents related to the Hindu Joint Family, as was held by the Supreme Court. The ordinary Hindu law is to be applied to Jains, in the absence of proof of special customs and usage varying that law. Those customs and usage must be proved by evidence, as other special customs and usage varying the general law should be proved, and in the absence of proof the ordinary law must prevail.

So the technically correct view appears to be at first sight that today, there is officially no Jaina law in India, since it was subsumed under Hindu law for the purposes of unification and codification of India's modern Hindu law. Perhaps there was Jaina law in the past, but it no longer exists. Yet a careful re-reading of the above quote shows that the abolition of Jaina law is not total and complete, since special Jaina customs and usages, if they can be proved, may still be legally recognised.

Since Mulla's *Hindu Law* and some other legal texts state so bluntly that Jainas have been governed by Hindu law at least since the 1950s, two further questions arise. First, when, how and why did this take-over by Hindu law happen? In other words, in what form did Jaina law exist before 1955–1956 and why was it abolished by the stroke of a pen? Second, given the official position that Jaina law has been taken over by Hindu law, what is the scope for arguing today that Jaina law still exists? Desai (1998: 826) provides some further hints about possible answers to the second question, indicating the scope for pleading specific customs:

> There is, however, nothing to limit the scope of the enquiry to the particular locality in which the persons setting up the custom reside. Judicial decisions recognising the existence of a disputed custom among the Jains of one place are relevant as evidence of the existence of the same custom amongst the Jains of another place, unless it is shown that the customs are different; and oral evidence of the same kind are [*sic*] equally admissible. Where, however, a custom is negatived by a judicial decision in one place, like Madras, the fact that among Jains in the other states such a custom has been upheld by courts does not warrant a general presumption of the prevalence of the custom in the Madras State.

This clearly indicates, again, that Jaina law may exist today, but only as a matter of local customary law, or as a second-tier type of law which cannot claim immediate legal recognition and remains subject to specific rules and constructions of evidence. So we need to ask a few more questions about Jaina customary law and proof of Jaina customs. Based on the earlier two quotes and on socio-legal analysis, my basic hypothesis therefore remains that Jaina law must be in existence, primarily because Jaina people exist. However, it appears that Jaina law has today become officially invisible in India, as have the Jainas themselves, to some extent. So there is maybe a need to remind the world – and even Jainas themselves – that Jainas and Jaina law exist?

The historical backdrop of Jainism

While this is not the main subject of this chapter, it is relevant as a contextualising element. I studied Jainism at Kiel University in Germany under the guidance of Professor Jagdish Chandra Jain, whose *Festschrift* contains several illuminating articles as well as an earlier exploration of Jaina law (Menski 1994). Here, a few brief points, relying to some extent on Jain (1926), are made as background to the subsequent legal discussion. It is a well-recognised fact that disputes between Jainas and Hindus go back to the earliest texts and the most basic concepts.

It is undisputed that Jainism is an ancient religion, arising and flourishing well before the start of Christianity. Quite how old its traditions are and how they relate to Hinduism continues to be debated. Jainism rejected the Vedic pantheon of gods and emphasised the importance of the *Tīrthaṅkaras*, the last of whom was Mahāvīra. The *Tīrthaṅkaras* were originally not seen as lawgivers in an Austinian or Napoleonic sense, more as outstanding role models in society, excellent personalities that achieved due spiritual reward. Later, it seems, positivist interpretations of legal aspects became more prominent.

Jainism as a philosophy and religion rejected the supremacy of the Vedas and, so we seem to assume, all that comes with it in terms of understanding the cosmic Order (*ṛta*) and the classical Hindu key concept of *dharma*. However, Jainism then developed its own concept of *dharma*, which is perhaps only marginally different from the understandings of this concept by the 'Hindus'. It has been difficult to draw boundaries since the ideals of Jainism do not really diverge greatly from those of Hinduism, unless one puts up a particular sectarian picture of Hinduism that is not representative of the whole. It appears that this is often done to illustrate the conceptual contrasts between Hinduism and Jainism, but this remains questionable academic methodology.

Hence, if we ask specifically what the ideas and ideals of Jainism are, as compared to those of Hinduism, much depends on what kind of Hinduism one looks at to compare and contrast with Jainism. The internal plurality of Hinduism clearly allows for an immense variety of perspectives and does not dogmatically determine anything that strictly binds all Hindus (see now Flood 2003). This radical pluralism is not recognised by many writers, and is often overlooked by lawyers. Refuting the argument that Jainas are merely Hindu dissenters, a leading writer on Jaina law (Jain 1926: 16–17) thus typically overplays and exaggerates the contrast by stereotyping Hindus and Hinduism in a particular way:

> The Jainas regard the world as eternal; the Hindus hold it to have been made by a creator. In Jainism worship is not offered to an eternal and eternally pure God, but to those Great Ones who have realised their high ideal and attained to Godhood themselves; in Hinduism worship is performed of one Lord who is the creator and the ruler of the world. The significance of worship in Hinduism is also not the same as in Jainism. In Jainism it is a kind of *idealatory* that is practised; there is no offering of food and the like; nor is a prayer made to the Deity for boons. In Hinduism the attainment of the object is by the will of certain divine beings who are to be propitiated. In respect of their scriptures, too, there are great differences between Hinduism and Jainism. Not one of the Books of the Hindus is accepted by the Jainas nor do the Hindus accept a single sâstra (Scripture) of the latter. The contents, too, of the Scriptures of the two religions differ. Not one part of the four Vedas and the 18 Puranas recognised in Hinduism is included in the Jaina scriptures. Nor is any part of the Sacred Books of the Jainas included clearly or expressly in the Hindu Books. The matters in respect of which there seems to be an agreement between the Jainas and the Hindus are merely social; their significance wherever they have a religious bearing is divergent.

Many aspects of Jaina philosophy, especially *ahiṃsā*, have also become an element of Hinduism and are, at any rate, not unknown to other people, especially communities residing together with Jainas. Conversely, it seems that Jainas have also retained or taken certain elements from various local Hindu forms of belief and practice. In this way, it becomes extremely difficult to say what is Hindu and what is Jaina.

Consequently, there are many similarities between Hindus and Jainas. For Hindus and Jainas, action (*karma*) and reaction seem to be at the core of the respective rule systems as a dynamising element. Hence it is difficult to identify elements exclusively specific to Jainas, given that *dharma* is also a key element of Jaina concepts. So where, if at all, does one draw lines between Jaina *dharma* and Hindu *dharma*? Should one assume that Jainas are merely a Hindu sect, or does one recognise them as a separate 'faith community', as we seem to be doing in multicultural Britain today? In terms of law, too, there are many unanswered questions, as shown in the following lines.

If accumulation of merit (which itself is questioned and even rejected as a dominant concern) for Jainas is, according to some authors (Jain 1991: 38), acquired through a combination of right conduct and right knowledge, and not merely by austerities and penances, it becomes at once doubly difficult to be a good Jaina. But is being a good Jaina the same as following Jaina law?

These few basic points and related questions indicate that we can forever argue about fine differences between Hinduism and Jainism; at the end of the day, many principles in both traditions actually appear to be shared elements. Far from wishing to throttle the debate about whether Jainas and Jaina law exist as a separate entity, I would therefore simply reiterate and assert here that Jainas and their ideas have influenced Hinduism itself so much that drawing any dividing line becomes almost impossible. And yet, in 'ethnic' terms, many Jainas continue to distinguish themselves from the Hindus around them, and are also perceived by many others as a separate group.[5]

Legal definitions

In law, too, the dividing lines between Hindu and Jaina elements are not well defined. Understandings of what Jaina law actually is show significant parallels with what Hindus are saying about their own traditional law. If, for Hindu law, Professor Kane claimed during colonial rule in his monumental *History of Dharmaśāstra* that the Hindus have long had law that can match Western ideas and ideals, the same has been done for Jaina law. The most prominent book on the subject of Jaina law remains the study by Champat Rai Jain (1926). It argues vigorously for the separate recognition of Jaina law at a time when court decisions were further restricting the scope for the application of traditional Jaina law, well before the important 1955–1956 reforms which submerged Jaina law into Hindu law.

It is interesting to see how Champat Rai Jain argued his case for the retention of Jaina law, showing parallels with how Hindus perceive their traditional law, namely as the result of some ancient lawgiving process. Such images are quite obviously modelled on the dominant Western ideas of legal positivism, so that 'proper' law is perceived as codified, an authoritative source, invariably related back to a male lawgiver. For Hindus and Jainas, the critical question is whether this could have been one personalised god, or rather a more diffuse power. It seems to me that the ambitious image of ancient lawgivers is deeply flawed by the inability to determine historical dates and definite personalities. Still, this has not prevented prominent Hindu law experts from fantasising about the revealed nature of Hindu law. Thus, we read in one such leading textbook (Diwan and Diwan 1993: 27–28):

> Hindu law is considered to be divine law, a revealed law. The theory is that some of the Hindu sages had attained great spiritual heights, so much so that they could be in direct communion with God. At some such time the sacred law was revealed to them by God Himself. This revelation is contained in *Sruti* or *Vedas*.

Such distortions of Hindu legal history, modelled on Judaeo-Christian elements, freely mixing images of the interaction of great men and God with South Asian concepts of texts as sources of law, create a confusing mess of concepts and impede analysis of legal reality. Even Diwan and Diwan concede, almost immediately (at p. 28), that the *śruti* is only considered to be the fundamental source of Hindu law in theory, while in practice 'its importance as a source of positive law is doubtful' (ibid.). At any rate, reliance on divine revelation as a defence against being reformed worked neither for Hindu law nor Jaina law.

Examining how C. R. Jain saw this matter in 1926, we find an instructive illustration of how legal writers tend to distort South Asian laws for an unsuspecting wider readership that is not familiar with internal debates about the nature of law among lawyers. Jain (1926: 3) opens his case immediately with the grand assertion that Jaina law is a separate entity and must be recognised as such. It is pure religious politics when he writes that '[t]he Jaina Law is an independent department of the science of Jurisprudence. Its original author, the first legislator, was Bharata Chakravarti, who was the eldest son of the first Tirthankara, Sri Rishabha Dêvaji'.

As a specialist on South Asian jurisprudence, I cannot help admiring such amazingly bold assertions. Jain claims here, logically correct in view of the Jaina refusal to recognise the authority of the Vedas, that Jaina law has a human author, an ancient legislator even, who laid down a legislated law in Napoleonic style, in other words a law code that positivists would recognise as law proper. What Jain thereby really claims, as P. V. Kane asserted a little later for Hindu law, is that Jainas are not inferior to other people and have developed something that Western observers should recognise as law. In other words, Jainas are not just an earthbound chthonic group living in close conjunction with nature (on chthonic laws, see Glenn 2000), but have a sophisticated, formally structured and separate law.

Quite significantly, the claim for Jaina law is not that it comes from a religious source or authority, as appears to be the case for Hindu law through the image of revelation from some divine source, and even God Himself.[6] None of that works for Jaina law, which cannot fall back on monotheistic models and therefore looks decidedly secular (as 'proper' positivist law should do), in that the lawgiver was, according to Jain (1926: 3) as cited earlier, the son of a Tīrthaṅkara, neither a prominent holy man nor a god or God. Jain (ibid.) carries on this assertive image of Jaina law in the next paragraph:

> The whole of the Jaina Law was composed at one time, and is, therefore, wanting in those marks which characterise the Judge-made Law, though it is not improbable that owing to the necessities of the community and the human intercourse slight changes, not affecting its basic principles, have been made in it from time to time.

These assertions carry on the theme and image of a complete, ancient codified law, which is therefore in danger of becoming somewhat outdated and inflexible because it is so old. Jain compares this to the familiar English concept of case-law, which has been able to build some modifications into its framework of rules through judicial intervention and simply asserts that because of the needs of the community, some changes must have been made 'not affecting its basic principles'. The next paragraph (ibid.) carries on this theme and provides some more detail about his vision of the original nature of Jaina law: 'The Jaina Law was originally a part of what is known as the Upāsakādhyāyāna Anga which is now lost. Its existing sources mainly are the books which are mentioned below.' This is another huge assertion, in principle familiar from Hindu law as well, namely that the original Jaina law could be identified as part of a larger body of text, all of which has been lost. Hence, without following any of the Hindu terminology, the assertion here is to the effect that the ancient Jaina law was founded on a textual basis that has not survived, but which much earlier generations of scholars still knew of. One may suspect that the author is trying to avoid the Hindu terms for 'revealed truth' (*śruti*) and 'remembered truth' (*smṛti*). He is certainly using those concepts without telling us so. One may deduce this from the way in which he discusses the 'existing sources', namely a number of 'law books'.

This shows that Jaina law probably faced the same problems as Hindu law in proving the links between the ancient 'heard' or 'revealed' material and what was later 'remembered'. In his brief description of what he perceives as the six major 'law books' of the Jainas, Jain (1926: 3–5) provides ample evidence that all of this material actually comes from a more recent era. It therefore constitutes at best what we should imagine as reconstructed 'bricks' of a much earlier tradition, originating more likely than not in a floating oral reservoir of rules which eventually coagulated into the named texts that we know today.[7] The following six 'Jaina law books' are listed by Jain (1926: 3–5) with some comments which are abbreviated here:

1 *Bhadrabāhu Samhitā:* Related to Bhadrabāhu (about 2300 years ago) but actually a much later work, composed between AD 1601 and 1609. Based on the ancient Code, composed by an unknown author.

2 *Arhan Nīti:* A Śvetāmbara work which is not very old. Its author declares that he remembered what he had heard and wrote it down. This is therefore clearly a *smṛti* work, whose title indicates the purpose of guidance.
3 *Vardhamāna Nīti:* Composed about AD 1011 by Sri Amitagati Ācārya. This has verses identical to *Bhadrabāhu Samhitā*, which Jain (1926: 4) takes as evidence that both texts must be based on an earlier book. But what if they are both simply based on a mass of floating oral text, which is equally likely?
4 *Indranandi Jina Samhitā:* Composed by Vasunandi Indranandi, apparently also based on the Upāsakādhyayana Aṅga, so that Jain (1926: 5) argues that this text consists of 'stray fragments' of the older text.
5 *Traivarṇikācāra:* Composed in AD 1611 by Bhaṭṭāraka Somasena.
6 *Ādi Purāṇa:* Composed by Sri Jinasena Ācārya in ninth century AD, a major Digambara text.

There are of course many more Jaina texts, and Jain (1926: 6) admits that the ones he mentions are therefore only stray parts of the ancient law, not a complete code of Jaina law. In effect, he simply asserts (ibid.) that this is a problem that has to be tolerated, and that what exists is good enough to reconstruct Jaina law

> These are chiefly the Law Books which are traceable now, but none of them contains the entire Law. Still I think that whatever portion has survived of it is quite sufficient for our jural purposes, though difficulties may have to be faced in the interpretation of it in the beginning.

Clearly, the debate over the legal status of those books remains undeveloped. It seems to be taken for granted that textual fragments can be used as evidence in a court of law, in other words, that textual rules and regulations may be treated as general legal rules, a mistake that was common under British rule. Grave reservations about such techniques of reconstructing law and the underlying assumptions are certainly in order. We know from the history of Hindu law, and particularly of Anglo-Hindu law, where the same problems arose, that one could therefore basically prove anything from any of the old texts, provided one could find the right textual statement to substantiate one's point. And if in doubt, a vague reference to 'the *śāstra*' might suffice. It could hardly be assumed that the above-listed six texts would, if taken together, constitute a coherent and consistent rule system, a code that could be used in legal practice.

Jaina law under British rule

Jain's study tells us virtually nothing about what happened to the application of such supposedly legal texts between the seventeenth century and the end of British rule. From the parallel history of Hindu law, it is known that the early British administrators tried in vain to make sense of what they assumed to be the Hindu law texts, which were in reality merely guidebooks on *dharma* and would not claim to lay down rules for uniform application in the way the British expected (Menski 2003). Given such fundamental problems of communication over basics, even those texts which the British had specifically commissioned only increased everyone's confusion, to the despair of many well-meaning administrators (Menski 2000: 179–181) and with far-reaching implications for the reconstruction of Hindu law (Menski 2003, chapter 4). Jain (1926: 6) highlights such problems of communication in the British Indian period, demonstrating that access to those texts, on account of ritual concerns, was sought to be restricted by the Jainas:

> When the British came, the Jains concealed their śāstras [*sic*] and objected to their production in courts. To a certain extent their action was justified, because in the courts the Scriptures of no religion are respected. The presiding officer at times and the court officials generally employ the saliva of their mouth for turning over the leaves of the books, which must cause pain to a devout heart. But the remedy for this is not the withholding of books altogether.

These observations are highly significant. It is not surprising that the British should have reacted to such uncooperative behaviour by concluding that the Jainas had no proper law books. Surely, if they were important for litigation, they would have been relied on and would have been brought into court? Thus, by giving more importance to ritual purity and protective isolation than public demonstration of their separate legal status, the Jainas soon lost the battle for recognition of a separate Jaina law. Jain (1926: 7) is quite clear on this:

> The result of the non-production of their Scriptures by the Jains has been that the courts have now held that they (the Jains) have no Law Books of their own... And this is notwithstanding the fact that as early as 1837 A.D. the names of certain Jaina Law books were mentioned in court... and even earlier than this in 1833 A.D. there was an allusion to Jaina works on Law.

This process of formal legal rejection by the British should probably be seen in the wider context of British dissatisfaction with the way in which all of Anglo-Indian law was developing at that time. Having employed *paṇḍit*s and *maulvī*s to help them make sense of Hindu law and Muslim law, the British would have required the services of some learned Jainas to unravel the contents of some of the Jaina works. But the Digambara Jaina Mahāsabhā repeatedly passed resolutions against printing any of the Jaina works (Jain 1926: 8) and pollution-conscious mendicants would not as readily engage with the polluting environment of the British courts as Hindu *paṇḍit*s. Hence there are several meaningful reasons for the lack of proper communication between the British authorities and the Jainas. Occasionally, though, Jaina *paṇḍit*s must have been consulted and

Jain (1926: 8) refers to one such case in 1869, even after the system of consulting such experts had been officially abandoned. So the British did try to assist, but the Jainas themselves were not cooperative enough in this venture.

A more complex problem, which the Hindu also *paṇḍit*s faced, concerns the interpretation of any texts deemed to be legal sources. The presumably correct strategy of tracing Hindu or Jaina law from the old texts inevitably had to run into enormous difficulties, since these texts did not speak with one voice and, more crucially, were not concerned with law, but with *dharma*. While such mismatches frustrated the British enormously when it came to Hindu law (Derrett 1968, chapters 8 and 9) and eventually led to the sacking of the *paṇḍit*s and reliance on judicial precedent as a major source of Anglo-Hindu law, we do not appear to know much about the communication problems between the British and the Jainas. Jain (1926: 7–8) exonerates the Anglo-Indian courts for the resulting marginalisation of Jaina legal texts:

> But the courts are not to be blamed for this; on the contrary they tried on each occasion to ascertain the Jaina Law or at least the Jaina customs, so that the disputes of the Jainas may be decided according to their own rules. Sir E. Montague Smith in the course of the judgment of their Lordships of the Privy Council in the case of *Sheo Singh Rai v. Musammat Dakho* (I.L.R., 1 Allahabad page 688) observed; – 'It would certainly have been remarkable if the courts had denied to the large and wealthy communities existing among the Jains, the privilege of being governed by their own peculiar laws and customs, when these laws and customs were, by sufficient evidence capable of being ascertained and defined; and were not open to objection on grounds of public policy or otherwise.'

It seems therefore that the reluctance among the Jainas to use their own texts as legal documents in public legal proceedings controlled by outsiders, manifesting itself both in private distancing and in obfuscation by the Jaina Mahāsabha, contributed much to the rapid waning of British interest in questions of Jaina law and the resulting formal de-recognition of Jaina law as well as its separate status as a personal law.

By the early 1920s, when some Hindu writing appeared that treated Jainas as Hindu dissenters in the context of law reforms, and thus sought to include them in the uniformising project of a Hindu Code, the Jainas became alarmed and started to protest, establishing a Jaina Law Committee (1921). This was composed of English-qualified lawyers as well as some *paṇḍits* and other learned men, but it achieved nothing. It appears that the Committee took the *anekāntavāda* philosophy too far and became a mere talking shop. Jain (1926: 10) is vaguely apologetic about why this Committee failed to accomplish its objectives. On the other hand, Jain (1926: 10–12) complained vigorously about the fact that in many cases Jain litigants had Hindu law rules applied to them. He set out his own programme, indicating that his compilation 'is prepared in the hope that the Jaina Law may once again raise its head independently, and the Jainas be enabled to observe the rules of their *Dharma* properly in obedience to their own Laws' (Jain 1926: 12). He also refused to question that it would necessarily be harmful for Jainas to have Hindu law applied to them, but provides an interesting example about gender relations in a footnote (ibid.):

> A single instance should suffice to illustrate the nature of the harm that will accrue to the Jaina community if not allowed to be governed by their own laws. The son in a Jaina household is placed in a subordinate position, and postponed before the wife, who takes the paternal property as absolute owner. She is at liberty to give it away to any one she likes and cannot be stopped by any one except as regards the maintenance of small children. The effect of this healthy rule is that the son has got to be well behaved, obedient and a model of virtue to win the favour of the mother. To invest the son with absolute ownership is to silence the mother's controlling voice effectively. The insignificant percentage of criminals among the Jainas – the lowest as compared with other communities – is a glowing tribute to the wisdom of the Jaina Legislator. If the Jainas are subjected to a system of Law in which the mother's controlling voice is silenced or deadened, the same excellence of moral goodness may not be expected of them.

I am not so sure about giving credit to the imagined 'Jaina legislator', but this particular rule about maternal control certainly makes a lot of social sense. There are, however, indications that this particular legal rule is not shared by all Jainas, so it may well be a matter of custom in certain Jaina communities rather than a binding rule of Jaina law as a whole. Anthropologists, in particular, might find it relevant to investigate to what extent matrilineal and patrilineal principles are intertwined here, because Jaina law applied also in many parts of South India and its customs will not have remained immune to local norms that might suggest a more equitable gender balance than is often found in North India.

Jaina customary law thus became a kind of unofficial legal system that developed many situation-specific methods of deciding contested matters outside the courts. The major problem in legal practice became therefore that whatever customs Jaina families and communities from all over India may have developed as sensible social norms within their local socio-legal contexts, these might not be recognised as law once a matter went to court. Serious problems arose in gauging the place of Jaina custom and Jain (1926: 13–14) discusses this in some detail, emphasising particularly the practical problems of evidence:

> And, it will not do to say that the Jaina Law can be enforced in the shape of special customs, so that matters may be allowed to continue as they have done hitherto. For every lawyer knows how difficult it is to prove

> a custom. Hundreds of witnesses have to be examined and instances to be established which are beyond the means of ordinary litigants and outside the scope of small cases. The chance of miscarriage of Justice is also very great, as is known to have happened more than once. The community, too, lives in a condition of insecurity, since nobody knows what will be the decision of the Court of Justice on a question of custom to be proved by oral evidence. This sense of insecurity is liable to become aggravated by wrong adjudication, since that means a pronouncement of law contrary to the actual prevailing practice. In ordinary cases miscarriage of justice, although reprehensible, may not matter much, as only the parties are affected by it. But in regard to general customs, the whole community is affected by such judgments.

These statements replicate evidence about the difficult role of custom which troubled Hindu lawyers, who could not help noticing that the official formal Anglo-Indian law diverged more and more from informal, unofficial local practices. Thus, while custom was in theory an important source of law, which could even override the text of the written law (Menski 1997: 42), in practical reality proof of custom was most difficult to achieve. The result, more so for Jainas than for other communities, perhaps, if we think of their moral value system and the major principle of *ahiṃsā*, might have been that less and less Jaina cases would actually come to the courts. This kind of avoidance reaction is not surprising, since it fits the historical evidence of Jainas hiding their legal sources from the British on account of fears about pollution as well as a desire to practise non-violent means of dispute settlement – among which one can certainly not count the Anglo-Indian judicial system. In addition, there must have been many local mechanisms for settling small disputes through *pañcāyat*s and other informal bodies, so the actual Jaina law would become more and more invisible. In other words, for a variety of reasons, under colonial rule Jaina law turned more clearly into an unofficial legal system, a system of rules that exists in social reality but is not brought to the notice of the state and is not formally recognised by it. Despite the formal recognition of Jaina customary laws in principle, informal processes of dispute management strengthened the trend towards making and keeping Jaina law officially invisible.

Jaina law under the umbrella of modern Hindu law

From there, it was only a small step to the early 1950s, when modernist reforms of Hindu law were being debated and the Jaina question inevitably came up again. In the end, the decision was made to agglomerate Buddhists, Jainas and Sikhs with Hindus for the purpose of codification and unification of modern Hindu law, irrespective of what these religious minorities thought about it (Derrett 1968: 44). Maybe the relative invisibility of Jaina and Buddhist law was one of the main reasons why modern Indian law makers decided with such apparent ease to amalgamate Hindu law with the personal laws of the Jainas, Buddhists and Sikhs to form the codified modern Hindu personal law of India. That process was completed in four major enactments in 1955–1956, instead of one comprehensive Code, which had been planned but was sabotaged by Hindu opposition to the perceived de-Hinduisation of the official law. The four statutes passed at that time all have a statement to similar effect, bringing Jainas formally under Hindu law. Thus, section 2 of the *Hindu Marriage Act*, 1955 provides:

> 2. Application of the Act.–
> (1) This Act applies –
> (a) to any person who is a Hindu by religion in any of its forms or developments, including a Virashaiva, a Lingayat or a follower of the Brahmo, Prarthana or Arya Samaj,
> (b) to any person who is a Buddhist, Jaina or Sikh by religion, and
> (c) to any other person domiciled in the territories to which this Act extends who is not a Muslim, Christian, Parsi or Jew by religion, unless it is proved that any such person would not have been governed by the Hindu law or by any custom or usage as part of that law in respect of any of the matters dealt with herein if this Act had not been passed.
>
> Explanation: –
> The following persons are Hindus, Buddhists, Jainas or Sikhs by religion, as the case may be:
> (a) any child, legitimate or illegitimate, both of whose parents are Hindus, Buddhists, Jainas or Sikhs by religion;
> (b) any child, legitimate or illegitimate, one of whose parents is a Hindu, Buddhist, Jaina or Sikh by religion and who is brought up as a member of the tribe, community, group or family to which such parent belongs or belonged; and
> (c) any person who is a convert or re-convert to the Hindu, Buddhist, Jaina or Sikh religion.

This, however, was by no means the end of Jaina law. It only signifies its formal demise as a separate personal law and thus relegates it still more clearly to an informal and unofficial status, hidden below the assumed formal uniformity of the new state-made Hindu law. Under this vast and wide umbrella of the modern codified Hindu law, however, there is in theory as well as practice plenty of scope for asserting individual claims that a particular matter should be governed by Jaina law.[8] However, as in the colonial period, the methods for achieving legal recognition of Jaina customs are dictated by the formal modern law, which regulates the processes of ascertaining and applying Jaina law through pleading Jaina custom.[9]

It is known that custom was extremely difficult to prove under Anglo-Indian law, which granted it a large role in theory, but restricted it in practice well beyond what Hindus and Jainas themselves saw as appropriate. One must wonder to what extent the situation may have changed under the modern enactments. No detailed research appears to have been done on this issue.[10] My tentative view, which is primarily based on an analysis of the scope for the recognition of Hindu customary marriage laws, is that post-colonial Hindu law, conscious of the fact that it governs such a widely divergent population, has actually facilitated the use of customs, but they will have to be pleaded and proved in the courts when disputes arise. To what extent such disputes will arise before any formal forum, in the first place, remains therefore a critical issue on which far too little is known with specific reference to Jainas.

Compared to the colonial period, however, the strictness of the test of custom has since been significantly relaxed. In the realm of the lower courts and their unreported cases, particularly in Gujarat and Karnataka, it should therefore be possible to locate much local evidence of the judicial recognition of Jaina customary law. Certainly in theory, if not in practice, the new Hindu law offers a chance for Jaina litigants to assert themselves and their personal law, particularly at the lower court level. It appears, however, that as in the nineteenth century, today's Jainas may be rather hesitant when it comes to using this legal facility in open court. In practice, many Jainas will either stay out of the state courts altogether, or they may be happy to see Hindu law applied to them officially to avoid undue complications. A viable balance may have to be found between spending extra legal fees on pleading specific Jaina customs in courts for the sake of asserting a religious identity and pursuing such claims in private informal negotiations and settlements.

Nobody appears to have studied these issues in any depth, nor have I conducted any systematic research on case law for the purpose of this particular chapter. It remains a challenging task to ascertain the extent of evidence that Jainas in India today are able to use customary laws to assert any claims to being governed by their own personal law. As indicated, the formal mechanisms for this exist within the Hindu statutory law itself, since the modern Hindu law is not as uniform as is widely believed, and as may appear at first sight. For example, section 3(a) of the *Hindu Marriage Act*, 1955 provides:

> 3. Definitions.–
>
> In this Act unless the context otherwise requires,–
>
> (a) the expressions 'custom' and 'usage' signify any rule which, having been continuously and uniformly observed for a long time, has obtained the force of law among Hindus in any local area, tribe, community, group or family:
>
> Provided that the rule is certain and not unreasonable or opposed to public policy; and provided further that in the case of a rule applicable only to a family it has not been discontinued by the family;

This innocuous section is extremely powerful, and far too few Indian and foreign observers seem to realise this. The old Anglo-Indian test of custom, as a rule or norm that was 'ancient' and applied 'from time immemorial' has clearly not been adopted by the modern Hindu law. Custom now has to be shown to be observed merely 'for a long time', hence opening up vast opportunities for enterprising plaintiffs and their lawyers to plead Jaina customs without going back for centuries. It appears that this happens a lot in practice, especially at lower court level, but we do not hear about such cases, which remain unreported. There are strong indications, however, even at Supreme Court level, that the superior Indian courts remain perfectly capable of handling such complex questions of customary law.[11]

The scope for unofficial Jaina law

Hence, it may be possible to argue that Jaina law has not totally lost its potential in terms of legal and social reconstruction. As in the nineteenth century, the community itself will actively need to use the existing mechanisms of the formal legal system to assert the separate status of Jaina law, now as Jaina custom under the wide umbrella of Hindu law. This scenario confirms that Jaina law may have officially disappeared, but has the potential to flourish as a largely unofficial law, in the sense of a system of rules that is not officially recognised by the state (Chiba 1986). This is the case in India as well as in Britain, where the scope for asserting the special qualities of Jaina law and life also exists, but is probably not utilised to the same extent by the community.

I have first-hand knowledge of a British case involving Jainas, in which some such arguments could have been used as a matter of 'cultural practice', as we would call it in Britain today. In *A. v. J.* [1989] 1 FLR 110, the basic facts were that a young Jaina couple had fallen out over a misunderstanding of proper behaviour for spouses who are legally married in England through a registered marriage, but have not yet undergone the religious rituals of marriage. We know that normally such couples are expected to defer cohabitation despite being legally married. In the present case, it appears that the young woman expected her husband to display at least some affection towards her and to behave more akin to a married man, while the clearly inexperienced husband thought it proper to keep a decent distance until after the 'real' marriage. For example, he sent his wife a Valentine's card, but she felt this lacked romance and feeling, given that he was her husband.

An application for nullity of the marriage was made by the wife, and this was granted after much argument, but there is not a word in the reported judgment to indicate that the spouses were Jainas. Of course, why should an English case report be interested in such cultural facts? But by keeping such a low cultural profile, Jainas do not help the cause of Jaina law, if indeed they see any such cause. So, I fear, we are still in the same scenario that C. R. Jain observed in the early twentieth century – unless Jainas assert their distinct cultural and religious identity, they will not even be noticed as a separate category of people.

This seems to be different in India, where a good number of reported cases concerning Jainas make rather a lot of this fact, and where interesting controversies have been reported. Derrett (1968: 460) refers to a case in the Bombay High Court during the late 1950s, *Chhotalal Lallubhai v. Charity Commissioner, Bombay* (1957) 59 *BomLR* 349, in which the claims of a Jaina charitable trust established for the welfare of animals were refused in what Derrett (ibid.) called an 'extremely negative attitude':

> We do not think that the other bequests can be regarded as religious. A bequest to Panjrapole, i.e. a home meant for maimed, aged and deformed animals, can by no stretch of imagination be regarded as a religious bequest. Similarly, a bequest for practising kindness to all forms of life cannot, in our judgement, be regarded as a religious bequest; and a bequest for providing food to pilgrims visiting temples or providing clothes to Jain male and female Sadhus and Sadhvis cannot also be regarded as a bequest for religious purposes.

Obviously, something went wrong here in the judge's understanding of religion itself, rather than of Jainism and its tenets, but this was such an obvious mistake that the Supreme Court, albeit only in 1965, rectified this matter (see *Shah Chhotalal Lallubhai v. The Charity Commissioner, Bombay* (1965) 67 *BomLR* 432 (SC).

The indications from Jain's study of 1926, as well as some specialist law books on Hindu law which contain stray references to Jainas, are that there are quite a few cases in which Jainas as litigants have felt that injustice was done to them through overlooking or disregarding even basic principles of Jaina law. This, too, will have contributed to attempts to keep disputes out of formal courts as much as possible. Only detailed research could tell us to what extent this is still an issue today and what the consequences have been. Manifestly, however, Jaina law continues to exist today, now under the formal cloak of Hindu law, and at an informal and almost invisible level. It is a classic case of an unofficial law within a formal legal environment, benefiting from the fact that no state legal system can totally control the socio-cultural field of all citizens. Unofficial Jaina law is therefore protected not only by reticence on the part of Jainas about their own laws, but also by the inherent limits of formal legal regulation.

The particular theoretical perspective taken here demonstrates, of course, that a purely legalistic, positivist approach would have yielded very different results, which would in all likelihood neither please the Jainas (because it would deny the existence of Jaina law altogether), nor accord with the social reality of unofficial laws as a universal phenomenon. The socio-legal methodology applied here inevitably yields the conclusion that Jaina law in India (and elsewhere) is today largely an unofficial legal system and will remain in that position. What effects this will have on assertions of Jaina identity and Jaina 'ethnicity' remains to be investigated in more detail.

Notes

1 There can be no doubt that Jaina law existed as a personal law before that and was applied by courts as such. Historical research on old cases would unearth a lot of material. For some details see Desai (1998: 825–830).

2 Notably, another method of considering 'Jain law' is based on the assumption that the texts and the men who know and use them, embody the law. This is a conceptual approach akin to the one in Hindu law that equates the *Manusmṛiti* to a kind of Napoleonic Code. In the present chapter this aspect is neither critiqued nor elaborated, but this is a topic for future discussion.

3 On the fashionable concept of transnational communities, which is now itself beginning to be challenged by terms like 'translocal', see the special issue of the *Journal of Ethnic and Migration Studies* (Vol. 27 Number 4, October 2001), edited by Steven Vertovec, one of the foremost writers on this theme.

4 In this regard, the general observations found in Ballard (1994: 1–34) about the reconstruction of Asian ways of life in the UK 'on their own terms' clearly also apply to Jainas.

5 I take the concept of 'ethnicity' here as a key element of identity formation and assertion of differences between groups of people who may otherwise, in certain respects, be rather similar. The main legal definitions of ethnicity were developed in English law through a case involving 'racial' discrimination against a Sikh schoolboy that went up to the House of Lords. For details of the historical and cultural criteria see *Mandla v. Dowell Lee* [1983] 1 All England Reports 1062. To my knowledge, no attempt has been made so far to argue that Jainas could also be defined as a 'racial group' under the *Race Relations Act*, 1976. The legal debates over Jaina identity and 'ethnicity' in India have probably taken quite a different route and seem to me, at least at this stage, undeveloped.

6 This method or process is most clearly argued in the case of Muslims, where the direct link of Allah and the Holy Prophet forms the core for all Muslim belief.

7 Peter Flügel rightly suggests that much more could be said about this particular selection, a view shared by Christoph Emmrich at the South Asia Institute in Heidelberg. I must leave this topic to better qualified people, at least for the moment.

8 For example, the Jaina customs of marriage would appear to be comprehensively preserved by section 7 of the *Hindu Marriage Act* of 1955, which has the effect that a Jaina couple may marry in accordance with the customary rites and rituals of the respective family or community. The modern Indian state has made no attempt whatsoever to impose a uniform secular system on every couple that wishes to marry. While formal registration of the marriage remains optional, a customary religious wedding in the midst of family and friends, thus *prima facie* a socio-cultural process, creates legal validity *per se*. For details see Menski (2001: 9–46).

9 It appears therefore that Derrett's observation (1968: 178) to the effect that Jainas became some kind of Hindu caste, is still an appropriate way of looking at this issue.

10 Derrett (1970: 123–124) only considers the much-contested question whether adoption among the Jainas is religious or secular.

11 A most instructive recent example is found in *M. Govindaraju v. K. Munisami Gounder*, AIR 1997 SC 10, where the Supreme Court of India recognised the legal effects of customary divorces in low caste communities in order to protect an individual's property rights.

Bibliography

Ballard, Roger (ed.) (1994). *Desh Pardesh. The South Asian Presence in Britain*, London: Hurst & Co.

Banks, Marcus (1994). 'Jain Ways of Being', in Ballard (ed.), pp. 231–250.

Chiba, Masaji (ed.) (1986). *Asian Indigenous Law in Interaction with Received Law*, New York and London: KPI.

Derrett, J. Duncan M. (1968). *Religion, Law and the State in India*, London: Faber and Faber.

——. (1970). *A Critique of Modern Hindu Law*, Bombay: Tripathi.

Desai, Satyajeet A. (ed.) (1998). *Mulla Principles of Hindu Law*, 17th edn, New Delhi: Butterworths.

Diwan, Paras and Diwan, Peeyushi (1993). *Modern Hindu Law*, 9th edn, Allahabad: Allahabad Law Agency, pp. 27–28.

Flood, Gavin (ed.) (2003). *The Blackwell Companion to Hinduism*, Oxford and Malden, MA: Blackwell Publishing.

Gale, Richard and Naylor, Simon (2002). 'Religion, Planning and the City: the Spatial Politics of Ethnic Minority Expression in British Cities and Towns', in Vol. 2 No. 3 (September 2002) *Ethnicities*, pp. 387–409.

Glenn, Patrick H. (2000). *Legal Traditions of the World. Sustainable Diversity in Law*, Oxford: OUP.

Jain, Champat Rai (1926). *The Jaina Law*, Madras: Devendra.

Jain, Jagdish Chandra (1991). *The Jain Way of Life*, Gurgaon: Academic Press.

Jones, Richard and Welhengama, Gnanapala (2000). *Ethnic Minorities in English Law*, Stoke-on-Trent and London: Trentham Books.

Menski, Werner (1994). 'Law and Religion: The Hindu and Jain Approach', in Bhattacharyya, N. N. (ed.) *Jainism and Prakrit in Ancient and Medieval India: Essays for Prof. Jagdish Chandra Jain*, New Delhi: Manohar, pp. 361–374.

——. (1997). *Indian Legal Systems Past and Present*, London: SOAS.

——. (2000). *Comparative Law in a Global Context: The Legal Systems of Asia and Africa*, London: Platinium.

——. (2001). *Modern Indian Family Law*, Richmond, VA: Curzon.

——. (2003). *Hindu Law. Beyond Tradition and Modernity*, New Delhi: OUP.

Örücü, Esin (ed.) (1999). *Critical Comparative Law: Considering Paradoxes for Legal Systems in Transition*, Kluwer: Deventer.

Parekh, Bhikhu (2000). *The Future of Multi-ethnic Britain*, London: Profile Books.

15

AHIṀSĀ AND COMPASSION IN JAINISM

Kristi L. Wiley

Ahiṁsā is one of the core ethical values in Jainism, as expressed in the oft-quoted phrase "*ahiṁsā paramo dharmaḥ* (nonviolence is the supreme form of religious conduct)." Padmanabh S. Jaini has observed that within Jainism there is a "preoccupation with *ahiṁsā*," for no other religious tradition "has carried it [*ahiṁsā*] to the extreme of the Jainas. For them it is not simply the first among virtues but the virtue."[1] Although in most religious traditions non-harming relates to other living beings, Jaini has noted that "for Jainas, however, it [*hiṁsā*] refers primarily to injuring oneself – to behavior which inhibits the soul's ability to attain *mokṣa*."[2] The reasoning here is that a tendency to intentionally harm other living beings that is motivated by strong passions (*kaṣāya*) causes the binding of harmful varieties (*pāpa prakṛti*) of karmic matter to one's own soul. These *karmas* cause rebirth in undesirable states of existence as hell-beings (*nāraki*) and animals (*tiryañca*) that are characterized by a preponderance of suffering and that are not conducive to spiritual progress, thereby prolonging the soul's journey in *saṃsāra*.[3]

Ahiṁsā and nonpossession (*aparigraha*), along with the doctrine of manifold aspects (*anekāntavāda*), are frequently viewed as cornerstones of a Jain world-view.[4] The concept of compassion is mentioned less frequently in most survey texts on Jainism. For example, in *The Jains* by Paul Dundas there is no entry for the word compassion in the index, and in *The Jaina Path of Purification* by P. S. Jaini, it is discussed briefly.[5] However, Jains sometimes associate *ahiṁsā* with compassion in their writings. For instance, in an essay entitled "Environmental wisdom in Ancient India," L. M. Singhvi states:

> Compassion and reverence for life are the sheet-anchor of the Jain quest for Peace, Harmony, and Rectitude, based on spiritual and physical symbiosis and a sense of responsibility and restraint arising out of the principle of cause and effect. Although the term *ahiṁsā* is stated in the negative (*a* = non, *hiṁsā* = violence), it is rooted in a host of positive aims and actions which have great relevance to contemporary environmental concerns. *Ahiṁsā* is an aspect of *dayā* (compassion,

> empathy and charity). . . . *Jiva-dayā* means caring for and sharing with all living beings, tending, protecting and serving them. It entails universal friendliness (*maitrī*), universal forgiveness (*kṣamā*) and universal fearlessness (*abhaya*). . . . It is the same sense of compassion and non-violence which is the basis of the ancient Jain scriptural aphorism *Parasparopagraho Jīvānām* (all life is bound together by the mutual support of interdependence).[6]

On a website for Jain pilgrimage sites, Jainism is described as being "synonymous with *ahiṁsā. Ahiṁsā* (non-violence) occupies the supreme place in Jainism. . . . Compassion (*dayā*) is the guiding force of non-violence. It is the positive way of life. It has been assigned an equally high place in Jainism – '*Dayā dharma kā mool*' (Compassion is the basis of religion)."[7]

Given the fact that compassion is mentioned along with *ahiṁsā* in contemporary writings such as these, it would be useful to investigate the textual basis for these statements in earlier Jain sources. In what contexts is compassion discussed in the *Tattvārtha-sūtra*, which is accepted by both Śvetāmbaras and Digambaras? Are views about compassion in the *Tattvārtha-sūtra* and its commentaries reflected in writings on lay and mendicant conduct and in texts on *karma* theory? Is there evidence of sectarian differences in views on compassion? How do the commentators define the various Sanskrit words such as *anukampā, dayā*, and *kāruṇya* that are translated into English as "compassion"?

Views on compassion in the *Tattvārtha-sūtra* and commentaries

Compassion is mentioned twice in the *Tattvārtha-sūtra* (= *TS*) itself, at *TS* 6.12 where *anukampā* is listed as one of the causes of binding *sātā-vedanīya karma* and at *TS* 7.6 (= *SS* 7.11) where *kāruṇya* is listed as one of the contemplations (*bhāvanā*) that strengthen the five lay vows (*aṇuvrata*) and the five mendicant vows (*mahāvrata*).[8] Compassion is mentioned in the commentaries on *TS* 1.2 where a proper view of reality (*samyak-darśana*) is defined as belief in existents (*tattva*) ascertained as they really are.[9] Two Śvetāmbara and three Digambara commentaries on the *Tattvārtha-sūtra* are examined here. The Śvetāmbara commentaries include the *bhāṣya* by Umāsvāti, which Śvetāmbaras believe is an autocommentary, and the *vṛtti* by Siddhasenagaṇi (*c.* seventh century), which is the most extensive Śvetāmbara commentary on both the *sūtra* and the *bhāṣya*. The three Digambara commentaries include the *Sarvārthasiddhi* of Pūjyapāda (sixth century), the *Tattvārthavārtika (Rājavārtika)* of Akalaṅka (eighth century), and the *Tattvārthaślokavārtika* of Vidyānanda (ninth century).[10] At the first occurrence of each Sanskrit word used by the commentators that may be translated into English as "compassion," the definitions from the Sanskrit–English dictionaries of Monier-Williams and Apte are included in the notes.

Compassion and samyak-darśana

In his commentary on *TS* 1.2, Umāsvāti lists four indicative signs of *samyak-darśana*: *praśama* (calmness), *saṃvega* (fear of worldly existence), *anukampā* (compassion), and *āstikya* (belief in the existents such as the soul, non-soul, and so forth), but he does not define any of these indicative signs. Siddhasenagaṇi defines *anukampā* as "*ghṛṇā* or *kāruṇya* towards living beings. For example, those who are desirous of happiness for all living beings and who are desirous of the cessation of suffering, having decided, 'I will not cause them any affliction, not even a little,' they strive for this with a tender heart."[11]

In Digambara commentaries on this *sūtra*, compassion (*anukampā*) is not defined by Pūjyapāda. However, Akalaṅka defines this term as "*maitrī* (friendliness, kindness) towards all beings"[12] and Vidyānanda defines it as "*dayā* towards all mobile (*trasa*) and immobile (*sthāvara*) beings."[13] The Digambara commentators state that there are two types of *samyak-darśana*: *sarāga samyak-darśana* (right belief with attachments) and *vītarāga samyak-darśana* (right belief without attachments). The indicative signs of *samyak-darśana*, namely *praśama, saṃvega, anukampā*, and *āstikya*, are associated with *sarāga samyaktva. Vītarāga samyaktva* is characterized only by the purity of the soul itself (*ātma-viśuddhi-mātra*).

There are slight variations in the wording of various Digambara commentaries. Pūjyapāda states that *samyaktva* is of two types "on account of a difference in the object (*sarāga-vītarāga-viṣaya-bhedāt*)."[14] It is not entirely clear to me what Pūjyapāda is saying here. One way to interpretet his statement is that when the object of perception is *sarāga*, in other words, when the object is a living being who has not overcome attachments and aversions, there would be compassion towards that person by someone who has attained *samyaktva*. There would be no compassion when the object is *vītarāga*. This would include a person who has overcome all attachments and aversions, and contemplation of the inner soul itself, which is characterized by innate purity and thus not affected by *karma* that causes attachment or aversion. Akalaṅka does not use word "object" (*viṣaya*). Instead, he mentions that *samyaktva* is of two types "on account of the distinction between *sarāga* and *vītarāga* (*sarāga-vītarāga-vikalpāt*)." Commenting on the phrase "*ātma-viśuddhi-mātra*," Akalaṅka states: "When the seven varieties of *karma* have entirely disappeared, there is only the purity of the soul. This is *vītarāga samyaktva*."[15] This phrase is somewhat ambiguous because there are no souls that are devoid of seven of the eight main varieties (*mūla-prakṛti*) of karmic matter. Apparently Akalaṅka is associating *vītarāga samyaktva* with a *kevalin*, who has destroyed all varieties of destructive (*ghātiyā*) *karma*s previously bound with the soul and for whom the *binding* of seven of the eight main varieties of karmic matter has disappeared (all *karma*s except for *sātā-vedanīya karma*).[16] The *kevalin* has thereby attained direct omniscient knowledge of all existents, including the soul itself, and has eliminated forever all attachment (*rāga*) and aversion (*dveṣa*). In his commentary on *TS* 1.2, Vidyānanda also associates *anukampā* with *sarāga samyaktva*. In the Hindi commentary on this verse, Paṇḍit

Māṇikcand explains that *praśama*, *saṃvega*, *anukampā*, and *āstikya* are good or auspicious attachments (*śubha-rāga*).[17] Vidyānanda clarifies another point by explicitly stating that the qualities of *saṃvega* and *anukampā* are not possible for those who have a false view of reality (*mithyādṛṣṭi*) and are thereby in the first *guṇasthāna*.[18]

Thus, according to Digambara commentators, compassion is associated with the *samyaktva* of those who are still subject to the binding of the eight main varieties of karmic matter, in other words, by those who are affected by conduct-deluding (*cāritra-mohanīya*) *karma*, which causes attraction (*rāga*) and aversion (*dveṣa*) in the form of the four passions (*kaṣāya*), namely anger (*krodha*), pride (*māna*), deceitfulness (*māyā*), and greed (*lobha*) in the three lesser degrees of intensity.[19] This would include those who have not taken any vows and are thereby in the fourth *guṇasthāna*, laypeople who have taken the lay vows thereby attaining the fifth *guṇasthāna*, and mendicants who have taken the mendicant vows thereby attaining the sixth *guṇasthāna*. However, these indicative signs of *samyaktva*, compassion and so forth, would not be associated with the *samyaktva* of a *sayoga kevalin* in the thirteenth *guṇasthāna*.

Compassion and sātā-vedanīya karma

Given the fact that compassion is associated with *samyaktva*, which is characterized by activities that minimize harm to other living beings and that lead to the binding of beneficial varieties of karmic matter (*puṇya prakṛti*) associated with well-being in this life and a good rebirth in the next life, it is not surprising that at *TS* 6.13 (= *SS* 6.12) compassion (*anukampā*) is listed as one of the causes of the influx of *sātā-vedanīya karma* (the *karma* that causes pleasant feelings).[20] In discussing the phrase "*bhūta-vrati-anukampā*" in the *sūtra*, Umāsvāti states that one should have compassion "especially for those who have taken the vows," and Siddhasenagaṇi explains that compassion for those who have taken the vows is preeminent. He glosses *anukampā* with *dayā* and *ghṛṇā* and states: "When one gives food, water, clothing, utensils, shelter, and so forth to the afflicted, the poor, and beggars, who have not renounced the household life, and to mendicants as well, there are fruits in the form of disassociation of various types of karmic matter. This brings about knowledge, faith, and conduct. Or, giving is showing compassion. It is viewing the suffering of others as if it were one's own. *Dāna* is giving away with the intent or wish of showing kindness or giving assistance to others."[21] The Digambara commentators agree that compassion towards mendicants is preemiment in this context, stating that this is the reason that those who have taken vows (*vratī*) are mentioned separately here. Pūjyapāda defines a compassionate person as "one whose heart is full of warmth and kindness (*anugraha*) and who views the afflictions of others as if they were one's own."[22]

In his translation of the *Tattvārtha-sūtra*, Nathmal Tatia has commented that in the *Tattvārtha-sūtra* the description of compassion has been expanded "to include positive acts of charity and also adds further factors, self-restraint, etc. as causes of the inflow of pleasure-producing *karma*." He notes that in the *Bhagavaī Viyāhapannatti-sutta* "the inflow of pleasure-producing *karma* is attributed solely to compassion for living things by desisting from inflicting pain."[23] Tatia is refering here to *Bhagavaī-sutta* 7.6.358, which states that *sātā-vedanīya karma* is bound by compassion (*anukampā*) for all living beings (*prāṇa*, *bhūta*, *jīva*, and *sattva*), by causing them no suffering (*aduḥkha*), no grief (*aśoka*), no emaciation of the body (*ajīrṇa*), no bitter weeping (*ati-atepanatā*), no affliction (*apīḍana*), and no bodily or mental distress (*aparitāpana*). What constitutes compassion here is not clear from the *sūtra* itself and unfortunately, in his commentary on this passage, Abhayadevasūri (eleventh century) is silent regarding compassion. Compassion could be interpreted as encompassing all of the following restraints, that compassion means causing all living beings no suffering, no grief, and so forth. However, one could also interpret this passage as a series of individual items, "by showing compassion for all living beings, and by causing them no suffering, and by causing them no grief," and so forth. This is how Deleu has interpreted this passage in his study of the *Bhagavaī-sutta*: "by compassion (*aṇukampā*) on all living beings *and* by not afflicting them (*adukkhaṇayā*), souls produce *karman* that will be experienced in a pleasant way."[24] While charitable acts are not mentioned in the context of binding of *sātā-vedanīya karma* here, in commenting on *Bhagavaī-sutta* 8.8.412, which discusses three opponents (*paḍiṇīya*) of various items including compassion (*aṇukampā*), Abhayadevasūri states that a compassionate person is "one who supports with food, water, and so forth those who have renounced the household life and are practicing asceticism, those who have recently renounced, and those who are not capable of renouncing on account of illness or disease."[25] It is possible that compassionate acts associated specifically with the binding of *sātā-vedanīya karma* may have been expanded by Umāsvāti in the *Tattvārtha-sūtra*. However, according to Abhayadevasūri, charitable acts are an aspect of compassion elsewhere in the *Bhagavaī-sutta*.

Compassion is associated with the binding of *sātā-vedanīya karma* in other texts on *karma* theory such as the Digambara *Gommaṭasāra Karma-kāṇḍa* of Nemicandra (ninth century) and the Śvetāmbara *Karmagrantha* of Devendrasūri (thirteenth century). However, the commentators do not elaborate on compassion here. At *Gommaṭasāra Karma-kāṇḍa* 801, *bhūta-anukampā* is defined as "a feeling of compassion (*dayā*) for all living beings," and at *Karmagrantha* 1.54, Devendrasūri defines *karuṇā* as "one whose mind is filled with compassion (*dayā*)." As in the *Tattvārtha-sūtra*, there are additional causes for the influx of *sātā-vedanīya karma*.

Compassion and the bhāvanās

Since compassion is associated with *samyaktva* and therefore would be an element in proper lay and mendicant conduct, *kāruṇya* is listed among the contemplations (*bhāvanā*) that strengthen all five lay and mendicant vows at *TS* 7.6

(= *SS* 7.11). This *sūtra* reads: "Friendliness (*maitrī*) towards all living beings (*sattva*), delight (*pramoda*) with those whose qualities are superior (*guṇādhika*), compassion (*kāruṇya*) for the afflicted (*kliśyamāna*), and equanimity (*mādhystha*) towards the ill-behaved (*avinaya*) [should be contemplated]." Here, Umāsvāti defines *kāruṇya* as *anukampā* and as rendering assistance (*anugraha*) to the afflicted (*dīna*). Siddhasenagaṇi defines the afflicted as those who suffer bodily pain or mental anguish and glosses *kāruṇya* with the terms *ghṛṇā, anukampā, dayā, kṛpā*, and *dīnānugraha*.[26] Likewise, Pūjyapāda defines *kāruṇya* as a disposition (*bhāva*) to render assistance (*anugraha*) to the afflicted (*dīna*), or those who suffer pain or anguish due to the rise of *asātā-vedanīya karma*. He concludes: "Those who have this disposition practice nonviolence and other vows completely."[27]

Views on compassion in the *Dhavalā* commentary of Vīrasena

The commentators on the *Tattvārtha-sūtra* do not discuss why compassion is associated with those who have attained *samyak-darśana* or why it is not manifested in those who have a false view of reality (*mithyātva*). Like the commentators on the *Tattvārtha-sūtra*, the Digambara commentator Vīrasena (eighth century) lists *anukampā* as one of the four indicative signs of *samyaktva* in his commentary on the *Ṣaṭkhaṇḍāgama* entitled *Dhavalā*.[28] Vīrasena clarifies his position by raising the following questions. "There is a cause for compassion. Why is it said that there is no *karuṇā karma*? (Answer): Because *karuṇā* is a modification that is associated with the inherent nature (*svabhāva*) of the soul, one cannot say that it is caused by karmic matter. (Question): There is a cause for lack of compassion (*akaruṇā*). Why is it correct to say that there is no specific *karma* that is the cause of a lack of compassion? (Answer): This is correct because *akaruṇā* is caused by the fruition of the *karma*s that destroy restraint (*saṃyama-ghātī karma*)."

What Vīrasena is saying here is that although compassion is often thought of as a feeling or emotion, it is not caused by the rise (*udaya*) any of the twenty-five sub-varieties (*uttara-prakṛti*) of conduct-deluding (*cāritra-mohanīya*) *karma*.[29] It is not caused by the sixteen sub-varieties of *mohanīya karma*s that generate the four "feelings" or passions (*kaṣāya*) of anger (*krodha*), pride (*māna*), deceitfulness (*māyā*), or greed (*lobha*) in any of the four degrees of intensity. Nor is it generated by the rise of the nine varieties of *mohanīya karma*s that cause the non-passions (*no-kaṣāya*), or "emotions" or "feelings," namely laughter (*hāsya*), prejudicial liking (*rati*), prejudicial disliking (*arati*), sorrow (*śoka*), fear (*bhaya*), disgust (*jugupsā*), and sexual cravings of the male (*puṃveda*), female (*strīveda*), and hermaphrodite (*napuṃsakaveda*). Like the four passions, as long as these nine emotions exist, it is impossible to attain the highest stages of spiritual perfection characterized by omniscience (*kevala-jñāna*) and perfect conduct (*samyak-cāritra*).

Therefore, according to Vīrasena, compassion is not a state of the soul (*bhāva*) that is caused by the rise of *karmas* (*audayika bhāva*). Compassion is a state of the soul that is manifested when the *karmas* that cause the strongest degree of passions (*anantānubandhī-cāritra-mohanīya karma*) associated with wrong views (*mithyādṛṣṭi*) and wrong conduct (i.e., the first *guṇasthāna*) have been suppressed or destroyed. Compassion is a characteristic of *samyaktva* in its preliminary stage (*kṣāyopaśamika-samyaktva*), and in its perfected forms, whether they are temporary due to the suppression of all *darśana-mohanīya karma* (*aupaśamika-samyaktva*) or permanent due to the destruction of all *darśana-mohanīya karma* (*kṣāyika-samyaktva*).[30] Those who have a proper view of reality have compassion for others. This includes humans, heavenly beings, and five-sensed rational animals.[31]

Conversely, a lack of compassion is caused by *karmas*, namely those that destroy restraint (*saṃyama-ghātī karma*). Here, Vīrasena apparently is referring to those in the first *guṇasthāna* in which the conduct-deluding (*cāritra-mohanīya*) *karmas* that generate passions in the strongest degree (*anantānubandhī-kaṣāya*) are manifested. These *karmas* always operate with *darśana-mohanīya karma*, and together they cause improper conduct and delusion regarding the proper view of reality.

Views on compassion in texts on lay and mendicant conduct

As in the commentaries on the *Tattvārtha-sūtra* and the *Ṣaṭkhaṇḍāgama*, the authors of the Śvetāmbara and Digambara *śrāvakācāra* texts, which discuss appropriate conduct for laypeople, list *anukampā* as one of the indicative qualities (*guṇa* or *liṅga*) of *samyaktva*.[32] Compassion also is listed in some texts as one of the qualities of an observant layperson (*śrāvaka-guṇa*). Compassion (*dayālu*) is mentioned in the earliest literary source for the twenty-one *śrāvaka-guṇas*, the Śvetāmbara *Dharma-ratna-prakaraṇa* of Śāntisūri (d. 1040) and also in the Digambara *Sāgāra-dharmāmṛta* of Āśādhara (thirteenth century).[33] In the Śvetāmbara *Yogaśāstra* of Hemacandra (1089–1172) *sa-dayā* is listed as one of thirty-five qualities of a layman. In his commentary on *Yogaśāstra* 2.15, which lists the indicative signs of *samyaktva*, Hemacandra defines compassion as "the desire to eliminate suffering: in this compassion for those in misery, no partiality may be shown, for even a tiger will manifest affection for its own offspring. In its material aspects this virtue takes the form of practical steps to remedy suffering where one has the power and in its non-material aspects it expresses itself in tenderness of the heart."[34]

Compassion also can be expressed in observing a variety of restraints. For example, in the Digambara *Ratna-karaṇḍa-śrāvakācāra*, Samantabhadra (*c.* fifth century) defines *rātri-bhojana* as abandoning food at night out of compassion for living beings (*jīva-dayā*).[35] Vāmadeva (Digambara, *c.* fifteenth century) in the *Bhāva-saṃgraha*, equates compassion for living beings (*jīva-dayā*) with abstention from eating various foods, from adultery, theft, gambling, and from eating after dark (*rātri-bhojana*).[36]

As mentioned previously in the *Tattvārtha-sūtra*, compassion is one of the contemplations (*bhāvanā*) that strengthen all five lay and mendicant vows. These four contemplations, including compassion (*karuṇā*), are described as prerequisites for analytic meditation (*dharma-dhyāna*) by Śubhacandra (Digambara, late ninth or early tenth century) in his *Jñānārṇava* and as sustainers of *dharma-dhyāna* by Hemacandra in his *Yogaśāstra*.[37] Here, Hemacandra defines compassion (*anukampā*) as the desire to eliminate suffering. It may be expressed in tenderness of heart or in practical steps to remedy suffering where one has the power to do so.[38]

Compassion is also mentioned in Śvetāmbara and Digambara texts in association with mendicant conduct. For instance, *Āyāraṃga-sutta* 1.6.5.2 states: "A saint, with right intuition (*samyak-darśana*) who cherishes compassion (*dayā*) for the world, in the east, west, south, and north, should preach, spread, and praise (the faith), knowing the sacred lore."[39] *Uttarajjhayaṇa-sutta* 21.13 says: "A monk should have compassion (*dayānukampā*) on all beings, should be of a forbearing character, should be restrained and chaste, and abstaining from everything sinful; he should live with his senses under control."[40] In discussing religious virtues in the *Praśamaratiprakaraṇa*, Umāsvāti states: "Compassion (*dayā*) is the root of sacred doctrine (*dharma*). A person who is devoid of patience or forgiveness (*akṣamāvān*) does not show compassion (*dayā*). Therefore, one who is devoted to patience attains the highest *dharma*."[41] Unlimited compassion (*karuṇāpara*) is listed among the fruits of practicing severe austerities in the Digambara *Ātmānuśāsana* of Guṇabhadra (ninth century).[42] In verse 107, the renunciant is urged to follow the path of compassion (*dayā*), self-control, renunciation, and equanimity.[43] Guṇabhadra observes: "When the shore of the ocean of the cycle of existence is close by, the fortunate man has aversion to sense-gratifications, has renounced all possessions, subjugates the passions, has tranquility, vows, self-control, practice of self-contemplation, pursuit of austerities, duly ordained mental activity, devotion to the conquerors, and compassion (*dayālutā*)."[44]

Views of Ācārya Bhikṣu on compassion

A disagreement over the issue of compassionate help was one of the reasons that Ācārya Bhikṣu (1726–1803) split with Ācārya Raghunātha (1710–1790) of the Śvetāmbara Sthānakavāsī tradition in 1760 and subsequently founded the Śvetāmbara Terāpanthī tradition.[45] Ācārya Bhikṣu maintained that compassion represents two feelings: worldly compassion (*laukika dayā*) and spiritual or religious compassion (*lokottara* or *dharma dayā*).[46]

In explaining Ācārya Bhikṣu's views on compassion, Ācārya Mahāprajña, the current leader of the Terāpanthīs, has written:

> When a strong person is moved at the suffering of the weak, this is sympathy of the strong towards the weak. The word compassion (*dayā*) is an expression of this feeling. When a person is moved at the suffering

> of the strong or the weak, this is the realization of the equality of one soul with all other souls. The word compassion is an expression of this feeling. Thus, the word compassion represents two feelings. After being so moved, there are two courses of action: to not cause suffering and to remove suffering. Everyone agrees that one should not cause suffering, but there is some question with respect to removing the suffering of the afflicted. Therefore, Ācārya Bhikṣu has said, "The *dharma* of compassion is proper, but salvation is attained only by those who have recognized it as it really is and have observed it properly."[47] He warns, "Do not be deceived in the name of compassion. Penetrate it in depth and investigate it."[48]

Ācārya Mahāprajña asks: "Why should one remove suffering? Whose suffering should be removed? How should one remove it?" He concludes that there is not a single answer to these questions. From the perspective of societal (*laukika*) *dharma*, suffering should be removed in order to make beings happy (*sukha*), by some means or another. The suffering of human beings should be removed and that of other beings as well if this presents no problems with respect to the welfare of humans. However, from the perspective of *ātma dharma* (or *lokottara dharma*), suffering should be removed only in order to make the soul pure and only by virtuous means. This should be done for everyone.[49] In the case of *laukika dayā*, the idea of restraint (*saṃyama*) or non-restraint (*asaṃyama*) is not predominant, only the feeling of compassion (*karuṇā*). However, where there is compassion that is informed by restraint, this is *lokottara dayā*. Therefore, worldly kindness (*laukika upakāra*) is to rescue someone who is being burned in a fire or to save someone who has fallen into a well. Spiritual kindness (*lokottara upakāra*) is to save someone who is without restraint and who is being burned in the fire of birth and death from falling into the well of evil (*pāpa*) by giving religious instruction.[50] To give money and goods to someone who is poor is worldly kindness.[51] To give peace (*śānti*) to someone who is burning in the fire of desire by giving religious instruction is spiritual kindness.[52]

Thus, according to Ācārya Bhikṣu, from the spiritual perspective, compassion is shown through acts of kindness that are expressed in giving religious instruction, thereby encouraging restraint in others, which leads to the lessening of suffering in the cycle of *saṃsāra*. It is also shown through one's own restraint by not causing suffering in others through acts of violence or through causing fear to arise in them. Ācārya Bhikṣu has said that nonviolence is restraint towards living beings. Compassion is the feeling of friendliness towards living beings and a trembling in the heart that comes in association with their being afflicted. Without compassion, *ahiṁsā* is not possible, and without *ahiṁsā*, compassion is not possible. In these two, there is an inseparable connection. The first *mahāvrata* is to abstain from killing all living beings. In this, the totality of compassion is absorbed.[53] To not cause distress from fear is giving freedom from fear. This is another name for compassion and *ahiṁsā*. Not killing, not causing another to kill, and not approving of the killing, this is giving freedom from fear, and this is compassion.[54]

In her ethnography on the Śvetāmbara Terāpanthī community at Ladnun, Anne Vallely explains: "Terāpanthī Jains sharply demarcate between social and spiritual action in a way that makes them distinct among the other Jain orders. Only religious guidance that leads to a 'positive change of heart' is truly spiritual and earns good *karma*. They argue that while acts of charity (feeding, clothing, healing, etc.) are social duties, they cannot be considered religious or spiritual acts."[55] Thus, the building of hospitals or animal shelters is a social activity, not a religious activity.[56] She states: "Jain compassion is not directed so much at the suffering in social life, but at the suffering of social life."[57] She was told, however, that householders should perform social duties such as these even though they do not cause the binding of good *karma*. She observes that it is hard to know whether the lay community believes that such actions do not cause the accumulation of merit. "When I spoke with members of the Terāpanthī Mahila Mandal (a women's organization) the majority believed – through a creative interpretation of their doctrine – that their efforts would benefit them karmically. As one woman explained, 'Perhaps the acts themselves are not *dharma*, but the compassion that drives them is, and this surely leads to *puṇya*.' And I knew of at least one *saman* who interpreted philanthropic acts in the same way."[58]

Conclusions

Although there several different Sanskrit words used for the concept of "compassion" such as *anukampā*, *dayā*, and *kāruṇya*, in the commentaries consulted here, these terms are not differentiated from each other. Instead, the commentators gloss one word for compassion with another, for example, *anukampā* is glossed with *dayā*. Therefore, all of these terms can be translated into English as "compassion."

The association of compassion with *ahiṁsā* expressed in contemporary writings by Jains is supported in classical Jain texts and commentaries, where compassion is associated with a proper view of reality (*samyak-darśana*, or the fourth *guṇasthāna*) but not with a false view of reality (*mithyātva*, or the first *guṇasthāna*). This association of compassion with *samyak-darśana* is also found in texts on lay and mendicant conduct. As P. S. Jaini has explained, compassion (*anukampā*) that is associated with a proper view of reality (*samyaktva*) is free from pity or attachment to its object. "It develops purely from wisdom, from seeing the substance (*dravya*) that underlies visible modes, and it fills the individual with an unselfish desire to help other souls toward *mokṣa*. If this urge to bring all tormented beings out of *saṃsāra* is particularly strong and cultivated, it may generate those auspicious *karma*s that later confer the status of Tīrthaṅkara upon certain omniscients. When present to a more moderate degree, *anukampā* brings an end to exploitative and destructive behavior, for even the lowest animal is now seen as intrinsically worthwhile and thus inviolable."[59]

The opinion of Jain authors, that true compassion is always accompanied by a proper view of reality (*samyaktva*) and that compassion is lacking in those with a false view of reality (*mithyātva*), might be associated with views of compassion held by other religious traditions. By definition, those who follow other religious traditions could not have *samyak-darśana* because one of its indicative signs is *āstikya*, or the acceptance of the Jain doctrine as the true creed. Phyllis Granoff has observed that medieval Jains were especially concerned with the Buddhist concepts of compassion and self-sacrifice. "[T]he Jains might be said to have defined themselves as the religion of compassion par excellence in medieval India, and to support their claim they needed to show that all possible rival claimants practiced a false compassion." They believed that "the Buddhist exemplified a wrong ideal of compassion that was in itself inherently violent."[60] Jains equated acts of self-sacrifice that were considered to be expressions of compassion by Buddhists, for example, of a Bodhisattva offering his body to save a living being or offering his body as food in times of famine, as misguided acts entailing violence that is tantamount to murder. As argued in texts devoted to lay conduct, acts of compassion do not entail killing under any circumstances whatsoever, even when it is perceived to alleviate the suffering of other living beings or to prevent them from killing others in the future. Jains also argued against the views of a group called the *saṃsāramocaka*s, who believed that it was meritorious to kill sinful or suffering creatures, and against the Mīmāṃsakas, who believed that the prohibition against killing animals did not apply in the context of the sacrifice.[61]

There is no disagreement over compassion when it is understood as restraint, by not causing suffering in others by refraining from acts of violence (*ahiṁsā*) or by refraining from acts that would cause fear to arise in others. However, the Śvetāmbara Terāpanthī Ācārya Bhikṣu disagrees with Digambara commentators and with the other Śvetāmbara commentators examined here, who believe that compassionate acts that are aimed at alleviating the physical suffering of those who are afflicted is karmically beneficial to oneself and is conducive to spiritual progress. He would disagree with the views expressed by Siddhasenagaṇi in his commentary on *Tattvārtha-sūtra* 6.13 and by Abhayadevasūri in his commentary on *Bhagavaī-sutta* 8.8.412 that material forms of giving by laypeople to those who are afflicted and have not renounced the household life are compassionate acts that have positive karmic effects. Ācārya Bhikṣu believes that the only compassionate acts of giving that are beneficial from a spiritual perspective are giving freedom from fear and giving religious instruction. Giving material support to those who give religious instruction, namely, giving to support the mendicant community is also considered spiritually beneficial by Śvetāmbara Terāpanthīs.

Digambara commentators on the *Tattvārtha-sūtra*, but not Śvetāmbara commentators, differentiate between two types of *samyak-darśana*: with attachment (*sarāga*) and without attachment (*vītarāga*). Digambara commentators associate compassion with *sarāga samyaktva* but not with *vītarāga samyaktva*.

This raises the question of how one might understand compassion in the context of the Tīrthaṅkara, who by definition must have *vītarāga samyaktva*. How could the soul of a Tīrthaṅkara, who has destroyed all destructive (*ghātiyā*) *karmas*, be devoid of compassion in the same way that the soul of a non-omniscient person (*chadmastha*) is devoid of compassion after it has fallen from a state of *samyaktva* to *mithyātva* due to the rise of *mithyātva-darśana mohanīya karma*? The apparent absence of compassion in the Tīrthaṅkara could not be associated with the rise of *karmas* that affect proper belief and proper conduct since these *karmas* have been eliminated from the soul. There is one definition of compassion that might be relevant here. In explaining the term *dayānukampā* in his commentary on *Uttarajjhayaṇa-sutta* 21.13, Lakṣmīvallabhagaṇi states: "A mendicant should have compassion for all beings. This means that the mendicant should be intent on observing compassion in the form of salutary instruction."[62] As discussed earlier, this is the view of compassion that Ācārya Bhikṣu understands as spiritual kindness (*lokottara upakāra*), which encompasses giving religious instruction and giving freedom from fear. Both of these are precisely what the Tīrthaṅkara does after attaining *kevala-jñāna* by preaching to those who have gathered in the assembly hall (*samavasaraṇa*) including his *gaṇadharas*, who interpret the utterances of the Tīrthaṅkara and compose the sacred scriptures on the basis of his teachings. The notion of giving for the benefit of others is expressed by Pūjyapāda when he states that on account of the destruction of *dānāntarāya karma* (the *karma* that prevents giving to others), the Tīrthaṅkara has the ability to give protection or fearlessness (*abhaya*) against the sorrows of *saṃsāra* to other beings through his preaching.[63] Śvetāmbaras believe that through the destruction of all of the *ghātiyā karmas* collectively the Tīrthaṅkara acquires the ability to influence for the better his immediate surroundings, giving freedom from fear and comfort to others. Perhaps in the case of the omniscient *sayoga kevalin* (*kevalins* and Tīrthaṅkaras in the thirteenth *guṇasthāna*), the quality that is expressed by the word compassion in the context of a non-omniscient being in the state of bondage (*chadmastha*) could be understood as an expression of perfect knowledge (*kevala-jñāna*). This is how some Digambara commentators have understood the soul's quality of infinite bliss (*ananta-sukha*). For example, on *Tattvārtha-sūtra* 10.4, which lists the four qualities that remain in the unembodied, emancipated soul (*siddha*) as *kevala-samyaktva, kevala-jñāna, kevala-darśana*, and *siddhatva*, Pūjyapāda states that other qualities of the soul are not excluded because there is an invariable concomitance between *ananta-jñāna/darśana* and *ananta-vīrya* (infinite energy) and so forth. [Infinite] *sukha* always accompanies [infinite] knowledge.[64] Thus, one could understand that the perfect knowledge of Tīrthaṅkaras, which is conveyed through their preachings, encompasses the concept of compassion, and that this compassion still exists in the world through their teachings and through the sight (*darśana*) of their images in temples, which are representative of the *samavasaraṇa*.

Notes

1 Jaini 1979: 167.
2 Jaini 1979: 167.
3 *Kaṣāyas* are caused by conduct-deluding (*cāritra-mohanīya*) *karma*. See Note 19. The *karmas* that cause birth as a five-sensed rational animal, human, and heavenly being are considered beneficial varieties (*puṇya prakṛti*). For a complete listing of the *pāpa* and *puṇya prakṛtis*, see Tatia 1994: 204–206. For a general discussion of the binding and the operation of *karma*, see Jaini 1979, chapter 4.
4 A number of works have been written on the doctrine of manifold aspects or a non-one-sided view of reality (*anekāntavāda*) and the associated doctrine of qualified assertion (*syādvāda*) and its sevenfold predication (*sapta-bhaṅgi-naya*). For example, see Mookerjee 1944. Non-harming (*ahiṁsā*) and nonpossession (*aparigraha*), which is interpreted for householders as placing limits on one's possessions, are two of the five minor vows (*aṇuvrata*) of a layperson and two of the five major vows (*mahāvrata*) of a mendicant.
5 Jaini 1979: 66, 150, and 163.
6 Singhvi 1998: 40–42.
7 http://www.jainpilgrimages.com/general/mahavir.htm (accessed December 15, 2001).
8 Numbering of the *sūtras* in the *TS* follows the Śvetāmbara version. A difference in the Digambara version is indicated by (= *SS*).
9 The *tattvas* as listed at *TS* 1.4 are the soul (*jīva*); the non-soul (*ajīva*); the influx (*āsrava*), bondage (*bandha*), stoppage (*saṃvara*), and disassociation (*nirjarā*) of karmic matter; and liberation (*mokṣa*). Here, merit (*puṇya*) and demerit (*pāpa*) are not listed but are implied in influx and bondage. *Samyaktva* is the state of having *samyak-darśana*. A person who has attained *samyak-darśana* is called a *samyak-dṛṣṭi*. This is also a designation given to the fourth *guṇasthāna*, or stage of spiritual development. For a listing of the fourteen *guṇasthānas*, see Jaini 1979: 272–273. Following Jaini 1979, I have used the spelling "*samyak*" in all terms, rather than the *sandhi* form with the phonological change, "*samyag-darśana*."
10 According to Ohira (1982: 146) dating of the *TS* ranges from 150 BCE (Datta) to 500 CE (Woods). In between these dates are 100 CE (Phūlcandra Siddhāntaśāstrī), 135–219 CE (J. L. Jaini), third to fourth century CE (Nāthūrām Premī), and third to fifth century CE (Sukhlāl Saṅghvī). Ohira believes it was written in the middle of the fifth century. Dating of Digambara commentators follows Dundas (2002: 87). Digambaras believe that Umāsvāmin was the author of the *sūtra* and therefore do not understand the *bhāṣya* by Umāsvāti to be an autocommentary. No date is given in the colophon of Siddhasenagaṇi's commentary, but on the basis of the works and authors mentioned, it could not have been written prior to the seventh century. In his introduction to his commentary on the *TS*, Sukhlāl Saṅghvī states that the commentary was written between the last quarter of the seventh century and the middle of the eighth century (Sanghvi 1974: 58–60). See also H. R. Kāpadīā's introduction to his edited edition of the *TS* (Kāpadīā 1926: 48–53 and 63–64). He believes that Siddhasenagaṇi's commentary is posterior to the *Sarvārthasiddhi* (= *SS*) and coexisting with, or anterior to, the *Tattvārtharājavārtika* (= *RV*) and the *Tattvārthaślokavārtika* (= *SV*), both of which he assigns to the ninth century.
11 Siddhasenagaṇi's commentary on *TS* 1.2. *Anukampā* is defined as "sympathy or compassion" by Monier-Williams and "compassion, commiseration, or pity" by Apte. *Ghṛṇā* is defined as "a warm feeling towards others, compassion, tenderness" by Monier-Williams and "compassion, pity, or tenderness" by Apte. *Kāruṇya* is defined as "compassion or kindness" by Monier-Williams and "compassion, kindness, or pity" by Apte.

12 *RV* 1.2.30.

13 *SV* 1.2.12 (vol. 2, p. 34). *Dayā* is defined as "sympathy, compassion, or pity" by Monier-Williams and "pity, tenderness, compassion, mercy, or sympathy" by Apte.

14 *SS* 12.

15 *RV* 1.2.31.

16 In the absence of passions (*kaṣāya*), activity (*yoga*) is the sole cause for the influx of *karma*. In this case, there is instantaneous inflow and bondage (*īryāpatha*) of only one variety of *karma*, *sātā-vedanīya karma*. However, the soul of the *sayoga kevalin* still has all four varieties of non-destructive (*aghātiyā*) *karma*s (*nāma*, *āyu*, *gotra*, and *vedanīya*) bound with it, which are rising and producing their effects. For details on the *aghātiyā karma*s, see Wiley 2000.

17 *SV* 1.2.12 (vol. 2, p. 30).

18 *SV* 1.2.12 (vol. 2, p. 36).

19 There are two main varieties of deluding (*mohanīya*) *karma*: those that cause delusion regarding the nature of reality (*darśana-mohanīya karma*) and those that cause delusion regarding conduct (*cāritra-mohanīya karma*). When *darśana-mohanīya karma* is operative, the soul is in the first *guṇasthāna*, or lowest stage of spiritual development. There are twenty-five sub-varieties (*uttara-prakṛti*) of conduct-deluding *karma*s. Sixteen sub-varieties generate the four passions (*kaṣāya*) of anger (*krodha*), pride (*māna*) deceitfulness (*māyā*), and greed (*lobha*). These *karma*s operate, or produce their effects, in four degrees of intensity. The strongest degree of intensity is *anantānubandhī* (pursuers from beginningless time). It operates with *darśaṇa-mohanīya karma*, causing the soul to remain in the first *guṇasthāna*. The three lesser degrees of intensity are *apratyākhyānāvaraṇa* (obstructers of partial renunciation), which prevent one from taking the lay vows (*aṇuvrata*), *pratyākhyānāvaraṇa* (obstructers of complete renunciation), which prevent one from taking the mendicant vows (*mahāvrata*), and *saṃjvalana* (smoldering), which prevent one from attaining complete right conduct (*yathākhyāta*). There are nine sub-varieties of *mohanīya karma* that cause the non-passions (*no-kaṣāya*) of laughter (*hāsya*), prejudicial liking (*rati*), prejudicial disliking (*arati*), sorrow (*śoka*), fear (*bhaya*), disgust (*jugupsā*), sexual feelings of a male for a female (*puṃveda*), sexual feelings of a female for a male (*strīveda*), and sexual feelings of a hermaphrodite (*napuṃsakaveda*). The first six *no-kaṣāya*s are not operative after the eighth *guṇasthāna* and the three *veda*s are not operative after the ninth *guṇasthāna*. The *saṃjvalana* degree of *krodha*, *māna*, and *māyā* are not operative after the ninth *guṇasthāna* and *lobha* is not operative after the tenth *guṇasthāna*. For varieties of *karma*, see Glasenapp 1942, chapter 2, and for the *guṇasthāna*s, see Glasenapp 1942, chapter 8.

20 Other causes for the influx of *sātā-vedanīya karma* listed here are giving (*dāna*), asceticism with attachment (*sarāga-saṃyama*), concentration (*yoga*), equanimity (*kṣānti*), and purity or freedom from greed (*śauca*).

21 Siddhasenagaṇi's commentary on *TS* 6.13.

22 *SS* 632.

23 Tatia 1994: 157.

24 Deleu 1970: 137 (emphasis on "and" is mine).

25 Abhayadevasūri's commentary on *Bhagavaī-sutta* 8.8.412. Cf. Deleu 1970: 151 (382a).

26 *Kṛpā* is defined as "pity, tenderness, or compassion" by both Monier-Williams and Apte. Neither Umāsvāti nor Siddhasenagaṇi state how one should render assistance to the afflicted here.

27 *SS* 683. Pūjyapāda does not state how one should render assistance to the afflicted here.

28 *Dhavalā* commentary on *Ṣaṭkhaṇḍāgama* 2.1.2 (vol. 7, p. 7). The Digambara *Ṣaṭkhaṇḍāgama* was written by Puṣpadanta and Bhūtabali (*c.* second century CE).

According to Hīrālāl Jain and A. N. Upadhye, its date is 683 years after Mahāvīra's death (*c.*156 CE) (*Ṣaṭkhaṇḍāgama*, vol. 1, p. 9 of the editorial section). This is the earliest extant Digambara text and it discusses the bondage of the soul by *karma*.

29 On *mohanīya karma*s, see note 19.

30 Three types of *samyak-darśana* are possible in the fourth *guṇasthāna*. *Aupaśamika-samyaktva* is due to the temporary suppression of all *darśana-mohanīya karma*. It lasts only for a short time (less than forty-eight minutes, or an *antarmuhūrta*). *Kṣāyopaśamika-samyaktva* is brought about by subsitence-cum-disassociation of *darśana-mohanīya karma*. It may be lost if the strongest degree of passions (*kaṣāya*) re-emerge, causing the soul to fall to the first *guṇasthāna*. *Kṣāyika-samyaktva* is the state that is attained when all *darśana-mohanīya karma* has been destroyed. It is always associated with the destruction of the conduct-deluding *karma*s that cause the strongest degree of passions (*anantānubandhī-cāritra-mohanīya karma*). This type of *samyak-darśana* can never be lost. The technical details regarding the processes of energy (*karaṇa*) associated with the attainment of the three types of *samyaktva* is beyond the scope of this paper. See Tatia 1951: 268–275.

31 On rare occasions, this can include hell-beings as well. Normally, a soul that has attained *samyaktva* is not born as a hell-being because such a soul (i.e., one in the fourth *guṇasthāna* or above) does not bind the sub-variety (*uttara-prakṛti*) of *āyu karma* that causes such a rebirth. However, it is possible for a human or animal to have bound *nāraka āyu karma* previously while in a state of *mithyātva* and to subsequently attain a proper view of reality that arises with the destruction of all *darśana-mohanīya karma* (*kṣāyika-samyaktva*). Once *āyu karma* has been bound, it is impossible to change its sub-variety (*uttara-prakṛti*) and thereby attain rebirth in another state of existence. However, since all *darśana-mohanīya karma* has been destroyed, it is impossible to fall back into *mithyātva*, even after rebirth as a hell-being. King Śrenika is an example of such a rebirth. See Wiley 2003.

32 See Williams 1963: 41.

33 Williams 1963: 259. For dates, see Williams 1963: 9 and 28.

34 As translated by Williams (1963: 42).

35 *Ratna-karaṇḍa-śrāvakācāra* v. 21, as cited in Williams 1963:108.

36 Williams 1963: 54. He dates this work sometime after 1350 CE, probably in the fifteenth century.

37 Tatia 1951: 285 and 290.

38 *Yogaśāstra* ii.15, as cited in Williams 1963: 42.

39 *Āyāraṃga-sutta* 11.6.5.2, as translated by Jacobi 1884: 60.

40 *Uttarajjhayaṇa-sutta* 21.13, as translated by Jacobi 1895: 109.

41 *Praśamaratiprakaraṇa* 168. Cf. *Sāgāra-dharmāmṛta* i.4, a *śrāvakācāra* text written by the Digambara Āśādhara (thirteenth century): "compassion is the root of the whole sacred doctrine," as cited in Williams 1963: 42.

42 *Ātmānuśānana* 68. Guṇabhadra, who was a pupil of Jinasena, was also the author of the *Uttarapurāṇa* and the last five chapters of the *Ādipurāṇa*.

43 *Ātmānuśānana* 107.

44 *Ātmānuśānana* 224 as translated by J. L. Jaini.

45 Peter Flügel has written extensively on the Śvetāmbara Terāpanthīs. See Flügel 1994, 1995–1996, and 2000.

46 His views are expressed in *Aṇukampā rī Caupaī*, written in 1787 in the local Marwāri language. Not having access to this text, I have relied on passages discussed by Muni Nathmal (now, Ācārya Mahāprajña) in *Bhikṣu Vicāra Darśana* (Nathmal 1964). Although this work has been translated into English (*Acharya Bhikshu: The Man and His Philosophy*, Adarsh Sahitya Sangh Publications, Churu, Rajasthan, 1968), I have translated from the Hindi text, which includes verses from the *Aṇukampā rī Caupaī* in the notes.

47 Nathmal 1964: 86, quoting *Aṇukampā* 8.1.
48 Nathmal 1964: 86, quoting *Aṇukampā* 1.4.
49 Nathmal 1964: 86.
50 Nathmal 1964: 87, quoting *Aṇukampā* 8.2–8.3.
51 Nathmal 1964: 87, quoting *Aṇukampā* 11.4.
52 Nathmal 1964: 87, quoting *Aṇukampā* 11.15.
53 Nathmal 1964: 88–89, quoting *Aṇukampā* 9.8.
54 Nathmal 1964: 89, quoting *Aṇukampā* 9.4.
55 Vallely 2002: 85.
56 Vallely 2002: 31.
57 Vallely 2002: 29.
58 Vallely 2002: 68.
59 Jaini 1979: 150.
60 Granoff 1992: 2.
61 Granoff 1992: 36–37. On *saṃsāramocaka*s, see Halbfass 1991: 98–129 and Granoff 1992: 3–4 and 41, note 13. According to Granoff, these arguments were most often advanced in the *śrāvakācāra* texts devoted to proper lay conduct. In this article, Granoff has translated portions of the *Śrāvakaprajñapti* attributed to Umāsvāti and its commentary attributed to Haribhadra. This is the earliest Śvetāmbara *śrāvakācāra* text. Williams (1963: 2–4) believes the Umāsvāti who wrote this text was not the author of the *Tattvārtha-sūtra*. He dates this text to sometime prior to the end of the fifth century and the commentary in the eighth century.
62 Lakṣmīvallabhagaṇi's commentary on *Uttarajjhayaṇa-sutta* 21.13. According to the introduction to vol. 2 (pp. 7–8), he was the pupil of Lakṣmīkīrtigaṇi of the Kharatara Gaccha and he lived in the late seventeenth century. According to Digambaras, giving protection also is associated with the rise of *Tīrthaṅkara nāma karma*.
63 *SS* 261 on *TS* 2.4.
64 *SS* 927 on *TS* 10.4.

Bibliography

Primary sources

Ātmānuśānana, of Guṇabhadra. Tr. by J. L. Jaini as *Atmanushasana: Discourse to the Soul*. Sacred Books of the Jainas, vol. 7. Lucknow: The Central Jaina Publishing House, 1928. Reprint New Delhi: Today and Tomorrow's Printers and Publishers, 1991.

Āyāraṃga-sutta (*Ācārāṅga-sūtra*). Tr. by Hermann Jacobi as *Jaina Sūtras*, pt. 1. Oxford: Oxford University Press, 1884. Reprint Delhi: Motilal Banarsidass, 1989.

Bhagavaī Viyāhapannatti-sūtra (*Bhagavatī-aṅga-sūtram* with the *ṭīkā* of Abhayadevasūri). *Āgamasuttāni*, vols 5–6. Ed. Muni Dīparatnasāgara. Ahmedabad: Āgama Śruta Prakāśana, 2000.

Dhavalā, of Vīrasena. See *Ṣaṭkhaṇḍāgama*.

Gommaṭasāra Karma-Kāṇḍa, of Nemicandra. Ed. Pt. Manoharlāl. Agas: Rājacandra Jain Śāstramālā, 1971.

Karmagrantha, of Devendrasūri (*Catvāraḥ Karmagranthāḥ* with *Svopajña-vṛtti*). Bhavnagar: Śrī Jain Ātmānanda Sabhā, 1934.

Praśamaratiprakaraṇa, of Umāsvāti. Tr. by Yajneshwar S. Shastri. L. D. Series 107. Ahmedabad: L. D. Institute of Indology, 1969.

Sarvārthasiddhi, of Pūjyapāda (The Commentary on Ācārya Gṛddhapiccha's *Tattvārtha-sūtra*). Sanskrit text with Hindi translation by Siddhāntācārya Phūlcandra Śāstrī. Jñānapīṭha

Mūrtidevī Jaina Granthamālā, Sanskrit Grantha, no. 13. Varanasi: Bhāratīya Jñānapīṭha, 1934. Tr. by S. A. Jain as *Reality: English Translation of Pūjyapāda's Sarvārthasiddhi*. Madras: Jwalamalini Trust, 1960. Reprint, 1992.

Ṣaṭkhaṇḍāgama, of Puṣpadanta and Bhūtabali (with the *Dhavalā-ṭīkā*, of Vīrasena). 16 vols. Ed. Hīrālāl Jain. Amaravati: Jaina Sāhityoddhāraka Fund, 1939–1959. Rev. third ed., Solapur: Jaina Saṃskṛti Saṃrakṣaka Saṅgha, 1992–1995.

Tattvārthādhigamasūtra, of Umāsvāti (with *Svopajña-bhāṣya* and the *ṭīkā* of Siddhasenagaṇi). 2 vols. Ed. Hīrālāl Rasikdās Kāpadīā. Śreṣṭhi Devcandra Lālbhāi Jain Pustakoddhāra, nos. 67 and 76, 1926 and 1930.

Tattvārthaślokavārtikālaṅkāra, of Vidyānanda. 7 vols. Sanskrit text with Hindi translation by Mānikcandra Kaundeya Nyāyācārya. Solapur: Ācārya Kunthusāgara Granthamālā, 1949–1984.

Tattvārtha-sūtra. Tr. by Nathmal Tatia as *Tattvārtha Sūtra: That Which Is*. San Francisco: Harper Collins, 1994.

Tattvārthavārtika (*Rājavārtika*), of Akalaṅkadeva. 2 vols. Jñānapīṭha Mūrtidevī Jaina Granthamālā, Sanskrit Grantha, nos. 10 and 20. Delhi: Bhāratīya Jñānapīṭha. First ed. 1953–1957. Second ed. 1982.

Uttarajjhayaṇa-sutta (*Uttarādhyayana-sūtra* with the *ṭīkā* of Lakṣmīvallabhagaṇi). 2 vols. Ahmedabad: Śāradā Prakāśana Kendra, 1984. Tr. by Hermann Jacobi as *Jaina Sūtras*, pt. 2. Oxford: Oxford University Press, 1895. Reprint Delhi: Motilal Banarsidass, 1989.

Secondary sources

Apte, Vaman Shivaram. 1957. *The Practical Sanskrit–English Dictionary*. Revised and enlarged edition. Ed. P. K. Gode and C. G. Karve. Poona: Prasad Prakashan. (Reprint Kyoto: Rinsen Book Company, 1978.)

Bālcandra, Siddhānta-Śāstrī, ed. 1972–1979. *Jaina Lakṣaṇāvalī*. 3 vols. Vīr Sevā Mandir Series, no. 15. New Delhi: Vīr Sevā Mandir.

Deleu, Jozef. 1970. *Viyāhapannatti (Bhagavaī): The Fifth Anga of the Jaina Canon: Introduction, Critical Analysis, Commentary, and Indexes*. Brugge: De Tempel, Tempelhof. Reprint Delhi: Motilal Banarsidass, 1996.

Dundas, Paul. 1985. "Food and Freedom: the Jaina Sectarian Debate on the Nature of the Kevalin." *Religion* 15: 161–198.

——. 2002. *The Jains*. Second ed. London: Routledge. First ed. 1991.

Flügel, Peter. 1994. *Askese und Devotion: Das rituelle System der Terapanth Svetambara Jains*. Doctoral dissertation, Johannes Gutenberg-Universität, Mainz.

——. 1995–1996. "The ritual circle of the Terāpanth Śvetāmbara Jains." *Bulletin d'Études Indiennes* 13: 117–176.

——. 2000. "Protestantische und Post-Protestantische Jaina a-Reformbewegungen: Zur Geschichte und Organisation der Sthānakavāsī I. *Berliner Indologische Studien* 13–14: 37–103.

Glasenapp, Helmuth von. 1942. *The Doctrine of Karma in Jain Philosophy*. Tr. G. Barry Gifford. Bombay: The Trustees, Bai Vijibai Jivanlal Panalal Charity Fund.

Granoff, Phyllis. 1992. "The Violence of Non-Violence: a Study of some Jain Responses to Non-Jain Religious Practices." *The Journal of the International Association of Buddhist Studies* 15: 11–43.

Halbfass, Wilhelm. 1991. *Tradition and Reflection: Explorations in Indian Thought*. Albany, NY: State University of New York.

Http://www.jainpilgrimages.com/general/mahavir.htm (accessed December 15, 2001).

Jacobi, Hermann. 1884. *Jaina Sūtras*, Part I. Sacred Books of the East, vol. 22. Oxford: Oxford University Press (Reprint Delhi: Motilal Banarsidass, 1989).

——. 1895. *Jaina Sūtras*, Part II. Sacred Books of the East, vol. 45. Oxford: Oxford University Press (Reprint Delhi: Motilal Banarsidass, 1989).

Jaini, Padmanabh S. 1979. *The Jaina Path of Purification*. Berkeley, CA: University of California Press.

Monier-Williams, Monier. 1899. *A Sanskrit–English Dictionary*. Oxford: Oxford University Press. Reprint 1992.

Mookerjee, Satkari. 1944. *The Jaina Philosophy of Non-Absolutism: A Critical Study of Anekāntavāda*. Delhi: Motilal Banarsidass. Second ed. 1978.

Nathmal, Muni. 1964. *Bhikṣu Vicāra Darśana*. Calcutta: Sāhitya Prakāśana Samiti.

Ohira, Suzuko. 1982. *A Study of the Tattvārthasūtra with Bhāṣya*. Ahmedabad: L. D. Institute of Indology.

Sanghvi, Sukhlal. 1974. *Pt. Sukhlalji's Commentary on Tattvārtha Sūtra of Vācaka Umāsvāti*. Tr. K. K. Dixit. Ahmedabad: L. D. Institute of Indology.

Singhvi, L. M. 1998. "Extract from Environment and the Ancient Indic Heritage." (Keynote address delivered at the Summit on Religions and Conservation in Atami, Japan, on April 7, 1995). In *Jainism: Give Life, Take Not*. Sri Chinmoy. New York: Agni Press, 39–48.

Tatia, Nathmal. 1951. *Studies in Jaina Philosophy*. Varanasi: Jaina Cultural Research Society.

——. 1994. *Tattvārtha Sūtra: That Which Is*. Translation of the *Tattvārtha Sūtra* of Umāsvāti/Umāsvāmi. San Francisco, CA: Harper Collins.

Varṇī, Jinendra. 1970–1973. *Jainendra Siddhānta Kośa*. 5 vols. Delhi: Bhāratīya Jñānapīṭha. Sixth ed. 1998.

Vallely, Anne. 2002. *Guardians of the Transcendent: An Ethnography of a Jain Ascetic Community*. Toronto: University of Toronto Press.

Wiley, Kristi L. 2000. "*Aghātiyā Karmas*: Agents of Embodiment in Jainism." PhD dissertation, University of California, Berkeley.

——. 2003. "The Story of King Śreṇika: Binding and Modification of *Āyu Karma*." In *Jainism and Early Buddhism: Essays in Honor of Padmanabh S. Jaini*. Ed. Olle Qvarnström, 337–358. Fremont, CA: Asian Humanities Press.

Williams, R. 1963. *Jaina Yoga: A Survey of Medieval Śrāvakācāras*. London: Oxford University Press. Reprint Delhi: Motilal Banarsidass 1991.

INDEX